1988

Flora (Ed.), Growth to Limits Vol.

European University Institute

Growth to Limits

The Western European Welfare States
Since World War II

Volume 2
Germany, United Kingdom, Ireland, Italy

Edited by

Peter Flora

1988

Walter de Gruyter · New York · Berlin

This book was originally published (clothbound) as part of the Series C (Political and Social Sciences, Vol. 6.2) of the European University Institute, Florence.

Library of Congress Cataloging-in-Publication Data

Growth to limits.
    Contents: v. 1. Sweden, Norway, Finland, Denmark --
v. 2. Germany, United Kingdom, Ireland, Italy.
    1. Europe--Social conditions--20th century. 2. Welfare state.
3. Europe--Politics and government--1945-
4. Europe--Economic conditions--1945-   I. Flora, Peter,
1944-
HN377.G76   1986   306.7'094   86-19938
ISBN 0-89925-266-4 (U.S. : v. 1)
ISBN 0-89925-398-7 (Paperback)

Cover Design: K. Lothar Hildebrand, Berlin. — Setting: Satz-Rechen-Zentrum, Berlin.
Printing: H. Heenemann GmbH & Co., Berlin.
Binding: Verlagsbuchbinderei Dieter Mikolai, Berlin.
Printed in Germany.

Preface

The five volumes *Growth to Limits - The Western European Welfare States Since World War II* represent only one stretch of a longer road. To understand the destination, it may be useful to get a picture of the whole distance. At the beginning stood an encounter with one of the leading social scientists of the postwar period, the late Stein Rokkan. I first met him in 1971 at the Lausanne 'Workshop on Indicators of National Development' which he had organized under the auspices of the International Social Science Council. The conference was one of his manifold efforts to advance comparative research in the social sciences. This as well as later encounters have had a great impact on my work, in giving my own predilections a more specific meaning and above all providing continuing encouragement in times of uncertainty.

Rokkan's message was simple:

- Most of the 'big old questions' referring to the evolution and future of the industrial society and the modern state, of capitalism and mass democracy, of war and peace, are still essential for the social sciences.

- The progress already made in the development of new techniques and organizations of social research must be further advanced and made productive for an analysis of the development of global societies.

- Comparison, over time and across countries, is the essential method in this kind of analysis, linking theory and empirical research at a conceptual level which is not too remote from everyday language and experience.

- Europe is the ideal place for this comparative research, as the laboratory of the modern world with basic concepts and models deriving from its experiences, as well as because of its persisting diversity.

- Europe, however, is more than a testing ground for scientific hypotheses, its study more than an academic concern. Its development will be relevant not only for the Europeans, but for the future of the entire world.

- Comparative research, the study of Europe, must be a collective endeavour, an enterprise of the scientific community, requiring large-scale organization as well as networks of friendship among social scientists across national borders.

More than any other social scientist I have known, the Norwegian Stein Rokkan has embodied this philosophy: a classical scholar and promoter of new research methods, an ingenious inventer of complex models and scrupulous student of national experiences, a true European from the Northern periphery, an eminent organizer and father-figure for younger social scientists. Sometimes personality is more important than arguments, even in science, or should it be said that personality *is* the argument?

Apart from this general view, Rokkan provided me with two more concrete stimuli which have had an impact on my life. First, I made the crazy decision to produce a huge historical data handbook on Western Europe since the early nineteenth century in order to - as Rokkan expressed it - 'pin down numbers on the European variations'. Second, I decided that his studies on the long-term development of the European mass democracies and nation states should be supplemented by analyses of the development of the European welfare states. Both purposes were served through the HIWED Project (Historical Indicators of the Western European Democracies), which I began with Wolfgang Zapf in 1973 in Mannheim and took with me to Cologne in 1977. Through its entire duration from 1973 to 1979, this project received generous financial support from the Volkswagenwerk Foundation.

We began the work on the data handbook with much enthusiasm - which everyone knows is only another word for naïveté. First, the sources for European statistics had to be determined. In this connection I published in 1977 a bibliography along with an institutional history of official statistics (*Quantitative Historical Sociology. Current Sociology 23.2.* Paris, Mouton). Later a bibliography of all census publications was added. Throughout the good ten-year period in which we worked on the completion of the handbook, our naïveté gradually faded and with it our enthusiasm. Finally in 1983 we published the first volume (subtitle: *The Growth of Mass Democracies and Welfare States*) of our data handbook entitled *State, Economy and Society in Western Europe 1815-1975* (Frankfurt, Campus; London, Macmillan, 1983). The second and concluding volume followed in 1986 (subtitle: *The Growth of Industrial Societies and Capitalist Economies*). As a by-product of our work on the data handbook, the West-European-Data-Archive (WEDA) was formed, consisting of a combination of an old-fashioned collection of data sources and a new-fashioned collection of computer tapes. Winfried Pfenning was responsible for the set-up of this archive from 1979 to 1984, and since then Franz Kraus has taken charge. Today WEDA is a part of the Institute of the Social Sciences at the University of Mannheim and should serve as an important instrument for this Institute's future research on Western Europe.

Concurrent with our work on the data handbook, we began with the analysis of certain aspects of the long-term development of the West European welfare states since the end of the nineteenth century. First results were published in a book which I edited together with Arnold J. Heidenheimer (*The Development of Welfare States in Europe and America.* New Brunswick and London, Transaction Books, 1981). The most important in the series of comparative studies were the works of Jens Alber on the development of social insurance (*Vom Armenhaus zum Wohlfahrtsstaat.* Frankfurt, Campus, 1982) which won him the Stein Rokkan Prize of the International Social Science Council, Jürgen Kohl on the development of public expenditure (*Staatsausgaben in Westeuropa.* Frankfurt, Campus, 1985), and finally Franz Kraus on the development of income inequality (*Income Distribution in Western Europe 1900-1980.* Forthcoming).

When I moved from Cologne to the European University Institute in Florence in Autumn 1979, it was also swith the intention of deepening our studies of the long-term development of the European welfare states (today I think perhaps I should have devoted myself more to the study of Renaissance art and Italian cooking). In Spring 1980, with the financial support of the European Community, I launched a comparative project on the growth of the European welfare states (Austria, Belgium, Denmark, Finland, France, Germany, Great Britain, Ireland, Italy, Netherlands, Norway, Sweden, Switzerland) since World War II, along with a group of social scientists from these countries.

I would like to thank at this point Hans Daalder most warmly. He had the courage to recruit me, then a rather young and unknown sociologist, for the European University Institute. And he encouraged the kind of comparative research which I then started in Florence. Having grown up myself in a slightly cynical Catholic culture, I have always admired his Protestant *Prinzipientreue*.

By the first project meeting in 1980 I had been successful (with Austria, Switzerland, and Belgium as exceptions) in recruiting social scientists from these countries who were prepared to collaborate on this extensive project. The majority were younger scientists, some old friends, and some only known to me through the literature. As in real life, so in scientific projects: you lose some people and win others. Competent contributors were found for the three remaining countries. On the other hand, new teams had to be formed subsequently for Austria and the Netherlands, and it was unfortunately impossible to replace our French colleagues who left the project after two years.

Thus 12 countries remained and were researched by the following persons or teams:

Austria	Anton Amann/ Wolfgang Weigel	University of Vienna
Belgium	Jos Berghman/ Jan Vranken	Univ. of Antwerp/Univ. of Tilburg University of Antwerp
Denmark	Lars N. Johansen	University of Odense
Finland	Matti Alestalo/ Hannu Uusitalo	University of Helsinki Helsinki School of Economics
Germany	Jens Alber	European Univ. Institute, Florence/ Univ. of Cologne
Ireland	Maria Maguire	European Univ. Institute, Florence/ OECD Paris
Italy	Maurizio Ferrera	European Univ. Institute, Florence/ Univ. of Pavia
Netherlands	Theo Berben/ Joop Roebroek/ Goran Therborn	University of Nijmegen
Norway	Stein Kuhnle	University of Bergen
Sweden	Sven Olson	University of Stockholm
Switzerland	Peter Gross	University of Bamberg (FRG)
United Kingdom	Richard Parry	University of Edinburgh

In Spring 1980 my old friend and colleague Jens Alber joined the project as additional support for the project coordination. At the same time I had the good fortune of acquiring a Swiss secretary, Ursula Nocentini, who proved to me that the old saying that the Swiss even 'sweep the fields clean' is no myth. In the true style of the Swiss, she was able to put some order into our multi-national chaos.

In respect to the goal setting of the project, my ideas were simple. It was not my intention to examine a specific hypothesis or study a particular limited area. Much more than that, I wanted to initiate broadly based studies on the postwar development of the welfare states in a number of European countries. These studies were to be based on the same questions, work with comparable data, and utilize the same methods. I thought that it would then be possible to draw a picture of the major variations between the European welfare states, thus laying the groundwork for further research.

Naturally I knew that the way to hell is paved with good intentions. In order to get started on the right track, I employed two means: first, sections of the entire studies were written step-by-step for one or two countries and, after discussion in subsequent meetings, served as models for the other countries. Secondly, I met with the project members on a regular basis in order to work on the text and data 'on location' and to attain a greater cohesion and comparability (in a sometimes viscious battle sentence by sentence). Some years of my life were spent on this, and therefore I keep telling myself that the work *must* have been somehow meaningful.

As is well-known, several languages are spoken in Western Europe. Thus, a common language had to be found, and this was pidgin English. And as I am only familiar with the Austrian version of pidgin English, it was necessary to recruit the services of native English speakers. Often up to five different versions of a text (which grew to a country average of almost 150 pages) were being worked on. The reader may thus understand that even the old myth of Sisyphos was of little consolation. I am sure that my periodic despair was shared by Clare Gardiner, who worked in Florence on the numerous versions of the various chapters, as well as by Margaret Herden, who took on this work in Mannheim with refreshing American optimism.

Scientific work is certainly not unimportant in the production of such books, and editorial work may also be useful. *Conditio sine qua non*, however, is the actual typing of the manuscripts, not to mention the patience and creativity necessary for the production of the hundreds of tables and graphs which embellish these volumes. Computer readable texts and tables were done with passionate devotion by the two Ursulas (Ursula Nocentini in Florence and Ursula Rossi in Mannheim) and the graphs were produced reluctantly but meticulously by our artist in residence, Siegbert Sussek.

The completed manuscripts would never have gone to print without the Publication Officer of the European University Institute, Brigitte Schwab. Our common Bavarian-Tyrolian view of the world has certainly facilitated our collaboration. I would also wish to thank President Maihofer, who not only followed the endless progress with fatherly understanding, but also offered his energetic support.

The monumental product of our multi-phase cross-national chaos consists of five volumes which, following the tradition of the publishing house de Gruyter, are at least aesthetically pleasing and thus convey a respectable impression: three volumes (I-III) with four country studies each, one Appendix volume (IV) containing for each country an institutional synopsis, an annotated bibliography and a collection of documented time-series data, and finally a comparative study (V) by the editor. The first three volumes contain the following country studies: Sweden, Norway, Finland, Denmark (I); Germany, United Kingdom, Ireland, Italy (II); Austria, Switzerland, Netherlands, Belgium (III). Volumes I, II and IV are being published in 1986; the two remaining volumes III and V are scheduled for 1987.

I both fear and hope that with the completion of these volumes only a 'stop-over' point is reached. On the occasion of the twentieth anniversary of the Mannheim Institute of Social Sciences, a symposium on 'Western Europe in Transition' was organized in Autumn 1985, the contributions of which will be published in German in 1986 (Peter Flora (ed.), *Westeuropa im Wandel*. Frankfurt, Campus) and in English in 1987 (*Europe in Transition*. London, Macmillan). With this symposium the Mannheim Faculty of Social Sciences has documented its intention to develop a new research centre on Western Europe in order to expand and systematize its previous research, and to assure a greater continuity of research in this important field.

Mannheim, July 1986   Peter Flora

Table of Contents

Introduction

PETER FLORA

Contents

Since the Second World War, Western European societies have undergone changes which deserve to be called revolutionary, even though they were accomplished without a mounting of barricades. Europe did not rise like a phoenix from the ashes of the war, but it recovered much faster than most observers had anticipated, reaching a fairly high degree of economic and political stability as early as the 1950s. From this foundation, the long-term process of modernization of Western Europe was able to accelerate, deeply transforming these societies. The development of the welfare state was an essential element of this modernization process, most obvious in the expansion of public services and transfer schemes, and with far-reaching consequences for the class structures, the functioning of the economy, and political stability.

The origins of the Western European welfare states reach back to the nineteenth century, some of their present institutional features predating the First World War. Their present format, however, is mainly a product of the 'golden age of the welfare state' from the early 1960s to the mid-1970s, when the world-wide economic crisis put an end to this historically unprecedented expansion. Today, though with great variations, the Western European welfare states seem to have approached their limits of expansion. Persistent high rates of unemployment and public deficits set economic limits; tax resistance and a neo-liberal mood set political limits; and a new arms race and increased technological competition set external limits.

Furthermore, the welfare states have matured to such a degree that a repetition of past growth rates appears unnecessary. The primary task has become the economic and political stabilization of the welfare states. Large welfare clienteles will prevent that stabilization necessarily implies a dismantling. The ageing of the population, the changing division of labour between the sexes and a more general change of values will require instead that stabilization involves reorganization, above all a more flexible harmonization of different life domains (in particular work and family) and different stages of the life cycle (in particular education, employment, and retirement).

In the project, our concern was not primarily an investigation of the most recent problems and changes, but rather an analysis of the long-term development of the European welfare states which has been characterized by common growth tendencies and similar developmental problems as well as persisting institutional variations. We were convinced, however, that such a study would also teach us something about the solutions to be found for the present and future challenges.

This introduction can only try to sketch the broader context of the project (a more comprehensive comparative analysis is provided in Volume V). It starts with some reflections on the common heritage of the European welfare states and on the early origins of their institutional variations. A brief account follows of the long-term growth to limits of the welfare state. Then an attempt is made to characterize its present situation by problems of institutional adjustment without clear-cut political cleavages. The introduction concludes with a description of the common structure of the twelve country chapters.

1. Common origins of the European welfare state

The modern welfare state is a European invention - in the same way as the nation state, mass democracy, and industrial capitalism. It was born as an answer to problems created by capitalist industrialization; it was driven by the democratic class struggle; and it followed in the footsteps of the nation state. Thus, we should understand the development of the European welfare state as an essential element in the transformation of European societies which started with the Industrial and the French Revolution. In a stricter sense, however, the 'take-off' of the modern welfare state occurred in the late nineteenth century, in the period extending roughly from the Italian and German unification to the First World War.

In retrospect, this development did not come as a surprise. The period witnessed the general breakthrough of industrialism, the decisive steps in the evolution of mass democracy and the culmination of the European nation state. Industrial breakthrough meant above all an unprecedented increase in both productivity and production, surpassing a population growth which was then the most rapid in European history. From around 1870 to World War I, the growth of European populations averaged somewhat more than 40 percent; it was the climax of their 'demographic transition'. The national product increased much faster in the same period; it quadrupled in some countries and tripled in most others [1].

This growth led to massive population shifts from agriculture to industry, from country to town. While around 1870 only one in six West Europeans lived in towns of 20,000 or more inhabitants, by 1910 this figure was one in three; the population in cities of 100,000 and more inhabitants tripled in these decades to almost 50 million. Industrialization spread from the core areas to other regions and even to the peripheries in the North, South and West, transforming employment and class structures everywhere. In the more industrialized countries such as Great Britain, Belgium, Switzerland and Germany, 40 percent or more of the labour force was working in the secondary sector at the eve of World War I, and in the more peripheral countries the figure was at least one fifth to one fourth.

Population shifts of such unknown dimension and speed must inevitably create immense social problems. Furthermore, these problems were shaped and intensified by the capitalist structure of the European economies and by the increasing impact of the business cycle. It is not difficult, therefore, to understand that this was a period of intensified class conflict, of the mobilization of the new working class and its organization in trade unions and labour parties. While the establishment of trade unions was facilitated by freedom of association, which most European countries had granted even prior to 1870, the development of workers' parties usually came about later, with the introduction of male suffrage. Such parties were established everywhere in Europe before the turn of the century and became the prototype of the modern mass party. Although the franchise was achieved much earlier, this period saw the greatest extensions of suffrage, and voting turn-outs reached high levels well before World War I. Parliamentary control of government was also introduced in this period, with the exception of Austria and Germany.

The mobilization of anti-system forces was moderated and mediated to some extent by an (at least rudimentary) institutionalization of industrial conflict, the more general 'institutionalization of class conflict' through the evolving parliamentary institutions, and finally by an increasing state intervention and the creation of new public institutions. Buoyed by economic growth, state revenues rose remarkably in absolute terms, and slowly the European states took a larger share of the national product. As this was a period of relative peace and only minor wars, the new resources could be used for development of the economic infrastructure, for internal order - and for social welfare.

The fact that the modern welfare state originated in the late nineteenth century in Europe may thus be simply explained by the comparatively high levels of industrialization and democratization achieved in this region of the world. In this sense, European developments indicated the direction in which the rest of the world would move once the process of modernization got started, just in the way Marx had thought that industrial England would mirror the future of the other countries. And indeed, with the spread of the industrial mode of production, and the diffusion of the nation state as the predominant form of political organization, the creation of public education, health and social security systems has become a world-wide phenomenon. In this respect, the evolution of the welfare state clearly represents a universal aspect of modernization. In a Durkheimian perspective, it is the increasing division of labour and the growing complexity and interdependence which require both a strengthening of the state as steering centre and a strengthening of individual rights as normative basis.

However, even if one is convinced that the evolution of the European welfare states exhibits some universal traits, three qualifications seem appropriate: (1) In Europe, the close relationships with the development of the *capitalist* market economy and the *democratic* nation state have produced a specific type of liberal welfare state. (2) European societies have some distinct *common historical preconditions*: above all, old nation states, specific family structures and strong industrial working classes, which have left their mark on the development of the European welfare states. (3) On the basis of common historical preconditions and within the broad limits of the liberal model, the European welfare states display a gamut of *institutional variations* which make generalized statements about the European welfare state often rather meaningless.

When industrialization started to transform the European societies and create problems of a completely new kind and order of magnitude, solutions were sought within a well-established form of political organization, the nation state. This form had already become predominant in Europe long before and differed from alternative forms (such as empires or trading networks) through its territorial consolidation, the degree of centralization, its differentiation from other organizations and the monopolization of the means of coercion [2].

Most important perhaps, was the development of relatively direct and close relationships between the political centre and the population, in long-term processes of subjection and counter-mobilization. These relationships became institutionalized in the form of obligations and rights, crystallizing in the concept of citizenship. The extension of rights as claims on the state was often preceded or accompanied, however, by the restriction of rights previously vested in other organizations such as manors, guilds, communities or estates.

The *early* development of nation states was probably facilitated by the weakness of corporate structures in Europe, especially those linked to kinship. The *later* development of welfare states was probably furthered by the specific European family structures. As we know today from historical research [3], pre-industrial Europe was quite unique for its relative predominance of simple family households. The nuclear family was less a product than a precondition of industrialization in this world area. And it was probably less adapted to cushion the impact of capitalist industrialization, which called for other collective forms of social security, above all state intervention, once the protective mechanisms of the manor and the guild had been destroyed.

Industrialization generally implies the emergence of an industrial working class. Only in Europe, however, was this class the dominant social category for a longer period of time. In this narrow sense, it is only in Europe that something like an 'industrial society' developed [4]. It is not surprising therefore that the modern welfare state started in Europe with an attempt to tackle the problems common to this new social class: loss of income through accident, sickness, invalidity, unemployment, and in old age. The solution was found in a new institution which broke with the principles of the century old European poor law: social insurance. As a consequence of this early development, the social security system still dominates the welfare state. This distinguishes Europe from America, the 'first new nation', which developed much later what is still a rudimentary system of social security, seeking instead to strengthen social citizenship much earlier and with greater enthusiasm than the Europeans, through an extension of education opportunities [5].

But the emergence of the European welfare state cannot be fully understood as a reaction to problems of the industrial working class. Its close connection with the evolution of mass democracy puts it into a much broader perspective in which the extension of political rights led to a democratic struggle for a more equitable share in the material wealth and cultural heritage of a nation [6]. In this perspective, the welfare state may be seen as a 'completion' of the nation state, to the extent that individual social rights become an essential element of citizenship as the main basis of political legitimacy.

However, it usually is a very imperfect completion. Only few social rights are citizen rights in a stricter sense. They are related much more often to employment status than to political status, and frequently welfare policies are not based on individual entitlements at all. The institutionalization of social rights is not only imperfect, but there are also principal limits to their extension. They derive from civil liberties connected with basic institutions such as the family or private property as well as from the imperatives of a society based on differentiation by achievement.

With all these limitations, the essence of the liberal European welfare state lies nevertheless in the idea of basic *rights* of individuals to state-provided benefits as principle elements of their *life chances*. Security and *equality* are the welfare state's central objectives, i.e. the attempt to stabilize the life chances of, in principle, the entire population and to make their distribution more equal.

The concept of 'life chances' was introduced by Max Weber in his analysis of class structures which he defined as specific structures of inequality in which the life chances of individuals are contingent upon their market position [7]. By the extent to which the welfare state influences the life chances of individuals and social groups independent of their market position, it reduces the 'class structuration' of society.[8] or rather introduces a new dimension of structuration [9].

Which life chances are referred to here? Max Weber speaks of *Güterversorgung* (procuring goods), *äußere Lebenstellung* (gaining a position in life), and *inneres Lebensschicksal* (gaining inner satisfaction), but without further exploring the latter aspects. It may thus be more useful to start with a somewhat different distinction made by Erik Allardt in his pioneer study, the Scandinavian Welfare Survey [10]. He differentiates three dimensions of life chances: *having* which basically refers to the 'level of living', *being* which points to the potential of 'self-actualization', and *loving* which is related to 'solidarity' and 'belongingness'. In his understanding, having, being, and loving represent opposite poles to poverty, alienation, and anomie.

The importance of different elements of individual life chances may of course vary greatly. The public guarantee of basic food supply, for instance, plays a role in developing countries today which it has lost in Europe since the early nineteenth century. Another example is the problem of housing supply which varied greatly in different phases of industrialization and population growth, and following war destruction. It seems reasonable to assume that with economic growth and increasing social security, the aspect of having becomes *relatively* less important and aspects of being and loving *relatively* more important. With regard to these aspects of welfare or life chances, however, the modern bureaucratic welfare state rapidly approaches its inherent limits. As different aspects of life chances may gain or lose in significance, the boundaries of the welfare state can also shift, but its historical core - the system of income mainte- nance and the public provision of certain services, especially in health and education- is very unlikely to change substantially.

The nationalization of industry or other sectors of the economy has not become a constitutive element of the liberal welfare state [11], which derives its basic character pre- cisely through its close relationships with the capitalist market economy and mass democracy. The liberal welfare state is based on the economic surplus produced in the market economy, and its structure must be adapted to the basic laws governing this economic system. At the same time it is also based on the political consensus pro- duced in the democratic mass polity, and its structure must reflect the basic nature of this consensus. Principle limits to the development of the welfare state lie only where it would begin to undermine these foundations. Thusfar, such *principal* tendencies have not become evident, despite predictions to the contrary [12]. The liberal welfare state has remained an essential element in the reconciliation of capitalism and de- mocracy.

As a basic type, the liberal welfare state can also be found outside of Europe, but the Western European welfare states have developed in addition some specific characteris- tics. These originate from the early state formation and from the weight of the indus- trial working class, reflected above all in the salience of bureaucratic organization *and* social rights. However, one must not exaggerate the common origins and characteris- tics and thereby overlook the obvious differences among the West European welfare states which are related, among others, to differences in the processes of state and class formation across Europe.

2. Early sources of diversity

If one tries to map major variations among the European welfare states and search for the origins of this diversity, Stein Rokkan's work on a macro-model of European political development is the most obvious starting point. No one else among social scientists has contributed more to our understanding of the systematic and enduring character of the structural and cultural variations across Europe [13].

Rokkan made a distinction between four basic processes of development which to some extent formed distinct time phases:

(1) *state formation*: the process of political, economic, and cultural unification at the elite level, and the establishment of institutions for the mobilization of resources, external defence, and internal order;

(2) *nation-building*: the process of bringing larger population groups into the system by means of conscript armies, compulsory education and mass media, strengthening the contacts between the population and the central elite;

(3) *participation*: the process of a growing active participation of the subject masses in the working of the territorial system, the establishment of political citizenship, the evolution of mass democracy;

(4) *redistribution*: the process of growth in public welfare services and social security systems for the equalization of economic conditions, the establishment of social rights, the evolution of welfare states.

Rokkan was mainly interested in explaining the differences between the European mass democracies and did not aim at studying the variations among the European welfare states. Nevertheless, he can teach us several lessons:

(1) To an important extent institutional variations among the European welfare states should be understood as offsprings of other - often much older - structural differences: above all the varying experiences and results of the early state formation and nation-building processes, which usually preceded the emergence of modern welfare institutions, but also the differences in the later evolution of mass democracies.

(2) Equally important, the diversity among the welfare states may be understood as a result of the different 'timing' in the creation of major institutions, 'time' defined not in chronological but in developmental terms. This is true above all with respect to the process of industrialization, where different levels were usually related to different problem pressures and varying constellations of collective actors.

(3) Many of the major institutional variations date back to early phases in the development of the European welfare states, often to the period prior to World War I. Once crucial decisions were taken, it became difficult to reverse them, and this often happened only under exceptional circumstances, e.g. in times of war and economic crisis.

For a long time the European welfare states have demonstrated an almost irresistible growth tendency, but this has not reduced their institutional variations. To some extent the persistence of diversity may simply be explained by the stability of other underlying differences such as more centralist or federalist political institutions or varying party systems. It is also explained by the fact that welfare institutions usually create new - often powerful - vested interests and reinforce underlying values.

When one speaks of a persistence of diversity, which diversity do we mean among the myriad of variations? Obviously, one has to look for basic principles persisting amidst institutional change. Furthermore, one should try to find those structural variations which may be relevant for the future institutional adaptation of the European welfare states to new challenges which will be discussed further below. I believe that at least two basic dimensions of the institutional infrastructure will be relevant:

(1) the degree to which the (central) state has 'penetrated' the welfare institutions, i.e. the *stateness* of the welfare state which defines the *Spielraum* (room for manoeuvre) for intermediary structures;
(2) the degree to which the welfare institutions reflect social differentiations, i.e. the *fragmentation* of the welfare state which defines the potential of conflict and change.

'Stateness' as defined by J.P. Nettl [14] means the degree to which the instruments of government are differentiated from other organizations, centralized, autonomous, and formally coordinated with each other. State penetration in this sense corresponds negatively with the *Spielraum* offered for the development of the various non-state 'intermediary structures' ranging from e.g. highly organized churches to loosely knit social networks. If one foresees a future trend towards a greater variety of more flexible institutions of a mixed private-public character, then the existing differences in the intermediary structures may be decisive. These differences reflect variations in state penetration with roots reaching far back into history.

A first and major root can be found in the diverse relationships between Church and State since the Reformation. The Church of Rome had traditionally assumed responsibility for the care of the poor and sick and for education. With the onset of the Reformation, divergent patterns evolved across Europe. The break with the Roman Church brought about a certain fusion of secular and religious powers in the Northern states, particularly in the Lutheran monarchies. The property of the Church and the religious orders was confiscated and the clergy was incorporated into the bureaucracy of the territorial state. Thus, a concept of public welfare provisions was able to develop relatively early in the North, at least partially legitimized by the Protestant Churches. The same may be assumed for the development of a concept of corresponding citizens' obligations towards the state, probably still an important factor in mobilizing the necessary resources without excessive state pressure.

In the Catholic South, the Church instead maintained separate welfare organizations (schools, hospitals, etc.) well into the twentieth century, thus impeding the development of a national welfare state, of an idea of legitimate public welfare provisions and corresponding citizens' obligations. Important for the socialization and social control of the population, these Catholic institutions were contested by secularizing nation-builders, but with quite varying success. Often they became subsidized by the state with little public control. If their autonomy survived the first stages of democratization, the welfare institutions became easily exploited by political parties seeking to secure the loyalty of their clienteles. A syndrome of political clientelism emerged as a result of the division of Church and State.

There is of course no clear dichotomy betwen Catholic and Protestant countries with respect to the 'stateness' of the welfare state. There are early variations among the Catholic countries with respect to the 'nationalization' of welfare institutions (schools in particular); there are differences with respect to the pro- or anti-state attitudes among the Protestant churches and sects, and finally there is the special category of the religiously mixed countries where the competition between the denominations seems to have promoted the development of welfare institutions, at the same time preventing their transformation into public institutions. The most interesting case is certainly the Netherlands where denominational welfare institutions became an essential element in state subsidized cultural segmentation - the famous *verzuiling*.

The varying state-church relationships had different effects in the various policy fields. They were perhaps most important in education where the Catholic Church has succeeded to this day (at least in some countries) to control a relevant part of the school system, especially in secondary education [15]. In general the Catholic Church continued to stress the principle of *Subsidiarität* which implies that smaller groups and voluntary organizations should be given priority over the state wherever possible. Thus, it is not surprising that in most Catholic countries the development of public poor relief was delayed much longer than in other countries [16]. On the other hand, the early attempts to develop a family income policy were mainly limited to the Catholic countries [17]. Only in the area of hospital health care are the differences somewhat less clear-cut, as throughout Europe the state (mainly the local communities) assumed responsibility for the poor sick very early on [18].

In addition to the state-church relationships, the characteristics of the state formation process *stricto sensu* are relevant in explaining the varying 'stateness' of welfare institutions. This refers primarily to two dimensions: the establishment of a more centralized or decentralized political structure, and the survival or destruction of civil liberties and representative institutions during the absolutist period which created different opportunities for the development of more decentralized and associative forms of welfare organizations.

With respect to the first dimension, the two cases where city-confederations developed into federal political systems, Switzerland and the Netherlands, are the most interesting, also for an analysis of possible future developments. In both countries, the 'stateness' of the welfare institutions has been rather low, but this long-standing structural similarity was related to very different growth patterns in the postwar period. In Switzerland, political decentralization, the referendum, local citizen participation, associative self-help, and finally the pervasive impact of the military reserve system culminated in a structure which slowed the development of the national welfare state to an extraordinary degree.

A comparison with the Netherlands is instructive. In no other West European country has the welfare state expanded to such an extent after World War II. An explanation for this striking difference appears to lie in the forms of funding and control of services in both countries. Financing and control at local and associative levels appears to result in a much slower and better balanced expansion than in the case of control by organizations which do not raise their own funding. This may be especially true when they are in competition with each other and use the institutions for clientelistic purposes.

The early formation of decentralized political structures may largely explain a relatively low level of 'welfare stateness' which offered opportunities for the development of 'intermediary structures' in the organization of welfare. Equally important for such opportunities was probably the extent to which civil liberties survived the age of absolutist state formation and were strengthened in the nineteenth century. These differences defined the *Spielraum* for the unfolding of organized bourgeois philanthropy as well as working class self-help which varied greatly across Europe [19]. Mutual benefit societies and other forms of voluntary organization assumed a prominent role in the late nineteenth century, especially in sickness and unemployment insurance, and thereby influenced the structure and extension of the later developing public institutions, in some cases to this day.

Different preconditions and experiences in the processes of state formation and nation-building explain many of the fundamental and long-lasting variations in the structure of 'social services' (education, health, poor relief) at the time of the 'take-off' of the modern welfare state and thereafter. They tell us much less, however, about the variations in the structure of 'social transfers', the social insurance or income maintenance system.

Social insurance schemes differ of course in manifold ways, but there is one dimension mentioned above which may be crucial in the mastering of current and future problems: the type and degree of institutional fragmentation along lines of social differentiation. Two questions may be distinguished in this context: (1) the extent to which claims for social transfers are based on citizen rights as opposed to employment and contribution records, and (2) the degree to which schemes are differentiated among occupational groups and social classes.

Most of the fundamental decisions on this subject were taken relatively early, many prior to the First World War. Today, a distinction is usually drawn between the Scandinavian-British welfare state with its relatively strong elements of social citizenship and relatively uniform and integrated institutions, and the continental welfare state with its much more fragmented institutions and smaller citizenship component. However, this is only a first and very crude distinction, the actual variations being more complex.

For an insight into the origins of these persistent differences, one must leave behind the framework of Rokkan's political development theory and turn to an analysis of the variations in class structure in the Western European countries. Three elements should be emphasized here: the homogeneity or heterogeneity of the blue-collar workers in manufacturing, their ties to the farmers, and their relationship to the white-collar employees.

Throughout Western Europe, as stated above, the modern welfare state originated as an answer to specific problems of the new industrial working class. The more homogeneous this class, i.e. the weaker the craft or anarchic-syndicalist traditions and the more influential big industry and centralized the trade union movement, the greater -ceteris paribus - were the chances for the development of a uniform system of income maintenance, at least for the industrial workers.

Bismarck cannot be credited with the invention of such a system, but he was the first to implement it. For long the dominant model, the German system was entirely centred around the industrial worker. No one considered including the farmers or agricultural workers. After the turn of the century a separate insurance was created for white-collar employees which effectively blocked the way to a uniform national system. This remains the case up to the present.

The opposite was the case in Scandinavia, where the introduction of a uniform and egalitarian national system can be traced to a class compromise between the industrial workers and the small farmers. It appears that these two groups were less remote from each other than on the continent and that they drew closer together through their fight for the extension of voting rights. Thus, the element of class compromise in the development of the Scandinavian type of welfare state is evident from the first Swedish pension system in 1913 to the Finnish sickness insurance scheme of 1964.

This proves how productive it could be to examine the implications of different agrarian structures for the development of welfare states, as Barrington Moore has done for the more general process of political modernization [20]. It also shows that the time point at which systems were introduced, the 'developmental time', is relevant in explaining characteristics of these systems. In comparison to most other European countries, in Scandinavia the percentage of the labour force working in the agricultural sector was relatively high when the first social insurance schemes were established. Around 1910, it varied from 39 percent in Norway to 43 percent in Denmark and 46 percent in Sweden, whereas only around 25 percent of the labour force in these three countries was employed in industry. Given an agricultural structure dominated by small farmers, this sectoral distribution required and facilitated a class compromise in the creation of welfare schemes.

Moving to the other major example of a uniform and egalitarian system of income maintenance - to Beveridge England, the argument of 'time' reappears at a different stage of development. Usually, the groundbreaking reforms during World War II and immediately thereafter have been explained by a combination of factors: the war situation and national consensus building, the antiquated structure of British welfare institutions, and not least the influence of Lord Beveridge. However, it must also be taken into consideration that at that time already around 90 percent of the labour force were dependent blue-collar workers or white-collar employees with much less institutionalized status distinctions than in Germany, offering a social basis for the creation of a uniform national system.

Institutional unification or fragmentation and 'stateness' have been defined here as the two major dimensions of variation among the Western European welfare states. How are these related to a typology of the welfare state? Most typologies start with the distinction made by Richard M. Titmus between three 'models of social policy' [21]:

(A)   the *residual welfare model* in which social welfare institutions come into play only after the breakdown of the private market and the family as the 'natural' channels for the fulfilment of social needs;

(B)   the *industrial achievement-performance model* in which social welfare institutions are adjuncts of the economy, and social needs are met on the basis of merit, work performance and productivity;

(C)   the *institutional redistributive model* in which social welfare institutions are an integral part of society, providing universalist services outside the market on the principle of need.

These may be understood as normative models or Weberian ideal types, but they have been frequently used as empirical classifications and even interpreted in a developmental perspective. In this second use, the typology poses at least two problems, even if one accepts that any typology neglects many of the variations across welfare programmes within a country and thus greatly reduces the complexity of national cases.

The first problem is that 'stateness' (underlying the distinction of model A versus B and C) and 'institutional fragmentation' (differentiating models B and C) are not conceived as two clearly independent dimensions of variation. Thus, we can find relatively unified but limited welfare states on the one side and highly developed but fragmented welfare states on the other, with strongly differing developmental problems and opportunities.

The second problem is that the 'residual' model or more general low 'stateness' is defined only in terms of a priority given to the family and the market, largely neglecting the variety of intermediary structures with important welfare functions, i.e. of non-public or semi-public subsidized forms of charity, cultural segmentation or self-organization. Variations in these structures persist to the present and will also play a definite role in shaping future developments.

3. Growth to limits

The modern European welfare states thus started out from very different preconditions and with a greatly varying institutional heritage. Yet most of them originated in the same period prior to World War I, and all of them demonstrated a similar growth momentum. The initial variations did not really subside in the general process of growth, but rather, old differences were transformed into new ones. If we neglect the variations for a moment and take social insurance as the major new institution, we can then characterize the (in a literal empirical sense) average European development from the turn of the century to the mid-1970s as having very modest beginnings, surprisingly continuous expansion, and extraordinary acceleration in the last 15 years [22].

The beginnings of the welfare state were limited indeed. Around the turn of the century, 12 countries had accident insurance covering an average of 20 percent of the employed population; 7 had a sickness insurance covering an average of 17 percent of the employed; a compulsory insurance for old age and invalidity existed only in Germany; 4 other countries had more limited systems; and none of the West European countries had unemployment insurance.

Since then the expansion has been surprisingly continuous with respect to the coverage of risks as well as to the inclusion of population groups. Neither the world wars nor the economic crisis of the 1930s stood in the way of this process. In the early 1930s, about half of the labour force on average was protected by accident, sickness, invalidity and old age insurances, but still not more than 20 percent by unemployment insurance; of course, this says little about the extent of protection. By the mid-1970s over 90 percent of the labour force was covered against income loss due to old age, invalidity, and sickness; over 80 percent was covered in case of accident, and 60 percent for unemployment [23].

Generally speaking, one can assume that the extension of social insurance schemes throughout Europe was connected with an absolute and relative growth of expenditure, even though detailed and comparative figures are largely lacking for the interwar period. Around 1930 average expenditure on social insurance amounted to probably less than 3 percent of GDP. By 1950 it had increased to 5 percent, by 1960 to 7 percent and by 1974 to 13 percent. If one takes the broader concept of social security expenditure (including all income maintenance programmes and public health), the relative growth becomes even more marked and one can see a clear acceleration of growth. At the same time, a persistence of different expenditure levels due to continuing institutional variations is evident. In 1950 social security expenditure in Western Europe averaged 9.3 percent of GNP, ranging from 5.9 percent in Switzerland to 14.8 percent in West Germany; in 1965 the average was 13.4 percent, from 8.8 percent in Switzerland to 17.6 percent in Austria, and by 1974 the average had risen to 19.2 percent, ranging from 13.9 percent in Switzerland to 24.8 percent in the Netherlands.

Measured in terms of percentage points, the average growth accelerated from 0.9 in 1950-55 and 1.4 in 1955-60 to over 1.8 in 1960-65 and 2.4 in 1965-70 to 3.4 in 1970-74. Most of the relative growth and its acceleration was due to the increased spending on pensions and health, which raised their respective shares in total social security spending from approximately one fourth in 1954 to around one third in 1974 (while spending on family transfers was halved in the same period from around 12 to 6 percent).

Finally, if one takes an all-embracive concept of social expenditure (including spending on education and housing), the growth of the welfare state is most obvious and impressive. Whereas in the early 1950s the share of social expenditure varied between more than 10 and less than 20 percent of GNP, it had grown by the mid-1970s to between one fourth and one third of GNP, and in some countries to considerably more than one third. This growth of social expenditure explains almost completely the increase of the 'state share' (measured by total public expenditure as a percentage of the national product). This share had started to increase in the late nineteenth century after a long period of stagnation. The increase was most pronounced during the First World War (to a lesser extent, during the Second World War), producing the so-called 'displacement effect' [24]. In 1950 the average share in Western Europe was around 25 percent and by the mid-1970s it had almost doubled to more than 45 percent.

As a result of the first and second oil crises and their consequences for continuing high levels of unemployment and public deficits, and enduring distortions of the world economy, the situation has changed substantially. At least one thing seems clear: the late 1970s witnessed the end of the 'golden age' of the European welfare state. But beyond this statement, the diagnosis of what happened and what will follow is much less clear.

Most probably the tremendous growth of the welfare state from the early 1950s to the mid-1970s cannot be repeated in the future; indeed this may not even be necessary. Has the 'golden age' come to an end because external conditions underlying the past growth have changed so dramatically, and/or because more inherent growth impulses have become exhausted? But has growth really ceased at all - can one even speak of a 'dismantling' or 'regression' of the European welfare state? Even if the objective is only a stabilization of the welfare state at present levels, will this be possible without far-reaching institutional changes? Questions on top of questions which are not easily answered.

Before one tries to explain changes in the long-term development of the European welfare states, one should first attempt to assess their concrete form. Although systematic data for more recent years are not yet available, the country studies contain some basic information on expenditure trends and institutional changes since the mid-1970s. The picture they offer is somewhat bewildering. The strong growth trend of the past is broken, but at the same time growth continues, and the differences across countries have widened. This makes a general assessment more difficult.

One should first distinguish between expenditure growth in absolute terms (total social expenditure at constant prices) and relative terms (expenditure as a percentage of GDP). In some countries the social expenditure ratio stagnated from the late 1970s to the early 1980s; in some it declined; in many it rose further (in some cases even rapidly), and all this in the face of persistent high levels of public deficit in most European countries. If one considers instead social expenditure in absolute real terms, an impression of slow but uninterrupted growth results. The same observation can be made with respect to average benefits (at constant prices) which in general have further increased, major exceptions being family allowances (mainly due to a lack of indexation), and unemployment benefits (mainly due to a longer duration and changing structure of unemployment).

From this one could conclude that forces exist, which will also be at work in the future, for a further expansion of the welfare state, especially when the currently unfavourable conditions once again improve. In this view only severe economic and political crises would be capable of halting a further expansion. I do not share this view. Rather I believe that as welfare states mature there will be a 'natural' tendency in their expansion to slow down or stagnate without such crises - similar to the slowdown of population growth in the course of the demographic transition and to the deceleration of the sectoral change of employment from an industrial towards a service society. Considering the long distance the welfare state has come, its major advances are most certainly behind it. The spread of social security schemes throughout the entire population, the significant absolute and relative increases of the major social transfer payments, the enormous expansion in the areas of health and education services - all this makes the growth rates of the past seem unnecessary.

However, this is a more evolutionary view which may contribute to our understanding of the long-term development of the welfare state *in nuce*, but less to an explanation of the concrete developments in the last decade or to reasonable guesses about changes in the near future. For this purpose one has to combine the evolutionary view with an analysis of the historical constellaton of forces which have supported the postwar growth of the welfare states, and which may have dissolved in the 1970s. This constellation consisted of a comparatively stable international system, a high level of internal consensus and institutional stability, and a historically unique economic growth.

As a by-product of the American leadership and as a result of the relatively peaceful conditions, defence expenditure as a proportion of GNP declined almost everywhere in Europe since the Korean War. This has precluded major conflicts over trade-offs between defence and social expenditure. A further decline, however, cannot be expected, given the increased tensions and arms race between the super powers and the pressures within NATO to redistribute defence expenditure towards Europe. If one includes the international transfers to developing countries under a broader category of security expenditure, it seems very likely that from this side the conditions for the future development of the welfare state will be less favourable than in the past.

The second crucial element in the favourable constellation was the outstanding internal political stability since World War II, which has successfully passed the test of the economic crisis from the mid-1970s. Despite everything said to the contrary, the overall legitimacy of the fundamental democratic institutions is not threatened: voting turn-outs do not signalize any large-scale alienation from the political process; the party systems on average demonstrate a mixture of stability and adaptability, and anxieties about a trend towards instable coalition cabinets or minority governments have not been confirmed.

To some extent, the relatively high level of political consensus may be seen as a precondition for as well as a result of the expansion of the welfare state. In his comparative study of the historical evolution of social security systems in Europe, Jens Alber has shown that up to 1900 these systems first developed in the more authoritarian states; from the turn of the century to World War I, the parliamentary democracies with liberal governments took the lead, and in the interwar period, the extension of these systems seems to have been linked to an increasing strength of socialist political forces. After 1945, however, these differences became blurred and the building of welfare institutions was carried forward by all relevant political forces [25].

Social policy is of course not an area without conflicts. We find cases of severe political confrontations well before the 1970s, but on the whole there was a broad political consensus. In the early 1970s, however, to the surprise of many observers, tax protest flared up in some countries, most prominently in Denmark. Social scientists [26] started to speak of a 'welfare backlash', although it was primarily a protest against taxation and bureaucracy and much less against social benefits and public services.

As a phenomenon of a certain period, leaving aside the important variations across countries, the protest may be understood as a result of the most rapid increase of the tax ratio in modern European history, with World War I as the only exception. As an indicator of the most 'visible taxes', the average ratio of income taxes and social security contributions to GNP almost doubled in Europe between 1960 and 1975, from 15 to more than 27 percent [27]. But tax protest in its manifest form has proved to be an ephemeral phenomenon. It has largely disappeared or perhaps has been replaced by other forms such as tax evasion and a black labour market.

With growing difficulties in the financing of welfare programmes since the mid-1970s, distributional conflicts have increased, but nothing similar to a 'cleavage' of larger population groups pro- and anti-welfare state has appeared. Survey results across Europe cited in our country studies - incomplete as they may be - create the image of a still vast and often overwhelming support for the welfare state, even if this support has somewhat declined over the years. This may be explained by the fundamental changes in the social structure and the electorate which will be discussed in the following section.

There seems to be a certain change in the political climate since the 1970s: a neo-liberal economic philosophy, a conservative interpretation of the state's role, and an anti-modernist critique of large-scale institutions have gained some ground. However, the articulated enemies of the modern welfare state have remained in the minority, with a chance of taking over government responsibility only under very specific conditions of the electoral system and party constellation.

The third and perhaps most important element of the favourable historical constellation was the unprecedented economic growth of the postwar period. The years from the Korean War to the first oil shock were, according to Angus Maddison, the 'golden age' of capitalism, characterized by rapid *and* stable growth [28]. The absolute growth of the national product formed the basis for the *relative* growth of the welfare state. Whereas on average the European economies grew between 1950 and 1980 by about 4 percent, the average growth rate of social expenditure was around 6.5 percent. However, the relationships between economic growth and social expenditure growth changed over time. If one classifies the years as to whether economic and/or social expenditure growth rates lay below or above the average of the entire period, a relatively uniform picture emerges, despite all cross-national variations shown in the country studies.

Whereas in the 1950s social expenditure growth was consistently below average even in years with very strong economic growth, the decade from the early 1960s to the early 1970s is seen as the high season of the postwar welfare state with real growth rates of the economy as well as of social expenditure far above the average. In these 10 to 12 years the European welfare states took on their modern shape. The two years following the first oil shock, 1974 and 1975, were then characterized by a combination of very high social expenditure growth rates and very low or even negative economic growth rates, indicating that the European governments were not able or not willing to respond immediately to the economic crisis by reducing social expenditure. Only afterwards did social expenditure growth rates start to fall, sinking below the level of the 1950s. Thus the changing relationship between economic growth and social expenditure growth formed a kind of 'postwar spiral'.

4. System disintegration without class conflict

The crisis of the world economy of the 1970s had two obvious consequences for the welfare states: it reduced revenues and increased expenditure, creating a structural deficit of the public households. These deficits accumulated to large public debts as most governments only started to respond to the financial problems after the second oil shock in the late 1970s. However, the current difficulties of the welfare states cannot be explained as a simple result of the economic crisis only. Rather they should be understood as the product of a historical coincidence of this economic crisis with the preceding extraordinary expansion of the public sector and with a demographic wave originating from the relatively high European birth rates between the late 1950s and mid-1960s.

Yielded by the demographic wave and pushed by the European revolution in higher education and an increasing female mobilization from the 1960s, more young people, highly educated people, and highly motivated women started to enter the labour market. This happened under increasing unemployment, in a situation in which European industry lost many jobs and in which the public deficits prevented a further extension of public employment. Thus in contrast to the 1930s, the situation today is characterized by above average unemployment rates of younger people and women.

This may explain why solutions are frequently sought in a greater flexibility of working and family life, and in an extension of the service sector.

On the one hand, the rationalization effects of an intensified international competition in the industrial sector and the stagnation of the public sector with lower turn over rates as a result of its previous rapid expansion do not allow much optimism for the immediate future. On the other hand, however, assuming a continuation of present economic growth and a further success in the consolidation of the public households, the strong decline in birth rates since the mid-1960s will ease the current problems considerably in the medium future. This will also be necessary because the welfare states must then be free for the solution of a future problem which is the opposite side of the declining birth rates: the pension systems.

It is not unlikely that by the early 1990s the European welfare states will have overcome the specific problems created by a historical coincidence of unfavourable developments. However, I believe that the troubles of the past ten years have also brought to the surface some more basic challenges which will require long and complex processes of institutional adaptation - which have already started. I would like to point to three challenges:

(1) the ageing of the population and the necessity of a new contract between the generations;
(2) the changing sexual division of labour and the necessity of a new contract between the sexes;
(3) the change of values and the necessity of a new contract between the state and the citizens.

Today European populations have entered the last phase of their 'demographic transition' which started in the nineteenth century. Essentially, this long-term process has represented a transition from limited population growth at high birth and death rates to low or zero population growth at low birth and death rates, after a longer period of accelerated population growth resulting from an interval in the decline of the death and birth rates. In principle a uniform process, this transition was superimposed in Europe by erratic demographic movements as a consequence of war losses and several violent oscillations of birth rates, both of which have distorted the age structure of most European populations.

As is well known, the slowdown of population growth leads to an ageing of the population, i.e. to an increasing share of older people as a result of declining birth rates and a still increasing life expectancy. This may not only imply a loss of adaptive capacity as social change is largely achieved through a succession of generations; it may also mean that the older generation continues to gain political weight and that the age dimension becomes more pronounced in distributional conflicts. This is most obvious with respect to the pension systems on a pay-as-you-go basis which represent the most notable redistributive machineries of modern societies.

There can be no doubt that with a significant increase in the share of old people a new contractual basis must be found for the pension systems; and it must be found before the ageing process gains more momentum, making solutions politically ever more difficult. Solutions will certainly be sought in a mixture of increases in contributions, cuts in benefits, and a raising of pensionable age; they may also be sought in a strengthening of the basic universal element of the pension systems while at the same time allowing for a greater variety with respect to other - public, occupational or private - elements. Finally, solutions may lie in a greater flexibility of work and retirement at a time when fewer young people will enter the labour market.

It will be even more important, however, to redefine the basis of the contract between the generations. In legal terms, it is only a contract between two generations, the employed who pay contributions and the retired who draw pensions. In reality the contract is based on the relationships between three generations, i.e. it includes the young people who are not yet employed but will be held responsible for paying the pensions in the future, without adequately institutionalizing these relationships. Given the altered demographic parameters, we are thus facing an institutional maladjustment with considerable explosive force, in which the changing relationships between the generations is interwoven with a change in the relationships between the sexes. The nodal point lies in the structural underevaluation of that part of necessary work which is not involved in market exchange and therefore is usually done without independent income and adequate social rights.

Child-raising is an essential part of necessary but undervalued work in our society. Not surprisingly, therefore, the striving of women for equality and independence has become a striving to leave the home. At the same time, the demographic development has increased the possibilities of non-domestic activities for women. There are fewer children today, and the phase in the family cycle dominated by child dependency has become much shorter. This 'demographic release' of women was related with a long-term equalization of education opportunities between the sexes throughout Western Europe, although with a conservation of the century-old gradiant from the Protestant North to the Catholic South.

Following an equalization of opportunities in education, female employment ratios have also started to increase slowly but steadily. This long-term trend was not even interrupted by the economic crisis of the mid-1970s, despite the fact that in most countries women were more affected by unemployment than men. Most significant perhaps in this general development is the tendency of younger women to return to their jobs after childbirth. This fundamental and irreversible change in the sexual division of labour requires an adaptation of many institutions, of marriage and family above all, but also of the institutions of the welfare state.

A first and obvious aspect of this process of adjustment is a further strengthening of independent and equal social rights for women, in particular with respect to old age pensions. The welfare state was originally built around the figure of the male provider of the family. Social rights of other family members were usually introduced much later and were derived from the provider's status and work. A greater equalization may be sought through an equalization of employment opportunities, but also by assigning rights to the work of child-rearing, or more generally, extending the universal elements of social rights.

Family policy, on the other hand, must be more than a policy for the equalization of opportunities and rights between men and women. An equalization of *individual* rights may even contradict the objective of making living conditions and social security of *families* more equal. From two-earner couples without children to one-parent families, there is today an increasing variety of family structures which will require a re-definition of many welfare institutions.

In order to combine a policy of sex equality and a policy of family stabilization with the objective of a more balanced population development, even more far-reaching institutional changes will be necessary. This refers above all to a more flexible co-ordination of work and family life, but also to a more flexible timing of the major life cycle phases: education, employment, and retirement. In its development, the welfare state has adapted itself to the strong tendencies of differentiation and standardization inherent in the evolution of industrial societies, and has further strengthened these tendencies. With the transition from industrial to service society it appears possible to rediscover, in different form, some of the flexibility found in pre-industrial societies with respect to the linkage of life domains and life phases. But this would also imply a fundamental reform of the welfare institutions.

Such a reform seems to be called for also by the changes in basic values which social scientists believe to have observed since the late 1960s and early 1970s, and which they relate above all to the growth of prosperity, the expansion of higher education and the extension of the service sector, but also to the long period of peace in Western Europe as well as to specific consequences of the economic crisis of the 1970s [29]. Despite all healthy scepticism of survey-based observations, the very fact of a change of values, in particular among younger people, seems to be undeniable. One finds a certain 'neo-liberal' renaissance in the sense of a greater emphasis on self-determination, self-responsibility and freedom of choice, but at the same time a desire for more solidarity in everyday life and a more direct participation in public affairs.

The direction of these value changes runs counter to some of the fundamental characteristics of the modern welfare state, namely its bureaucratization, 'monetarization', and professionalization [30]. In principle these developments are irreversible, but to some extent the welfare state institutions can and must be adapted to the changing values to avoid a loss of legitimacy. This may imply a new 'contract' between the state and the citizens, according to which the citizen would no longer be reduced to a tax and contribution payer (and a recruit), but would also offer some services, in fields and forms of a mixed private-public character.

Thus, the ageing of the population, the changing division of labour between the sexes, and value changes challenge the adaptive capacity of welfare state institutions. Solutions will have to be sought in a greater flexibility of family and working life, and a more varied mix of public, semi-public, and private organizations. More individual responsibility and mobility will be necessary, but this will require at the same time a strengthening of the universal elements of the welfare state, of a basic social security.

It has been a classic idea in sociology (maintained by Marx in particular) to relate problems of 'system integration' and 'social integration' [31], i.e. to search for cases of increasing maladjustment of institutions which produces social conflicts with a tendency towards a polarization of major population groups. It is my contention that the present situation is indeed characterized by serious problems of institutional adjustment, but *without* the emergence of relevant political cleavages. This judgement may be supported by the survey data included in the country chapters, but it is primarily derived from simple observations of changes in the employment structure and the growth of welfare clienteles.

A first simple fact is that strong legions have grown up around the welfare state, even if they have not yet become organized. This is especially true for two population groups: the recipients of transfer incomes, particularly pensioners, and those who provide social services in the widest sense. If we consider these two groups in relation to the electorate, the share of the pensioners grew on average from 10 percent in 1950 to 25 percent in 1980, while the number of those employed by the welfare state often increased to 10 percent or more. To illustrate this general observation with an extreme example: in Sweden, more than half of the electorate today draws a transfer income or an earned income from the welfare state.

Another simple fact is that the employment structure has thoroughly changed from 1950 to 1980. Whereas in 1950 on average two-thirds of the labour force in Western

Europe were either blue-collar workers or white-collar employees, this share had grown to more than four-fifths, and in some countries more than 90 percent, thirty years later. The expansion of enfranchised 'welfare clienteles' thus coincides with the structural elimination of the 'natural enemies' of the welfare state, namely the mass of self-employed in agriculture, trade and crafts.

A structural basis for a 'pro- or anti-welfare state cleavage' seems to be lacking therefore, although the necessity to stabilize and reorganize the welfare state will certainly result in a variety of distributional conflicts. The risk of institutional immobility appears much greater than the danger of large-scale polarization.

Very probably, the direction and extent of institutional reforms will strongly depend on the stance taken by the new middle classes. Their position is characterized by a combination of dependent employment status *and* relatively extended individual resources. They stand between collective interest organizations and state regulation on the one side, individual mobility and freedom of choice on the other. Institutional reforms combining a strengthening of basic rights with a greater flexibility may well find their political support, but the more concrete steps will depend on the very different ways in which the middle classes articulate and aggregate their heterogeneous and ambivalent interests. The direction and extent of institutional reforms will furthermore depend on the structure of the institutions themselves which may create very different obstacles or opportunities for reforms. It is therefore important to carefully examine the institutional variations, on the basis of the analyses given in the twelve country chapters.

5. The structure of the country chapters

Each of the twelve country chapters is divided into five sections. The various analyses usually refer to the years 1950-1980. This period was selected mainly for practical reasons as data are often incomplete for the years immediately following World War II as well as for more recent years. The reforms carried out in many countries in the second half of the 1940s serve as a point of departure for analyses and are not treated as a subject in themselves.

The whole study is, however, embedded in a somewhat longer time period. The first of the five sections (I. Historical Synopsis) begins with an overview of the historical development of each national welfare state from the turn of the century, and the last section (V. Present Problems and Policy Choices) concludes with an analysis of the most recent changes from the second half of the 1970s to the first half of the 1980s. The three remaining sections tend to have a descriptive (II. Resources and Clienteles), evaluative (III. Achievements and Shortcomings), and explanatory (IV. Correlates and Causes) character.

In principle the definition of the welfare state is understood in relatively broad terms, despite the fact that the social security system is the focus of the major part of our analyses. This is especially true for Sections II and IV, while in Section III the various social services are more specifically addressed.

Section I

By way of introduction, the first section provides an overview of the long-term development of the welfare state of each country. The specific national characteristics of the welfare state and its historical background are explored in this section, and a brief survey of the central institutional changes and fundamental development trends after 1945 is given.

Section II

The second more descriptive section is only modestly exciting, but nevertheless fundamental. It attempts to trace growth and structural change through two central aspects: the public household and the population groups affected by the various programmes. Emphasis is placed on a description of the quantitative changes, but an attempt is also made to relate these to institutional changes. In order to facilitate the reading of this data-ridden section, a graphic representation was decided upon (the sources for the data contained in the graphs, as well as in the tables appearing in the texts, are listed at the end of each country chapter; the figures for the graphs can be found in Volume IV). An attempt was usually made to characterize developments in terms of both absolute data and percent distributions.

The major part of Section II is devoted to the development of public expenditure. (For the treatment of the problems of deflating time series on public expenditure, the Appendix Volume IV should be consulted). The description of public expenditure development begins with a brief analysis of the share of total public expenditure in the national product and a breakdown of the total public expenditure by major purpose, economic category and level of government. Then social expenditure is analysed according to its major categories: usually income maintenance, education, health, and housing.

A detailed study of individual programmes follows, supplementing the examination of the aggregates and major expenditure categories. It begins with a description of the qualitative and institutional development of the various income maintenance programmes and concludes with a brief account of developments in public education, health, and housing.

The relatively extensive investigation of the development of public expenditure is accompanied by a brief overview of the development of public revenues: first, the development of total revenues and public deficits, then the major sources of public revenues, and finally, the financing of individual programmes through the state, employees, and employers.

The second central aspect of the expansion of the welfare state examined in Section II refers to these population groups affected by the programmes. The term 'clienteles' was chosen for these groups, despite its somewhat negative connotation deriving from the concept of 'clientelism'. In our context it is thought of as a purely neutral term. It refers to the fact that the welfare of ever-increasing population groups has become the result of political rather than market mechanisms.

The expansion of these clienteles has been reconstructed for the different income maintenance programmes in five-year intervals in absolute numbers, as well as in relation to the relevant population groups (e.g. the population over 60 years or children at a certain age). In order to compare the relative weight of the diverse clienteles across countries, the development of their respective shares of the total population has been graphically represented.

The political significance of clienteles is certainly not only a function of their number, but also of the relative weight of the respective social transfers, i.e. their importance in relation to earned income. Section II therefore concludes with a specification of the various social transfers according to three types of indicators: (a) legally fixed earnings-replacement ratios, (b) standard benefits at current and constant prices, and (c) average benefits, which have simply been calculated by dividing total expenditure by the number of beneficiaries; they are presented at constant prices and as a percentage of average income (which, however, is defined differently from country to country).

Such systematic information has never before been available for any of the twelve countries under investigation and is an essential precondition for an empirically based analysis of the development of the welfare state. Nevertheless, it is still far from the theoretically desirable. What we would need for a more detailed understanding of the interest structure of the national welfare states is a type of 'interest matrix' in which we could enter, for the most important social categories, the respective costs and benefits of the various programmes and their change over time.

Section III

Whereas the description of the development of welfare state resources and clienteles in Section II refers mainly to *aggregates* and averages, the more evaluative analysis of Section III is also based on statistics on the *distribution* of social transfers and services. This section contains numerous additional tables which have not been included in the Appendix Volume. Because of their much greater complexity, these tables refer to much shorter time periods, or merely single points in time.

Of course, in order to evaluate achievements and shortcomings, one needs criteria. Do such general criteria actually exist? Certainly they do not exist in the sense of general values, i.e. values shared by all, which could be used to evaluate welfare state developments. In this section it is not possible to assess 'welfare' in any fundamental sense, or to discuss its complex relationships to other basic values. The section also does not deal with the complicated question of whether certain services could not be better supplied by non-state institutions such as private enterprises or the family. Finally, it does not deal with an evaluation of unintended consequences such as the effects of welfare state programmes on the functioning of the market economy or the growth of public bureaucracy.

The goal is much more modest. It lies in the assessment of long-term developments according to criteria which are 'inherent' to the welfare state. The two criteria applied here are the 'adequacy' of the social transfers and services and their impact on the distribution of the life chances of the population.

With respect to the transfer payments, the adequacy is defined in terms of 'income replacement'. The question is to what extent these payments adequately replace income from work. In studying this question, a considerable problem results from the fact that alternative income sources (e.g. from private or occupational pensions) are normally insufficiently recorded. In reference to social services, the 'adequacy' is measured primarily through the level and development of the average provision of services for the population. Here the major assessment problem, especially at higher developmental levels, involves the question of to what extent an improved provision, (e.g. of hospitals) results in greater 'welfare' (in this case: health).

A change in the inequality of life chances is the second central criteria for the evaluation of welfare state development. Without doubt one of the most frequently put questions in the literature is to what extent the welfare state balances out the inequalities created by the market and the family. Yet our knowledge in this area is still insufficient today, and varies greatly from country to country. In all the chapters a distinction is made between problems of poverty in a narrow sense and inequality in a broader sense. The analysis of poverty has to overcome considerable data problems, as well as conceptual difficulties resulting from the varying concepts of relative poverty. In the analysis of inequality, the data problems increase as one progresses from the inequality of primary incomes to the incidence of taxes, social transfers and social services.

Section IV

Section IV attempts to provide explanations for certain aspects of the development of welfare states. These developments are of course very complex phenomena, and 'causality' is a difficult concept in the social sciences. Our goal has therefore been relatively limited. Various methods are applied to examine certain demographic, economic, and political factors and correlates in welfare state development. The influence of the demographic and economic factors is examined using strictly quantitative methods, the demographic factors with the 'component method', and the economic factors with the help of a regression and correlation analysis. In contrast, the analysis of the political factors and correlates is based mainly on qualitative interpretations and illustrative data. Two types of 'dependent variables' were utilized as *explanandum*: social expenditure items and institutional changes of the welfare programmes.

The various welfare programmes have a varying impact in the different phases of the individual and family life cycle. This means that demographic changes, especially changes in the size of families and the age structure, have direct effects on the size of clienteles, and thus on the development of social expenditure. In a series of studies in the 1970s, the OECD utilized a so-called component method to measure the weight of demographic factors in the development of various social expenditure items [32]. We have adopted this method in order to be able to compare our results with those of the OECD studies which comprise a greater number of countries, but are based on more limited data for a shorter time period.

The component method may be applied whenever a social expenditure aggregate can be defined as the product of various multiplicands or components. It may be utilized for decomposing the level or change of expenditure in absolute terms (i.e. in money terms at current or constant prices) or in relative terms (i.e. as a share of GDP or more general of available resources). Here the method has been used mainly for analysing *changes in expenditure ratios*.

For a study of the impact of demographic changes on social expenditure one of the components must of course be a demographic parameter in the stricter sense (e.g. a parameter of the age structure). The respective expenditure aggregate (e.g. pension expenditure) is then usually analysed in terms of three components: demographic structures, beneficiaries in a given 'target' group, and average payments per beneficiary. For an analysis of expenditure ratios, these components must also be expressed as ratios:

(a) a *demographic ratio*, i.e. the 'relevant' population (e.g. people aged 65 and over) as a percentage of total population;

(b) an *eligibility ratio*, i.e. the beneficiaries (i.e. old age pensioners) as a percentage of the 'relevant' population;

c) a *transfer ratio*, i.e. the payments per beneficiary (e.g. total pension expenditure divided by the number of pensioners) as a percentage of 'average income' (calculated as GDP per head).

The component method makes it possible to find out how much a change in one component (or a combination of changes in two or more components, the so-called interaction effect) has contributed to an increase (or decrease) of social expenditure. This means that one can decompose, for a given period, the relative weight of demographic changes, the extension or restriction of welfare programmes, and the improvements or curtailment of benefits, for the expenditure development.

The enormous expansion of the welfare state after the Second World War would obviously not have been possible without the historically unparalled economic growth of this period. What results, however, when one investigates the short-term correlations instead of those of the entire time span? To arrive at an answer to this question, an analysis of the correlation between the annual real growth rates of the national product as the independent variable and various social expenditure items was carried out. Relatively low correlation coefficients were the usual outcome, indicating the possibility of varying period-specific relationships. This possibility was investigated in a graphic regression analysis of the relationships between the annual economic growth and the annual growth of total social expenditure. The resulting country-specific periodizations were then interpreted in relation to political developments.

The inquiry into the political factors and correlates is more complex than the demographic and economic developments and utilizes more qualitative and illustrative methods. An attempt is made not only to trace the influence of political changes as reflected in party platforms, election results, parliamentary strength of parties, or the party composition of the government, but also the influence of certain interest groups or even the Catholic Church on the institutional development of the welfare state.

Because of the complexity of the subject and the differing availability of data, this part of Section IV shows the greatest variations between the country chapters. The relationship between the party composition of government and the development of social expenditure is investigated in almost all of the chapters, and in many, institutional changes are incorporated in this analysis (based on a listing and brief description of 'core laws' governing the various welfare programmes since 1945 provided in the Appendix Volume). Furthermore, for some countries the development of party platforms and/or of parliamentary voting on social welfare legislation are studied. In the case of Italy, a very extensive roll-call analysis of pension legislation after 1945 is attached as a special appendix to the country chapter. Finally, some of the country chapters also include case studies on crucial reforms, in which the specific national context of the welfare state development and its place in the political process and system are examined.

Section V

The focus of our project lay in the long-term development of the European welfare states and not on their most recent changes. It was to be expected, however, that the problems faced by the welfare states since the second half of the 1970s would be of particular interest to the reader. A systematic treatment of recent changes was difficult due to the often insufficient data and the gradual step-by-step production of the chapters which would have made a later updating of the whole text very difficult. For this reason a concluding section on the developments and problems of the welfare states from the end of the 1970s into the early 1980s was added to the three central sections.

The basic issue of this section is whether the economic and political framework of the European welfare states has fundamentally changed since the late 1970s. To go into greater detail, the following questions were posed:

(a) In which way and to what extent have the European governments responded to the problems of growing public deficits by cutting social benefits and through other institutional adjustments?

(b) What are the scenarios for the future development of social expenditure under varying economic and demographic assumptions, on the basis of the existing institutions or with certain institutional changes?

(c) Has public opinion changed with respect to the legitimacy of the welfare state in general and the structure and functioning of single welfare programmes in particular? And based on these data, can one discover certain latent conflicts between social groups or even some polarization?

(d) What are the options regarding the future development of the welfare state currently under public debate or under discussion among the political parties?

On the basis of this information and the preceding analyses, the country chapters conclude with a cautious and necessarily speculative look into the future.

Notes

[1] Cf., also in the following, Peter Flora, Franz Kraus and Winfried Pfenning, *State, Economy and Society in Western Europe 1815-1975*, Vol. II: The Growth of Industrial *Societies and Capitalist Economies*. Frankfurt, Campus; London, Macmillan, 1986.

[2] Cf. Charles Tilly (ed.), *The Formation of National States in Western Europe*. Princeton, Princeton University Press, 1975; esp. chapters 1 and 9.

[3] Cf. e.g. Peter Laslett and Richard A. Wall (eds), *Household and Family in the Past*. New York, Cambridge University Press, 1972.

[4] This argument was developed by Hartmut Kaelble, 'Was Prometheus most unbound in Europe?'. *Journal of European Economic History*, 14, 1985.

[5] Cf. Arnold J. Heidenheimer, 'Education and social security entitlements in Europe and America', pp. 269-304 in: Peter Flora and Arnold J. Heidenheimer (eds), *The Development of Welfare States in Europe and America*. New Brunswick and London, Transaction Books, 1981.

[6] The first and most famous exponent of this view was T.H. Marshall, *Class, Citizenship, and Social Development*. New York, Doubleday, 1964.

[7] Cf. Max Weber, *Wirtschaft und Gesellschaft*. 5th ed., Tübingen, Mohr, 1976.

[8] This concept was developed by Anthony Giddens, *The Class Structure of the Advanced Societies*. London, Hutchinson, 1973.

[9] This is the argument of Rainer M. Lepsius who introduced the concept of *Versorgungs-klassen*, in the sense of welfare clienteles. Cf. his 'Soziale Ungleichheit und Klassenstrukturen in der Bundesrepublik Deutschland', pp. 166-209 in: Hans-Ulrich Wehler (ed.), *Klassen in der europäischen Geschichte*. Göttingen, Vandenhoeck and Ruprecht, 1979.

[10] Cf. Erik Allardt, About Dimensions of Welfare. An Exploratory Analysis of a Comparative Scandinavian Survey. Research Group for Comparative Sociology, University of Helsinki. Research Report No. I, 1973.

[11] There are no systematic relationships between the expansion of the welfare state and the extent of nationalization, as shown by Anthony King, 'Ideas, institutions and the policies of governments: a comparative analysis'. *British Journal of Political Science* 3, pp. 291-313 and 409-423.

[12] Cf. e.g. John O'Connor, *The Fiscal Crisis of the State*. New York, 1973, and Ian Gough, *The Political Economy of the Welfare State*. London, St. Martins Press, 1979.

[13] For a synthesis see Peter Flora, 'Stein Rokkans MakroModell der politischen Entwicklung Europas: Ein Rekonstruktionsversuch'. *Kölner Zeitschrift für Soziologie und Sozialpsychologie* 33, 3, pp. 397-436.

[14] Cf. J. Peter Nettl, 'The state as a conceptual variable'. *World Politics*, 20, 1968, pp. 559-592.

[15] Cf. Margaret S. Archer, *The Social Origins of Educational Systems*. London, Sage, 1979.

[16] See the article 'Armenwesen', pp. 1-169 in *Handwörterbuch der Staatswissenschaften*, 3rd ed. 1909.

[17] Cf. Sheila B. Kamerman and Alfred J. Kahn (eds), *Family Policy*. New York, Columbia University Press, 1978.

[18] See Brian Abel-Smith, 'The history of medical care', pp. 219-240 in: E.W. Martin (ed.), *Comparative —Development in Social Welfare*. London, Allen and Unwin, 1972.

[19] Not only the absolutist break with old liberties was important, however, but also the 'liberal break' with old forms of social protection under the impact of capitalist industrialization. Cf. Gaston V. Rimplinger, *Welfare Policy and Industrialization in Europe, America and Russia*. New York, John Wiley, 1971. Cf. also Reinhard Bendix, *Nation-Building and Citizenship*. New York, John Wiley, 1964, pp. 80ff., who points to the important variations in the continuance of traditional organizations of crafts into the modern period.

[20] Barrington Moore, *Social Origins of Dictatorship and Democracy*. Boston, Beacon Press, 1964.

[21] Cf. Richard M. Titmus, *Social Policy*. London, Allen and Unwin, 1974; for earlier formulations see his *Essays on the Welfare State*. London, Allen and Unwin, 1958, and Commitment to *Welfare*. London, Allen and Unwin, 1968. For a discussion of his typology cf. above all R. Pinker, *Social Theory and Social Policy*. London, Heinemann, 1971 and R. Mishra, *Society and Social Policy. Theoretical Perspectives on Welfare*. London, Macmillan, 1977. Ugo Ascoli has invented the more appropriate term 'meritocratic-particularistic' for Titmus' 'industrial achievement-performance model'; cf. Ugo Ascoli (ed.), *Welfare State all'Italiana*. Roma-Bari, Laterza, 1984.

[22] Cf. in the following the data on the evolution of social insurance collected by Jens Alber in Peter Flora et al., *State, Economy and Society in Western Europe 1815-1975*, Vol. I: *The Growth of Mass Democracies and Welfare States* Frankfurt, Campus; London, Macmillan, 1983. For data on the social expenditure development, see the country chapters and the Appendix Volume.

[23] In judging these percentages, one should take into account that the labour force data also include the self-employed and family workers.

[24] This concept was developed by Alon T. Peacock and Jack Wiseman, *The Growth of Public Expenditure in the United Kingdom*. Princeton, Princeton University Press, 1961.

[25] Jens Alber, *Vom Armenhaus zum Wohlfahrtsstaat*. Frankfurt, Campus, 1982.

[26] Cf. e.g. Harold L. Wilensky, *The Welfare State and Equality*. Berkeley, University of California Press, 1975 and *The 'New Corporatism', Centralization, and the Welfare State*. London, Sage Publications, 1976.

[27] Cf. Peter Flora, 'Solution or source of crises? The welfare state in historical perspective', pp. 343-389 in: W.J. Mommsen (ed.), *The Emergence of the Welfare State in Britain and Germany*. London, Croom Helm, 1981.

[28] Angus Maddison, *Phases of Capitalist Development*. Oxford University Press, 1982.

[29] As an introduction to the vast literature on value change, see e.g. Helmut Klages and Peter Kmieciak (eds), *Wertwandel und gesellschaftlicher Wandel*, Frankfurt and New York, Campus, 1979.

[30] Cf. Christian von Ferber, *Sozialpolitik in der Wohlstandsgesellschaft*, Hamburg, Zeitverlag, 1967.

31 Cf. David Lockwood, 'Social integration and system integration', pp. 244-257 in: George K. Zollschan and Walter Hirsch (eds), *Explorations in Social Change*. London 1964.

32 Cf. above all the OECD studies *Public Expenditure on Income Maintenance Programmes*. Paris 1976, and Public Expenditure *Trends*. Paris 1977. The component method has also been applied to an analysis of education and health expenditure; cf. the studies *Public Expenditure on Education*. Paris 1976, and *Public Expenditure on Health*. Paris 1977.

Germany

JENS ALBER

Contents

I Historical synopsis

1. The German approach to the welfare state

In terms of expenditure on social programmes, Germany certainly qualifies as a modern welfare state. As a political concept, however, the term 'welfare state' usually has negative connotations in Germany denoting excessive state intervention, and the term 'social policy' is considered preferable. In the German tradition the core of social policy is defined in a limited way by 'social insurance plus labour legislation'. This definition pervades most of the standard literature on social policy which usually excludes education and says little about health and housing. It is also reflected in the governmental division of labour which limits the competence of the Ministry of Labour and Social Affairs to the social transfer schemes and to labour law.

On the programmatic level, the term 'social market economy' is frequently used in place of 'welfare state'. In this sense, the role of the state is to supplement the market as the best mechanism for the allocation of productive resources by social benefits, compensating for market failures in the distribution of incomes. The intervention, however, should be limited and not interfere too much with the incentive structure of the free market economy. This limited definition of state activity originated in the political philosophy of neo-liberalism and the social ethics of Catholicism, but should also be understood as a reaction to the bureaucratic state control experienced in the Nazi period and the presence of Communist collectivism in East Germany. Since the late 1950s even the Social Democrats (*Sozialdemokratische Partei Deutschlands*, SPD) have been moving, albeit reluctantly, towards acceptance of the social market economy model in an attempt to widen their electoral support.

Given the lack of political support for the construction of a broadly defined welfare state, German social programmes have developed within a relatively stable institutional framework. There are four main features of German social policy.

The fragmentation of programmes

Social programmes are fragmented into a large number of uncoordinated and decentralized schemes. At the national level, income maintenance, health, housing and education are dealt with by four different Ministries: Labour and Social Affairs; Youth, Family and Health; Building, Regional Planning and Urban Development; and Education. The administration and supply of services is further decentralized in a large number of autonomous carrier organizations: for different types of benefit (e.g. various social insurance programmes); for different beneficiary groups (e.g. workers, the self-employed, etc.); and for different regions or districts (in the case of education, social assistance).

The emphasis on cash benefits

Most benefits are income maintenance cash payments, which leave consumption decisions to the beneficiary and stress the importance of the private provision of services. With the exception of education, the state provision of services is of limited importance. Outside hospitals, which may be public or private, medical goods and services are mainly provided by private suppliers (the pharmaceutical industry, private doctors and dentists, etc.). In the housing sector, state support is limited to subsidizing the supply of private housing, the provision of housing allowances for low-income families, rent regulation, and tenant protection.

The reliance on social insurance

Individuals are not normally entitled to income maintenance benefits in their capacity as citizens, but as members of social insurance programmes who have a certain contribution record. Benefits are usually earnings-related and seek to maintain the standard of living attained by the recipient during his working life. Income maintenance programmes are financed by the insured and their employers, with only a small amount of state financing.

The importance of labour legislation

All social programmes must be seen in the context of labour legislation which establishes a high degree of regulation regarding working conditions, dismissals and co-determination at the plant level. This aspect will not be dealt with further here.

2. Social protection in defence of traditional authority: the origins of the welfare state in Imperial Germany

The present structure of German welfare state institutions is not the result of a unified plan for social reorganization, but the product of long-term historical developments. The industrial revolution, which arrived relatively late in Germany, transformed society rapidly. The number of industrial workers more than doubled to 2 million in the period 1850-1867, and had risen to 6 million by 1895 [1]. This growth was accompanied by a significant increase in the organizational capacity of workers. In 1863 Ferdinand Lassalle founded the first German Labour party. In 1875 the party merged with the SPD, founded in 1869 by Bebel and Liebknecht. During the second half of the 1860s, the first trade unions were organized, and the 'social question' (*Soziale Frage* became a crucial political issue.

The Prussian state had for a long time relied on repression as the only way of reacting to the mobilization of workers. The Industrial Codes of 1845 and 1869 limited the freedom of association, and workmen's organizations were repeatedly disbanded. Nevertheless, the SPD continued to grow in parliamentary strength. Although universal male suffrage had been introduced from the outset of German unification, the government sought to combat the electoral success of the SPD with anti-socialist legislation that banned the political organization of workers and which remained in effect from 1878 until 1890 [2].

After Bismarck had opted for an interventionist economic policy with high protective tariffs for industry and agriculture, thus considerably increasing the cost of living for the working class, he realized that repression alone was not sufficient to prevent the political mobilization of the workers. With the establishment of public social insurance programmes he hoped to create a tight bond between the state and workers and to split the opposition of the SPD and the Liberals in the Reichstag who were pressing for the realization of parliamentary government.

Education never entered into Bismarck's plans for social reform. The principle of compulsory education was introduced in Prussia as early as 1717, and had become effective in all Prussian territory by 1825. The Prussian state had gained effective control of the education system by 1872 after fierce battles with the Catholic Church. The democratization of (primary) education had thus already been achieved before the political mobilization of workers began to gain momentum: nearly all workers' children attended public primary school in the last quarter of the nineteenth century, and Germany had the highest educational enrolment figures in Europe [3]. This fact may help to explain why education is not usually considered an element of German social policy.

Bismarck's social insurance bills were only passed after heated debate and several modifications. When the compulsory insurance schemes against sickness (1883), industrial accidents (1884), and invalidity or old age (1889) were finally adopted, they were the outcome of a series of compromises rather than the result of a consistent reform plan. The consideration of a broad spectrum of interests may be one of the reasons why the German social insurance schemes displayed such remarkable institutional longevity. These three programmes embodied the basic principles of present day social insurance provision: that insurance is made compulsory by law, but administered by a plurality of autonomous bodies with representatives of employers and the insured; that entitlement to benefits is based on past contributions rather than on need; that benefits and contributions are earnings-related; and that financing should, on aggregate, be tri-partite (the insured, the employer, and the state).

The successful functioning of the new social protection schemes for workers soon generated feelings of relative deprivation among other social categories. In 1901, salaried employees established an association and demanded that social insurance coverage be extended to salary earners. Pressure from the association eventually led to an important reform of the social insurance system. In 1911 the three compulsory insurance laws were consolidated in a single uniform National Insurance Code (*Reichsversicherungsordnung*). The Code included the introduction of survivors' pensions for widows and orphans [4]. In the same year, another law established a pension insurance scheme for salaried employees. Although heavily amended, the 1911 legislation is still in force today.

The provisions for salaried employees were in many respects more generous than those for workers. Employees were entitled to: an invalidity pension in cases where their earning capacity had been reduced by half (two-thirds for workers); an old age pension from the age of 65 (70 for workers); and an unconditional survivors' pension for widows of the insured (for workers, only where the widow was disabled). Employees' coverage for sickness was also preferential. The 1891 Industrial Code and the 1897 Commercial Code established full wage continuation for employees in the case of sickness lasting for a period of six weeks. Workers, instead, were only entitled to sickness insurance benefit which covered 50 percent of earnings up to a certain maximum. By institutionalizing the differentiation between workers and employees, the establishment of special social rights for salaried employees became an important element in the fragmentation of the German working class.

Apart from the revision of 1911, a second modification was the reform of sickness insurance. The Sickness Insurance Law did not regulate the relationship between insurance funds and doctors - an area which became extremely prone to conflict. In 1892 the funds won the right to determine which doctors were to be licensed with the insurance system, and to draw up individual contracts with them. The doctors, in turn, pressed for unlimited access to licenses and the collective negotiation of contracts in order to strengthen their position vis-a-vis the funds. In 1900 they formed a central association (*Hartmannbund*) in order to pursue these aims. After a series of strikes they succeeded in reaching a national agreement with the insurance funds in 1913 which introduced a system of collective bargaining. Doctors became recognized as the contracting partners of the insurance funds, the number of licences issued was regulated on the basis of the number of insured persons per district, and doctors' fees became subject to collective bargaining between the funds and doctors' associations. Although repeatedly modified, this system is still effective today.

Bismarck did not succeed in his objective of undermining the political mobilization of workers by the introduction of social reforms. The SPD voted against the social insurance bills, and by 1912 it had become the strongest faction in the *Reichstag* Nevertheless, the new social protection schemes, although not halting the growth of the SPD, effectively strengthened its revisionist wing. The administrative bodies of the social insurance schemes gave party members access to power positions and gave workers the opportunity for upward mobility to white-collar status. When an amendment to the Invalidity Insurance Law was discussed in 1899, the SPD began to vote in favour of the insurance bills. Later, at the 1902 Munich Congress, it even endorsed a public unemployment insurance scheme which was still regarded with suspicion by the unions [5]. The fact that social insurance and public education were well developed long before a Labour Party participated in government may be considered one of the reasons why the development of the German welfare state differs from that of, for example, the Scandinavian countries.

In addition to social insurance, the German *Reich* had a fairly developed public assistance scheme. In 1870, the earlier Prussian laws were transformed into a consolidated Public Assistance Law which was extended to (almost) all regions of the *Reich* after the unification. The federal structure of the Empire and the limited share of revenues accorded to the central government, however, set tight limits to the development of further initiatives in social policy. The supervision of health conditions lay within the competence of the single states. An Imperial Health Office (*Kaiserliches Gesundheitsamt*) established in 1876 only operated in an advisory capacity.

Despite very severe housing problems - especially in the rapidly growing cities - the state remained remarkably inactive in the field of housing legislation. Until World War I all initiatives to subject the housing market to a certain degree of state regulation failed. Central government activities remained limited to the granting of modest public loans to building societies, paid for the first time in 1901.

In the field of education a series of national school conferences in 1873, 1890 and 1900 sought to standardize the federally fragmented school system. The rigid differentiation between primary and secondary schooling was confirmed. Although the depression of 1873 led to a slowdown of expansion in the post-primary sectors, Germany maintained its position as one of the leaders in public education until World War I [6].

By 1913, educational expenditure (1,265 million RM) still accounted for the bulk (46 percent) of social expenditure. Outlays for social insurance and social assistance together amounted to 1,181 million RM (43 percent). Public expenditure on health (272 million RM), and housing (31 million RM) remained modest. Total social expenditure (2,749 million RM) corresponded to 37 percent of all public expenditure or scarcely 5 percent of GDP (see Graph 1).

World War I stimulated state intervention in previously neglected areas. Immediately after the onset of hostilities a federal decree introduced measures to protect tenants and control the housing market which were subsequently tightened during the war. A law of 1918 empowered the central government to subsidize the supply of housing. The state also took first steps to develop a labour market policy. In 1914 a central labour exchange was established in the Ministry of the Interior, and parts of the state's war loans were used to finance assistance payments for the unemployed. Social insurance benefits were also extended. Thus in 1916 the age limit for the receipt of old age pensions under the workers' insurance scheme was fixed at its present (regular) level of 65 years, bringing it into line with the employees' scheme.

Shortly before the end of the war in 1918, collective bargaining was recognized. In the same year a special Ministry of Labour was established. Headed by a former trade union leader, it assumed the responsibility for social policy formerly held by a department of the Ministry of the Interior. This symbolized a change in the role of social policy, from being an instrument of social order to one of social change.

3. Social policy and the democratic class struggle: the Weimar Republic

The collapse of the monarchy in November 1918 was not accompanied by a basic change in societal power structures. The change in political regime was the result of a series of compromises between old and new elites rather than of a victorious revolutionary upheaval. As plans for the nationalization of key industries were soon abandoned, social reforms to calm public unrest became necessary. Important reforms of labour relations had already been realized as part of the transition from a war to a peace economy immediately after the establishment of the Republic. Decrees of 1918 established the eight-hour working day, set up a public labour exchange, recognized collective bargaining for determining wages and working conditions, and issued rules for the formation of arbitration committees.

Labour legislation of 1923 empowered the state to declare the results of collective bargaining legally binding and to settle unresolved labour conflicts by means of obligatory arbitration. The system of local labour offices, factory inspection and arbitration committees set up under the Ministry of Labour was completed in 1926 by the introduction of special labour courts, thus creating a differentiated machinery of state intervention in labour conflict [7]. The heavy involvement of the state in labour conflicts led to an enhanced politicization of the collective bargaining process, as the conflicting parties now increasingly sought to gain control over the Ministry of Labour.

In the context of fierce domestic conflicts during the postwar economic crisis of 1919-1923, the government - led by centre-left coalitions throughout most of this period - felt constrained to implement social reforms despite a lack of resources. In the field of labour legislation, a law of 1920 consolidated the wartime provisions on workers' co-determination by making the establishment of workers' councils obligatory in all firms with more than 20 employees. In the same year another law established a nationwide corporatist Economic Council with advisory functions in economic and social matters.

Other important innovations were made in the fields of housing and education. A federal school law of 1920 abolished private primary schools preparing for entry to the *Gymnasium* and introduced a four-year comprehensive system of primary schooling for all pupils. This law led to a considerable increase in *Gymnasium* attendance [8]. In the housing sector, a law of 1920 subjected the housing market to administrative controls. Other laws to regulate rents and to strengthen tenant protection were passed in 1922 and 1923. A 1921 law introduced a special tax (subsequently extended in 1924) for the financing of the public promotion of housing construction.

The most important income maintenance reforms included the introduction of war victims' benefits (1920), which temporarily accounted for a third of the central government's budget; and the transformation of the emergency postwar unemployment relief system into a regular assistance programme, financed by employees' and employers' contributions (1923). The 1913 agreement between doctors and the insurance funds was incorporated into the National Insurance Code in 1923. The 1922 Youth Welfare Act established the basis for the present programmes for young people.

With the stabilization of the currency in late 1923, a period of economic recovery began which lasted until 1928. In the context of economic growth and a strengthened position of the unions, the social legislation of the new centre-right governments concentrated on the development of the income maintenance schemes, whilst considerably reducing the control of the housing market. A law of 1924 set up a modern public assistance scheme which replaced the old poor relief legislation of 1870, strengthening the legal position of recipients. The scope of the social insurance system was broadened through extensions to additional occupational groups and repeated increases of the income limits for compulsory coverage. The most important reform, however, was the introduction of a compulsory unemployment insurance scheme in 1927.

In late 1928 a period of economic downswing began, and the new unemployment insurance ran into financial difficulties. Its deficits had to be covered by the central government, which had itself faced deficits for several years. This generated a fierce debate in the newly formed centre-left government as to the appropriate strategy of financial consolidation. As the level of unemployment benefits sets limits to potential wage reductions, the controversy became linked to fundamental distributional conflicts. The SPD, backed by the unions, supported an increase in contribution rates, whereas the other coalition parties, supported by the employers' associations, favoured a reduction in benefits. The cabinet subsequently voted in favour of the latter, and the SPD withdrew from government. This opened the way to the replacement of parliamentary decision making by a system of presidential emergency decrees.

The new governments - first headed by Brüning - tried to balance the budget through a deflationary policy. A series of emergency decrees in 1930, 1931, and 1932 cut the public housing construction programme and drastically reduced practically all income

Graph 1

The long – term growth of total public and social expenditure
as a % of GDP

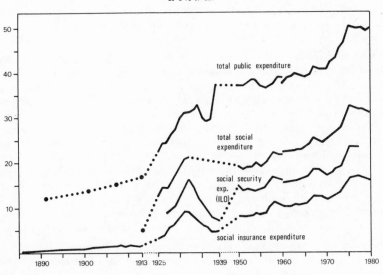

maintenance benefits. In the unemployment insurance scheme, the level of benefits was halved between 1930 and 1932, and entitlement was considerably restricted. In 1933 only 10 percent of the unemployed were in receipt of insurance benefits, and another 28 percent were in receipt of unemployment assistance payments [9].

On aggregate, social expenditure fell from 15.8 billion RM in 1930 to 12.0 billion in 1932. Social insurance expenditure (including unemployment insurance) was reduced from 10.5 to 8.5 billion RM [10]. However, as GDP shrank even faster than social expenditure, the social expenditure ratio rose, reaching an unprecedented level in 1932 (see Graph 1).

In the context of high unemployment, curtailed transfer payments and parliamentary stalemate, the National Socialist opposition increased its share of the vote in the national elections from 2.6 percent in 1928 to 37 percent in 1932. Together with the Communists it now held a majority of the seats in the *Reichstag*. Despite a setback of four percentage points at the second 1932 elections, the National Socialists came to power in 1933, and the Weimar Republic collapsed a few weeks later.

4. Social policy as an instrument of totalitarian control: the National Socialist regime

Once in power the National Socialists transformed German society rapidly. By mid-1933 all rival political parties had been dissolved. The unions were destroyed and collective bargaining was replaced by a tight bureaucratic control of the labour market. In comparison with other institutions, the body of social programmes remained remarkably intact. The fragmented structure of the social insurance system resisted all unifying and centralizing tendencies of the new regime, but its administration and functions underwent significant changes.

A law of 1934 abolished the autonomous self-administration of social insurance by employees and employers. Each social insurance fund became headed by a 'leader' chosen by the new state authorities. The high contribution rates and reduced benefit levels fixed during the depression were preserved even when economic recovery increased the funds' resources. The funds were compelled to invest a sizeable part of their surplus in government loans. In the Nazi war economy, social insurance contributions were used as an additional source of government revenues and as a means to reduce the purchasing power of the masses. The social expenditure ratio fell far below the levels of the Weimar period (see Graph 1).

The Nazi period, however, was not merely one of welfare state dismantling. The scope of social insurance was repeatedly widened. When the intensive production of heavy armaments led to a labour shortage in the late 1930s, thus strengthening the bargaining position of the working class, the regime made some improvements in social benefit levels [11]. In 1937 the option of voluntary membership of the pension insurance scheme was introduced [12]. In 1938 compulsory insurance was extended to artisans as the first major category of self-employed persons to be so covered. Pensioners were included in sickness insurance coverage in 1941. In 1942 industrial accident insurance was extended to all wage-earners regardless of occupation. Benefit levels were improved when the restrictions imposed during the economic depression were lifted, and by the extension of entitlements. Among the most important innovations were the extension of the period of sick care (unlimited duration), and the introduction of a maternity allowance for a period of six weeks before and after the birth (1942).

From the outset, the regime paid special attention to family policy. In 1933 loans to newly-wed couples were introduced with the idea of reducing female employment. A social insurance reform which increased benefits and contributions and made some tax reform of 1934 provided sizeable tax credits for large families. A year later an extraordinary benefit was introduced, being payable to families with more than four children. In 1936 this was transformed into a regular child allowance for the fifth child and any further children. Payment of this allowance presupposed 'faithful service to the German people', and similar mechanisms for social control were incorporated into legislation on youth welfare. A law of 1938 regulating the conditions of child employment made the minimum length of holidays dependent upon membership of, and participation in, the *Hitlerjugend* [13].

Reorganization of the social assistance system was also used to cultivate loyalty to the party. The autonomous public assistance organizations were dissolved, and the system was centralized under the leadership of a National Socialist organization established in 1933 (*Nationalsozialistische Volkswohlfahrt* NSV). Administrative guidelines specified that the function of assistance was to promote collective rather than individual well-being and to educate recipients in National Socialist thinking.

In the health sector, a law of 1934 established health offices, still in existence today, to supervise medical standards throughout the country. In the sectors of housing and education, the state remained deliberately inactive. As all available resources were channelled into the war effort, public investment on housing was significantly reduced. Contrary to political promises, annual housing construction fell to below the levels reached in the Weimar period [14].

Educational expenditure was reduced in real and even nominal terms [15]. In the period 1930-1939, the number of university students fell by more than half [16]. Enrolment ratios fell below the Weimar levels and also dropped to beneath the West European average [17]. Once a 'leader' in education, Germany was now becoming a 'laggard'. The 'educational catastrophe' discovered in the mid-1960s thus originated in the Nazi period.

Although the regime subjected the education system to strict central control and established standardized curricula, the structure of the school system remained remarkably stable. Apart from the establishment of some new types of secondary schools, the rigid differentiation between primary and secondary education was maintained. The number of private schools was drastically cut, however, and religious schools were almost completely replaced by non-denominational schools [18].

After the defeat of the Nazi regime, the financial resources of the social insurance system were depleted, the universities were drained, and health and housing conditions were disastrous. Many able social administrators were either dead or had emigrated [19].

5. Security and opportunity in the social market economy: the Federal Republic

After the defeat of the Hitler regime most of the existing social programmes remained intact. Only child allowances and some other special schemes established under Nazi rule were discontinued. In 1946, however, the Allied Control Commission drafted a plan for the establishment of a unified national insurance scheme based on the Beveridge model. The project immediately met with strong opposition from German interest groups, including the trade unions. With the onset of the 'Cold War' the Western allies lost interest in its implementation.

In the Western zones the allied authorities began to shift legislative functions to German parliamentary bodies which were then being built up. In late 1948 the newly established assembly (*Wirtschaftsrat*) in the Anglo-American zone passed a law on

Table 1   Major institutional changes in the German welfare state, 1949-1980

Pensions

1957   Indexation of pensions; compulsory insurance for independent farmers
1967   Abolition of income-limit for compulsory coverage
1972   Introduction of flexible age limit and other extensions of entitlements
1977   Modification of pension formula

Sickness insurance and health

1955   Regulation of relationship between doctors and insurance funds
1957   Reform of sickness insurance with partial wage-continuation for workers
1969   Full wage continuation for workers; constitutional reform strengthening the role of the federal
        government in the health sector
1970   Indexation of income-limit for compulsory coverage; introduction of preventive medical check-ups
1972   Compulsory sickness insurance for independent farmers; regulation of hospital financing with
        participation of federal government
1977   Introduction of corporatist "concerted action" to contain cost explosion in the health sector

Occupational injuries insurance

1963   Reform of occupational injuries insurance with indexation of benefits

Unemployment insurance

1956   Reform of unemployment insurance with sizeable benefit increases
1969   Major re-organization of unemployment insurance introducing instruments for an active labour
        market policy

Families and children

1954   Introduction of employer financed child allowances
1961   Youth Welfare Act
1964   Re-organization of child allowances shifting financing to federal government
1974   Introduction of universal child allowance scheme

Social assistance

1961   Major re-organization of social assistance replacing legislation of 1924
1969   Reform of social assistance extending entitlements

War consequences

1950   New benefit scheme for war victims
1952   Fund for equalization of burdens for refugees

Housing

1950   Federal subsidies for housing production; promotion of social housing
1960   De-regulation of housing market
1965   Introduction of housing allowances
1971   Legislation on tenant protection

Education

1964   Agreement among the single states to standardize the school system; compulsory education extended
        to 9 years
1969   Constitutional reform empowering federal government to legislate on education; introduction of
        education allowances
1976   First nationwide legislation on universities

structural changes to the existing schemes. The 1949 Constitution deliberately did not contain any commitment to a specific economic and social order. The result of the first national elections clearly indicated, however, that the majority of voters did not favour a socialist planning of the economy. The Communists and SPD together captured only 36.5 percent of the seats. The coalition government, formed by Christian Democrats (*Christlich Demokratische Union, Christlich Soziale Union*, CDU/CSU), FDP (*Freie Demokratische Partei*), and a conservative splinter party, opted for a liberal economic policy. Only the housing market remained subject to state controls.

The first social policy initiatives dealt mainly with a programme of subsidized housing construction, and with measures for the integration and compensation of war victims and refugees. A series of laws restored the social insurance principles of the Weimar Republic. The traditional self-administration by employers and employees was re-introduced [20]. Union and SPD plans for the establishment of a unified national insurance scheme were crushed when the first elections to the new administrative boards were overwhelmingly won by those advocating the differentiation of workers' and employees' schemes [21].

The subsequent re-establishment of a special pension insurance scheme for employees signalled the persistence of the fragmented structure of German social insurance. Two 1955 laws confirmed the traditional structure of the health system with its dominance of private suppliers, collective bargaining between doctors and insurance funds, and the limited supervisory role of the public health services. Educational matters remained the sole competence of the single states.

At the beginning of the second legislature, Chancellor Adenauer announced his intention to introduce a fundamental social reform which would restructure the highly complex welfare system. A group of experts drafted a reform plan (*Rothenfels Denkschrift*) and several academics, committees, interest groups, and parties produced a mass of elaborate proposals. In this connection a General Secretariat of Social Reform was set up within the Ministry of Labour in 1955.

In practice, few of these ambitious reform plans were implemented. This was mainly due to the deep cleavage within the CDU, between the Social Christian Workers' wing and that of the neo-liberal employers. In the cabinet this cleavage took the form of a split between the Ministry of Labour and that of Finance, with the latter advocating a highly selective social policy based on means tests. Under these circumstances, and after Adenauer had sided with the workers' wing, the idea of a complete remodelling of the welfare state gave way to the gradual extension of single programmes. Adenauer not only needed the electoral support of the growing number of pensioners, but also wished to link the extension of political rights to broader political considerations. The rebuilding of the German army needed to be balanced by improvements in social policy in order to overcome opposition from the SPD and the unions to rearmament [22].

With the sails thus set for a course of expansion, a new child allowance scheme was introduced in 1954. Subsidies to private builders were increased, with priority being given to the construction of family housing. Unemployment benefits were improved. The extension of benefits culminated in a thorough reform of pension insurance in 1957. This reform increased benefits, equalized entitlements for workers and employees, and introduced a pension scheme for farmers. Following a political strike by the unions, another law of the same year introduced partial wage continuation in the case of sickness, thus narrowing the gap between workers' and employees' entitlements.

During the third and fourth legislatures (1957-1965), reforms of social assistance (1961), child allowances (1961, 1964), and occupational injuries insurance (1963) considerably broadened the scope of individual entitlements. The deregulation of the housing market in 1960 was followed by the introduction of housing allowances for low-income families. Union demands for a further equalization of workers' and employees' sickness benefit entitlements led to an extension of workers' wage continuation in 1961. More fundamental plans to restructure sickness insurance and to introduce private cost-sharing were abandoned after a decade of contention with the unions and doctors' associations.

The mid-1960s marked the end of the expansion phase and the beginning of a period of transition. This change was linked to important political and economic changes. The rate of economic growth had declined considerably during the 1960s. The coalition government of Christian Democrats and FDP headed by Erhard, sought to develop mechanisms for increased social and economic planning. A standing committee of economic advisors (*Sachverständigenrat zur Begutachtung der gesamtwirtschaftlichen Entwicklung*) was set up to issue annual analyses of economic policy. In preparation for a reform of social policy, a committee was set up to examine the workings of social programmes. The resulting report initiated the publication of an annual governmental 'social budget', designed to link the planning of social and economic policy more closely.

In the meantime, an important political realignment brought an end to the long period of polarization between the bourgeois and social democratic camps, making all parties possible coalition partners. After a series of conflicts, the FDP moved away from the Christian Democrats. The SPD replaced its old manifesto of 1925 with a new party platform in which it reconciled itself to the social market economy and the country's integration into the Western alliance.

When a sudden recession in 1966/67 led to unresolvable conflicts between FDP and Christian Democrats over the budget, a 'grand coalition' (*Grosse Koalition*) of Christian Democrats and SPD was formed. To combat the economic crisis, the new government intended to shift public expenditure from social consumption to social investment. Various transfer payments were curbed, and for the first time, educational issues were given political priority. A wider access to higher education institutions was pursued as an investment in human capital and as a means to promote equal educational opportunities. The new coalition initiated a reform empowering the federal government to pass educational legislation and to participate in the provision of health services. A federal Ministry of Education and Science was established [23], new universities were constructed and education allowances were introduced for low-income families. Changes in income maintenance schemes met some of the long-standing demands of the SPD. As a first step towards a more active labour market policy, the competence of the unemployment insurance scheme was extended to include the promotion of vocational training. A new system of wage continuation equalized the entitlements of workers and employees, and the pension schemes of both groups were financially consolidated by an obligation to mutually balance liquidity reserves.

The drive for a new social policy gained momentum when a SPD/FDP coalition was formed in 1969 and when the renewed growth of the economy replenished federal resources. In promising to 'democratize society', the new government sought to transform social policy into a tool for active social engineering. Several commissions were set up to develop broad-based reform plans. Special attention was given to the improvement of working conditions. Social services were expanded, particularly in sickness insurance with the introduction of preventative treatment. In the educational sector, allowances were improved. Income maintenance entitlements were extended by reforms of all social insurance schemes, most notably pensions. Child allowances were increased and extended to all families with children. Housing allowances were improved and tenant protection was strengthened.

The new social policy suffered a sudden setback when the recession of the mid-1970s combined with deficits in the pension insurance scheme and a cost explosion in the health sector. Since 1975, the government has sought to bring the growth rate of social expenditure into line with that of economic growth. In this new phase of financial consolidation, most social benefits were cut (see Section V). Once again steps towards a systematic reform were initiated when the government set up a transfer inquiry commission in 1977 to examine the workings of welfare schemes and to issue recommendations for their reform. Up to the present, however, all attempts to reform the old-established fragmented system have failed. The growth of the German welfare state has therefore taken place within a fairly stable institutional order.

II   Recources and clienteles: descriptions

1.   The postwar growth of public and social expenditure

After World War II the Federal Republic was faced with enormous economic problems. Around two million dwellings had been destroyed, almost ten million refugees had immigrated to the Republic from the former Eastern regions of the *Reich*, and unemployment was very high. Despite this, and despite the constitutional option of nationalizing private property, the new government led by the Christian Democrats chose a liberal economic policy, and sought the reconstruction of the economy by stimulating private initiative rather than by the imposition of state regulation.

In this context, the public expenditure share of GDP remained modest. Contrary to Peacock and Wiseman's famous 'displacement effect' hypothesis, public expenditure ratios even fell below the levels reached in the interwar period. In its most inclusive definition, the share of the consolidated public sector amounted to 37 percent of GDP in 1950 (see Graph 2) as compared with 39 percent in 1938. Excluding social insurance, public outlays claimed 29 percent of GDP in 1950 as against 34 percent in 1938 [24].

During the 1950s the volume of public expenditure more than doubled in real terms (see Graph 3). As annual growth rates corresponded closely to those of GDP, the expenditure ratio remained fairly constant at around 38 percent. Since 1960 there has been a growing disparity between the growth of public outlays and the rate of economic growth. Although both growth rates were subject to a downward trend, in most years public expenditure grew much faster than GDP, so that the expenditure ratio increased sharply. During the economic recession of the mid-1970s the threshold of 50 percent was passed for the first time, and the expenditure ratio has since stabilized at this level. Graph 3 shows that absolute growth in real terms has been much steadier than the growth of the expenditure ratio. In the entire postwar period, public expenditure has shown a sixfold (real) increase, as compared with a fivefold increase in GDP.

During the 1950s and 1960s the growth of the public expenditure ratio was almost exclusively due to the increase in social insurance outlays. Whereas the social expendi-

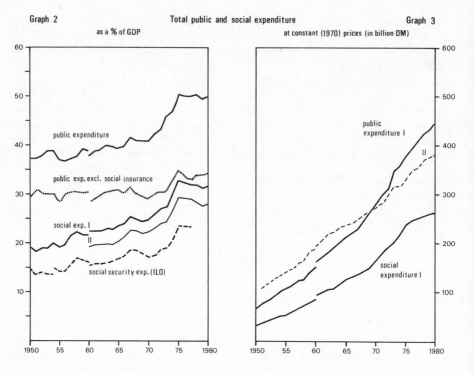

Graph 2 — Total public and social expenditure — as a % of GDP

Graph 3 — at constant (1970) prices (in billion DM)

ture ratio (see Graph 2) grew by about five percentage points, the ratio of government spending (excluding social insurance) stagnated at about 29 percent. In the early 1970s public authorities began to expand their outlays at a rate far exceeding that of economic growth. During this period a debate on 'government overload' started, fuelled by an SPD long-term programme which advocated a further increase in the state share. In the second half of the decade, however, public budgets were partially curbed, and their growth rates were again brought into line with the rate of GDP growth.

In a federal system of government like that of West Germany, it would be misleading to interpret public expenditure development simply as a function of political decisions at the national level. The central government share has never exceeded 50 percent of total government expenditure in the postwar period (see Graph 6). Contrary to Popitz' 'law' of an increasing centralization of public spending, the central government share of total public outlays has even declined [25], while the regional government share increased. Institutionally, the legislative competence of the federal government has been strengthened, however, as the financial reform laws of 1955 and 1969 transformed many previously single state competences (e.g. building of universities and the promotion of regional economic development) into joint tasks of federal and single state governments.

The increase in the volume of public spending was accompanied by significant changes in its composition (see Graph 5). The increasing share of regional government spending is to a large degree due to the growth of educational expenditure. Since 1950 outlays on education, science and culture doubled their share of total government expenditure (excluding social insurance) from 8.5 to 17.4 percent.

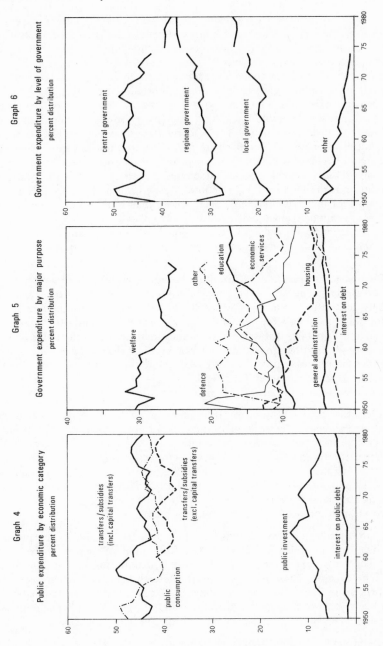

Graph 4

Public expenditure by economic category
percent distribution

Graph 5

Government expenditure by major purpose
percent distribution

Graph 6

Government expenditure by level of government
percent distribution

Educational expenditure thus became the second most important expenditure item after welfare spending. The latter consists of social transfers and health expenditure financed from general revenues, but does not include the bulk of social insurance payments financed from contributions [26]. The various outlays reported as 'other expenditure' (i.e. civil servants' pensions, expenditure on war damages and on counter-cyclical economic programmes, etc.) form a third important expenditure category, which has increased its share from 11 to 20 percent. Public outlays for economic services have been subject to considerable fluctuation. Increasing in relative importance throughout the 1960s, they declined in the 1970s to their original shares. The share of housing expenditure was high in the immediate postwar years, but has since declined from 13 to 6 percent. Defence expenditure has experienced the most conspicuous decline in relative importance. Having initially amounted to about a fifth of total government expenditure, it declined to a postwar low of 8 percent in 1980. The defence budget of 41 billion DM thus amounted to scarcely more than one half (56 percent) of the outlays for education, science and culture, which it had surpassed twofold in the early 1950s. Expenditure on public administration has remained fairly constant, at 4 percent. In recent years even the interest on debt has claimed a larger share of expenditure.

The distribution of public expenditure by economic category (see Graph 4) shows that the increase in public debt payments has in recent years been accompanied by a conspicuous decline in public investment. By 1980 the debt service already accounted for slightly more than half the amount spent on investment purposes. During the early years of the Republic, investment expenditure had grown noticeably faster than total public outlays. Starting from a level of 6 percent, its share rose to 14 percent in 1964. Since then its rate of growth has fallen far below the annual increases in total spending. In the recession year of 1967, and between 1974 and 1977, investment expenditure was even reduced in nominal terms.

However, the declining share of investment in public expenditure was not accompanied by a similar decrease in the proportion of government investment in total gross fixed capital accumulation. As private investment grew more slowly than government investment for several years, the share of state investment even reached a peak of 19 percent in 1975. In subsequent years the share fell to its long-term average of between 16 and 17 percent, where it has remained fairly constantly since 1977. As about two-thirds of all public investment is made by local government, the influence of the federal government on total public investment is marginal.

The share of transfers and subsidies has remained fairly stable in the postwar period. Including capital transfers [27] it fluctuated at around 45 percent between 1950 and 1980. The temporary increase in the 1950s is mainly due to the pension reform of 1957. The category comprises social insurance cash benefits, but excludes social insurance benefits in kind, which appear under public consumption in national accounts statistics. National accounts data therefore do not give an adequate picture of the increasing importance of public transfer schemes in the postwar period.

Public consumption originally claimed almost one half of total public expenditure. Its share was reduced to 40 percent during the 1950s when income maintenance schemes were improved and public investment expanded dynamically. Since the mid-1960s consumption has grown much faster than investment. Its share of total expenditure subsequently increased again and levelled off at about 43 percent in the late 1970s. More than half of public consumption expenditure is presently spent on wages and salaries for public employees. Personnel expenditure has tripled in real terms since 1960, thus outpacing the growth of other expenditure categories. This growth was due to significant increases in salaries, changes in personnel structure (a reduction of blue-collar jobs and an expansion of higher civil service positions), and to a sweeping expansion of the number of jobs. Table 2 describes the growth of public employment for the period 1950-1980.

Table 2   Public employment in the Federal Republic

	1950	1960	1970	1980
Full-time personnel in public employment (a)				
in 1,000s	2 104	2 639	3 113	3 614
as % of the labour force	9.8	10.0	11.6	13.4
Full-time government personnel (b)				
in 1,000s	1 282	1 799	2 260	2 807
as % of the labour force	5.9	6.8	8.4	10.4
Personnel by level of government:				
Federal government				
in 1,000s	65	211	305	316
as % of total govt. personnel	5.1	11.7	13.5	11.2
Single states				
in 1,000s	661	946	1 214	1 517
as % of total govt. personnel	51.5	52.6	53.7	56.0
Local government				
in 1,000s	556	642	740	920
as % of total govt. personnel	43.4	35.7	32.8	32.8
Personnel by sector:				
Education and science				
in 1,000s	245	352	570	826
as % of total govt. personnel	19.1	19.6	25.2	29.4
Social services and health				
in 1,000s	165	285	345	484
as % of total govt. personnel	12.9	15.8	15.3	17.2
General administration and public order				
in 1,000s	493	642	722	852
as % of total govt. personnel	38.5	35.7	31.9	30.3
Economic services				
in 1,000s	344	435	452	474
in % of total govt. personnel	26.8	24.2	20.0	16.9
Defence (c)				
in 1,000s	35	86	171	172
in % of total govt. personnel	2.7	4.8	7.6	6.1

(a) Personnel of government, railways, postal service and special communal agencies (excl. social insurance and
    other indirect public services)
(b) All government levels excluding railways, postal service and special communal agencies
(c) All government levels excluding soldiers

Full-time public employment, including the railways, postal service and special local government agencies, almost doubled between 1950 and 1980. Its share of the total labour force increased from 10 to 13 percent. The number of government employees *strictu sensu* has grown even faster, with an almost twofold increase of its share of the total labour force from less than 6 to over 10 percent. If we include part-time employment, the number of people employed in the public sector amounted to 3.9 million or 14.6 percent of the labour force in 1980.

The federal government increased its personnel mainly in the 1950s. The single states, which have always accounted for over half of all public employees, had their highest increases in staff numbers after 1960. Although continuing to grow in absolute numbers, local government employment has been declining in relative importance. The heavy expansion of public employment in regional government is also reflected in the distribution of public employment by function. The educational sector, which is controlled by the single states, has witnessed the greatest expansion. In 1950, this sector offered only half the number of positions provided by general administration (including police and courts), but by 1980 it had practically caught up with this traditionally leading sector of public employment. In absolute numbers, educational personnel more than tripled in the postwar period. Social services and health experienced a similar steep increase in number of personnel. Together with education, they accounted for almost half (47 percent) of total government employment in 1980. In contrast, the relative importance of employment in the economic services sector has declined drastically. The defence sector, which expanded most heavily during the 1950s and 1960s, has been at an almost complete standstill since 1970.

The data thus indicate a change in government functions from the maintenance of public order and external security to the provision of welfare. This change is further revealed if we take a closer look at the development of the volume and structure of social expenditure.

In its first years, the Federal Republic's expenditure on income maintenance, health, housing and education represented less than one half of total public spending. Social expenditure grew faster than total public expenditure in most subsequent years, and its share surpassed 60 percent in 1974. Although the financial consolidation legislation of the late 1970s considerably curbed the rate of growth, the proportion of public expenditure devoted to social purposes has remained above this 60 percent mark. Expressed as a ratio of GDP, the growth of social expenditure was even more impressive, having increased from a fifth to almost a third during the postwar period (see Graph 2).

With the expansion in volume, the structure of social expenditure has undergone considerable changes (see Graph 7). According to a popular sociological critique, the welfare state in Germany is characterized by an increasing monetarization of benefits [28]. Contrary to this thesis, however, the relative importance of income maintenance benefits has been constantly declining in the postwar period. Although social transfer payments still represent the lion's share of total social expenditure, their proportion decreased, from about two-thirds in 1950 to about one half in 1980. The public promotion of housing has been similarly subject to a relative decline. In the years of postwar reconstruction more than 10 percent of social expenditure was channelled into the housing sector. By the mid-1960s the share had been halved, and subsequently fell to below 3 percent in 1980.

In recent years the German welfare state, which has traditionally been dominated by the income maintenance schemes, has been moving in the direction of a social service state. Benefits in kind and general services have grown faster than cash benefits, and their share of total social expenditure rose slightly from 7 to 8 percent. Education and health expenditure have expanded more dynamically. Up to the mid-1960s the proportion of education expenditure had stagnated at around 11 percent. The then comparative backwardness of the German educational system became an issue of public debate, and considerable funds were channelled into its expansion. Consequently the share of educational expenditure grew to about 16 percent. Although not given similar political priority, health expenditure [29] has grown at an even faster rate. During the postwar period its share of social expenditure doubled. Today almost a fifth of

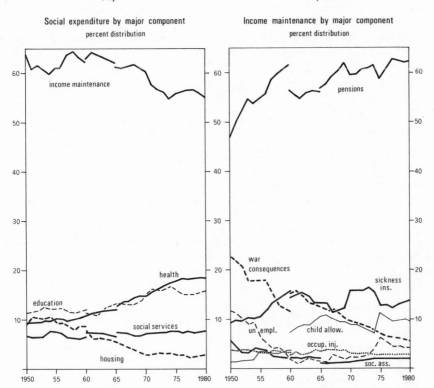

Graph 7

Social expenditure by major component
percent distribution

Graph 8

Income maintenance by major component
percent distribution

social expenditure is spent on health purposes. Taken together, education and health presently amount to almost two-thirds of the outlays for income maintenance, as compared with a third in 1950. This contrast clearly demonstrates that the hypothesis of an increasing monetarization is without any empirical basis.

Within the income maintenance programmes, pensions have become increasingly dominant (see Graph 8). Limited to less than half of total income maintenance in the early 1950s, they now account for almost two-thirds of all cash payments. Since the late 1950s the share of sickness cash benefits (including wage continuation) has fluctuated around the 15 percent level. Child allowances, which were repeatedly extended by federal legislation, have increased their share to about 10 percent of income maintenance expenditure [30]. Unemployment benefits were a heavy financial burden during the postwar period of economic reconstruction when unemployment rates were particularly high. With the economic recovery they declined considerably in relative importance. During the recent economic recession they again increased to 4 percent of total outlays on income maintenance (1980). Benefits to war victims [31] claimed a quarter of all cash benefits in 1950, but have since decreased to 5 percent in 1980. Cash benefits for the victims of industrial accidents have always been of only modest relative importance. Following a slight downward trend their share has fluctuated at around 2-3 percent. The relative importance of social assistance payments has also declined. Their share dropped from 5 to 1 percent during the 1960s. After a reform in 1969, this share slightly increased, and with the onset of the economic recession it has risen to about 2 percent. The other social compensation payments have been of only marginal importance, consistently remaining below the one percent level. These relative changes, however, do not reveal expenditure developments in real terms. For a better understanding of the dynamics of welfare state expansion, we should look at the development of expenditure for single programmes.

2. The development of single programmes

Pensions

Pensions are the most important item of social expenditure. Together, the three pension insurance schemes for workers, employees and miners, the farmers' scheme, and the two civil service schemes accounted for 183 billion DM in 1980, as compared with 6 billion DM in 1950. The GDP share of pensions thus doubled from 6 to 12 percent in the postwar period. Graph 9 shows that this increase is mostly due to the expansion of the three pension insurance schemes [32]. Pension insurance today accounts for three-quarters of total pension expenditure. Civil servants' pensions have also increased, but their share of total pension cash benefits has declined from 40 to 20 percent. Farmers' pensions and the supplementary scheme for non-tenured civil servants are of limited importance. In 1980 about 59 percent of all cash benefits under pension insurance were old age pensions, 12 percent were invalidity pensions, and 29 percent were survivors' pensions [33].

In real terms, pension outlays increased twelvefold in the period 1950-1980 (see Graph 10). Up until the mid-1970s the annual rates of increase ranged from 5 to 10

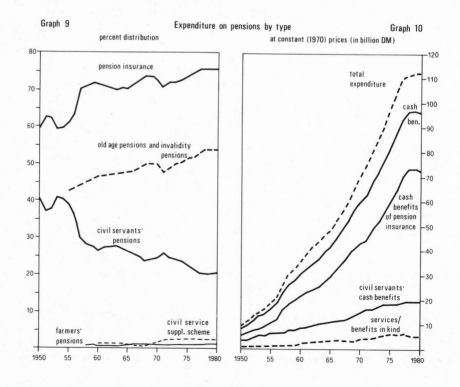

percent. Growth rates of 20 percent and more occurred in 1952 and in 1957/58, related to extensions in entitlement. In the early 1950s, pensions were repeatedly augmented in order to bring them into line with prices, a major increase of this sort being legislated in 1951. A 1957 law then introduced a thorough reform of pension insurance. As the wars and two major waves of inflation had considerably weakened the value of private savings, pensions had become the major source of income for a large part of the retired population. In addition, pensioners now represented a significant proportion of the electorate. Departing from the traditional principle of subsistence benefits, pensions were now designed to be the main source of income. The benefits of the three insurance schemes for workers, employees and miners were significantly increased and indexed to wage changes. Pensions became more closely linked to contributions. Entitlements under the workers' and employees' schemes were equalized. In the year of the reform, total pension expenditure increased by 4 billion DM or 26.5 percent in real terms.

In 1972, a second major pension insurance reform was implemented. Individual entitlements were extended by the introduction of a minimum pension component which raised benefits for low-income groups, and by the introduction of a flexible age limit, lowering pensionable age to 63. The scope of the insurance scheme - already widened by the abolition of the income limit for employees in 1967 - was further extended by the introduction of voluntary membership for previously non-insured groups, particularly the self-employed and housewives. The cost of the 1972 reform was estimated at around 10 billion DM annually [34].

Expansion in pension policy came to a halt in the second half of the 1970s when the insurance system ran into deficit. Since 1977, a series of curtailments have been introduced which have significantly curbed the rate of growth (see Graph 10 and Section V). In real terms the level of pension expenditure remained fairly constant, but the GDP share declined by one percentage point in the period 1977-1980.

Sickness insurance and health

This is the second largest item of social expenditure. Total health sector spending amounted to 120 billion DM or 8.1 percent of GDP in 1980, as compared with 2.9 billion DM and 3 percent in 1950. The aggregate amount consists of expenditure for the following schemes: sickness insurance (71 percent), wage continuation (23 percent), civil service health benefits (5 percent), and the public health service (1 percent). Graphs 11 and 12 regroup these expenditure items under income maintenance and health services.

Cash benefits presently present less than a third of total health expenditure (wage continuation and sickness insurance cash benefits, being 22.6 and 6.5 percent respectively in 1980). In the early 1950s wage continuation was only payable to employees, and workers had to rely on sickness insurance cash benefits. The right to a full wage continuation was gradually extended to workers by reforms taken in 1957, 1961 and 1969. The increase in wage continuation expenditure and the concomitant decline in sickness insurance cash benefit expenditure at the end of the 1960s (Graph 11) are largely accounted for by these institutional changes [35].

Expenditure on health benefits and services has grown more consistently and more rapidly than income maintenance expenditure (Graph 12). In 1980 benefits in kind and services represented 71 percent of total health sector spending as compared with 62 percent in 1950. The bulk of these outlays consists of medical benefits and services

Graph 11

Expenditure on sickness cash benefits
at constant (1970) prices (in million DM)

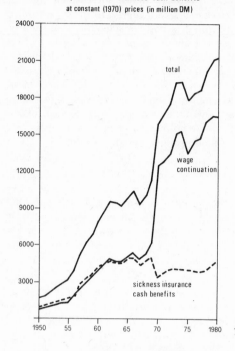

Graph 12

Expenditure on health
at constant (1970) prices (in million DM)

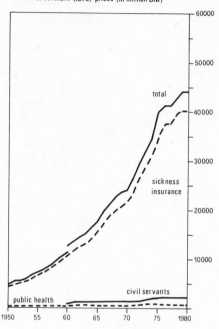

of the sickness insurance scheme. Benefits for civil servants and expenditure on the public health sector claim small and decreasing shares of health expenditure.

The growth of sickness insurance expenditure began to accelerate conspicuously in the early 1970s when the government passed several reforms improving benefits. Innovations in medicine and the rapid increase in the number of doctors from the mid-1960s [36] also contributed to rising expenditure.

For five consecutive years (1971-1975), the annual growth of sickness insurance expenditure was over 10 percent with a peak of 17 percent in 1971. As economic growth had, on average, fallen to below 3 percent in the same period, attempts were made in the second half of the 1970s to contain the 'cost explosion' in the health sector. Some benefits were cut, private cost-sharing was extended, and a corporatist form of 'concerted action' was established which obliged doctors associations and insurance funds to link negotiations on medical fees more closely to the development of wages. These measures curbed the growth rate of sickness insurance expenditure which fell to an average of 3 percent (in real terms) in the second half of the 1970s (see Graphs 11 and 12).

Occupational injuries insurance

Compared with other social programmes, occupational injuries insurance is of limited economic importance. Throughout the postwar period its GDP share has varied at around 0.6 percent. In real terms, however, expenditure (including transfers) has increased sixfold since 1950 (see Graph 13). Particularly high annual rates of growth were recorded in the 1950s and early 1960s, when five-year averages reached 10 percent. This expansion is attributable to legislative changes, and to a sharp increase in the number of industrial accidents (from 1.3 million in 1950 to 2.9 million in 1961). Since this time the number of accidents has consistently declined, and has remained below 2 million since 1974.

Graph 13

Expenditure on occupational injuries
at constant (1970) prices (in million DM)

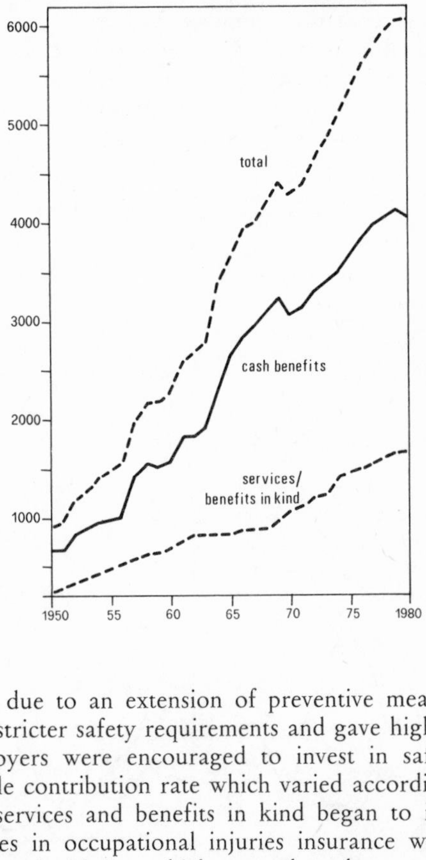

This decrease is partly due to an extension of preventive measures. In 1963 a basic reform law introduced stricter safety requirements and gave higher priority to rehabilitation measures. Employers were encouraged to invest in safety protection by the introduction of a flexible contribution rate which varied according to the frequency of accidents. Outlays on services and benefits in kind began to increase markedly (see Graph 13). The changes in occupational injuries insurance were accompanied by a series of reforms in labour legislation which strengthened protective measures [37].

The unsteady development of cash benefit expenditure is largely attributable to institutional changes. Increases in the 1950s are the result of occasional improvements in benefit levels legislated in 1952 and 1957. The 1963 reform indexed pensions to wages. The temporary drop in real expenditure in 1970 was due to the inbuilt time-lag in the indexation formula. Low rates of annual adjustment, legislated in 1978, account for the decline in expenditure in 1979/80 (see Graph 13). The extension of accident insurance to pupils and students only affected outlays marginally (about 3 percent of total expenditure) [38].

Unemployment

Expenditure on unemployment is, of course, closely related to the fluctuations in the business cycle. In the early 1950s unemployment rates [39] were very high, ranging above 10 percent. They declined to below 3 percent in 1959 and full employment prevailed until 1974 when the recession led to renewed mass unemployment. After a sudden peak in 1975, unemployment rates remained above 4 percent up to 1978. Following a temporary decline in subsequent years they have, since 1981, again risen to above 5 percent.

The decline in expenditure between 1950 and 1965 and the significant increase afterwards (see Graph 15), are thus partly explained by labour market developments. Since outlays have also increased during the period of full employment between 1965 and 1974, however, changing levels of unemployment do not tell the entire story. A comparison of years with similar rates of unemployment indicates the importance of legislative changes. Rates of 3.7 percent in 1957 and 1958 were accompanied by outlays amounting to 0.8 and 0.9 percent of GDP respectively. In 1980 an almost identical level of unemployment (3.8 percent) claimed almost twice this share (1.5 percent) of GDP.

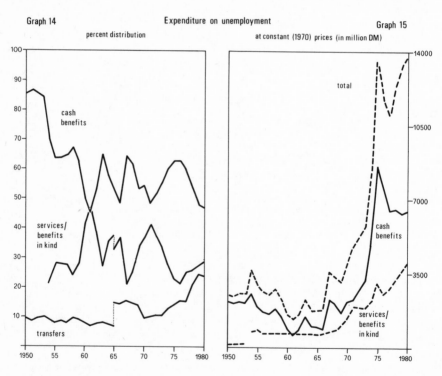

Graph 14   Expenditure on unemployment   Graph 15

percent distribution   at constant (1970) prices (in million DM)

Showing the composition of total expenditure Graph 14 may serve as a first indication of the institutional changes which occurred. The proportion of outlays claimed by income maintenance payments - whose annual fluctuations closely correspond to the level of unemployment - has been subject to a conspicuous long-term decline. Presently the classical insurance and assistance cash benefits represent less than a half of total outlays on unemployment. Income maintenance today is only one among several functions fulfilled by the Federal Employment Institution. Other functions include counselling and placement services, the preservation of jobs through various subsidies, and the promotion of employment.

A major shift from a traditional to a more active labour market policy occurred in 1969. A thorough legislative reform extended the services to vocational training, the reintegration of handicapped persons, and the prevention of unemployment through counselling, research and subsidies for job creation. This legislation was followed by a sizeable increase in outlays for general services and benefits in kind (see Graph 15).

The gradual extension of functions also led to changes in the composition of cash benefits. Important increases of the insurance and assistance benefits were legislated in 1956, 1967 and 1974. In addition, these classical forms of earnings replacement were supplemented by benefits in the construction industry during the winter months (1959 and 1969), allowances for vocational training courses (1969), and redundancy allowances in cases of bankruptcies (1974). The transfers reported in Graph 14 consist of contributions to other social insurance schemes. Whereas the employment institution paid contributions to sickness insurance from the outset, contributions to pension insurance were introduced in 1977. The decline in cash benefits in the late 1970s is not only related to the gradual reductions in unemployment, but also to a series of curtailments and entitlement restrictions introduced since 1975.

Child allowances and youth services

In contrast to its pioneering role in the development of other social programmes, Germany has been a 'laggard' with respect to the introduction of child allowances. The limited benefits for larger families introduced under National Socialist rule were discontinued after the war. Only civil servants remained entitled to special child supplements. For an extended period, the family policy of the Federal Republic relied mainly on tax credits. As these favoured higher income earners, they were challenged by the unions and the SPD.

In 1954 the system of tax credits was complemented by a limited scheme of flat-rate allowances for the third child and further children, financed and administered by employers. In 1961, allowances financed from general revenues were introduced for families with two or more children. A 1964 reform then shifted the responsibility for the entire system of child allowances to the federal government and increased benefits significantly. In 1974 the Social-Liberal coalition abolished the dual system of tax credits and direct payments in favour of a universal child allowance scheme with flat-rate benefits payable for all children.

The expenditure development shown in Graph 16 largely reflects these institutional developments. The outlays for child allowances grew conspicuously in the years when the reforms took place and after legislated benefit increases in 1957, 1959, 1961 and 1970. Data for the civil service are incomplete prior to 1960. The decline in expenditure in 1975 was due to the replacement of the special civil service child supplements by the general child allowance scheme. Post-1975 outlays refer to family-related components of civil servants' salaries. In 1980, total public expenditure on families (excluding tax credits) amounted to 31 billion DM, or 2.1 percent of GDP, as compared with 3.5 billion DM or 1.2 percent in 1960. Of total expenditure, 57 percent is claimed by the general child allowance scheme, 24 percent by the civil service income supplements, and 19 percent by the youth welfare programme.

Graph 16

Expenditure on child allowances and youth assistance
at constant (1970) prices (in million DM)

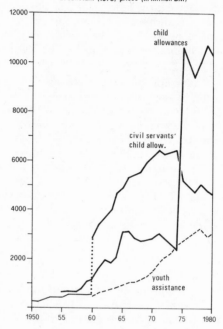

Expenditure on youth welfare consists mostly of services and benefits in kind. The 1961 Youth Welfare Act, which replaced the old legislation of 1922, considerably extended the counselling and supervisory functions of local authorities. The marked increase in expenditure since 1970 is mostly due to the expansion of day-care services and subsidies to voluntary youth welfare organizations [40]. The data on youth welfare also include income maintenance benefits (introduced in 1979) for single parents, in cases where the liable parent does not meet his responsibilities.

Social assistance

Despite the expansion of other social programmes, social assistance is still important as a form of 'last resort', and has even increased its economic importance in recent years. In real terms, expenditure doubled in the period 1950-1969, and again in the 1970s (see Graph 18), amounting to 0.9 percent of GDP in 1980. In 1954 a federal administrative court decision established an individual right to assistance benefits. A 1961 reform law (which replaced the 1924 legislation), considerably extended entitlements, and increased benefits, the latter now designed to provide culturally 'necessary' rather than merely economically 'indispensable' means. A second thorough reform took place in 1969, improving benefits in kind and services. Sizeable increases in benefits were also legislated in 1965 and 1974. The steep rise in expenditure during the 1970s is partially attributable to these reforms, as well as to the downswing of the economy. The number of beneficiaries, which had consistently decreased throughout the 1950s and had remained stagnant during the 1960s, began to rise steeply in the context of rising unemployment from 1971 onwards.

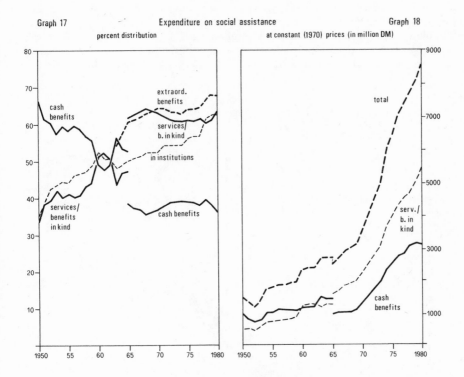

The growing volume of expenditure was accompanied by significant increases in its composition (see Graph 17). Cash payments have consistently decreased in importance, from two-thirds to a third of total expenditure. The bulk of benefits is now accounted for by general services and benefits in kind (assistance for the handicapped, day-care for those requiring nursing services, and support for the sick not covered by sickness insurance).

The increasing importance of such 'extraordinary benefits' bears witness to the policy of freeing social assistance from standard tasks, such as income maintenance, in order to provide coverage for particular circumstances of need. The growing proportion of expenditure for residents in institutions is, however, an indication of the rise of a new standard risk (rather than of an increasing degree of repressive control): the increase in life expectancy, together with the weakening of family ties has made a growing number of old people dependent upon institutional day-care. As the cost of such nursing care far exceeds normal pension levels, social assistance has become increasingly important as a supplement to pensioners' income. Thus the share of expenditure accounted for by payments to people in institutions for the old, blind or handicapped (including children) nearly doubled from 34 to 63 percent between 1950 and 1980 (see Graph 17).

Expenditure on war consequences

In the Federal Republic, expenditure on war consequences is still of much greater importance than in other Western European countries. The 16.9 billion DM spent for this purpose in 1980 corresponded to 1.1 percent of GDP, the corresponding percentage for 1950 being 3 percent. Total expenditure consists of outlays for three separate programmes: benefits to war victims, the equalization of burdens (*Lastenausgleich*), and political reparation payments (*Wiedergutmachung*). In real terms, expenditure for these schemes grew dynamically up until the mid-1960s, but has remained fairly stagnant since (see Graph 20) and is expected to decline markedly in the future.

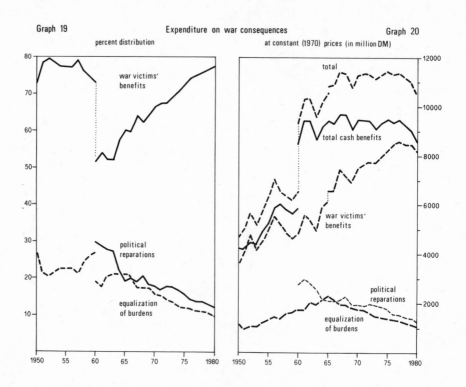

Graph 19   Expenditure on war consequences   Graph 20
                  percent distribution   at constant (1970) prices (in million DM)

Of the three programmes, benefits to war victims are the most important expenditure item (see Graph 19). They consist of widows' and orphans' pensions, invalidity pensions, and rehabilitation services. The first law of the Federal Republic replacing the old legislation of 1920 was passed in 1950. Political pressure from two powerful interest groups with several million members [41] led to several amendments in subsequent years which considerably improved benefits. A first major reform came about in 1960, a second - preceded by a spectacular mass demonstration of war victims in Bonn - was passed in 1964. An amending act of 1966 provided for an annual adjustment of pensions, but became effective only after the passage of a further reform act in 1969. The repeated improvements in benefits help to explain why expenditure on the scheme continued to grow despite a conspicuous decline in the number of recipients, which amounted to more than four million in the early 1950s, but to less than two million in 1980 [42].

The equalization of war burdens inflicted upon civilians is a historically novel policy programme. It was introduced in 1952 after a previous emergency law of 1949 (*Soforthilfegesetz*) had given the approximately ten million refugees only the most urgently needed assistance. The benefits are designed to indemnify civilian war victims. They consist of various forms of pensions, compensations for loss of property, special lump sum payments to relieve hardship, and loans and subsidies to promote economic activities. On paper, the programme entailed a rather drastic redistribution, as it was to be financed by a special 50 percent property tax on all private property existing in 1948 [43]. The original 1952 Act was amended several times. The twenty-eighth and final amendment was passed in 1977. Pension payments have been indexed to wages since 1974. Following official estimates, the cumulative cost of the programme including the compensation for lost property will sum up to some 140 billion DM [44]. The expenditure data reported here only apply to consumptive transfer payments. These outlays kept growing steeply up to the mid-1960s. Their decline in subsequent years is mostly due to the decreases in the number of refugees.

A scheme for political reparation payments to the victims of the Nazi dictatorship was introduced by the Federal Indemnification Law (*Bundesentschädigungsgesetz*) in 1953. It became effective only after the passage of an amending act in 1956. Benefits are designed to provide partial compensation for the survivors of murdered persons, invalids, former political prisoners, or persons who suffered a loss of property or of career opportunities under Nazi rule. They consist predominantly of pensions which are presently paid to some 200,000 persons living for the most part in foreign countries [45]. Entitlements were extended by amending acts of 1965 and 1980. Expenditure data are available only since 1960 [46]. They refer to transfer payments, but do not include payments for the restitution of property [47]. The decline in outlays is due to the decreasing number of recipients [48].

Housing

Housing expenditure grew at a much lower speed than outlays for other social programmes. In real terms, total spending barely tripled between 1950 and 1980 (see Graph 22). In the same period, its GDP share declined from 1.7 to 0.8 percent. Aggregate expenditure consisted of three major components: subsidies for housing supply [49], premiums on private savings for housing construction, and housing allowances for low-income families which subsidize demand.

The subsidization of housing supply is by far the most important policy tool (see Graph 21). During the war almost a fourth of the dwellings in the area of the Federal Republic had been destroyed [50]. As private capital was in short supply during the immediate postwar years, the promotion of construction became an imperative task of public policy. A 1950 law provided for loans, grants and subsidies at lower interest rates for builders who accepted certain public standards, as well as for sizeable tax credits for all private builders. Dwellings erected for low-income tenants under the so-called social housing programme of the law received the largest subsidies. Amending acts of 1956 and 1965 then targeted the subsidization programme more specifically on family houses and private rather than collective dwellings for low-income groups. Public loans and grants were now increasingly being replaced by subsidies to lower the debt burden. Together with the decrease in construction activities, this change led to a sizeable decline in public outlays [51]. From 1966, subsidies to lower the interest on debt in the social housing programme were gradually extended to higher earnings groups building owner-occupied housing [52]. A 1971 law then considerably raised the income-limit for social housing. It also extended entitlements to the subsidization of the debt burden to builders surpassing the regular income-limit by up to 40 percent. As a consequence, public outlays for the subsidization of supply outlays began to grow markedly again (see Graph 22).

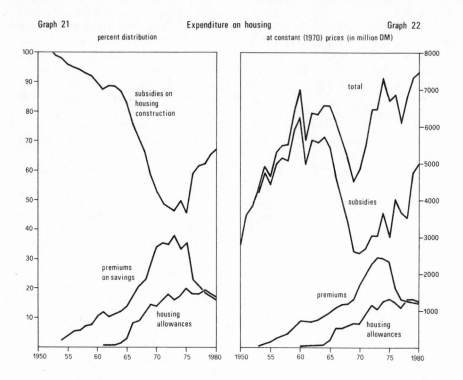

Graph 21

percent distribution

Expenditure on housing

at constant (1970) prices (in million DM)

Graph 22

Premiums on private savings for construction are a second instrument to promote the supply of housing. They were introduced in 1952 as a means of combining housing policy with the bourgeois government's attempts to spread private property. A 1969 law passed under the 'Grand Coalition' (CDU/SPD) then introduced special higher rate premiums for low-income groups. Since 1974, the premiums programme was subject to a series of curtailments (passed in 1974, 1975 and 1981), which generally limited entitlement to groups below an income limit, and successively lowered the rates of subsidization. Consequently aggregate expenditure was more than halved in real terms.

For an extended period, the demand for housing remained unsubsidized. In the immediate postwar period, a strong regulative legislation, based on the 1946 law passed by the allies, subjected the housing market to tight administrative controls. Tenants could be allocated housing by public authorities, and were additionally safeguarded against rent increases and eviction notice by protective tenant legislation. These controls were gradually loosened during the 1950s. After fierce parliamentary struggles between the bourgeois coalition government and the SPD opposition, a 1960 law almost completely deregulated the housing market. In the same year a system of limited subsidies was introduced in order to compensate tenants, covering specific groups whose rents exceeded a bearable burden. Laws of 1963 and 1965 then extended this limited subsidization to a regular system of housing allowances for all families under an income limit. Increases in the allowance rates were legislated in 1970 and 1977 and led to sizeable increases in expenditure (see Graph 22). Nevertheless, the subsidization of housing supply still represents more than two-thirds (67 percent) of total public expenditure on housing, amounting to 12.3 billion DM in 1980. As this figure does not include another 9 billion DM which are spent on indirect subsidies such as tax credits, the actual subsidization of housing supply is even higher [53].

Education

In real terms, educational expenditure increased from roughly 6 to 38 billon DM between 1950 and 1980. Its GDP share rose from 2.1 to 4.9 percent. The growth in aggregate spending was accompanied by some significant changes in the composition of expenditure [54]. Whereas the relative importance of the school sector declined, that of education allowances increased in the 1970s. Post-secondary, pre-school and adult education gained slightly in importance (see Graph 23). The growth in total expenditure was rather discontinuous with marked phase-specific variations (see Graph 24).

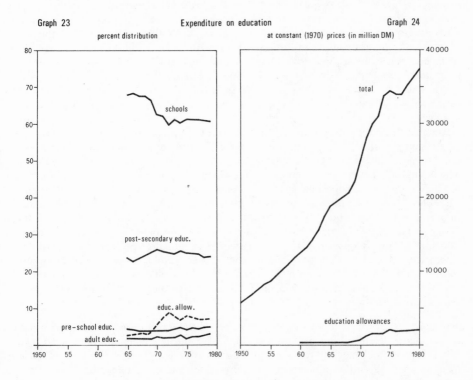

During the 1950s outlays for education grew only moderately faster than GDP, increasing their share by half a percentage point from 1950 to 1959. Under the 1949 Constitution, legislative and administrative responsibility for education remained the jurisdiction of the single states. The traditional structure of the German education system, with its rigid differentiation between primary and secondary schooling, was restored soon after the war, after the Allied Powers had given up their original plans for the construction of a more comprehensive school system. To co-ordinate the federally fragmented educational policies, the state ministers of education established a permanent conference in 1949 which has periodically convened since 1951 (*Ständige Konferenz der Kultusminister*). A special co-ordinating body was set up for the post-secondary sector (*Westdeutsche Rektorenkonferenz*) in 1949. A 1955 agreement by the state ministries then issued first guidelines for a standardization of the school system (*Düsseldorfer Abkommen*) [55].

A gradual process of centralization started during the second half of the 1950s. The foundation of a Federal Ministry of Nuclear Energy and Cultural Policy in 1955 was accompanied by the creation of a parliamentary committee for cultural affairs. The growing number of university students - which was largely due to demographic factors - led to a first sizeable expansion in the number of university personnel [56], and to the introduction of a limited scheme of study allowances for talented students (*Honnefer Modell*) in 1955. In 1957 a Central Science Council (*Wissenschaftsrat*) was established with the task of issuing recommendations for co-ordinated reforms of the post-secondary sector.

During the early 1960s, educational policy rapidly gained priority as a political issue. Economic growth rates had considerably declined, the immigration of well-educated refugees from East Germany had come to a halt after the construction of the Berlin Wall in 1961, and the superpowers' space race had drawn attention to the importance of technological innovation. Investments in the education system were now perceived as a major precondition for the mobilization of human capital, for technological progress, and for economic development. In 1962 a Federal Ministry of Scientific Research was established. A statistical analysis of the functioning of the education system carried out by the Conference of Education Ministers in 1963 produced alarming results regarding the shortage of educational facilities. A special parliamentary session on cultural policy one year later drew attention to the shortage of academics. The political debate was stimulated by widely circulating media reports and books which suggested that an imminent educational catastrophe would jeopardize the nation's economic competitiveness [57]. This primarily economic debate later combined with public concern for a fairer distribution of educational opportunities [58]. For the first time, educational questions were now perceived as being an integral part of social policy [59]. In 1965 the single states and the federal government agreed upon the establishment of an Educational Council (*Deutscher Bildungsrat*) for the planning of embracive educational reforms. After the earlier emphasis on the promotion of science, public resources were now increasingly channelled into the expansion of the school system as well, and in 1965 the GDP share of expenditure surpassed the 3 percent level for the first time.

The quick recovery of the economy after the 1966/67 recession [60], and the formation of the centre-left coalition provided the basis for the implementation of more extensive reforms. A change of the Constitution in 1969 empowered the federal government to pass legislation concerning the universities and education allowances. Several states established a number of comprehensive schools to overcome the traditional rigidity of the German school system [61]. In 1970 both the Educational Council and the federal government issued embracive plans for a co-ordinated reform of the educational system. Federal laws of 1969 and 1971 introduced an extensive system of education allowances for pupils and students from low income families. Several new universities were built, the size of school and university teaching staffs was substantially increased. For several years educational spending had the highest priority in public budgets. Between 1969 and 1974, its GDP share rose from 3.4 to 5 percent.

With the recession of 1974/75 this expansive phase came to an end. In 1973 an agreement between the single states had already established a central admissions office for university entrance which restricted access to certain subjects, making admissions contingent upon the applicant's previous school performance (*numerus clausus*). A federal university law subjected academic studies to a tighter degree of administrative regulation and control by establishing ground rules governing admissions and the length of studies. The expansion in the number of academic staff came to an abrupt end in 1975, and in some years the number of positions was even reduced [62]. Former plans for fundamental structural reforms of the school system were formally discarded when the Education Council was abolished in 1975 because the various states could not reach a new agreement on its continuation. Between 1975 and 1977 aggregate expenditure on education declined in real terms. Although it started to grow again in 1978, its GDP share has since remained stagnant. In the early 1980s the drive for more equal educational opportunities increasingly gave way to a new debate on the desirability of a more rigidly differentiated school system and a more selective promotion of elite education.

3. State revenues and public deficits

The expansion of state functions and the steep increase in public expenditure necessitated a massive growth in public revenues. During most of the postwar period, state revenues grew considerably faster than GDP. In the early 1950s total public receipts

Graph 25

Public revenues and public debt
as % of GDP

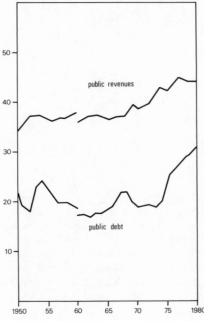

amounted to less than 34 percent of GDP [63]. Since then the ratio has been rising fairly consistently (Graph 25). In 1973 it surpassed the 40 percent threshold for the first time, and reached a peak of 45 percent in 1977. The ratio has been declining slightly since 1977, but has not fallen below the levels reached in the early 1970s.

The high growth rate of public revenues was not sufficient to keep pace with the steep increase in expenditure however. As shown in Graphs 26 and 27, balanced growth patterns only continued up to the mid-1960s. The public sector in a broad sense (central, regional and local government, social insurance) recorded a continuous surplus up to 1964. Thereafter revenues only surpassed expenditure in the years 1969, 1970, and 1973. Since 1975 the annual deficits consistently amounted to more than 5 percent of expenditure. For the public sector, in a stricter sense (i.e. excluding social insurance), the ratio of deficit spending was even higher (Graph 27).

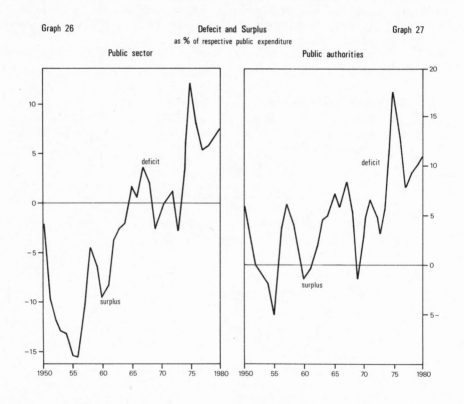

Graph 26   Defecit and Surplus   Graph 27
                          as % of respective public expenditure
              Public sector   Public authorities

The annual development of the deficits is only partly related to conscious policy choices. It must be remembered that aggregate statistics for public finance are the sum of the financial transactions of some 10,000 independent bodies [64]. The federal government pursued a very restrictive fiscal policy throughout the 1950s. At the end of this decade it initiated a change of policy and started to consciously use the budget as a counter-cyclical instrument [65]. In subsequent years deficits were usually increased or reduced according to the state of the economy. Since 1974, however, the development of deficits could no longer be controlled, and the second half of the 1970s saw imbalances of unprecedented magnitude.

The widening gap between revenues and expenditure led to a massive increase in public debt (see Graph 25). Public debt amounted to 21 percent of GDP in 1950 compared to 32 percent in 1980. In absolute terms the level of debt had roughly doubled in the 1950s and 1960s. Since economic growth rates were similarly high, the debt ratio remained fairly constant throughout both decades. In the 1970s the level of indebtedness almost quadrupled, and the debt ratio increased by 12 percentage points between 1974 and 1980. In most years up to the early 1970s, local authorities were primarily responsible for the public debt. The federal government usually ranked second, with the individual states as a distant third. Following the financial reform of 1969 which considerably improved the solvency of the local authorities, the situation changed. Since 1974 the federal government has accounted for the greatest annual increases in debt, now consistently followed by the individual states.

The rapid growth of public indebtedness led to rising expenditure for the debt service. Expressed as a percentage of total government expenditure, interest on debt tripled from 2 percent in 1950 to 6 percent or 29 billion DM in 1980. The respective figures for the public sector (including social insurance), are 1.7 and 4.1 percent. More than half of the state's net borrowing of 55 billion DM in 1980 was thus spent on the payment of interest for past liabilities. In this situation the consolidation of the public household became one of the prime political targets.

All parties seem cautious to advocate increases in revenues as a solution due to the widespread impression that the burden of taxation is approaching its upper limit. For dependent workers the rate of direct taxation rose from 5 percent in 1950 to 12 percent in 1980. If one includes social insurance contributions, the tax burden increased

Graph 28

Tax ratios
as % of GDP and gross earnings

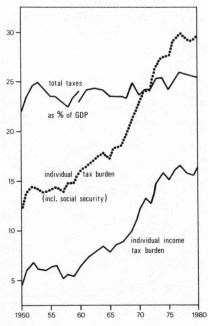

from 13 to 30 percent (see Graph 28). Given the effect of inflation upon wages, many workers found themselves in higher income-tax brackets, even though the legal rates remained unchanged. Repeated reforms of the tax system have sought to counteract this tendency by lowering tariffs, smoothing the course of progression or increasing tax credits.

Contrary to the individual tax burden, the aggregate tax ratio has remained remarkably stable. Displaying only a weak upward trend, it ranged around 25 percent, a value which it also assumed in 1980 (Graph 28). The seeming inconsistency between the steep rise of the individual tax burden and the much more constant aggregate tax ratio is explained by the fact that the aggregate tax ratio also includes indirect taxes and that various forms of income are subject to widely discrepant levels of taxation. Thus, the fiscal authorities claim tax on 82 percent of the incomes of employees and workers, but only on 74 percent of the national income. The respective figures for agricultural earnings and income from independent work are 16 and 35 percent [66]. About one fourth of all income earners or 5.5 million persons are not subject to any direct taxation [67]. These figures demonstrate the important role which open or hidden tax credits play in the German welfare state.

Graph 29 explains why the ratio of total revenues has been increasing despite a stagnant aggregate tax ratio: the share of taxes in total revenues decreased continuously.

Graph 29

Total revenues by major component
percent distribution

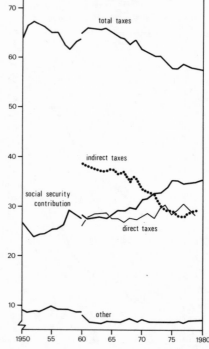

Between 1952 and 1980, it dropped from 67 percent to 58 percent. Originally indirect taxation constituted the largest source of public revenues, but its importance has been continuously declining. Today direct and indirect taxes each provide about an equal share of total tax receipts [68]. The declining share of taxes in total revenues is a reflection of the rapidly growing importance of social insurance contributions. Whereas the contributions originally accounted for only a quarter of total revenues, this share had increased to more than a third in 1980. This development will now be analysed in more detail.

Table 3   The financing of public welfare programmes

Scheme	Institutional regulations (a)	Financing shares (1980) (b)	%
Pension insurance	Equal contributions by employees and employers plus state subsidies; transfers from unemployment and sickness insurance	Employees Employers State Transfers	38 38 21 3
Farmers' pensions	Insured persons' contributions; heavy state subsidies	Insured State	21 79
Public employees' supplementary pensions	Public employers' contributions and general subsidies	Public employees Public employers State Other	1 54 10 34
Civil servants' schemes	Financed from public revenues	Public employers State Transfers Other	55 35 2 7
Sickness insurance	Equal contribution by employers and employees; small state subsidies; transfers from unemployment and pension insurance	Employees Employers State Transfers	41 35 2 20
Public health	Only general revenues	State Other	73 27
Unemployment insurance	Equal contributions from employees and employers; state subsidies	Employees Employers State Transfers	38 44 16 1
Occupational injuries insurance	Only employers' contributions (students' and pupils' insurance: general revenues)	Employees Employers State Others	2 86 4 8
Family allowances	Only general revenues	State	100
Youth assistance	Only general revenues	State Other	93 7
Social assistance	Only general revenues	State Other	84 11
War + other compensation (c)	Only general revenues	State	100
Housing	Only general revenues	State	100
Education	Only general revenues	State	100

(a) Minor groups may be subject to special regulations
(b) Other sources (income on capital etc.) are only listed if over 5%
(c) War victims, equalization of burdens, political reparation, and other compensations

4. Social security contributions and financing of welfare programmes

The German welfare state is predominantly financed by contributions from the insured and the employers. Public authorities carry the cost of education, housing and public health, but play a minor role in the financing of social security. Only a few of the less important schemes, which together account for about a third of total social security expenditure, are financed through general revenues (see Table 3). The major social insurance programmes are mainly financed by special contributions from employees and employers who contribute equal shares to pension, sickness and unemployment insurance. The cost of industrial accident insurance is exclusively born by employers. The role of the state is limited to the subsidization of the insurance schemes. In pension insurance, general revenues account for about a fifth of total receipts. In the unemployment insurance scheme, the federal government carries the cost of unemployment assistance and assumes a limited liability for the coverage of deficits. In sickness insurance, it provides limited subsidies for maternity allowances and student insurance.

Given the broadest definition of public welfare programmes, including education and housing, general revenues account for 40 percent of total financing. In the social

Table 4   Contribution rates and contribution ceilings in social insurance schemes

Year	Contribution rates as % of gross earnings (a)				Contribution ceilings in DM and as % of average gross earnings						Maximum monthly amount (DM)	Year
	Total	Pens. ins.	Sickn. ins. (b)	Unempl. ins.	Pension insurance DM	%	Sickness insurance DM	%	Unemployment insurance DM	%		
1950	20.0	10.0	6.0	4.0	600	247	375	154	375	154	97.50	1950
1951						212		133		133		1951
1952					750	246	500	164	500	164	125.00	1952
1953						232		155		155		1953
1954	20.2		6.2			221		147		147	126.00	1954
1955		11.0		3.0		199		133		133	128.50	1955
1956						189		126		126		1956
1957	23.8	14.0	7.8	2.0		180	660	158	750	180	171.48	1957
1958	24.4		8.4			169		149		169	175.44	1958
1959					800	171		141		160	182.44	1959
1960					850	166		129		146	189.44	1960
1961	24.4		9.4		900	159		117		133	203.04	1961
1962	25.0		9.6	1.4	950	154		107		122	206.86	1962
1963					1 000	153		101		115	213.86	1963
1964			9.7	1.3	1 100	154		84		105	227.77	1964
1965	25.2		9.9		1 200	154	900	116		96	266.85	1965
1966	25.3		10.0		1 300	156		108	1 300	156	288.90	1966
1967	25.4		10.1		1 400	162		104		151	303.80	1967
1968	26.5	15.0	10.2		1 600	175		98		142	348.70	1968
1969	27.8	16.0	10.5		1 700	170	990	99		130	392.85	1969
1970	26.5	17.0	8.2(b)		1 800	157	1 200	105	1 800	157	427.80	1970
1971					1 900	148	1 425	111	1 900	148	464.55	1971
1972	27.1		8.4	1.7	2 100	150	1 575	113	2 100	150	525.00	1972
1973	28.9	18.0	9.2		2 300	147	1 725	110	2 300	147	611.80	1973
1974	29.2		9.5		2 500	143	1 875	108	2 500	143	670.63	1974
1975	30.5		10.5	2.0	2 800	150	2 100	112	2 800	150	780.50	1975
1976	32.3		11.3	3.0	3 100	155	2 325	116	3 100	155	913.73	1976
1977	32.4		11.4		3 400	159	2 550	119	3 400	159	1 004.70	1977
1978					3 700	165	2 775	124	3 700	159	1 093.35	1978
1979	32.2		11.2		4 000	169	3 000	127	4 000	169	1 176.00	1979
1980	32.4		11.4		4 200	166	3 150	125	4 200	166	1 241.10	1980

(a) Total rates payable by employees and employers together; (b) average rates of all sickness insurance funds; 1950–69 workers' schemes only with lower rates in employees' schemes; lower rates in 1970 due to introduction of wage continuation.

security schemes (following the ILO definition), the state share amounts to 29 percent of the cost. Of their total revenues, 70 percent stem from employees' and employers' contributions. The legal contribution rates for employees and employers have been raised considerably over time, from an initial 20 percent for all systems together, to 32.4 percent in 1980 (see Table 4). More recently only unemployment insurance contributions have remained below the levels reached in the early 1950s. Sickness and pension insurance contributions were first raised substantially in 1957, and then again after 1967 following a decade of relative stagnation. Since the contribution ceilings have also been raised considerably, the maximum payable monthly contribution rose from 97.50 DM in 1950 to 1,241 DM in 1980 [69].

The increase in contribution rates for employees and employers was accompanied by a conspicuous decline of the state share in financing (see Graph 30). In particular the pension insurance system and unemployment insurance had to cope with a substantial reduction in state subsidies. In the pension insurance schemes for workers and employees, the state share sank to a third of the initial value between 1955 and 1975 [70]. For all pension schemes taken together, it sank from 25 percent in the 1950s to 20 percent in 1980. In unemployment insurance, the state share characteristically varies with the level of unemployment and the concomitant liquidity of the insurance fund. In the context of high unemployment in the early 1950s, public authorities contributed about one half of the total cost. In the context of similar high unemployment in the recession of 1975, state subsidies amounted to only 29 percent of total revenues. By 1980 their share had even declined to 17 percent.

While reducing its share in the financing of schemes, the government also shifted some new functions (alien to the original concept of insurance), to the social security system. Thus, the unemployment insurance system became responsible for carrying

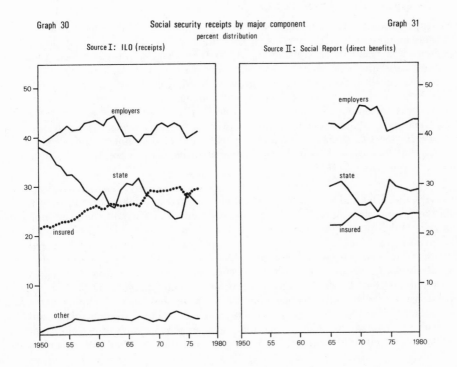

Graph 30   Social security receipts by major component   Graph 31
                                            percent distribution
            Source I: ILO (receipts)   Source II: Social Report (direct benefits)

out general labour market policies (e.g. vocational training), and the pension insurance system was obliged to recognize certain periods when no contributions were made (e.g. periods of military service) in the calculation of pension entitlements. This combination of decreasing state subsidies and extended functions is one of the sources of the recent fiscal problems of the social insurance system.

Up to the mid-1960s the social security system had been able to avoid deficits. Considerable financing gaps first appeared in 1967 and 1968. The quick recovery of the economy and some consolidation measures in subsequent years soon led to a renewed surplus. Following the recession of 1975, however, deficits of a previously unknown magnitude began to occur. Since that time the fiscal crisis in the social security system has been a topic of public debate (see Section V).

The marked decline of state subsidization together with the extension of the functions of the insurance schemes have made the contributors to both pension and unemployment insurance the 'losers' of recent social policy developments. In contrast, the existing regulations clearly favour civil servants. This group does not pay contributions, but nevertheless receives more generous pensions than workers and employees in the private sector. In addition, civil servants do not run the risk of unemployment as they hold tenured positions, and continue to draw their salaries in the case of sickness. Farmers constitute a second group which benefits from the current welfare provisions. As the decline in agricultural employment has led to a very unfavourable relationship between contributors and beneficiaries with regard to the pension scheme, the state carries 80 percent of its cost. The structure of privilege and underprivilege in the German welfare state is revealed more closely if we examine the benefit levels under the various programmes.

5. The expansion of the welfare clienteles

One explanation for the growth of welfare expenditure lies in the fact that an ever-increasing number of people have been drawing benefits. The growth of the welfare clienteles is a result of several factors. Apart from demographic and socio-economic changes, legislative extensions of eligibility for benefits and the introduction of new schemes have all contributed to this growth. As shown in Section II.2, the classical social insurance schemes were successively complemented by new types of income maintenance programmes such as child, housing and education allowances in the 1960s and early 1970s. Social insurance coverage has been widened mainly since the late 1960s (see Graph 32). Prior to this period, the income limit for the compulsory coverage of employees had only been adapted to changes in the wage level in 1952 and 1957 (see Table 5) [71].

The level of the income limit has always been an intensely debated political issue. Whereas the SPD and the unions advocated unlimited coverage, the Christian parties and the Liberals favoured a rather low income limit which would stimulate individual initiative and leave ample room for private insurance. Their policy was supported by the private insurance companies and the employers' associations who feared that extensions in coverage would not only lead to increasing labour costs, but that it would also bring about a reduction of occupational pension funds which represented an important and tax-credited form of capital accumulation [72]. Deliberate political non-decisions freezing the income limit were the easiest way of coping with these demands. Under the bourgeois coalition governments, the income limit for compulsory coverage in sickness, pension and unemployment insurance thus remained constant between 1957 and 1965. When the recession of 1967 led to unbalanced

Table 5

Extension of social security coverage

Year	Extension by social category — Pensions	Sickness insurance	Occupational injuries (b)	Child allowances	Extension of income limit (a) — Pensions/unempl.(c) DM	%	Sickness DM	%	Child allow. DM	%	Year
1950(d)					600	247	375	154			1950
1951						212		133			1951
1952					750	246	500	164			1952
1953						232		155			1953
1954				Third child		221		147			1954
1955						199		133			1955
1956						189		126			1956
1957	Compulsory farmers' insurance	Workers' (partial) wage continuation			1 250	300	660	158			1957
1958						282		149			1958
1959						267		141			1959
1960				Second child		244		129	600	106	1960
1961						221		117		97	1961
1962						203		107		92	1962
1963						191		101		91	1963
1964						175		93	650	84	1964
1965					1 800	231	900	116		78	1965
1966						216		108		75	1966
1967						209		104		71	1967
1968					Abolition of income limit			98		65	1968
1969		Workers' full wage continuation					990(e)	99		95	1969
1970			Students and pupils				1 200	104	1 100	97	1970
1971							1 425	111	1 250	89	1971
1972	Voluntary membership for housewives, self-employed and others		Compulsory farmers' insurance				1 575	112	1 400	90	1972
1973							1 725	111	1 530	88	1973
1974							1 875	108	Universal coverage		1974
1975	Handicapped persons	Handicapped persons/students		First child			2 100	114			1975
1976							2 325	118			1976
1977							2 550	121			1977
1978							2 775	125			1978
1979							3 000	128			1979
1980							3 150	126			1980
1981	Independent artists	Independent artists					3 300	126			1981

(a) In DM at current prices and as % of average gross earnings of the dependent labour force; (b) there is no income limit for occupational injuries insurance; (c) the income limit for pension and unemployment insurance is identical; (d) regulations existing in 1950; (e) indexation of income limit to contribution ceiling in pension insurance.

public budgets, the Grand Coalition government of Christian and Social Democrats abolished the income limit for pension and unemployment insurance in order to increase the financial resources of the schemes. The income limit for compulsory sickness insurance was indexed to changes in the wage level in 1970. Presently, less than 5 percent of all employees remain above this limit[73]. The majority of self-employed categories still find themselves outside the compulsory coverage. Civil servants are protected under special schemes.

Graph 32

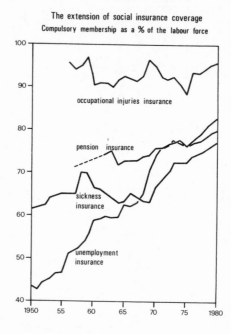

The extension of social insurance coverage
Compulsory membership as a % of the labour force

In the 1970s the scope of social insurance was increasingly extended beyond the economically active population. In 1971 students and pupils became incorporated into the accident insurance scheme which has covered almost the entire labour force since the early 1950s[74]. Besides economically active persons, sickness insurance also covers the family members of the insured (on an obligatory basis since 1930), pensioners (1941), students and some marginal groups such as the handicapped (since the 1970s)[75]. Including family members and the voluntarily insured, about 90 percent of the population are presently protected under the general sickness insurance scheme[76]. The coverage ratios reported in Graph 32 only relate to the development of compulsory coverage. The scope of pension insurance was widened in 1972 when the scheme was opened-up to the voluntary membership of housewives and other uncovered groups.

The impact of entitlement extensions on the growth of the welfare clienteles, independent of demographic or socio-economic changes, is best expressed by eligibility ratios. These show which percentage of persons exposed to a given risk actually receive benefits. Table 6 gives a synopsis of the number of beneficiaries in each of the cash benefit schemes and reports the relevant eligibility ratios. For a comparison of the various schemes, Graph 33 expresses the number of welfare recipients as a percentage of the population.

Graph 33

The clienteles of the major welfare schemes
as a % of total population

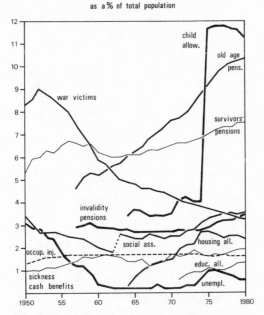

Pensioners are by far the largest group among the welfare clientele. In 1980, 13.1 million pensions were paid. Among the various pensions, old age pensions are not only the largest but also the most rapidly increasing category. Their dynamic growth is not merely a function of demographic changes. In 1960 only about a third of the population over the age of 60 drew an old age pension, but in 1980 more than half of this group received benefits (see Table 6) [77]. The steep increase in eligibility ratios in the 1970s reflects the introduction of a flexible age limit (1972) which permitted a reduction in the retirement age from 65 to 63 [78]. Among old age pensions the proportion of pensions drawn at the regular retirement age of 65 declined from 96 percent in 1960 to 62 percent in 1980 [79].

The lowering of the average retirement age is also a consequence of the shortage of vacancies in the labour market. In recent years retirement frequently occurred in two steps. Many elderly unemployed persons withdrew from the labour market, making claims for invalidity pensions which are transformed into old age pensions once they reach regular retirement age. Presently more than half of the newly issued pensions per year thus consist of invalidity pensions [80]. The total number of invalidity pensions which had remained fairly constant during the 1960s, grew continuously throughout the 1970s [81]. In 1980, 2.1 million invalidity pensions were paid. The number of survivors' pensions has also grown steeply, from 2.5 million in 1950 to 4.6 million in 1980 [82].

Since the generalization of the child allowance scheme in 1974, families receiving child allowances are the second largest group among the welfare clientele. More than seven million families or 85 percent of all families with children under 18, have been receiving benefits since that time. The remaining 15 percent usually draw special child supplements under the pension or accident insurance schemes or under the social assistance scheme.

Table 6   The clienteles of the major welfare schemes

	1950	1955	1960	1965	1970	1975	1980
Pensions (a)							
Old age pensions							
in thousands			2 901	3 645	4 585	5 703	6 349
as % of population 60+	2 786	3 661	32.7	34.5	39.3	46.0	53.4
Invalidity pensions							
in thousands	42.4	49.2	1 628	1 595	1 657	1 822	2 141
as % of population 60+			18.4	15.1	14.2	14.7	18.0
Survivors' pensions							
in thousands	2 547	3 285	3 447	3 597	3 969	4 314	4 617
as % of population 60+	38.7	44.2	38.9	34.0	34.0	34.8	38.8
Occupational injuries (b)							
Pensions in thousands	636	830	916	1 011	1 018	1 018	1 005
as % of labour force	2.9	3.5	3.5	3.7	3.8	3.9	3.8
Sickness (c)							
Recipients of cash benefits							
in thousands	(477)	(621)	(902)	(850)	(1 003)	(1 014)	(1 176)
as % of compulsorily insured	3.6	4.0	5.1	4.9	5.6	5.3	5.7
Unemployment (d)							
Recipients of cash benefits							
in thousands	1 455	890	226	109	113	817	576
as % of unemployed	77.8	82.9	83.4	74.1	75.8	76.1	64.5
War victims							
Pension recipients in thousands	3 939	4 165	3 276	2 813	2 587	2 318	1 981
as % of total population	8.3	8.3	5.9	4.8	4.3	3.7	3.2
Social assistance							
Recipients of ordinary benefits (e)							
in thousands				760	749	1 190	1 322
as % of total population				1.3	1.2	1.9	2.1
Recipients of ordinary or special benefits							
in thousands	1 633	1 328	1 134	1 404	1 491	2 049	2 144
as % of total population	3.4	2.6	2.0	2.4	2.5	3.3	3.5
Child allowances							
Supported families in thousands				2 171	2 113	7 253	6 967
as % of families with children under 18				27.4	24.8	82.6	82.9
Supported children in thousands				4 826	5 176	14 027	12 663
as % of all children under 18				30.9	31.5	87.3	88.1
Education allowances							
Aided students in thousands		1.5	32	46	200(f)	345	340
as % of all students		1.3	11.0	12.0	33.4	41.0	32.6
Aided pupils in thousands					160(f)	320	490
as % of secondary level pupils					24.1	35.2	40.7
Housing allowances							
Households receiving benefits							
in thousands				395	908	1 666	1 486
as % of all households				1.9	4.1	7.0	6.0
Welfare recipients (g)							
in thousands			7 200	7 799	9 087	10 538	11 195
as % of all income receivers			21.3	22.3	25.2	28.2	28.7

(a) The data refer to the number of pensions paid under the workers', employees' and miners' scheme; one person may draw several pensions.

(b) The data refer to the total number of pensions including survivors' pensions.

(c) The percentages refer to the proportion of compulsorily insured persons reporting sick; absolute numbers are calculated from these percentages.

(d) Number of persons drawing unemployment insurance benefits or unemployment assistance benefits.

(e) For a definition of ordinary benefits (Hilfe zum Lebensunterhalt) see the Institutional Synopsis.

(f) 1971.

(g) The data refer to persons dependent on pensions or similar payments as their main source of income.

There are four other categories of welfare recipients numbering more than one million each. Over two million people, or 3.5 percent of the population, received social assistance payments in 1980. After a decline in recipients in the 1950s and fluctuations around a fairly constant level of 1.5 million throughout the 1960s, numbers rose again in the 1970s, especially after the mid-decade economic recession. The recession years of 1966/67 and 1973-75 each saw over-proportional increases of assistance recipients [83]. Scarcely two million persons still receive payments under the benefits for war victims scheme. In the early 1950s their number had exceeded four million with a peak of 9 percent of the population in 1952. Since that year the number of beneficiaries has been consistently declining, falling below two million for the first time in 1980.

About 1.5 million households or 6 percent of all households are in receipt of housing allowances. Since the introduction of regular benefits in 1965, their absolute number and proportion have more than tripled. In 1980, 1.1 million persons drew sickness cash benefits. The proportion of compulsorily insured persons reported sick has increased continuously in the postwar period. Averaging 4 percent in the 1950s, it rose to 4.4 in the 1960s, and 5.5 percent in the 1970s [84]. Another million persons draw a pension from the occupational injuries scheme. After a continuous increase throughout the 1950s and the first half of the 1960s, their number has remained fairly constant since 1965.

In the two remaining categories, the number of beneficiaries is much more limited. The number of persons maintained on unemployment benefits (insurance or assistance) correlates closely with the fluctuations in the business cycle. It is remarkable, however, that the proportion of unemployed people receiving benefits has been declining sharply in recent years (see Section III.1). Unemployed persons who remain without compensation have either exhausted their entitlements [85] or have not contributed long enough in order to satisfy the minimum qualification requirements.

Education allowances are granted independently of previous contributions. Nevertheless, the proportion of students in receipt of allowances has also been declining since 1975. During the phase of educational expansion in the early 1970s, around 41 percent of all students drew benefits. In the second half of the decade, the absolute number of beneficiaries remained stagnant at about 330,000, but as a proportion of the total number of students, it continuously declined to a low of 33 percent in 1980. The number of pupils in receipt of allowances continued to grow in absolute and relative terms. In 1980, 490,000 pupils drew allowances as compared with 160,000 in 1971. This corresponded to 24 and 41 percent respectively of all full-time pupils at secondary stage II [86].

6. The development of benefits

By and large, welfare recipients have been able to keep pace with the living standards of the economically active population. In some cases they could even improve their relative position (see Tables 7 and 8, and Graph 34). To give welfare recipients a share in the increasing prosperity of the economy has always been an explicit policy goal of German governments [87]. Originally it was accomplished by occasional revisions which - often with considerable delay - sought to adapt benefit levels to the development of prices or wages. In the case of the income replacement schemes, these revisions later gave way to indexation procedures.

Indexation of benefits was first implemented for pension insurance. Following intense political struggles, the 1957 pension reform provided for annual pension increases according to changes in wage levels. As the development of the pensioners' standard of living had previously been dependent on the stability of prices, but was now immediately tied to the results of the collective bargaining process, the reform effectively contributed to a homogenization of the interests of the economically active and the retired population. Pensions under the occupational injuries insurance scheme were indexed in 1964. Sickness and unemployment benefits are automatically tied to the wage level, since individual entitlements are expressed as percentages of lost earnings. If they are paid for periods of more than one calendar year, they are also indexed. Benefits for war victims and payments under the equalization of war burdens fund were indexed in 1970 and 1974 respectively.

The benefits of the schemes which serve as income supplements rather than income replacements are not indexed, but occasionally adapted to changing economic conditions. During the most recent period this adaptation has in some cases also taken the form of cuts (see Section V). The standard rates (*Regelsätze*) of the social assistance scheme have been revised annually since 1957. Child allowances have only been increased at irregular intervals. Housing allowances are occasionally adapted to changing income or rent levels. Sizeable augmentations were legislated in 1970, 1977 and 1980. The rates of education allowances have been re-examined biennially since 1974.

All benefits have increased substantially in purchasing power over time, but the degree of generosity varies considerably among schemes (see Tables 7 and 8). The legal rates are highest for the short-term income replacements for the economically active population. Sickness cash benefits originally amounted to 50 percent of lost earnings, but reforms in 1957 and 1961 pushed them up to a full wage continuation for six weeks. The legal earnings replacement ratios of unemployment insurance benefits increased from about 40 percent in 1950 [88] to 68 percent of net earnings in 1980. The per capita unemployment insurance benefits have sizeably increased in purchasing power during the postwar period. The fluctuations over time reported in Graph 34 are unrelated to legislative changes and do not lend themselves easily to a substantive interpre-

Graph 34

Average benefits of major welfare schemes
as a % of average net earnings

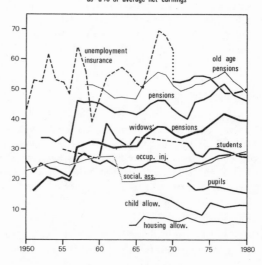

Table 7   Average benefits of the major welfare schemes (a)

	1950	1955	1960	1965	1970	1975	1980
Pensions (b)							
Average pension (old age or invalidity)							
at constant prices (1976)	173	211	352	421	542	671	705
as % of average net earnings	34	34	45	42	43	48	47
Average old age pension (age 65)							
at constant prices (1976)			391	472	638	746	742
as % of average net earnings			50	47	51	53	49
Average widows'/widowers' pension							
at constant prices (1976)	82(d)	129	248	311	437	534	601
as % of average net earnings	16	21	32	31	35	38	40
Occupational injuries							
Average benefits at 1976 prices	121	134	195	242	294	370	429
as % of average earnings	26	22	25	24	24	26	28
Unemployment (e)							
Average benefits at 1976 prices	196	325	367	527	655	755	762
as % of average earnings	43	52	47	52	52	54	50
Social assistance (f)							
Average ordinary benefits							
at constant prices (1976)				143	183	221	236
as % of average net earnings				14	15	16	16
Average benefits (ordinary or special)							
at constant prices (1976)	104	154	212	196	260	357	445
as % of average net earnings	23	25	27	19	21	25	29
Education							
Average benefits for students							
at constant prices (1976)		185	209	346	429(g)	423	395(h)
as % of average net earnings		30	27	34	32	30	27
Average benefits for pupils							
at constant prices (1976)				69	253	245	214(h)
as % of average net earnings				7	19	17	15
Child allowances							
Average benefits per family							
at constant prices (1976)				149	157	172	174
as % of average net earnings				15	13	12	11
Housing allowances							
Average benefits per household							
at constant prices (1976)				49	77	87	90
as % of average net earnings				5	6	6	6

(a) In general, average benefits are benefits per capita obtained by simply dividing aggregate expenditure by the number of beneficiaries; percentages are calculated on the basis of current figures.

(b) All figures are averages of the workers', employees' and miners' schemes; they have been obtained by taking the average benefits for each scheme from official sources and weighing them by the number of beneficiaries of the respective scheme. They always refer to the end of the stated year.

(c) 1952.

(d) 1951.

(e) Insurance benefits only, i.e. excluding unemployment assistance; 1970 change in statistical definitions.

(f) For a definition of ordinary and special benefits see Appendix Volume; between 1960 and 1965 change in official statistics on social assistance.

(g) 1972.

(h) 1982.

Table 8   Standard benefits and earnings replacement ratios

	1950	1955	1960	1965	1970	1975	1980
Pensions (old age):							
Standard earnings replacement ratio (a)			67.5	67.5	67.5	67.5	67.5
Standard pension (b), at current prices			271	378	550	929	1 232
at constant prices (1976)			487	592	770	970	1 063
as % of average net earnings			63.0	59.0	62.0	69.0	70.0
Sickness:							
Earnings replacement ratio (c)	50.0	50.0	90.0	100.0	100.0	100.0	100.0
Unemployment:							
Earnings replacement ratio (d)	(40.0)	(47.0)	(50.0)	55.0	62.5	68.0	68.0
Social assistance:							
Standard benefits (e), at current prices			84	118	155	252	309
at constant prices (1976)			151	185	217	263	266
as % of average net earnings			19.0	18.0	17.0	19.0	18.0
Child allowances:							
Standard benefits for							
1st child: at current prices						50	50
at constant prices (1976)						52	43
as % of av. net earnings						4.0	3.0
2nd child: at current prices				25	25	70	100
at constant prices (1976)				39	35	73	86
as % of av. net earnings				4.0	3.0	5.0	6.0
3rd child: at current prices (f)		25	40	50	60	120	200
at constant prices (1976)		49	72	78	84	125	172
as % of av. net earnings		8.0	9.0	8.0	7.0	9.0	11.0

(a) Earnings replacement ratio according to pension formula (cf. Appendix Volume) for a beneficiary with 45
    contribution years and life-time earnings corresponding to average earnings of the insured population.
(b) Actual pension drawn by a pensioner fulfilling the conditions of note (a).
(c) Legal earnings replacement ratio during the first six weeks of illness.
(d) Since 1975 legal earnings replacement ratio; in previous years earnings replacement ratio obtained by a single
    beneficiary with average earnings. For the period 1950-1960 calculated from legal benefit tables.
(e) Rates to which single persons below 65 are entitled if without other income; persons above 65 receive 30% more
    (until 1964: 20% more).
(f) Since 1975 rates for 3rd child and further children; between 1964 and 1974 benefits for the fourth child, the fifth
    child or further children had special higher rates.

tation, because pre-1970 data include transfers to other insurance schemes and restitutions to foreign unemployment insurance funds [89].

Among the long-term income maintenance benefits (occupational injuries pensions, invalidity, survivors' and old age pensions) the legal rates of the occupational injuries insurance scheme are highest. In the case of permanent incapacity, they amount to two-thirds of lost gross wages which in most cases corresponds to net earnings. The per capita benefits are much lower than these standard rates because they refer to statistical averages which lump full pensions together with partial pensions and survivors' pensions. Changes over time since the 1957 reform reflect the distribution of previous earnings from work among the beneficiaries and the severity of accidents suffered.

Legal benefit rates in the pension insurance schemes have basically remained unchanged since 1957. The reform of that year homogenized the entitlements of workers and employees, but established a closer link between pension levels and recipients' earnings records. In the standard case of an average earner with a contribution record of 45 years, old age pensions amount to 67.5 percent of recent average gross earnings [90]. Invalidity and widows' pensions are lower, in standard cases amounting to 52.5 and 21 percent respectively of average wages [91]. The average old age pension is lower than the standard pension because many pensioners only have short contribution records or life-time earnings are below the average wage. The average old age pension drawn at the age of 65 has more than doubled in purchasing power since 1960 and has been fluctuating at around 50 percent of average net earnings since the 1957 reform.

The annual fluctuations of per capita benefits shown in Graph 34 are largely the result of the time-lag in the indexation procedure. As the increase of pensions depends on the increase in wages in preceding years, the relative level of pensions typically varies in a counter-cyclical fashion. This effect was particularly strong in the years following the recession of 1966/67 and 1974/75. The decrease in the late 1970s, however, also reflects the impact of the cutback legislation of 1977 and 1978 which seriously curbed the rate of pension growth. The statistically typical pension which the majority of male pensioners in the workers' scheme actually receive amounted to 1,096 DM or 62 percent of average net earnings of the dependent labour force in 1980 [92].

The cash benefits of the other schemes serve as income supplements which do not usually replace, but augment, other sources of income. With the exception of child allowances, they therefore vary with the recipient's income in the sense that lower income leads to higher benefits. Increasing per capita benefits may in these cases therefore indicate growing poverty gaps. The legal rate of the standard social assistance benefit (*Regelsatz*) has doubled in purchasing power since 1957 and fluctuated at around 19 percent of average net earnings (see Table 8). The fact that assistance benefits have generally kept pace with the development of wages, indicates that the standard rates may be interpreted as a quasi-official definition of poverty in relative terms. As the beneficiaries usually receive various supplements (especially for the cost of housing) which double the amount of the standard rate, the quasi-official poverty line is drawn at roughly 40 percent of average net earnings [93]. Since 1977, however, benefits have not only been growing significantly slower than earnings, but have also been decreasing in real terms [94]. The per capita ordinary benefits (*Hilfe zum Lebensunterhalt*) have maintained a fairly constant relationship to wage levels, fluctuating at around 15 percent. The fact that total assistance payments per capita have grown faster than earnings largely reflects the increasing costs and growing relative importance of institutional care.

Education allowances have not kept pace with the development of wages. The average benefit for university students fluctuated at around a third of net earnings in the early 1960s, but in the second half of the 1970s it fell to below 30 percent (1978: 28, 1982: 27 percent). In this more recent period, student grants were even subject to a cut in purchasing power. The same applies to pupils' allowances which amounted to 19 percent of net wages in 1972, as against 15 percent in 1982. Although they have not been growing as dynamically as the other expenditure categories, education allowances are on a surprisingly high level when compared with other benefits. In the early 1950s the per capita benefits for a university student on a public scholarship were higher than the average pension under the workers' scheme [95]. In the 1970s the average education allowance (for students or pupils) was consistently higher than the standard rate for a social assistance recipient [96].

Child allowances frequently suffered setbacks in their purchasing power. The standard rates for the second child were not increased between 1961 and 1974. The rates for the first child have remained constant since their introduction (1975). The rates for the third child and further children were occasionally revised, but did not keep pace with the development of wages. The average payments per family therefore dropped from 15 percent of average net earnings in 1965 to 11 percent in 1980. As benefit rates increase with the number of children, the shrinking size of the family also contributed to a lowering of the benefits per family. Housing allowances are the lowest of the social transfer payments. Since the 1960s, the average allowance per household maintained a fairly constant relationship with the average wage, of about 6 percent.

Since several benefits may be drawn by one person at the same time, the discussion of single schemes cannot serve to develop a clear picture of the relative importance of welfare clienteles as a whole. Since the late 1950s, however, the central statistical office has carried out an annual microcensus which allows us to make an approximate assessment of the number of persons relying on social transfers as their main (but not necessarily only) source of income. In 1960, 7.2 million citizens, or 21 percent of all persons who received income, drew their income largely from welfare schemes. In 1974 their number surpassed 10 million for the first time, and in 1980 it had risen to 11.2 million, or 29 percent of all income recipients. By the early 1980s, there were in fact half a million more persons living from public transfer payments in West Germany than blue-collar workers [97].

The size of the various welfare clienteles and the average level of benefits which they receive may give some first indication of the quality of German welfare provisions. A sounder assessment of the effectiveness of the schemes, however, requires further information on the distribution of transfer income and services, and on the position of groups which the welfare state does not cover despite serious need. These questions are dealt with in the following section.

III Achievements and shortcomings: evaluations

Institutions which spend close to one third of GDP and two-thirds of public expenditure should be subject to routine assessment of their effectiveness. Public authorities in Germany have failed, however, to develop a systematic set of data which would allow such an analysis [98]. Only in recent years, some limited attempts have been made to provide the necessary information. The following account is therefore confined to the presentation of some basic indicators of the achievements and shortcomings of the major income maintenance schemes, the health system, housing policy, and the system of public education.

1. The adequacy of the income maintenance schemes

Following the policy statements of various federal governments and the platforms of the major political parties, the German income maintenance schemes have three basic aims: to prevent poverty, to provide social security in the sense of helping people to preserve their social status in the case of lost earnings, and to reduce inequalities in living conditions. Although the exact meaning of these goals may be subject to debate, there is fairly widespread consensus as to their desirability. The report of the Transfer Enquete Commission established by the federal government ranks all three aims among the basic goals of the transfer system [99]. Consensus is probably highest on the first goal. A public responsibility for the prevention of poverty even follows from the Constitution (see Articles 1, 20 and 28). We will therefore first analyse how poverty is defined in West Germany and to what extent the welfare state has succeeded in eliminating it.

Poverty and the effectiveness of social assistance

The German social assistance scheme rests on the premise that no citizen should fall below an official poverty line. This is defined by the money value of the basket of goods considered necessary for a life in keeping with human dignity. A list of such necessary goods was first established in 1955 and modified in 1961 and 1971. The official definition of poverty also has a relative element in that social assistance benefits, including the cost of housing, are designed to be below the average net earnings of the lower wage categories.

Graph 35 shows how the official poverty line has developed in absolute and relative terms since 1957. The absolute definition of poverty has been substantially upgraded over the past decades. Between 1957 and 1980 the purchasing power of the official

Graph 35

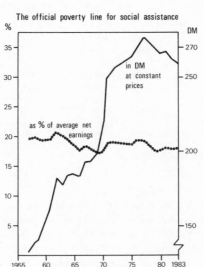

minimum doubled. In relative terms, the poverty line rose faster than the average net earnings of the dependent labour force in some periods (1957-1961, 1971-1977) but more slowly in others (1962-1970, 1978-1980). In the long run, it has declined slightly, but by and large the official minimum for the poor has developed at a speed similar to that of the net earnings of the dependent labour force.

Definitions of poverty are always to some extent arbitrary. We will therefore not discuss the adequacy of the German definition, but will analyse instead to what extent the welfare state is successful in reducing the number of people falling below this poverty line. As we have seen in Section II.5 (see Graph 33) the number of assisted people declined continuously from 3.4 percent of the population in 1950 to 1.8 percent in 1962. In a new statistical definition, it then remained fairly constant at a level of around 2.5 percent between 1963 and 1971, but since 1972 it has again risen to the size of the early 1950s [100]. Given the considerable expansion of the income maintenance schemes for standard risks in the last decades, the constant or even increasing number of social assistance recipients is noteworthy. It may be interpreted as a first indication of sizeable gaps in social security which have persisted despite the remarkable growth of welfare state programmes. An analysis of the internal composition of the 'registered' poor may help to identify where these gaps are.

The high sensitivity of poverty estimates to minor variations in income, and the limited size of the poverty gap, also appears if we look at a definition of poverty in relative terms. As Table 10 shows, the proportion of people identified as poor increases sharply if the relative definition of poverty is gradually made more lenient. Only two percent of all households live in severe poverty as defined by 40 percent of the average standard of living [113], but three times as many have to settle with moderate conditions (50 percent of the average), and one fifth to one fourth of all households live in mild poverty (60 percent of the average). The conclusion seems warranted that a sizeable minority of the West German population has to cope with living conditions close to the official poverty line (which roughly corresponds to the 40 percent standard).

Table 10   Households and persons in relative poverty according to different poverty standards

Standards (a)	Households/persons in thousands			As % of all households/persons		
	1963	1969	1973	1963	1969	1973
Households						
40% standard	860	515	480	4.3	2.5	2.3
50% standard	2 256	1 668	1 573	11.4	8.1	7.4
60% standard	4 364	3 520	3 492	22.1	17.1	16.5
Persons						
40% standard	3 018	1 582	1 507	5.3	2.8	2.6
50% standard	8 051	5 414	5 087	14.1	9.7	8.9
60% standard	15 331	11 516	11 135	26.9	20.6	19.5

(a) Percentage of average standard of living.

The question of who the hidden poor are, and why they live in poverty, can only be analysed on the basis of representative surveys of the income of private households carried out in 1963, 1969, 1973, and 1978 [114]. From Table 11, it is evident that poverty hits the economically inactive population most. Their risk of falling below the social assistance standard is almost three times higher than the average risk for all households. In contrast more than 99 percent of the households of employed persons manage to remain above the official poverty level. This also applies to worker households. In this sense the assertion of Geissler and other proponents of Christian Democratic social policy that the 'old social question' of a poor proletariat has been successfully solved, contains an element of truth [115]. It may even be shown that on average, self-employed groups have a higher poverty risk than worker households [116].

Table 11   Poverty risks of various types of households (a)

Type of household	1963	1969	1973
Economically active heads of household	0.9	0.3	0.2
Workers	1.1	0.2	0.3
Economically non-active heads of household	9.5	4.5	5.6
Single male	3.7	2.8	3.0
Single female	10.7	4.9	5.3
Married couples without children	3.2	1.4	2.6
Married couples with children	1.4	0.3	0.4
Others	2.8	1.7	2.0
Age of heads of households			
under 25	.	.	.
25-35	0.8	0.2	0.4
35-45	1.9	0.5	0.4
45-55	1.7	0.5	0.5
55-65	4.1	1.2	1.1
65+	10.3	5.1	6.9
Total households	3.6	1.7	2.2

(a) Percentage of households in hidden poverty below the social assistance standard.

A closer analysis by type of household shows the elderly and single women to be the groups most threatened with poverty. Contrary to common assumptions, statistical analysis does not reveal that families with children have an over-proportionate poverty risk [117]. The question to what extent the rising unemployment of the past decade has led to an increasing number of poor persons will be taken up below. In addition to the groups covered by the income surveys of private households, various marginal groups live in poverty without drawing social assistance benefits. These include some 100,000 tramps and an estimated half million homeless persons [118].

In summary, roughly 3 percent of all households or 2 percent of the population have to rely on regular social assistance benefits. Another group of about the same size lives below the official poverty line, but does not claim assistance benefits. Economically inactive groups, elderly persons, single women (especially the old), and single-parent families are the groups with the highest poverty risk. In many cases, members of these groups are in receipt of benefits from other income maintenance schemes which, however, are not sufficient to avoid poverty as defined by official standards. This indicates considerable shortcomings of the programmes designed to cover the standard risks of income loss. The effectiveness of these schemes, first of the unemployment compensation programme, and then of pension insurance, will now be analysed.

The adequacy of the unemployment benefit system

During the 1950s the initially very high level of unemployment could be reduced continuously, as the number of openings in the labour market expanded much more rapidly than the size of the labour force. From 1960 to 1973 practically full employment prevailed (see Graph 36). Between 1974 and 1977 unemployment quickly increased despite a shrinking labour force, because in the recession the number of jobs was reduced by almost one million. Since 1977 demographic changes have led to a heavy increase in the demand for jobs, as the labour market entrance of the large age cohorts born during the baby boom years (1961-1967) [119] combined with the shrinking numbers of withdrawals in the retiring generation decimated by the war. From 1977 to 1980 the expansion of the labour force was accompanied by a rising supply of jobs. This was not sufficient, however, to meet the growing demand. Since 1980 further increases in demand have even been accompanied by a shrinking supply as the number of jobs decreased by one million.

Graph 36

The development of the labour force
in millions

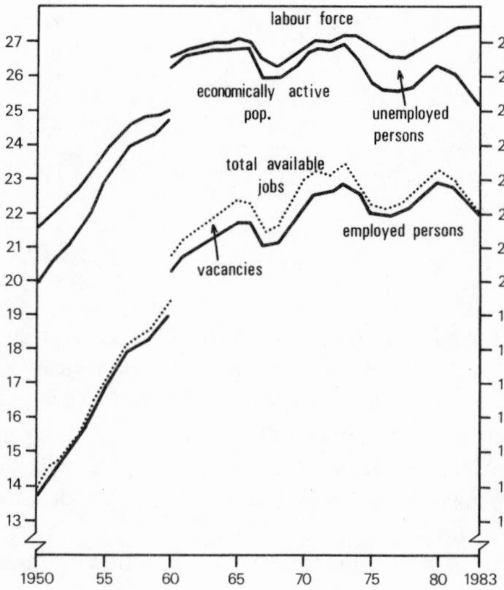

Regular social assistance benefits (*Hilfe zum Lebensunterhalt*) go predominantly to households with economically inactive heads of family who represent about 90 percent of all recipient households. Major categories receiving benefits include those over the age of 60 (about one third), single persons, especially women (about one third), and single-parent families (about one fifth) [101]. The composition of recipient groups remained practically constant during the 1960s, but underwent considerable changes in the 1970s. In the context of rising unemployment, especially the proportion of recipients in younger age cohorts, of families with children, and of persons in receipt of unemployment benefits increased heavily [102]. A 1981 survey by the Federal Statistical Office identified the following predominant causes for the dependence on social assistance: insufficient pensions (27.6 percent), insufficient income among other economically inactive groups (27.4 percent), insufficient means of single-parent families (17.0 percent), and unemployment (10.5 percent). In contrast, insufficient earnings from work played only a minor role (2.7 percent of all cases) [103]. In most cases poverty was not merely a transitory episode, but a rather permanent condition. In 1981, 75 percent of all recipient households had drawn benefits for more than one year, and 53 percent for more than three years [104]. The data suggest that considerable gaps still exist in the pension insurance programmes, the child allowance scheme, and the unemployment compensation system.

This conclusion is sustained if we analyse the poverty risks of various types of households (see Table 9). Single persons and single-parent families have an over-proportionate poverty risk. Pensioners (especially female pensioners) represent a high proportion of single-person households. The poverty risk of families with children is generally below average, but increases with the number of children. Single parents with children are subject to conspicuously high poverty risks, especially if they have to care for several children. The introduction of the 1979 maintenance security scheme reduced this risk to a considerable yet still insufficient degree.

Table 9 — Households in receipt of social assistance by type of household as % of all respective households

Type of household	1963	1969	1970	1971	1972	1973	1974	1975	1976	1977	1978	1981
Single persons												
male		2.7	2.5	2.6	2.7	2.9	3.7	4.5	4.7	5.0	5.3	6.2
female		4.6	5.0	4.7	5.2	5.1	5.0	5.1	5.0	4.9	4.8	4.6
Married couples												
without children		0.8	0.8	0.8	0.8	0.9	0.9	0.9	0.9	0.9	0.8	0.7
Married couples with												
1 child		0.1	0.1	0.1	0.2	0.2	0.3	0.3	0.4	0.5	0.4	0.5
2 children		0.1	0.1	0.1	0.1	0.2	0.3	0.4	0.5	0.5	0.5	0.5
3 or more children		0.4	0.4	0.4	0.4	0.5	0.8	1.0	1.1	1.2	1.0	0.7
Single parents with												
1 child		1.8	1.8	2.0	2.3	2.5	3.3	4.2	4.9	5.4	5.8	6.0
2 children		6.4	6.9	7.4	8.1	8.4	11.0	12.5	14.0	13.7	13.8	11.6
3 or more children		13.4	14.8	14.6	16.0	16.9	19.5	18.9	21.1	20.3	19.5	13.8
Total households	2.2	1.9				2.2					3.0	3.0
Total persons as % of total population	1.4	1.2				1.4					2.1	2.0

Following the official definition of poverty, all persons in receipt of social assistance payments are no longer below the poverty line. It could therefore be argued that the assistance scheme successfully bridges the gaps left by other welfare state programmes. In fact, increasing numbers of recipients do not necessarily indicate growing gaps in other schemes, but may also be an expression of more generous eligibility criteria. In this sense, the 1974 reform, which limited the potential liability to repay assistance benefits to first degree relatives, presumably contributed to an increasing number of claims. The public debate on poverty which started in the early 1970s therefore primarily centered on the question of how many people were living below the social assistance level without receiving benefits.

A 1976 publication by Heiner Geissler, a leading Christian Democratic politician, aroused widespread concern, stating that 9 percent of all private households with altogether 5.8 million persons were living below the official poverty line [105]. This opened up a lively debate in which widely discrepant estimates of the size of the poor population were produced, ranging from 0.7 to 20.3 percent of all households in various years between 1969 and 1975 [106]. These astounding discrepancies mainly arise from differences in the methods of calculating the official poverty standard (based on different assumptions as to the cost of housing and the size of single lump-sum payments), from different ways of weighting the needs of additional household members, from differences in assessing the amount of private property to be deducted under the means test, and from the use of different income statistics.

The national poverty report published in 1981 arrived at estimates of 3.6 percent of all households in 1963, 1.7 percent in 1969, and 2.2 percent in 1973 [107]. It concluded that the number of persons living in 'hidden' poverty is roughly the same as the number of assistance recipients, so that the 'real' poverty ratio is about twice as high as the official ratio derived from social assistance statistics [108]. The decrease of the poverty ratio since 1963 may be interpreted as evidence of an increasing effectiveness of the welfare state programmes, but during the 1970s the proportion of those living in hidden poverty does not seem to have decreased [109].

The social assistance scheme thus fulfills its function as an ultimate safety net only partially. The great variability in the estimates of the poor population indicates, however, that the gap between the income of poor persons and the standards of the social assistance scheme cannot be very large. Following the results of the national poverty report, the means of the hidden poor in 1973 were on average about 13 percent (or 85 DM per month) under the official standard [110]. This would imply that an effective elimination of poverty below the social assistance level would only have cost an additional half billion DM corresponding to 8.8 percent of actual social assistance expenditure [111]. It may well be, however, that the gap separating potential beneficiaries from the assistance standard is so small in actual practice that most persons do not bother to make a claim which would be connected with considerable social controls [112].

Throughout the 1970s and early 1980s the demand for public action for the unemployed expanded. Employment programmes initiated by the federal government in 1973 led to the annual creation or preservation of some 200,000 jobs between 1974 and 1978 [120]. These measures reduced the level of unemployment by between one seventh to one fifth [121], but they were not sufficient to prevent mass unemployment. Consequently, the demand for unemployment benefits grew rapidly, but at the same time, the proportion of unemployed persons in receipt of benefits declined drastically (see Graph 37). In the most recent period less than two-thirds of the unemployed received

Graph 37

Unemployed persons with or without
unemployment benefits
percent distribution

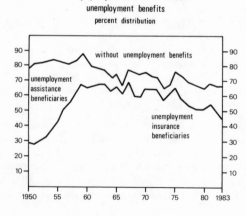

benefits. The structure of beneficiary groups also underwent considerable changes. A growing proportion of recipients only received unemployment assistance benefits which are considerably lower than insurance benefits. In the early 1980s, scarcely half of the unemployed drew insurance benefits, one fifth received assistance benefits, and one third did not receive any benefit at all [122]. Welfare gaps of a similar magnitude had only existed in the early 1950s.

The worsening situation of the unemployed is mostly due to an increasing duration of unemployment, but curtailments of entitlements from 1975 have also had an impact. In the early 1970s, unemployment was only temporary for the overwhelming majority of the unemployed, the average duration being two months; almost two-thirds of the unemployed were without a job for less than three months, and only 8 percent were unemployed for more than one year. In contrast, the average duration of unemployment in 1983 was 7 months, with only 29 percent being unemployed for less than three months, 54 percent for more than half a year, and 29 percent for more than a year [123]. Since unemployment insurance benefits are only paid for a maximum period of one year, and the duration of benefits is dependent upon the previous contribution record, the increase in long-term unemployment was accompanied by a relative decrease in the number of beneficiaries. Legislation in 1981 and 1982 (see Section V) which extended the contribution periods necessary for the receipt of benefits of a certain duration, exacerbated this development even further. The tightening linkage between entitlements and employment record in a situation where employment opportunities were rapidly diminishing may be considered a paradox of recent German social policy.

These recent developments raise the question of to what extent the system of unemployment compensation provides social security. Unemployed persons receiving benefits are much better off today than in the 1950s, because benefit levels have been repeatedly improved (especially in 1953, 1956, 1967, and 1974). The great majority of recipients therefore do not fall below social assistance standards [124]. A 1981 survey showed that only 7.8 percent of all private households would sink below the official poverty line if all workers and employees had to live from unemployment benefits [125]. Another survey carried out in 1975 showed that the average reduction in disposable household income is limited to 25 percent for households with unemployed heads of family [126]. This is because a sizeable proportion of the unemployed lived in households with a second or third earner. Thus, 40 percent were married with an economically active spouse [127].

Such crude averages, of course, are not particularly suited to identifying problem groups. Since the overwhelming part of the unemployed comes from low-income groups [128], even a reduction of only 25 percent of disposable household income may lead to serious hardship. A representative survey held in 1978 showed that one fourth to one half of all households of long-term unemployed (depending on household size) remained below or near the poverty line of the social assistance scheme [129]. The poverty risk was highest for single person households (43 percent), and for households with four (39 percent), or five and more persons (49 percent).

The authors of the national poverty report estimated that some 50,000-70,000 households were living in poverty due to unemployment in 1978, and that 20 percent of all households of long-term unemployed were below the social assistance standard [130]. In February 1984, 40 percent of recipients had unemployment insurance benefits below 800 DM per month, 65 percent remained below 1,000 DM, and only 14 percent received more than 1,200 DM. The respective percentages for recipients of unemployment assistance benefits were 63, 89, and 4 percent. These data must be compared with average net earnings of the dependent labour force, which amounted to 1,930 DM in 1983 [131].

The gaps in the social security schemes for the unemployed are also evident from social assistance statistics. Among all households receiving regular assistance benefits, the percentage of those in receipt of unemployment benefits increased from 1 to 10 percent between 1973 and 1982 (see Table 12). To the extent that the data allow such inferences, we may say that in almost one out of ten cases (8 percent), unemployment benefits were not high enough to prevent poverty [132]. The proportion of the unemployed not receiving compensation, but living from social assistance, is estimated at 10-20 percent [133].

Table 12   Recipients of social assistance and unemployment benefits

Year	Households receiving regular social assistance in 1,000s	% receiving also unemployment benefits	Recipients of assistance and unemployment benefits as % of	
			total unemployed	unemployment benefit recipients
1973	505 000	1.2	(2.2)	(3.4)
1974	568 000	3.5	(3.4)	(5.1)
1975	633 173	5.8	(3.4)	(4.5)
1976	674 198	6.7	(4.3)	(5.8)
1977	715 478	7.4	(5.1)	(7.3)
1978	716 803	8.0	(5.8)	(8.5)
1979	723 325	6.6	(5.4)	(8.2)
1980	759 916	6.1	(5.2)	(8.0)
1981	756 485	7.7	(4.6)	(6.7)
1982	908 104	10.2	(5.1)	(7.6)

We may conclude that the West German unemployment compensation schemes fulfill their functions only partly. Although the great majority of beneficiaries manage to avoid outright poverty, unemployment always leads to sizeable reductions in the standard of living. In recent years a growing minority of the unemployed has even fallen below the official poverty line. Single persons and heads of households with three or more dependents are particularly jeopardized. This situation is partly the result of the institutional structure of the compensation schemes. Although the earnings-replacement ratios are relatively high, the absence of a minimum component which would keep benefits above the social assistance level, and of child supplements for large families [134] exacerbates the poverty risk for specific groups.

The adequacy of pension insurance

As shown in Section IV, the proportion of elderly persons drawing old age pensions has greatly increased over the last decades (see Table 6). This increase is partly attributable to the lowering of the retirement age for specific groups and to the introduction of a flexible age limit in 1972. Whereas in 1970 only 16 percent of all old age pensions under the pension insurance scheme went to persons under 65, in 1983 the respective figure was 46 percent [135]. If we include another million persons drawing pensions under the farmers' and the civil servants' schemes [136], about two-thirds of the population over 60 appear on the payroll of public pension programmes. The remaining third are still economically active [137], or do not fulfill the qualifying conditions for the receipt of benefits. The latter group includes self-employed persons not covered by compulsory insurance schemes who live from private pensions or from capital returns. It also includes former members of compulsory schemes who have not made sufficient contributions. This group mainly consists of women, many of whom are in receipt of a survivor's pension.

The exact proportion of elderly persons who are economically inactive and not in receipt of a pension is not known. According to the national poverty report (see Table 11), 7 percent of all households with heads of family over the age of 65 were living in poverty in 1973. Thus, it is obvious that the German pension system has some considerable gaps. In an attempt to narrow these gaps the contribution period for old age pensions was lowered from 15 to 5 years in 1983.

The extension of entitlements still does not guarantee, however, adequate benefit levels. Graph 38 shows the development of the standard pension and of average pensions in the workers' and the employees' scheme, expressed as percentages of average net earnings of the insured population. In recent debates on the adequacy of the pension insurance scheme the federal government usually points out that the level of the standard pension has risen to unprecedented heights. In fact, the level of the standard pension has been fluctuating around an all-time high of 65 percent since 1977. Compared with the economically active population, pensioners have apparently been able to pass through the economic crisis in relatively favourable terms despite the recent cutback legislation.

Graph 38

Standard and average pensions

as % of average net earnings of the insured population

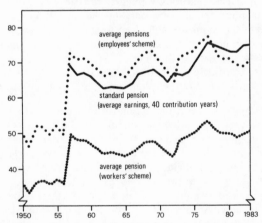

A comparison with the development of average pensions shows, however, that the standard pension drawn by a pensioner with a contribution record of 40 years and life-time average earnings is not totally representative. In recent years, even the average pension of the relatively privileged employees' scheme has fallen below the level of this standard pension [138]. The average pension of the workers' scheme has always remained at a much lower level. Although the pension reforms of 1957 and 1972 considerably improved benefit levels, the average workers' pension has never risen far above the standard rates of regular social assistance benefits [139].

Of course, such averages only give a sketchy impression of the adequacy of pensions. A closer evaluation clearly requires more information on the stratification of pensions and on the living conditions of the recipient households. As a first step, Table 13 presents some data on the distribution of pensions for selected years [140].

Only a smaller part of all pensions may be considered generous in that they amount to 60 percent or more of the average net earnings of the insured population. Before the pension reform of 1957, pensions at this level were very unusual (5 percent of all pensions in 1953). After the reform the economic situation of pensioners improved considerably. In 1968 about one fourth of all pensions had reached generous levels and by 1982 this proportion had grown to almost one third [141]. The proportion of low pensions has declined considerably over time, particularly after the pension reforms of 1957 and 1972. The great majority of pensions, however, remain below the level sufficient to maintain the status obtained by the recipient during his working life. Moreover, nearly one half of all pensions barely exceed the social assistance poverty line [142].

The fact that the majority of pensions are of a mediocre standard is mostly due to the inequality between male and female entitlements and between workers' and employees' pension entitlements. Low pensions are predominantly paid to beneficiaries of the workers' scheme and to female pensioners. Nearly two-thirds of male pensions, but only one tenth of female pensions, may be considered generous. The majority of female pensions (72 percent in 1982) are in fact close to social assistance levels. The 1972 pension reform improved this situation to a sizeable, but hardly sufficient degree.

Employees' pensions are generally much higher than workers' pensions. More than 75 percent of male employees' pensions were generous in 1982, in the workers' scheme only 57 percent. Including female pensions, one half of all workers' pensions and one third of all employees' pensions are still close to the social assistance level. Even in the employees' scheme the majority of female pensions are low, and 11 percent of all male pensions still do not exceed this level. As the legal entitlements of these various social categories are, in principle, identical, the data indicate the remarkable extent to which the German pension insurance system reproduces labour market inequalities.

We should bear in mind, however, that administrative data on the stratification of pension payments cannot give an adequate picture of the living conditions in recipient households, because pensions are not necessarily a beneficiary's only source of income. Thus, one household or even one person may be in receipt of several pensions, and pensions may coincide with earnings from work, with private or occupational pensions, or with capital returns. An assessment of the adequacy of German pensions therefore requires more detailed information on the combination of various sources of income. An attempt to provide such information has recently been made by the Transfer Enquete Commission which analysed the data from the 1973 government survey of household incomes [143].

The Commission found that in most cases pensions were supplemented by other sources of income. On average, pensions represented only 36.5 percent of the disposable income in the beneficiary households [144]. One fifth of the beneficiaries lived in households with economically active heads of family. For 80 percent of the recipients, however, pensions constituted the main (but not only) source of income. Among those households predominantly living from pensions the average disposable household income per month amounted to 1,052 DM [145]. The overwhelming majority of these households received additional income from capital returns [146]. Another one to two million persons also received occupational pensions.

Table 13   Percent distribution of pensions by pension level (a)

Pension level		1953	All direct pensions (b)				Old age and full invalidity pension			
		1953	1968	1972	1975	1982	1968	1972	1975	1982
					Workers' pension scheme					
'Low':	male		25.2	28.0	20.4	21.0		26.2	19.3	20.4
	female		87.0	93.5	82.7	81.7		93.0	81.7	81.2
	total	78.9	56.1	61.4	52.8	52.6	53.8	59.8	51.3	52.0
'Modest':	male		37.2	25.5	26.9	22.4		25.1	26.6	22.1
	female		12.4	5.9	16.7	17.4		6.4	17.6	17.8
	total	20.3	24.8	15.6	21.6	21.0	25.4	15.7	22.0	21.1
'Generous':	male		37.7	46.4	52.7	56.5		48.6	54.1	57.5
	female		0.6	0.5	0.6	0.9		0.6	0.7	1.0
	total	0.8	19.1	23.1	25.6	26.3	20.7	24.5	26.7	26.9
Average pension (DM)		.	273	346	532	737				
No of recipients (1,000)		2 239	3 737	4 599	5 051	5 509	3 396	4 303	4 820	5 385
					Employees' pension scheme					
'Low':	male		9.7	11.9	9.0	10.5		10.6	8.1	10.1
	female		46.6	57.7	49.4	52.7		54.9	47.1	52.0
	total	33.4	26.6	33.9	29.2	33.5	23.5	31.5	27.3	32.7
'Modest':	male		19.8	13.4	14.1	12.6		12.7	13.7	12.4
	female		31.7	19.8	29.0	25.8		20.9	30.1	26.1
	total	45.2	25.3	16.5	21.5	19.8	25.5	16.6	21.8	19.8
'Generous':	male		70.5	74.7	76.9	76.9		76.7	78.2	77.6
	female		21.8	22.5	21.7	21.5		24.1	22.8	22.0
	total	21.4	48.1	49.6	49.3	46.8	51.0	51.9	50.9	47.4
Average pension (DM)		.	457	573	843	1 096				
No of recipients (1,000)		592	1 168	1 531	1 813	2 607	1 089	1 452	1 747	2 568
				Workers' and employees' pension schemes						
'Low':	male		21.3	23.9	17.3	17.7		22.1	16.2	17.0
	female		77.9	85.0	74.2	72.3		83.9	72.8	71.8
	total	69.4	49.1	54.5	46.5	46.5	46.5	52.7	44.9	45.8
'Modest':	male		32.8	22.4	23.5	19.3		21.8	23.1	19.0
	female		16.7	9.3	19.8	20.1		9.9	20.8	20.5
	total	25.5	24.9	15.8	21.6	20.6	25.4	15.9	21.9	20.7
'Generous':	male		45.9	53.8	59.2	63.0		56.0	60.7	64.0
	female		5.4	5.8	6.0	7.6		6.2	6.3	7.8
	total	5.1	26.0	29.7	31.9	32.9	28.1	31.4	33.2	33.5
Average pension (DM)		.	317	403	614	852				
No of recipients (1,000)		2 831	4 905	6 130	6 863	8 117	4 485	5 755	6 567	7 952

(a) On the basis of official data pensions have been reclassified as (1) 'low' if they amounted to less than ca.
40 percent of average net earnings, i.e. to less than DM 100 in 1953, 250 in 1968, 400 in 1972, 500 in
1975 and 700 in 1982; these pensions were below or close to the social assistance standard which is about
twice the social assistance standard rate if housing costs and lump sum payments are included; the social
assistance rate (in DM) was in 1968: 131, 1972: 203, 1975: 252, and 1982: 338; (2) 'modest' if they amounted to around 40-60 percent of average net earnings, i.e. to DM 100-150 in 1953, 250-450 in 1968, 400-600 in
1972, 500-800 in 1975, and 700-1,100 in 1982; (3) 'generous' if they amounted to more than about 60 percent of average net earnings, i.e. to more than DM 150 in 1953, 450 in 1968, 600 in 1972, 800 in 1975, and
1,100 in 1982. Average net earnings (in DM) were in 1953: 277, 1968: 735, 1972: 1,062, 1975: 1,355, and
1982: 1,889.
(b) Excluding survivors' pensions.

Of pensioner households, 36 percent were in receipt of additional public transfer payments such as housing allowances or social assistance. The receipt of more than one pension is the exception rather than the rule. The 1977 microcensus reported that 72 percent of beneficiaries received only one pension, 20.2 percent received two (in most cases a combination of direct pensions and survivors' pensions), 4.4 percent drew an additional civil servants' pension, and 1.6 percent received supplementary social assistance benefits. Only 1.6 percent were in receipt of three or more pensions.

The cumulation of several transfer payments and other sources of income make the actual living conditions of pension recipients much more comfortable than data on the stratification of pensions would suggest. The lower the individual pension, the lower the proportion of the disposable household income it represents. In 1973, 24 percent of all recipients had pensions below 250 DM per month, and another 26 percent had benefits between 250 and 500 DM. In the former group the pension represented 9 percent of the disposable household income, which on average amounted to 638 DM per capita. In the latter case the respective figures are 27 percent and 722 DM. It appears that gaps in the pension insurance are to a significant degree compensated by private provisions. On average, the post-retirement income of male pensioner households with two persons amounted to around 73 percent of the pre-retirement income of comparable households.

Since average values conceal the considerable variation in the income of pensioner households, we must assume that a sizeable proportion of pensioners fall short of this level of social security. The inequality of pension entitlements is illustrated by the high standard deviation of pensioner household incomes which amounted to 62 percent of the mean in 1973 [147]. Five percent of pensioner households had means which fell below the official poverty standard. Single women are the group with the most inadequate pensions. In 1973, 17 percent of the 2.1 million single women mainly dependent upon pensions had disposable household incomes below 500 DM. This means that they were living below or very close to the social assistance poverty line, set at 437 DM by the Commission, including the estimated cost of housing.

Obviously the German pension insurance system falls short of its basic goals. In cases of lost earnings it is only possible to preserve the previous standard of living when public transfers are supplemented by private means. In an affluent society with high private incomes this may be considered a typical or even a politically desirable situation. It runs counter, however, to the proclaimed goals of the German transfer system. The fact that these schemes aim at income maintenance, but do not even effectively prevent poverty among beneficiaries must be considered a significant failure. This leads to the more general question of to what extent the growth of the transfer system has contributed to realizing the goal of reducing income inequality.

Redistributive effects of the transfer system

The steep growth of public and social expenditure in the postwar period considerably modified the structure of material rewards in West German society. Today, the life chances of the population are no longer a mere function of market position, but are increasingly determined by transfers and services provided by the state. In 1978, 17.7 million or 80 percent of all private households were in receipt of public transfer payments. Even if we exclude child allowances, this leaves one half of all households dependent, though to varying degrees, on public transfers [148].

In a longitudinal perspective, the proportion of disposable household income derived from social transfer payments has increased strikingly (see Graph 39). In the early

1950s transfers accounted for less than 15 percent of total disposable household income, but since the second half of the 1950s this proportion has grown dynamically to 27 percent or more in the 1970s. The question now is to what extent this growing importance of public transfers has contributed to a more equal distribution of income.

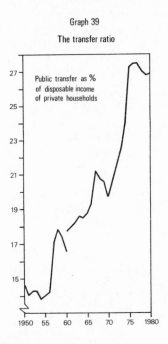

Graph 39

The transfer ratio

Table 14 shows that the distribution of disposable household income has changed only slightly over the last three decades. A relatively marked tendency towards greater equality during the 1950s was reversed in the 1960s. Although the 1970s again witnessed equalizing tendencies, the long-term changes remained very limited. The overall degree of inequality as measured by the Gini coefficient decreased by only 6 percent between 1950 and 1975. The income share claimed by groups in the lowest and highest quintiles were also remarkably stable. The gap between the average income of workers and the self-employed even increased [149].

The growing volume of social transfer payments has thus not had a markedly increased redistributive effect. Obviously the vertical redistribution of income does not rank among the major achievements of the German transfer system. This does not mean, however, that the system merely shifts money from one of the citizen's pockets to the other. In order to assess the redistributive effect of the welfare state, we need to make a closer comparison of income inequality before and after redistribution [150]. Official data measuring the effectiveness of the transfer system in these terms are in surprisingly short supply (see Table 15) [151].

Within specific social categories disposable income (after redistribution) is much more equally distributed than factor income (see the Gini coefficients) [152]. With the exception of farmers in 1978, this holds true for all socio-economic groups and for all years for which data are available. The transfer system also markedly reduces the difference in average household income between various social categories. Thus in 1950,

Table 14   The distribution of disposable household income

	1950	1955	1960	1964	1968	1970	1975	1978	1980
Mean									
– at current prices (DM per month)	357	586	838	1 089	1 330	1 581	2 378	2 795	3 158
– at constant (1976) prices	773	1 154	1 507	1 762	1 959	2 211	2 482	2 634	2 722
Median									
– as % of mean	79.3	80.7	80.8	80.3	78.2	77.9	78.0	.	80.6
Gini coefficient	0.396	0.384	0.380	0.380	0.387	0.392	0.371	.	.
Distribution by quintiles (%)									
1st	5.4	5.8	6.0	6.1	6.2	5.9	.	.	6.9
2nd	10.7	10.7	10.8	10.8	10.5	10.4	.	.	11.2
3rd	15.9	16.2	16.2	16.1	15.7	15.6	.	.	16.2
4th	22.8	23.2	23.1	22.9	22.5	22.5	.	.	22.5
5th	45.2	44.1	43.9	44.1	45.1	45.6	.	.	43.3
Average income (a) of									
Workers	0.93	0.94	0.93	0.95	0.93	0.96	0.95	0.95	0.93
Employees	1.19	1.18	1.16	1.15	1.17	1.17	1.10	1.10	1.10
Civil servants								1.10	1.24
Farmers	1.59	1.60	1.70	1.77	1.97	2.07	2.38	1.58	1.26
Self-employed								2.72	2.85
Pensioners	0.57	0.58	0.60	0.60	0.61	0.58	0.60	0.59	0.58
Civil service pensioners								0.80	0.81

(a) Average income of selected social groups as multiple of general mean.

the difference between the average income of worker and self-employed households was 762 DM before, and 639 DM after redistribution. For 1980, the respective figures were 7,794 DM and 6,053 DM.

In a longitudinal perspective, the growing volume of social transfers has not led to a consistently increasing redistribution. This becomes clear if we compare the Gini coefficients before and after redistribution. For the dependent labour force the redistributive effects of taxes and transfers were greatest in 1978, but they decreased between 1962 and 1969 despite a growing volume of transfers. For the self-employed, the redistributive effect was even greater in the 1960s than in 1978.

A comparison of average household income before and after redistribution may give some first indications of the direction of redistributive effects and of the structure of privilege in the transfer system. As could be expected, disposable incomes are higher than factor incomes only in the case of retired persons. For all economically active categories they fall far below factor incomes. This illustrates that the German transfer system is redistributive mainly in the horizontal sense, shifting incomes from the economically active to the inactive population. However, the relationship between disposable and factor income also differs markedly among the various categories of the labour force. Since workers and employees carry the major burden of social insurance scheme financing, their disposable income is significantly below their factor income. For civil servants and farmers who pay either small or no contributions, but who are entitled to draw sizeable benefits, the relationship between factor and disposable income is more favourable. The self-employed, who usually neither contribute to, nor benefit from the transfer schemes, hold an intermediate position between these two extremes.

For 1980, the extent of the vertical redistribution achieved by the transfer system is revealed by data on the distribution of income by quintiles before and after redistribution (see Table 16). The transfer system obviously benefits the lower income levels most [153]. The two lowest quintiles increased their share of total income to a consider-

Table 15   Distribution of monthly household income before and after redistribution (a)

Average income

	1955 A	1955 B	1960 A	1960 B	1970 A	1970 B	1978 A	1978 B	1980 A	1980 B
Workers	600	516	920	761	2 065	1 470	4 005	2 645	4 455	2 947
Employees					2 375	1 695	4 705	3 075	5 503	3 482
Civil servants					2 185	1 800	3 970	3 065	4 862	3 912
Employees and civil servants	785	657	1 231	977						
Farmers					2 555	2 330	4 910	4 430	4 474	3 969
Self-employed					4 890	3 625	10 495	7 605	12 249	9 000
Self-employed incl. farmers	1 362	1 155	1 881	1 600						
Pensioners					300	885	475	1 650		1 829
Civil service pensioners					225	1 250	350	2 240		2 564
Pensioners incl. civil service	137	361	222	557						
Total private households	640	611	942	884	1 785	1 550	3 300	2 795	3 756	3 158

Multiples of mean income

	1955 A	1955 B	1960 A	1960 B	1970 A	1970 B	1978 A	1978 B	1980 A	1980 B
Workers	0.94	0.84	0.98	0.86	1.16	0.95	1.21	0.95	1.19	0.93
Employees					1.33	1.09	1.43	1.10	1.47	1.10
Civil servants					1.22	1.16	1.20	1.10	1.29	1.24
Employees and civil servants	1.23	1.08	1.31	1.11						
Farmers					1.43	1.50	1.49	1.58	1.19	1.26
Self-employed					2.74	2.34	3.18	2.72	3.26	2.85
Self-employed incl. farmers	2.13	1.89	2.00	1.81						
Pensioners					0.17	0.57	0.14	0.59		0.58
Civil service pensioners					0.13	0.81	0.11	0.80		0.81
Pensioners incl. civil service	0.21	0.59	0.24	0.63						
Total private households	1.00	1.00	1.00	1.00	1.00	1.00	1.00	1.00	1.00	1.00

Gini coefficients

	1962 A	1962 B	1962 C	1969 A	1969 B	1969 C	1978 A	1978 B	1978 C
Workers	.220	.202	8.2%	.214	.206	3.7%		.248	12.4%
Employees	.291	.284	2.4%	.277	.271	2.2%		.260	5.3%
Civil servants	.212	.202	4.7%	.219	.211	3.7%		.244	14.4%
Farmers	.286	.261	8.7%	.262	.235	10.3%	.178	.183	+2.6%
Self-employed	.542	.459	15.3%	.510	.418	18.0%	.318	.311	2.2%
Pensioners								.355	
Civil service pensioners								.308	
Pensioners incl. civil service	.746	.408	45.3%	.728	.364	50.0%			
Total private households	.497	.360	27.6%	.500	.352	29.6%		.364	

(a) A = before redistribution (factor income), B = after redistribution; C = reduction of Gini coefficient
calculated as a percentage of the total possible reduction.

able degree. The third quintile also improved its position, but only marginally. The incomes share dropped slightly in the case of the fourth quintile and drastically in the case of the fifth quintile.

Table 16   Distribution of income before and after redistribution in 1980

Quintiles	Percent distribution of total income by quintiles	
	Before redistribution	After redistribution
1st	0.2	6.9
2nd	4.9	11.2
3rd	15.5	16.2
4th	25.8	22.5
5th	53.6	43.3

We can get a more accurate idea of the structure of privilege if we look at the positive transfers drawn by various groups and compare them to their negative transfers, i.e. taxes and social security contributions. Table 17 shows the average annual amounts which selected types of households contribute and receive, together with the proportions of aggregate transfers they account for.

Almost three-quarters of all positive transfers go to households of retired persons who contribute only 5 percent of all negative transfers. During the 1970s this balance further changed in their favour [154]. Worker households receive roughly 15 percent of the benefits, but pay one third of the direct taxes and social security contributions. Their balance is clearly negative, and has become less favourable over time. White-collar employees and civil servants together contributed the highest proportion of negative transfers in 1980 (40 percent), but received only one tenth of all cash benefits. Their growing share in negative transfers is largely a consequence of the sharp increase in white-collar employment. Their share of positive transfers increased much less, because they are not covered by all social insurance programmes and frequently exceed the limits of income-tested schemes. With the declining number of self-employed (including farmers), their share of total transfer payments has also declined. In 1980 they received only 2 percent of all cash benefits, but contributed 18 percent of the negative transfers, and this balance has increasingly developed to their disadvantage.

To sum up, the income maintenance schemes redistribute income in a predominantly horizontal direction, from the economically active generations to the retired. Transfers from the economically active to the temporarily inactive (sick, unemployed, etc.) and transfers from households without children to those with children are other forms of horizontal income redistribution, for which, however, detailed data are not available [155]. In comparison, vertical redistribution between various income strata is of secondary importance. As the pronounced differences in the transfer balances of the various economically active categories indicate, however, some vertical redistribution does occur. Thus, worker households have a much more favourable balance between positive and negative transfers than white-collar households, and these, in turn, fare better than the self-employed. In 1980 workers received back about one fourth of their total contributions, whereas white-collar households received only one sixth, and the self-employed received less than one tenth of the sums they contributed.

The vertical redistribution achieved by the public transfer system may further be analysed in terms of the balance between positive and negative transfers by income strata.

Table 17   Redistribution in the transfer system

		1955	1960	1970	1978	1980
Type of household		Transfers per household (in DM)				
Workers	Positive transfers	631	1 148	1 965	5 639	5 663
	Negative transfers	1 638	3 063	9 083	21 938	23 760
	Balance	-1 007	-1 915	-7 118	-16 299	-18 097
Employees and civil servants	Positive transfers	604	685	1 354	3 341	4 114
	Negative transfers	2 145	3 726	8 672	20 843	25 378
	Balance	-1 541	-3 041	-7 318	-17 502	-21 264
Self-employed incl. farmers	Positive transfers	459	563	1 004	2 836	2 699
	Negative transfers	2 961	4 018	12 576	31 051	34 410
	Balance	-2 502	-3 455	-11 572	-28 215	-31 711
Pensioners incl. civil service	Positive transfers	3 007	4 564	9 114	17 516	19 047
	Negative transfers	318	544	1 332	2 379	2 243
	Balance	2 6	4 020	7 782	15 137	16 804
Total households	Positive transfers	1 262	1 936	4 009	9 159	9 979
	Negative transfers	1 599	2 635	6 845	15 216	17 095
	Balance	-337	-699	-2 836	-6 057	-7 116
		Transfers as a percentage of total transfers				
Workers	Positive transfers	17.2	20.2	15.4	16.7	15.2
	Negative transfers	35.3	39.6	41.6	39.1	37.3
Employees and civil servants	Positive transfers	9.7	7.4	8.8	9.9	11.2
	Negative transfers	27.1	29.6	32.9	37.1	40.3
Self-employed incl. farmers	Positive transfers	6.3	4.7	2.6	2.7	2.3
	Negative transfers	32.0	24.9	19.2	18.0	17.5
Pensioners incl. civil service	Positive transfers	66.8	67.7	73.2	70.7	71.2
	Negative transfers	5.6	5.9	6.3	5.8	4.9
Total transfers (in million DM)	Positive transfers	20 660	33 720	87 800	212 500	238 400.
	Negative transfers	26 180	45 880	149 900	353 000	408 400
		Percent distribution of households				
Workers		34.5	34.0	31.4	27.1	26.8
Employees and civil servants		20.2	21.0	26.0	27.1	27.2
Self-employed incl. farmers		17.3	16.3	10.4	8.8	8.7
Pensioners incl. civil service		28.0	28.7	32.2	37.0	37.3
Total number of households (1,000)		16 370	17 415	21 900	23 200	23 890

Following the results of the Transfer Enquete Commission, for 1978 positive transfers are largely concentrated in low-income strata, whereas negative transfers are largely progressive [156]. As a result, the balance becomes less favourable as factor income increases [157]. In some special cases, increasing factor income may even lead to decreasing disposable income due to the combined effect of progressive taxation and income-tested benefits. In actual practice, however, this combined effect is limited to over-proportionate increases in the rate of marginal taxation which narrow, but do not nullify gains in factor incomes [158].

We may summarize that the German transfer system achieves a high degree of horizontal redistribution, with the additional effect that the distribution of disposable income is noticeably less skewed than the distribution of factor income. In a longitudinal perspective the markedly growing volume of transfers does not seem to have led to any significant increase in vertical redistribution.

2. The adequacy of the health services

As shown in Section II, expenditure for health services more than tripled its GDP share in the postwar period, while the coverage of the sickness insurance scheme was considerably widened. Presently more than 90 percent of the population are directly or indirectly covered by the general sickness insurance scheme. Persons outside the scope of this scheme are either members of private insurance (about 7.5 percent of the population [159]) or of special occupational schemes. Only 0.2 percent of the population are without any institutionally provided protection.

The heavy expansion of health spending led to considerable improvements in the supply of medical services. In 1982 about one million persons - 40 percent more than in 1973 - were employed in the health sector [160]. This corresponded to 4.1 percent of the labour force, as compared to 1.5 in 1950, 1.7 in 1961, and 2.4 in 1970 [161]. The supply of physicians, pharmacists and hospital beds increased substantially (see Table 18). Between 1952 and 1982 the number of medical doctors doubled from 68,135 to 146,221. In relative terms - i.e. compared to population size - the supply of doctors remained fairly stagnant up to the late 1960s, but grew sizeably thereafter. Statistically, one medical doctor had to care for 442 inhabitants in 1980, as compared to 732 in 1952. The number of physicians in free practice also increased both in absolute and relative terms [162], but the expansion of the medical profession favoured hospital doctors and specialists over general practitioners. The number of dentists increased at a slower rate. Even though absolute numbers rose by 5700 (20 percent) between 1952 and 1983, the number of inhabitants per dentist increased up to 1973, and has declined only moderately since. In contrast, the absolute number of pharma-

Table 18		The supply of medical services (number of inhabitants per service)			
Year	Physicians	Physicians in free practice	Dentists	Pharmacies	Hospital beds
1952	732	1 265(a)	1 783	7 775	93
1956	718	1 235	1 678	7 614	92
1960	699	1 126	1 705	6 044	95
1965	688	1 175	1 864	5 709	93
1970	609	1 196	1 946	5 262	89
1975	521	1 110	1 946	4 455	85
1980	442	993	1 852	3 790	87

(a) 1953

cies almost tripled between 1952 and 1982, while the number of inhabitants per pharmacy was almost halved.

The number of hospital beds increased by some 200,000 in the postwar period. In relative terms, the supply was stagnant up to 1965, but has considerably improved in subsequent years. Since the late 1970s, oversupply became an increasing public concern which led to deliberate reductions. On average only about 85 percent of all hospital beds are actually occupied [163]. Within hospitals the supply of services has been sizeably expanded. Whereas in 1956 the number of beds per member of the nursing staff amounted to six, by 1970 it had been reduced to four, and by 1981 to 2.5. The number of beds per hospital doctor similarly decreased from 19 in 1956 to 15 in 1970, and 9 in 1981 [164].

The aggregate data and national averages conceal considerable discrepancies between urban and rural areas in the supply of health services [165]. By and large, however, the sick person's chances of finding medical assistance have considerably improved in the postwar period. The question now is to what extent the improvements in the medical infrastructure have led to more satisfactory health conditions.

The most basic indicator of health conditions is the length of life expectancy (see Table 19). For men at age 60 the remaining length of life stagnated at around 16 years. Between 1950 and 1970, it even decreased by one year, but rose again thereafter. As the life expectancy of women continuously increased in the same period, the differences between the sexes became much more marked. The sex specific longevity at age 30 developed at similarly discrepant rates. Life expectancy at birth sizeably increased for both sexes, but the growth of more than eight years for women was accompanied by an increase of less than six years for men.

Table 19	Life expectancy at various ages						
	1949/51	1958/59	1960/62	1964/66	1970/72	1974/76	1980/82
At birth							
male	64.6	66.8	66.9	67.6	67.4	68.3	70.2
female	68.5	71.9	72.4	73.5	73.8	74.8	76.9
Age 30							
male	41.3	41.4	41.1	41.2	41.0	41.4	42.4
female	43.9	45.3	45.5	46.0	46.3	47.0	48.4
Age 60							
male	16.2	15.7	15.5	15.5	15.3	15.6	16.5
female	17.5	18.3	18.5	18.9	19.1	19.7	20.8

To a large extent the increasing life expectancy at birth is a result of the remarkable decline in infant mortality from 56 to 11 per 1000 live births between 1950 and 1982. The decline in mother mortality is even more impressive. It fell from 206 to 18 per 100,000 live births in the postwar period. The question to what extent this remarkable success is related to the expansion of health services cannot be answered easily. One of the puzzling findings about the German health system is, in fact, that infant and mother mortality are higher in the city states than in the other *Länder* although the former offer much better health services than the latter [166].

Data on morbidity indicate a far-reaching continuity of health conditions. In survey research conducted since the early 1970s, 15-20 percent of the population generally report suffering from an illness [167]. The most recent official survey (1980) arrived at 16 percent [168]. The administrative data from the sickness insurance scheme report a fairly constant sickness ratio of 4.5 to 5.5 percent among compulsory members since the late 1950s (see Graph 40). The number of sickness days per year and per member of local sickness funds shows phase-specific variations without a clear long-term trend. Since the late 1950s it has been fluctuating between 17 and 23 days. The number of hospitalized persons increased in every year during the period 1956 to 1980 [169]. In the same period the average number of hospital days per inhabitant and year remained practically constant [170]. In public debates on the German health system, the length of hospitalization (20 days per patient in 1980 [171]) is frequently criticized as excessively long by international standards.

Graph 40

Sickness rate and working days lost

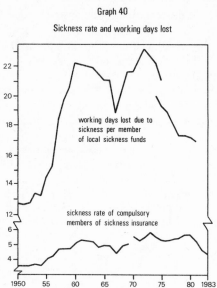

The available morbidity data thus indicate remarkably stagnant health conditions despite the heavy growth of health services. The causes of death, however, underwent significant modifications as Table 20 shows. Particularly, cardio-vascular diseases and cancer have come increasingly to the fore. In 1950 these two groups accounted for less than one half of all deaths, but in 1982 for almost three quarters. In contrast, infectious diseases have dwindled in importance and the number of fatal accidents was also reduced [172].

Considerable success in the combat against infectious diseases and accidents was thus counteracted by the rise of new 'civilization diseases', frequently of a chronic character and rooted in changing lifestyles which can hardly be influenced or controlled. In the absence of countervailing tendencies, these developments must lead to rising costs in the medical sector.

If an immediate translation of rising inputs in the health sector into improving health conditions can thus not be expected, the question is still whether the expansion of public services has contributed to a more equal distribution of health. Unfortunately, the state of epidemiological research in Germany is very poor [173]. The few regional studies and administrative data which do exist indicate higher morbidity and mortality in the lower strata. For example, members of the workers' pension scheme die on average two years earlier than members of the employees' scheme, and their invalidity

Table 20   Major causes of death

Diseases	1950		1960		1970		1980		1982	
	1,000	%	1,000	%	1,000	%	1,000	%	1,000	%
Infectious diseases (a)	43.8	8.4	31.9	5.0	24.7	3.4	14.7	2.1	17.3	2.4
Cardio-vascular diseases	171.6	33.0	256.2	39.8	324.1	44.1	359.5	50.3	360.6	50.4
Cancer	85.3	16.4	112.0	17.4	134.4	18.3	148.1	20.7	150.7	21.0
Diseases of digestive organs	31.7	6.1	36.0	5.6	40.1	5.5	.	.	.	.
Decrepitude	36.6	7.0	30.0	4.7	12.5	1.7	6.6	0.9	6.1	0.9
Accidents and poisoning	21.4	4.1	31.2	4.8	39.0	5.3	27.7	3.9	26.7	3.7
Suicide	9.9	1.9	10.8	1.7	13.0	1.8	12.9	1.8	13.1	1.8
Other	119.3	23.0	134.9	21.0	147.0	20.0	144.7	20.3	141.3	19.7
Total deaths	519.6	100.0	643.0	100.0	734.8	100.0	714.1	100.0	715.6	100.0

(a) Tuberculosis and pneumonia.

risk is twice as high [174]. On average, workers also lose more working days due to ill-ness, and they become victims of occupational accidents eight times more frequently than employees [175]. Infant and mother mortality are also higher in the lower strata [176]. Regional studies on the incidence of specific diseases document socio-economic differ-entials in morbidity and mortality especially for liver cirrhosis, cancer, and myocardial infarction [177]. In contrast, survey research on subjective health has not found a clear relationship between income and the frequency of health complaints [178]. Some diseases are reported more frequently by lower income groups, others seem to be positively correlated with the respondents' household income [179].

The extension of sickness insurance coverage has led to an equalization of entitle-ments with an almost general access to health services. This far-reaching institutional equality is only distorted by regional disparities in the supply of medical services. However, the utilization of services appears to be correlated positively with income. Thus, the higher income strata visit physicians more frequently than lower earning groups. This is especially true for consultations with specialists [180].

An attempt by the Transfer Enquete Commission to assess the flow of medical bene-fits arrived at similar results. Following its analysis, the health system favours the households of self-employed persons, farmers, and civil servants, and places pensioners and employees at a disadvantage. Workers' households are close to the average [181]. As the commission points out, however, the paucity of available data makes the results of such analyses highly dependent on different model assumptions about service utilization. In fact, an attempt to analyse the redistributive process in the general sickness insurance scheme in 1971 arrived at the conclusion that redistribution occurs from higher to lower earning groups, from the young to the old, from men to women, from single living persons to married couples, and from small to large fami-lies [182].

In summary, the expansion of welfare state schemes has made access to health services much more equal. The degree to which they are actually utilized, however, is largely beyond the control of public institutions [183]. The heavy expansion of health expenditure contributed to improvements in medical infrastructure which were accom-panied by a significant decline in various diseases and by very heavy reductions of infant and mother mortality. At the same time, however, several new health risks have developed which are partly rooted in changing lifestyles of the population. Their elimination would require a control of risk-involving behaviour for which public programmes in a free society usually lack the instruments.

3. Achievements and shortcomings of housing policy

The reduction in housing production during the Nazi period and the heavy war destruction of dwellings led to a severe housing shortage in the immediate postwar years. The supply of adequate housing at a bearable cost therefore became one of the foremost policy goals. Other central aims of housing policy included the upgrading of housing standards, the more widespread distribution of housing property, and the protection of tenants [184]. In the pursuit of these goals, the Federal Government channelled sizeable resources into the housing sector (see Section II and Appendix Table 14).

The supply of housing has improved substantially in the postwar period (see Graph 41). The annual number of newly contructed dwellings quickly increased to more than half a million in the early 1950s. From 1954 to 1966 it remained close to 600,000 thus surpassing the levels attained in the Weimar Republic more than twofold [185]. A temporary decline due to the 1967 recession was followed by a new building boom with record production figures in the early 1970s. The mid-decade recession then led to another slow-down pushing the annual output below the levels of the early 1950s.

Graph 41

Annual housing construction

in 1,000s

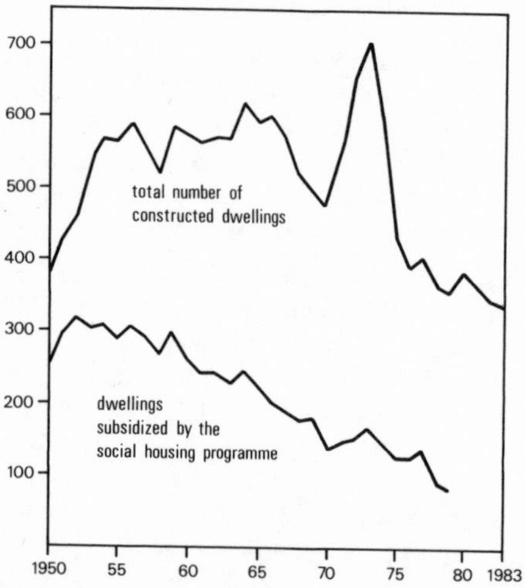

The heavy subsidization of housing production was an important catalyst for the long-lasting building boom. Throughout the postwar period, only about ten percent of all dwellings were constructed without any public subsidies or tax credits [186]. 41 percent of the dwellings built from 1949 to 1980 were subsidized under the social housing programme [187]. In the early 1950s this programme even accounted for roughly two thirds of all newly erected dwellings. Step by step its share diminished to one half in the late 1950s, one third in the late 1960s, and about one fifth to one fourth in the 1970s (see Graph 41).

In 1950 the number of private households still surpassed the available number of dwellings by almost six million (see Table 21). More than one third of all households were subtenants. During the 1950s and early 1960s the situation quickly improved. The proportion of subtenant households fell to below 10 percent. By 1967 the housing stock had doubled, but since the number of households had also grown rapidly, a considerable shortage remained. During the 1970s the number of dwellings approximated the number of households, and since 1980 there has even been a modest statistical oversupply of dwellings.

Table 21	Housing shortage and housing supply						
	1950	1956	1961	1965	1970	1975	1980	1982
No of dwellings (1,000)	9 512	12 864	16 762	18 550	20 608	23 014	25 406	26 076
No of private households (1,000)	15 342(b)	16 492(b)	19 399	21 211	21 991	23 722	24 811	25 336
Statistical shortage of dwellings (1,000) (a)	5 830	3 628	2 637	2 661	1 383	708	-595	-740
Dwellings per household	0.62	0.78	0.86	0.87	0.90	0.97	1.02	1.03
Subtenant households (%)	35.6	20.7	13.4	9.0	5.8(c)		3.1(d)	

(a) Number of private households exceeding the number of dwellings; (b) calculated from the ratio dwellings per household; (c) 1972; (d) 1978.

In the light of aggregate data the postwar housing policy must be termed a remarkable success. A closer analysis suggests three qualifications, however. First, the official data on housing supply are based on extrapolations of past censuses and therefore lack reliability. In the past, the extrapolated figures have usually exceeded the more accurate census or sample survey data by considerable margins [188]. Second, housing experts estimate that around 3 percent of all dwellings are not occupied. A balanced market would therefore require a statistical oversupply of at least 3 percent. Even according to the currently available (overestimated) data, this target is not yet realized. Third, aggregate data do not grasp the undersupply of various regions or specific groups. As the boom in housing construction was accompanied by heavy price increases and a sizeable reduction in the number of old houses let at low rents, the housing market began to split into various submarkets. The present aggregate oversupply thus coincides with a serious undersupply of low cost dwellings, especially in the big cities. In some cities the registered number of persons in search of housing surpassed 10,000 in 1980 [189].

The early 1980s therefore saw rising concern about a new housing shortage ('neue Wohnungsnot') which was not only indicated by statistical data, but also by spectacular mass demonstrations and several hundred illegal occupations of empty houses [190]. The partial undersupply particularly affects low-income groups, pensioners, one or two person households in younger age cohorts, and large families [191]. Since the age cohorts born during the baby boom years of the late 1950s and the 1960s now begin to raise families and to enter the housing market, the present gaps are likely to persist up to the mid-1990s.

The quality of German housing has been sizeably upgraded in the postwar period. On average, dwellings have become larger, less densely populated, and more comfortable (see Table 22). In the 1950s many dwellings were overcrowded, as the number of persons far exceeded the number of available rooms. By the late 1960s the standard 'one room per person' was achieved. Since then there have always been more rooms than persons and the average living space per person has increased. Between 1950 and 1978 it almost doubled. This quantitative upgrading of housing standards was accompanied by substantial improvements in fixtures and fittings. Whereas in 1950 the vast majority of dwellings did not have a bath, in 1978 the majority had baths, lavatories and central heating as well.

Table 22		Housing quality				
	1950	1956	1960	1968	1972	1978
No of persons per dwelling	4.7	3.7	3.6	3.0	2.8	2.6
Average size of dwellings (m^2)	68	.	67(a)	71	74	79
Size per person (m^2)	14.9	.	19.7	23.8	25.2	(28.1)
No of rooms per person	0.63	0.73	.	1.04	1.08	(1.21)
Dwellings with bath, lavatory, and central heating (%)	.	11.4(b)	10.3	29.8	41.9	58.7
Dwelling without bath (%)	80.3	52.8(b)	53.3	28.5	17.7	11

(a) 1961; (b) 1957.

Despite all improvements, sizeable groups are still living in conditions below these modern housing standards. 18 percent of all households occupied dwellings with less than one room per person in 1978 [192]. In particular, large families frequently have to live in overcrowded apartments. Dwellings with insufficient fixtures and fittings are mostly occupied by small households (especially pensioners), by low income groups, or by foreign workers [193]. The various deficiencies of housing conditions thus affect different social groups.

The sizeable upgrading of housing standards was accompanied by steep rent increases which far exceeded the development of the general cost-of-living index [194]. In 1978 private households spent an average of 22 percent of their net income on housing costs [195]. Among tenant households, rents claimed 14 percent of the household income. However, 22 percent of the tenants had to spend more than one fifth, and 17 percent more than one quarter of their net income on rent [196]. Low earning groups bear even higher relative costs, as the rent burden varies inversely with household income [197]. Housing experts consider a rent burden of 20 percent a critical threshold. Measured by this standard, the goal to provide adequate housing at a cost bearable by all population strata has not yet been realized.

There are several reasons for the present imbalances. Firstly, the volume of social housing construction has decreased substantially in recent years (see Graph 41). Presently the number of social housing dwellings for tenants amount to some 4 million, corresponding to less than one third of the number of tenant households [198]. Within the social housing programme, owner-occupied houses represent an increasing proportion of the total number of constructions. In the 1970s their proportion doubled from roughly 30 to 60 percent [199]. This change is a consequence of the shift in public promotion from tenement houses to owner-occupied buildings which occurred in the 1960s (see Section II). As Graph 42 shows, the proportion of dwellings constructed by public-interest corporations steeply decreased, while the share of private households building mostly owner-occupied houses increased from less than one half to two thirds. Public housing has always been of only marginal importance.

Graph 42

Annual housing construction by type of builder

percent distribution

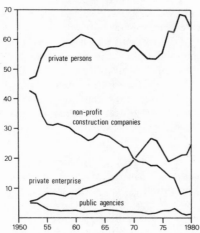

Secondly, the shift in public promotion from grants to the subsidization of annuities led to successive rent increases in social housing, because the degree of subsidization decreases year by year. As a result, social housing rents which start out at around one sixth to one third lower than market rents gradually approximate market rents in the course of a decade. Thirdly, the social housing programme does not always benefit groups with the most urgent needs, because it is targeted inadequately. The income-test for tenant entitlements is set at a relatively high limit allowing about 50 percent of all households to make claims [200]. In addition, income is only tested before the dwelling is occupied, so that once moved in, tenants may keep their dwellings even if they surpass the income limits. It is estimated that today roughly one third of all occupants exceed the income limit by more than 20 percent [201]. Many low-income households thus find themselves barred from social housing apartments and compelled to pay burdensome market rents.

As a consequence, the number of households claiming housing allowances has been growing (see Section II). Presently one tenth of all tenant households receive allowances [202]. About one half of these occupy dwellings of the social housing programme [203]. Here a considerable irrationality of German housing policy becomes evident. It can hardly be the goal of a programme aiming at the supply of low cost dwellings to make the occupants of such dwellings dependent upon public housing allowances. Many observers therefore demand that the subsidization of construction be replaced by better targeted allowances for low-income tenants [204]. The effectiveness of the existing allowance scheme may be considered satisfactory. Depending on household size, the reduction of the rent burden through housing allowances varies between one third and one fourth. The size of the reduction increases with household size [205]. Curtailments in the most recent period have somewhat narrowed the effectiveness of the scheme.

The question as to which social groups have benefited most from German housing policy cannot be answered easily. Following the report of the Transfer Enquete Commission, different studies have led to discrepant results. An analysis by Rudi Ulbrich arrived at the conclusion that housing transfers predominantly benefit the higher earning groups. According to his study, the average transfer per household consistently increases with household income [206]. Another study by Klaus Mackscheidt et al. found an inconsistent relationship between household income and the amount of benefits drawn. Average transfers were highest for the lowest income bracket, decreased in the next category, increased again among middle brackets, and decreased in the highest earning groups [207]. Following this analysis, low earning households benefited predominantly from housing allowances, the middle groups from premiums on savings and tax credits including the social housing programme. The reduction in the highest income strata may be due to the surpassing of income limits and to the fact that they are already in possession of houses, thus benefiting less frequently from subsidies to new constructions. As the commission notes, the results of empirical studies are highly dependent upon the types of transfers included and on various model assumptions concerning their distribution.

Even if the results of empirical analyses are ambivalent, there can be litle doubt that German housing policy has been concentrating more on the stimulation of housing supply than on social redistribution. Even in the social housing programme the lion's share of benefits goes to the builders. Whereas they receive subsidies bridging the difference between market rents and cost bearing rents, the tenants profit only from the bridging of the smaller gap between cost rents and approved social rents [208]. Outside the social housing programme, builders receive subsidies which amount to between one third and one half of the invested capital [209]. The effectiveness of this heavy subsidization is doubtful, because most of the private building takes place in rural areas whereas the shortage is greatest in the cities. Besides, the Federal Government estimates that 90-95 percent of the private builders would also build in the absence of subsidies [210].

Given the rising rent burden and the regional imbalances with partial undersupply, housing security becomes an important issue. Obviously the most effective safeguard against the loss of housing is private ownership. Measured by international standards, the Federal Republic has a rather low proportion of house ownership. Following the most recent official survey (1978) only 36 percent of all households own the dwellings they live in [211]. Private opinion polls asking about house ownership (including tenant-occupied and non-occupied dwellings) usually arrive at an ownership ratio of close to 50 percent [212]. Due to the intensive private building activities in recent years, the proportion of owner-occupied houses is likely to increase. Presently, however, a two thirds majority of private households live in tenement houses.

Tenant protection legislation followed a path of stop and go in the postwar period. It has always been subject to fierce poltical struggles. Whereas the Social Democrats favour a strengthening of tenant protection, the Christian Democrats and the Liberals perceive a balanced market or moderate oversupply as the best form of tenant protection. Since the latter two consider a strong protective legislation an impediment to private construction, they have recently weakened the degree of regulation and introduced new incentives for private builders (see the Institutional Synopsis and Section V).

In summary, there have been sizeable increases in housing supply and an impressive upgrading of housing standards. The substantial narrowing of the housing shortage despite a rapidly growing number of private households must be considered a remarkable success. However, the social component of German housing policy has always been rather weak. The proportion of public housing is marginal, and the various subsidization programmes benefit builders more than tenants. In recent years the rent burden for tenants has substantially increased. For low income groups and certain urban areas there are still considerable imbalances of supply and demand.

4. The impact of educational policy

As shown in Section II, educational expenditure has been one of the fastest growing public expenditure items in the postwar period. Its GDP share more than doubled from 1950 to 1980 with particularly heavy increases occurring between 1965 and 1975. A large proportion of total expenditure was spent on the expansion of teaching staffs. Up to 1960 the teaching personnel of schools and universities accounted for less than one percent of the labour force. In the following decades the ranks of teachers more than doubled, increasing their share in the labour force from 0.9 percent in 1960 to 2.1 percent in 1980 [213].

The heavy investments in the educational sector were accompanied by a rapid expansion of educational enrolment (see Table 23). The absolute number of pupils grew consistently from the mid-1950s to 1975 when a postwar peak of 10 million pupils was reached. In subsequent years, the declining size of age cohorts contributed to a reduction of school enrolment by one fifth [214]. The number of students in post-secondary institutions has continued to grow up to the present. Between 1950 and 1983, it increased roughly eightfold. The expansion and partial contraction of the educational system is to a large extent influenced by demographic waves which are an important characteristic of the German social structure. However, demographic changes alone cannot explain the postwar educational development. This becomes evident if we look at enrolment ratios expressing the number of pupils and students as a percentage of the relevant age cohorts (see Graph 43).

Table 23				Enrolment in educational institutions				
				Number of pupil/students (in 1,000s)				
	1951	1955	1960	1965	1970	1975	1980	1983
Primary schools (a)	5 849	4 636	5 291	5 607	6 348	6 425	5 044	4 247
Secondary schools (b)	880	1 099	1 222	1 497	2 233	3 177	3 690	3 400
All general schools (c)	(6 729)	(5 735)	6 655	7 302	8 938	10 066	9 127	7 990
Universities (d)	135(f)	160	238	300	410	680	824	977
Total post-secondary (e)	152(g)		291	384	511	841	1 044	1 273

(a) Excluding special schools for handicapped persons; (b) Gymnasien, intermediary schools (Realschulen) and comprehensive schools; (c) including special schools and evening schools; (d) including teachers' colleges; (e) including technical colleges; (f) 1950; (g) 1952.

Public efforts to promote educational opportunities already set in at the pre-primary level. In an attempt to provide for more equal opportunities and as a response to the growing proportion of female employment, the number of kindergarten places was greatly expanded. The absolute number of places increased from 817,000 to 1.4 million between 1960 and 1981 [215]. In relative terms, i.e. in relation to the number of children aged 3-5, this meant an increase from 34 to 79 percent [216].

Among the school age population, a substantial shift from primary to secondary schooling took place. Up to the mid-1960s, 70 percent or more of the population at age 15 left the school system after the minimum period of compulsory schooling [217]. A

Graph 43

Educational enrolment ratios

Pupils /students as % of various age groups (in brackets)

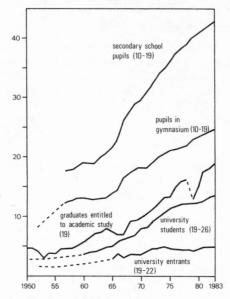

massive campaign advocating the advantages of higher education then soon produced results. The enrolment in secondary schools rapidly grew, and by 1983 the proportion of those leaving school early had dropped to 46 percent. As Graph 43 shows, the proportion of those in the age group 10-19 attending secondary schools increased from 18 to 43 percent between 1957 and 1983 [218]. In the same period enrolment in the traditional *Gymnasium* doubled from 12 to 25 percent. The increase in the number of secondary school graduates with an entitlement to academic studies was even steeper. Expressed as a proportion of the population at age 19, the number of graduates quadrupled from 4.7 to 19.1 percent between 1950 and 1983.

As the overwhelming majority of the graduates entered the universities, the enrolment revolution in secondary schools soon also affected the post-secondary sector [219]. Up to 1960 the proportion of persons in the age group 19-22 beginning academic studies remained fairly stagnant at approximately 2 percent. Then it began to rise continuously up to 5 percent in the mid-1970s. With minor variations, it has since remained close to this level. The total number of university students grew to an even greater extent, partly because the average duration of studies increased [220]. Expressed as a proportion of the age group 19-26, the number of post-secondary students increased almost fivefold between 1950 and 1983, from roughly 3 to 14 percent. When students in technical colleges (*Fachhochschulen*) are included, a full 18 percent of the population aged 19-26 presently attends institutions of higher learning.

To what extent has the expansion of the post-secondary sector been paralleled by an increase in the number of successful graduations? Exact data on the development of academic success and failure would require longitudinal studies of the academic careers of various student cohorts. Such studies are non-existent [221]. Presently, the majority of students bring their studies to a successful end, but the number of graduations has been growing to a lesser degree than the total number of students or the number of university entrants [222]. In 1982 there were 131,000 graduations as compared to 48,000 in 1960. In the same period the number of doctorates increased from 6,200 to 13,000 [223].

The postwar expansion of the educational system led to a substantial upgrading of the educational status of the population, which some observers have termed a social revolution. In past decades the overwhelming majority of the German people had accomplished only a basic school education. In the 1982 microcensus, 84 percent of the population aged 65 or over reported to have passed only the ordinary school, while 5 percent of this group were in possession of a diploma entitling to academic studies. In contrast, only 58 percent of the age group 25-30 had to settle with an ordinary school degree, while 21 percent had secondary school diplomas, and another 21 percent had graduated from intermediary school [224].

The substantial upgrading of educational standards was certainly not only an achievement of educational policies, but also the result of social mobilization. However, public efforts have contributed to the process. Hundreds of new secondary schools and several new universities were built in regions previously deprived of institutions of higher learning. Various institutional reforms since the 1960s facilitated the access to educational institutions. These included the abolition of fees for the attendance of secondary schools, the provision of school books free of charge, the introduction of education allowances, and the creation of comprehensive schools and universites. Since private schools are of only marginal importance in West Germany, most of the educational expansion actually occurred in public schools. In 1983 a mere 1 percent of all primary pupils and 10 percent of the secondary pupils attended private schools [225].

To what extent has the increase in the number of teachers kept pace with the enrolment revolution? In the primary sector, the number of teachers has grown faster than

Graph 44

Pupils and students per teacher

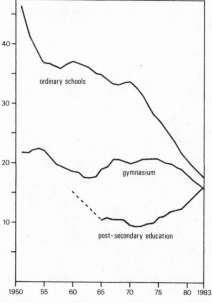

the number of pupils (see Graph 44). During the 1950s, the number of pupils per teacher fell from 46 to 37, mainly due to a decline in the number of pupils. From 1957 to 1972, the number of pupils was growing, but as the teaching personnel expanded at an even faster speed, the pupil/teacher ratio was further reduced. During the 1970s and early 1980s, a rapid decline in the number of pupils combined with further expansions of the teaching personnel so that the pupil/teacher ratio was almost halved from 34 in 1970 to 18 in 1983. In the secondary sector, the heavy increases in the number of pupils were by and large balanced by the growth of the teaching personnel up to the mid-1970s. In subsequent years, the growth in personnel clearly outpaced the growth in the number of pupils so that the pupil/teacher ratio fell from 21 to 16. In the entire postwar period, the number of teachers in the *Gymnasien* roughly quadrupled, whereas the number of teachers in the entire secondary sector increased sixfold from 37,000 in 1951 to 216,000 in 1983 [226]. In the post-secondary sector, the growth in teaching personnel kept pace with the heavy increases in the number of students only up to the mid-1970s. In subsequent years an almost stagnant number of teachers (around 78,000) coincided with further increases in the number of students so that the student/teacher ratio rose from 11 in 1975 to 16 in 1983 [227].

To what extent has the public promotion of education led to a reduction in the inequality of educational opportunities? This question is usually analysed with reference to two social categories which are notoriously underrepresented in German institutions of higher learning, i.e. working class children and women (see Table 24). Among university students (including teachers' colleges but excluding technical colleges), the proportion of working class children has roughly quadrupled since the early 1950s. Most of the educational mobilization of workers' children occurred during the last 10-15 years. Since 1975 the proportion of university entrants of working class background has remained stagnant. Further increases in the relative number of working class students thus appear unlikely. This means that a serious underrepresentation of workers' children will persist in the post-secondary sector despite the recent improvements. In 1975 only 8 percent of the working class children at university entrance age actually began academic studies, as compared to 39 percent of civil servants' children, 24 percent of employees' children, and 20 percent of the children of the self-employed [228].

Table 24   Indicators of educational inequality (a)

	1950	1955	1960	1965	1970	1975	1980	1982
Proportion of working class students (%)	4.4(b)	5.0	5.2(c)	5.9(d)	6.7(e)	11.5(f)		16
Proportion of workers' children among university entrants				10.3	11.9 .	14.9 18.2	14.7 17.7	14.5 18.0
Proportion of female pupils in the Gymnasium	40.5		44.2 39.9	41.3	43.9 43.9	47.9	50.1	50.7(g)
Proportion of female graduate with entitlement to academic studies	32.4	.	35.9	.	40.3 39.3	39.8	45.4	46.3
Proportion of female university entrants	18.0		27.4 34.0	39.8	40.6 38.1	41.0	43.4	41.2(g)
Proportion of female students	16.9		22.5 27.9	30.9	31.1 30.8	35.8	38.3	40.1(g)

(a) Different rows per category refer to different statistical definitions or sources; (b) 1952/53; (c) 1958/59; (d) 1963; (e) 1967/68; (f) 1973; (g) 1983.

Women have increased their representation in institutions of higher learning much more substantially. Their share among secondary pupils increased by ten percentage points between 1950 and 1983. Women presently account for 51 percent of all pupils and for 49 percent of the population aged 10-19. Among secondary school graduates with entitlement to academic studies, the female share increased from 32 to 46 percent in the postwar period. Sex-specific inequalities in secondary education are thus gradually disappearing. In 1982 the proportion of women at age 19 graduating from a secondary school almost equalled the proportion of men (25.3 as compared to 27.6 percent) [229]. In the post-secondary sector the proportion of female students more than doubled between 1959 an 1983. Nevertheless a slight female underrepresentation persists, as women represented 48 percent of the age cohort 19-26 in 1983, but only 40 percent of all students. Among post-secondary graduates, the proportion of women increased from 21 percent in 1960 to 35 percent in 1982 [230]. Since women have caught up with men in secondary schooling, it is to be expected that their underrepresentation on higher levels of learning will soon disappear.

In summary, educational opportunities have improved substantially in the postwar period. Enrolment in institutions of higher learning increased. The expansion of teaching staff largely kept pace with or even surpassed the growth in the number of pupils and students. Inequalities of educational opportunities diminished. Nevertheless, some sizeable inequalities persist, especially with respect to the educational chances of working class children. In addition, the massive expansion of higher education has itself created some new problems.

Firstly, the ordinary school, which for a long time was the dominant type of schooling for the overwhelming majority of the population, increasingly moves into the position of a residual school for underprivileged strata. This implies the risk of the development of an educational underclass with severely hampered employment or mobility chances in the labour market. The risk of marginalization is particularly high for those roughly 100,000 persons who leave the ordinary school each year without any formal degree. This long-term trend presently combines with cyclical problems in the labour market. The age groups below 25 years currently have the highest ratio of unemployment, and those without an ordinary school examination represent a high proportion of youth unemployment [231]. Critics of educational policy therefore argue that the long lasting emphasis on higher education has led to an undue neglect of ordinary and vocational schooling which should be given higher priority.

A second problem arises from the lack of co-ordination between the university system and the employment system. The annual output of post-secondary graduates by far exceeds the number of qualified openings in the labour market. The civil service and especially the educational system, major sources of job opportunities for university graduates in the past, are now practically closed to new employees. Since most new teaching positions during the enrolment revolution of the 1970s were filled with young candidates, access for the present generation of graduate teachers will remain blocked [232]. The number of graduates from post-secondary institutions in unemployment tripled from roughly 30,000 in 1975 to 105,000 in 1983. In the latter year graduates represented 5 percent of the unemployed [233]. This increasing unemployment may develop into a serious political problem.

IV   Correlates and causes: explanations

Our attempts to identify some determinants of the enormous welfare state expansion in the postwar period will proceed in four steps. First, we inquire whether the growth of welfare state schemes was a continuous process or whether we can identify specific phases of accelerated or decelerated expansion. In three separate analyses, we then examine to what extent demographic changes, economic growth and political constellations have shaped the postwar pattern of growth.

1.   Phases of welfare state development

If we look at the growth of social expenditure, we can identify four rather distinct phases (see Graph 45 and Table 25). During the first two legislatures of the Federal Republic (1949 to 1957), annual real growth rates of social spending exceeded 10 percent. Although the economic product also grew rapidly during the postwar reconstruction boom, the GDP share of social outlays increased by only two percentage points between 1950 and 1957. Social security and housing outlays recorded the highest annual growth rates, while health and education spending also increased at an above average rate. These years may therefore be labelled the 'take-off phase' of the West German welfare state.

Graph 45

Annual real growth rates of social expenditure

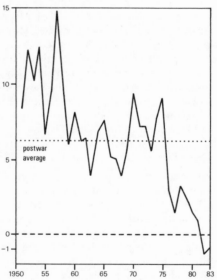

In institutional terms, this initial period may be subdivided into a reconstruction phase (1949-1953) and an extension phase (1953-1957), corresponding to the first two legislative periods. The reconstruction of the welfare state began with the Social Insurance Adaptation Law passed under Allied control in 1949, and proceeded with the restoration of self-administrative bodies in the social insurance schemes in 1951. The build-up of traditional schemes was accompanied by the establishment of novel programmes for war victims and by a very active new housing policy based on generous

Table 25   Phases of welfare state development and social expenditure growth

Phases of development	Years	Average real growth rate of social expenditure	Stand- ard devia- tion	Average annual in- crease in GDP share(a)	Average real growth rate of			
					Social security	Health	Hous- ing	Educa- tion
Take-off	1949-57(b)	10.6	2.6	0.29	11.5	8.8	11.4	8.8
Consolidation	1958-69	6.3	1.6	0.15	6.6	7.9	-1.1	6.8
Expansion	1970-75	7.8	1.3	1.38	7.7	8.7	7.2	7.7
Austerity	1976-83	1.3	1.6	-0.18	1.3	2.3	0.9	0.4
Average	1951-83	6.3	3.7	0.35	6.5	6.9	3.5	5.9

(a) Percentage points; (b) data refer to 1951-1957.

subsidies for builders. Despite the dynamic growth of these new schemes, the GDP share of total social spending remained fairly constant at around 19 percent up to 1953.

The second legislature opened with the announcement of extensive social reforms [234]. The adoption of a child allowance scheme in 1954 was followed two years later by extensions of the social housing programme and the unemployment compensation scheme. Finally in 1957 the major pension insurance reform was passed along with improvements in sickness benefits. These extensions led to a steep increase in the social expenditure ratio by almost three percentage points between 1956 and 1958, when the annual adjustment of pensions was implemented.

During the following three legislative periods (1957-1969), the growth of social pro- grammes slowed down. The years 1958 to 1969 may therefore be termed a 'consolida- tion phase' of the welfare state. The GDP share of social expenditure increased only moderately by an average of 0.15 percentage points per year. Only education and health spending grew at a speed distinctly above the postwar average, the former mainly during the early 1960s, the latter particularly in the second half of the decade. Housing outlays declined in real terms, while the GDP share of the income mainte- nance programmes stagnated. Institutional reforms of some importance only occurred in minor programmes such as the social assistance scheme and the occupational injuries insurance scheme.

Under the social-liberal coalition government formed in late 1969, a new 'expansion phase' began which lasted from 1970 to 1975. In this period, the social expenditure ratio increased by eight percentage points or an average of more than one percentage point per year. Income maintenance, health, housing, and education outlays all grew at rates distinctly above the postwar average. Health and education expenditure recorded particularly heavy increases. Educational reform laws, passed by the previous government in 1969, were implemented and further extended by legislation in 1971 and 1974. A series of benefit extensions in the income maintenance schemes culminated in the 1972 pension reform.

The mid-decade recession then ushered in an 'austerity phase' in social policy which lasted from 1976 to 1983. The series of benefit curtailments began with a Budget Con- solidation Law in late 1975. The GDP share of social spending declined by 1.4 percen- tage points between 1975 and 1983, but in absolute terms social expenditure con- tinued to grow until 1981. Its growth rates reached unprecedented low margins, how- ever, and in the two last years of the period the volume of social outlays declined to the level reached in 1979.

An attempt to analyse this pattern of growth should take at least three basic explanatory factors into account: 1) the potential need for welfare state benefits, which is largely shaped by socio-demographic developments, 2) the availability of resources,
which hinges upon the growth of the economy, and 3) the political power struggle in
which diffuse aspirations are transformed into specific political demands.

2. The impact of demographic factors

The social structure of the Federal Republic has been greatly affected by a sequence
of demographic waves which have shaped developments in the labour market and the
welfare state schemes to a considerable extent (see Table 26 and Graph 48). Up to the
early 1960s more than two-thirds of the population were of working age (15-65).
From 1961 to the mid-1970s, the proportion of the working age population declined
by almost four percentage points, but since 1975 it has risen again to a postwar peak
of 69 percent in 1983. Among the population of dependent age, the number of elderly
persons has roughly doubled since 1950. The number of children below 15 years
increased up to the early 1970s, but has since drastically decreased to a record low in
1983. The steep growth in the proportion of elderly persons has thus been
counteracted by a decrease in the proportion of minors. The shrinking number of the
elderly population in the early 1980s is only a temporary effect of the demographic
consequences of the First World War.

Table 26   Demographic developments in the post-war period

	Age groups as % of total population					
	1950	1961	1970	1975	1980	1983
Working age population (15-65)	67.3	67.2	63.6	63.7	65.9	69.3
Children under the age of 15	23.3	21.7	23.2	21.8	18.2	16.5
Elderly persons above the age of 65	9.4	11.1	13.2	14.5	15.9	14.2
Dependent population	32.7	32.8	36.4	36.3	34.1	30.7
Dependent pop./working age pop.	0.49	0.49	0.57	0.57	0.52	0.44

An impression of the impact which changes in the age structure have upon public policy may be gained from Graph 46 which gives the numerical strength of various age
groups in absolute terms. The number of minors (an important determinant of the
expenditure on education and child allowances) has been subject to very heavy fluctuations. In the 1960s this number increased by roughly two million. It remained almost
constant for some years, but has decreased by three million since 1972. Demographic
waves of such magnitude put the educational system under heavy strain. The school
age population (ages 6-19) declined by half a million during the 1950s, increased by
three million up to 1975, and decreased by 2.5 million again between 1975 and 1983.
Within the secondary sector (ages 10-19) and the post-secondary sector (ages 19-26)
the variation between demographic boom and bust was even more marked. In contrast, the pension system was faced with a steep and fairly consistent growth in the
number of persons above age 60. The temporary decline during the late 1970s has,
since 1979, already given way to renewed growth.

The component method developed by the OECD provides a useful tool to specify the
effects of demographic factors upon social expenditure. Following the OECD
approach, the proportion of GDP allocated to a given social programme may be

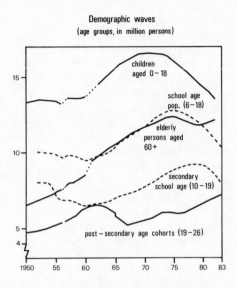

Graph 46

Demographic waves
(age groups, in million persons)

expressed as the product of three factors, i.e. the demographic ratio showing the proportion of the population exposed to a given risk, the eligibility ratio showing which proportion of this target group actually receives benefits, and the transfer ratio expressing the average benefit per beneficiary as a proportion of per capita GDP [235]. Here we can apply this method to an analysis of the development of pension expenditure and child allowance outlays.

In real terms, expenditure for invalidity and old age pensions increased fourteenfold from 3.6 billion DM in 1950 to 51.7 billion DM in 1980 (see Graphs 47 and 48).

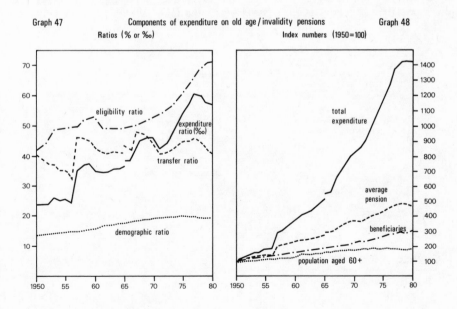

Graph 47   Components of expenditure on old age / invalidity pensions   **Graph 48**
Ratios (% or ‰)   Index numbers (1950=100)

Most of this increase is due to the sizeable upgrading of average benefits which grew almost fivefold in real terms from 1950 to 1980, accounting for 37 percent of the total increase in pension outlays per capita of the population (see Table 27). As the number of beneficiaries tripled and that of elderly persons less than doubled, extensions of eligibility and demographic factors were only of secondary importance, explaining 7 and 4 percent of the total growth, respectively. The combined effect of upgraded benefits and extended eligibility accounts for 25 percent of the growing volume of pension expenditure per capita. The interaction of demographic change and benefit increases contributes roughly 14 percent, and the joint effect of demography and extended entitlements accounts for 3 percent. The remaining 10 percent of the total increase is due to the combined effect of changes in all three components. In this analysis, benefit improvements and extensions of eligibility thus appear as the crucial determinants of pension expenditure, while demographic factors exert only a marginal influence.

A somewhat different picture results if we ask which factors explain the growing GDP share of pension outlays. Between 1950 and 1980 expenditure for invalidity and old age pensions grew from 2.4 to 5.7 percent of GDP. Almost one half of this growth is explained by increases in the eligibility ratio which rose from 42 to 71 percent. The increase in the proportion of elderly persons in the population accounts for 28 percent of the growing GDP share of pensions. The joint effect of changes in eligibility and demography explains 19 percent of the total growth. Increases in average benefits exceeded increases in per capita GDP only marginally (with an increase in the transfer ratio from 40.6 to 41.4 percent) accounting for little more than one percent of the growing GDP share of pensions. The remaining two percent are explained by the various interactions of the three components. The growing GDP share of pensions is thus almost exclusively due to extensions of eligibility and to demographic changes. The frequently legislated benefit increases merely helped pensioners to keep pace with the development of the economy.

A closer analysis shows that the impact of the single components has varied considerably in different phases (see Table 27). From 1950 to 1956 average benefits grew at a slower rate than per capita GDP. Nevertheless the GDP share of pensions increased

Table 27   Components of growth of expenditure on invalidity and old age pensions

Phase	Total change	due to single components			due to interaction effects			
		Demogr. change	Eligib. change	Transfer ratio change	Demogr./ Eligib.	Demogr./ Transfers	Eligib./ Transfers	All three components
1956-80	154.6	-1.5	130.9	4.0	-15.1	-0.5	41.6	-4.8

Growth of per capita expenditure (DM at 1970 prices)

Change in GDP share (percentage points) (a)

Phase	Total change	Demogr. change	Eligib. change	Transfer ratio change	Demogr./ Eligib.	Demogr./ Transfers	Eligib./ Transfers	All three components
1956-80	0.90	-0.03	2.40	-0.12	-0.28	0.01	-1.23	0.14
1956-65	0.37	0.00	0.69	-0.08	0.00	-0.00	-0.24	-0.00
1965-74	-0.29	-0.00	0.04	-0.31	-0.00	-0.00	-0.02	0.00
1974-75	1.08	-0.00	0.51	0.22	-0.01	-0.00	0.36	-0.00
1975-80	-0.25	-0.14	0.01	-0.13	-0.00	0.01	-0.00	0.00

(a) Discrepancies between total and sum of components due to rounding errors.

because extensions in eligibility and, to a lesser degree, demographic effects resulted in a growing number of recipients. The 1957 pension reform then caused a steep increase in the GDP share of pensions, almost exclusively due to the augmentation of benefits. In the subsequent period from 1957 to 1971, the transfer ratio declined (with the exception of the 1966/67 recession), whereas the GDP share of pensions continued to grow by almost one percentage point. Most of this relative growth was due to demographic factors, but increases in eligibility also contributed to the process [236]. From 1971 to 1977 pension outlays rapidly expanded their GDP share by almost two percentage points. In this period the extension of entitlements to previously uncovered groups was the most important factor accounting for 55 percent of the growing GDP share. Another 33 percent is explained by increases in the transfer ratio and 7 percent by the joint effect of both components. The long-term growth of the GDP share of pensions came to an end in 1977 when the financial consolidation legislation began to curb the growth of benefits. From 1977 to 1980 the GDP share of old age and invalidity pensions declined. Most of this decline was due to the decreasing transfer ratio, but a temporary decline of the proportion of elderly persons also had an impact.

The same method may also be applied to analyse the development of child allowance expenditure. In this case, however, one must be aware of a methodological problem. The extension of benefits to families with only one or two children results in a lowering of the transfer ratio, because benefits for the first and the second child are lower than those for the third or further children. From 1955 to 1980 expenditure on child allowances increased seventeenfold in real terms from 0.6 to 10.3 billion DM (see Graphs 49 and 50), or from roughly 13 to 167 DM per capita of the population. The increase in per capita outlays is almost exclusively due to extensions in eligibility (see Table 28). The eligibility ratio increased elevenfold from 8 to 88 percent. Average benefits increased only marginally in real terms by a growth factor of 1.3 [237], whereas the demographic ratio even declined from 26 to 23 percent. Extensions of eligibility

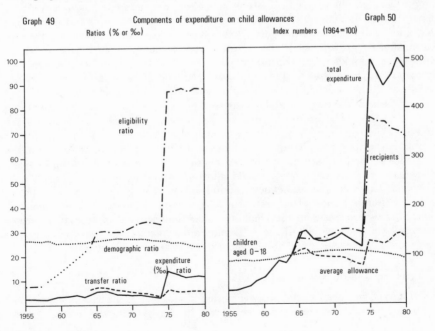

Graph 49   Components of expenditure on child allowances   Graph 50
            Ratios (% or ‰)   Index numbers (1964=100)

and the joint effect of widened entitlements and slightly increased average benefits thus account for the growth of child allowances in absolute terms.

Table 28   Components of growth of expenditure on child allowances

| Phase | Total change | Growth of per capita expenditure (DM at 1970 prices) | | | | | | |
| | | due to single components | | | due to interaction effects | | | |
		Demogr. change	Eligib. change	Transfer ratio change	Demogr./ Eligib.	Demogr./ Transfers	Eligib./ Transfers	All three components
1950–80	764	30	52	280	22	112	192	76

Change in GDP share (percentage points) (a)

Phase	Total change	Demogr. change	Eligib. change	Transfer ratio change	Demogr./ Eligib.	Demogr./ Transfers	Eligib./ Transfers	All three components
1950–80	3.34	0.95	1.62	0.05	0.65	0.02	0.03	0.01
1950–56	0.04	0.21	0.41	-0.48	0.03	-0.04	-0.08	-0.01
1956–57	1.14	0.05	0.02	1.03	0.00	0.02	0.01	0.00
1957–71	0.74	0.96	0.35	-0.47	0.09	-0.13	-0.05	-0.01
1971–77	1.77	0.07	0.97	0.57	0.02	0.01	0.13	0.00
1977–80	-0.35	-0.12	0.46	-0.65	-0.01	0.01	-0.05	0.00

(a) Discrepancies between total and sum of components due to rounding errors.

The GDP share of child allowances increased by roughly one percentage point between 1955 and 1980. The declining number of children and the sluggish development of average benefits which could not keep pace with the growth of per capita GDP would normally have led to a lowering of the GDP share of child allowances. While the demographic ratio shrank by three percentage points, the transfer ratio declined by almost six points between 1955 and 1980 [238]. The joint effects of these two components were countered, however, by the heavy extension of entitlements which was made complete by the introduction of the universal scheme in 1975.

A more detailed phase-specific analysis shows that demographic factors contributed to a growth in child allowances only in the period 1956 to 1965. Even in this phase, however, their influence was marginal. Extensions of eligibility appear as the decisive determinant of growth, while the transfer ratio declined, because benefits were only adjusted occasionally. Entitlements at a lower rate were introduced for the second child in 1961. From 1965 to 1974 a marked decrease in the transfer ratio was accompanied by a slight decline in the demographic ratio. The GDP share of child allowances decreased, although eligibility was further extended by successive upgradings of the income limit. The implementation of the universal scheme in 1975 marks a milestone at which the heavy extension of eligibility coincided with a sizeable increase in benefits surpassing the growth of per capita GDP. The demographic ratio slightly declined, but the joint effects of widened entitlements and upgraded benefits made for an increase in the GDP share of child allowances by one percentage point between 1974 and 1975. In the subsequent period up to 1980, almost equally important decreases in the demographic ratio and the transfer ratio were accompanied by a minor statistical increase in the eligibility ratio (independent of legislative measures), resulting in a declining GDP share. Demographic factors and benefit increases thus played a negligible role in the development of child allowance outlays.

3. Economy and the welfare state

In a historical perspective, the postwar period stands out as a phase of unprecedented economic growth. Between 1950 and 1980 the gross domestic product increased almost fivefold in real terms. This long-term growth was accompanied by intensive short-term fluctuations (see Graph 51). Up to 1982 economists have identified eight business cycles in the history of the Federal Republic [239]. A ninth cycle began in 1983.

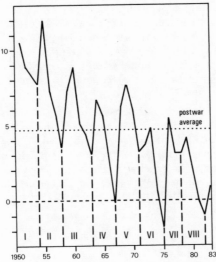

Graph 51

Annual real growth rates of GDP

Record growth rates were reached during the reconstruction period with an average of 8 percent during the first two business cycles from 1951 to 1958 (see Table 29). Although the war had done distinctly more harm to urban housing than to industrial plants [240], industrial production in the immediate postwar years fell below the level reached in 1913 [241]. Industrial plants were dismantled by the occupation powers and German patents lost their protection in international markets. When increasing East-West tensions made for a change in the policy of the victors, the liberal economic policy pursued in the Western zones with massive financial aid from the United States set the sails for a rapid economic recovery. During the first two business cycles in the Federal Republic (1951-58), the annual real growth rates of GDP averaged 8 percent (see Table 29).

Table 29   Phases of economic growth

	Average annual real growth rate		
Phase	Mean	Range	Standard deviation
Cycles 1 and 2 (1951-1958)	8.0	3.5-12.0	2.5
Cycles 3 and 4 (1959-1967)	4.8	-0.2- 8.9	2.6
Cycles 5 and 6 (1968-1975)	3.8	-1.8- 7.8	3.0
Cycles 7 and 8 (1976-1982)	2.4	-1.0- 5.5	2.1
Post-war period (1951-1982)	4.8	-1.8-12.0	3.3

Once the postwar reconstruction was accomplished, these high levels of growth could no longer be maintained. In 1959 total economic output surpassed the level attained in 1938 for the first time [242]. During the next two cycles (1959-1967), the annual growth rates of GDP fell to an average of 4.8 percent. The recession of 1967 led to the first actual reduction in the economic product. Although the slump could quickly be turned into renewed expansion, the growth rates during the next two cycles (1968-1975) remained distinctly below the earlier levels, reaching on average 3.8 percent. The 1975 recession even brought a sizeable reduction in GDP by almost two percentage points. During the subsequent two cycles (1975-1982) annual growth rates settled at an average of 2.4 percent. In 1981 and 1982 the economic product failed to grow in two successive years for the first time in the history of the Federal Republic. Although a new upswing began in 1983, total output remained limited to the level reached in 1980. The postwar economy is thus marked by two outstanding developments: a steep long-term growth in the economic product, and a marked downward trend in annual growth rates.

The structure of the economy underwent significant changes (see Table 30). In 1950 the primary sector still contributed 10 percent of the gross domestic product and employed more than one fifth of the economically active population. Its importance quickly declined during the 1950s, when the heavy industrial growth attracted a large part of the rural manpower to the cities. The shrinkage of the agricultural sector also continued in the subsequent decades, but the increasing productivity upheld the level of self-sufficiency attained in 1950 [243].

Table 30	Sectoral change of the economy				
Sector	1950	1960	1970	1980	1983
	Percent distribution of GDP at factor cost by sector				
Agriculture etc.	10.2	5.8	3.4	2.2	2.1
Industry	49.6	53.2	51.7	44.8	42.3
Services	40.2	41.0	44.9	53.0	55.6
GDP at 1970 prices (in billion DM)	186.1	400.6	678.8	895.1	
	Percent distribution of the labour force by sector				
Agriculture etc.	22.1	13.7	8.5	5.5	5.5
Industry	44.7	47.9	48.9	44.2	41.8
Services	33.2	38.3	42.6	50.3	52.7
Total labour force (in million)	23.5	26.1	26.6	26.3	25.1

The industrial sector continuously increased its share in the gross domestic product up to the early 1960s. Its share of the labour force even grew until the beginning of the 1970s. In the first half of the 1960s, a severe shortage of manpower led to a massive recruitment of foreign labour. The number of foreign workers surpassed one million for the first time in 1964 [244] and kept growing to a peak of 2.6 million or 12 percent of the dependent labour force in 1973. In that year the active recruitment of foreign labour was discontinued. Since then the number of foreign workers almost consistently declined to 1.8 million or 9 percent of the dependent labour force in 1982 [245]. While the German labour market became increasingly affected by the migration of foreign workers, German industry became increasingly dependent upon developments in foreign markets. In the early 1950s only some 15 percent of GDP went into exports. During the 1960s the export ratio climbed to above 20 percent, and in the early 1980s exports even absorbed one third of GDP [246]. This growing dependence upon exports gave rise to concern that the increasing labour costs linked to the expansion of welfare state schemes might hamper the competitiveness of German products in international markets [247].

During the 1970s the Federal Republic joined the ranks of post-industrial societies in the sense that more than half of its economic product was produced in the service sector. Since 1980 this sector has also employed more than half of the labour force. The growing economic importance of the service sector is partly related to overproportionate price increases. It is also due, however, to a real expansion which was particularly marked in the fields of credit institutes, insurance companies, and state services [248]. The massive welfare state expansion in the sectors of health and education has contributed to the process.

The growth of the service sector was accompanied by significant changes in the employment structure. The proportion of bluecollar workers in the labour force continuously declined. The number of white-collar employees and civil servants surpassed the number of workers for the first time in 1976. In 1983, 39.9 percent of the economically active population were blue-collar workers, 47.3 percent were white-collar employees or civil servants, 9.3 percent were self-employed, and 3.5 percent were family workers [249].

In a historical perspective, the coincidence of welfare state expansion and unprecedented economic growth is remarkable. In an influential article on social policy, a German economist once argued that all social outlays must be financed from the resources made available by the current national product [250]. He noted that in modern middle mass societies the potential for a redistribution of consumption expenditure is limited, while a curtailment of investments does not seem advisable. Consequently, increases in the economic product are the only source available for a sizeable augmentation of social outlays.

If policy-makers actually follow this reasoning, we would expect a strong positive correlation between the annual growth rates of GDP and social expenditure. However, since social outlays are usually based on statutory regulations and changes in legislation require some time, it is also possible that expenditure responds to changes in the economic product only after a time-lag. If policy-makers base their budgetary decisions on counter-cyclical considerations, this may also produce a time-lag in the correlation of economic and social expenditure growth, given an average length of a business cycle of 4-5 years.

Table 31 shows that increases in social outlays are correlated positively with economic growth rates and that the association is strongest if a time-lag is introduced into the analysis. Without a time-lag, only the correlation between education expenditure and economic growth is high enough to reach statistical significance [251]. Whereas the other

Table 31   Correlation between annual real growth rates
             of GDP and social expenditure, 1951-1983

Annual growth of	Annual growth of GDP			
	Lag 0	Lag 1	Lag 2	Lag 3
Total social expenditure	.49(a)	.68(b)	.73(b)	.45(a)
Social security	.31	.66(b)	.68(b)	.41(a)
Health	.28	.38(a)	.64(b)	.56(b)
Housing	.32	.27	.40(a)	.27
Education	.52(b)	.65(b)	.55(b)	.32

(a) Significant at .05 level; (b) significant at .01 level.

types of social expenditure are most closely associated with changes of the economy two years ago, changes in educational outlays correlate highest with the growth rates of the economy in the preceding year. The special pattern of educational spending may be related to the fact that decisions on educational matters are made primarily at the *Länder* level.

Since pensions represent the bulk of social security spending, the time-lag built into the adjustment formula of German pensions presumably accounts for the delay with which economic growth rates are reflected in the annual variations of social security outlays. Changes in health expenditure are also most closely related to GDP changes in previous years, but this pattern lends itself less easily to a straightforward interpretation. Since sickness rates of the insured population tend to co-vary with the ups and downs of the economy, and doctors' fees are negotiated on the basis of current wage developments, a more immediate correspondence with economic growth could have been expected. A sound interpretation of the pattern of association would require a more detailed analysis of the annual changes in the single components of health expenditure. Housing outlays have developed in a very erratic fashion, with wide variations between annual increases and decreases. Their correlation with economic growth rates therefore remains comparatively low. Countercyclical considerations, taking the state of the construction industry into account, may be more prominent in this sector than in other realms of the welfare state.

For a better understanding of the relationship between economic growth and social expenditure development, a closer inspection of the pattern of association is necessary. Graph 52 reports the annual deviations between economic growth and social expenditure growth, while the scatterplot in Graph 53 visualizes their relationship. The annual differences between the growth rates of GDP and social outlays show a phase-specific pattern which closely corresponds to our distinction of four social policy phases at the beginning of this section.

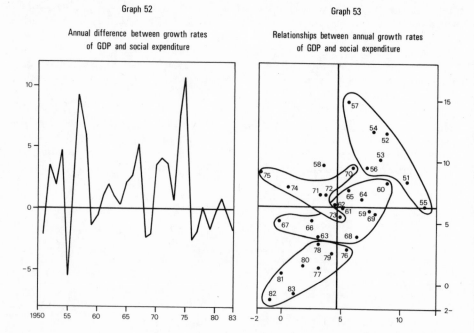

Graph 52

Annual difference between growth rates
of GDP and social expenditure

Graph 53

Relationships between annual growth rates
of GDP and social expenditure

From 1951 to 1957 the growth in social expenditure exceeded the growth in GDP by wide margins. Only in 1951 and 1955 (the two years when GDP growth reached its record heights above 10 percent) did social expenditure growth fall short of GDP increases. Even in these years, however, the volume of social outlays was greatly expanded, with annual growth rates of roughly eight and seven percent respectively. On average, the annual growth rates in social expenditure surpassed the growth rate in GDP by 2.6 percentage points in this period (see Table 32).

Table 32   Phase-specific correspondence between annual real growth
               rates of GDP and social expenditure

Phase	Annual difference between GDP and social expenditure growth rates	Correlation between GDP and social expenditure growth rates
1951-1957	+2.1	-.85 (a)
1958-1969 (1959-1969)	+1.2 (+0.7)	.27 (.51)
1970-1975	+5.0	-.30
1976-1983	-0.9	.84 (b)

(a) Significant at .05 level; (b) significant at .01 level.

From 1958 to 1969 the growth in social expenditure was brought much closer into line with the growth in GDP. The marked increase in 1958 is an exceptional vestige of the previous phase which is due to the postponed implementation of the pension adjustment legislated in 1957. In subsequent years the growth in social expenditure exceeded the growth in GDP by a wide margin only in the recession of 1967 when the GDP was shrinking. On average the increases in social expenditure closely approximated the increases in GDP in this period.

In contrast, from 1970 to 1975 social expenditure developed quite independently from economic growth. On average its annual growth rate exceeded the growth rate in GDP by five percentage points. The period 1976 to 1983 stands out as the only phase in which social outlays increased at a slower rate than the economy. On average their growth fell almost one percentage point behind the annual growth rate in GDP.

A similar phase-specific pattern results from the scatterplot in Graph 53. It shows that the annual relationship between social expenditure growth and economic growth varies according to an almost perfect chronological order. In the take-off phase from 1951 to 1957, social outlays expanded heavily irrespective of the growth rate of the economy. As Table 32 shows, the association between the annual variation of both magnitudes is even negative in this phase. In the consolidation phase from 1958 to 1969, changes in social outlays were brought into closer correspondence with changes in the economic product. In this period both growth rates approximated average levels and their association turned positive. With the exception of 1958, in which deviation from the general pattern may be explained by the postponed effects of the pension reform, the correlation coefficient even amounts to r = .51.

From 1970 to 1975 social outlays once again developed independently from the growth of the economic product. While economic growth rates fell below the postwar average, social expenditure grew at an above average speed. As welfare state schemes were expanded even when the economy was declining, the correlation coefficient for this period is negative. In the austerity phase from 1976 to 1983, increases in social outlays were curbed and closely tied to the rate of growth of the economy. The high positive correlation coefficient makes this most recent period almost appear as the mirror image of the take-off phase in the 1950s.

The clear-cut division of the postwar development of the German welfare state into four distinct phases is noteworthy and calls for interpretation. One element, conspicuously common to the two phases in which welfare state schemes grew irrespective of the constraints of the economy, is that both periods were the initial years after a change in political regimes. The early 1950s mark the formative years of parliamentary democracy after the defeat of a totalitarian regime and the period of foreign occupation. The early 1970s are the initial years of the social-liberal government after the first occurrence of a democratic regime change in the postwar period. This invites the speculation that new regimes seek to enhance their legitimacy by expanding social benefits irrespective of economic resources. The following section will therefore take a closer look at the political context of welfare state development.

4. The politics of welfare state development

The aftermath of World War II led to significant changes in the structure of German politics. Prior to the Nazi regime, the German party system had consisted of four major groupings: 1) a conservative-authoritarian political formation rooted in the agrarian and Protestant population segments in North and East Germany, 2) a liberal camp primarily centred in the Protestant urban population and divided into a nationalist and a democratic wing, 3) a Catholic camp represented by the Centre Party, and 4) the socialist labour movement which in the Weimar Republic split into a Social Democratic and a Communist party [252].

The division of the country following World War II was partly responsible for the erosion of the social bases of the traditional political line-up. With the loss of the agrarian regions east of the Elbe river, the conservative-authoritarian camp lost its social basis. The exclusion of Prussia led to an almost balanced quantitative relationship between the religious denominations in West Germany, the Catholic population losing its former minority status [253]. Cleavages based on class or religion were now translated into a new arrangement of political forces. The Catholic Centre Party was replaced by the Christian Democratic Union (CDU), designed to represent Catholics and Protestants in a common party. However, a regional differentiation between the Christian Social Union (CSU) in Bavaria and the CDU elsewhere persisted. The Liberals also united to form the Free Democratic Party (FDP). The Social Democratic Party (SPD) was re-established in 1945 and resisted the invitation to unite with the Communists. Deprived of their former strongholds in Eastern Germany, the Communists declined to the status of a splinter party. In 1956 their party organization was ruled unconstitutional.

In the first elections to the Bundestag in 1949, the three major formations (CDU/CSU, SPD, FDP) captured 72 percent of the votes (see Graph 54). Among the eight other parties represented in parliament, only the Communists polled more than 5 percent of the votes. The subsequent years saw a marked concentration of the party system. In the 1953 elections only three more conservative parties joined the major formations in parliament. The major parties captured 83.5 percent of the votes. The Christian Union absorbed a sizeable portion of the conservative splinter parties. Since 1961 the three major party formations were the only forces to be represented in parliament, consistently attracting more than 94 percent of the valid votes. This situation only changed in 1983 when the Greens established themselves as a fourth political group [254].

Up to 1969 the Christian Union parties won all elections, although since 1953 the Social Democrats had been continuously increasing their electoral strength. *Genosse*

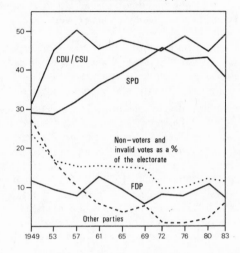

Graph 54

Election results

Percent distribution of votes by party

1949 53 57 61 65 69 72 76 80 83

Trend, as this development was called, helped the party to exceed 30 percent of the vote for the first time in 1957 and pushed it over 40 percent by 1969. In the 1972 election, the Social Democrats succeeded for the first time in outrunning the Christian Union at the polls. In subsequent years *Genosse Trend* abandoned the party. The Christian Union parties increased their share of the votes up to 1957 when they became the first political group in German history to poll an absolute majority. In subsequent elections they attracted roughly 45 to 49 percent of the vote. The Liberals captured around 10 percent of the vote up to 1965. Later their share somewhat declined, exceeding 10 percent only in 1980.

The major parties are related to distinguishable social clienteles. Whereas the Social Democrats have strong ties to bluecollar workers and white-collar employees with union affiliations, the Christian parties draw overproportionate support from the self-employed, farmers, and from segments of the dependent labour force with strong church affiliations [255]. They are also more dependent upon the older generation than the Social Democrats. The Liberals are primarily tied to self-employed categories outside agriculture and to highly trained white-collar groups including those in the civil service. To win election, all parties need to attract votes from the new middle class which is not only the most dynamically growing category, but also most heterogeneous in its political loyalties with a marked tendency for issue-specific voting.

The shifting political loyalties of the new middle class also affected the formation of coalition governments. Although the Christian parties had captured an absolute majority of the seats in 1953 and 1957, the Federal Republic has always been ruled by coalition cabinets [256]. The Liberal party was represented in all cabinets with the exception of short interludes from 1957 to 1961 and 1966 to 1969. Throughout the 1950s the voters were confronted with two political blocks representing clear-cut policy alternatives. The governing Christian and Liberal parties stood for the social market economy and the country's integration into the Western alliance; the Social Democratic opposition advocated a socialist planned economy, neutrality in international affairs, and disarmament. This situation changed when the Social Democrats, in a new party platform in 1959, accepted the social market economy and shortly afterwards also Germany's integration into NATO.

The new strategy paid off in considerably widened electoral support especially among middle class voters. Theoretically all major parties were now available for alternative coalitions. In 1963, under Liberal pressure, Chancellor Adenauer was replaced by Ludwig Erhard, the major proponent of a liberal economic policy among the Christian parties. His cabinet lasted until 1966 when a recession led to budgetary deficits which the Liberals refused to cover with tax increases. The Liberals withdrew from the coalition and a new right wing party scored considerable success in state elections.

In response to this first political crisis situation in the Federal Republic, the Christian Union parties and the Social Democrats formed the 'Grand Coalition' government. The Social Democratic Party's participation in government further promoted its appeal to middle class voters. In the 1969 election it polled almost 43 percent which proved enough to form a coalition government with the Liberals; this was confirmed and strengthened in the 1972 election. In 1974 Helmut Schmidt replaced Willy Brandt as Chancellor, and his social-liberal coalition government was confirmed in the elections of 1976 and 1980. It broke up in 1982 when conflicts over budgetary deficits and economic policy led the Liberals to opt for a new coalition with the Christian parties. The new governing parties scored a convincing victory at the polls in 1983.

The history of the Federal Republic may thus be divided into two phases with varying political control: a period of Christian Union domination from 1949 to 1969, and a period of Social Democratic control from 1969 to 1982. The years 1966 to 1969 mark a transition period in which both major parties joined in a coalition. Throughout most of the two major phases, the Liberal Party exerted control as the junior partner in coalition cabinets. Since the major parties have noticeably different political clienteles, we will examine in the following what impact the variations in government control had on welfare state policies.

If we look at the GDP share of social spending as the most conventional but also crudest measure of welfare state development, the social-liberal coalition government appears as a much more active promoter of welfare state expansion than the bourgeois coalition governments (see Table 33). From 1950 to 1983 the GDP share of social spending increased by roughly 12 percentage points [257]. Almost two-thirds of this increase (7.5 percentage points) occurred under the social-liberal government. Pushing the expenditure ratio up by 4.4 percentage points, the bourgeois coalition governments in control up to 1966 accounted for 38 percent of the total increase. The Grand Coalition government contributed another three percent to the growth of the

Table 33   The growth of the social expenditure ratio under various governments

| Governments | Increase in the GDP share of expenditure for | | | | |
	Total social expenditure	Social security	Health	Housing	Education
Christian Union/Liberal coalition (1951–1966)	4.4	2.1	1.4	−0.3	1.3
Grand coalition (1966–1969)	0.4	0.3	0.3	−0.5	0.2
Social-Liberal coalition (1969–1982)	7.5	3.5	2.5	0.2	1.5
Christian Union/Liberal coalition (1982–1983)	−0.6	−0.4	0.0	−0.1	−0.2
Total post-war period (1951–1983)	11.7	5.5	4.2	−0.7	2.8

social expenditure ratio, whilst under the new bourgeois coalition government formed in 1982, the GDP share of social spending declined. A similar pattern of relative social expenditure growth results in the fields of social security, health and housing. Only the GDP share of education spending increased almost as heavily under the bourgeois governments as under the social-liberal coalition.

The overproportionate increase of the GDP share of social spending under Social Democratic rule does not mean that the CDU governments refrained from expanding welfare state schemes. The real annual growth rates of social expenditure (at 1970 prices) were in fact much higher under the bourgeois governments up to 1966 than under the social-liberal coalition (see Table 34). However, this was largely due to the fact that economic growth was also much higher when the former were in office. As the table shows, the CDU governments expanded social outlays in much stronger correspondence with the available economic surplus than the governments led by the Social Democrats. We have seen above that both major periods of varying political control may be subdivided into phases with strong and weak associations between economic growth and social expenditure growth. We can now detect two more general patterns. Under the CDU governments welfare state growth came about primarily as a by-product of economic growth, whereas, to a much greater degree, the Social Democrats pursued expansionist social policies independent of economic conditions.

Table 34   Annual real growth rates of social expenditure under various governments

Governments	Annual growth rates of expenditure for					Annual difference between the growth rates of GDP and expenditure for				
	Total social	Social security	Health	Hous- ing	Educa- tion	Total social	Social security	Health	Hous- ing	Educa- tion
Christian Union/Liberals (1951-1966)	8.4	8.9	8.7	6.0	8.1	1.4	1.0	3.8	-2.8	3.2
Grand coalition (1967-1969)	4.9	5.6	6.0	-9.9	4.6	0.5	0.4	3.6	-15.3	2.5
Social-Liberal (1970-1982)	4.4	4.4	5.3	4.3	4.0	2.3	1.7	4.5	1.7	3.2
Christian Union/Liberals (1983)	(-0.8)	(-0.8)	(0.8)	(-5.9)	(-2.1)	(-1.9)	(-1.7)	(-0.6)	(-7.3)	(-3.5)
Post-war average (1951-1983)	6.3	6.5	6.9	3.5	5.9	1.6	1.1	4.0	-1.7	2.9

On the basis of aggregate data, the role which both major political forces played in welfare state development may be perhaps best illustrated, if we look at the increase of social spending in absolute terms (see Table 35). From 1950 to 1983 social outlays grew by roughly 226 billion DM (at 1970 prices) [258]. 41 percent of this total increase occurred up to 1966 under governments headed by the Christian Democrats. The period of social-liberal rule accounted for 51 percent of the total augmentation, while the years of the Grand Coalition government contributed another 9 percent. Under the new bourgeois coalition, total social outlays declined by more than 2 billion DM in 1983.

These data suggest that the social-liberal government was a more active promoter of welfare state expansion than the bourgeois governments. If we standardize for the number of years each party was in office, the CDU governments up to 1966 increased social outlays by an average of 5.7 billion DM per year, while the social-liberal coali-

Table 35   The growth of social expenditure under various governments

| Governments | Increase of expenditure at constant (1970) prices (in million DM) for | | | | |
	Total social	Social security	Health	Housing	Education
Christian Union/Liberals (1950–1966)	91 704	60 695	13 789	3 503	13 718
Grand coalition (1966–1969)	20 620	15 540	3 798	−1 657	2 938
Social Liberal (1969–1982)	115 583	75 992	22 414	2 983	14 194
Christian Union/Liberals (1982–1983)	−2 359	−1 537	358	−439	−741
Entire post-war period (1950–1983)	225 548	150 690	40 359	4 390	30 109

tion recorded an average increase of 8.9 billion DM per year (at constant prices). Under the joint government of both leading parties, social expenditure grew by 6.9 billion DM on average. A second conclusion is similarly noteworthy, however. If we consider that the Grand Coalition was headed by the Christian Democratic party, it appears that both major political forces contributed roughly similar shares to the total growth of welfare state schemes in the postwar period. This is also confirmed by an analysis of expenditure developments in single welfare state dimensions. Only health expenditure grew predominantly under Social Democratic rule. In summary, the Social Democrats tended to pursue a more expansionist course in social policy, but the long-term growth of the welfare state in the postwar period can only be understood as the result of common efforts made by both leading political parties.

An analysis of legislative activities also shows that the postwar development of the welfare state was to a large extent built on consensus (see Table 36 and the list of core laws in the Appendix volume). From 1950 to 1983, 130 core laws were passed in the major welfare state schemes [259]. 46 percent of these laws were passed under the social-liberal coalition, 45 percent under bourgeois coalition governments, and 9 percent under the Grand Coalition. If we distinguish between laws bringing about welfare state extensions, curtailments or merely re-organizations, a similarly balanced pattern results. In each of these dimensions, 'bourgeois' and 'left' governments enacted an almost identical number of core laws.

Within single policy areas, the legislative activity of the various governments is less evenly distributed. The core of the social security schemes was predominantly built up by the CDU governments. Only the responsibility for the curtailments of the most recent period is divided roughly equally between both types of coalition governments. In contrast, most core laws and the lion's share of the extensions in sickness insurance and health were passed while the social-liberal coalition was in office. Since responsibilities for educational matters were only shifted to the federal government in 1969, the social-liberal coalition also accounts for the major part of federal education laws. In housing, the governments led by the CDU or the SPD passed a similar number of core laws. Whereas the activities of the social-liberal coalition centred on an extension of state regulations, however, the bourgeois governments predominantly legislated extensions of housing allowances and subsidies, while they de-regulated the housing market.

If we look at the annual legislative activity scores rather than at the total number of core laws, the social-liberal coalition once more appears as a more active force in social policy than the bourgeois governments. Whilst the former legislated an average number of almost five core laws per year, the latter enacted only three. In social security and in housing, both leading parties were similarly active while in office, but

Table 36   The enactment of welfare state core laws under various governments (a)

	Extensions	Curtailments	Other	Total
	Total core laws			
Social-Liberal	34 (2.6)	17 (1.3)	9 (0.7)	60 (4.6)
Grand coalition	8 (2.7)	2 (0.7)	2 (0.7)	12 (4.0)
Christian Union/Liberals I	34 (2.0)	3 (0.2)	7 (0.4)	44 (2.6)
Christian Union/Liberals II	0 (0.0)	13 (6.5)	1 (0.5)	14 (7.0)
Christian Union/Liberals Total	34 (1.8)	16 (0.8)	8 (0.4)	58 (3.1)
Total	76 (2.3)	35 (1.0)	19 (0.5)	130 (3.8)
	Social security (income maintenance)			
Social-Liberal	15 (1.2)	9 (0.7)	3 (0.2)	27 (2.1)
Grand coalition	5 (1.7)	1 (0.3)	1 (0.3)	7 (2.3)
Christian Union/Liberals I	25 (1.5)	0 (0.0)	3 (0.2)	28 (1.6)
Christian Union/Liberals II	0 (0.0)	8 (2.0)	1 (0.5)	9 (4.5)
Christian Union/Liberals Total	25 (1.4)	8 (0.4)	4 (0.2)	37 (1.9)
Total	45 (1.3)	18 (0.5)	8 (0.2)	71 (2.1)
	Sickness insurance and health			
Social-Liberal	6 (0.5)	3 (0.2)	4 (0.3)	13 (1.0)
Grand coalition	1 (0.3)	1 (0.3)	1 (0.3)	3 (1.0)
Christian Union/Liberals I	3 (0.2)	0 (0.0)	4 (0.2)	7 (0.4)
Christian Union/Liberals II	0 (0.0)	2 (1.0)	0 (0.0)	2 (1.0)
Christian Union/Liberals Total	3 (0.2)	2 (0.1)	4 (0.2)	9 (0.5)
Total	10 (0.3)	6 (0.2)	9 (0.3)	25 (0.7)
	Housing			
Social-Liberal	7 (0.5)	3 (0.2)	0 (0.0)	10 (0.8)
Grand coalition	1 (0.3)	0 (0.0)	0 (0.0)	1 (0.3)
Christian Union/Liberals I	6 (0.4)	3 (0.2)	0 (0.0)	9 (0.5)
Christian Union/Liberals II	0 (0.0)	2 (1.0)	0 (0.0)	2 (1.0)
Christian Union/Liberals Total	6 (0.3)	5 (0.3)	0 (0.0)	11 (0.6)
Total	14 (0.4)	8 (0.2)	0 (0.0)	22 (0.6)
	Education			
Social-Liberal	6 (0.5)	2 (0.2)	2 (0.2)	10 (0.8)
Grand coalition	1 (0.3)	0 (0.0)	0 (0.0)	1 (0.3)
Christian Union/Liberals I	0 (0.0)	0 (0.0)	0 (0.0)	0 (0.0)
Christian Union/Liberals II	0 (0.0)	1 (0.5)	0 (0.0)	1 (0.5)
Christian Union/Liberals Total	0 (0.0)	1 (0.1)	0 (0.0)	1 (0.1)
Total	7 (0.2)	3 (0.1)	2 (0.1)	12 (0.4)

(a) Number of laws; in brackets: number of laws per year ('legislative activity score').

in health and education the social-liberal coalition displayed considerably greater legislative dynamics. It is noteworthy, however, that the overproportionate legislative
activity of the SPD-led governments includes curtailments as well as extensions. This
is probably due to the fact that a large proportion of their years in office was marked
by economic austerity, while most of the Christian Democratic rule coincided with a
period of prosperity. It is obvious, however, that neither extensions nor curtailments
of the German welfare state can be understood as a monopoly of a specific party government.

An analysis of the mere number of laws passed under each coalition government may
even underestimate the degree of consensus in the establishment of welfare state
schemes, because it neglects the extent to which the respective opposition party partici-

pated in the legislative process. A roll-call analysis of the final reading of the most important bills shows that there was, in fact, a high degree of cooperation between government and opposition (see Table 37) [260]. 57 percent of 39 of the major 68 core laws examined here were passed with the votes of both leading parties. 37 percent of these laws were even passed unanimously.

Table 37   Parliamentary voting on the major welfare state core laws

	Total number of laws	Passed with the votes of the major opposition party	Passed against the votes of the major opposition party
Extensions	38	33	5
Curtailments	20	1	19
Organizational laws	10	5	5
Total major core laws	68	39	29

A closer analysis distinguishing between the various types of laws is particularly revealing. With the exception of one bill enacted under the Grand Coalition, all curtailments of welfare state schemes had to be passed against the dissent of the major opposition party. The major organizational laws were also rather embattled. Five of the ten most important re-organizations had to be enacted against the resistance of the major opposition party. In contrast, 85 percent of the most important welfare state extensions were based on broad political consensus. Only five of the 38 major extensions met with resistance from the major opposition party. In two of theses cases, the opposition demanded even further extensions (1954 child allowances, 1971 education allowances). In two other cases organizational questions or the priorities for various forms of public promotion were at stake (1956 Housing Act, 1961 Social Assistance Act). The 1971 Tenant Protection Act is the only example of a welfare state extension which the major opposition party challenged on principle as an interference in individual responsibilities or liberties which was too far-reaching.

The roll-call analysis thus confirms the impression that the expansion of the German welfare state was to a large extent built on political consensus. All major parties usually sustained the extension of public schemes, whereas the responsibility for curtailments had to be assumed by the governing parties alone. Of course, it must be considered, that the final reading of a bill takes place only after the decisive battles in parliamentary committees. Therefore, the high degree of consensus on extension bills does not mean that the welfare state expanded entirely free of political conflicts, or that the major parties advocated identical models of welfare state development. As we have seen, the German parties are tied to distinguishable social clienteles. In addition, they also maintain diverse ties to the major interest groups. Whereas the trade unions are closely linked with the Social Democrats for whom several of their functionaries hold parliamentary seats, the employers maintain a close network of personal and organizational relations with the Christian parties and the Liberals [261].

Both the unions and the employers' associations have frequently issued petitions and manifestos on social policy, because welfare state developments heavily affect the balance of power between them. In order to avoid a split-up of the dependent labour force into segments with differential welfare entitlements, the unions have always pressed for the abolition of income limits for compulsory coverage in the income

Table 38   Basic social policy outlooks of the major parties

S P D	C D U / C S U	F D P

Income maintenance

Preference for universal schemes; aboliton of income limits in social insurance; harmonization of entitlements for various occupational groups; integration of differentiated schemes for a better pooling of risks and a more effective linkage of benefits to need; for generous benefits to preserve standard of living; higher state share in financing of schemes; strengthening of self-administrative bodies enabling them to function as centres of citizen welfare	Advocation of income-limits in compulsory insurance; preservation of differentiated schemes for various occupational categories; earnings-related benefits based on equivalence principle in social insurance, but linked to economic prosperity; financing to be based on individual contributions rather than general revenues in order to stress individual responsibility and personal dignity	Accentuation of individual responsibility as basis of a free society; occasional advocation of more selective schemes centering on prevention of hardship; defence of income-limits in compulsory insurance and traditional differentiation of schemes; general affirmation of earnings-related benefits, but occasional considerations to shift from earnings-related to national minimum pensions; priority of low tax burden over generous benefits; financing to be based on individual contributions following the equivalence principle; state share as limited as possible

Health

Public responsibility for the promotion of preventive rather than curative health care; integration of hospitals and new medical-technical centres into the supply of ambulant services in order to improve services and to combat the cost explosion; stricter public control of the pharmaceutical market by the Federal Health Office	Strengthening of private responsibility of health through cost sharing; preservation of the position of private doctors as providers of ambulant services; regulation of the pharmaceutical market through voluntary self-control of the pharmaceutical industry	(Basically in accordance with CDU/CSU)

Housing

Preferential promotion of social housing; strong tenant protection in order to strengthen the market position of tenants; higher land taxes as an incentive to increase the supply of purchasable land; more generous housing allowances	Preferential promotion of family housing; de-regulation of tenant protection to stimulate investment; oversupply perceived as the most effective form of tenant protection; de-regulation of public building norms impeding private construction	De-regulation of the housing market; shift from the subsidization of housing supply to housing allowances targeted to low income groups; increase of land supply through privatization of public land

Education

More equality of opportunity through introduction of comprehensive schools and education allowances for pupils and students; standardization of fragmented federal school system; integration of vocational training into system of public education	Preservation of traditional differentian of the German school system; limitation of education allowances to grants for students; preservation of federal pluralism; preservation of dual system of vocational training	Return to defence of differentiated school system after temporary advocation of comprehensive schools in the 1970s; limitation of education allowances to grants for students; standardization of fragmented federal system, but more autonomy for universities; preservation of dual system of vocational training

maintenance schemes, whereas the employers sided for limited programmes which keep labour costs low and generate divided interests [262]. For the same motive, employers also defend the organizational segmentation of the welfare state into schemes for various occupational categories, whereas the unions press for more unitary schemes forging the interests of the dependent labour force together. The administration of social insurance schemes has also been an area of contention between the major interest groups. To give union representatives privileged access to authority positions in social policy, the unions pressed for a majority representation of the beneficiaries on administrative boards, whereas the employers advocated a representation according to the distribution of contributions which strengthened their influence.

The social policy proposals of the major parties reflect to a large extent their relationships to the various clientele groups and interest organizations. The different positions on welfare state issues emerging from party manifestos are summarized in Table 38 [263]. Of course, this synopsis simplifies rather complex political debates. It shows, however, that the Liberal party's position on social policy is much closer to the position of the Christian parties than to that of the Social Democrats. In income maintenance and housing policy, the Liberals even tend to be noticeably more restrictive than the Christian parties. In health policy, the positions of the two bourgeois parties largely coincide. Educational policy may be considered the only field where the Liberals were at least temporarily closer to the Social Democrats than to the Christian parties.

Using concepts developed by Titmuss and by Korpi [264], we may say that the Social Democrats advocate an 'institutional' model of the welfare state in which public transfers and services supplement the market and private households are a major mechanism of distribution. The bourgeois parties, on the other hand, champion a more 'residual' model where state schemes are confined to a subsidiary role only activated when the market and private households fail. Generally, the Christian parties and the Liberals stress the need to limit the role of the state, because they perceive the principle of compulsion in most welfare state measures as an encroachment upon individual liberties and responsibilities. In contrast, the Social Democrats perceive social security as a substantive precondition of human freedom and dignity, and they propagate an 'active' social policy which not merely compensates for risks once they have developed, but also seeks to modify societal conditions giving rise to risks. More specifically, the social policy efforts of the Social Democrats usually centre on the regulation of work conditions, on the promotion of full employment, and on social security, whereas the social policy of the bourgeois parties primarily seeks to strengthen the self-help potential of families and to promote a more widespread capacity for property formation (*Vermögensbildung*). Thus all parties may contribute to the expansion of social programmes, but in doing so they still seek to extend different models of the welfare state.

The discrepant conceptions of social policy usually do not become apparent in the final reading of a bill. Only detailed case studies of the parliamentary decision-making process could reveal the extent to which different conceptions shape final decisions. We can only refer here to two major examples for which detailed historical studies are available. The first one concerns the basic reforms in pension insurance, the second one relates to the failure of the sickness insurance reforms in the late 1950s and early 1960s [265].

The pension reform of 1957

When pensioners fell increasingly behind the standard of living of the working population during the postwar reconstruction boom, all parties agreed that a reform of the pension scheme was necessary. In 1952 the Social Democrats published an embracive 'social plan' which largely followed the principles of the Beveridge plan. One year later the government responded with the announcement of a thorough reform. The plan for pension insurance was to link pension levels to wage increases, while preserving the traditional principles of the German social insurance model.

When the government failed to introduce a reform bill in parliament for several years, the Social Democrats in early 1956 brought in a pension insurance bill which now followed the more pragmatic lines of the government's proposals. Shortly afterwards the government brought in its own bill. The two bills coincided in the following major points: compulsory coverage should be extended to all persons in dependent employment without an income-limit; the organizational differentiation between a workers' and an employees' scheme should be preserved, but entitlements should be equalized; benefits should be strictly tied to past contributions and function as earnings-replacements, largely maintaining the standard of living attained during working life; running pensions should be periodically adjusted; the financing of the scheme should largely be put on a pay-as-you-go basis.

However, there were also major divergences. These concerned the relationship between pensions and earnings in the new pension formula, the financing, and the scope of the scheme. The Social Democrats wanted to link pension entitlements directly to the earnings of the dependent labour force, by making the general computation basis of pensions equal to the average earnings in the year immediately preceding the pension claim, and by providing for an automatic indexation of pensions following the development of wages without any time-lag. In addition to the principle of earnings-related benefits, they wanted to introduce an element of minimum security based on need rather than merit, by introducing a fictitious minimum computation basis for low earning strata. In contrast, the government bill provided for a more indirect linkage between pensions and earnings by expressing the general computation basis as a moving average of earnings in the three years preceding the pension claim, and by adjusting running pensions only every five years following the advice of an expert committee which was to take the development of productivity into account. All benefits were to be strictly related to past earnings and contributions. With respect to financing, the Social Democrats intended to increase the state share, whereas the government bill provided for higher individual contribution rates. In contrast to the government bill, finally, the Social Democratic bill provided for an opening of the coverage of the scheme to the voluntary membership of economically inactive groups.

The fierce struggles during the parliamentary readings of the bill were described in the press as a 'pension war'. The abolition of the income-limit for compulsory coverage and the linkage between pensions and earnings proved to be the most controversial issues. With respect to coverage, both the general trade unions and the special employees' union (*Deutsche Angestelltengewerkschaft*) advocated the extension of the scheme to the entire dependent labour force. On the other side, the employers' association, the private insurance companies, and the association of higher level white-collar employees (*Union der leitenden Angestellten*) rallied to thwart the plan. Their argument was that an extension of compulsory coverage would threaten individual liberties, ruin the private insurance companies, overburden employers with excessive labour costs and damage industrial capital formation. In parliament the Liberal party - whose core had defected from the government after a split in 1956 - sided with these interests. In the Christian parties the traditional cleavage between a social Christian workers' wing and a neo-liberal employers' wing became manifest. Only the former backed the government bill. Finally, a compromise was reached under which the income-limit for the compulsory coverage of employees was raised.

Together with the associations of banks and savings banks, the employers' associations and the private insurance companies also rallied against the plan to link pensions to wages. They argued that this would give pensioners an immediate interest in wage increases which would encourage the unions to make higher wage claims that would fuel inflation. They also maintained that the indexation of pensions would lead to a reduction in private savings. The unions, on the other hand, sided with the Social Democrats in demanding a direct linkage between pensions and wages. The Liberals voiced the arguments of the critics, while the internal division between the workers' wing and the employers' wing brought the Christian parties close to a rupture. Under the compromise which was finally formulated, the general computation basis for new pension claims remained linked to the average of earnings in the three year period preceding the claim, but an additional time-lag of one year was introduced. Pension adjustments were made contingent upon special legislation without any explicit linkage to wages in the general law. However, the government was obliged to issue annual reports on the potential for adjustments based on the advice of an expert committee whose recommendations were to consider the development of the economy. In actual practice, this meant that pension adjustments linked to the development of wages were subsequently legislated in every year between 1958 and 1977. The final bill was passed with the votes of the Christian parties and the Social Democrats against the opposition of the Liberals [266].

The common support for the pension insurance reform bill did not impede the Social Democrats and the Christian parties from again developing divergent initiatives once the reform had been implemented. Prior to the 1965 elections, the Social Democrats came up with a new master plan for the creation of a universal pension scheme, whilst the Christian parties introduced a bill which - among other new regulations - provided for the introduction of an income-limit for coverage even in the workers' scheme. Neither of these plans materialized. The SPD initiative was abandoned when the party lost the election; the government bill found a parliamentary majority only after the clause on the income-limit had been cancelled. The fiscal problems faced by the Grand Coalition government then helped both parties to find a compromise solution for pension insurance coverage. In an attempt to cover the deficit in the federal budget, the state share in financing was reduced, but to compensate for the resulting gap in pension finances, compulsory coverage was extended to all employees.

When the social-liberal coalition came to office and financial forecasts showed an abundant surplus of resources in the pension scheme, the Social Democrats set out to implement a second major pension reform which would realize some of their old conceptions. The new bill provided for the complementation of earnings-related pensions with entitlements based on a fictitious minimum income for the lowest earning groups, and for the opening of membership to the voluntary coverage of housewives and self-employed persons. The latter proposal met with trade union resistance, but besides bringing the Social Democratic idea of universal coverage closer to realization, it also served as a concession to the electoral clientele of the liberal coalition partner. Other central features of the government bill foresaw an optional lowering of the retirement age to 63 years (flexible age limit) and the introduction of a 'baby-year' which would accredit women with an extra year of contributions for each child.

In an attempt to appeal more directly to pensioners in the approaching elections, the Christian Democratic opposition introduced an alternative bill that centred on an upgrading of pensions. Since the time-lag in the pension adjustment procedure and the mounting inflation rate made for an increasing gap between the standards of living of pensioners and workers, the Christian Democrats proposed to antedate the annual adjustment of pensions by half a year, and to fix a statutory minimum relationship between a standard pension and average earnings which future adjustments would have to take into account. With respect to voluntary membership and the flexible age limit, the bill largely concurred with the government bill. In contrast to the latter, however, it neither provided for entitlements based on a minimum income nor for a 'baby-year' for women.

The final reading of the bill took place on the penultimate day of the legislative period when the governing parties had lost their parliamentary majority due to several defections after conflicts over foreign policy. Based on the votes of the new Christian Democratic majority and the governing parties, the law which was finally passed combined elements of both previous bills. The upgrading of pensions advocated by the opposition was adopted together with all reform proposals of the government except for the 'baby-year'. The reform led to a marked increase in pension insurance outlays almost half of which was due to the antedated pension adjustment [267]. This is the only example of a social reform law which combined extension proposals of all major parties trying to outbid each other prior to an election.

In order to improve our understanding of the politics of welfare state development, case studies of the legislation of major acts should be combined with case studies of non-decisions which prevented major institutional changes. The outstanding example of this latter case is the history of the failure of the sickness insurance reforms proposed by the Christian Democratic governments between 1957 and 1965.

The failure of sickness insurance reforms

In the mid-1950s the cost of medical care had rapidly grown. Upon union pressure which included a massive regional strike, the government had in 1957 enacted a law which increased sickness insurance cash benefits and introduced a partial wage continuation for workers as a first step toward an equalization of workers' and employees' entitlements. In combination with the increasing incidence of sickness, the additional benefits led to mounting financial difficulties of the sickness funds.

After the Christian parties had won an absolute majority of parliamentary seats in the 1957 election, Chancellor Adenauer announced a thorough reform of sickness insurance in order to contain medical expenditure. He also stressed that after the implementation of the pension insurance reform his government was resolved to promote the idea of self-help and private initiative in order to prevent slipping into a total welfare state.

In October 1958 the government drafted a reform bill which was formally submitted to the legislature one year later. The bill provided for cost sharing in the form of a a private fee for every medical service (doctor's care, hospital care, drugs). This strengthening of individual responsibilities was to be combined with more generous cash benefits, a shorter waiting period, mandatory hospital care for an indefinite period, and a series of mandatory preventive measures. The central idea was to shift the emphasis of public protection from minor ailments to major illnesses and to foster a stronger sense of responsibility among the insured. In order to reduce the incidence of sickness and to promote preventive measures, a supervisory body of consultant physicians was to be established. In response to long-standing demands of the doctors' associations, the traditional system of remuneration based on a uniform fee per capita was to be replaced by a differentiated fee-for-service system which would be based on a federal fee schedule to be issued by the Ministry of Labour. Finally, the traditional licensing procedure limiting admission to sickness fund practice would be abolished in favour of free admission.

The compound reform package was designed to neutralize countervailing pressures of various interest groups. The coupling of cost-sharing with more generous cash benefits was to make the bill palatable to the unions, while to the doctors cost-sharing was presented as a necessary corollary to the new fee-for-service system which required giving the patients a certain degree of control over the services that were being offered.

Immediately after the publication of the bill a storm of protest set in which proved the governments' hopes to be unrealistic. Among the major interest groups, only the employers' associations and the private insurance companies endorsed the bill. Split into several rival associations, the medical profession did not develop a uniform stance. However, the Federal Association of Sickness Fund Physicians (*Kassenärztliche Bundesvereinigung*), which is the most important medical organization, resisted the plan outright. Although they were not hostile to the idea of cost-sharing on principle [268], the physicians resented the concept of an individual fee for doctor's care, arguing that this would induce patients to shy away from necessary consultations and would overburden the physicians with administrative tasks. Their main thrust was against the intended re-organization of medical services which they perceived as a first step toward a dictatorial control of the health system. The association feared that the establishment of a control mechanism on consultant physicians would undermine their monopoly in the supply of medical services and that a governmental fee schedule would threaten the organization's autonomy as a broker between individual doctors and insurance funds.

The physicians' resistance against the bill combined with the rigid opposition of the trade unions. The unions perceived any cost-sharing as a restriction of their social achievements. The moralistic undertones of the bill, which suggested that the working class needed the stimulus of cost-sharing in order to foster a sense of responsibility, helped them to mobilize their rank and file on a massive scale. Hundreds of thousands of workers signed petitions against the bill, and the year 1960 was marked by a long series of protest marches and mass demonstrations against the government's policy.

In parliament, the German party (*Deutsche Partei*) and the Liberals supported the position of the employers' associations, but the Liberals criticized the cost-sharing provisions for not going far enough. The Christian parties were once again divided between their workers' and their employers' wings. The workers' wing demanded that cost-sharing be complemented by wage continuation provisions that would further equalize workers' and employees' entitlements. The Social Democrats resisted the concept of cost-sharing on principle. They advocated higher benefits, a system of wage continuation that would put workers fully on par with employees, and an extension of the income limit for compulsory coverage. Their tactic was to delay the deliberations of the bill in a way that would force the government to enact at least its extensive provisions once the election date drew near.

Backed by the mutually reinforcing resistance of the trade unions and the medical profession, the tactic of the Social Democrats was successful. Without a chance of concluding the deliberations in the current legislative period, the standing committee on social policy dropped the government bill from its agenda in February 1961. The government then brought in a new bill which provided for some extensions basically in line with an earlier SPD bill on urgent measures in sickness insurance [269]. Six weeks prior to the election, this bill was passed with the joint votes of the Christian parties and the Social Democrats. Despite the large parliamentary majority of the government, the opposition forces had thus scored a decisive victory. The unions had successfully resisted the introduction of cost-sharing, the medical profession had kept its organizational autonomy and bargaining power intact, and the Social Democrats had succeeded in realizing at least some of their proposals for further extensions.

In the subsequent elections the Christian parties lost their absolute majority and were forced to form a coalition government with the Liberals. The new government announced that it would make another try at a comprehensive reform which would strengthen individual responsibility and check the trend toward ever increasing incidence of sickness. In 1962 it introduced a new bill which contained a supposedly well-balanced package deal. The introduction of cost-sharing was to be linked with the equalization of workers' and employees' entitlements, including a full wage continuation without any waiting period. However, this included the introduction of an income limit for compulsory coverage also for workers, and the granting of wage continuation coupled with more stringent controls on sick reporting by the medical control service of the sickness funds. To compensate the employers for the increasing labour costs, the financial responsibility for the child allowance scheme would be shifted from the employers to the federal government.

Though hostile to the idea of a wage continuation for workers, the employers endorsed the new bill in priniciple. The unions and the Social Democrats resisted the reform plan, because they considered cost-sharing, the income-limit for workers, and the more stringent controls too high a price for the introduction of an equal wage continuation for workers and employees. The government parties were internally divided. While the Liberals pressed for increased cost-sharing and a more limited scheme of wage continuation, the workers' wing of the Christian parties advocated a fully equal wage continuation scheme and a raising of the income-limit for compulsory coverage. As a consensus could not be found, the reform package was finally dissolved. The child allowance reform bill was passed alone in 1964. In the subsequent year, a sickness insurance act was passed which largely conformed with a bill prepared by the Social Democrats. The new law provided for an upgrading of the income-limit for the compulsory coverage of employees, and for higher cash benefits in case of long-term illness. Thus also the second attempt at an embracive reform of sickness insurance had failed. Whereas the first bill had to be buried because of the fierce resistance of extra-parliamentary interest groups, the second one primarily failed because of the disunity among the governing parties in parliament.

These case studies show that social policy developments were highly conflict-prone, notwithstanding the frequent consensual passage of final bills. They also suggest, however, that the politics of welfare state development cannot be understood simply as a function of party ideologies or class interests. Although the parties do have discrepant welfare ideologies and maintain differential links to the major interest groups, the chances of a particular class association of shaping policies vary even under identical governments. The employers' associations were much more successful than the unions in influencing the provisions of the 1957 pension reform, but they lost to the latter in the struggle for sickness insurance reform, although in both cases the Christian Democratic party was in office. This differential success cannot be attributed to the changing balance of class forces [270]. The decisive factor in the sickness insurance debates was that the unions were able to find a powerful ally in the medical profession, and that the government was not able to overcome the joint resistance of these two groups.

This suggests consideration of status groups as a third unit of analysis in social policy studies in addition to parties and classes. Whereas the parties advocate discrepant conceptions of the just social order, and class associations represent antagonistic material interests in distributional conflicts, the status groups typically mobilize their members in defense of their organizational independence and autonomy in conflicts over the distribution of institutional competences. In the corporatized German welfare state [271], status groups of this nature are not only formed on the supply side of services (e.g. sickness fund physicians vs. private doctors), but also on the demand side (e.g. workers' and employees' funds).

The case studies also suggest an image of government as not merely a broker of party ideologies, but partially as an independent actor with autonomous interests that may be at variance with the stance assumed by the parliamentary factions of the governing parties. It seems that, independent of party ideologies, every government seeks to combine the highest possible degree of organizational control over a given welfare state programme with the lowest possible financial obligations [272]. In addition, every government interested in its re-election must mobilize voters beyond its party members or core clienteles. Together with the veto power exerted by major interest groups and the fiscal interests common to all governments, this necessity to win the electoral support of numerically strong blocks of voters helps to explain why basic differences in party ideologies do not necessarily translate into similarly stark differences in actual policy output. The changing composition of the electorate must therefore be considered a fifth independent determinant of welfare state politics.

Electorate and election cycle

As Table 39 shows, the social structure of the German electorate underwent considerable changes in the postwar period [273]. Today no single social category accounts for a clear-cut relative majority of the voters. Instead there are several social blocks with almost equal numerical strength. On the whole, the members of the dependent labour force, whose social security hinges upon public transfers, have maintained a fairly stable leading position in the electorate. Within this broad category, however, white-collar strata have surpassed blue-collar workers as the numerically strongest block of voters. Pensioners living for the most part from welfare state schemes represent an ever-growing proportion of the electorate. On the other hand, self-employed categories, which formed the traditional stronghold of opposition against welfare state expansion, have declined in electoral importance. To a sizeable extent, their decrease is due to the shrinking number of farmers. The twin processes of a vanishing strength of traditional opposition groups and a growing electoral strength of welfare state clienteles enhanced the importance of social policy as a means to win the political loyalty of voters. Given the changing structure of the electorate, no party aiming to win a parliamentary majority can afford to neglect these interests in favour of extended welfare state schemes.

If democratic pressures actually blur differences in party ideology, we should expect that the course of welfare state developments also reflects the election cycle to a vis-

Table 39   The social structure of the electorate

Year	Self-employed	Employees and civil servants	Workers	Pensioners	Other (a)
	Major social categories as % of the electorate				
1949 (b)	21.3	15.5	38.4	.	.
1957	17.4	18.5	37.8	.	.
1961	15.9	20.8	35.0	19.3	9.0
1965	13.8	22.9	33.6	20.3	9.4
1969	12.4	24.4	32.1	22.6	8.5
1972	9.8	25.7	29.4	23.1	12.0
1976	8.3	26.8	26.0	25.7	13.2
1980	7.5	28.3	26.3	25.9	12.0
1983 (c)	7.2	28.5	25.1	26.3	12.9

(a) Calculated difference to 100 percent (mainly housewives, pupils and students above the age of 18); cf note 273.
(b) Data on social categories for 1950 related to electorate in 1949.
(c) Data on social categories in 1982 related to electorate in 1983.

ible degree, i.e. that extensions of welfare state benefits are predominantly legislated in election years, while curtailments cluster in post-election years. Table 40 reports the legislative activity (absolute number of laws) in election years, in post-election years, and in intermediate years. The figures in brackets are activity scores showing how many laws were passed on average in the respective type of year. If we look at the total number of welfare state core laws, we cannot detect any election cycle effects. Throughout the legislative period, an almost identical number of roughly four laws per year is passed. A more differentiated analysis shows, however, that the election date does have an impact. Welfare state extensions clearly cluster in election years, whereas cutbacks are predominantly enacted in post-election years. Only the enactment of organizational regulations is distributed fairly evenly throughout the legislative period [274].

Table 40   The enactment of welfare state core laws in the election cycle (a)

	Election years	Post-election years	Intermediate years	All years
Extensions	27 (3.0)	13 (1.3)	36 (2.3)	76 (2.2)
Curtailments	1 (0.1)	16 (1.6)	18 (1.1)	35 (1.0)
Other	6 (0.7)	5 (0.5)	8 (0.5)	19 (0.6)
Total	34 (3.8)	34 (3.4)	62 (3.9)	130 (3.8)

(a) Number of laws; in brackets: number laws per year ('legislative activity score').

Of course, a simple chronological distinction between years preceding or following an election date may be too schematic. Table 41 therefore presents a more refined analysis which examines the timing of legislation under the various governments and counts all acts passed within twelve months prior to the election date as 'election year laws' [275]. Under the CDU led governments up to 1966, the timing of social legislation closely followed the election cycle. The annual number of laws providing for welfare state extensions sharply increased when the elections drew near, but conspicuously declined afterwards. The output of social laws not providing for extensions shows no similar influence on the election cycle. As economic growth made for an abundant flow of resources, curtailments of welfare state provisions hardly occurred at all. The only three acts classified as curtailments provided for de-regulations of the housing market. Under the Grand Coalition, welfare state extensions were similarly concentrated in the election year 1969, but the period was too brief to allow any generalizations.

Table 41   Election cycle and enactment of welfare state core laws
                                under various governments (a)

	Election years	Post-election years	Intermediate years	Total
Christian Union/Liberal coalition 1950–1966				
Extensions	19 (4.8)	3 (0.6)	12 (1.5)	34 (2.0)
Curtailments	1 (0.3)	0 (0.0)	2 (0.3)	3 (0.2)
Other	1 (0.3)	0 (0.0)	6 (0.8)	7 (0.4)
Total	21 (5.3)	3 (0.6)	20 (2.5)	44 (2.6)
Grand coalition 1967–1969				
Extensions	6 (6.0)	0 (0.0)	2 (1.0)	8 (2.7)
Curtailments	0 (0.0)	0 (0.0)	2 (1.0)	2 (0.7)
Other	2 (2.0)	0 (0.0)	0 (0.0)	2 (0.7)
Total	8 (8.0)	0 (0.0)	4 (2.0)	12 (4.0)
Social-Liberal coalition 1969–1982				
Extensions	6 (2.0)	10 (2.5)	18 (3.0)	34 (2.6)
Curtailments	3 (1.0)	11 (2.8)	3 (0.5)	17 (1.3)
Other	4 (1.3)	4 (1.0)	1 (0.2)	9 (0.7)
Total	13 (4.3)	25 (6.2)	22 (3.7)	60 (4.6)
Christian Union/Liberal coalition 1982–1983				
Extensions	0 (0.0)	0 (0.0)	0 (0.0)	0 (0.0)
Curtailments	8 (8.0)	5 (5.0)	0 (0.0)	13 (6.5)
Other	0 (0.0)	1 (1.0)	0 (0.0)	1 (0.5)
Total	8 (8.0)	6 (6.0)	0 (0.0)	14 (7.0)
Entire post-war period				
Extensions	31 (3.4)	13 (1.3)	32 (2.0)	76 (2.2)
Curtailments	12 (1.3)	16 (1.2)	7 (0.4)	35 (1.0)
Other	7 (0.8)	5 (0.8)	7 (0.4)	19 (0.6)
Total	50 (5.6)	34 (3.4)	46 (2.9)	130 (3.8)

(a) Number of laws; in brackets: number of laws per year ('legislative activity score').

Under the governments headed by the Social Democrats, the annual output of social laws was much more evenly distributed. Only the legislation of curtailments reflects the election cycle, as cutbacks were predominantly enacted in the months immediately following an election. The new bourgeois government formed in 1982 has yet to pass through an entire election cycle. Its legislative activity can therefore not yet be fully assessed. In its first two years, however, which were marked by serious fiscal problems, the new government sharply deviated from previous patterns. While not legislating any welfare state extensions, it did not hesitate to enact a series of curtailments immediately prior to the election.

The general pattern of welfare legislation in the postwar period is thus composed of two distinct sub-patterns under different regimes. Welfare state extensions were visibly applied as a tool to win the electoral support of voters only under the conservative governments. The governments headed by the Social Democratic party legislated extensions much more steadily. Welfare state curtailments, on the other hand, were legislated in correspondence with the election cycle only under the Social Democrats, who are apparently more reluctant to advertise curtailments before their voters than their bourgeois rivals.

Institutional changes affect social expenditures only in combination with many other factors and also become effective only after some time-lag. The impact of the election cycle on aggregate outlays is therefore less visible (see Table 42). The growth rates of social expenditure are distributed fairly evenly throughout the legislative period. Only the intermediate years of an election cycle stand out as having growth rates distinctly below the general average. Of course, we must consider that changes in social outlays are also influenced by the amount of available resources. To control for this factor, the table also shows the annual relationship between the growth rates of social spending and the growth rates of the economy. These data do show a certain impact on the election cycle. While the increases in social expenditure outpaced economic growth most heavily in post-election years, they were brought into closer correspondence with the growth rates of the economy in intermediate years. This concurs with our analysis of the timing of legislative decisions, if we assume that institutional changes affect aggregate outlays with a time-lag of one year.

Table 42   Growth rates of social expenditure in the election cycle
                              under various governments (a)

Governments	Real growth rates (1970 prices)					Annual difference between the growth rates of GDP and social expenditure				
	Election years	Post-elect. years	Inter-mediate years	Pre-elect. years	Average	Election years	Post-elect. years	Inter-mediate years	Pre-elect. years	Average
Christian Union/Liberals (1950-1966)	9.8	8.5	6.3	9.3	8.4	3.3	4.0	-2.8	1.0	1.4
Grand coalition (1967-1969)	(5.8)	-	(5.1)	(3.9)	(4.9)	(-2.2)	-	(5.8)	(-2.0)	(0.5)
Social-Liberal coalition (1970-1982)	3.9	4.3	4.3	4.4	4.4	1.1	1.3	3.1	3.3	2.3
Christian Union/Liberals (1983)	(-0.8)					(-1.9)				
Entire post-war period	6.2	6.4	5.3	6.5	6.3	1.4	2.6	0.8	1.7	1.6

(a) The years before the special elections of 1972 and 1983 were counted twice as intermediate years
    and pre-election years.

At least partly, the aggregate data also confirm the differences between the two major government periods. During the reign of the Social Democrats, social expenditure grew fairly steadily independent of the election cycle. Under the Christian Democratic governments, in contrast, the growth pattern was much more varied. When the Christian parties were in office, social outlays increased over-proportionately in election years, but at a pace far below average in intermediate years.

If we account for variations in the flow of economic resources, the differences become even more marked. Under the CDU governments social expenditure growth far exceeded the growth rates of the economy in election years and post-election years, but was brought into close correspondence with economic growth rates in the remaining years. For the SPD governments, no similar effects of the election cycle can be discerned. This concurs with the results of our institutional analyses and confirms the assumption that differences in party ideology did not translate into similarly strong differences in policy output, because the ideologically more restrictive Christian parties also expanded social programmes in an attempt to win the political support of the voters.

In summary, we may conclude that the postwar expansion of the West German welfare state was to a large extent built on political consensus. Both leading parties contributed roughly similar shares to the extension of welfare state schemes. However, the Social Democrats promoted the expansion more actively and also more steadily than the Christian Democrats. The former are ideologically committed to an institutional model of the welfare state which they perceive as an important supplement to the distributive mechanisms of the market. The latter are ideologically committed to the market economy and champion a more residual model of the welfare state. These differences in policy conceptions are to a certain extent blurred by the impact of interest group pressures and by the democratic pressures of the electorate, growing shares of which live from welfare state schemes. Whereas the Social Democrats apparently pursue expansionist social policies out of a basic commitment, the Christian parties tended to instrumentalize the expansion of schemes primarily as a vote-getting device as long as economic resources were abundantly available. In the most recent period of economic austerity, however, the Christian parties and the Liberals not only propagated but also enacted curtailments of welfare state schemes even immediately prior to an election. Whether this was merely a necessary adaptation to a situation of severe fiscal problems or a programmatic turning point ushering in a phase of welfare state dismantling will be examined in the concluding section.

V   Present problems and policy choices

1.   The fiscal crisis of the welfare state

When the long-standing period of prosperity came to an end in the early 1970s, the welfare state came under heavy fiscal and political strain. Since the oil crisis, economic growth rates have been close to zero in several years, the inflation rate tripled to levels above 5 percent and unemployment has been increasing steadily, in recent years affecting more than two million people. As the budget of the public sector remained in the red without interruption from 1974 to 1983, the resources channelled into the debt service multiplied. The pension insurance schemes recorded deficits from 1975 to 1979 and again in 1982 and 1983. In the sickness insurance scheme and the unemployment compensation system, expenditure surpassed revenues in 1975 and again in 1979 and 1980 [276]. In this situation, fiscal consolidation became a foremost task of federal policy-making. Since Helmut Schmidt became Chancellor in 1974, all federal governments have publicly subscribed to four goals: 1) to reduce the public debt, 2) to shift public expenditure from consumption to investment, 3) to alleviate the burden of taxation in order to stimulate private initiative and investment, and 4) to curb inflation. Under this new policy of austerity, several welfare benefits were to be curtailed.

The series of curtailment acts started with the Budget Structure Law of December 1975 which restricted entitlements to unemployment compensation, curbed the public premiums on savings for housing purposes, and transformed education allowances par-

Table 43   Curtailments of the German welfare state in the period 1975-1983

Pension insurance

1977   Half-year postponement of pension indexation; lowering of the general computation basis for pension
       claims leading to lower benefits; other minor restrictions
1978   Suspension of standard indexation procedure in favour of lower discretionary increases for three years;
       higher contribution rates; other minor restrictions
1981   Curtailment of federal subsidy by 3.5 billion DM; introduction of individual contributions to pensioners'
       sickness insurance; return to regular indexation procedure; contribution rates lowered to 18%
1982   Half-year postponement of pension indexation; lowering of federal subsidy by 0.9 billion DM; reduction
       of pension insurance contributions by the employment office for the unemployed, lowering the financial
       obligations of the federal government vis-à-vis the employment office
1983   New calculation method for the general computation basis (now tied to wage developments in the preceding
       year) leading to lower pension entitlements; replacement of child supplements by lower general child
       allowances; stricter qualifying conditions for invalidity pensions; higher contributions through new
       calculation of creditable earnings; shorter qualification period for pension entitlements (5 instead
       of 15 years)

Sickness insurance and health

1976   (Extented planning capacities for doctors' associations and insurance funds improving the means for cost
       containment)
1977   Introduction of corporatist 'concerted action' for cost containment; higher individual fees for pre-
       scriptions (1 DM); higher private share in cost of dental prostheses; restricted coverage for family
       members through income-limit for dependants; (steps towards financial integration of separate funds)
1979   (Regulations on the administration of the assets of funds in an attempt to promote financial solvency)
1981   Higher individual fees for prescriptions (DM 1.50); higher private cost sharing for dental prostheses;
       stricter qualifying conditions for rehabilitation; reduction of hospitalization period for mothers after
       birth; (law on hospital cost containment to reduce the over-supply of hospitals and beds)
1982   Higher individual fees for prescriptions (DM 2.00); private cost-sharing in hospital care (5 DM per day
       during first two weeks); private cost sharing in rehabilitation (10 DM per day); list of drugs no longer
       covered by insurance
1983   Indirect lowering of sickness insurance cash benefits through deductions for pension and unemployment
       insurance

Unemployment insurance

1975   Stricter definition of suitable employment; restricted entitlements to unemployment assistance; restrict-
       ed access to promotion of vocational training and curtailment of vocational training allowance (80%);
       higher contribution rates (3%)
1977   Stricter controls of beneficiaries; normal duration of unemployment assistance limited to one year with
       subsequent re-examination of claims
1981   Doubling of qualification period to one year; curtailment of benefits through new calculation of credit-
       able earnings; restricted entitlements to unemployment assistance benefits; reduction of vocational
       training allowances (now 68% of net earnings); stricter controls through longer disqualification periods
       in case of abuse; higher contribution rates (4%)
1982   Longer qualification period; curtailment of allowances in case of special rehabilitation training (from
       75 to 70%); higher contribution rates (4.6%)
1983   Reduction of earnings replacement ratio for singles (by 5 percentage points for insurance benefits, and
       2 points for assistance benefits); higher contributions through new calculation of creditable earnings;
       other minor restrictions

Family allowances

1981   Curtailment of allowances for second child by 20 DM or 17%, and for third child by 20 DM or 8%
1982   Curtailment of allowances for high income groups above an income-limit by 30 DM or 30% for the second
       child, and by 80 DM or 36% for the third child
1983   Curtailment of maternity vacation allowance by 32% (from 750 to 510)

Social assistance

1978   (Adjustment of standard benefits below the inflation rate)
1979   (Adjustment of standard benefits below the inflation rate)
1980   (Adjustment of standard benefits below the inflation rate)
1981   Legislated adjustment of standard benefits by 3%, i.e. below the inflation rate; curtailment of supple-
       ments for special groups by one third; entitlements limited through stricter means-test
1982   Legislated adjustment of standard benefits by 2%, falling short of the inflation rate; half-year post-
       ponement of benefit adjustment
1983   Legislated adjustment of standard benefits not exceeding the inflation rate; curtailment of supplements
       for housing; greater administrative discretion in dealing with claims

Table 43 (contd.)

Housing and housing allowances

1975   Reduction of premiums on private savings for housing purposes by 5 percentage points
1981   Restricted entitlements through new calculation procedure of income-limits; reduction of premiums on
       savings by 4 percentage points
1982   Restricted entitlement through less favourable calculation of income-limits; curtailment of allowances
       amounting to an average reduction of around 24%; abolition of housing allowances for students; weakening
       of tenant protection

Education allowances

1975   Transformation of allowances for post-graduates into loans; increase of proportion of loans in student
       allowances
1981   Upgrading of allowances combined with increased proportion of loans and stricter calculation of (now
       upgraded) income-limit
1982   Abolition of allowances for most categories of pupils; transformation of student allowances into loans

tially into loans (see Table 43). It continued in 1977, with a lowering of pension entitlements brought about by the first major change of the pension formula enacted in 1957, with increases in private cost-sharing in the sickness insurance scheme, and with tightened controls of the recipients of unemployment compensation. Pensions were further curbed through a suspension of the regular indexation procedure in 1978, and controls of the unemployed were further tightened in 1979. A second Budget Structure Law and a series of other laws passed in 1981 then introduced cutbacks in every major welfare state scheme. The federal subsidy to pension insurance was reduced, and private cost-sharing in sickness insurance further extended; entitlements to unemployment compensation, housing and education allowances were narrowed, and child allowances and social assistance benefits curbed. Again in 1982 all major schemes were subjected to cutbacks. Pensions were lowered; private cost-sharing in sickness insurance was increased; access to unemployment compensation was limited; child allowances were curbed for families above an income-limit, and social assistance benefits and housing allowances cut; education allowances for pupils were abolished and those for students were entirely transformed into loans. Further restrictions enacted in 1983 once again cut the level of pensions, curbed the level of sickness insurance cash benefits, maternity allowances, and social assistance benefits, and reduced the level of compensation for the unemployed.

In institutional terms, the mid-1970s thus stand out as a watershed in social policy developments. Our data on institutional changes in the Appendix volume identify 130 core laws in the postwar period [277]. 78 core laws were passed up to 1974, 52 in subsequent years. Among the 78 laws of the former period, only 8 percent brought about cutbacks; 81 percent initiated extensions, and 11 percent brought organizational modifications which cannot be classified as curtailments or extensions. In contrast, 56 percent of all core laws passed since 1975 instituted cutbacks, 17 percent brought about organizational changes and merely 27 percent can be classified as extensions. More than four-fifths of all postwar curtailments of the welfare state have thus been legislated in the most recent period of austerity.

The long series of cutbacks left a clear mark on long-term trends in aggregate public and social spending. In 1975 the postwar growth of the public expenditure ratio and the social expenditure ratio came to a halt (see Graph 2 above). It is equally noteworthy, however, that both ratios have since been stagnating rather than declining. A temporary decrease of the GDP share of social spending by close to two percentage points between 1975 and 1979 was almost matched by a renewed increase between 1979 and 1982 [278]. Following the change of government in the latter year, the ratio once more declined by the same margin as in 1976, i.e. 0.6 percentage points. With respect to aggregate expenditure ratios, a rupture in long-term social policy trends thus appears to have occurred under the social-liberal coalition government in 1975, rather than under the bourgeois government formed in 1982.

The fact that the GDP share of social spending remained more or less at its historical peak during the past years indicates that the recent period of curtailments has been a phase of consolidation rather than of dismantling. The data on institutional develop- ments also sustain this conclusion, as benefit extensions were also legislated. These included the adoption of a compulsory sickness insurance scheme for students and for handicapped persons (both in 1975), the extension of education allowances to tenth grade pupils (1978), the creation of a maintenance security system for single parents not in receipt of maintenance payments from the liable parent (1979), and the estab- lishment of a compulsory sickness and pension insurance scheme for independent artists (1982). In an historical perspective, the recent period of austerity thus bears closer resemblance to the consolidation phase from 1959 to 1969 than to the phase of welfare state dismantling in the inter-war period. From 1932 to 1938 social outlays had been radically curtailed so that the social expenditure ratio of the German Reich declined by roughly nine percentage points (see Graph 1 above). In contrast, social outlays continued to grow in the most recent period, but were now brought into closer correspondence with the growth rates of the economy. Only when economic growth came to a standstill did the expansion of social spending also come to a halt.

At constant prices, public expenditure and social expenditure continued to grow throughout the 1970s despite all cutbacks (see Table 44) Whereas in relative terms, the year 1975 appears as a watershed in welfare state development, in absolute terms, the early 1980s mark a turning point. Social spending (at 1976 prices) reached a peak of 422 billion DM in 1981, but subsequently declined to 414 billion DM in 1983. Total public outlays culminated at 610 billion DM in 1982, but decreased by 1.5 bil- lion DM in the following year.

A closer look at the development of single programmes shows that the turning points differed across programmes. In the pension insurance schemes, the curtailment legisla- tion of 1977 appears as the major break with a visible impact on aggregate outlays. Since 1978, pension insurance outlays have remained more or less stagnant in real terms, although the number of beneficiaries kept increasing by almost one million from 1978 to 1983. The postponement of the pension indexation, legislated after the change of government in 1982, then functioned as a second brake. In sickness insur- ance, the 1977 curtailments had much less noticeable effects on aggregate spending. Only the more recent cutbacks of 1981 and 1982 changed the pattern. Child allow- ance expenditure reached its peak in 1979. The sizeable reduction in aggregate out- lays in subsequent years can be only partly related to the cutback legislation of 1981 and 1982 because the number of beneficiaries has declined by 1.4 million since 1979 [279]. Aggregate spending for the unemployment compensation schemes and for social assistance continued to grow up to 1983, because the rising number of benefi- ciaries concealed the effects of the cutbacks. Education expenditure declined markedly from 1975 to 1977 and from 1980 to 1983. Most of this decrease is due to the decline in number of personnel. Cutbacks in education allowances affect aggregate spending only marginally, representing merely 7 percent of total expenditure. Housing allow- ances, which represent around 20 percent of total housing outlays, shrank in 1980 and in 1983. Total housing expenditure, after marked annual variations, reached a peak in 1981.

Table 44 The development of social expenditure during the period of austerity

	1975	1976	1977	1978	1979	1980	1981	1982	1983
					As % of GDP				
Public expenditure	49.6	48.7	48.6	48.2	48.1	48.9	49.7	49.9	49.0
Social expenditure	34.6	34.0	33.5	33.2	32.8	33.1	33.9	33.8	33.2
Aggregates				Expenditure in million DM at constant (1976) prices (a)					
Public expenditure	528 970	545 700	556 150	572 550	591 650	602 290	607 190	610 000	608 500
Social expenditure	370 056	380 985	386 205	399 367	410 389	416 917	421 995	416 796	414 124
Social security	241 669	249 620	256 093	264 237	270 391	272 135	274 612	271 889	270 512
Health	63 005	66 321	66 645	69 007	71 223	73 656	75 807	74 728	75 340
Housing	9 426	9 651	8 581	9 496	10 263	10 438	11 060	10 574	9 952
Education	55 956	54 921	54 886	56 627	58 512	60 688	60 476	59 605	58 320
Selected schemes				Expenditure in million DM at constant (1976) prices (a)					
Pension insurance	106 252	114 900	121 389	122 662	123 681	124 127	123 478	124 475	122 883
Sickness insurance (b)	83 123	87 107	88 298	93 692	98 338	106 678	100 614	93 562	93 136
Unemployment compensation	18 868	16 237	15 038	17 046	18 328	19 692	25 550	29 867	31 585
Child allowances	15 280	14 359	13 594	14 322	15 800	15 180	15 607	13 079	11 751
Social assistance	9 683	10 560	11 079	11 798	12 356	13 042	13 666	14 195	15 041
Housing allowances	1 893	1 759	1 567	1 839	1 861	1 750	2 194	2 295	2 182
Education allowances	2 410	2 005	2 128	2 164	2 307	2 715	2 579	2 407	1 790

(a) Deflators: public consumption deflator for public expenditure, health, education; private consumption
deflator for total housing; cost of living index for pensioners and social assistance recipients for
pension insurance, social assistance, housing allowances; cost of living index for dependent workers
for all other social expenditures; (b) including wage continuation.

In summary, since 1975 the German welfare state has seen a series of curtailments which left a clear mark on the development of aggregate expenditure. Since 1976 social outlays have by and large increased at a speed below the rate of economic growth, and in the early 1980s social spending even declined in real terms. However, the cutbacks merely led to a freezing of aggregate expenditure at a level which had never been reached before the great surge of expansion during the early 1970s. At the level of aggregate data, therefore, the recent period appears as a phase of consolidation rather than of dismantling. The question then is whether the turn in social policy has been so farreaching as to diminish the fiscal crisis of the state (see Table 45).

The tax ratio, i.e. direct and indirect taxes as a percentage of GDP, reached a postwar peak of almost 27 percent in 1977. In subsequent years, it declined by one and a half percentage points, but this moderate reduction did not drive it back below the high levels reached during the phase of welfare state expansion in the early 1970s. Including social security contributions, the burden of taxation even remained distinctly above the levels reached before the curtailment legislation set in. A peak of 43 percent was reached in 1977. In subsequent years, the expansion was brought to a halt, but in 1983 the total burden of taxation was still one percentage point higher than in 1975, when the welfare state had reached its greatest expansion. Despite this high level of taxation, public debt, which had more than doubled between 1969 and 1975, doubled once more from 256 to 546 billion DM between 1975 and 1981. In the years following, the speed of expansion was curbed, but the debt volume continued to increase to

Table 45   Fiscal effects of the austerity policy

	1975	1976	1977	1978	1979	1980	1981	1982	1983
Inflation rate	6.0	4.3	3.7	2.7	4.1	5.5	5.9	5.3	3.0
As % of GDP									
Tax ratio	24.8	25.5	26.5	26.1	25.7	25.7	25.0	24.7	24.9
Ratio of taxes and social security contributions	41.0	42.3	43.2	42.6	42.2	42.4	42.4	42.5	42.3
Debt ratio	25.0	26.5	27.5	28.9	29.7	31.6	35.3	38.4	40.3
In billion DM at current prices									
Volume of debt	256.4	296.7	328.5	370.8	413.9	468.6	545.6	614.8	671.7
Annual new debt	64.0	40.3	31.8	42.3	43.1	54.7	77.0	69.2	56.9
As % of public expenditure									
Interest on debt	2.8	3.2	3.5	3.5	3.6	4.0	4.6	5.5	6.1
Annual deficit	11.5	7.1	5.0	5.2	5.6	6.4	7.7	6.9	5.6

672 billion DM in 1983, the debt ratio rising from 25 percent of GDP in 1975 to 40 percent in 1983. Consequently expenditure for the debt service also continued to rise. As a percentage of total public spending, the interest on debt doubled from roughly 3 percent in 1975 to 6 percent in 1983. In the latter year, the interest on debt thus roughly equalled the defence budget, and devoured larger sums than the unemployment compensation schemes, the housing allowance scheme and the education allowance scheme taken together.

Only the annual increase in debt could be reduced in some years. The annual augmentation of debt had reached a postwar peak of 64 billion DM in 1975. In the two subsequent years, the amount was cut in half, but in 1981 it rose to a new peak of 77 billion DM. The consolidation measures of 1982 and 1983 then helped to reduce the amount of new debt once again to the level of 1980. Expressed in relative terms, the deficits could be reduced more successfully. Whereas in 1975 the deficit spending amounted to 11.5 percent of total public sector spending, it was more than halved in subsequent years. After renewed temporary increases from 1978 to 1981, it settled to 5.6 percent in 1983. Even this degree of deficit spending, however, had never been approximated before the mid-1970s.

In the on-going debates on the nature of the present economic problems, neo-conservative critics of the welfare state interpret the limited success of the government's fiscal policy as proof that the cutbacks in social legislation have not been far-reaching enough. For the defenders of the welfare state, however, the fact that the debt burden continues to grow even though benefits have been curbed proves that the present fiscal crisis is not inherent in the welfare state, but contingent upon a specific constellation in which structural changes of the economy merge with demographic problems. They argue that the fiscal problems of the state are primarily due to the current extent of unemployment which represents a tremendous drain both on public expenditure and revenues, and to the extraordinarily high interest rates which are largely due to developments in the United States [280].

The development of the inflation rate suggests that it would indeed be mistaken to attribute all economic problems simply to the welfare state. In recent years the inflation rate has declined considerably even though the public debt has kept growing. In the first half of the 1970s, it had risen from a mean of 2 percent in the period 1951 to

1969 to a record average of 6 percent. Between 1974 and 1978, it was reduced from 7 to 2.7 percent. In subsequent years, inflation again rose to almost 6 percent in 1981, but was halved once more in 1983 [281].

The defenders of the welfare state further argue that while the relationship between welfare spending and economic performance is far from being clarified, the cutbacks of welfare schemes have given rise to a 'new poverty', demanding painful sacrifices from pensioners, unemployed persons and social assistance recipients [282]. An impression of the social costs of the recent austerity measures may be gained if we leave the level of macro-data and examine how the position of these welfare state clients has changed during the past decade.

Pensioners were affected by two major entitlement curtailments. First, the established pension formula was modified in favour of a new calculation method that lowered the general computation base for all pension claims. This new formula was legislated in 1977, but was one year later suspended in favour of a temporary discretionary procedure which further lowered entitlements during the years 1979 to 1981. In 1982 the new formula was re-instituted, only to be soon replaced by another less favourable formula legislated in 1983. In addition to these changes, the annual adjustment of pensions was twice postponed by half a year in 1977 and 1982.

Table 46 shows the effects which the modification of the pension formula had in the standard case of a claimant of a new pension who had average earnings and a contribution record of 40 years. In 1984 the standard pension was 231 DM or 15 percent lower than it would have been on the basis of the original pension formula. Whereas such a comparison is merely of a hypothetical nature, the table shows that the standard pension which was actually granted declined in real terms. In 1978 it had still grown by 22 DM or 2 percent despite the cutbacks, but since then the purchasing power of the pension slightly decreased up to 1981. In the two subsequent years, it rose again to the level attained in 1979. Recipients of the standard pension thus reached a peak standard of living in the history of the Federal Republic in 1978, but have since suffered a setback of some 3 percent. The average pension of all three pension insurance schemes (at 1976 prices) reached a historical peak of 745 DM in 1977. Up to 1982 it then diminished by 53 DM or almost 8 percent [283].

Table 46   The effects of the cutback legislation on pension levels (a)

	General computation basis prior to / after cutbacks		Monthly standard pension prior to / after cutbacks		size of reduction	Pension levels at 1976 prices standard pension	average pension
1977	20 161	20 161	1 008.10	1 008.10	0.0	974	745
1978	21 841	21 068	1 092.10	1 053.40	38.70	996	725
1979	23 363	21 068	1 168.20	1 053.40	114.80	963	725
1980	24 841	21 911	1 242.10	1 095.60	146.50	955	713
1981	26 291	22 787	1 314.60	1 139.40	175.20	938	696
1982	27 804	24 099	1 390.20	1 205.00	185.20	941	692
1983	29 357	25 445	1 467.90	1 272.30	195.60	963	.
1984	30 861	26 310	1 543.10	1 315.50	227.60	.	.

(a) In DM; data on standard cases refer to new pension claims in the given year.

In the unemployment compensation schemes, the most important cuts consisted of a narrowing of the access to benefits and a reduction of benefit levels. Access to benefits was first limited by the Acts of 1975 and 1977 which tightened the qualifying conditions for the receipt of insurance and assistance benefits. The Acts of 1981 and 1982 then prolonged the qualification period for claims. As Table 47 shows, the minimum contribution period was doubled, while the duration of benefits was reduced. The level of benefits was cut indirectly in 1982 through the introduction of a less favourable method for the calculation of creditable earnings, and directly in 1983 through the reduction of the earnings replacement ratios for singles by 5 percentage points in the insurance scheme, and by 2 points in the assistance scheme.

Table 47   Reduction of entitlements to unemployment benefits (a)

Years						
	Contribution period (no of months)					
	6	9	12	18	24	36
	Duration of benefits (no of months)					
1969–1981	3	5	6	9	12	
1982 (Act of 1981)	–	–	6	9	12	
1983 (Act of 1982)	–	–	4	6	8	12

(a) Changes of the required contribution record for varying duration
    of benefits.

As shown in Section III (see Graph 37), the stricter qualifying conditions, which combined with extensive increases in the average duration of unemployment, led to a drastic decline in the proportion of unemployed people receiving benefits. Similar proportions of unemployed persons barred from compensation had only existed in the depression years from 1930 to 1933. Compared to the situation in the Weimar Republic, where benefit levels were halved between 1930 and 1932, the curtailments in the Federal Republic remained relatively limited, however. The average unemployment insurance benefit has slightly decreased in purchasing power since 1975, but has not fallen below the levels of the early 1970s. Following the most recent cutback legislation, it declined by some 7 percent between 1981 and 1983.

The level of the standard benefit for social assistance recipients is determined by the authorities of the single *Länder* as long as the Federal Government does not decide to intervene. Since 1981 the federal lawmakers issued three acts limiting the annual increases of the standard assistance benefit to 3 percent in 1982, 2 percent in 1983, and to the increase of the cost-of-living index in 1984, and postponing the 1983 augmentation by half a year. This meant that the benefit increases were not sufficient to match inflation.

As shown in Section III (see Graph 35), the purchasing power of the standard assistance benefit has in fact been decreasing since 1977. Between 1977 and 1983 its real value declined by some 6 percent. In comparison, the average net earnings of the dependent labour force kept growing in real terms up to 1979, and have since been subject to a setback in purchasing power of some 4.5 percent. Whereas the dependent workers thus fell back to the standard of living attained around 1977/78, assistance recipients were driven back to the level they had reached around 1972/73.

Graph 55 compares how the standard of living of various social categories developed during the recent years of economic crisis. Relatively speaking, members of the dependent labour force passed through the crisis most favourably, although they too had to accept setbacks in purchasing power in the 1980s. This contrasts with the situation in the first half of the 1970s when social transfer payments had grown faster than earnings from work. In 1983, average gross earnings were 10 percent higher in real terms than in 1975. As a major part of this progress was taxed away, average net earnings were only 4 percent higher in 1983 than in 1975. Among the welfare clienteles, only pensioners were able to keep more or less pace with the dependent labour force. The standard pension roughly followed the course of gross earnings to which it is institutionally linked with a time lag. The average pension developed at a much less favourable speed than gross earnings, but did not fall far behind the development of net earnings. Despite the cutbacks, the purchasing power of the average pension was in 1982 still 2.5 percent higher than in 1975. In contrast, the unemployed and social assistance recipients had to accept cutbacks which pushed their standard of living below the 1975 level. Among the welfare clienteles studied here, pensioners thus appear as a relatively privileged category which had to make distinctly smaller sacrifices in the years of austerity than the other two groups.

Graph 55

Average earnings and transfers

Index (1975=100) of incomes
at constant (1976) prices

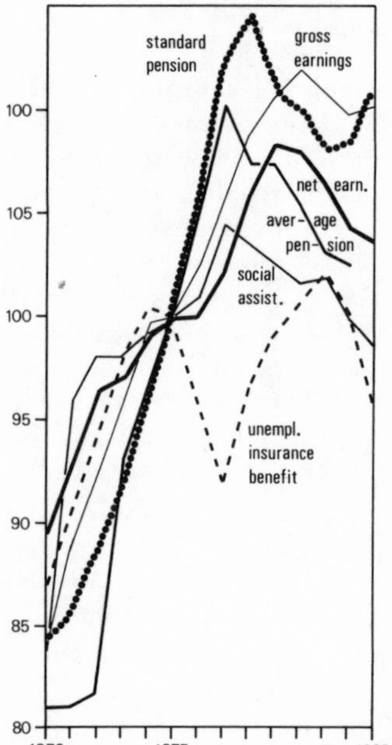

In summary, the trend toward runaway social spending which had set in during the early 1970s has clearly come to an end. Although the recent consolidation measures helped to improve the financial situation of the public sector, they did not resolve the fiscal crisis of the state, which may largely be interpreted as a concomitant of the present mass unemployment. For the recipients of welfare state transfers as well as for dependent workers, the austerity policy led to painfully visible setbacks in the standard of living. Therefore we should examine what consequences the recent policy had for the social integration of German society.

2. The citizens' reactions to the cutback legislation

Our study of the consequences of the recent cutback legislation in terms of social integration will proceed in three steps. Firstly, we will examine if there was a resurgence of class conflict as indicated by the frequency of strikes. Secondly, we will examine how the voters reacted to parties advocating a policy of austerity. Thirdly, we will take a look at the reactions voiced by citizens in public opinion polls.

At the level of the major industrial interest groups, the policy of fiscal restraint has led to an increasing polarization. In 1982 the Association of German Employers (BDA) issued guidelines for the development of the social security system in which they demanded a series of cuts in pension insurance and sickness insurance. A few months later the Association of German Industry (BDI) seconded with a memorandum advocating a policy of stricter fiscal restraints. The unions, on the other hand, accused the government's financial consolidation measures of exacerbating unemployment and pressed for an expansionist course in public finance based on further deficit spending. When the social-liberal coalition government drafted its budget proposal for 1983, the unions accused it of being socially unbalanced and detrimental to the labour market. Newspaper commentaries spoke of a rupture of the alliance between the labour unions and the Social Democratic party. After the change of government in the autumn of 1982, the unions twice staged mass demonstrations against the alleged welfare state dismantling, with some two hundred thousand participants in major German cities.

In contrast to the mobilization in the headquarters of the organizations, the strike front remained remarkably quiet. In fact, the austerity years 1980-1983 stand out as the four-year period with the lowest strike frequency in postwar German history, notwithstanding the unprecedented series of curtailment laws in this phase. On average, only 61,000 working days were lost, as compared to an average of 121,000 days in the second most peaceful four-year period witnessed from 1964 to 1967 [284]. An examination of the long-term strike pattern in the postwar period shows that strikes were more intensive during the two phases of welfare state expansion from 1950 to 1958 and 1970 to 1975 than in the two phases of consolidation from 1959 to 1969 and 1976 to 1983. In the former two periods, the average number of working days lost amounted to 1,086,000 and 740,000 respectively, in the latter two to 205,000 and 454,000. The overall association between social expenditure growth and strike activity in the postwar period is clearly positive ($r = .39$). This does not seem compatible with the assumption that cuts in social transfers necessarily lead to enhanced civil strife in capitalist countries.

An examination of the recent election results also fails to support this view. In 1976, the voters confirmed the social-liberal coalition government in office, although it had enacted visible cutbacks in unemployment compensation, in housing, and in education allowances less than one year prior to the election. After the series of severe curtailments in all major social insurance schemes between 1977 and 1979, the coalition government won an even more convincing victory at the polls in 1980, increasing its combined share of the vote by three percentage points. In 1983, the new bourgeois coalition won the election with the extraordinary margin of 12 percentage points over the opposition parties, although it had enacted severe curtailments three months prior to the election and had announced even harsher cuts for the years to come. The Social Democratic party, which criticized the new policy as an attack on established welfare entitlements, scored its lowest election result since 1965, falling below 40 percent of the votes. Does this mean that the political support for the welfare state is declining and that there is a welfare backlash which some observers consider typical for a modern middle mass society? [285]. To examine this question, we must take a closer look at the results of recent opinion polls.

Contrary to neo-conservative assumptions about a distemper of citizens and a revolution of rising welfare aspirations, the survey data suggest that the new bourgeois government was able to mobilize widespread support for its policy of fiscal restraint. A 1983 survey, held a few months after the change of government and in the midst of an electoral campaign in which the new ruling parties made the fiscal crisis a major issue, showed that the citizens were now much more willing to tolerate curtailments of welfare programmes than in previous years. When they were asked in 1975 and 1978 in which policy fields the government should 'by no means' reduce its outlays, an overwhelming majority of more than 70 percent of the respondents answered: social services (hospitals, homes for the aged, kindergartens, etc.), social transfers, and the fight against crime. Environmental protection and energy supply stood out as two additional fields in which a majority of the respondents refused to accept curtailments (see Table 48). In 1983, the percentage of respondents resisting cuts declined sharply in practically all fields. Only in internal security and environmental policy a majority of the citizens still refused curtailments. The percentage of stern defenders of welfare schemes drastically declined by almost 30 percentage points. Less than one half of the respondents now perceived the existing social services and transfer schemes as sacrosanct.

Table 48   Refusal to accept curtailments in various policy areas

	Percentage of respondents saying that the state should "by no means" reduce its provisions		
	1975	1978	1983
Social services	71	76	48
Social transfers	67	73	44
Education	39	46	38
Internal security	71	71	65
Environmental protection	60	59	62
Energy supply	47	51	45
Public transport	25	34	32
Highway construction	20	26	16
Foreign aid	8	18	18
Defense expenditure	14	18	11

In the present situation of fiscal strain, a reduction in expenditure seems to be more popular than an augmentation of the tax burden. Two surveys carried out by different institutes in 1981 and 1983 showed that a clear majority of the respondents, when

Table 49   The popularity of different measures for fiscal consolidation

	1981	1983	
	IfD Allensbach	Infratest	
	(What to do if the state is in financial difficulties)	(Most acceptable method to ensure the solvency of the social security system)	
Measure	% in favour of respective measure	% ready to accept	% who would rather refuse
Curtail expenditure	67	43	23
Raise taxation	5		
taxes		23	7
social sec. contrib.		14	34
Both	18		
Increase public debt		15	34
No answer or undecided	10	5	2

asked to choose between various strategies of fiscal consolidation, opted for a curtailment of spending rather than for an increase of taxes or social security contributions. Further increases of the public debt seem to be the least popular strategy (see Table 49).

More specific questions about the best ways of safeguarding the financial solvency of single welfare schemes arrived at similar results in 1983. Thus, the majority of the respondents advocated a curtailment of pensions in order to ensure the solvency of the pension scheme, whereas only a minority opted for higher contributions (see Table 50).

Table 50   Best ways to safeguard the financial solvency
of the pension scheme (1983)

| | Percentage of respondents | | |
	for	against	undecided
Higher social security contributions	23	40	33
Slower augmentation of pensions	51	21	28
Taxes on pensions	61	20	19

The citizens seem to be willing to tolerate cuts in social programmes, if they are perceived as necessary to restore the financial solvency of the state. This does not mean, however, that they are also in favour of a welfare state dismantling. In 1984 only a small minority advocated further cuts of the social security system (see Table 51). A large relative majority now opted for a preservation of the status quo, while a sizeable minority even recommended further extensions. A breakdown by occupational categories shows that there is fairly general consensus that further curtailments are not advisable. Even among the self-employed only a small minority calls for further restrictions. Skilled workers, white-collar employees and civil servants appear as a fairly homogeneous block in defence of current welfare provisions. This does not seem compatible with the assumption of a welfare backlash. In the German 'Arbeitnehmergesellschaft' (employees' society), the middle mass is obviously in favour of the modern welfare state.

Table 51   Support for the social transfer system in 1984 (a)

| | Percentage of respondents in favour of | | | No | No |
	curtailment	preservation	extension	opinion	answer
Unskilled workers	2.0	36.9	24.8	35.6	0.7
Skilled workers	8.1	46.8	18.7	26.4	0.0
Employees	11.7	52.4	16.4	18.8	0.7
Civil servants	12.0	54.9	19.0	14.1	0.0
Self-employed	15.6	58.1	10.6	13.8	1.9
Farmers	14.3	42.9	23.8	19.0	0.0
Pensioners	5.2	50.5	16.5	27.5	0.3
Total	7.8	48.5	19.5	23.7	0.5

(a) Question: Should social transfers in the future be curtailed, preserved as they are or extended?

This impression is also confirmed by longitudinal data (see Table 52). Although, due to the different phrasing of the question, the 1977 survey is not fully comparable with those of the subsequent years, the results indicate that there is a growing resistance against further welfare state curtailments throughout all social categories. Even among the most skeptical groups, advocates of cuts are a small and shrinking minority. Skilled workers, white-collar employees, and civil servants once again appear as a homogeneous block professing similarly strong preferences for the preservation of existing provisions as pensioners. Thus, there is absolutely no indication of a growing middle mass reaction against the welfare state.

Table 52   The intensity of welfare state resentment or commitment

Scale	1977		1982		1984	
	— Percent distribution of all respondents by scale value					
1 (Strong resentment)	8.2		2.7		1.9	
2	8.4	28.1	4.8	18.3	3.3	13.2
3	11.5		10.8		8.0	
4	28.3	28.3	18.8	18.8	20.0	20.0
5	14.5		16.5		14.1	
6	13.1	41.2	15.8	51.3	16.4	56.0
7 (Strong commitment)	13.6		19.0		25.5	
No answer	2.4		11.7		10.8	
Mean scale value	4.3		4.9		5.3	

Mean values of occupational groups (b)

	1977		1982		1984	
Workers	4.4	(25)				
unskilled			5.1	(18)	5.4	(10)
skilled			4.9	(18)	5.1	(14)
Employees	4.3	(30)	4.8	(19)	5.1	(15)
Civil servants	4.3	(28)	4.8	(24)	5.0	(16)
Self-employed	3.6	(40)	4.3	(26)	4.5	(26)
Farmers	3.8	(30)	4.8	(20)	4.2	(25)
Pensioners	4.3	(25)	4.9	(16)	5.2	(13)

(a) 7 point-scale; in 1977 the scale extended from 1: "Already too much is done for social security, the cost for the individual is too high" to 7: "There must be done more for social security even if the individual citizen must contribute more to the costs"; in 1982 and 1984 the scale extended from 1: "The state should reduce its social benefits in order to curtail social expenditure" to 7: "It is important that the state continues to deliver the present social services even if this means that no savings in social expenditure are possible";
(b) in brackets: percentage of respondents with welfare resentment (scale values 1-3).

It would also be misleading to interpret the toleration of curtailments which the citizens displayed up to now as an indication of a preference for private provisions. Asked whether it is the responsiblity of the state or the individual to provide for social security, the overwhelming majority of the respondents support a state obligation. Although the results of various surveys show that the opinions are fluid enough to be heavily affected by the phrasing of the questions (which also hampers longitudinal comparisons), there is sufficient consistency to conclude that only a small minority of the German citizens is in favour of enhanced individual responsibilities (see Table 53). Again, workers, employees and civil servants appear as a solid block which unites with pensioners in the quest for state provided security. In summary, the results of recent opinion polls seem to indicate that the policy of legitimate curtailments is approximating its limits and that an attempt at deliberate welfare state dismantling would not get a majority in a society consisting mostly of employees.

Our data on the changing social structure of the electorate (see Table 39) also confirm this view. The two groups harbouring the greatest resentment against the welfare

Table 53   The perceived state responsibility for social security

	1977 (a)	1975 (b)	1978 (b)	1984 (c)
	Percentage of respondents opting for state or individual responsibility			
State	58	77	74	90 (55)
Individual	19	20	24	9 (2)
Undecided	21			
No answer	2	3	2	1
	Percentage opting for state responsibility, by occupational status			
	(Mean scale value)			
Workers	(5.0)			
unskilled		81	78	95 (68)
skilled		87	75	94 (68)
Employees	(4.9)			89 (48)
lower		79	75	
higher		70 (d)	71 (d)	
Civil servants	(5.1)	82 (e)	77 (e)	88 (54)
Self-employed	(4.4)			78 (39)
small		69	68	
large		62	58	
Farmers	(4.4)	87 (f)	67 (f)	95 (f) (40)
Pensioners	(4.7)			91 (57)

(a) 7-point scale extending from 1: "Every citizen must himself take care of his social security"
    to 7: "It is the task of the state to provide social security for all citizens". The percent-
    ages reported here combine the scale values 1-3, and 5-7.
(b) The respondents were asked to choose between two statements arguing for state responsibility
    ("the state guarantees everyone social security, the cost is born by the citizens") or for pri-
    vate responsibility ("everyone can decide for himself whether he wants to get insured or not").
(c) The respondents were asked if they agreed/disagreed fully or mainly with the statement: "The
    state must take care that everyone has a decent living also in case of sickness, need, unem-
    ployment and old age"; percentage of respondents in agreement (in brackets: full agreement).
(d) Including higher civil servants.
(e) Excluding higher civil servants.
(f) The number of farmers in the samples is usually very small.

state - farmers and the self-employed outside agriculture - are declining in electoral importance while those social categories which defend the prevailing welfare state institutions represent an ever-growing proportion of the electorate. This must be considered an important safeguard against a welfare state dismantling.

More recent political developments sustain these assumptions. In 1984 and 1985 no further curtailments were legislated. Two laws of 1984 even enacted some minor corrections mitigating the adverse effects of the cutback legislation. For unemployed persons above age 50, the entitlement to unemployment insurance benefits was extended from 12 to 18 months; for the younger age cohorts among the unemployed, the age limit for the receipt of child allowances was raised to 21 years. This was not sufficient, however, to match the failure of an important element of the policy of austerity. In November 1984 the Supreme Court declared the extraordinary tax levied on the higher income brackets as unconstitutional, and ruled that it be reimbursed to the tax payers. When the new bourgeois government was formed in 1982, it had agreed upon this tax in an attempt to demonstrate the 'social symmetry' of its austerity policy. The government's policy could now be convincingly attacked as a 'class struggle from above', violating the principles of social equity.

In two regional elections of the Spring of 1985 the Christian Democratic Union suffered severe defeats. In his mid-term address to Parliament, Chancellor Kohl hastened to declare that the government's successful budgetary consolidation also opened up leeway for improvements in the social transfer schemes. Soon after a law was passed which upgraded housing allowances. A social assistance benefit increase was drafted, and the introduction of a new type of family allowances for parents of new born babies was announced. The budget draft of the Federal Government for 1986 foresaw overproportionate increases in social expenditure [286]. It seems that after one decade, the policy of welfare state curtailments has come to an end.

3. Future problems and choices

So far the government's austerity policy can be characterized as crisis management in the sense of a muddling-through, resulting from short-term fiscal considerations rather than long-term reform perspectives. As increases and decreases in contribution rates and federal subsidies were shifted back and forth between various social insurance schemes, critical observers characterized the recent social legislation as a 'switch yard' without conception [287]. However, the patchwork of governmental interventions was accompanied by a revival of fundamental debates over social policy in intellectual circles and in the media.

As a model of social order, the welfare state has always been contested in Germany. Even prior to the 1957 pension reform, influential Christian Democratic politicians such as Ludwig Erhard or Eugen Gerstenmaier had warned in party convention speeches that 'the utmost limits of social legislation' had now been reached [288]. The critics usually attack the welfare state on two fronts. On economic grounds they argue that extended welfare state benefits encourage idleness and weaken the competitiveness of German industry in international markets. On political grounds they argue that extended state responsibilities lead to bureaucratic control and weaken associational self-help, favouring the rise of a new authoritarianism. As a reaction to the embracive reform designs of the social-liberal coalition government in the early 1970s, especially criticisms of the latter kind became prominent in intellectual circles [289]. When the welfare state later met with increasing financial problems, these concerns of a political liberalism combined with the argument of economic liberalism claiming that the excessive burdens on the economy would lead to the country's decline. As it is almost certain that future challenges will put the welfare state under heavy strain, it is to be expected that such fundamental criticisms will continue to be raised.

Especially the two big spending welfare programmes - pension insurance and sickness insurance - are likely to run into severe financial problems in the years to come. In a pension scheme based on a pay-as-you-go system of financing, pension levels and contribution rates can only be kept constant if the quantitative relationship between pensioners and contributors does not change. However, the number of pension recipients is bound to increase by several million once the large age cohorts born during the baby booms of the mid-1930s and the early 1960s enter into pensionable age. This will happen in the mid-1990s and in the 2020s. At the same time the steep decrease in marriage and birth rates since the early 1970s will lead to a sizeable shrinkage in the number of contributors.

The politicians have been aware of this problem for several years now. In 1979 the Ministry of Labour set up an expert committee for the study of long-term problems in the pension scheme. The committee issued its three-volume-report in 1981 [290]. According to its projections, the ratio of elderly persons above age 60 to the population of working age (20-60) will begin to increase in the 1990s from its present 35 percent to 41 percent in 2000, 50 percent in 2020 to a peak of 68 percent in 2035 (see Graph 56). A preservation of the present level of benefits would therefore require a raise in contribution rates from 18 percent in 1980 to above 20 percent after the turn of the century up to a peak of almost 35 percent in 2035. If, on the other hand, the present level of contributions were to be preserved, the level of the standard pension would have to fall from its present 45 percent of gross wages to below 40 percent after the year 2000, below 30 percent after 2020, and even to below 25 percent in the 2030s.

Graph 56

Projections of pension insurance development

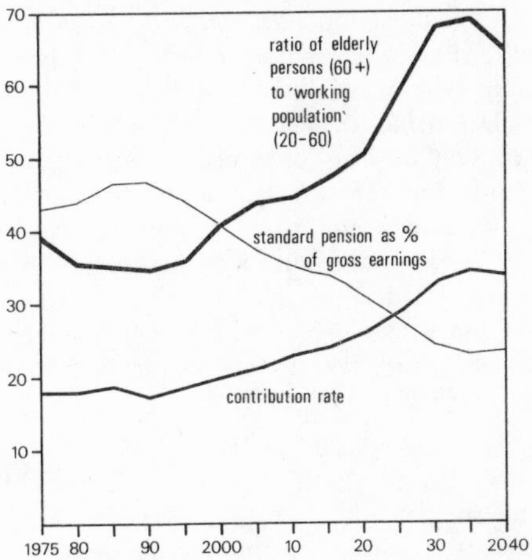

As neither of these two extreme scenarios seem politically acceptable, several reform plans are being drafted. The most radical proposals advocate the replacement of the present earnings-related pension scheme by a national insurance system with flat-rate benefits. It is noteworthy that these proposals come from prominent members of the Liberal and the Christian Democratic parties rather than from sections of the Labour movement. In 1985, Martin Bangemann, the leader of the Liberal party and present Minister of Economic Affairs, expressed his preference for a national pension scheme in several public speeches, while a research institute established by Kurt Biedenkopf, one of the key figures in the Christian Democratic party, came up with an elaborate reform plan showing how the shift from the present system to a universal flat-rate scheme could technically be implemented. The trade unions as well as the Social Democrats immediately declared their opposition to such plans, confirming their commitment to the preservation of the traditional system. Their plans to safeguard the financial solvency of the pension scheme centre on the introduction of a new system of financing which would replace the employer-paid payroll contributions with a new type of contribution linked to the firms' returns. They also advocate incorporation of civil servants into the social security schemes [291].

The expert commission followed neither of these plans but drafted some more pragmatic proposals aiming at a distribution of the burdens with respect to both expenditure and revenues. On the revenue side, this implies a linkage of the federal subsidy to pension expenditures rather than to the general computation basis, and an increase of the subsidy from its present level of roughly 18 percent of total outlays to 20-30 percent. On the expenditure side, it suggests a modification of the indexation procedure which would link pension adjustments to changes in gross earnings diminished by the pension contribution, or by levying a tax on pensions amounting to half of the contribution rate. Increases of the pensionable age could further contribute to a financial consolidation. Thus, an increase of 2 years would lower the necessary contribution rates by six percentage points [292]. Since the Social Democrats as well as the core of the Christian Democrats, including the Minister of Labour, are committed to the principles of the present pension scheme, gradual reforms along these pragmatic lines appear much more likely than a basic system change.

The financial situation of the sickness insurance scheme has also given rise to concerns. The attempts to contain the cost explosion in the health sector through the establishment of the Concerted Action (*Konzertierte Aktion*) in 1977, which brought together the government, the trade unions, sickness funds and various suppliers of medical services, has only been partially successful. Although the sickness incidence among the insured population has decreased (see Graph 40), the benefit expenditure of the sickness insurance scheme has continued to rise slightly faster than the economic product. Consequently the contribution rates for sickness insurance were higher in 1983 than in 1977. Especially the cost of hospital care and of dental services increased sharply. In 1970 hospitals had only claimed one fourth of total benefit expenditure of the sickness funds, but in 1983 their share amounted to one third. Dental care increased its share from 10 to 15 percent between 1970 and 1980. In the 1980s, the proportion spent on dental care somewhat declined, while the share flowing to hospitals continued to increase [293].

Long-term changes on the demand side as well as on the supply side make it likely that the costs of sickness insurance in general and of hospital care in particular will continue to rise. On the supply side, improvements in technology and facilities fuel the cost of medical services, whereas the increasing density of physicians intensifies the competition among doctors, inciting them to search for patients and to raise the number of services per treatment. On the demand side, the growing number of elderly people increases the financial burden, because elderly persons fall ill more frequently and for longer durations [294]. Increases in life expectancy will also contribute to a growing number of very old persons requiring long-term institutional health care. Between 1950 and 1982 the proportion of persons above age 70 doubled to 11 percent. In the latter year there were 6.6 million people in the Federal Republic aged 70 years or more [295]. As their number is expected to increase sharply after the turn of the century, special provisions for long-term care may become necessary.

Two alternative strategies in prevention of a renewed cost explosion in sickness insurance are being discussed. The first one, more prominent among the political left, is primarily an attempt to control the supply side. In this perspective, sickness fund physicians and other supplier groups are in an overprivileged position, because the doctors' associations hold a state-guaranteed monopoly over the supply of ambulant services, and are not confronted with an independent demand. As the fees are determined in collective bargaining so that the patients cannot exert an effective price control, a permanent oversupply is stimulated. Reform proposals departing from this analysis recommend bureaucratic controls limiting the autonomy of the suppliers, such as checklists evaluating the effectiveness of drugs, and a competition in supply by allowing sickness funds or hospitals to offer ambulant services. The second strategy, more prominent in liberal and conservative circles, is primarily an attempt to control the demand side. In this perspective, the cost explosion is primarily due to the free-rider effects of the social insurance system. Since an abstention from the utilization of medical services does not yield any individual advantage, the prevailing system stimulates a permanent over-demand. Therefore a private cost sharing is recommended.

Given the organizational strength of the interest groups on the supply side, the first strategy for reform would probably be much harder to realize than the second. The failure of the intended sickness insurance reform in the 1950s and 1960s shows, however, that even the second approach will be difficult to realize. The most likely scenario, therefore, is that the sickness insurance scheme will only be gradually restructured by piecemeal reforms. The problem of long-term health care and nursing services for disabled elderly will presumably require special solutions, however. In recent years, conceptual debates over the appropriate reform strategy have intensified. The Social Democrats favour the adoption of a new social insurance scheme for long-term care (*Pflegeversicherung*), whereas the Christian Democrats argue that the social insurance solution would stimulate excessive demand and thus create further financial problems. They advocate an expansion of ambulant communal services and a strengthening of the capacity of private households to care for elderly persons through tax incentives and extended counselling services. The latter proposal is linked to a more general debate about the proper margins of self-help and state help.

4. From welfare state to welfare society?

There seems to be a widespread impression that the prevailing welfare state institutions are sub-optimal in size and structure and that the welfare functions of the state should be better combined with the neglected welfare production in private households, associations, and markets [296]. It is argued that the centralized bureaucracies are too distant from the concerns of the citizens. This implies that social administration becomes limited to compensation functions without being able to exert control over conditions giving rise to claims, be it detrimental living conditions and life styles or benefit abuse. It also implies that the citizens are confined to the role of passive clients without effective chances to participate in the delivery of services. The rigid differentiation of welfare schemes according to specific contingencies or causes of need lacks flexibility. As complex and particular personal needs are compartmentalized and transformed into judicial cases, the communication between clients and administrators is hampered and feelings of alienation rather than security are fostered. In the social security schemes, the differentiation also leads to highly unequal levels of compensation for similar needs. Therefore a decentralization and de-differentiation of welfare institutions is recommended which would move the provisions closer to the citizens. According to the critics, however, a mere restructuring of welfare state schemes is not enough. They also advocate a mobilization of two presumably under-utilized potentials for welfare production, namely associational networks and private households. In recent years reform proposals of this kind have become prominent especially among sociologists [297]. The common denominator of the various reform concepts seems to be that it is necessary to move from the welfare state to the welfare society providing for a new and better mix of state help and self-help in households and associational networks.

These ideas have in the meantime diffused into the political sphere where they find proponents in all major parties. Yet the emphasis given to various strategies of reform differs. Somewhat oversimplifying, one might say that the Social Democratic formula for the future is 'extended state help plus associational solidarity', whereas the Christian Democratic strategy centres on 'necessary state help plus primary group solidarity'. The emphasis of the Social Democrats is clearly on state help. Basically, they advocate a widening of the functions of self-administrative bodies in social insurance and a decentralization of the delivery of services by establishing integrated or at least co-ordinated units of social administration on the local level. Both measures are designed to reduce the social distance between welfare bureaucracies and clients and to improve the preventive capacities of social policy [298]. A minority faction of the party led by Johano Strasser advocates more unconventional approaches centering on the mobilization of associational networks. The key to this strategy is more participation in the spheres of production, bureaucratic planning and provision of services [299]. In addition, support for the self-help activities in community groups and alternative movements through public subsidies and counselling is propagated.

Among the Christian Democrats, the workers' wing also seems to rely on the established welfare state institutions as the principal source of social security. However, a strong minority based on the liberal market economy wing, also advocates a more selective targeting of welfare state schemes to groups in need and a limitation of state responsibilities in favour of a stronger reliance on the self-help potential of families and private households. This group, most strongly represented by Kurt Biedenkopf and the director of his research institute, Meinhard Miegel, argues that the steep increase in the income and property of private households in the postwar period make the extended scope of public welfare programmes obsolete as it allows a majority of the citizens to provide for their own social security [300]. The social transfer schemes should therefore concentrate on the provision of effective minima. In the sphere of social services, the state should primarily seek to activate the self-help potential of families through tax incentives rewarding the care of disabled family members and through extended ambulant services in local social facilities.

The idea that there are under-utilized potentials for welfare production which might relieve the welfare state is already beginning to become concrete policy [301]. The federal government is currently supporting research activities investigating the self-help potential of families and associational networks. The results of various surveys indicate that the modern family, far from being reduced to a mere consumption unit, is an active producer of various household services, and that there is an extended network of mutual assistance in kinship groups and neighborhood circles [302]. However, the significance of these findings must not be exaggerated [303]. Even if it may be true that there are developmental trends in post-industrial societies which strengthen the associational self-help potential, there are other long-term trends which counteract these tendencies. The proportion of single elderly persons, especially widows, and of incomplete families is constantly increasing. As birth rates are declining, a growing proportion of marriages remain childless or with only one child [304]. This means that a growing number of elderly persons is confronted with a declining number of younger family members able to provide assistance. However, there are not merely statistical limits to the revitalization of self-help activities. Widened responsibilities of the extended family and of neighborhood communities would also mean an extension of social controls which would perhaps clash with individual liberties more sharply and more visibly than bureaucratic public services. Therefore, not too much should be expected of a revival of private and associational assistance. It may perhaps complement welfare state provisions, but it cannot effectively substitute them. In historical perspective, the institutional inertia displayed by German welfare state programmes is striking. It seems safe to conclude, therefore, that the welfare state has become a constituent element of German social structure which is most likely here to stay.

Notes

1   Detlev Zöllner, *Ein Jahrhundert Sozialversicherung in Deutschland.* Berlin, 1981, p. 16.

2   This legislation formally prohibited the revolutionary activities of existing working class organizations, but left the party free to participate in elections.

3   See the data by Reinhart Schneider in Peter Flora, *State, Economy and Society in Western Europe 1815-1975,* Vol. I. Frankfurt, London, Chicago, 1983.

4   For a systematic summary of the most important legislative developments see Zöllner, *op. cit.*

5   Zöllner, *op. cit.*, p. 103, and Gaston V. Rimlinger, *Welfare Policy and Industrialization in Europe, America, and Russia.* New York, London, Sydney, Toronto, 1971, p. 129.

6   See Hartmut Kaelble, *Soziale Mobilität und Chancengleichheit im 19. und 20. Jahrhundert Deutschland im internationalen Vergleich.* Göttingen, 1983; see also Arnold J. Heidenheimer, 'Education and social security entitlements in Europe and America', *In* Peter Flora and Arnold Heidenheimer (eds), *The Development of Welfare States in Europe and America.* New Brunswick and London, 1981, pp. 269-304.

7   Ludwig Preller, *Sozialpolitik in der Weimarer Republik* Düsseldorf, 1978; see also Albin Gladen, *Geschichte der Sozialpolitik in Deutschland.* Wiesbaden, 1974.

8   The proportion of 10 year olds entering the first class of the Gymnasium was 18 percent in 1928 as compared with 9 percent in 1910; see Karl Dietrich Erdmann, *Die Weimarer Republik*, Gebhardt Handbuch der deutschen Geschichte, Vol. 19. Munich, 1983, p. 226.

9   As another 38 percent received local government relief payments, one million persons or a quarter of the unemployed population, remained without any form of support from public funds. Calculated from the *Deutscher Bundestag 2. Wahlperiode*, Drucksache 1274.

10   The social expenditure data are from Suphan Andic and Jindrich Veverka, 'The growth of government expenditure in Germany since unification', *Finanzarchiv N.F.* 23, 1963/64, pp. 169-287; the social insurance data are from Detlev Zöllner, *Öffentliche Sozialleistungen und wirtschaftliche Entwicklung.* Berlin, 1963, p. 18. Both types of data are at nominal prices.

11   See Timothy W. Mason, *Sozialpolitik im Dritten Reich* Opladen, 1977. For more specialized accounts of social insurance see Gladen, *op. cit.*, especially pp. 108-113, and Volker Hentschel, *Geschichte der deutschen Sozialpolitik 1880-1980.* Frankfurt, 1983, especially p. 144.

12   The option of voluntary insurance was abolished by the 1957 pension reform, but re-introduced in 1972.

13   See Heinz Lampert, 'Staatliche Sozialpolitik im Dritten Reich', *In* Karl Dietrich Bracher, Manfred Funke, Hans-Adolf Jacobsen (eds.), *Nationalsozialistische Diktatur 1933-1945. Eine Bilanz.* Düsseldorf, 1983, pp. 177-205.

14   See Heinz Lampert, *Sozialpolitik.* Berlin, Heidelberg, New York, 1980, p. 146.

15   Kaelble, *op. cit.*, p. 141.

16   See the data by Schneider in Flora, *op. cit.*, p. 589.

17   See Reinhart Schneider, 'Die Bildungsentwicklung in den westeuropäischen Staaten 1870-1975', *Zeitschrift für Soziologie*, 11.3.1982, pp. 207-226.

18   Karl Dietrich Erdmann, *Deutschland unter der Herrschaft des Nationalsozialismus*, Gebhardt Handbuch der deutschen Geschichte, Vol. 20. Munich, 1982, p. 168.

19   See Stephan Liebfried and Florian Tennstedt, *Berufsverbote und Sozialpolitik 1933.* Bremen, 1981.

20   Deviating from the traditional practice and following the new concept of 'social partnership' between capital and labour, workers were now also represented on the boards of occupational injuries insurance, but lost their two-thirds majority representation in sickness insurance.

21   Employees' pensions had been administered jointly with the workers' scheme since 1945.

22 On the political motives behind the social policy reforms see Hans Günter Hockerts, *Sozial-politische Entscheidungen im Nachkriegsdeutschland.* Stuttgart, 1980.

23 A Federal Ministry of Science had already been established in 1962.

24 The figures for 1938 are from Jürgen Kohl, in Flora, *op. cit.*, p. 385, and from Horst Claus Recktenwald, 'Umfang und Struktur der öffentlichen Ausgaben in säkularer Entwicklung', *In* Fritz Neumark et al. (eds.), Handbuch der *Finanzwissenschaft,* Vol. I. Tübingen, 1976, pp. 713-752 (here p. 719).

25 The break in statistical definitions in 1974/75 does not allow for comparisons over the entire time-span. However, the trend for the central government share for the years 1950-74 is negative (b = -0.74), and the share does not increase in the subsequent years with a consistent statistical definition.

26 Post-1974 data only report figures including social insurance schemes.

27 Capital transfers consist of undistributed profits of public undertakings with an independent legal status, of certain payments under the equalization of war burdens' fund, of subsidies for private investment, and of various specific premiums for private sector activities. They are included in the figures on transfers and subsidies in Appendix Table 2, as they have only been reported independently since 1960.

28 See for example Christian von Ferber, *Sozialpolitik in der Wohlstandsgesellschaft.* Hamburg, 1967; and Michael T. Greven, 'Soziale Probleme und politische Antworten - Sozialpolitische Konzeptionen und Konflikte der siebziger Jahre', *In* Michael T. Greven, Rainer Prätorius, Theo Schiller, *Sozialstaat und Sozialpolitik. Krise und Perspektiven.* Neuwied, 1980, pp. 91-196.

29 Health expenditure is here defined as the sum of benefits in kind and services in sickness insurance, of public health spending and of reimbursements of medical fees for civil servants.

30 The increase in 1960 is due to a change in statistical definitions.

31 The figures refer to three schemes: war victims' benefits, equalization of burdens, and political reparation payments.

32 The graph refers to cash benefits only.

33 Since official statistics only provide detailed breakdowns for selected years, Graph 9 gives the share of old age and invaldity pensions together. The share of invalidity pensions has remained practically constant throughout the 1970s (see Appendix Table 7). As shown in Section IV, the proportion of invalidity pensioners in the annual number of new beneficiaries has nevertheless conspicuously increased. This is not reflected, however, in increasing expenditure figures,as invalidity pensioners are shifted to the category of old age pensioners once they reach pensionable age.

34 Cf. Der Bundesminister für Arbeit und Sozialordnung, *Sozialbericht 1972.* Bonn, 1972, p. 6.

35 The steep rise of total income maintenance outlays following the 1969 reform has led to public debate on absenteeism and benefit abuse. Analyses of the impact of the new legislation are impeded by the fact that wage continuation expenditure data are only (official) estimates, and also because there are no consistent statistics on sickness rates due to a change in statistical procedures in 1970.

36 The number of doctors per 10,000 inhabitants increased from 13.6 to 14.5 between 1952 and 1965, but shot up to 22.1 in 1979. See Eike Ballerstedt and Wolfgang Glatzer, *Soziologischer Almanach.* Frankfurt, 1979, p. 151; Presse- und Informationsamt der Bundesregierung, *Gesellschaftliche Daten 1982.* Bonn, 1982, p. 41.

37 This reform legislation was so extensive that by 1976 all protective labour legislation passed prior to 1968 had been either abolished or replaced (cf. Helmut Schüssler, 'Bedeutung und Stellenwert des Arbeitsschutzes im sozialpolitischen Kräftespiel der Bundesrepublik nach 1945', *In* Reinhart Bartholomäi et al. (eds.), *Sozialpolitik nach 1945.* Bonn, 1977, pp. 315-323).

38 Pupils' and students' accidents represent a rising share in the total number of accidents (cf. *Sozialbericht 1980,* pp. 103-104). This makes the decline in the total number of accidents mentioned above even more remarkable.

39 Expressed as percentages of the dependent labour force.

40 Pre-1960 expenditure data are not available.

41 The two organizations are: Reichsbund der Kriegs- und Zivilgeschädigten, Sozialrentner und Hinterbliebenen, and Verband der Kriegsbeschädigten, Kriegshinterbliebenen und Sozialrentner Deutschlands (VdK). For an account of their activities and membership see Karl Weishäupl, 'Die Bedeutung des VdK für die Nachkriegsgeschichte der deutschen Sozialpolitik', In Reinhart Bartholomäi et al. (eds.), *Sozialpolitik nach 1945*. Bonn, 1977, pp. 489-498, and Rudolf Kleine, 'Die Geschichte des Reichsbundes in ihrer Bedeutung für die Nachkriegsentwicklung der Sozialpolitik', in *ibid.*, pp. 497-511.

42 The figures are from Gerhard W. Brück, *Allgemeine Sozialpolitik*. Cologne, 1976, p. 266, and from Der Bundesminister für Arbeit und Sozialordnung, *Sozialbericht 1983*. Bonn, 1984, p. 102.

43 Since this tax had to be paid in quarterly instalments over a period of 30 years, it actually amounted to annual payments of 1.66 percent of the property held in 1948.

44 See Lisa Korspeter and Walter Haack, 'Politik für Vertriebene, Flüchtlinge, Kriegsgeschädigte, Heimkehrer, politische Häftlinge und Aussiedler', In Bartholomäi et al. (eds.), *op. cit.*, pp. 275-293.

45 *Die Zeit* No. 41, 1984, p. 36. This article is the best short summary of the workings of the scheme and its development.

46 This fact explains the break in the statistical series in Graphs 19 and 20.

47 The total outlays made under the scheme and several accompanying restitution acts (*Bundesrückerstattungsgesetze*) amount to an estimated aggregate of 70 billion DM; see *Die Zeit*, op. cit.

48 Taken altogether about one million persons have made claims under the scheme; cf *Die Zeit*, op. cit.

49 The data on subsidies also include the financial participation of public authorities in public interest construction corporations.

50 See Uwe Wullkopf, 'Wohnungsbau und Wohnungsbaupolitik in der Bundesrepublik Deutschland', *Aus Politik und Zeitgeschichte* Vol. B 10, 1982, pp. 11-25.

51 For details, see Michael Hecht, *Subventionsformen in der Wohnungswirtschaft*. Munich, 1978, especially p. 112.

52 This refers to the so-called second branch of the social housing programme (2. Förderungsweg). See Kurt H. Biedenkopf and Meinhard Miegel, *Wohnungsbau am Wendepunkt* Bonn, 1978, p. 32, and Wullkopf, *op. cit.*, p. 15.

53 In this context attention must be drawn to the important role played by public interest building corporations. About a fourth of all dwellings built after the war were constructed by such corporations which are frequently controlled by public authorities. Public bodies (mostly local authorities, but also state governments, the postal service and railways, and social insurance funds) hold roughly two-thirds of the majority shares in these corporations. See Werner Nowak, *Das gemeinnützige Unternehmen als Instrument der Wohnungspolitik*. Berlin, 1973, especially p. 18. For more concise summaries see Brück, *op. cit.*, p. 330, Hecht, op. cit., p. 52 and Lampert, *op. cit.*, 1980, p. 346, and pp. 355-356.

54 Unfortunately detailed data in a standard form are only available from 1965.

55 For a concise summary of postwar developments in educational policies see Rolf Arnold and Fritz Marz, *Einführung in die Bildungspolitik*. Stuttgart, Berlin, Cologne, Mainz, 1979.

56 For a documentation and discussion of this first expansion see Jens Naumann, 'Entwicklungstendenzen des Bildungswesens der Bundesrepublik Deutschland im Rahmen wirtschaftlicher und demographischer Veränderungen', In Max-Planck-Institut für Bildungsforschung, Projektgruppe Bildungsbericht (ed.), *Bildung in der Bundesrepublik Deutschland. Daten und Analysen* Vol. I, Reinbek, 1980, pp. 21-102 (here p. 71).

57 See especially Georg Picht, *Die deutsche Bildungskatastrophe*. Munich, 1965 (first edition 1964).

58   This aspect was stressed by sociological contributions; see for example Ralf Dahrendorf, *Bildung ist Bürgerrecht* Hamburg, 1965; and Ralf Dahrendorf, *Arbeiterkinder an deutschen Universitäten.* Tübingen, 1965.

59   Thus, Picht, *op. cit.*, p. 21 explicitly refers to 'school policy as today's social policy'.

60   In the context of the recession the limited scheme of education allowances for pupils, which had been introduced as an 'election gift' in 1965, was abolished by the budgetary consolidation legislation of 1967.

61   The first comprehensive school was established in Berlin in 1968; see Arnold and Marz, *op. cit.*, p. 26.

62   For data see Naumann, *op. cit.*, p. 79.

63   This definition of public revenues corresponds to the definition of public expenditure given in Appendix Table 2 (public expenditure by economic function). Broadly defined, total public revenues include special financial transactions and are identical with total expenditure as given in Appendix Table 1.

64   The official publication *Bundesrepublik Deutschland-DDR Systemvergleich 3* (Materialien zum Bericht zur Lage der Nation), Bundestagsdrucksache 7/2423 mentions 16,000 independent public budgets. Another source (Alfred Stobbe, *Volkswirtschaftslehre I.* Volkswirtschaftliches *Rechnungswesen.* Berlin, Heidelberg, New York, 1976, p. 56) speaks of 11,200 government budgets and 1,800 social insurance budgets in 1975. A third source (Richard A. Musgrave, Peggy B. Musgrave, Lore Kullmer, *Die öffentlichen Finanzen in Theorie und Praxis*, Vol. 4. Tübingen, 1975, p. 167) reports that the regional reform reduced the original number of 22,500 local authorities to 8,550, plus some independent cities and counties.

65   See Bundesministerium der Finanzen, *Finanzbericht 1961* Bonn, 1961, especially pp. 65-98.

66   Earnings of industrial employers have the same registration ratio as workers' income. The data are from Christof Helberger, 'Strategien der Verteilungspolitik ohne Gefährdung des Wachstums?', *In* Hans-Jürgen Krupp, Wolfgang Glatzer (eds.), *Umverteilung im Sozialstaat* Frankfurt, 1978, pp. 315-349.

67   This information relates to the situation in 1972; see Horst Claus Recktenwald, 'Gerechte Einkommens- und Vermögensverteilung', *In* Richard Löwenthal and Hans-Peter Schwarz (eds.), *Die zweite Republik. 25 Jahre Bundesrepublik Deutschland. Eine Bilanz.* Stuttgart, 1979, pp. 762-790 (here p. 771).

68   Different sources give widely discrepant information on the share of direct and indirect taxes because they follow different classification procedures. The figures reported in Graph 29 are based on national accounts statistics. The data in Appendix Table 15 rely on the classification used in financial statistics. Both types of data demonstrate a trend towards an increasing importance of direct taxes, but they deviate from each other by more than 10 percentage points in single years.

69   In 1983, 1,598 DM; calculated from Der Bundesminister für Arbeit und Sozialordnung, *Materialband zum Sozialbudget 1983.* Bonn, 1984, pp. 239-240.

70   See Der Bundesminister für Arbeit und Sozialordnung, *Übersicht über die soziale Sicherung.* Bonn, 1977,p. 111.

71   Workers are subject to compulsory coverage regardless of income.

72   On the politics of the income limit see Viola Gräfin von Bethusy-Huc, *Das Sozialleistungssystem der Bundesrepublik Deutschland.* Tübingen, 1965, especially pp. 121-130; see also Hockerts, *op. cit.*, especially pp. 373-377.

73   See Press- und Informationsamt der Bundesregierung (ed.), *Gesellschaftliche Daten 1982.* Bonn, 1982, p. 51. Including voluntary members only 4.6 percent of male, and 2.5 percent of female employees remain outside the general sickness insurance scheme.

74   German statistics on the coverage of social insurance schemes are generally poor. The figures for the accident insurance scheme are only estimates relating to man-years, i.e. a statistical concept translating the total number of insured persons into full-time workers in order to eliminate the effects of irregular or part-time employment (excluding pupils and stu-

dents). Exact statistics on the scope of pension insurance are only available since the institutionalization of the microcensus. Sickness insurance figures refer to annual averages of compulsory members (excluding pensioners). The unemployment insurance data refer to compulsory contributors at a fixed day in October. Generally the number of contributing members fluctuates with the business cycle.

75 The extension of prisoners foreseen in a law of 1976 has not yet been implemented.

76 See *Gesellschaftliche Daten 1982*, p. 51.

77 These ratios actually overestimate the proportion of pensioners because the official statistics refer to the number of pensions paid, and one person may draw several pensions.

78 Special groups such as women, the seriously handicapped or unemployed may retire at the age of 60.

79 See Appendix Tables.

80 Their proportion among direct pensions (*Versichertenrenten* excluding survivors' pensions) rose from 46 percent in 1969 to 51 percent in 1982. Calculated from *Rentenanpassungsbericht 1980*, Bundestagsdrucksache 8/3845, pp. 57-58, and from Der Bundesminister für Arbeit und Sozialordnung, *Sozialpolitische Informationen* 17 (No. 13), 1983, p. 4.

81 Between 1957 and 1968 the total number of invalidity pensions fluctuated at around 1.6 million. In 1970 it reached a previously unknown level of 1.66 million and has been rising consistently since.

82 Almost 90 percent of survivors' pensions are widows' or widowers' pensions, so that their expression as a proportion of elderly people seems justified, despite the fact that they also include payments to orphans.

83 About one third of the beneficiaries are older than 65. Roughly a fourth are children below the age of 14. Cf. Der Bundesminister für Arbeit und Sozialordnung, *Sozialbericht 1978*. Bonn, 1978, p. 126.

84 Different official sources, however, report widely discrepant figures for the 1950s and 1960s; cf. Der Bundesminister für Arbeit und Sozialordnung, *Übersicht über die soziale Sicherung 1977*. Bonn, 1970, p. 100; see also *Hauptergebnisse der Arbeits- und Sozialstatistik 1970* Bonn, 1970, p. 107. In addition, a break in statistical definitions which occurred in 1970 impedes comparisons over time (for a description see Bernhard Knoblich, 'Krankenstand, Diskussion versachlichen', *Bundesarbeitsblatt* 9, 1982, pp. 5-13). Since 1980 sickness ratios have again declined.

85 The duration of insurance benefits depends on the recipient's previous contribution record (see the Institutional Synopsis). Unemployment assistance benefits are in principle paid for an unlimited duration, but claims are re-examined after one year.

86 The governmental social budget (*Sozialbericht 1980*, p. 125, and *Sozialbericht 1983*, p. 110) reports ratios of 30 and 34 percent for 1972 and 1980, because it relates the number of beneficiaries to the number of pupils in those educational institutions which qualify for benefits under the law.

87 See the collection of policy statements by Klaus von Beyme, *Die grossen Regierungserklärungen der deutschen Bundeskanzler von Adenauer bis Schmidt*. München, 1979.

88 The legislation in effect in 1950 did not specify an earnings-replacement ratio. The reported ratio expresses the cash amount to which a single earner of average earnings was entitled as a percentage of net earnings.

89 The steep increase in the late 1960s presumably reflects growing restitution payments for re-migrating foreign workers who received payments without figuring among the registered number of beneficiaries.

90 The percentage actually refers to the proportion of the general computation base which reflects average wages only with a time lag (see the Institutional Synopsis).

91 Invalidity pensions vary with the degree of incapacity and the length of the contribution record. The cited standard case assumes full incapacity occurring below the age of 55 and contributions from the age of 20. The widows' pension is legally defined as 60 percent of

the pension to which the deceased would have been entitled in the case of occupational incapacity ('Berufsunfähigkeitsrente'). The mentioned rate applies if death occurred below the age of 55, contributions were paid from the age of 20 and the earnings of the deceased corresponded to the average wage.

92   The majority of male pensioners in the workers' scheme have a contribution record of 40 years or more, and life-time earnings which correspond to the average wage (see *Rentenanpassungsbericht 1980*, Bundestagsdrucksache 8/3845, pp. 64, 68). The pension for average earners with a personal computation base of 100 percent and a contribution record of 40 years amounted to DM 1,095.60 in January 1980 (see *Sozialbericht 1983*, p. 249).

93   See Richard Hauser, Helga Cremer-Schäfer, Udo Nouvertné, *Armut, Niedrigeinkommen und Unterversorgung in der Bundesrepublik Deutschland*. Frankfurt, 1981, pp. 42, 113.

94   The 1977 standard rate of DM 287 corresponded to DM 277 at constant (1976) prices as compared with merely DM 266 in 1980.

95   The average worker's pension (old age or invalidity) was DM 89.70 in 1955, whereas the per capita benefits for students amounted to DM 94 according to the data published in Der Bundesminister für Arbeit und Sozialordnung, *Übersicht über die soziale Sicherung 1977*, p. 277.

96   The beneficiaries of the assistance scheme, however, usually receive some additional supplements.

97   In 1982, 11.59 million persons lived mostly from transfer payments as compared with 11.06 million blue-collar workers. The number of transfer recipients includes a small proportion of persons living from capital returns (less than 5 percent), but excludes 1.43 million economically active persons living mostly from transfer payments (e.g. unemployed or handicapped persons). See Der Bundesminister für Arbeit und Sozialordnung, *Arbeits- und Sozialstatistik - Hauptergebnisse 1983*, p. 11, and *Statistisches Jahrbuch für die Bundesrepublik Deutschland 1983*, p. 96.

98   According to the findings of the Transfer Enquete Commission, the data and research situation is 'unsatisfactory'; see Transfer Enquete Kommission, Das *Transfersystem der Bundesrepublik Deutschland*. Stuttgart, 1981, p. 11.

99   *Ibid.*, Zur Einkommenslage der Rentner. Zwischenbericht der *Kommission*. Stuttgart, 1979, pp. 29-33; see also the collection of federal government policy statements edited by Klaus von Beyme, *op. cit.*

100   This refers to all recipients including those only receiving unique lump sum payments. The number of recipients of regular assistance benefits (*Hilfe zum Lebensunterhalt*) amounts to about 60 percent of the total with the same phase-specific variation.

101   The information is taken from the national poverty report produced for the Commission of the European Communities; see Richard Hauser, Helga Cremer-Schäfer, Udo Nouvertné: *Armut, Niedrigeinkommen und Unterversorgung in der Bundesrepublik Deutschland*. Frankfurt, 1981, pp. 49, 55, 56.

102   See Hauser et al., *op. cit.*, pp. 47, 58. For developments in the early 1980s see Dieter Deininger, Laufende Hilfe zum Lebensunterhalt. Ergebnisse einer Zusatzstatistik zur Statistik der Sozialhilfe im September 1981, *Wirtschaft und Statistik* 35, 1983, pp. 254-264; Dieter Deininger, Sozialhilfeempfänger 1981, *Wirtschaft und Statistik* 35, 1983, pp. 505-511; Richard Hauser, Armut im Wohlfahrsstaat - empirischer Befund und Lösungsansätze, in Heinz Lampert and Gerhard Kühlewind (eds.), *Das Sozialsystem der Bundesrepublik Deutschland*. (Beiträge zur Arbeitsmarkt- und Berufsforschung 83). Nürnberg, 1984, pp. 214-263.

103   See Deininger, *op. cit.*, p. 258.

104   *Ibid.*, p. 257.

105   See Heiner Geissler, *Die neue soziale Frage*. Freiburg, 1976, pp. 48-49.

106   For summaries of the literature see Hauser et al., *op. cit.*, pp. 63-91; Frank Klanberg, Materielle Armut in Perspektive, in Hans-Jürgen Krupp, Wolfgang Glatzer (eds.), *Umverteilung im Sozialstaat*. Frankfurt, 1978, pp. 113-158; Klaus Kortmann, Zur Armutsdiskussion in der

Bundesrepublik, *SPES Arbeitspapier Nr. 50.* Frankfurt, 1976 (mimeo); Hans Peter Widmaier (ed.), *Zur Neuen Sozialen Frage.* Berlin, 1978.

107   Hauser et al., *op.cit.,* pp. 76, 307.

108   *Ibid.,* pp. 73-74. A sample survey of low income groups arrived at the same result; see Otker Bujard and Ulrich Lange, *Theorie und Praxis der Sozialhilfe. Zur Situation der einkommensschwachen alten Menschen,* Schriftenreihe des Bundesministers für Jugend, Familie und Gesundheit, Band 56. Stuttgart, Berlin, Köln, Mainz, 1978, p. 162.

109   In the absence of more recent data this conclusion made by the authors of the national poverty report is based on some plausible guesses, see Hauser et al., *op. cit.,* p. 308.

110   Hauser et al., *op. cit.,* p. 86. Klanberg 1978, op. cit., p. 146 arrives at similar results.

111   Hauser et al., *op. cit.,* p. 89.

112   This interpretation is suggested by Klanberg 1978, *op. cit.,* p. 146.

113   All data relate to weighted average household incomes taking the size of household into account; relative definitions of poverty in terms of crude average incomes would lead to much higher poverty ratios; for relative poverty ratios in these crude terms see Eike Ballerstedt, Wolfgang Glatzer, *Soziologischer Almanach.* Frankfurt, 1975 (first edition), p. 380, where 21.6 percent of all households are shown to have fallen below the 50 percent poverty line in 1969.

114   At the end of 1984 the results of the 1978 survey were not available.

115   See Geissler, *op. cit.,* esp. pp. 13-14.

116   See Transfer Enquete Kommission 1979, *op. cit.,* pp. 100-101 with data for 1973.

117   As Klanberg, *op. cit.,* p. 150, shows, even the poverty risk of families with several children is not over-proportionately high. This is due to the fact that the higher income strata tend to have more children. Within given income brackets, an increasing number of children does increase the risk of falling below the official poverty standard; see Hermann Scherl, Absolute Armut in der Bundesrepublik Deutschland: Messung, Vorkommen und Ursachen, in Hans Peter Widmaier (ed.), *op. cit.,* pp. 79-126, here p. 112.

118   See Hauser et al., *op. cit.,* pp. 186, 188. Estimates of the number of homeless persons range from 260,000 to 800,000. Only about one fifth of these are estimated to receive social assistance benefits.

119   In these years the number of births was consistently above one million; see Statistisches Bundesamt, *Bevölkerung und Wirtschaft 1872-1972.* Stuttgart and Mainz, 1972, p. 108.

120   See Hauser et al., *op. cit.,* p. 217.

121   Calculated on the basis of data presented by Hauser et al., *ibid.*

122   Among the non-recipients, young persons in search of a first job are over-represented. In recent years about 10 percent of the unemployed were under 20. Annual data on the age distribution of the unemployed are published in the series: Der Bundesminister für Arbeit und Sozialordnung, *Arbeits- und Sozialstatistik Hauptergebnisse*

123   The average values are taken from Richard Hauser, Ingo Fischer, Thomas Klein, Verarmung durch Arbeitslosigkeit? Sonderforschungsbereich 3, *Arbeitspapier Nr. 154* Frankfurt, 1984 (mimeo); all other data are calculated from figures published in various editions of *Arbeits- und Sozialstatistik Hauptergebnisse*

124   Hauser, Fischer, Klein, *op. cit.,* p. 34.

125   *Ibid.,* p. 35.

126   Hauser et al., *op. cit.,* p. 137.

127   *Ibid.,* p. 61.

128   During the late 1970s and early 1980s about 85 percent of all unemployed persons had below average earnings from work; about one fifth to one fourth had earnings below 50 percent of the average earnings of the dependent labour force; data calculated from various editions of the series *Arbeits- und Sozialstatistik Hauptergebnisse.* The fact that the unemployed are largely recruited from low income strata can also be seen if the institutional earn-

ings-replacement ratio of 68 percent is compared with the level of average benefits which has been fluctuating around 50 percent of average net earnings of the dependent labour force in the 1970s (see Graph 33, Section IV).

[129] Hauser et al., *op. cit.*, p. 99. These data refer to households with an unemployment duration of more than four months.

[130] *Ibid.*, pp. 98, 101.

[131] Data on unemployment benefits are from the Bundesanstalt für Arbeit as reported in Süddeutsche Zeitung, 28./29. July 1984. Average net earnings are from Materialband zum Sozialbudget 1983, *op. cit.*, p. 238.

[132] The data allow only tentative conclusions in this direction, because the official social assistance figures relate to proportions of households (in selected regions), whereas the data on unemployment compensation recipients (insurance or assistance benefits) relate to persons.

[133] Hauser, Fischer, Klein, *op. cit.*, p. 28.

[134] Unemployed persons receive only the general child allowances which are lower than the child supplements of the social assistance scheme.

[135] Figures calculated from *Arbeits- und Sozialstatistik Hauptergebnisse* 1984, p. 114.

[136] In 1983, 413,000 persons were in receipt of old age pensions under the farmers' scheme (including widows), and 608,000 persons drew civil service pensions (cf. *Arbeits- und Sozialstatistik Hauptergebnisse* 1984, p. 139, and Werner Breidenstein, Versorgungsempfänger des öffentlichen Dienstes am 1. Februar 1983, *Wirtschaft und Statistik* 35, 1983, pp. 573-576).

[137] The employment ratio of persons in the age categories 60-65 amounted to 39 percent in 1983; see *Arbeits- und Sozialstatistik Hauptergebnisse* 1984, pp. 20 and 27.

[138] The comparatively sharp decrease in the employees' system is presumably due to the fact that the proportion of female pensioners has been growing faster than in the workers' scheme.

[139] As shown in the previous section, assistance rates correspond to roughly 40 percent of average earnings if the cost of housing and lump sum payments are included. Since the data on pensions refer to cases, not households, recipients of low pensions are not necessarily entitled to assistance benefits.

[140] The table shows the distribution of old age and invalidity pensions (*Versichertenrenten*). Partial invalidity pensions may coincide with earnings from work. As a comparison between the left side and the right side of the table shows, the exclusion of partial invalidity pensions changes the distribution only marginally in favour of higher pension levels.

[141] The 1968 value is comparatively too low, because the limits of the income brackets could only be set at roughly similar relative levels (see the rows under 'definitions' in Table 13).

[142] Again the 1968 value is relatively low, because the class limit had to be set at a relatively low standard.

[143] See Transfer Enquete Kommission, *Zur Einkommenslage der Rentner. Zwischenbericht der Kommission.* Stuttgart, Berlin, Köln, Mainz, 1979. If not stated otherwise, all data in the following paragraphs are from this report.

[144] In the following, the terms '(pension) recipients' and 'beneficiaries' always refer to beneficiaries of the pension insurance schemes or the occupational injuries insurance scheme (which could not be differentiated). The term 'pensioners' refers exclusively to recipients who predominantly live from pensions.

[145] The average disposable income per month of all private households amounted to DM 2,096 in 1973 (calculated from *DIW Wochenbericht* 46, 1979 (no 29), pp. 302, 304). In the same year the average net earnings of the dependent labour force were at DM 1,152 (calculated from Materialband zum Sozialbudget 1983, p. 238). Households predominantly living from civil servants' pensions had an average household income of DM 2,022, but their benefits were subject to taxation.

[146] The commission reports a proportion of 87 percent of all households living predominantly

from public transfers. Of these households, 85 percent were in receipt of social insurance pensions.

147 This refers to the income of all households predominantly living from public transfers. These consist mostly of pensioners.

148 See the final report of Transfer Enquete Kommission, *op. cit.*, pp. 108, 111.

149 This is largely due to structural effects. The reduction in the number of self-employed persons led largely to the elimination of the low-earnings groups in this category - see Deutsches Institut für Wirtschaftsforschung, *DIW Wochenbericht* 40, 1973 (No. 34), p. 307.

150 'After redistribution' here refers to disposable household income after the payment of taxes and social security contributions ('negative transfers'), and after the receipt of cash benefits ('positive transfers').

151 The paucity of available data is criticized in the final report of the Transfer Enquete Kommission, *op. cit.*, p. 11.

152 The heavy reduction in the overall income inequality reported for 1962 and 1969 is largely a statistical artefact, due to the inclusion of pensioners. Since they are covered by public insurance schemes, pensioners have usually abstained from making contributions to private pension schemes during their working lives so that they draw only small (or no) factor incomes.

153 Again, the inclusion of pensioners overstates the magnitude of redistributive effects. Data on the vertical distribution of incomes before and after redistribution for the labour force have not been available.

154 Pre-1970 data are not fully comparable, as they have been taken from a different source.

155 See Deutsches Institut für Wirtschaftsforschung, *DIW Wochenbericht* 50, 1983 (no.30), pp. 380-381.

156 See Transfer Enquete Kommission, *op. cit.*, pp. 39-40, 103, 109.

157 *Ibid.*, p. 51.

158 *Ibid.*, pp. 221-226.

159 See Gesellschaftliche Daten, *op. cit.*, p. 50.

160 See Ulrich Brasche, 'Strukturwandel am Arbeitsmarkt', *Aus Politik und Zeitgeschichte* B45, 1984, pp. 18-30, here p. 23.

161 *Ibid.*, and Bernhard Badura and Peter Gross, *Sozialpolitische Perspektiven.* München, 1976, p. 71.

162 The declining numbers of patients provided an economic incentive for doctors to raise the number of prescriptions.

163 Gustav Grillmaier, Krankenhäuser 1981, *Wirtschaft und Statistik* 35, 1983, pp. 343-346, here p. 346.

164 Figures for 1956 to 1974 are from Christof Helberger, 'Ziele und Ergebnisse der Gesundheitspolitik in der Bundesrepublik Deutschland', *In* Wolfgang Zapf (ed.), Lebensbedingungen in *der Bundesrepublik 1950-1975.* Frankfurt, 1977, pp. 567-631, here p. 601; more recent data have been taken from various editions of the statistical yearbook.

165 For data see Der Bundesminister für Jugend, Familie und Gesundheit, *Daten des Gesundheitswesens.* Stuttgart, 1983.

166 See Uta Gerhardt and Klaus-Uwe Kirchgässler, *The influence of social and administrative structures on the distribution of health care and health risks in West Germany* Contribution to the Meeting on the Health Burden of Social Inequities organized by the World Health Organization. Copenhagen, 1984 (mimeo), p. 20.

167 Helberger, *op. cit.*, p. 580, and Sabine Lang, Maria Müller-Andritzky, 'Gesundheit und soziale Indikatoren', *In* Wolfgang Glatzer and Wolfgang Zapf (eds.), *Lebensqualität in der Bundesrepublik.* Frankfurt, 1984, pp. 141-156, here p. 142.

168 Gustav Grillmaier, 'Fragen zur Gesundheit. Ergebnis des Mikrozensus April 1980', *Wirtschaft und Statistik* 35, 1983, pp. 127-132, here p. 128.

169 In 1981 it declined for the first time since 1956; see Grillmaier, *op. cit.*, p. 344.

170 The data presented by Helberger, *op. cit.*, p. 585 show a fluctuation around 3.6 days between 1956 and 1973; calculations based on Grillmaier, *op. cit.*, p. 343, arrive at 3.6 for 1980 and 3.5 for 1981.

171 Grillmaier, *op. cit.*, p. 343.

172 The number of people killed in traffic accidents rose from almost 13,000 to above 19,000 between 1950 and 1970, but was reduced to 11,715 in 1982; see *Bevölkerung und Wirtschaft*, op. cit., p. 206, and the statistical yearbook of 1984.

173 For a summary account, see Gerhardt and Kirchgässler, *op. cit.*

174 Helberger, *op. cit.*, pp. 595-596.

175 *Ibid.*, pp. 594, 595.

176 See Gerhardt and Kirchgässler, *op. cit.*, pp. 10, 28.

177 *Ibid.*, p. 9.

178 See the results of the 1978 welfare survey in Lang and Müller-Andritzky, *op. cit.*, p. 145.

179 See the summary of a study by Ralph Brennecke in Hauser, Cremer-Schäfer, Nouvertné, *op. cit.*, pp. 157-162.

180 These are the results of Brennecke's study as reported in *ibid.*, pp. 162-166.

181 See the final report of the Transfer Enquete Kommission, *op. cit.*, p. 65. These results are not standardized for differences in household size.

182 See Norbert Andel, 'Verteilungswirkungen der Sozialversicherung am Beispiel der gesetzlichen Krankenversicherung der Bundesrepublik Deutschland', *In* Norbert Andel and Helmut Schneider, Öffentliche *Finanzwirtschaft und Verteilung III.* Berlin, 1975, pp. 39-82, here p. 71.

183 As an example, participation in the cancer prevention programme established in 1970 never exceeded 35 percent of the eligible population; see Gerhardt and Kirchgässler, *op. cit.*, p. 13.

184 For a summary of the goals of German housing policy, see Wolfgang Glatzer, *Wohnungsversorgung im Wohlfahrtsstaat* Frankfurt, 1980, pp. 33-73.

185 In the Weimar Republic, the (net) number of annual constructions averaged 190,000 from 1918 to 1932 with a peak of 318,000 in 1929. During the Nazi period, the average for the years 1933-1943 amounted to 187,000 with a peak of 320,000 in 1937; see Carl Johannes Fuchs, 'Wohnungsfrage und Wohnungswesen', *In* Ludwig Elster and Adolf Weber, *Handwörterbuch der Staatswissenschaften*, 4. Auflage, Ergänzungsband. Jena, 1929, pp. 1098-1160, here p. 1146 (data for 1918-1927), and Länderrat des amerikanischen Besatzungsgebiet (ed.), *Statistisches Handbuch von Deutschland 1928-1944.* München, 1949, p. 340.

186 See Biedenkopf and Miegel, *op. cit.*, (note 52), p. 52. Dwellings without public promotion exceed the prescribed sizes.

187 See Gesellschaftliche Daten 1982, *op. cit.*, p. 265.

188 For a discussion, see Glatzer, *op. cit.*, pp. 78ff, and Rainer Dringenberg, 'Tendenzen der Wohnungspolitik in den 80er Jahren', *Sozialer Fortschritt* 7, 1983, pp. 152-158, here p. 154. According to these sources the overestimation amounted to 715,000 dwellings in 1968, and to 1.3 million in 1978.

189 See Dietmar Görgmaier, 'Haben wir wieder eine Wohnungsnot?', *Aus Politik und Zeitgeschichte* B10, 1982, pp. 26-37, here p. 28.

190 In February 1981 about 100 houses were occupied in the city of Berlin; see Renate Petzinger and Marlo Riege, *Die neue Wohnungsnot.* Hamburg, 1981, p. 7.

191 These are the results of the national welfare survey of 1978; see Martin Diewald and Wolfgang Zapf, 'Wohnbedingungen und Wohnzufriedenheit', *In* Wolfgang Glatzer and Wolfgang Zapf (eds.), *op. cit.* (note 168), pp. 73-96, here p. 84. Another study arrived at practically identical results, see Görgmaier, *op. cit.*, pp. 28-29.

192   Diewald and Zapf, *op. cit.*, p. 75.

193   *Ibid.*, p. 76, and Wullkopf, op. cit. (note 50), p. 19.

194   For data see Gesellschaftliche Daten 1982, *op. cit.*, p. 275.

195   This data presumably refers to the total cost of housing (including the cost of heating), see Diewald and Zapf, *op. cit.*, p. 82.

196   These data are from Rainer Neef, 'Wohnungsversorgung und *neue Wohnungsnot*', *Leviathan* 9, 1981, pp. 332-353, here p. 346, and Wullkopf, *op. cit.*, p. 19; the figures are based on the official housing survey of 1978 and refer to rents excluding other expenditure for housing. Time series data on the rent burden of specific groups are presented in Glatzer, *op. cit.*, pp. 103-109.

197   See Diewald and Zapf, *op. cit.*, p. 82; Glatzer, op. cit., p. 105.

198   The absolute figure is from Wullkopf, *op. cit.*, p. 14; the number of tenant households is given in Statistisches Bundesamt (ed.), *Das Wohnen in der Bundesrepublik Deutschland*, Ausgabe 1981. Stuttgart und Mainz, 1981, p. 33.

199   See Wullkopf, *op. cit.*, p. 14.

200   *Ibid.*; Petzinger and Marlo, op. cit., p. 119 give an absolute number of 14 million tenants formally entitled to social housing.

201   Wullkopf, *op. cit.*, p. 14.

202   See Jürgen Forster, 'Bei Mietzuschüssen regiert jetzt der Rotstift', *Süddeutsche Zeitung*, March 5-6, 1983.

203   This proportion is reported by Petzinger and Riege, *op. cit.*, p. 106.

204   See, for example, Biedenkopf and Miegel, *op. cit.*, p. 82.

205   These are the results of an investigation by the Federal Statistical Office as reported in *Süddeutsche Zeitung* October 25, 1984.

206   See Rudi Ulbrich, *Verteilungswirkungen des Förderungssystems für den Wohnungsbau*, 2. Teil: Subventionen nach Einkommensklassen der privaten Haushalte. Gutachten des Deutschen Instituts für Wirtschaftsforschung im Auftrag des Bundesministers für Raumordnung, Bauwesen und Städtebau. Berlin, 1979. This study refers to 1972; its results are here cited from the final report of Transfer Enquete Commission, *op. cit.*, p. 70.

207   See the summary of this study in Transfer Enquete Commission, *op.cit.*, p. 66.

208   See the institutional synopsis, and Biedenkopf and Miegel, *op. cit.*, pp. 40-42.

209   These are the results of a study by the Deutsches Institut für Wirtschaftsforschung as reported in *Süddeutsche Zeitung* February 25, 1983.

210   See Wullkopf, *op. cit.*, p. 22

211   See Statistisches Bundesamt, *op. cit.*, p. 49. Compared with 1957 this is an increase of 7 percentage points, see Glatzer, *op. cit.*, p. 113. For international data see Ballerstedt and Glatzer, *Soziologischer Almanach*, op. cit., p. 119.

212   See Biedenkopf and Miegel, *op. cit.*, p. 139.

213   The teaching staff of schools and universities numbered 173,000 persons in 1951, 229,000 in 1960, 366,000 in 1970, and 573,000 in 1980 (see the Appendix table on educational personnel).

214   In addition to the pupils in general schools, some 2.7 million pupils attended vocational schools in 1983 (as compared to 1.9 million in 1960) - see Der Bundesminister für Bildung und Wissenschaft (ed.), *Grund- und Strukturdaten*, ed. 1984/85. Bonn, 1984, p. 25.

215   For data see *Grund- und Strukturdaten*, op. cit., (various editions, especially 1984-85, p. 12).

216   Almost three quarters of all kindergartens are privately organized, but they are subsidized by local authorities, and the proportion of public places increased from 20 to 29 percent between 1960 and 1981 - see *ibid.*, p. 15.

217   See *ibid.*, p. 60. In 1965, 53 percent left ordinary schools with a degree, 17 percent left without a degree; the corresponding percentages in 1983 were 37 and 9.

218   This includes *Gymnasien*, comprehensive schools, and intermediary schools. Pre-1957 data on pupils exclude several regions and were therefore not considered.

219   The proportion of secondary school graduates entering post-secondary institutions varied around 90 percent between the late 1950s and 1973. Thereafter it declined from 89 percent in 1973 to 80 percent in 1975. Since 1976 it has remained close to 75 percent, see Wissenschaftsrat, *Zur Lage der Hochschulen Anfang der 80er Jahre.* Köln, 1983, p. 29.

220   Official data on the average length of university studies are only published since 1977. A study by Hitpass of the student class 1958 arrived at an average length of 12 semesters in the early 1960s (see Rainer Ruge, 'Bildung', *In* Wolfgang Zapf (ed.), Lebensbedingungen in der *Bundesrepublik 1950-1975*, op. cit., pp. 633-729, here p. 683). Following the official data, the average duration increased from 6.3 to 6.7 years between 1977 and 1983 (see Ludger Viehoff, 'Zur Entwicklung der Soziologie an den Hochschulen der Bundesrepublik Deutschland von 1960 bis 1981', *Zeitschrift für Soziologie* 13, 1984, pp. 264-272, here p. 270, and Wissenschaftsrat, *Eckdaten zur Lage der Hochschulen. Stand 1984.* (Drucksache 6690/84). Köln, 1984, p. 22.

221   For a discussion of available studies and an attempt to create an indicator of academic success based on official cross-sectional data, see Ruge, *op. cit.*, pp. 681-683.

222   See Wissenschaftsrat, *op. cit.*, 1984, p. 5.

223   See *Grund- und Strukturdaten 1984/85*, op. cit., p. 158. The number of graduations refers to all examinations including teachers' colleges and technical colleges. The number of university diplomas rose from 20,000 to 51,000.

224   *Ibid.*, p. 246.

225   Calculated from *ibid.*, p. 34.

226   The data on the number of pupils and teachers are from Statistisches Bundesamt, Bevölkerung und Wirtschaft, *op. cit*, pp. 127-128 (1951-1968) and from Statistisches Bundesamt, *Bildung im Zahlenspiegel 1984.* Stuttgart und Mainz, 1984, p. 43 (1969-1983).

227   See *Grund- und Strukturdaten* ed. 1978, op. cit., p. 132, and ed. 1984/85, p. 163. Data presented in the statistical yearbook on the scientific personnel of universities and teachers'colleges (excluding technical colleges) are much higher than the total number of scientific personnel reported in *Grund- und Strukturdaten*. However, also the data in the statistical yearbooks yield increasing student/teacher ratios from 7 in 1972 to 9 in 1982 (see *Statistisches Jahrbuch für die Bundesrepublik Deutschland* 1981, p. 341, and 1984, p. 357).

228   See Ballerstedt and Glatzer, *Soziologischer Almanach op. cit.*, p. 299.

229   Calculated from graduation data in Table 24 and population data in *Grund- und Strukturdaten 1984/85*, op. cit., p. 233.

230   Calculated from *ibid.*, pp. 158-159.

231   See Der Bundesminister für Arbeit und Sozialordnung, *Sozialpolitische Informationen* 19, 2, 1985, p. 3.

232   In the social sciences 60 percent of all university professors are below 45 years, 83 percent are below 51 - see Viehoff, *op. cit.*, p. 271.

233   Calculated from *Grund- und Strukturdaten* 1984/85, op. cit. p. 258.

234   See Klaus von Beyme (ed.), *Die großen Regierungserklärungen der deutschen Bundeskanzler von Adenauer bis Schmidt.* München, 1979, pp. 75-102.

235   See OECD, *Public Expenditure on Income Maintenance Programmes.* Paris, 1976, pp. 19-20. The GDP share of a given programme is then expressed in the equation $S/GDP = R/P \times B/R \times S/B/GDP/P$, where S refers to total spending, R to the population under risk, B to the beneficiaries, and P to the total population.

236   A more detailed analysis which takes the 1965 break in statistical definitions into account, shows that from 1957 to 1965 demography was the most important component of growth, whereas from 1965 to 1971 changes in the eligibility ratio played the decisive role.

237   The average benefit for 1956 calculated from aggregate data on cash benefit expenditure and beneficiaries is misleadingly high, however. It amounts to 37 DM per month, whereas

the legal benefit rate actually was 25 DM; cf. Der Bundesminister für Arbeit und Sozialordnung (ed.), *Übersicht über die soziale Sicherung in der Bundesrepublik Deutschland*. Bonn, 1960, p. 87. For the development of the legal rates at constant prices see Section II.6.

238 The information given in the previous note suggests that the decline in the transfer ratio may partly be a statistical artifact.

239 See Werner Glastetter, Rüdiger Paulert, Ulrich Spörel, *Die wirtschaftliche Entwicklung in der Bundesrepublik Deutschland 1950-1980*. Frankfurt, 1983, p. 47.

240 For data see Alfred Grosser, *Deutschlandbilanz*. München, 1970, p. 93.

241 See Walther G. Hoffmann et al., *Das Wachstum der deutschen Wirtschaft seit der Mitte des 19. Jahrhunderts*. Berlin, Heidelberg, New York, 1965, p. 452.

242 *Ibid.*

243 About three quarters of the foodstuff consumed in the Federal Republic stem from domestic production; see Heinrich Niehaus, 'Sorgenkind Landwirtschaft: Verwandlung oder Ende der Bauern?', *In* Richard Löwenthal and Hans-Peter Schwarz (eds.), *Die zweite Republik. 25 Jahre Bundesrepublik Deutschland - eine Bilanz*. Stuttgart, 1973, pp. 728-761, here p. 730.

244 See Heinz-Herbert Noll, 'Soziale Indikatoren für Arbeitsmarkt und Beschäftigungsbedingungen', *In* Wolfgang Zapf (ed.), *Lebensbedingungen in der Bundesrepublik*, op.cit., pp. 111-222, here p. 130.

245 The data are taken from Institut der deutschen Wirtschaft, *Zahlen zur wirtschaftlichen Entwicklung der Bundesrepublik Deutschland*. Köln, 1984, Table 10b.

246 For time-series data on exports see Statistisches Bundesamt, *Bevölkerung und Wirtschaft 1872-1972*, op.cit., p. 266, and Deutscher Bundestag, *Jahresgutachten 1984/85 des Sachverständigenrates zur Begutachtung der gesamtwirtschaftlichen Entwicklung*, Drucksache 10/2541. Bonn, 1984, p.278.

247 To discuss such concerns, the Friedrich-Ebert Foundation linked to the Social Democratic party organized a symposium on 'International Competition and the Welfare State' in 1984.

248 See Glastetter, Paulert, Spörel, *op.cit.*, p.86f.

249 The percentages are calculated from the data in Der Bundesminister für Arbeit und Sozialordnung, *Arbeits- und Sozialstatistik Hauptergebnisse 1984*. Bonn, 1984, pp. 33-34.

250 See Gerhard Mackenroth, 'Die Reform der Sozialpolitik durch einen deutschen Sozialplan', *In* Berhard Külp and Wilfrid Schreiber (eds.), *Soziale Sicherheit*. Köln, Berlin, 1971, pp. 265-275. The article was first published in 1952.

251 Although our data do not constitute a random sample in any meaningful sense, we have followed the common practice of reporting significance levels for the correlation coefficients. Since in this time-series analysis both GDP and social expenditure growth rates are subject to a downward trend, all reported correlation coefficients are to a certain extent misleadingly high.

252 This description follows Lepsius' work; see e.g. M. Rainer Lepsius, 'From fragmented party democracy to government by emergency decree and national socialist takeover', *In* Juan J. Linz and Alfred Stepan (eds.), *The Breakdown of Democratic Regimes*. Baltimore and London, 1978, pp. 34-79.

253 See M. Rainer Lepsius, 'Sozialstruktur und soziale Schichtung in der Bundesrepublik Deutschland', *In* Richard Löwenthal and Hans-Peter Schwarz (eds.), *op. cit.*, pp. 263-288.

254 For information on the Greens, see Wilhelm P. Bürklin, *Grüne Politik*. Opladen, 1984, and the re-evaluation of the available evidence by Jens Alber, 'Modernisierung, neue Spannungslinien und die politischen Chancen der Grünen', *Politische Vierteljahresschrift* 26, 1985, pp.211-226.

255 For data see Franz Urban Pappi, 'Parteiensystem und Sozialstruktur in der Bundesrepublik', *Politische Vierteljahresschrift* 14, 1973, pp. 191-213; Kendall L. Baker, Russell J. Dalton, Kai Hildebrandt, *Germany Transformed*. Cambridge, Mass. and London, 1981; Statistisches Bundesamt, Wahl zum 9. Deutschen Bundestag am 5. Oktober 1980, *Fachserie 1* (Bevölke-

rung und Erwerbstätigkeit) Heft 9. Stuttgart, Mainz, 1982. See also Infas, *Infas-Report Wahlen Bundestagswahl 1983*. Bonn-Bad Godesberg, 1983. The Infas institute distinguishes five social categories with fairly homogeneous voting behaviour which it somewhat misleadingly labels 'workers', 'employees and civil servants with union ties', 'new middle class' (upwardly mobile groups including self-employed categories), 'old middle class' (inter-generationally stable members of white collar strata and self-employed categories), and 'Catholic tradition milieu' (workers and middle class groups with strong church affiliations).

256 In 1953 German rearmament required a modification of the constitution which needed a two-thirds majority. In 1957 the German Party entered parliament only on the basis of a political deal with the CDU which left some constituencies uncontested in order to ensure that its coalition partner would strengthen the conservative forces in parliament. (German electoral law requires a party to poll five percent of the votes or to win three constituencies in order to be represented in parliament). In 1960 the cabinet members of the German Party defected to the CDU.

257 This total increase is the sum of increases in constant statistical definitions which is not identical with the crude difference between the GDP shares of social spending in 1950 (19.2%) and 1983 (33.2%).

258 Again this refers to the increase in constant statistical definitions eliminating the various breaks in statistical concepts.

259 This excludes the laws on the civil service and on war consequences for which detailed institutional data could not be compiled.

260 The analysis refers to a selection of the 68 most important laws among the postwar core laws listed in the Appendix Volume. A roll-call analysis of West German legislation is complicated because the exact result of parliamentary voting is recorded only in exceptional cases. Usually voting occurs by a show of hands without any exact counting. Therefore information on party-specific voting must be painstakingly compiled from the concluding declarations of the parties' main speakers reported in the parliamentary minutes.

261 German employers are organized in two major interest groups. The Federation of German Industry (BDI) unites about 90 percent of industrial enterprises and seeks to influence the government's macroeconomic policy. The Federation of German Employers (BDA) represents the employers' side in collective bargaining and is responsible for all issues concerning labour relations and social policy. The trade unions are organized in the unified DGB, a federation of seventeen industrial unions. Separate unions compete for the support of white-collar employees and civil servants. Roughly 40 percent of the dependent labour force are unionized; about 85 percent of all union members are organized in the DGB.

262 For summaries of the positions of the major interest groups on social policy, see Viola Gräfin Bethusy-Huc, *Das Sozialleistungssystem der Bundesrepublik Deutschland* Tübingen, 1965, pp. 101-116; Gerhard W. Brück and Harald Eichner, *Perspektiven der Sozialpolitik*. Schriften der Kommission für wirtschaftlichen und sozialen Wandel Band 41. Göttingen, 1974; and Max Richter, *Die Sozialreform*. Dokumente und Stellungnahmen, Vols. 7-8, Bad Godesberg, 1970.

263 The table is largely based on the sources named in the previous note. For housing and education, see the articles by Wolfgang Glatzer and Rainer Ruge in Wolfgang Zapf (ed.), *Lebensbedingungen in der Bundesrepublik*, op. cit.

264 See Richard M. Titmuss, *Social Policy*. London, 1974, pp. 30-31; Walter Korpi, *The Democratic Class Struggle*. London, 1983, pp. 188-192.

265 The account of the pension insurance reform largely follows the detailed study by Hans Günter Hockerts, *Sozialpolitische Entscheidungen im Nachkriegsdeutschland* Stuttgart, 1980. In addition, it is based on the articles by Kurt Jantz, 'Die Rentendynamik 1957 als Vorbild im Sozialleistungsrecht', and Dieter Schewe, 'Von der ersten zur zweiten Rentenreform 1957-1976 - Die Entwicklung der Gesetzgebung in der Rentenversicherung', *In* Reinhart Bartholomäi et al. (eds), *Sozialpolitik nach 1945. Geschichte und Analysen*. Bonn-Bad Godesberg, 1977, pp. 102-123 and 183-190, by Klaus Nieder, 'Zur Sozialpolitik in der 6. Legislaturperiode des Deutschen Bundestages', *In* Institut für Politikwissenschaft der Univer-

sität Münster (ed.), *Wahl '72*. Opladen, 1972, pp. 28-43, and by Helga Michalsky, 'Parteien und Sozialpolitik in der Bundesrepublik Deutschland', *Sozialer Fortschritt* 33, 1984, pp. 134-142. The account of the sickness insurance bills is based on three books, i.e. William Safran, *Veto Group Politics. The Case of Health Insurance Reform in West Germany*. San Francisco, 1967; Max Richter and Albert Müller, *Kampf um die Krankenversicherung 1955-1965*. Bad Godesberg, 1967; Frieder Naschold, *Kassenärzte und Krankenversicherungsreform. Zu einer Theorie der Statuspolitik*. Freiburg, 1967.

266 The vote of the German party was split.

267 See Schewe, *In* Bartholomäi, op. cit., p. 187.

268 The doctors'· associations advocated a limitation of compulsory coverage as the most effective form of cost sharing.

269 The major features of the bill included an upgrading of sick-pay for workers, a reduction of the waiting period to one day, and extended preventive care and hospital care on a mandatory basis.

270 It is true that the deliberations of the sickness insurance reform took place in a context of full employment and high trade union strength. However, unemployment had been declining throughout the 1950s, and during the deliberations of the pension reform in 1956 and 1957 it was also rather low (4.4 and 3.7 percent, respectively).

271 This term is borrowed from Arnold Heidenheimer in Arnold J. Heidenheimer, Hugh Heclo, Carolyn Teich Adams, *Comparative Public Policy*. 2nd ed., London, 1983, p. 65.

272 For an analysis of German social policy from the perspective of autonomous state interests, see Thomas Stahl and Michael Zängle, *Die Legende von der Krise des Sozialstaats*. Frankfurt, 1984.

273 As the labour force also includes persons below voting age, the table gives only a crude impression, somewhat overstating the electoral importance of economically active groups. Roughly 5 percent of the labour force are below 18 years; see Der Bundesminister für Arbeit und Sozialordnung, *Arbeits und Sozialstatistik. Hauptergebnisse*. Bonn, 1984, p. 18.

274 The only cutback here classified as a curtailment in an election year may be considered a special case. It refers to the 1953 loosening of housing controls which had been instituted by the Allied Powers. A similar pattern of legislative activities following the election cycle was found in a detailed study of social legislation up to 1968 by Hans-Peter Bank, *Sozialpolitik und Wahlpolitik*. Berichte des Deutschen Industrieinstituts zur Sozialpolitik 11. Köln, 1968.

275 With the exception of the March election of 1983 all German federal elections were held in Autumn.

276 See Der Bundesminister für Arbeit und Sozialordnung, *Materialband zum Sozialbudget 1983*. Bonn, 1984.

277 This excludes the laws passed under the control of the Allied Powers, the laws on civil service and public employees benefits which have not been analyzed in detail, and the 1969 constitutional amendment merely entitling the federal government to legislation in the educational sector.

278 This is based on the revised official data published in the 1983 social budget (see Der Bundesminister für Arbeit und Sozialordnung, *op. cit.*) and in Deutscher Bundestag, *Jahresgutachten 1984/85 des Sachverständigenrates zur Begutachtung der gesamtwirtschaftlichen Entwicklung* Bundestagsdrucksache 10/2541. Bonn, 1984 (GDP data). These revised data deviate somewhat from the figures in the older official sources presented in Appendix Tables 1 and 3.

279 See Der Bundesminister für Arbeit und Sozialordnung, *Sozialbericht 1983*. Bonn, 1984, p. 91.

280 In 1981 the average interest rate on the federal government's debt amounted to 12 percent; see Dieter Schäfer, 'Anpassung des Systems der sozialen Sicherung an Rezession und Unterbeschäftigung', *Sozialer Fortschritt* 32, 1983, pp. 121-134, here p. 129. In the presence of a federal debt of 273 billion DM in 1981, a reduction of the interest rate by two percentage points would have led to savings of roughly 5.5 billion DM which is almost equal to the

sums spent on education allowances and housing allowances together. The total cost of unemployment presently amounts to some 50 billion DM per year, if the reductions in tax revenues and social security contributions are added to the expenditure for unemployment compensation.

[281] The ups and downs of the inflation rate coincide almost perfectly with the changes in government from the Grand Coalition to the social-liberal government in 1969, from chancellor Brandt to Schmidt in 1974, and from social-liberal government to the new bourgeois coalition in 1982. It would be misleading, however, to blame or credit national policy-makers for these developments. As a comparison with the average inflation rate in 13 Western European countries shows, the development of the German cost-of-living index exactly reflects the fluctuations in the international environment, albeit on a much lower level.

[282] In a series of articles two scholars affiliated with the trade unions have analyzed and criticized the effects of the cutback legislation in detail; see Wilhelm Adamy and Johannes Steffen, *Sozialabbau und Umverteilung in der Wirtschaftskrise - Zum Vergleich der Wirtschafts- und Sozialpolitik in Bonn und Weimar*. Köln, Seminar für *Sozialpolitik*, 1983; and Wilhelm Adamy, Gerhard Naegele, Johannes Steffen, 'Sozialstaat oder Armenhaus?', *Sozialer Fortschritt* 32, 1983, pp. 193-200.

[283] More recent data have not been available.

[284] For strike data see Statistisches Bundesamt, *Bevölkerung und Wirtschaft 1872-1972*. Stuttgart, Mainz, 1972, p. 149, and Der Bundesminister für Arbeit und Sozialordnung, *Statistisches Taschenbuch 1984*. Bonn, 1984, Table 3.4.

[285] For the concept of welfare backlash, see Harold L. Wilensky, *The Welfare State and Equality*. Berkely, 1975, and Harold L. Wilensky, *The 'New Corporatism', Centralization and the Welfare State*. Beverly Hills, 1976.

[286] Total federal spending is planned to increase by 2.4 percent in 1986. In contrast, the budget of the Ministry of Labour is scheduled to grow by 3.5 percent, the budget of the Ministry of Family, Youth and Health even by 13.3 percent; see *Süddeutsche Zeitung*, July 1, 1985.

[287] See Adamy and Steffen, *op. cit.*

[288] For more complete quotations, see the documentation in Max Richter, *Die Sozialreform-Dokumente und Stellungnahmen*. Bad Godesberg, 1970, here volume G I 7, p. 27.

[289] In the early 1970s the prominent sociologist Helmut Schelsky published widely circulating pamphlets criticizing the new bureaucratic tutelage of the citizens; see his collection of articles and speeches in the period 1973 to 1975 in Helmut Schelsky, *Der selbständige und der betreute Mensch*. Stuttgart-Degerloch, 1976. In a more scholarly yet influential article, the sociologist Horst Baier characterized the welfare state from a Weberian perspective as a new type of domination, promoted by the interests of new 'distributional elites' - see Horst Baier, 'Herrschaft im Sozialstaat. Auf der Suche nach einem soziologischen Paradigma der Sozialpolitik', *In* Christian von Ferber and Franz-Xaver Kaufmann (eds), *Soziologie und Sozialpolitik*. Kölner Zeitschrift für Soziologie und Sozialpsychologie, Sonderheft 19. Opladen, 1984, pp. 128-142. At the same time translations of Ivan Illich's critical accounts of the disabling effects of professional experts became bestsellers in Germany.

[290] See Sozialbeirat, *Langfristige Probleme der Alterssicherung in der Bundesrepublik Deutschland*. Bonn, 1981, 3 vols.

[291] See *Die Zukunft des Sozialstaats*. Zwischenbericht der Arbeitsgruppe 'Sozialpolitisches Programm der SPD'. Bonn, 1984.

[292] See Winfried Schmähl, 'Geburtenentwicklung, Altersgrenze und Beitragssätze in der Rentenversicherung', *Sozialer Fortschritt* 32, 1983, pp. 217-220, here p. 219.

[293] For data on sickness insurance expenditure, see Der Bundesminister für Arbeit und Sozialordnung, *Statistisches Taschenbuch 1985*. Bonn, 1985, Table 8.2.

[294] See Karl Schwarz, 'Auswirkungen der rückläufigen Bevölkerungsentwicklung auf das Gesundheitswesen', *In* Bundesminister für Jugend, Familie und Gesundheit (ed.), *Konsequenzen des Geburtenrückgangs für ausgewählte Politikbereiche*. Band 58 der Schrif-

tenreihe des Bundesministers für Jugend, Familie und Gesundheit. Stuttgart, Berlin, Köln, Mainz, 1978, pp. 78-96.

295 *Statistisches Jahrbuch für die Bundesrepublik Deutschland 1984*, p. 61.

296 The following considerations owe much to two articles by Wolfgang Zapf. See Wolfgang Zapf, *The Welfare State and Welfare Production.* Stanford University, 1980; and Wolfgang Zapf, *The Future of the Welfare State: The German Case.* Sonderforschungsbereich 3, Arbeitspapier Nr. 148. Frankfurt/Mannheim 1984.

297 The sociological critique of the inflexibility of bureaucratic welfare state structures goes back to Hans Achinger, *Sozialpolitik als Gesellschaftspolitik.* Hamburg, 1958 (2nd ed. 1971), and Christian von Ferber, *Sozialpolitik in der Wohlstandsgesellschaft.* Hamburg, 1967. In 1980 the German Research Council initiated a large research programme under the topic 'State, intermediary structures, and self-help'. Sociological spokesmen of the current interest in self-help include Bernhard Badura, Peter Gross, Franz-Xaver Kaufmann, and Eckart Pankoke. For useful review articles of current debates, see Peter Gross, 'Der Wohlfahrtsstaat und die Bedeutung der Selbsthilfebewegung', *Soziale Welt* 33, 1982, p. 26-48, and Adrienne Windhoff-Héritier, 'Selbsthilfe-Organisationen. Eine Lösung für die Sozialpolitik der mageren Jahre?', *Soziale Welt* 33, 1982, pp. 49-65.

298 See the draft of a new social policy programme 'Die Zukunft des Sozialstaats', *op. cit.*

299 See Johano Strasser, *Grenzen des Sozialstaats?* Köln, 1983, 2nd ed.

300 See Meinhard Miegel, *Die verkannte Revolution (1)* Stuttgart, 1983.

301 The city of Berlin is currently subsidizing self-help groups including initiatives within the new alternative movements.

302 See Wolfgang Glatzer, 'Haushaltsproduktion', *In* Wolfgang Glatzer and Wolfgang Zapf (eds), *Lebensqualität in der Bundesrepublik. Objektive Lebensbedingungen und subjektives Wohlbefinden* Frankfurt, 1984, pp. 366-388; and Friedhelm Neidhardt, *Soziale Netzwerkhilfen und Unterstützungsprobleme in der Bevölkerung.* Bericht für das Bundeskanzleramt. Köln, 1985.

303 The surveys usually show that some two thirds of the respondents have at least once provided or received support from/for relatives or neighbours in recent years. Apart from the fact that this leaves a sizeable minority of people not integrated into informal networks of assistance, this does not indicate how regularly people could rely on assistance in case of need.

304 Presently roughly one fifth of all married couples have no children, more than one fourth have merely one child; see Deutscher Bundestag, *Die Lage der Familien in der Bundesrepublik Deutschland - Dritter Familienbericht* Bundestagsdrucksache 8/3120. Bonn, 1979, especially pp. 95-100.

Notes to and sources for tables and graphs

List of numbered sources

(1)   Appendix Table 1

(2)   Appendix Table 2

(3)   Appendix Table 3

(4)   Appendix Table 4

(5)   Appendix Table 5

(6)   Appendix Table 6

(7)   Appendix Table 7

(8)   Appendix Table 8

(9)   Appendix Table 9

(10) Appendix Table 10

(11)   Appendix Table 11

(12)   Appendix Table 12

(13)   Appendix Table 13

(14)   Appendix Table 14

(15)   Appendix Table 15

(16)   Appendix Table 16

(17)   Appendix Table 17

(18)   Appendix Table 18

(19)   Institutional Synopsis, Appendix Volume

(20)   *Allgemeine Bevölkerungsumfrage Sozialwissenschaften 1982* (Zentralarchiv für empirische Sozialforschung Köln No 1160).

(21)   *Allgemeine Bevölkerungsumfrage Sozialwissenschaften 1984* (Zentralarchiv für empirische Sozialforschung Köln No 1340).

(22)   S. Andic and J. Veverka, The Growth of Government Expenditure in Germany since the Unification, *Finanzarchiv* N.F. 33, 1964, pp. 169-278.

(23)   E. Ballerstedt, W. Glatzer (eds), *Soziologischer Almanach* Frankfurt, 1979.

(24)   V. Gräfin Bethusy-Huc, *Das Sozialleistungssystem der Bundesrepublik Deutschland.* Tübingen, 1965.

(25)   G. Brück, H. Eicher, *Perspektiven der Sozialpolitik* (Schriften der Kommission für wirtschaftlichen und sozialen Wandel 41). Göttingen, 1974.

(26)   Bundesministerium der Finanzen, *Finanznachrichten* 34, 1981.

(27)   Bundesministerium für innerdeutsche Beziehungen, *Deutschland 1971* (Bericht und Materialien zur Lage der Nation). Bonn, 1971.

(28)   Der Bundesminister für Arbeit und Sozialordnung, *Arbeits- und Sozialstatistik Hauptergebnisse.* Bonn, various years.

(29)   Der Bundesminister für Arbeit und Sozialordnung (ed.), *Bürger und Sozialstaat* (Forschungsbericht Sozialforschung 22). Bonn, 1980.

(30)   Der Bundesminister für Arbeit und Sozialordnung (ed.), *Herausforderungen der Sozialpolitik* (Forschungsbericht Sozialforschung 92). Bonn, 1983.

(31)   Der Bundesminister für Arbeit und Sozialordnung, *Materialband zum Sozialbudget.* Bonn, various years.

(32)   Der Bundesminister für Arbeit und Sozialordnung, *Sozialbericht.* Bonn, various years.

(33)   Der Bundesminister für Arbeit und Sozialordnung, *Statistisches Taschenbuch.* Bonn, various years.

(34)   Der Bundesminister für Arbeit und Sozialordnung, *Übersicht über die soziale Sicherung.* Bonn, various years.

(35)   Der Bundesminister für Bildung und Wissenschaft, *Bildungsbericht '70.* Bonn, 1970.

(36)   Der Bundesminister für Bildung und Wissenschaft (ed.), *Das soziale Bild der Studentenschaft in der Bundesrepublik Deutschland* (10. Sondererhebung des Deutschen Studentenwerkes). Bonn, 1983.

(37)   Der Bundesminister für Bildung und Wissenschaft, *Grund- und Strukturdaten.* Bonn, various years.

(38)   Deutscher Bundestag, *Jahresgutachten 1982/83 des Sachverständigenrates zur Begutachtung der gesamtwirtschaftlichen Entwicklung* (Bundestagsdrucksache 9/2118). Bonn, 1982.

(39)   Deutscher Bundestag, *Jahresgutachten 1984/85 des Sachverständigenrates zur Begutachtung der gesamtwirtschaftlichen Entwicklung* (Bundestagsdrucksache 10/2541). Bonn, 1984.

(40)   Deutscher Bundestag, *Rentenanpassungsbericht* (Bundestagsdrucksache). Bonn, various editions.

(41)   Deutscher Bundestag, *Verhandlungen des Deutschen Bundestages, Stenographische Berichte*. Bonn, various years.

(42)   Deutsches Institut für Wirtschaftsforschung, *DIW Wochenbericht*. Berlin, various editions.

(43)   P. Flora et al., *State, Economy, and Society in Western Europe 1815-1975* Vol. I. Frankfurt 1983.

(44)   W. Glatzer, *Wohnungsversorgung im Wohlfahrtsstaat*. Frankfurt, 1980.

(45)   M. Groser and W. Veiders, *Die Neue Soziale Frage*. Melle, 1979.

(46)   R. Hauser, Armut im Wohlfahrtsstaat - empirischer Befund und Lösungsansätze, in H. Lampert and G. Kühlewind (eds), *Das Sozialsystem der Bundesrepublik Deutschland* (Beiträge zur Arbeitsmarkt- und Berufsforschung 83). Nürnberg, 1984, pp. 214-263.

(47)   R. Hauser, H. Cremer-Schäfer, U. Nouvertné, *Armut, Niedrigeinkommen und Unterversorgung in der Bundesrepublik Deutschland*. Frankfurt, 1981.

(48)   R. Hauser, I. Fischer, T. Klein, *Verarmung durch Arbeitslosigkeit?* (Sonderforschungsbereich 3, Arbeitspapier Nr. 154). Frankfurt, 1984.

(49)   C. Helberger, Ziele und Ergebnisse der Gesundheitspolitik in der Bundesrepublik Deutschland, in W. Zapf (ed.) *Lebensbedingungen in der Bundesrepublik 1950-1975*. Frankfurt, 1978, pp. 677-741.

(50)   H.-J. Krupp, Das monetäre Transfersystem in der Bundesrepublik Deutschland - Elemente einer Gesamtbilanz, in H.-J. Krupp and W. Glatzer (eds), *Umverteilung im Sozialstaat*. Frankfurt, 1978, pp. 21-69.

(51)   R. Neef, Wohnungsversorgung und 'neue Wohnungsnot', *Leviathan* 9, 1981, pp. 332-353.

(52)   E. Noelle-Neumann and D. Piel (eds), *Allensbacher Jahrbuch der Demoskopie 1978-1983*. München, 1983.

(53)   Presse- und Informationsamt der Bundesregierung, *Gesellschaftliche Daten*. Bonn, various years.

(54)   R. Ruge, Bildung, in W. Zapf (ed.), *Lebensbedingungen in der Bundesrepublik 1950-1975*. Frankfurt, 1978, pp. 743-841.

(55)   K.-D. Schmidt, U. Schwarz, G. Thiebach, *Die Umverteilung des Volkseinkommens durch den Staat in der Bundesrepublik Deutschland 1955 und 1960*. Tübingen, 1965.

(56)   Sozialbeirat, *Langfristige Probleme der Alterssicherung in der Bundesrepublik Deutschland* Vol. I. Bonn, 1981.

(57)   Statistisches Bundesamt, *Bevölkerung und Wirtschaft 1872-1972*. Stuttgart-Mainz, 1972.

(58)   Statistisches Bundesamt, *Bildung im Zahlenspiegel.* Stuttgart-Mainz, various years.

(59)   (Statistisches Bundesamt), Das Personal der öffentlichen Verwaltungen und Betriebe, *Wirtschaft und Statistik* 3, 1951 (no 12), pp. 482-485.

(60)   Statistisches Bundesamt, *Das Wohnen in der Bundesrepublik Deutschland*. Stuttgart-Mainz, 1981.

(61)   Statistisches Bundesamt, *Die sozialen Verhältnisse der Renten- und Unterstützungsempfänger* (Statistik der Bundesrepublik Deutschland Band 137). Stuttgart-Köln, 1955.

(62)   Statistisches Bundesamt, *Statistisches Jahrbuch für die Bundesrepublik Deutschland*. Stuttgart-Mainz, various years.

(63)   Transfer-Enquete-Kommission, *Das Transfersystem in der Bundesrepublik Deutschland*. Stuttgart-Berlin-Köln-Mainz, 1981.

(64)   E. Wiegand, W. Zapf (eds), *Wandel der Lebensbedingungen in Deutschland*. Frankfurt, 1982.

(65)   Wissenschaftsrat, *Empfehlungen zu Umfang und Struktur des Tertiären Bereichs*. Köln, 1976.

(66)   D. Zöllner, *Öffentliche Sozialleistungen und wirtschaftliche Entwicklung*. Berlin, 1963.

Sources for tables

Table 1:	19
Table 2 :	26, 59
Table 3 :	31, 32
Table 4 :	31, and own calculations
Table 5 :	31, 34, and own calculations
Tables 6-7 :	28, 32, 33, 34, 37, 62, and own calculations
Table 8 :	19, 33, and own calculations
Table 9 :	46, 47
Tables 10-11 :	47
Table 12 :	48, and own calculations
Table 13 :	Own calculations based on raw data in 28, 34, 61
Table 14 :	23, 42 eds. 40, 1973 (no 25), 45, 1978 (no 32-33), 46, 1979 (no 29), 49, 1982 (no 4), and own calculations
Table 15 :	42, 50, 55, 63, and own calculations
Table 16 :	42 ed. 49, 1982 (no 4)
Table 17 :	Own calculations based on raw data in 42 eds. 46, 1979 (no 29) and 49, 1982 (no 4); 55
Table 18 :	Calculated from raw data in 49, 53, 57, 62
Table 19 :	62
Table 20 :	57, 62
Table 21 :	28, 44, 57, 60, 62, and own calculations
Table 22 :	27, 44, 51, 53, 60, and own calculations
Table 23 :	35, 37, 65
Table 24 :	23, 36, 37, 54, 58, and own calculations
Table 25 :	Calculated from data in 3, 4, 32, 39
Table 26 :	Calculated from data in 62
Table 27 :	Own calculations based on 1, 7, 28, 34, 62
Table 28 :	Own calculations based on 1, 11, 28, 33, 34, 62
Table 29 :	Calculated from data in 1, 39
Table 30 :	39, 57
Tables 31-35 :	Own calculations based on 1, 3, 31, 39
Table 36 :	Calculated from raw data in 19
Table 37 :	Own analysis based on 19, 41
Table 38 :	24, 25, 44, 54
Table 39 :	Own calculations based on 28, 57, 62
Tables 40-41 :	Calculated from raw data in 19
Table 42 :	Calculated from data in 3, 31
Table 43 :	19
Table 44 :	31, 33, 39, and own calculations
Table 45 :	39, and own calculations
Table 46 :	Own calculations based on 28, 33
Table 47 :	Laws listed in 19
Table 48 :	29, 30
Table 49 :	30, 52
Table 50 :	30

Table 51 :   21
Table 52 :   21, 20, 45 (and unpublished material from this survey kindly supplied by Konrad-Adenauer-Stiftung)
Table 53 :   21, 29, 45

Sources for graphs

Graph 1 :   Expenditure shares calculated from data in 1, 4, 7, 8, 9, 10, 22, 43, 57, 66
Graph 2 :   1, 2, 4
Graph 3 :   1, 3
Graphs 4-6 :   2
Graph 7 :   4
Graph 8 :   6
Graphs 9-10 :   7, 8 (raw data deflated with cost-of-living deflator)
Graphs 11-12 :   9 (raw data deflated with public consumption deflator)
Graph 13 :   8 (raw data deflated with cost of living deflator)
Graphs 14-15 :   10 (raw data deflated with cost of living deflator)
Graph 16 :   11 (raw data deflated with cost of living deflator)
Graphs 17-18 :   12 (raw data deflated with cost of living deflator)
Graphs 19-20 :   13 (raw data deflated with cost of living deflator)
Graphs 21-22 :   14 (raw data deflated with private consumption deflator)
Graphs 23-24 :   14 (raw data deflated with public consumption deflator)
Graph 25 :   15, 17
Graph 26 :   15
Graph 27 :   16
Graphs 28-29 :   15
Graphs 30-31 :   18
Graph 32 :   Calculated from raw data in 28, 34, 62
Graph 33 :   Calculated from raw data in 28, 32, 33, 34, 62
Graph 34 :   Calculated from raw data in 28, 31, 33, 34, 40, 62
Graph 35 :   Calculated from raw data in 31, 33, 34
Graph 36 :   28, 38, 57
Graph 37 :   Calculated from data in 28, 33
Graph 38 :   Calculated from data in 28, 31, 33
Graph 39 :   Calculated from data in 33, 38
Graph 40 :   28, 33, 62 (raw data), 64, and own calculations
Graph 41 :   53, 62
Graph 42 :   53
Graph 43 :   Calculated from data in 35, 37, 54, 57, 62, 65
Graph 44 :   Calculated from data in 37, 57, 58, 62
Graph 45 :   Calculated from data in 3, 31, 37
Graph 46 :   37, 62
Graphs 47-48 :   Calculated from data in 1, 7, 28, 33, 62
Graphs 49-50 :   Calculated from data in 1, 11, 28, 32, 34, 62
Graph 51 :   1, 39, and own calculations

Graphs 52-53 :   Calculated from data in 1, 3, 31, 37, 39
Graph 55 :   62
Graph 55 :   Calculated from data in 28, 31, 33, 39
Graph 56 :   56

United Kingdom

RICHARD PARRY

Contents

I Historical synopsis

1. The modern British welfare state: a product of World War II

The welfare state is an essential and continuing concept for understanding postwar British public policy, but it is no longer truly a contemporary concept. Rather, it expresses the British national experience in the 1930s and 1940s, representing an alliance of political rhetoric and mass bureaucratic processes at a specific historical period - World War II. The United Kingdom in the early 1980s is a very different polity and society. Economic difficulties, high unemployment and the persistence of poverty have replaced previous expectations of prosperity. Ideological divisions between the political parties have sharpened. As this chapter will show, the postwar years have seen a loss of political salience for the concept of welfare and, in most sectors, the relative stagnation of resource input relative to the rest of the economy. Institutional change has been minimal, and extension of clienteles has tended to be forced by economic and demographic pressures. Welfare programmes have entrenched themselves into public policy, supported by both political expectations and bureaucratic interests, but the ideal of the welfare state is no longer at the heart of British politics.

At the same time, the idea of the welfare state is the clue to a whole generation of British ideology and bureaucratic culture, promoting the idea of consensual social cohesion. The British welfare state rests on a fusion of traditions, a fact reflected in the character of commentaries and ideological perspectives on the welfare state. Following such writers as Parker (1975), George and Wilding (1978), Room (1979), and Pinker (1979), it is possible to distinguish two influential sets of attitudes: social democratic and administrative rationalist [1]. More ideologically thorough attitudes, like the neo-liberalism of Hayek and Friedman and the critical socialism of Marxist-oriented thinkers, have by contrast had little influence, although their scepticism about the ameliorative potential of the welfare state has enjoyed a recent intellectual resurgence.

The social democratic tradition is for many the characteristic expression of the British welfare state. Its giants - R.H. Tawney, T.H. Marshall, Richard Titmuss, Anthony Crosland and the Fabian movement - promoted new ideas of social policy, non-judgmental assessment of needs, and the mobilization of altruistic motivation. The achievement of social democratic thought was to elevate welfare provision from a set of economic transfers and motivators into a vision of new kinds of social behaviour. The extent to which this kind of vision might be disappointed in practice is all too clear, and the evolving thought of Richard Titmuss shows how this most penetrating of thinkers became aware of the limitations of the British achievement [2].

Administrative rationality is a less noble vision but in practice a more significant contribution to the British welfare state. People like William Beveridge, J.M. Keynes and a host of politicians and civil servants - what George and Wilding call the 'reluctant collectivists' - have produced a tradition of elitist, pragmatic state action. This is basically congenial to capitalism, and unites compassion to a distaste for the waste of resources inherent in unemployment and sickness. As Heclo emphasized, it is the British civil service that has been the guardian of political learning and the arbiter between interest groups [3]. The 'reluctant collectivist' set of assumptions has tended to absorb and neutralize the social democratic tradition and resist liberal and socialist critique.

For historical reasons, the British welfare state is broadly defined (comprising a comprehensive approach to life chances, including education, housing and personal social services, as well as income maintenance and health) and relies on public institutional provision of services rather than the regulation and subvention of private sector organizations. Allied to the comprehensive British system of public expenditure planning and control, comprising all levels of government, this means that the main welfare programmes provide an acceptable definition of welfare state activity, as long as some attention is paid to tax expenditures on housing and pensions.

At the start of the twentieth century, primary education was the only major social programme made available to an entire client group by the State. The 1870 Education Act set up local school boards in response to the weakness of the church schools, education becoming compulsory and free in 1891 and placed under local authorities in 1902. The first major departure from a minimalist welfare policy came with the 1906 Liberal government, which introduced old age pensions in 1908 and social insurance against unemployment and sickness in 1911. Although this scheme covered only a minority of the workforce, the ideological principle was conceded, and the following 30 years saw the gradual relaxation and extension of eligibility, mainly to keep the unemployed out of the Poor Law (the residual public relief system) at a time of economic depression. Although progress was made in public education, health and housing, the creative impulse of the welfare state progressed little from the 1910s to the 1940s.

The total national mobilization required to fight World War II was also conducive to a programme of social reconstruction. If there is a prototypical figure of the British welfare state it is William Beveridge, a master of the technical tasks of an expanding bureaucracy - assembling information, identifying complexities and proposing rational solutions. Beveridge had, as a civil servant, already organized the first labour exchanges in 1909-10 and had high-level responsibility for manpower and food policy during World War I, even before his academic interest in social insurance culminated in his chairmanship (and later sole author of the report) of the Committee on Social Insurance and Allied Services in 1941-42 [4]. This proposed an integrated, contributory, flat-rate and universal social insurance system covering unemployment, sickness, invalidity and retirement benefits, and buttressed by a national health service, family allowances and full employment economic policies. The Committee had been conceived as an administrative rationalization of the confused income maintenance system. Despite its immediate popular impact, Beveridge's programme was limited and carefully costed, designed to rely on private saving (especially because of its flat-rate nature), and inheriting administrative practices from the 1911 system.

As well as the Beveridge proposals, the Labour government of Clement Attlee, which won a striking victory in the general election of July 1945, inherited a remarkably positive spirit of reconstruction from the wartime coalition. In 1944 a Reconstruction Priorities Committee of the Cabinet had been established, and during 1944 a series of proposals was published. There were white papers on the National Health Service (NHS), and on full employment, marking the acceptance of the Keynesian regulation of demand and investment. The passage of the 1944 'Butler' Education Act giving free compulsory education from the ages of 5 to 15, an emergency housebuilding programme, and the acceptance of the principles of the Beveridge Report were also secured. Finally, the coalition government introduced the first universal non-means tested benefits - family allowances - in early 1945 [5].

The Labour government inherited a structure of expectations traumatized by disappointments after 1918 and during the 1930s, and having modest aims of protection and security. Labour had been influenced by a corporatist approach to politics during the war, when class interests, particularly organized labour, were absorbed into technocratic decision making; its cautious, patriotic leadership of 'authentic' working class leaders like Ernest Bevin and Herbert Morrison was not disposed to go beyond the economic constraints of the postwar situation. The wartime welfare state plans were implemented, with National Insurance and the National Health Service coming into operation in July 1948. Compared with the original proposals, Labour enacted more generous eligibility for pensions, rather more restrictive scale rates for welfare benefits, and the takeover of voluntary hospitals as one of the outcomes of Health Minister Aneurin Bevan's negotiations with medical interests. The result was that all income maintenance and hospital functions, previously administered through local government, became a central responsibility.

Welfare state legislation was not opposed by the Conservative Party in parliament (although they were unhappy about the organization of the National Health Service). The main effect of Labour implementation of the post-1945 welfare state was to secure an integrated public organization of the social services. This broke decisively with the tradition of public support for privately-organized services. The welfare state was enacted by the party ideologically more congenial to it, but on the basis of broadly consensual policies. The basic structure was accepted by both major parties. Many areas of social policy were insulated from the sharpest political debate, and never recaptured the central position in British public policy they enjoyed in the 1940s. Welfare policy has become increasingly disarticulated from economic questions, with the impulses to policy development being frustrated by the lack of resources. For long, and especially in the 1965-75 decade, welfare policy sought a trajectory of growth autonomous of the economy as a whole, but the return of a Conservative government in 1979 made the retrenchment of public sector activity a major theme of policy.

2. Major institutional developments since 1945: continuity and stagnation

1945 was not 'year zero' for the British welfare state. It marked a continuation of wartime policies and of progressive and consensual policy developments which reflected the political lessons of the 1930s and administrative lessons extending back decades. But in the postwar period the main institutional characteristic of the British welfare state was a relative absence of change. Table 1 shows that the major institutional arrangements for the social services date from the 1940s; and while the flat-rate basis of the income maintenance programmes has been amended, other changes have centred on administrative reorganization and left eligibility and financing little altered.

The institutional basis of the 1946 welfare state persists. At its core is the National Insurance contribution by all employees and employers (about 40 percent) and the state (about 20 percent), which gives entitlement to unemployment, sickness, maternity and industrial injury benefit and retirement pensions. The contribution includes a small element for the National Health Service, but this is financed largely from general taxation, and treatment is free without conditions, as is school education. The National Insurance system is supported by cash child benefits, means-tested public assistance and a variety of personal social services. The welfare state services have developed in scale and detail, but not in basic character. The greatest institutional changes have been within the framework of each service and each level of government; and many have

Table 1   Major institutional changes of the British welfare state, 1945-1982

Income Maintenance

1945   Universal flat-rate family allowances for all but first child in family
1948   National Insurance system: flat-benefits for retirement, widows, sickness and unemployment, with flat-rate contributions
1948   National Assistance: means-tested social assistance on uniform national scales
1961   Graduated state pension on money purchase basis for workers without occupational pension
1966   Earnings-related supplement for first 6 months of unemployment or sickness benefit
1966   Supplementary benefit, with legal entitlement, replaced national assistance
1971   Invalidity pensions introduced
1974   National insurance contributions earnings-related; pensions uprated anually in line with earnings or prices, whichever greater
1977   Child benefit for all children replaced family allowances and child income tax allowances
1978   State earnings-related pension scheme (SERPS), reflecting increases in earnings and prices, replaced graduated pensions
1980   Pensions indexed to prices only
1982   Earnings-related supplement to sickness and unemployment benefit abolished

Health

1948   National Health Service: free, universal health care, with hospitals managed by central government
1952   Charges for drug prescriptions and optical and dental treatment
1974   Major reorganisation of National Health Service: hospitals, family practitioner and community health services integrated under regional and area boards
1982   Further reorganisation, with area tier abolished

Education

1944   Education Act increased school-leaving age to 15; organised system into primary, secondary and further sectors; selective education according to ability to be the norm for secondary pupils
1965   Government request for local authorities to organise secondary schools on a comprehensive, all-ability basis
1971   School-leaving age increased to 16
1976   Public grants to some independent (direct-grant) schools ended

Housing

1946   New subsidy system for local authority housing, with contributions from central government, local taxations, and rents paid by tenants
1972   National rent rebate system to give means-tested assistance to public and private sector tenants
1980   Right for local authority tenants to buy their house at a discount according to length of residence
1982   Means-tested assistance with rent and rates (Housing Benefit) integrated under local authority administration

Personal social services

1970   Establishment of integrated Social Services Departments in local authorities to provide non-cash residential and home-based services to children, the elderly and others

been implemented slowly and incrementally. The clearest example is the replacement of selective secondary education by 'comprehensive' schools catering for all levels of ability, which was achieved by advice and exhortation from central government, especially in 1965, and by changing norms within the teaching profession rather than by Act of Parliament. Major changes in government organization - such as the creation of large, conglomerate central departments (e.g. the Department of Health and Social Security, and the Department of the Environment) between 1968 and 1970, or the reorganization of local government in 1974 - which reduced the number of authorities and redistributed powers between tiers - have tended to leave the structure and style of service delivery within each function intact.

It is a testament to the developed nature of the postwar welfare state that universal eligibility for public health, education and social security was achieved in the 1940s. There have been no takeovers of private sector functions on the scale of hospital and welfare functions in 1948. Private provision functions freely in all welfare sectors, but covers less than 10 percent of the relevant population in education and health services. 70 percent of houses were privately owned, and 52 percent of the employed population were covered by an occupational pension scheme in 1983 (against about 85 percent and 25 percent in 1950), but private provision here has been encouraged by fiscal policy. Nor has the distribution of social functions between levels of government greatly changed, the only major shift being the loss of local authority community health functions to the National Health Service in 1974.

Two major organisational changes have occurred. In 1970, local authority child care and personal welfare services were merged into unified social services departments, with a unified social work profession dealing with cases in a 'generic', non-specialized way. In 1974 the previously 'tripartite' organization of the National Health Service into hospital boards, general practitioner executive committees and local authority medical services was integrated under health authorities appointed and financed by central government. It is significant that the form of health service reorganization was dictated largely by negotiation with professional interests, and received little subsequent political or popular enthusiasm [6]. Similarly, the introduction of corporatist management techniques into local government before and during the 1974 reorganization, in an attempt to define objectives and processes in an integrated, non-departmentalist manner, produced little payoff for welfare services. The organization of welfare is not a prominent theme in British politics.

The most important new welfare benefit came with the enactment in 1975 of an earnings-related state pension scheme to provide a second pension (in addition to the national insurance retirement pension) to all those not covered by occupational schemes offering at least as good a benefit. The new scheme was due to come into operation over a period of 20 years from 1978 and reinforced the bias in the welfare system to pensions, which since 1973 have been increased at a faster rate than other benefits [7]. The other prominent change in income maintenance, the replacement of national assistance by supplementary benefits in 1966, was more cosmetic than real and did not alter the operation of the means-tested system; this, and a simplification of the scheme in 1980, served to make it rather less discretionary and stigmatising. A more insidious development has been the proliferation of other means-tested benefits, many delivered under health, housing and education programmes (such as free school meals or exemption from drug prescription charges).

Changes in methods of financing are of importance. Local government services are heavily supported by central grants, and these have gradually been consolidated into block grants allocated on the basis of needs indicators; over the years the proportion of central financing has increased, but since the late 1970s conflict between levels about aggregate spending has intensified, with local social expenditure - the predominant part of local authorities' budgets - a main target for expenditure cuts.

The British welfare state has always relied on financing from general taxation rather than charges at the point of service: the imposition of charges for drug prescriptions and medical and dental treatment in 1951 caused political controversy disproportionate to the sums raised, and there is a long-standing political reluctance to pursue this course. The most important change was the replacement of flat-rate by earnings-related national insurance contributions in 1974. This reflected a wish to make the contribution system less regressive and to make it possible to raise greater sums from insured persons and employers.

The change was paralleled by a shift from a flat-rate to an earnings-related approach to benefits. For long opposed by the Labour Party, because it would enshrine income differentials, and by the Conservatives, because it compromised the minimalist basis of welfare, it was forced on the parties by the growth of occupational pension schemes and the electoral payoff from going beyond flat-rate benefits. A minimal graduated (earnings-related) pension scheme was introduced in 1961, but this offered a poor rate of benefit and was replaced by the new, more comprehensive state pension scheme in 1975. Earnings-related supplements to sickness and unemployment benefits were introduced in 1966. In general, the need to finance increasing welfare expenditure dictated the levying of earnings-related contributions which are effectively an additional slice of income tax, without a corresponding level of benefit.

The sharpest point of discontinuity came with the election of Margaret Thatcher's Conservative government in 1979, and its confirmation in office in 1983. For the first time since the 1940s, a party in power sought seriously to re-evaluate the purpose and structure of the welfare state. Some changes were significant. Public sector house tenants were given the right to buy their homes at a discount in 1980; earnings-related supplements to sickness and unemployment benefits were abolished in 1982; flat-rate state pensions were indexed to prices, not earnings; the amount, though not the range, of health service charges was increased. Major proposals were made in 1985 to reduce the generosity of the state earnings-related pension scheme, in favour of compulsory private insurance, and to increase work incentives for social assistance recipients [8].

But in all the main areas of social policy, apart perhaps from housing, the continuity of organization, financing and entitlement with the 1940s has remained. The safety-net of social assistance supports many more people, especially the unemployed, but it has not been breached. The Conservatives have identified themselves with criticisms of the welfare state and its financial demands, but have wished to perpetuate the health, education and income maintenance services it offers. In the long time perspective, the forces of persistence and continuity remain stronger than those of change and disruption.

II   Resources and clienteles: descriptions

1.   Summary of public and social expenditure

Aggregate data on public expenditure and public employment provide a first approach to the place of the welfare state in the British polity and economy. Both indicators share common features: a high starting level after the immediate postwar innovations, and subsequent low but uneven growth. Public expenditure (Graph 1) was, at current prices, 34.9 percent of GDP in 1950 (having been 41.8 percent in 1946). After a peak of 38.0 percent in 1952, associated with high defence expenditure during the Korean war, the ratio declined until 1955 (33.7 percent). A slow increase then took it up to 36.3 percent in 1964, when a more unstable pattern takes over. A sharp rise to 42.2 percent in 1968, which coincided with the first years of the Labour government, was followed by stability until 1973. A combination of still rising public expenditure and falling real GDP then caused the two years of sharpest postwar increase (up to 49.6 percent in 1975), to be followed by the two years of sharpest postwar decline (to 43.3 percent in 1977) as the directions were reversed; modest growth then resumed. The

overall growth in the public element of national expenditure over the 30-year period
was less than 10 percentage points: there was no irreversible public sector encroachment on the economy.

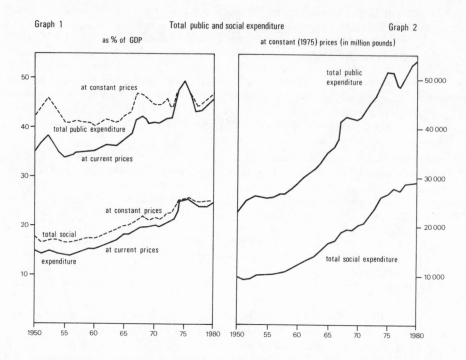

Graph 1   Total public and social expenditure   Graph 2

as % of GDP   at constant (1975) prices (in million pounds)

Public sector relative growth largely disappears when the measure is in constant prices. This represents the real volume of public services rather than their cost, and
allows for the relative price effect - the long-run tendency for the cost of government
services to rise at a faster rate than prices in the economy as a whole because of fixed
supply or lack of labour productivity growth. On this measure, the peaks in 1952,
1967 and 1975 are still evident, but overall growth is modest - from 42.2 percent in
1950 to 47.2 percent in 1980 (Graph 1). Most of the apparent increase in the relative
size of the British public sector is accounted for by the pattern of price movements[9].
The increase in the public share has been concentrated in only a few years, and in
four years (1954, 1969, 1976, and 1977) public expenditure has declined in real terms.
In absolute terms, both GDP and public expenditure have more than doubled - GDP
from UKL 54 billion in 1950 to UKL 114 billion in 1980, public spending (Graph 2)
from UKL 23 billion to UKL 54 billion (at 1975 prices). Graphs 1 and 2 show that
growth in social expenditure has been even faster and steadier, more than trebling
from UKL 9 to UKL 29 billion in constant prices, or from 17.5 to 25.5 percent of
GDP. These aggregate expenditure data are, of course, products of a variety of
internal movements, which are most appropriately analysed by socio-political function
(Graph 3), economic function (Graph 4), and level of government (Graph 5).

Graph 3 shows movements in the percentage share of public expenditure (at current
prices) by three main categories: social, economic growth (agriculture, industry,
employment and transport) and defence. The remaining 20 percent of the total comprises a heterogeneous group of functions, including law and order, debt interest and

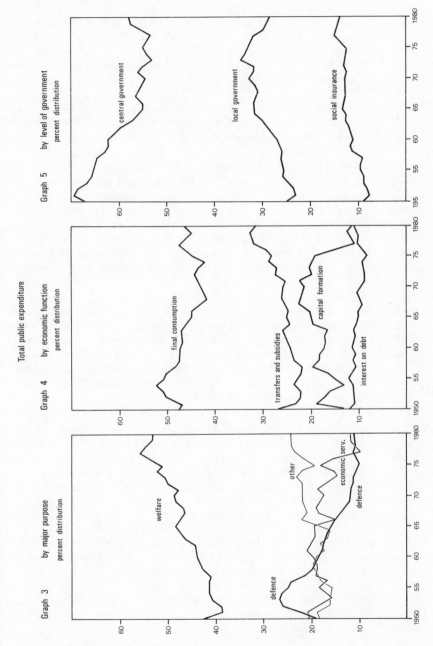

Total public expenditure

Graph 3
by major purpose
percent distribution

Graph 4
by economic function
percent distribution

Graph 5
by level of government
percent distribution

overseas aid, which have tended to increase in recent years. Social spending grew relative to the other categories in two phases: 1958 to 1966 and 1971 to 1977. Since 1972 it has accounted for over half of public spending. The share of defence spending declined almost continuously after 1957, and its 1980 level of 11 percent is almost half that of 1950. The most volatile category has been economic growth, heavily influenced by capital expenditure, which lost ground in most years - especially sharply after 1976 - punctuated by periodical upturns. Overall, social expenditure has been the gainer from the changing mix of public spending policies, but throughout the postwar period it has been the dominant category.

Disaggregation of public expenditure by major economic categories (Graph 4) provides an important clue to the changing character of British public policy. Four categories may be distinguished - final consumption, current grants and subsidies, debt interest, and capital formation. The largest is government final consumption (60 percent of which is accounted for by the salaries and wages of public employees), which declined as a proportion of public expenditure from 52.3 percent in 1954 to 41.8 in 1968 before a relative increase in the early 1970s to 47.3 percent in 1977 and 46.6 percent in 1980 - a pattern which is a central explanatory variable of the place in society of the public sector, because it measures how much is consumed within the governmental system.

Current grants and subsidies, or transfer payments (70 percent of which are social security payments) have been on an upwards track since 1957: over the whole period they increased from 24.4 to 32.3 percent of public expenditure, and 9.4 to 14.4 percent of GDP. A particular acceleration is evident from 1971 onwards. Constant price analysis reinforces the increasing prominence of public transfer payments, because price inflation in consumers expenditure (the most appropriate deflator for transfers spent by individuals) has been less than in government consumption (between 1956 and 1979, 374 percent as against 614 percent).

Debt interest is a more stable though still substantial slice of public expenditure at around 10 percent, although it has increased from 8.2 to 10.9 percent between 1975 and 1980 as large public borrowings at high rates of interest impose a funding burden for the future. The most striking pattern is in public capital investment, the most volatile economic category because of its ease of curtailment or expansion in the interests of economic policy. After a five percentage point fall as a share of public expenditure between 1951 and 1954, and a similar recovery by 1957, a stable trend persisted until 1963 when, for Keynesian motives of economic expansion shared by both main political parties, an investment spurt began which took its share up from 16.5 to 22.4 percent of public spending by 1968. After relative stability until 1975, the capital spending share then collapsed from 19.4 to 10.9 percent by 1977 before the decline was checked. In real terms the category declined from UKL 9.5 billion in 1974 to UKL 5.2 billion in 1977 (at 1975 prices). Until 1971, the size of transfer payments was similar to that of capital investment: by 1980 they were nearly three times as great. The trajectory of aggregate public expenditure during the 1960s and 1970s was largely accounted for by changes in capital investment, and in recent years the category has come to be used as a residual one for manipulation in order to secure cuts. The wider implications of the changing balance between capital and current expenditure have not been addressed systematically during this process.

Changes by level of government are analysed under three headings in Graph 5: central government; local government (elected local authorities which administer most of the non-cash social programmes); and the National Insurance Fund [10]. Three time phases may be distinguished. Firstly, from the early 1950s to the mid-1960s the balance between central and local government was shifting steadily to the local level (which rose from 24 to 32 percent of the total), not through any major decentralization of task but because the functional components of local expenditure were growing at a faster rate than public expenditure as a whole. Secondly, a more fluctuating pattern is evident from the mid-1960s to the mid-1970s, but with the trend to the local level continuing. Thirdly, since 1973, however, the local share has declined from the high 1973 level of 34.2 percent, and since 1975 there has been an absolute fall in local government expenditure in real terms; by 1980 the local share was no more than 28.4 percent.

Meanwhile, the National Insurance Fund has been on an almost continuous upwards trend, from 9 percent in the early 1950s to 13 percent in the mid-1960s before stabilizing. An acceleration in 1975-77 was caused by higher payouts of pensions at a time when other public expenditure was stable or falling. National Insurance Fund payments have continued to rise even in the years when other central government expenditure has fallen in real terms (1953-55, 1969, 1976-77), reflecting the expanding claims of entitlement programmes. Their trajectory is independent of the aggregate fluctuations at central and local level - but these should not be misinterpreted. The apparent centralization since 1973 is the reverse of the 1950s process: expenditure categories managed by central government have been growth areas. The fact that public expenditure as a whole is managed by central government - which provides over half the funds for local authorities - provides the centre with a great deal of scope for altering the balance between levels; but choices about public expenditure on a functional basis (with planning in terms of overall public sector programmes for defence, education, housing, etc.) are much more significant than any policy for centralization or decentralization.

Social expenditure

When the growth of social expenditure is disaggregated by service (Graph 6), it can be seen that income maintenance accounts for nearly half the total increase in constant price terms. From roughly similar real expenditure levels, income maintenance has run well ahead of health - though the latter has nearly doubled - and somewhat ahead of education, especially since 1970. Housing expenditure is more irregular, but with net growth over the period; personal social services had a concentration of growth in the 1965-75 period. It is noteworthy, though, that in the late 1970s two categories - education and housing- were tending to real decline and that income maintenance was maintaining the upward trend in social expenditure as a whole.

Within the total of social expenditure, the relative position of the main services fluctuated, but has not changed markedly when measured in current prices (Graph 7). Income maintenance took up 35 percent of the total in 1950 and reached 40 percent in 1980 after an irregular pattern of growth. Education and health had comparable shares in both 1950 and 1980 (at 20-25 percent), but between those dates education was the higher priority for public expenditure. It stood at over 25 percent of the social expenditure total from 1956 to 1973, but has since declined. Health's share fell from 25 percent in 1950 to 19 percent in 1969, but has since increased slightly.

Housing is the most volatile category, because it has a large component of capital expenditure which can change rapidly from year to year. Its share has been within the 12-20 percent range, falling markedly in the early 1950s and late 1970s. Personal social services has a small share of the total (under 4 percent), but this doubled between 1968 and 1974.

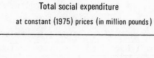

Graph 6

Total social expenditure

at constant (1975) prices (in million pounds)

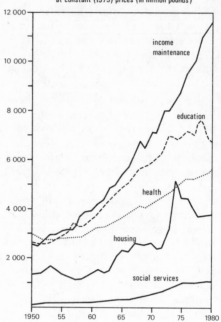

Graph 7

Total social expenditure

percent distribution

Graph 8

at current prices

at constant (1975) prices

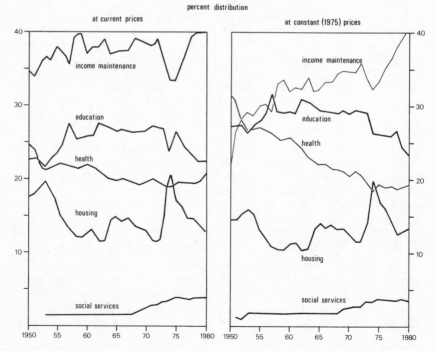

When the analysis is in constant (1975) prices (Graph 8) a rather different picture emerges. Income maintenance has increased, and education and health declined. The three services all had 25-30 percent of the total in the early 1950s, but since then a ranking of income maintenance first, education second and health third has appeared. This is because the rate of price increases for government consumption (principally the pay of public employees) has been faster than for prices as a whole. As a result the real value of services in labour-intensive education and health has fallen relative to that of the cash transfers in income maintenance.

Public employment

Data on public employment show a similar pattern of low but uneven growth from a high initial base, and comparable functional shifts over time. Over the postwar years the public sector has accounted for all the net gains in jobs in the British economy: between 1951 and 1981, 1.3 million public sector jobs were added, while the total employed workforce increased by no more than 0.7 million. Moreover, the growth is entirely concentrated in the decade 1966-76. Between 1951 and 1966 the public sector share of employment fell from 26.6 to 24.3 percent; from 1966 to 1976 it rose by seven percentage points, or 1.6 million jobs, over 1.2 of which were in the main social services (Table 2). As other sections of the public sector workforce have tended to decline, for instance, defence (military and civilian) from 1,228,000 in 1951 to 561,000 in 1981, social policy fields have become increasingly important. Their share of the workforce has nearly trebled, from 5.4 percent in 1951 to 14 percent in 1981, and is now nearly half of public employment.

Table 2			Public employment				
	1951	1956	1961	1966	1971	1976	1981
			in 1,000s				
Education	618	700	833	1 087	1 393	1 671	1 616
Health	492	549	627	727	839	1 190	1 316
Personal social services	116	142	170	228	276	320	370
Social security	58	47	54	61	72	92	100
Total social	1 284	1 438	1 684	2 103	2 580	3 273	3 402
Total public	6 284	6 150	5 940	6 161	6 821	7 802	7 632
Total workforce	23 602	24 515	24 457	25 355	24 399	24 765	24 323
			as % of total workforce				
Total social	5.4	5.9	6.9	8.3	10.6	13.2	14.0
Total public	26.6	25.1	24.3	24.3	27.9	31.5	31.4

Of the 3.4 million social employees, 2.5 million are women, over half of them part-timers. Within the total, education, health and the personal social services have increased at comparable rates, but a noteworthy feature is the stability of education employment since 1975. Staff administering social security have increased far more slowly despite the increase in the volume of payments and number of beneficiaries. Overall, the level of social employment in the workforce remains at only about half that of social expenditure in the GDP, because so much of income maintenance expenditure is in the form of transfer payments without direct employment implications.

But the rate of growth of employment has been faster, and in practice the public social services have been the most dynamic sector of the labour market, providing both public services and employment opportunities.

2. Single programmes: expenditure and institutional change

Public expenditure on welfare in Britain is not planned in an integrated approach to client groups and their social needs. It is rather an amalgam of programmes, institutions and delivery systems, even though the social problems they confront are frequently similar. In particular, benefits in cash and in kind tend to be planned and administered separately, and the various professions in health, education and social work have a distinct institutional identity. While social conditions integrate human need, public policy fragments it; and so much discussion of the welfare state needs to be in terms of single programmes - cash benefits in the form of pensions and sickness, unemployment, family and social assistance, and services in kind in education, health and personal social services, and housing.

Income maintenance

All social programmes have grown in real terms in the postwar period, but the largest and fastest growing sector is that of income maintenance. In real terms it has increased fourfold over the period, from 4.8 to 9.8 percent of GDP and from 27 to 40 percent of social expenditure. Graph 6 shows the steady acceleration of growth until 1968; growth with some interruptions from then until 1976, and marked and continuous growth since 1976 fuelled by the indexation of benefits, the replacement of child tax allowances by cash child benefit, and high unemployment.

Income maintenance has two components: 65 percent (up from 58 percent in 1950) is paid from the National Insurance Fund, which provides flat rate benefits in return for predominantly earnings-related contributions. The present scheme dates from 1948 and replaced earlier, less comprehensive schemes which started with Lloyd George's 1912 scheme. It covers the entire workforce, including the self-employed; funds come roughly equally from the insured and their employers, with a contribution of about 20 percent from the state. Adjustment of these shares is at the discretion of Parliament. Payment requires the satisfaction of minimum contribution conditions (broadly, a continuous record during the previous year). Some benefits are only paid for a limited period (notably unemployment benefit for up to one year), and additions to benefit are paid for adult and (sometimes) child dependants. The remaining expenditure is on non-contributory benefits, mostly child benefit (payable in cash at a flat rate to the mothers of all infant and school-age children) and supplementary benefit (public assistance payable to the non-working needy, most of whom are the elderly or unemployed lacking a national insurance entitlement). The distinction between the two income maintenance categories is one of entitlement rather than of administration or clientele. Central government administers both (through the Department of Health and Social Security), and in practice non-contributory benefits fill the gaps in the national insurance system up to a similar level of financial support.

Pensions

The components of income maintenance expenditure are disaggregated in Graphs 9 and 10. About half of the total is spent on retirement pensions, which have increased

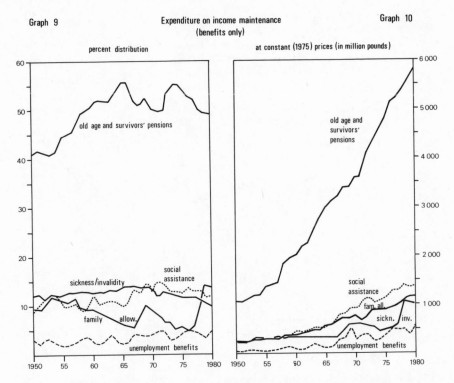

Graph 9   Expenditure on income maintenance   Graph 10
(benefits only)

percent distribution   at constant (1975) prices (in million pounds)

fivefold in constant prices. The dominance of retirement pensions within all long-term pensions is illustrated in Graph 11. These account for nearly all national insurance benefit for the elderly, since they replace widows' and invalidity pensions at retirement age (65 for men, 60 for women). The right to a pension in old age has always been the centrepiece of the British welfare state. In a departure from the Beveridge suggestion that the right to a pension should be phased-in, immediate payment was made to the great majority of the elderly in 1948 on the basis of contributions paid under a 1925 scheme. The exceptions were those over 55 in 1948 who lacked contributions: it was agreed that these 'late-age entrants' would qualify for a pension after ten years, and 400,000 were admitted in 1958, but a new group who were already retired in 1948 had to wait until 1970 when the 128,000 still alive were granted a pension on a non-contributory basis. In 1948, 4.3 million persons qualified for retirement pensions, but 470,000 in the non-qualifying groups had to rely on a means-tested national assistance benefit. There were also more than 1 million war pensioners.

Cash payments to the elderly have three components: the basic flat-rate pension under the 1948 scheme; earnings-related additions under schemes of 1961 and 1975; and means-tested supplementary pensions for those whose needs, including housing costs, still exceed what they receive. The 1948 scheme followed Beveridge's idea of a flat-rate pension (though at a higher rate for married couples) in return for flat-rate contributions. But an increasing number of the retired also received an earnings-related occupational pension from their employers: in 1983, 52 percent were covered, concentrated in white-collar occupations, including recipients of the non-contributory civil service scheme, against 27 percent in 1953 [11]. In 1961 a minimal state graduated scheme was introduced to provide supplementation for those not so covered, but the

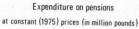

Graph 11

Expenditure on pensions

at constant (1975) prices (in million pounds)

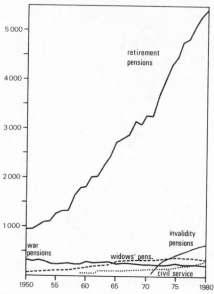

build-up of benefits was slow and the amount paid small and non-indexed: by 1980 it was no more than 2 percent of the flat-rate pension.

Political pressure for a more ambitious approach mounted, especially after the Labour Party abandoned its earlier commitment to flat-rate pensions in its policy document of 1957, *National Superannuation*. The first two initiatives failed to come into effect. Labour's National Superannuation and Social Insurance Bill was lost at the 1970 general election, and the Conservatives' 1975 Social Security (Pensions) Act was not implemented. Conflict between the parties and with private pension interests was a continuing undercurrent of the debate, and the State Earnings-Related Pension scheme (SERPS) that came into operation in 1978, on the basis of Labour's 1975 Social Security (Pensions) Act, was a compromise. Less strictly funded than the 1973 scheme but more generous to private pensions than Labour's earlier one, it pays a pension on the basis of the best 20 years' contributions during the recipient's working life (and is thus favourable to many women), is earnings-related up to one and a half times average earnings, and inflation-proofed. Employers may contract their employees out if they offer an occupational scheme which is at least as good as the state scheme; the inflation-proofing of this 'guaranteed minimum pension' is underwritten by the state. Most such schemes are funded, but that for civil servants is financed directly out of taxation (Graph 11).

The third component of cash assistance to the elderly - means-tested supplementary pensions - provides additional support to a substantial minority of pensioners, although its importance has declined in the 1970s as the real value of retirement pensions has increased. Although the income threshold for supplementary benefit is less than the basic pension (UKL 34.10 against UKL 35.80 for a single person in 1984), the former benefit also pays actual housing costs, and so many elderly with no resources other than their state pension are eligible. The former role of means-tested pensions as a fallback for the elderly without any other entitlement is now minimal since the reforms of 1958 and 1970, and the amount received is typically small. In 1980, 1.7 million of the 9 million retirement pensioners were receiving a supplementary pension, compared with 1.8 million out of 7.5 million in 1970. Part of this apparent fall is due to the transfer of many pensioners to means-tested housing benefits administered by housing authorities, and by a failure of eligible persons to claim [12].

The elderly also receive substantial assistance in kind through the personal social services departments of local authorities in the form of residential care, day care, home helps and meals. Since 1970 these services have been organised alongside those for physically and mentally handicapped children and adults and the socially deprived in the social service departments of local authorities, directed by professional social workers. They have only a very restricted right to make direct cash payments. 'Community care' has become an object of policy, but in practice integration between health, housing, social security and personal social services is weak.

Sickness and invalidity benefits

The next largest income maintenance category is sickness and invalidity benefits, which accounted for UKL 2.9 million or 13 percent of the total in 1980. Sickness benefit was, until 1982, paid after three waiting days, to national insurance eligible persons incapable of work through sickness or disability. Those incapacitated through industrial injury or disease receive an injury benefit at a higher rate. From 1948 to 1971 sickness benefit was the only non-means-tested benefit available to those sick and disabled from causes not related to work, although it was payable without a time limit. In the 1970s, provision for this group - whose numbers showed no signs of declining - was expanded. In 1971, a national insurance invalidity pension was introduced to take over from the sickness benefit after a period of six months at a rate some 25 percent higher: more people now receive this than the older benefit. A gap in the system was filled in 1975 when a non-contributory invalidity pension was introduced for those without a national insurance entitlement - usually because they were too ill ever to have worked - although the rate was much lower. Other major new benefits were the attendance allowance (payable from 1971 to disabled people requiring constant attention) and the mobility allowance (a cash payment, from 1976, to assist the disabled to get about, and which may be applied to the purchase of a car under a special scheme). As a result, cash support for the sick and disabled increased by 73 percent in real terms between 1971 and 1980. Nevertheless, a contrary tendency is evident from 1980 with the abolition of earnings-related supplement to sickness benefit (first paid in 1966) and the introduction in 1982 of a 'statutory sick pay' scheme which transfers to employers the responsibility for paying benefit on a flat-rate basis during the first eight weeks of sickness. This latter scheme reflects the fact that many employers already maintained salary during initial periods of sickness.

Unemployment insurance and employment policy

Unemployment benefit, accounting for 5 percent of income maintenance expenditure, or UKL 1.1 billion in 1980, covers an important area of personal contingency but is of small weight in social policy provision. This is because many of the unemployed fail to qualify for it. It is paid for a maximum of one year (at the same rate as sickness benefit) on the normal national insurance condition of having paid contributions through all the previous financial year. This excludes the long-term and young unemployed, two groups which have increased in recent years: the proportion of the unemployed receiving this benefit declined from 70 to 40 percent in the period 1961-1979. Most of the remainder receive supplementary benefits which yield at least the same amount since the earnings-related supplement on unemployment was abolished in 1982 (see Graph 12). Since the amount of supplementary benefit paid to the unemployed has been calculated separately (from 1976), it has always exceeded unemployment benefit, and was three times as great in 1984. Still, expenditure on unemployment benefit has been sensitive to the rapid rise in the number of unemployed to over 3 million by 1982: it doubled in real terms between 1973 and 1976, and rose by a real 47 percent in 1980 alone. This is a faster rate of growth than retirement pensions despite less favourable indexation since 1974 which broke the previous parity of benefit between the two. Unemployment benefit remains the most volatile category of cash support even though the total number of unemployed is more volatile yet.

Graph 12

Expenditure on unemployment
at constant (1975) prices (in million UKL)

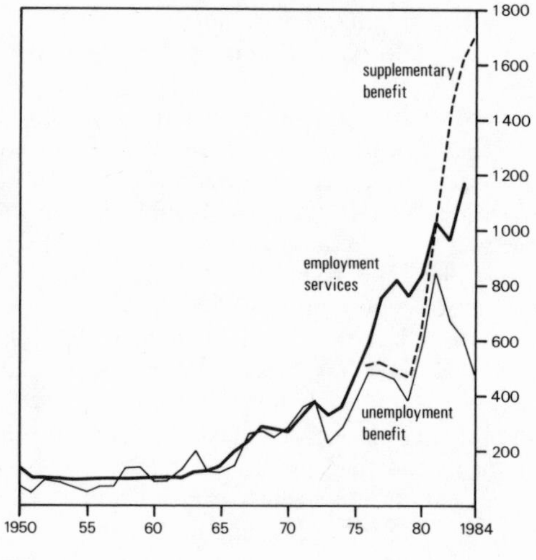

Of comparable expenditure size are the various services in kind provided for the unemployed. Expenditure on them trebled in real terms between 1974 and 1981 (see Graph 12). These have two forms: a long-established network of employment exchanges to match job seekers with employers' vacancies, with special services for the young school-leavers and the disabled; and special employment and training measures developed since 1975 to cope with high unemployment. Some of these latter have been little more than unemployment substitutes, such as the job creation programme (1975-78), the temporary employment subsidy (1975-80), and short-time working compensation (1980). The policy trend has been to promote schemes with a long-term training element, notably the Youth Opportunities Programme (1976) which by 1981 was providing work experience for 360,000 unemployed school-leavers, and was replaced in 1983 by the more comprehensive Youth Training Scheme (YTS). This, and other government-sponsored training schemes are sponsored by the Manpower Services Commission, whose expenditure increased by 70 percent in real terms in the period 1975-1981[13].

Families and children

Family support has occupied the most variable position in British income maintenance programmes (see Graph 13). Currently, it accounts for 18 percent of the total, second only to support for the elderly [14]; but until the mid-1970s it ranked below both unemployment and sickness support. The category includes maternity grants and allowances, which amounted to UKL 163 million in 1980; these are normally based on a husband's national insurance contribution. There is also, since 1975, a statutory right to unpaid maternity leave. Much more important is the UKL 2.9 billion paid in 1980 in child benefit, a flat-rate cash payment without contribution conditions paid to the mothers of all children. Phased-in from 1977 to 1979, this replaced family allowances (a smaller cash benefit paid from 1946, but not for the first child) and tax relief for children on a wage-earner's income tax bill. Upratings of family allowances were infrequent, and the total real value of the two benefits declined steadily.

Graph 13

Expenditure on family benefits
at constant (1975) prices (in million UKL)

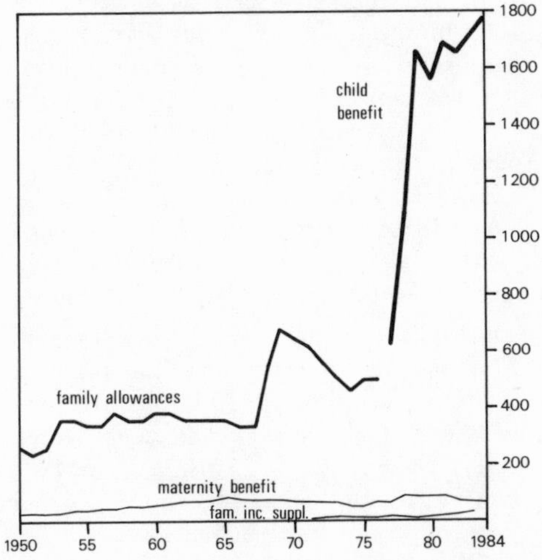

This changed in the 1970s. Awareness of the key role of child support in assisting the working poor led to the introduction of the consolidated child benefit payable to the mother alone and at a higher rate. Real cash expenditure increased from UKL 0.6 billion in 1977 to UKL 1.65 billion in 1979, but about UKL 0.5 billion of this represents the shift from tax to direct expenditure. Unlike other cash benefits, child benefit is not automatically index-linked, and since 1979 increases have been irregular and have not always matched prices.

A by-product of the same concern with child poverty is the Family Income Supplement (FIS), payable to poor families where the head of the household has been employed since 1971. Although coverage and costs are low (less than UKL 27 million in 1980), reflecting the means-tested nature of the scheme, its low qualifying limit and poor take-up rates, it is notable as one of the few means of regular additional cash support to those in work - always a weak area in the theory and practice of the British welfare state. Intended as a temporary measure before a full income tax credit scheme could be introduced, FIS has become a permanent scheme. In expenditure terms, it is eclipsed by other kinds of family assistance delivered through education and social services programmes: subsidized school meals and milk (UKL 400 million in 1980), higher education maintenance awards (over UKL 800 million), and residential care for deprived children (over UKL 250 million). Conceptually disparate, these programmes represent a commitment of public resources which is not clearly targeted to need.

Social assistance

The social assistance safety-net of the British income maintenance system is supplementary benefit (previously known as national assistance until 1966). Although the name has changed and benefit is a legal right theoretically without stigma, the concept remains the same: a cash payment to heads of households out of work to bridge the gap between income (from all sources, including other welfare benefits) and an officially defined poverty line. This line is composed of a scale rate for notional household needs (according to the number of dependents and with a higher rate for long-term recipients, except the unemployed) and actual housing costs. The use of actual housing costs reflects the wide range of rent levels which do not conform to a single scale. Supplementary benefits have come to serve as a permanent fallback for the coverage deficiencies inherent in the inflexible rules of national insurance: they are neither a systematic response to poverty nor a dwindling residuum. Expenditure increased six-fold in real terms between 1950 and 1980, the share of income maintenance total rising from 9 to 12 percent. Until the mid-1970s, growth was steady, and fastest after 1966 when take-up was encouraged. Subsequently, the main influence has been the trend of unemployment. There has been a long-run trend for supplementary benefit recipients who are unemployed or single-parent families to increase, and those who are sick and elderly to stabilize and tend to decrease: this reflects the improvement in the other cash benefits available to the latter two groups.

Three recent institutional changes in the supplementary benefit system are notable, even before the major Conservative review of 1985. In response to its growing cost, and especially a reliance on discretionary additions to the scale rates to meet occasional or regular needs (e.g. high heating bills, special diet and clothing, etc.) a team of officials produced a review, Social Assistance, in 1978 [15]. This suggested a rationalization of the scheme at no net extra cost, and this was implemented in part in 1980. At the same time, the Supplementary Benefits Commission, an appointed body that had administered the scheme since 1966, was abolished and staff reported directly to the Department of Health and Social Security. Thirdly, a major rationalization of housing benefit took place in 1982, involving the transfer of all housing support to rent rebate schemes operated by local authorities since 1968 [16]. Previously, the two slightly different means-tested housing schemes had run parallel to each other. A variety of other means-tested benefits exist outside the social security system, such as free school meals and student grants.

Health services

The fact that the United Kingdom has a free, universal National Health Service without eligibility conditions and with no charges for hospital services has reduced the importance of sickness cash benefits. Health service expenditure, most of which is accounted for by the salaries and wages of employees, amounted to UKL 11.5 billion in 1980, almost four times as great as sickness benefit. This represents 21 percent of social expenditure and 5.4 percent of GDP. The growth trajectory since 1950 has been stable and positive, with expenditure doubling in real terms, but it has failed to match the growth rate of aggregate social expenditure, with its share declining from the 31 percent held in 1950. This reflects the stability of policy since the National Health Service came into operation in 1948. The structure of the service represented a compromise with medical interests, though the Minister of Health at the time, Aneurin Bevan, secured a high degree of public corporate organization: all the previous voluntary and local authority hospitals were organized under boards appointed by central government, with hospital doctors becoming salaried employees. For 25 years there was no institutional change. The main political issue was the marginal one of charging for some services. In 1951 the Labour government compromised the free National Health Service by introducing charges for part of the cost of drug prescriptions outside hospitals, and dental and optical treatment. Drug charges were abolished in 1965 but reintroduced, with wider exemptions, in 1968. By 1980 charges amounted to only 3 percent of the gross cost of the National Health Service, though present policy is to increase the contribution they make.

The main preoccupation of the National Health Service during the 1960s and 1970s was managerial. During the 1960s the personal social services (the child care and welfare (non-cash) services of local authorities) developed into the social work profession. Unified departments were formed in 1970, and expenditure doubled in real terms betweej 1968 and 1973 (by 1980 it had reached UKL 2.1 billion, 3.8 percent of the social total). Health service reorganization followed in 1974, the culmination of proposals issued in 1968, 1970 and 1971. The effect of the policy debate, crossing a change of government, was to strengthen a regional tier of organization and provide safeguards for the professions. The new structure of regional and area health authorities integrated the various parts of the National Health Service at the price of organizational complexity, with parallel structures for each profession. Subsequent disillusionment about the effect of the reorganization on patient care, expenditure cutbacks and industrial disputes led to the appointment of a Royal Commission which in 1979 recommended greater emphasis on the role of preventative medicine, simplified administration, and a review of arrangements for negotiating pay and settling disputes [17]. The Conservative government of 1979 abolished one tier of administration, rescinded plans to phase-out private 'pay beds' from National Health Service hospitals, and encouraged the growth of private health insurance.

Education

Education expenditure more than trebled in real terms in the period 1950-1980, thus growing more slowly than social security and faster than health or housing, and rising from 3.3 to 5.5 percent of GDP. As a proportion of social expenditure it reached its peak in 1957 at 27.4 percent, declining to 22.4 percent by 1980 following the start of a definite downwards trend in 1973. Since 1978 education expenditure has fallen both in real terms and as a proportion of GDP. Uniquely among the social services, the principles of education organization were settled before the end of the war (by the 1944 Education Act), and have not changed in fundamentals since: education is free, compulsory from the age of 5 to 15 (16 since 1971), and divided into primary and secondary schools, operated by the local authorities, and several sorts of higher education, all with substantial public financing. Private sector education is of limited importance and accounts for only 6 percent of all pupils.

The two main educational issues have been the expansion of higher education and the principle of secondary school organization. By the 1960s the Labour Party was backing comprehensive secondary schools catering for all abilities in place of the 1944 system of selection to a 'grammar' or 'secondary modern' school by examination (the 11-plus, taken at that age, which sought to grade children by ability). Through circulars, the Labour government requested authorities to submit plans for comprehensive reorganization (1965) and the Conservatives adopted a more permissive approach (1970). It was only in 1976 that a Labour government passed legislation to insist on their policy, and this was repealed in 1979.

The expansion of higher education was a principal policy aim for 20 years, from the mid-1950s to the mid-1970s, the main impetus coming from a series of official reports on the grounds of both social equity and national economic efficiency. In 1958-59 the government approved the foundation of seven new universities, and in 1963 the Robbins Report [18] called for university places to be made available to all qualified applicants and Colleges of Advanced Technology (run by local authorities) to be given university status. In 1966 a 'binary' system of higher education was introduced, with non-university institutions organised into polytechnics and able to offer a wide range of degree level courses. In 1971 the Open University was established, offering non-residential degrees without formal entrance requirements though part-time correspondence, radio and television courses and summer schools. It was not until the mid-1970s that the policy climate changed. In 1975 there were major cutbacks in the intake to teacher training, and in 1981 a curtailment of public financing of universities, to amount to 8 percent in real terms over three years, was instituted.

Housing

The most variable element of social expenditure is housing, which has fluctuated at around 10-15 percent of the total, representing real growth of 175 percent between 1950 and 1980. There is also considerable tax expenditure in the form of mortgage interest relief, which by 1980 amounted to over a quarter of the total of direct expenditure on public housing construction and rent subsidies; there is also relief from capital gains tax when a principal residence is sold (see Graph 14). Major housebuilding programmes were pursued in the early 1950s, mid-1960s and mid-1970s which accounted for the peaks in housing expenditure in those years. The main areas of political conflict were the generosity of rent subsidy to public housing and the degree of rent and tenure control of private rented sector. Both of these tended to increase until the return of the 1979 Conservative government. The coincidence of a housebuilding programme and a rent freeze pushing up subsidies caused housing expenditure to exceed that on health for the only time in 1974. Subsequently, direct housing expenditure moved into sharp decline in real terms, falling by 29 percent between 1974 and 1978, with the subsidies element of the total increasing from 17 percent to 31 percent as cuts were concentrated on investment (Graph 14).

3. Financing

Given the predominant position of the social services in the British public policy, the expenditures that they generate must have a corresponding impact on the revenue side. Financing the welfare state has required higher levels of taxation, the develop-

Graph 14

Expenditure on housing
at constant (1975) prices (in million UKL)

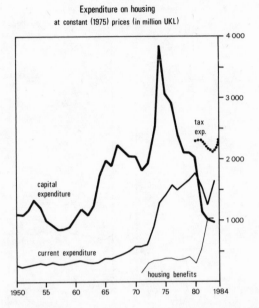

ment of new kinds of taxes, the extension of social insurance contributions, and higher levels of public borrowing. What have been avoided are heavy charges at the point of use. Fees for drug prescriptions and dental and optical treatment account for about 10 percent of the total of family practitioner health services, and rents are naturally the main element of current revenue for public sector housing, but elsewhere charges to users are minimal. The general pattern has been one of fiscal pressure on taxpayers as a whole to meet the cost of benefits which are increasingly universal in character.

Analysed as a proportion of GDP, total public revenue falls into three distinct periods. From 1950 to 1966 it was in the 33-37 percent range; from 1966 to 1970 it increased rapidly to nearly 50 percent, as a means of deflating domestic demand as well as raising revenue, only to fall back to 41 percent by 1972; and since then there has been stability within the 38-42 percent range (Graph 15). Taxes on capital are only a small part of this (less than 1 percent in most years); the bulk of revenue is in current receipts, made up of direct taxes (principally personal income tax, but also including corporation tax on company profits), indirect taxes (value-added tax, local property tax ('rates') and a variety of specific duties on the pleasures of life (motoring, alcohol, tobacco and betting)) (Graph 16).

The chief impulse to this revenue pattern came from the need to finance public expenditure; the British political system has always been preoccupied by a wish for strict accounting. The success in doing this is reflected in the relatively low size of the public sector deficit [19]. In the 1950s and early 1960s the deficit fluctuated according to the stage of the economic cycle at around 2-3 percent of GDP. In 1967 it rose to 4.3 percent, but was entirely eliminated by the deflationary tax increases which followed the devaluation of the pound in 1967; in 1970 there was a budget surplus. From 1972 onwards the expansionary policies of both Conservative and Labour governments, which they sought unsuccessfully to reconcile with tax cuts, caused the deficit to rise,

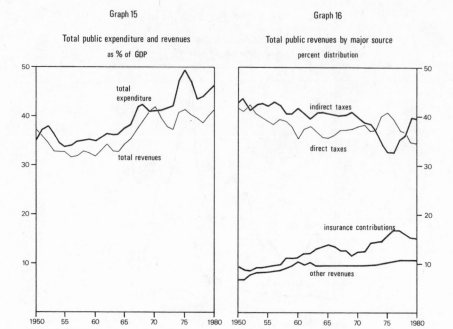

Graph 15

Total public expenditure and revenues
as % of GDP

Graph 16

Total public revenues by major source
percent distribution

to a high of 8.2 percent of GDP in 1975, equivalent to 16.6 percent of government expenditure. Thereafter, the deficit has been contained, though at a higher level than in the 1950s. The IMF-inspired cuts of 1976 reduced it to 3.4 in 1977, and a subsequent upwards movement was rolled back by the 1979 Conservative government under their 'medium-term financial strategy'. By 1981 it was back to 3.4 percent, a unique response to recession by a Western government.

Britain has an efficient tax collection system which provides high predictability of the effects of policy decisions. For income tax, pay-as-you-earn (PAYE) automatically deducts tax from gross pay through the employer without, in most cases, employee self-assessment. This system is aided by the apparently small size of the 'black economy' by international standards (although this appears to be increasing). As well as standard deductions for single and married persons, there are important tax expenditures on the interest on mortgage loans for house purchase, and on occupational pension schemes. Those are estimated to amount to UKL 3.5 billion each in 1984-85 [20].

The main indirect tax until 1973 was purchase tax, levied at the point of sale on what were defined as 'luxury' goods, principally consumer durables. The introduction of value-added tax to conform with European Community practice created a potentially higher revenue base, although this was not realized at first because of the low uniform rate (10 percent) and the wide range of exemptions. National insurance contributions, the only earmarked welfare tax, has become a further, though more regressive, slice of income tax, collected through the PAYE system. The main areas of failure in the British fiscal system are in company taxation - where a wide range of reliefs has become the rule - and inheritance tax - where a move from estate duty to capital transfer tax in the early 1970s was made subject to generous exemptions. Attempts by Labour governments to devise a wealth tax have also failed. As a result the main fiscal burden has fallen on the average taxpayer.

Graph 16 shows that the British fiscal structure has been one of comparable levels of direct and indirect taxes, with a lower level of social security contributions. The level of direct taxation is closely associated with the party in government; it fell from 14 to 11 percent of GDP during the 1951-64 Conservative government, increased to 14 percent by 1970 under Labour, and fell again to 12.6 percent by 1973. The highest postwar level (16 percent) was reached in 1975 under the impact of economic recession and tax increases, but thereafter the proportion fell back. A main cause of this was an amendment to tax law, passed against government advice in 1977, which index-linked tax thresholds and so prevented the semi-automatic increase in yields as money incomes rose. Despite the wish of the 1979 Conservative government to reduce income tax, and their reduction of the highest marginal rate from 83 to 60 percent, the proportion of national product taken in direct taxes has risen marginally. The yield from indirect taxes has also been boosted by the increase in the rate of VAT to 15 percent in 1979. Rates - the other main indirect tax - have also increased as central government financial support for local authorities has been reduced.

National insurance contributions were never intended to cover the cost of all income maintenance benefits, and even for national insurance benefits a subvention from general taxation was assumed. Over time, they have become even less of an insurance entitlement now that claimants who lack the contribution record to give them unemployment or sickness benefit may receive means-tested benefit to a similar level.

The total yield from national insurance contributions was about 3 percent of GDP in the mid-1950s but has been over 6 percent since 1974. Although this revenue source is tending to increase in yield, it is still not greatly in excess of the miscellaneous other items of revenue, like rents, interest and dividends. The proportion of national insurance benefit payments that it covers has been around 80 percent since the mid-1950s, with a higher state subsidy in the early 1960s (when the late-age pensioners had been admitted to the scheme) and the late 1970s (under the impact of high unemployment). Graduated contributions under the 1961 scheme became increasingly important, and from 1966 were payable (though at a lower rate) even by those contracted out of the graduated pension scheme; by 1974, they accounted for 43 percent of receipts. Contributions were put on a fully earnings-related basis in 1975.

The split between employers' and employees' contributions has tilted towards the former under the earnings-related system (Table 3). Until the late 1960s, employee contributions were higher. The graduated pension scheme of 1961 had the curiosity that the contracted-out minority paid a higher contribution than those contracted-in, as a subsidy to the system from those with an occupational pension. When fully graduated contributions were introduced in 1975, the differential of employers' over employees' contributions was increased from 19 to over 50 percent (8.5 percent against 5.5 percent). But from 1978 the differential narrowed as employee contributions were increased from 6.5 percent in 1977 to 8.75 percent in 1982, while employers' rose to only 10.2 percent from 10.0 percent. A complication is the 'national insurance surcharge', a payroll tax levied on employers since 1976 which goes to general taxation rather than the national insurance fund (and is counted with indirect taxes in Graph 16). This has meant that the tax burden on employers has increased even though their share of national insurance specific funding has declined in favour of higher employee contributions, on the argument that those in work should pay more towards benefits to the non-working population. The surcharge was reduced from 3.5 to 2 percent in 1982, and abolished in 1985; although a convenient source of revenue, the surcharge's disincentive to employment was recognized.

Table 3   National insurance contribution rates

Flat-rate and graduated contributions in pounds per week

At end-year	Flat-rate contrib. by employers for employees contracted-out	employees not contracted-out	Flat-rate contributions by employees contracted-out	employees not contracted-out	Graduated contributions (a) employees contracted-out	employees not contracted-out
1950	0.21		0.25			
1951	0.22		0.25			
1952	0.25		0.29			
1953	0.25		0.29			
1954	0.25		0.29			
1955	0.30		0.34			
1956	0.30		0.34			
1957	0.31		0.37			
1958	0.41		0.50			
1959	0.41		0.50			
1960	0.41		0.50			
1961	0.49	0.43	0.61	0.53	0	0.25(0.25)
1962	0.49	0.43	0.61	0.53	0	0.25(0.25)
1963	0.60	0.48	0.70	0.58	0	0.38(0.33)
1964	0.60	0.48	0.70	0.58	0	0.38(0.33)
1965	0.79	0.67	0.80	0.68	0	0.38(0.33)
1966	0.79	0.67	0.80	0.68	0.10(0.05)	0.49(0.43)
1967	0.79	0.67	0.90	0.78	0.10(0.07)	0.49(0.45)
1968	0.97	0.85	0.95	0.83	0.10(0.07)	0.49(0.45)
1969	1.02	0.89	1.00	0.88	0.43(0.29)	0.82(0.67)
1970	1.07	0.95	1.00	0.88	0.43(0.29)	0.82(0.67)
1971	1.07	0.95	1.00	0.88	1.08(0.59)	1.47(0.97)
1972	1.07	1.05	1.00	0.88	1.47(0.88)	1.85(1.26)
1973	1.31	1.19	0.96	0.84	1.87(1.19)	2.25(1.57)
1974	1.84	1.72	0.87	0.75	2.53(1.73)	2.91(2.12)

Contribution rates as a percentage of gross earnings (b)

	Contributions by employers for employees contracted-out	employees not contracted-out	surcharge on pay-roll	Contributions by employees contracted-out	not contracted-out	Earnings limits (pounds per week) lower	upper
1975	8.5			5.5		11.00	46.67
1976	8.75		2.0	5.75		13.00	56.33
1977	8.75		2.0	5.75		15.00	65.00
1978	6.5	10.0	3.5	4.0	6.5	17.50	75.83
1979	6.5	10.0	3.5	4.0	6.5	19.50	84.50
1980	6.7	10.2	3.5	4.25	6.75	23.00	99.67
1981	6.7	10.2	3.5	5.25	7.75	27.00	117.00
1982	6.7	10.2	2.0	6.25	8.75	29.50	127.83

(a) Payable from 1961 by both employers and employees, at the same rate, in addition to flat-rate contributions; the amounts given are the maximum payable; the amount payable for a man on average earnings is in brackets.
(b) No contributions are levied for employees earning less than the lower earnings limit; for others, the percentage rate is levied on all earnings up to the upper earnings limit.

National insurance contributions are levied not on total income but only on the amount up to the so-called upper earnings limit. There is also a lower earnings limit; those earning less pay no contributions. These limits are revalued annually in line with general wage movements; the lower limit is designed to exclude part-time workers; the upper limit is set at about one and a half times average industrial earnings. The effect is a regressive one which increases the relative tax burden on lower-paid workers. From November 1985 the upper earnings limit on employers contributions was removed and the percentage rate related to income. The justification for the upper earnings limit for employees is that the maximum level of the state earnings-related pension is similarly limited. Contracted-out employees pay significantly less (in 1982, 6.25 percent against 8.75 percent), but, as the absolute percentage increases since 1978 have been the same for both, the differential is effectively decreasing. Although advice on rates is given by the government actuary, decisions on them are part of fiscal politics.

The general pattern on the revenue side in Britain is one of balanced growth without excessive public sector deficits, except for the brief period of deficit financing in the mid-1970s. Total tax yield as a proportion of GDP has increased from around 30 percent in 1960 to 40 percent in 1980, with both direct and indirect taxation contributing to this. Tax-cutting objectives, especially of the 1979 Conservative government, have been frustrated by a cautious fiscal policy. National insurance contributions have proved to be a useful source of revenue; they have risen sharply since the mid-1970s and bear most heavily on average-income taxpayers, though they still amount to little more than 6 percent of GDP and represent only a small part of the total social security budget.

The reliance of the British welfare state on general tax revenues makes it difficult to talk of gainers and losers between schemes. Basically, those whose personal circumstances make them consumers of education or health services, or who are old, disabled, sick or unemployed, gain benefit whatever their occupational group or contributions record. Notions of insurance rights and entitlement in the British system have been eroded over time, and the careful and minimalist approach of British social security administration avoids windfall gains or multiple benefits. As the costs of the welfare state have risen, taxes have followed them to reach a level high by international standards. Even Conservative governments have been unable to reduce the tax burden, and recession - and the consequential rise in 'unfunded' payments to the unemployed - has compounded the problem in the early 1980s.

4. The welfare clienteles

The growth of the British welfare state has led to an increase in the number of people drawing cash benefits. This increase has three components: an extension of the proportion of the population eligible for coverage under existing schemes; an increase in the numbers whose personal circumstances qualify them for benefit under these schemes; and the introduction of new types of benefit. The characteristic progression in many European countries is to extend the range of occupational groups included in the schemes; but in Britain the changes under the first and third of the above categories have been relatively limited. The National Insurance system of 1948 covered the entire workforce, employed and self-employed, although the latter pay lower contributions and receive fewer benefits. The original right of married woman workers to opt-out and rely on their husband's insurance has been restricted since 1975. Although national insurance contributions include a notional element to finance the National Health Service, access to the service is freely available to all.

The range of contributory benefits has not been extended markedly from the 1948 structure of retirement, unemployment, sickness, widows' and industrial injury benefit payable at a flat-rate. The main change has been the introduction of earnings-related retirement pensions for the whole employed workforce under state schemes of 1961 and 1978; this supplements the flat-rate pension, which continues as conceived in 1948. The main new clientele have been those injured or disabled for reasons other than industrial accidents, who gained in the 1970s from benefits like invalidity pension, attendance allowance and mobility allowance. New means-tested schemes in education and housing, such as students' allowances (1962) and rent rebates (1967) are important but non-universal. The main growth in clientele has been in the long-established benefits to the retired, unemployed and sick, and chiefly through an expansion of the underlying social group rather than an extension of eligibility.

Table 4 shows the number of people receiving the main benefits and the proportion of the relevant population that they represent. Graph 17 provides an annual series as a proportion of the total population. Much the largest group are retirement pensioners: the number receiving has increased from 4.2 million in 1951 to 9.3 million in 1981, or from 8.4 percent to 16.7 percent of the total population. The retirement age has remained the same - 65 for men and 60 for women, with the pension not paid in full until 70 or 65 if the recipient has not retired from work. The ratio of pensioners to the 65 + age group has risen from 77 percent (1951) to 110 percent (1981). The main increase in this ratio occurred in 1958 when, after a ten-year period, retirement pensions were extended to virtually all of the age-group irrespective of their pre-1948 contribution record. The numbers drawing means-tested social assistance pensions, the indicator of the gap in the contributory scheme, fell from 471,000 in 1949 to 75,000 in 1965.

Of the 9.3 million retirement pensioners in 1981, most had an additional entitlement to an earnings-related pension. In 1979, 3.7 million were receiving pensions from occupational schemes run by their former employers; 62 percent of these pensions were from public sector schemes. Those not covered by a satisfactory occupational scheme are contracted into the state earnings-related scheme intended to be phased in between 1978 and 1998. This is calculated on the best 20 years of earnings during a working life and, if fully implemented, would provide for average-paid workers a pension of about half earnings when the flat-rate pension is taken into account. It is inflation-proofed, unlike the old graduated scheme (1961) it replaced, which relates benefits to contributions paid. In 1981, 5.3 million pensioners were receiving some graduated pension, but the average amount was only UKL 0.81 per week. A further 500,000 had some benefit from the new scheme, still building up, with an average of UKL 1.54 per week. Of the total insured population of 25.5 million in 1981, 20.2 million were employees and 8.8 million of these were contracted-out of the state earnings-related scheme.

The second-largest group of recipients are of child benefit: the number of families receiving increased from 3.2 million in 1951 to 7.3 million in 1981, the number of children represented from 7.5 to 13 million. Mothers (or single parents or guardians) entitled to a child benefit rose from 6 per cent to 13 percent of the population. The main variable here is the extension of benefit to the first child in a family in 1977, when integrated child benefit replaced family allowances and child income tax allowances. Other fluctuations are related to the number of births and the numbers leaving school. But despite its universal coverage and take-up child benefit is a supplement and not a substitute to income; the rate per child in 1981 is only 4.3 percent of average earnings. The same objection applies to Family Income Supplement, payable from 1971 to low-paid workers with children, whose coverage has barely risen above 100,000 families.

The most important personal contingency against which the national insurance scheme offers protection is sickness. The numbers sick (at a single time) have been remarkably stable at about 1 million, or 4 percent of the numbers insured; the trend has been slightly upwards, but there has been neither a proliferation of people seeking benefit nor an improvement of the sickness record of the workforce. Until 1971 sickness benefit was paid without time limit and so included many long-term invalids;

Table 4 — The clienteles of the major welfare schemes (a)

	1951	1955	1960	1965	1970	1975	1981
Retirement pensioners (b)							
in 1 000s	4 229	4 633	5 676	6 493	7 649	8 249	9 342
as % of population 65+	77.3	80.4	92.5	98.6	106.1	105.4	110.2
Invalidity pensioners (c)							
in 1 000s						557	783
as % of pop. 20-65						1.8	2.5
Widows' pensioners							
in 1 000s	447	450	557	610	560	527	433
as % of pop. 20-65	1.5	1.5	1.8	2.0	1.8	1.7	1.4
Injury benefit recipients							
in 1 000s	64	60	62	76	68	46	43
as % of labour force	0.3	0.2	0.3	0.3	0.3	0.2	0.2
Ind. disablement pensioners							
in 1 000s	60	137	175	201	211	203	200
as % of labour force	0.3	0.6	0.7	0.8	0.8	0.8	0.7
Sickness ben. recipients							
in 1 000s	942	957	927	1 033	1 105	585	657
as % of labour force	4.0	3.9	3.8	4.1	4.4	2.3	2.5
Unemployment ben. recipients							
in 1 000s	244	154	213	188	327	464	1 206
as % of labour force	1.0	0.6	0.9	0.7	1.3	1.8	4.5
as % of unemployed	80.8	68.1	60.5	58.6	54.7	41.4	52.2
Social assist. recipients							
Heads of household (d)							
in 1 000s	1 695	1 759	1 903	2 012	2 840	2 897	3 873
as % of population	3.5	3.5	3.7	3.8	5.1	5.2	5.3
Total persons							
in 1 000s					4 339	4 620	5 145
as % of population					7.8	8.3	9.2
Sole benefit recip. (e)							
in 1 000s	773	663	581	535	720	1 013	1 849
as % of population	1.6	1.3	1.1	1.0	1.3	1.8	3.3
Child allowance recipients							
Supported families							
in 1 000s	3 219	3 382	3 659	3 958	4 387	4 603	7 313
Aided students (f)							
in 1 000s					468	509	586
as % of all students					75.3	69.3	74.6
Rent rebate recipients							
in 1 000s					350	940	1 305

(a) Numbers receiving at a single time during the year, usually November/December.
(b) Takes over from other pensions at age 65 for men, 60 for women.
(c) Includes both contributory (introduced in 1971) and non-contributory (introduced in 1975) pensions; previously these groups received sickness benefits or social assistance.
(d) Defined as those over 16, their dependant spouses and children under 16.
(e) Not receiving any other income substitute benefit.
(f) In universities and other institutions of higher learning.

when a more generous invalidity pension was introduced for those absent as a result of sickness for more than six months, 40 percent transferred to it. A non-contributory invalidity pension was introduced in 1975 to widen coverage. Invalidity pensioners have subsequently increased at a faster rate (from 557,000 in 1975 to 783,000 in 1981) and the numbers receiving each benefit were comparable until 1983, when a new Statutory Sick Pay scheme transferred responsibility for paying benefit at a pre-scribed rate during the first 8 weeks of sickness to employers. Occupational injury

Graph 17

Welfare clienteles

as % of total population

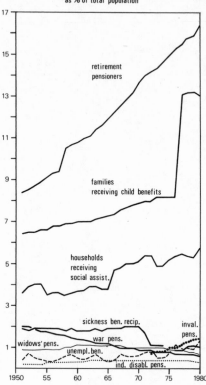

benefits are an older-established category, predating the 1948 scheme and paid at a higher rate; the number receiving has been stable since the 1960s at 1 percent of the labour force.

The numbers receiving unemployment benefit were smaller until the early 1980s because the contingency was less common than sickness and because of restrictions on eligibility; they amounted to no more than 1 percent of the population. But by 1981 1.2 million were receiving, against 0.5 million in 1979. Just as noteworthy is the decline in the proportion of the unemployed receiving the benefit, from 81 percent in 1951 to 52 percent in 1981 (and 30 percent by late 1984 as long-term unemployment increased) (see Graph 20 below). This is because benefit is payable for a maximum of one year and only to those who have paid contributions during the previous fiscal year, so excluding the long-term unemployed and those who have never worked.

Social assistance (known in Britain as supplementary benefit and before 1966 as national assistance) is the residual category. The failure of its original conception as a dwindling safety-net for the non-working uninsured is documented by the data on clientele. The number of heads of households receiving rose from 1.7 million in 1951 to 3.9 million in 1981, or from 3.5 percent to 6.9 percent of the population. In 1981 about 19 percent of households were receiving supplementary benefit. The total number - including children - in households receiving supplementary benefit was 5.1

million in 1981, or 9.2 percent of the population. The majority of these are receiving a national insurance benefit but, having a total income lower than the scale rates, are entitled to a supplement which may be small; this usually occurs in families with several children. An alternative indicator is of those receiving supplementary benefit and no other - but this shows an even more disconcerting trend, doubling between 1965 and 1975 after a decline in the 1950s, and then increasing from 1.1 million to 1.8 million (3.3 percent of the population) between 1979 and 1981.

An important additional means-tested benefit is rent rebate for public sector tenants (there are also rent allowances for private tenants). The numbers receiving have increased rapidly since introduction by local authorities in the 1960s; over 1.7 million were paid in 1981. Since 1982 all housing cash benefit - except to owner-occupiers - has been paid through this, rather than the supplementary benefit system. Rent rebates are the most prominent of the 50 or so means-tested benefits that have been instituted by education, health, social services and housing agencies. Most are paid to those in as well as out of work, but create problems of take-up and overlap. Also important in terms of cost and numbers are maintenance allowances for higher education students, with 586,000 covered in 1981; others are more numerous (notably the 1.3 million children receiving free school meals) but of smaller value.

A synoptic view of British welfare clientele requires an operational concept that is not recognised in official statistics. The most plausible approach is to aggregate those who receive an income substitute benefit from the state. This excludes small cash supplements like child benefit; deals only with payments under the social security system, so excluding public employment and job maintenance schemes; and requires a netting-out of persons receiving more than one benefit. The result (Graph 18) refers to a single time-point in the year in question. It should not be interpreted as the number wholly dependent on the state as many will receive an occupational pension, private sick pay, or other private income, in addition.

Graph 18

Welfare clienteles

Recipients of income substitutes as

% of population aged 20 and over

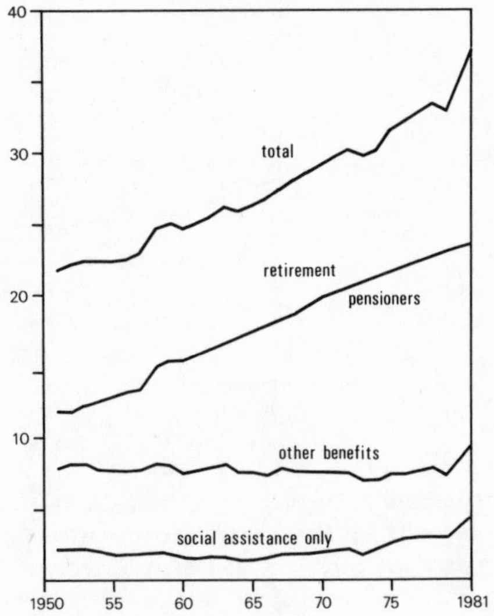

The data show that an increasing proportion of the British population aged 20 or more is a welfare client - 22 percent in 1951 rising to 37 percent in 1981. The children and dependants of these clients are not included in this ratio. The increase has been a steady one marked by an acceleration in certain years - 1958 (the extension of retirement pensions), 1967 (the new supplementary benefits scheme) and 1975 and 1981 (higher unemployment during recessions). The share of retirement pensioners in the total has increased from 54 to 62 percent and they are the dominant component. The safety-net group - those receiving only social assistance - has overtaken the 10 percent of the total that it was in 1951, after a decline to 5.4 per cent in 1965. The constituency of the welfare state continues to expand as a reflection of new benefits and continuing social need.

5. The improvement of benefits

The value of benefits in Britain is defined in terms of periodically adjusted cash levels rather than of earnings replacement ratios. Some earnings-related elements have been introduced, notably in the supplements to short-term national insurance benefits in 1966; but these were abolished for unemployment and sickness beneficiaries in 1982, and it will be 1998 before the new pension scheme provides for all a retirement pension related to earnings in the range up to 1.5 times the national average. A flat-rate cash approach raises the danger of the erosion of benefits by inflation, and in cases like the 1961 graduated pension, the national insurance death grant, and family allowances, this has happened. But Graph 19 and Table 5 make it clear that welfare benefits have far exceeded the rise in prices and in the main matched the rise in average earnings, while remaining well below the absolute level of earnings. The only benefits that can exceed 50 percent of such earnings for a single person are invalidity pensions for occupational or wartime injury.

Graph 19

Average benefits

as % of average earnings of male industrial workers

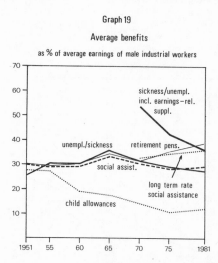

The evidence of real gain for beneficiaries comes from a comparison with prices. Most benefits have at least doubled in value in these terms since the national insurance scheme started - from 1951 to 1981, retirement pensions by 132 percent, unemployment benefit by 107 percent, and the social assistance scale rate (the official 'poverty line') by 93 percent. But the trend over time and the relationship between benefits is not stable. All adult benefits suffered an initial loss of value as the 1948 rates were maintained for too long, but after upratings they remained stable relative to earnings during the 1950s, rose in the early 1960s, but declined in the late 1960s and early 1970s. Until 1974 unemployment and sickness benefit generally matched retirement pensions, with social assistance lagging slightly behind.

Table 5

Average benefits (a)

	1951	1955	1960	1965	1970	1975	1981
Retirement pension							
- at current prices	2.50	3.25	4.63	6.50	9.70	21.20	47.35
- at constant (1982) prices	21.75	24.52	29.41	36.40	38.25	47.01	49.33
- as % of average earnings (b)	30.4	29.9	30.7	34.8	31.6	35.4	38.8
Sickness/Unemployment benefit (c)							
- at current prices	2.10	3.25	4.63	6.50	9.70	18.00	36.40
incl. earnings-related supplement (d)					16.48	26.47	47.44
- at constant (1982) prices	18.27	24.52	29.41	36.40	38.25	39.91	37.92
incl. earnings-related supplement					64.99	58.69	49.42
- as % of average earnings	25.7	30.2	30.7	35.1	31.6	29.1	27.7
incl. earnings-related supplement					53.7	42.8	36.1
Social assistance scale rate (e)							
- at current prices	2.50	3.15	4.50	6.28	9.45	17.75	37.75
longterm rate (f)					9.95	21.55	47.35
- at constant (1982) prices	20.33	22.45	27.46	33.79	36.23	38.08	39.23
longterm rate					38.15	46.23	49.21
- as % of average earnings	30.4	29.9	29.9	33.6	30.8	28.7	28.7
longterm rate					32.4	34.8	36.0
Child allowances (g)							
- at current prices	2.23	2.99	2.86	3.35	4.17	6.10	15.75
- at constant (1982) prices	20.35	22.51	18.19	18.34	16.80	15.11	16.41
- as % of average earnings	27.8	27.5	19.0	17.7	14.2	11.0	12.0

(a) As payable to a married couple without children previously on average earnings.
(b) Gross earnings of average male worker.
(c) These are payable at the same rates.
(d) As payable at average earnings.
(e) The income level guaranteed by social assistance.
(f) The longterm rate is payable to all retired people, and to other beneficiaries except the unemployed after one year.
(g) The total value of cash benefit and income tax allowances for a family with three children aged under 11.

From 1966, the introduction of earnings-related supplement for the first 6 months substantially improved the value of unemployment and sickness benefit, to over 50 percent of earnings for the average worker. The introduction in 1966 of a 'long-term rate' of supplementary benefit, giving an increase to all except the unemployed after two years and payable from the start to pensioners, also improved the position of beneficiaries. Although additions on all these benefits are payable for children in the household, universal child benefit (expressed as the net value of family allowances and tax relief) fell almost continuously in relation to earnings; it lost half of its relative worth between the early 1950s and early 1970s and also lost value compared with prices, especially in the late 1950s. All benefits suffered from the 'saw-tooth' effect of irregular adjustment at the initiative of the government, with value declining between upratings.

The most important change of trend came in the 1970s with the political acceptance of four principles. The first was that benefits should be uprated annually to maintain their value, and this was done from 1971. Secondly, from 1974 benefits have been index-linked (until 1983 on the government's forecast of price rises in each Novem-ber-November period, which occasionally fell short of full indexation, but now on the May-May actual figure). Thirdly, the long-run fall in the value of child benefit has been checked; this was secured when child benefit was fully implemented in 1979, but there is still not automatic annual indexation.

The fourth principle was that long-term benefits (retirement, widows' and invalidity pensions) should rise at a faster rate than short-term unemployment and sickness benefit. This was achieved from 1974 to 1980 by indexation to earnings rather than prices, and from 1980 (when price indexation only was reintroduced) by making short-term benefits liable to income tax. As a consequence relative values have diverged, especially now that earnings-related supplements to unemployment and sick-ness benefits have been abolished, and the long-term rate of supplementary benefit (since 1980 paid after one year) is over 25 percent more generous than the short-term. Pensions were at their highest-ever real value (39 percent of average earnings for a married couple) in 1981, but the short-term benefits, at 27.7 percent, were well down on the 1965 ratio of 35.1 percent (Table 5).

The result of these changes of principle is to redistribute social security benefits in favour of the retired and towards means-tested in place of contributory benefits. The increase in real value achieved since the mid 1970s has now been halted but the princi-ple of maintaining the relationship to prices remains intact despite some doubts on the part of the Thatcher government. Most welfare recipients have maintained or improved their relative economic position, but since 1980 a tightening of eligibility has combined with the economic recession to extend the numbers receiving while cutting earnings replacement ratios. By 1980 direct cash benefits amounted to 15 percent of the income of the average British household, an increase from 9 percent in 1967, but this average conceals major and often divergent changes of policy about the treatment of various client groups (see Tables 11 and 13 below). Most of the benefits are universal entitlements paid on grounds of age to the retired and for children, and pay-ments targeted to specific social needs are subsidiary elements only.

III   Achievements and shortcomings: evaluations

The question of the success or failure of the postwar British welfare state may be addressed at a number of levels. At its most basic is the question of whether funda-mental human deprivations have been corrected. The principal of these is poverty - the lack of a sufficient income to meet necessary expenditure (however this may be defined). This relates to the adequacy of coverage of clienteles, and to the interaction of the tax and benefit systems, which in Britain have produced the phenomena known as the unemployment and poverty traps. These basic issues are considered in the first part of the section.

At a higher level of abstraction is the distributional effect of the welfare state - on the inequality of wealth and income, on the overall impact of taxes and benefits (in both cash and kind) on various household groups, and of the incidence of consumption of the social services by socio-economic group. These are discussed in the second part.

At a lower level of abstraction is the output record of individual services, notably health, education and housing. For these, a variety of performance indicators are avail-able for each stage of the policy process, some intrinsic to government (like expenditure and staffing levels), others (like health status or educational ability) less directly an 'output' of public policy. Both the results and the limitations of these indicators are discussed in the third part.

Finally, an assessment needs to be made of the overall success of the British model of the welfare state, which has had so much influence in the rest of Europe. The British system is both universal and public in character, and has had high continuity over time. It is therefore particularly well suited to the evaluation of the potential and limitations of state welfare.

1. Poverty and the income maintenance system

The record of poverty

The most striking accusation against the British welfare state is that it has not succeeded in eliminating poverty. From the mid-1950s, the idea of 'the rediscovery of poverty' entered British political debate. It was originated by Peter Townsend and Brian Abel-Smith, who pointed out that the number of households around or below the social assistance threshhold seemed to be increasing during the 1950s[21]. Subsequently, Townsend conducted a major survey of the needs and resources of 2,000 households in 1968-69, whose findings were published as *Poverty in the United Kingdom* in 1979[22]. Another major survey of 1,200 households was made in 1983 and published as *Poor Britain* in 1985[23]. These produced rather similar results, claiming that over 20 percent of the population fall within a broad definition of being 'in poverty' (Table 6).

Table 6	Estimates of the numbers in poverty in million (m) and as % of population					
Definition	1968-69 official standard		relative deprivation standard		1983	
	m	%	m	%	m	%
'In poverty'	3.3	6.1	12.5	22.9	7.5	13.8
'Margins of poverty'	11.9	21.8			4.6	8.4

Townsend's 'official standard' is the state's supplementary benefits threshhold ('in poverty') or less than 40 percent above it ('margins of poverty'). His 'relative deprivation' standard is based upon an estimate of the resources necessary to sustain socially customary participation. Mack and Lansley's definition is based upon the lack of any of 18 housing or social necessities (like heating and carpets, or the means to take a holiday or give presents); those lacking one are on the margins of poverty, those lacking three or more in poverty.

These findings are consistent with other analyses of poverty in Britain during the twentieth century. A reanalysis of Rowntree's data for York in 1950 showed that 5.8 percent of the population were in poverty and 7.2 percent on its margins[24]. Layard's calculation from Family Expenditure Survey data suggest that 5.5 million, 10 percent of the population, were in poverty in 1975[25]. After an examination of the evidence, Brown and Madge conclude that 'although it would seem that the numbers of the very poor have decreased markedly since the turn of the century, a small consistent proportion of the population has remained in relative poverty until the present day'[26].

The figures produced by Townsend, and Mack and Lansley, are higher than those beneath the income threshhold for social assistance, conventionally taken to be the 'poverty line'. This threshhold has doubled in real terms, and as a relative measure it is liable to perpetual redefinition. As Conservative critics point out, increased poverty may be purely a statistical artefact. Nevertheless, as the threshhold is broadly related to income the proportion of the population falling beneath it ought to remain roughly constant. But as Table 7 shows this proportion increased from 3.4 percent in 1972 to 5.3 percent in 1981. Of this latter total, 680,000 were in work, 1,120,000 over pensionable age and the remainder in other out-of-work categories like the disabled and unemployed.

Table 7   Individuals with incomes below social assistance threshold, Great Britain

	in 1,000s	as % of population
1960	1 990	3.8
1972	1 780	3.4
1977	2 020	4.0
1981	2 810	5.3

Table 8 expands the analysis for the working poor to show how their numbers increased from 1979 to 1981 with the impact of high unemployment and how many more are within 40 percent of the supplementary benefits threshhold.

Table 8   Working families with low incomes

Income in relation to supplementary benefit level	Individuals in claiming units (in 1,000s)		
	1977	1979	1981
under 100 percent	500	480	680
100-120 percent	1 080	2 410	3 840
120-140 percent	2 060	1 310	2 090
Total	3 640	2 410	3 840

Many of the non-working poor are kept above the state's poverty line by means-tested social assistance (since 1966 known as supplementary benefit). The numbers receiving it have increased over three times between 1950 and 1982, from 1.35 million to 4.27 million; this latter figure represents provision for 7,068,000 claimants and dependants, or 13 percent of the population. Graph 20 shows that there has been a shift from the elderly to the unemployed, and that a new group of single- parent families has become a major recipient category. In 1966, 73 percent of recipients were elderly; in 1982 it was 42 percent, barely more than the proportion of unemployed.

More significantly, there has been a rapid increase in the numbers for whom social assistance is the sole source of income rather than a topping-up of contributory benefit. This is especially true of the unemployed, who lose their contributory entitlement after a year out of work (and such long-term unemployed now form 40 percent of the total); and single parents, who are not required to register for work. Such

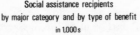

Graph 20

Social assistance recipients
by major category and by type of benefit
in 1,000 s

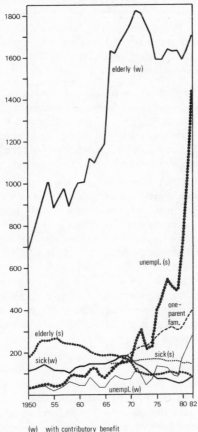

(w)   with contributory benefit
(s)   sole benefit

recipients lose benefit pound-for-pound if their earnings are above the low threshhold of only UKL 4 a week (3 percent of average earnings, though the rule is a little more generous for single parents). The reason for this increase is that the qualifying conditions for national insurance benefit can no longer be satisfied by many of those in poverty.

The contrasts in the estimates of the numbers in poverty between Tables 6 and 7 reflect the fact that the state's definition of poverty does not capture the full subtlety of the causes and characteristics of the phenomenon. This is why Townsend developed a more sociological definition of poverty. He offered three alternatives:

(1) subjective and social definitions based on normative public opinion of what it is to be poor: in the absence of evidence this is taken to be the state's supplementary benefits threshold;

(2) the relative income standard, based on the share of mean income for each type of household;

(3) Townsend's preferred 'relative deprivation' standard, defined as 'the lack of the resources necessary to permit participation in the activities, customs and diets commonly approved by society' [27]. This is operationalised by the assumption that there is a threshold of income deficiency which causes a rapid withdrawal from these customary social patterns. By means of a 'deprivation index' constructed from responses to survey questions about social participation, Townsend locates this threshold at about 150 percent of the supplementary benefits level, though he assesses it separately for each type of household [28].

These measures produce the data given in Table 6. Using a household rather than a population basis, Townsend also calculated that 25 percent of households fall beneath the relative deprivation standard, as against 7 percent (and a further 24 percent on the margin) falling below the state's standard. Evidence on income distribution is used to suggest that this conclusion, based on a 1968-69 survey, remains valid and that the long-run trend is at least to maintain the proportion in poverty [29].

Mack and Lansley's more recent survey has suggested that poverty (here defined as the enforced lack of socially defined necessities) is diffused widely through the lowest 40 percent of income earners; it found that as many as 16 percent of the fourth decile lacked five or more basic necessities [30]. The difference of this approach from Townsend's is that it starts from an evaluative position of what families should not lack, rather than from empirical evidence of what they do lack. The reasons for the 7.5 million in poverty and 2.5 million the authors define as being in intense poverty seem to be structural ones, related to poor housing, and the availability of support networks and child care. This relates to the theme of 'multiple deprivation', first identified in the 1970s, where lack of income is associated with poor housing and health in spatially concentrated areas. The approach is basically similar to Townsend, being sociological rather than economic.

Townsend has had many critics. His idea is of 'proselytisation of life-styles' from rich to poor, through which standards and styles of living are constantly redefined: what was a civilised social minimum in terms of possessions and activities in past decades may have been overtaken today [31]. This has been vulgarised into a purely relative view of poverty, which exaggerates the ability of social scientists to transform the statements of respondents into robust indicators. Social scientists sympathetic to the anti-poverty cause have perceived the weakness of Townsend's quest [32]. Conservatives have challenged the suggestion that a continuing upward revision of expectations will induce a limitless demand for social policies.

Nevertheless, the intensive research on poverty in Britain has served to isolate some of the practical reasons for the paradox of poverty alongside real income growth. Firstly, there are structural weaknesses in the construction of social assistance scales. These were derived from 1930s data and were not corrected for relative wartime price movements; in particular, the child allowances in the scales have always underestimated the cost of childrens' needs. Among those dependent on long-term state benefits, the elderly have done better than those of working age in terms of their expenditure needs and their income from other resources.

Secondly, the 'cost of being poor' appears to be increasing as a result of the totality of welfare policies. The material standards of housing construction seem to be declining, making them expensive to run: heating is a particular problem, as much public housing requires expensive heating systems designed before the post-1973 fuel price rises (and in Britain, particularly high increases in the prices of nationalised fuel utilities have been forced by government decision since the mid-1970s). Food prices have risen faster than nutritional content because of new styles of packaging; urban dwelling makes it difficult to grow food. For those without cars, standards of public transport have declined, making access to shops, hospitals and schools expensive and difficult. Environmental and social disturbance imposes both direct and psychological costs. Locational disruption of social networks reduces the scope for help from families and friends. Brown and Madge have documented the studies that show how a lack of food and equipment, problems of money management, and the fear that children will be taken into care, remain pressing realities for the poor [33]. The trend of political debate on poverty in recent years has been to emphasise the inadequacy of approaches that are based on the absolute level of social assistance.

The gaps in the coverage of clienteles

The data on the recipients of welfare benefits show that poverty is concentrated in particular household types. For long, the clearest such category was that of retirement pensioner households with no other income. Over time, though, more generous pension levels and eligibility have improved the relative position of pensioners. Now, some other categories may face a deficiency of income and public services whose extent is not perceived by public policy. Townsend's survey documented some of these groups, selecting 13 for special study. Together, these constituted 34 percent of households in poverty. The largest proportions in poverty were among the elderly incapacitated (61 percent), families with four or more children (51 percent) and one-parent families (44 percent) [34].

Relating Townsend's findings to the circumstances of the 1980s, four groups seem to represent a gap in the full coverage of social need:

(1) The unemployed, especially the long-term (by 1985, over 1.3 million had been unemployed for over one year) and those with discontinuous employment. The poor coverage ratio of unemployment benefit, and the cost of life-styles whose standards assume an income from employment, pose severe problems, especially for families with children.

(2) The low-paid: the inadequacy of income support measures paid to those in work (child benefit and Family Income Supplement) creates another large group of the poor, especially when high unemployment reduces the possibilities of a second, female, household income.

(3) A disabled person in a household, whether as head or as a supported adult or child, is a large and probably underestimated correlate of deprivation. 12.2 percent of Townsend's sample had a marked or specific reduction of activity [35]. Although state benefits to the disabled improved during the 1970s, with the introduction of attendance allowance and invalid care allowance, eligibility conditions are tight. It was not until 1984 that housewives no longer required to be incapable of 'normal household duties' before qualifying for an invalidity pension. Help through the social services to the families of the disabled is also intermittent.

(4) Single heads of households: one-parent families (usually headed by the mother) have been an emergent social category with the rise in divorce; there were 916,000 of them at the 1981 census, against 515,000 in 1971 and 367,000 in 1961 [36]. Their earning capacity is low, and although they receive a higher rate of child benefit, they are twice as likely as two-parent families to be in poverty [37]. A separate problem are

the elderly living alone: they are again twice as likely to be in poverty as are corresponding married pairs [38].

An important variable, fully documented in the Townsend survey, is the tendency of these four characteristics to interact to produce an underclass isolated from society and the market economy. Many workers, especially manual ones, have unstable employment conditions, with fluctuations in earnings, poor working conditions, and discontinuous periods of employment. They may depend on a wife's earnings to supplement the family income; they are vulnerable to the loss of their job through sickness and disablement. The social opportunities of those living, or bringing up children, alone are dependent on a high health or employment status. The discrimination necessary to direct special help to such cases is often not possible within the structure of the social services.

Even when people are entitled to assistance, they may not take it up. Low take-up is a continuing problem of the more complex benefits. For supplementary benefits in 1981 it was estimated to be 67 percent for pensioner households and 75 percent for non-pensioners; for Family Income Supplement 50 percent, and for One-Parent Benefit 70 percent [39]. Some of the amounts lost to claimants would be small, and are perhaps reckoned not to be worth the cost of time and loss of self-esteem involved. Although the stated aim of government action is to encourage take-up through publicity campaigns and the simplification of regulations, part of the depression of demand serves as a rationing device to restrain the cost of benefit.

The unemployment and poverty traps

The operation of the British income maintenance system has produced two phenomena which encourage behaviour contrary to the aim of the system to increase work incentives and reduce poverty through earnings from employment rather than state benefits: the so-called poverty and unemployment traps.

The poverty trap occurs when a rise in income leads to the withdrawal of means-tested benefits to the extent that an effective high marginal rate of taxation operates - above 100 percent in some theoretical cases in some years. This is because there is only a very limited opportunity to retain income from benefit alongside income from employment. One substitutes for the other, but at a near-constant level of income which leaves many households in poverty.

The unemployment trap leaves heads of households little better off in work than out of work: it is caused by the restriction of supplementary benefit (which also serves as an entry hurdle to health, housing and education benefits) to those out of work, and the low income threshold for the payment of income tax. This was more than average gross earnings in the early 1950s but declined to less than half by the mid-1970s as a result of a failure to realign tax brackets in line with the growth of earnings. Since then the position has stabilised through a legislative commitment to index tax allowance in line with prices; this has been respected by government in most years.

The result has been that, even at average earnings, benefits receivable when out of work are a high proportion of after-tax income - for an average family head unemployed for 13 weeks, 87 percent in 1968 and 73 percent in 1980, though falling to 60 percent in 1983; the proportion with more than a 90 percent replacement rate fell from 40 percent in 1968 to 3 percent in 1983 [40]. The fall is largely due to the removal of earnings-related supplement to unemployment benefit in 1982. For those with lower earnings the income benefit from working is even less, although the theoretical effect of the traps is unlikely to operate in practice to that extent because many means-tested benefits may not have been claimed at all and are often not withdrawn immediately when income rises. Official estimates for 1981 suggest that 260,000 working families (less than 2 percent of the total) would receive a net benefit of less than half of a UKL 1 increase in gross earnings [41].

This is confirmed by the detailed Department of Health and Social Security cohort study of 2,000 unemployed persons in 1978. It demonstrates that cases of 'profit' from unemployment are abnormal, but do exist. For 46 percent of the sample, benefits replaced less than half of earnings (a proportion which will since have increased because of the abolition of earnings-related supplement) - but 6 percent had higher benefits than earnings. On a wider definition of family income, including wife's earnings, occupational pensions, housing benefit and income tax rebates, about one-third of the sample replaced more than 80 percent of their income [42]. The main variables involved are the prevalence of low-paid jobs, the burden of taxation and national insurance contributions at low levels of income, and the poor take-up by those in work of the means-tested benefits to which they are entitled. The problem is not the level of welfare benefits but the weakness of pay and employment in the economy. The British welfare state cannot conceal this and the perverse outcomes of the unemployment and poverty traps bear testament to it.

2. Inequality and the welfare state

The impact of the welfare state on individuals and households is made through transfers of taxes and benefits. Income from employment and investment (including that generated by the holding of wealth) is subject to income and capital taxation, but is supplemented by cash benefits. Expenditure is subject to indirect taxation, which cannot be varied according to the circumstances of the consumer. Benefits in kind, like education, health and housing are received, again without full reference to the income level of recipients. Final income, taking into account all these transfers, is a product of both public finance and public expenditure. A variety of policies are involved, which are constructed on different criteria and may cancel each other out.

The search for equality has been a major goal of the British welfare state; but it has been convenient to politicians to leave the concept diffuse. On the economic side, Le Grand has suggested that there are five types of equality: of expenditure (between all relevant individuals); final income (after taxes have been paid and benefits received); use (the equal allocation of resources to those in equal need); cost (a proxy for barriers of access to a service); and outcome (in terms of ultimate personal status) [43]. On the sociological side, there are important distinctions between equality of opportunity and of outcome, and between consumption and social position. Not all of these can realistically be attained through public social policies. What is important is the broad direction of public policy, and the correspondence of outcome to aim.

The record of wealth and income equality

The broadest indicators of equality are data on the share of total income and wealth held by quintile groups of the population. These show a gradual move towards equality, but there are still marked differences between strata which are not much corrected by the tax system and have tended to increase under the 1979 Conservative government. The pattern is of a restratification from the very rich to the strata below them rather than a redistribution through all the population.

Inequality is greater on wealth, where the top 10 percent hold more than half the total (69 percent in 1966, declining to 54 percent in 1979, but increasing to 56 percent in 1982) (see Table 9). During the 1966-79 period the Gini coefficient (of inequality) on wealth declined from 81 to 69 percent, only to increase to 74 percent in 1982. But the most substantial gains were made by the second decile (the top 11-20 percent) and the share of the bottom 80 percent has changed little since the Second World War [44]. The attribution of pension rights, however, considerably evens out the distribution, with the bottom 80 percent approaching 50 percent of the total.

Table 9						The distribution of wealth			
Percent of wealth owned by top	Excluding pension rights					Including pension rights			
	1966	1971	1976	1979	1982	1971	1976	1979	1982
1 percent	33	31	24	22	21	21	14	13	11
5 percent	56	52	45	40	41	37	27	25	24
10 percent	69	65	60	54	56	49	37	35	34
25 percent	87	86	84	77	81	67-72	58-61	56-59	56-69
50 percent	97	97	95	95	96	85-89	80-85	79-83	78-82
Gini coefficient	.81	.80	.76	.69	.74	.59-.64	.48-.53	.45-.50	.45-.50

Income distribution is more even than that of wealth, but less subject to change over time. Both before and after tax, the top 25 percent of the population have had about 50 percent of total income throughout the postwar years. The effect of taxation, and the loss of share over the years, is marked only among the top 1 percent: between 1949 and 1982, their share fell from 11.2 to 6.0 percent (before tax) and 6.4 to 4.6 percent (after tax) (see Table 10). Inequality has increased marginally since the end of the 1970s, with the share of the bottom 50 percent falling by one percentage point both before and after tax.

Table 10				The inequality of income (a)			
Percent share of income before tax (after tax)	1949	1961	1966	1971-2	1976-7	1976-7	1981-2
Top 1 percent	11.2 (6.4)	8.1 (5.5)	7.7 (5.1)	6.5 (4.6)	5.4 (3.5)	5.5 (3.9)	6.0 (4.6)
Next 9% percent	22.0 (20.7)	20.8 (19.6)	20.8 (19.4)	20.8 (19.5)	20.4 (18.9)	20.7 (19.3)	22.3 (21.0)
Next 40 percent	46.9 (46.4)	51.2 (51.7)	47.8 (48.7)	49.3 (50.0)	49.7 (50.0)	49.7 (49.9)	49.2 (49.2)
Lowest 50 percent	23.7 (26.5)	23.3 (23.2)	23.7 (26.8)	23.4 (25.9)	24.5 (27.6)	24.1 (26.9)	22.7 (25.2)
Gini coefficient	.41 (35.5)	.39 (34.9)	.39 (33.7)	.38 (34.2)	.37 (31.5)	.37 (32.6)	.40 (36.0)

(a) The basis of calculation was changed in 1976 to include mortgage interest payments.

Between 1961 and 1976, the after tax Gini coefficient for income distribution fell only marginally, from .349 to .315, during years when Labour governments committed to greater equality were in power for most of the time. What redistribution there was fell within the top 50 percent of the population, and even this tended to slow in the 1970s. By 1981-82, inequality had increased even beyond its level of 1961. The effect of public policy on the distribution is much greater in wealth (by guaranteeing pension rights) than in income (by the operation of the income tax system). This is despite the failure of the 1974 Labour government to introduce a wealth tax. But in neither case has the welfare state induced a substantial shift in the relative position of the average household or taxpayer, and redistributionary aims have been abandoned by the 1979 Conservative government.

The overall impact of taxes and benefits

To take the analysis beyond the data on income and wealth, we need an indicator of the impact of government policies, both taxes and benefits, on various types of households and income groups. This is provided by the annual government analysis of the effect of taxes and benefits on household income, using data from the Family Expenditure Survey. This is open to the criticism that it covers only part of government activity - in 1983, 59 percent of revenue and 49 percent of expenditure. It omits much collective goods expenditure and corporate taxation, which is likely to be attributable fairly equally across the population, thus reducing the total redistributive effect.

Once again, the incidence of taxes and benefits varies according to household type; Table 11 gives average effects. The data show that a marked reduction in inequality of final income compared with original occurs only in households of the retired and those with many children. For two retired adults, the Gini coefficients are respectively .67 and .22, but for two adults with a youngest child under 5 they are only .34 and .24 [45].

Table 11   Effects of taxes and benefits on household income, 1983

Quintiles of	in UKL						
original income recipients	Original income	+ Cash benefits	+ Benefits in kind	– Direct taxes	– Indirect taxes	Final income	Final inc. as % of original inc.
Top	18 640	600	1 570	4 510	3 380	12 920	69.3
2nd	10 570	730	1 470	2 340	2 280	8 160	77.2
3rd	6 880	1 100	1 470	1 410	1 850	6 190	89.9
4th	2 580	2 250	1 250	410	1 270	4 400	170.5
Bottom (a)	120	3 020	1 740	10	840	3 360	2 800
(b)	1 440	2 730	1 670	190	1 210	4 400	205.6
Average	7 760	1 540	1 420	1 740	1 920	7 060	91.0

(a) Bottom quintile of all households.
(b) Non-retired households within the bottom quintile.

Nor are differentials being reduced over time. Table 12 shows that the inequality of original income increased between 1975 and 1983. This was counteracted by the effect of cash benefits, which benefitted low income households most, but partly reinstated by changes in the effect of taxation, which benefitted them least. Cash benefits are more important than the tax system in moderating income inequality: the effect of the former reduces the share of total household income of the top fifth from 48 to 40 percent, but the latter only from 40 to 39 percent [46].

Table 12   The effects of cash benefits and taxation on income inequality

	Gini coefficients				
	1975	1977	1978	1981	1983
Original income	.43	.44	.45	.47	.49
Incl. cash benefits	.35	.34	.35	.36	.36
Final income	.31	.21	.32	.32	.33

Detailed examination of the data by income group reveals the limited nature of state transfers. The bottom quintile, with virtually no original income (because most of them are retired) receives UKL 3,020 from the state, but still pays UKL 840 indirect taxes. If we distinguish the 35 percent of this group who are not retired (up from 19 percent in 1975 as unemployment has increased), their average original income of UKL 1,440 is almost matched by the UKL 1,400 taxes they pay [47]. By the second quintile direct taxes are being paid and final income is less than twice that of the original. By the third quintile the net effect of taxes and benefits is to reduce income, but the progressivity of this reduction is slow. Even the top quintile retains 70 percent of its original income and receives some benefits in both cash and kind.

An index of the efficiency of these transfers may be provided by relating the net amount transferred (after taxes and benefits are taken into account) to the total turnover of taxes and benefits. A low index reveals a 'churning' effect: cash and benefits in kind are being exchanged between state and household without substantial final effect. The index falls from 62 percent for the bottom quintile to 12 percent for the third (and 11 percent for the average household) before rising to 57 percent for the top quintile. At the extremities of the income distribution, the direction of movement is clear; in the centre, the values nearly cancel each other out.

The 'churning' effect has been increasing over time. The index for the average household was 28 percent in 1967 (the first year for which the calculation is available) and 23 percent in 1971 before falling to 15 percent in 1974, since when it has fluctuated (see Table 13). The principal variable has been the increase in cash benefits, which were 11 percent of the final income of the average household in 1967, but 22 percent in 1983. Between 1967 and 1983 the final post-transfer income of the average household was always rather less than the original income, fluctuating between 83 and 91 percent, but the level of transfers in both directions has increased. In 1967 the average household lost 38.0 percent of its income in taxation and recovered 21.2 percent in benefits; in 1983 the proportions had risen to 47.2 and 25.3 percent.

Table 13		Transfers for the average household		
			in UKL	
	Original income	Final income	Net amount redistributed	'Churning' indicator (a)
1967	1 394	1 161	233	28
1968	1 453	1 233	220	25
1969	1 519	1 271	248	26
1970	1 656	1 383	273	26
1971	1 802	1 544	258	23
1972	1 997	1 764	233	19
1973	2 309	2 078	231	17
1974	2 719	2 448	271	15
1975	3 386	3 000	386	16
1976	3 781	3 354	427	16
1977	4 230	3 810	420	14
1978	4 830	4 410	420	13
1979	5 220	4 690	530	13
1980	6 350	5 630	720	15
1981	7 130	6 350	780	14
1982	7 380	6 620	760	13
1983	7 760	7 060	700	11

(a) Net amount transferred as a percentage of the total turnover of taxes and benefits.

The countervailing movements have had no great redistributive effect, except towards the very poorest. Rather than rationalise the tax and benefits systems, governments have preferred to increase the range and size of benefits, leaving taxation to pay for them; tax reforms and reductions have tended merely to shift the balance between direct and indirect forms. This imbalance between activity and effect is a central criticism of the operation of the British welfare state.

The incidence of services

For all its apparent failure to direct help at the most needy, it might be expected that the effect of the welfare state had been to produce a more equal consumption of social services than would otherwise have been the case. The use of need and merit as an allocation principle in housing, health and education, and the lack of a cash nexus in most social services, would seem to rule out any great disparity in the distribution of services between income groups once they have been standardised for need. And yet there is evidence - from a service-by-service breakdown of the household data quoted in the previous section - that the use of public welfare services follows a pattern of distribution similar to that of private goods and services.

The most systematic argument of this thesis is by Julian Le Grand in *The Strategy of Equality* (1982). He contends that a prime objective of the welfare state was to redistribute resources by differentially high public expenditure on lower income groups; and that data on consumption patterns show that in fact welfare services are consumed disproportionately by higher income groups. Le Grand perhaps exaggerates the place of expenditure-led redistribution as a primary rather than an incidental objective of policy; he also confines himself to health, housing, education and transport, the last of which is not specifically defined as a social service, not including income maintenance benefits. But he does identify how, through accident or design, many welfare programmes benefit the affluent many rather than the needy few.

Le Grand found, using data from the late 1970s, that the most unequal service is transport, where the richest fifth in the income distribution receive 17 times as much subsidy per household on private transport, and 10 times as much on rail transport, than the poorest fifth. Even bus subsidies are marginally unequal. Education is less unequal - an overall balance of three times by the top over the bottom quintile, wholly accounted for by differential expenditure on the over-16s, rising to a five-fold advantage on university expenditure. Next is housing, where the effect of tax expenditures more than cancels out that of direct spending on housebuilding and rent subsidies, leaving the richest stratum nearly twice as well off. Housing support is biased towards those with high incomes and high housing costs. The most equal service is health, not surprisingly given the poor health record of lower socio-economic strata, but there is a disparity when the amount of expenditure per ill person is considered - here the richest groups are 40 percent better off [48].

The rich receive a higher amount of social services in kind than the poor. The mean value of social services in kind in 1983 was UKL 1,550 per household; for the richest 20 percent it was UKL 902 and the next-to-poorest 20 percent UKL 670. The poorest 20 percent disturbed the trend by receiving an average of UKL 691, caused by much higher housing benefit (see Table 14). The official figures, however, by ignoring tax expenditures on housing and not including students in their parents' households, give an incomplete impression of the extent of the inequality of distribution.

Central to Le Grand's thesis is the contention that these absolute sums are the important indicator. Were they to be expressed as proportions of the original income, they

Table 14		Service expenditure by income group, 1983				
			in UKL			
Income group	Health	Education	Housing	Other	Total	Index
Top 20 percent	600	790	20	130	1 570	101
Next 20 percent	600	800	40	70	1 550	100
Middle 20 percent	630	730	60	60	1 520	98
Next 20 percent	630	650	80	60	1 440	93
Bottom 20 percent	650	840	130	50	1 670	108
Mean	610	760	50	70	1 550	100

would be of greatly different significance - less than 10 percent for the top quintile, more than 80 percent to the bottom. It is not surprising that the development of welfare policies has tended to involve a diffusion of support across the electorate. A claim for equity between different types of house tenure, or for making higher education places available to all qualified applicants, is difficult to resist. Means-tested schemes that benefit the poor more precisely tend to be less acceptable politically than are universal benefits. Again, an apparently perverse outcome to welfare state policies is implicit in the political purpose of these policies.

3. Social services output

Evaluation of individual programmes requires a careful definition of what the objectives of a programme are and how they are to be measured. For most social services, input (the commitment of resources, personnel and political attention) is taken as a proxy for output achievement; and intermediate output (the quantity and type of services produced) displaces final output (the desired social and political states) as a measure of performance. Output definition has two overriding problems: defining measures which reflect the policy itself and are not contaminated by other variables; and ensuring that the measures chosen are the politically appropriate ones. These will be explored in three services: health, education and housing.

Health

The record of health policy can be assessed on two levels: intermediate output in terms of staff (doctors, nurses and other support) and indicators of patient load (hospitals and numbers of beds); and some notion of final output, or health status. The causal connection between the two seems to be weak, and it would be wrong to posit mortality and morbidity statistics as evidence of the success or failure of the British National Health Service.

The evidence on caseload assembled in Table 15 shows that the number of hospital inpatients increased by 48 percent between 1960 and 1983 through a reduction in the length of stay, which nearly halved, from 37.6 days in 1960 to 18.7 days in 1980. The number of hospitals and beds has actually decreased, especially during the 1970s. The number of out-patients increased to a lesser degree. Despite this the hospital waiting list has continued to rise.

Table 15	Indicators of caseload			
	1960	1970	1980	1983
Number hospital beds (in 1,000s) (GB)	549	525	441	429
Average length of stay (days) (England)	37.6	25.6	18.7	16.8
Number of inpatients (in 1,000s) (GB)	4 852	6 020	6 810	7 197
Number of outpatients (in 1,000s) (GB)	8 631(a)	9 279	9 053	9 856
Hospital waiting list (in 1,000s) (England)	520	607	640	703
Average GP list (in 1,000s) (England)	2 343(b)	2 478	2 247	2 116

(a) 1964; (b) 1963.

The number of hospital staff has doubled, but this crude measure needs to be refined. As Table 16 shows, the increase of 63 percent in health service staffing between 1961 and 1981 is reduced to 56 percent when allowance is made for changes in health service tasks and in the number of hours worked. The number of doctors has doubled, and the input of nursing staff has increased by a net 50 percent.

Table 16	Health service staffing (a)					
	1961	1971(b)	1971(c)	1976	1976(c)	1981
Medical and dental	19	27	28	34	34	39
Nursing and midwifery	239	309	320	342	365	392
Administrative	47	69	72	99	99	109
Other	198	243	244	268	268	283
Total	503	648	664	743	765	822

(a) Full-time equivalents in thousands, England only.
(b) 1961 basis.
(c) Comparable with 1981 in terms of tasks and hours worked.

The problem in evaluating health policy is to make the transition from health care provision to health itself, which is a matter of subjective well-being as well as objective capacity. Indicators of health status provide an ambiguous picture (Table 17). Average life expectancy has increased by four years for men and five for women, but most of this was concentrated in the first decade of the NHS. Infant mortality has been dramatically reduced to one-third of its 1950 level, but is influenced by nutrition and housing as well as the health care system. Working days lost through sickness have continued to mount: this is an unreliable measure of health, but a better one of its relationship to perceived ability to work.

Table 17	Indicators of health status				
	1950	1960	1970	1980	1983
Working days lost		313(a)	327	345	361
Life expectancy: male	66.4	68.1	68.6	70.2	71.1
female	71.2	73.9	74.9	75.2	77.0
Infant mortality rate	31.2	22.4	18.5	12.2	10.1

(a) 1966

Self-reported health status, as measured by the General Household Survey, shows that 30 percent of the sample have some chronic complaint, and over 10 percent some recent restriction of activity; these proportions seem to have risen since the question was first asked in 1972 (Table 18), when only 20 percent of the sample reported a chronic complaint. This may most plausibly be explained not as a deterioration in levels of health, but of an increase in the perceived level of acceptable well-being.

Table 18   Self-reported health status

Percentage reporting:	Males			Females		
	1972	1979	1982	1972	1979	1982
Long-standing illness, disability or infirmity	20	27	28	21	28	31
As above and limiting activities	n/a	16	17	n/a	18	19
Restricted activity in 14 days before interview	7	12	10	8	14	13

The British health services, providing over 90 percent of health care and mostly free at the point of need, ought to be able to eradicate the differences of class and territory which all health care systems are liable to involve. This makes the variation in the distribution of health care facilities, their utilization, and morbidity, by territory and class, a particular problem. The Black report, published in 1980, showed that higher social classes have a better mortality record, and their advantage has even increased over time (see Table 19). While the mortality of professional men declined from 86 percent of the average in the early 1970s, that of unskilled men remained at least 20 percent above the average.

Table 19   Mortality by occupational group (a)

Occupational group	1949-53	1959-63	1970-72
I (Professional)	86	76(75)	77(75)
II (Mangerial)	92	81	81
III (Skilled)	101	100	104
IV (Semi-skilled)	104	103	114
V (Unskilled)	118	143(127)	137(121)

(a) Standardized mortality of men; figures in brackets are for occupational classifications comparable with 1949-53.

Confirming Le Grand's findings, the data suggest that, while there is no particular evidence that consumption of health resources varies according to class, there is an advantage for higher social classes when health need is taken into account [49]. Another source of inequality is the territorial unevenness of health provision; although steps have been taken since the late 1970s to reallocate funds between health authorities on the basis of standardised mortality rates, these are slow to take effect. In general, there has been a failure in Britain to understand how resource inputs to health are transformed into the desired service output.

Education

In education, indicators of intermediate output show success. Pupil-teacher ratios
have fallen as more teachers have been recruited - between 1960 and 1983, by 24 percent in primary schools and 20 percent in secondary (see Table 20). For primary
schools, the most rapid improvement was in the 1970s, for secondary schools in the
1960s.

Table 20	Pupil/teacher ratios			
	1960	1970	1980	1983
Primary education	28.9	27.7	22.3	22.0
Secondary education	20.0	17.7	16.4	16.0

The choice of appropriate indicators for education output is difficult. An initial
approach is through the kinds of education consumed. A major objective of policy is
to induce pupils to remain at school longer and to provide academic opportunities for
a wider range of ability. The proportion of secondary pupils at comprehensive (all-
ability) rather than selective secondary schools increased from less than one percent in
1954 to 84 percent in 1981, representing a major success for the aims of education
policy. The number of school-leavers with passes in public examinations increased
from 39 percent in 1967 to 54 percent in 1981. Even so, there has been a decline in
the proportion of the 16-18 age group in full-time education since the mid-1970s. At
the other end of the age range, the proportion of children under 5 being educated has
nearly tripled since 1966 to more than half the age-group.

Table 21	Education final output		
	1960	1970	1981
Children under 5 in school as % of all aged 3-4	15.0(a)	20.5(c)	44.3
Percentage of all aged 16-18 in full-time education		36.5(d)	32.0
Percentage of secondary pupils in comprehensive schools	4.7	32.0	83.7
Percentage of school-leavers with exam passes	38.5(b)	42.8	54.7

(a) 1966; (b) 1967; (c) 1971; (d) 1975.

These aggregate figures conceal differences in consumption by class. Estimates of educational access by social class for the earlier part of the period were made by the
Oxford Mobility Project, whose authors conclude that though the fastest rates of
growth almost always accrue to the working class, the greatest absolute increments of
opportunity go to the service class [50]. Table 22 shows how this has operated in terms
of entrance to university: class differentials narrowed slightly between the 1940s and
1960s, but professional families took up most of the expansion in places.

Table 22	Attendance of university by father's class and birth cohort (percentage entering university)		
	Birth cohort		
Father's class	1923-31	1933-42	1943-52
Professional and managerial	15.9	23.7	26.4
Non-manual	4.0	4.1	8.0
Manual and agricultural	1.2	2.3	3.1
All	3.4	5.4	8.5

Table 23 uses General Household Survey data to show how the class gradient of educational qualification has not diminished over time. About half of the children of professionals receive full-time education after leaving school, but only about 10 percent
of those of unskilled manual workers.

Table 23		Full-time post-school education 1981–82, by father's class, sex and age (a)					
Sex	Age	Father's class					
		Professionals, employers, managers	Junior non-manual	Skilled manual	Semi-skilled manual	Un-skilled manual	Total
Male	25–29	47	32	19	18	8	26
	30–39	41	31	14	12	11	22
	40–49	29	25	10	5	7	14
Female	25–29	49	40	21	19	10	28
	30–39	49	32	17	14	9	25
	40–49	38	27	13	9	5	18

(a) Percentage having full-time education after leaving school.

When it comes to educational status - levels of literacy, learning and skill - the indicators are as ambiguous as they are for health, but they do not give substance to any
notion of a general improvement in the educational standard of the population. A
survey found literacy problems among 10 percent of the 23 year olds [51], and the Bul-
lock Report which investigated the matter in the mid-1970s was unable to find evidence of a general improvement in reading skills [52]. A trend towards a greater vocational content in further and higher education courses became evident in the early
1980s and reflects a scepticism about the purpose of an academic education.

Housing

The most characteristic physical expression of the welfare state was the building of
millions of dwellings. The private sector contributed most of this since 1959: public

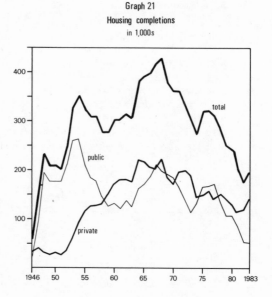

Graph 21

Housing completions
in 1,000s

housebuilding reached its peak at 261,000 in 1953 and 1954, then fell off and was stepped up in the mid-1960s to a peak of 210,000 in 1967. Under the present Conservative government it has fallen even further, from 108,000 completions in 1979 to 55,000 in 1983.

When the components of change in the housing stock are examined, it becomes evident that the net increase in houses is considerably less than the number of new buildings because of losses through slum clearance. Nevertheless the number of dwellings overtook the number of households in Britain in the early 1960s, and by the 1980s there was a crude surplus of over one million. Net additions to the housing stock were at their fastest rate in the late 1960s and only began to fall off markedly in the early 1980s.

Table 24   Components of change in the housing stock (a)

Year	New building	Conversion gain	Slum clearance	Other losses	Net increase
1951-55	1 252	48	92	72	1 136
1956-60	1 298	51	271	95	983
1961-65	1 504	34	322	119	1 096
1966-70	1 716	25	363	136	1 242
1971-75	1 381	44	308	100	1 017
1976-80	1 243	46	187	45	1 057
1981-84	698	53	71	38	643

(a) England and Wales only; in thousands.

A major success of housing policy has been to improve the physical state of dwellings. The total number of unsatisfactory houses fell from 9.7 million (73 percent of the stock) in 1951 to 4.1 million (24 percent of the stock) in 1971 (see Table 25). Most of this improvement reflects the fact that new houses invariably included basic facilities (inside toilet, bath and hot water), and that the housebuilding programme has reduced the sharing of dwellings by more than one household. The number of overcrowded households continued to fall in the 1970s, from 226,000 in 1971 to 109,000 in 1981 [53]. Nevertheless, physical defects like damp and structural weakness have become increasingly prevalent, especially in system-built multi-house units.

Table 25   Households unsatisfactorily housed, 1951-1971 (a)

Type of unsatisfactory condition	1951	1961	1971
Multi-person sharing	1 442	582	380
One-person sharing	430	448	440
Concealed households	935	702	426
Overcrowded	664	415	226
Lack of amenities	7 500	4 700	2 846
Net total	9 700	6 400	4 100
As % of total households	73.2	43.5	24.4

(a) England and Wales only; in thousands.

The more recent data in Table 26 show that, while the number of unsatisfactory houses (in terms of being structurally unfit or lacking a basic amenity) continues to fall, the number requiring major repairs is increasing, by 20 percent during the 1970s. The apparent problem - lack of amenities - has been very largely solved, only to be replaced by one of unexpected deterioration in the physical qualities of the stock itself.

Table 26	Unsatisfactory houses 1971-1981 (a)		
Type of unsatis- factory houses	1971	1976	1981
Unfit	1 276	1 162	1 115
Needing major repairs	864	859	1 049
Unfit and in disrepair	538	464	475
Lacking amenities only	1 642	666	316
Total unsatisfactory	2 815	1 531	910

(a) England only; in thousands.

At the same time, homelessness has become a problem. Despite the surplus of dwellings over households, it became clear in the 1960s that certain groups - the rootless young and the victims of family discord or sudden loss of income - were suffering from the lack of any kind of house. Until 1977 these were dealt with by social services departments, but the Housing (Homeless Persons) Act of that year placed a statutory duty on housing departments to house those who were unintentionally homeless and had a local connection with the area.

The overall record of housing is of apparent physical success but of ultimate failure to achieve satisfactory housing for all. Despite the 9 million dwellings constructed, far too many were of a kind susceptible to physical deterioration and located in an environment that proved socially unacceptable. This applies particularly to the high-rise flats built in large numbers by the public sector in the 1960s. Many of these used non-traditional building techniques and materials like aluminium and concrete which have proved to require costly repairs. The reasons for this are complex, but represent misguided thinking by the architectural and planning professions and a political wish to complete the housebuilding programme quickly and economically[54]. The result is that the one social service that seemed the closest to success now represents the greatest trouble for the future.

Taken as a whole, single programme indicators present two messages. Increased resource input has been translated into visible signs of service like buildings and staff; but there is less clear evidence of effectiveness or results, let alone the eradication of unwanted social conditions. The reason for this is that political attention is concentrated on intermediate output, where results can be achieved quickly. It is very difficult to plan for final output, because the time-scale is longer and the connection between policy and outcome is not easy to trace. It is only in the 1970s that the apparent lack of success in single-service output came to be noticed, but few remedies were offered except resource input better targeted to need, whose achievement has been frustrated by general expenditure restraint and the difficulty of disturbing the gainers from present service patterns.

4. The British welfare state: a success?

The central question in evaluating the British welfare state is not so much whether it has been a success as whether its aim was large-scale social change or merely the improved delivery of services. The former aim would imply a redistribution of income and wealth and the use of the social services to change patterns of power and social relationships. The latter would aim primarily at objectives of coverage and efficiency and at the extension of opportunity.

Stated in this way, the evidence of this chapter suggests relative failure on the former criteria but relative success on the latter. The record on redistribution is a mixed one, because the momentum of equalization of income and wealth has not been maintained. Labour governments have not found it possible to pursue fiscal instruments radical enough to ensure a significant redistribution, and the 1979 Conservative government has reversed the trend towards equality. Just as serious is the distribution of services in cash and kind towards the more affluent income groups. Relatively deprived geographical areas and socio-economic groups have not received the support their circumstances warrant. In their efforts to improve social services without a sufficiently strong economic base, governments have neglected distributional outcomes, the interaction of the tax and benefit systems, and the difficulties of transforming resource inputs into service outputs.

On criteria of technical efficiency, the British welfare state has stronger claims to success. The establishment of the national insurance system and the National Health Service in 1948 provided universal services in a structure of political accountability. There were no class or occupational barriers to access; private sector management was swept away; the highest standards of service were to be found in the public sector. With a public sector presence in education and housing high by international standards, the post-war British welfare state was able from the start to pursue its objectives and enforce political control. Even today there are two clear manifestations of this: the relatively low proportion of national resources devoted to health, reflecting not so much poor service as strong control of the resource claims of the health care professions, and a comprehensive open-ended system of social assistance for those out of work without a contributory benefit entitlement.

The relative weight to be given to these contrasting pictures of failure and success depends on a political interpretation of British welfare as either a radical or a conservative force. Certainly there have been elements of manipulation and social control from Lloyd George's 1912 scheme onwards, which have been prevalent in social policy towards the unemployed up to the present day. And yet the idealistic and innovative elements remain the most impressive. The aim in the late 1940s was to extend the wartime spirit of social solidarity into peacetime conditions. This reflected both the success of national mobilization during the war and the discrediting of many of the social policy structures of the 1930s. The development of new structures that would further reinforce a perceived sense of social solidarity among the British people was a motive force for much of postwar social policy, and it continued through to the search for proper housing and pensions in the 1960s.

The limiting factor on this idealistic spirit is that it was bound up with the theme of reconstruction, in an almost physical sense. The welfare state was to construct the framework of a responsible social life and then retire, its task complete. The Beveridge report was not so much about the virtues of public welfare as about the support and promotion of private responsibility. The state was fitted to run the national insurance scheme not because it was the state, but because it alone could do so with full efficiency and probity. Similarly, British social policy proved much better suited to the physical tasks of house, school and hospital building programmes than to the continuing problems of operation and management. It was assumed that equality of opportunity would be enhanced by an increase in the supply of services, and evidence that the distribution of benefit was little changed was ignored.

This made the crisis of the 1970s all the more difficult to manage. At the time when social policy might have passed its peak of consumption of national resources, it seemed to be demanding yet more. The fact that income maintenance benefits for the elderly, unemployed and children were on an upward trend for demographic and political reasons was combined with pressure for better pay and conditions from public employees. The welfare state seemed to be pre-emptive and uncontrollable. The essential identity of interest between government and people was lost: social services were valued, but not necessarily at the price of increased taxation; forces restricting expenditure became predominant in government.

It became clear in the 1970s that the British model of the welfare state is an exercise in the subordination of social services to public sector norms. This has both strengths and weaknesses. Incorporating service delivery into the public sector helped to achieve economy of cost and social integration; it also provided political goods for politicians, and promoted a culture of expertise and social responsibility. Its vulnerability was to the growing evidence that such the more ambitious aims of policy were not really working. It has not been possible for politicians to distance themselves from social policy or to abstract its products from general issues of public expenditure and taxation. This is why the economic and political correlates of social policy - to be explored in the next section - offer explanations of both achievements and shortcomings.

IV   Correlates and causes: explanations

The relative institutional stability of the British welfare state makes it all the more important to identify the links between patterns of expenditure and various developments extrinsic to social policy. These indicators include the demographic (the structure of age groups in the population and the demands on services that they make), the economic (the rate of growth or stagnation in the economy), and the political (the policies of the party forming the government at the time). This section examines each of these categories in turn, and seeks to provide an explanatory framework for the stages of welfare growth in Britain.

1.   Demographic development

The planning of social policy in Britain has frequently been influenced by projections of population change - most often by projections of growth which have turned out to be optimistic. In reality, however, population growth in most periods has been modest. For instance, the central projection made in 1965 for 1980 was of a total population of 61.2 million, while the actual figure was 55.9 million; the number of births, projected to be 1.5 million by 2000, is now less than 700,000 [55]. The pressure from a high birth rate for increased social provision has been less than was assumed in the 1960s.

The population of the United Kingdom increased from 48.4 million in 1951 to 55.9 million in 1980. The postwar increase was fastest in the 1960s (by over 3 million), but the population has been virtually stable since 1972. Among European Community nations, only Germany has had slower growth since the 1970s.

The main explanatory factor is the fluctuation in the birth rate. After a postwar baby boom, which reached a peak in 1947, the birth rate fell by a quarter by 1951, but then increased steadily to a postwar maximum in 1964. This 'bulge' was a principal motivation for the development of public education and housing policies at this time, and seemed to suggest a continuing increase in household formation which called for a policy response. But the subsequent downturn in births was continuous. In 1973 fertility fell below replacement levels, and in 1976 and 1977 there were more deaths than births. The birth rate recovered slightly after 1977, but since 1980 it has once again declined.

In terms of age groups, the proportion of the population under 20 increased from 20.5 percent in 1951 to 23.9 percent in 1977 before starting to decline; in absolute numbers, an increase from 10.3 to 13.3 million. This relatively low and stable proportion of school-age population contrasts with the number of those aged over 65, which increased from 5.5 million in 1951 to 8.3 million in 1980, or from 10.8 to 14.7 percent of the population. The number of the those aged 75 and over has doubled between 1951 and 1984. The total number of elderly will remain stable over the next two decades, due to the low birth rates of the 1920s and 1930s, but its age profile will become older and thus increasingly burdensome to the health and social services.

The total dependent population reached a peak of 72 percent of the working age population in 1974, but has since declined to less than 65 percent [56]. Even given increasing female participation in the labour force, demographic and educational developments, reinforced in recent years by economic recession, have held the ratio of employed workers to the total population stable: 45.8 percent in 1951, and 44.0 percent in 1980. Despite this, the declining birth rate and stable number of retired people will reduce the demands of the dependant young and old until the postwar generation reaches retirement age - armed with generous pension entitlements - in the second and third decades of the twenty-first century.

Migration has not been a major element in British population change. There has been a small net outflow of less than 100,000 a year except from 1955-61 when there was substantial immigration by Commonwealth citizens, whose right of abode was progressively restricted after 1962. By 1981, 5 percent of the population was self-reported by the EEC Labour Force Survey to be other than 'white', and 8 percent of births were to mothers themselves born in former British colonies in Africa, Asia and the Caribbean [57]. While immigration has been a major political issue, in which alleged pressure on social services has been used as a proxy for racial prejudice, it has had a less significant real impact on population or labour market aggregates.

As a variable relatively detached from the economic policy of government, demographic changes have reinforced changing pressures for expansion and contraction in social provision. But population trends have been stable by comparison with many countries and have not in themselves dictated or pre-empted political choice on the development of services and the application of economic growth.

2. Components of change

The next section uses the OECD component analysis method to separate growth in expenditure into three components: demographic (the share of the relevant population group in the total population); eligibility (the share of beneficiaries in the relevant population); and transfer (the value of the benefit, defined as the average payment per beneficiary as a percentage of per capita GDP) [58].

Old age pensions

The OECD method is most useful for old age pensions. Graphs 22 and 23 show that the growth in the expenditure ratio to GDP was steady from 1950 to 1973 when it accelerated. The sharp increases in 1958 and 1974 are associated with an extension of pension entitlement ten years after the introduction of national insurance in 1948 (evident in the eligibility ratio), and the index-linking of pensions to wages by the 1974 Labour government (evident in the transfer ratio). The demographic ratio has increased from 11 to 15 percent as a consequence of the high level of fertility in the decades before World War I. The eligibility ratio was high, from 75 percent upwards, especially once virtually all the elderly had established a title to benefit under the 1948 scheme. The fact that since the 1940s women with contribution records have been entitled to a pension at the age of 60 lifts the eligibility ratio above 100 percent.

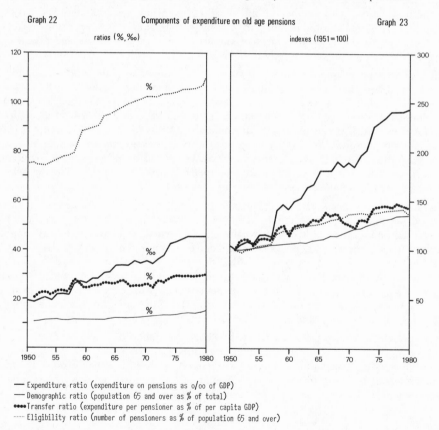

Graph 22   Components of expenditure on old age pensions   Graph 23

ratios (%,‰)   indexes (1951=100)

—— Expenditure ratio (expenditure on pensions as o/oo of GDP)
—— Demographic ratio (population 65 and over as % of total)
●●●●Transfer ratio (expenditure per pensioner as % of per capita GDP)
······· Eligibility ratio (number of pensioners as % of population 65 and over)

The main variable affecting the eligibility ratio is not entitlement but choice of retirement date. Pensions are paid to men aged 65-70 only if they have retired from work, and deferment of retirement enhances the eventual pension. In the 1950s less than half of men retired at 65, and about 20 percent worked until 70 (when pension is paid automatically). From 65 to 70 the pension is subject to reduction if earnings are above a threshold which is about half the male average - the so-called 'earnings rule'. But the economic activity rate for the 65-69 age group has declined markedly, especially during the 1970s when it fell from 30 to 13 percent. As a result the eligibility ratio is continuing to increase, and the main policy variable - the admission of late age entrants in 1958 - accounts for only 9 of the 30 percentage point rise in the ratio over the period.

The transfer ratio has increased by one-third from 20.3 to 29.3 percent, indicating that the average pension has grown faster than GDP. The increases in the late 1950s and the early 1970s are a function of both the real value of the pension and of the extent to which beneficiaries had contribution records which entitled them to a full pension.

Child allowances

The relevant population here is the 0-19 age group, since child benefit (referred to as family allowances until 1977) is paid to all children up to 19 provided they remain in full-time education. Graphs 24 and 25 show that the proportion of GDP devoted to child allowances has remained low - 0.49 percent in 1951 and 1.33 percent in 1980.

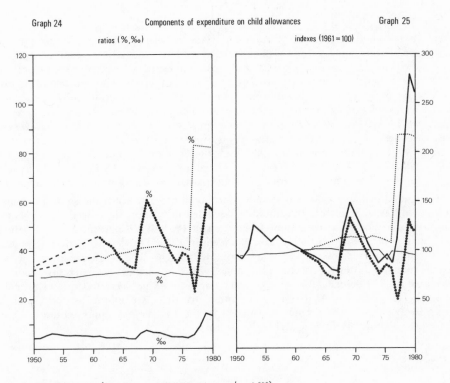

Graph 24   Components of expenditure on child allowances   Graph 25

ratios (%,‰)   indexes (1961=100)

—— Expenditure ratio (expenditure on child allowances as o/oo of GDP)
—— Demographic ratio (population aged 19 or under as % of total)
•••• Transfer ratio (expenditure per child beneficiary as % of per capita GDP)
········ Eligibility ratio (beneficiaries as % of population aged 19 or under)

The increase since 1976 is exaggerated because of the transfer from tax expenditure. A similar caveat applies to the increase in the late 1960s which was partly 'clawed-back' through the income tax system. The demographic ratio has remained remarkably stable, in the range of 29-31 percent, as successive baby booms have worked their way through. The transfer ratio has fluctuated from as low as 0.03 percent of per capita GDP in 1967 to 0.06 percent in 1980 (the low figure of 0.023 percent in 1977 is due to the extension of benefit to the first child in April of that year). In general, the transfer ratio parallels the expenditure ratio, but with sharper increases and decreases.

This leaves the eligibility ratio as the main explanatory variable. Its movements may be accounted for in two ways: the increase in those above the school leaving age who remain in education and so attract benefit; and the extension of benefit to the first child in 1977, which doubled the ratio. If this latter effect is excluded, the record on child benefit is one of stagnation, with a decline in the expenditure and transfer ratios in the early 1960s and early 1970s. Because of growing political awareness of the importance of child benefit to the relief of poverty, its value is now generally maintained in line with prices, though it is not index-linked by law, and the increase in 1985 was well below inflation. This is likely to stabilise the transfer ratio, and the continuing decline in the demographic ratio since 1973 will moderate the overall cost of the benefit.

Education

Here, as for child benefit, the demographic ratio is relatively stable. The proportion of the population aged 5-19 was 20.5 percent in 1951 and 23.3 percent in 1980. It rose slowly to 22.9 percent in 1971 and then rapidly to a peak of 23.9 percent in 1977. The beneficiary ratio (the proportion of the age group who are school pupils) rose fastest between 1967 (69.3 percent) and 1975 (78.0 percent) in a movement associated with, but not totally dependent on, the raising of the minimum school-leaving age from 15 to 16 in 1971. Available data suggest that the transfer ratio (the average cost of education per pupil as a proportion of per capita GDP) rose from 12.5 percent in 1971 to 15.9 percent in 1980 for primary pupils, while that for secondary pupils fell from 22.4 to 20.9 percent in 1979 before rising to 22.6 in 1980 [59]. Changes in the ratio tend to reflect primarily relative class sizes as school populations fluctuate.

This suggests that the major variable in educational expenditure is the shift in demand between different levels of education. As discussed in Section II, educational expenditure as a share of GDP rose from 4.5 percent in 1951 to 6.6 percent in 1973, before beginning a decline which took it to 6.0 percent in 1980. The demographic and beneficiary rates increased less sharply - by about 15 percent. The more expensive sectors have expanded fastest; between 1961 and 1978 the number of university students increased by 159 percent, that of secondary pupils by 46 percent, and that of primary pupils by 15 percent [60]. As a result, the fastest growth in expenditure is caused not so much by aggregate demographic pressure as by the widening of opportunities to enter the more expensive secondary and higher sectors.

Conclusion

All three services for which the component method is appropriate emphasize the low contribution of demographic factors. In old age pensions, the increase in expenditure is a result of the political decision to make pensions available to the entire age group

at levels increasingly generous relative to per capita GDP. In child benefit, the important factors are the extension of benefit to the first child and the political decisions to
increase benefit annually and to avoid most of its erosion by inflation. In education,
the main variable is increasing participation in the more expensive sectors. In all cases,
conscious political decisions were more important than pressure from socio-demographic factors outside the political system.

The timing of the increases in the ratios is worth commenting on. In each of the services studied here it can be seen that transfer and eligibility ratios were held steady in
the 1950s. Once the political changes necessary to increase them (e.g. the index-
linking of pensions or the raising of the school-leaving age), were conceded in the
late 1960s and early 1970s, there was insufficient economic growth to finance them
painlessly, and so expenditure ratios rose. Transfer ratios also increased, as indexation
to prices became an accepted principle. Component analysis suggests that, in Britain,
causes and correlates may best be sought in political rather than demographic explanations.

Education gives a further dimension of explanation, because here the unit cost per
pupil is bound up with the efficiency and mix of cost inputs to the service, and not
just with the generosity of the transfer. In this respect, education is akin to those
social services (health, housing and personal social services) which are less amenable
to component analysis. An important element here is the relative price effect, the tendency in most years for public sector inputs (principally pay, but also land, buildings
and equipment) to rise in price faster than general inflation. In this sense, growth as a
share of GDP may involve a lesser improvement in the real quality of service than in
income transfers where the final choice of expenditure is left to the recipient. Quality
of welfare cannot necessarily be equated with the expenditure indicators used in the
component method.

3. Economic correlates of social policy

British economic development since World War II has been based on a mature economic structure shifting from manufacturing to services (including the public social
services). Table 27 shows that the services sector has become increasingly important to
GDP and, especially, to employment. Agriculture is a relatively small sector in Britain,
accounting for only 4.1 percent of GDP in 1961 and 2.2 percent in 1981, and an even
smaller share of the workforce. Manufacturing has fallen sharply, especially as its 38
percent share of GDP in 1981 included 5.3 percent from North Sea oil, which gener-
ates little employment. Services, many of them in the public sector, now account for
around 60 percent of both employment and output.

Table 27		GDP and workforce by sector				
			percent distributions			
Sector	GDP			Workforce		
	1961	1971	1981	1961	1971	1981
Agriculture	4.1	2.8	2.2	3.2	2.0	1.6
Manufacturing	46.7	42.3	38.0	50.1	45.6	36.5
Services	49.2	54.9	59.8	46.7	58.2	61.9

Two patterns of growth may be distinguished: from 1950 to 1974 an annual average
of 2.8 percent growth (the most consistent growth performance in the modern history

of the British economy); and since 1974 an annual average of 1.4 percent, with two recessionary contractions (see Appendix Table 1). In the early period social policy was able to use the product of this growth, which was assumed to be a minimum that could be increased by the right economic policies; in the second, it had to come to terms with an insufficiency of economic resources to meet its policy pretensions. If we relate the economic record to the policies pursued by governments, the time since 1950 may be divided into four periods (see Table 28).

Table 28   Periods in the development of the English welfare state

Years		Annual average real growth rates of GDP	Standard deviation
1950–1955	Reconstruction	+ 3.0	1.86
1956–1964	Stop-go	+ 2.9	1.82
1965–1972	Search for growth	+ 2.5	0.76
1973–1980	Recessionary cycle	+ 1.8	3.03

Each of these phases corresponds to a particular view of Britain's economic position. The first period represented the emergence from wartime regulation and resource shortages, and the growth record was similar to that of the 'stop-go' period (1956-64) in that attempts to achieve self-sustaining and non-inflationary growth were repeatedly frustrated by balance of payments crises, although downturns were modest and real growth was always maintained. From 1965 to 1972 growth was slower but more stable (hence the lower standard deviation). Increasingly bold policy measures (devaluation, the floating of the pound, and compulsory wage and price controls), were tried in order to stimulate economic growth. The result was instead a 'stagflation' of declining growth rates and inflationary pressures. This culminated in the much sharper cyclical pattern from 1973 onwards, with a standard deviation which was much higher than average growth. At the end of the decade a sharp recession reduced manufacturing output by nearly 15 percent which, allied to the ideology of the 1979 Conservative government, imposed severe strains on the British welfare state.

The relation between economic growth and social expenditure might follow three patterns: coincident, independent or lagging. The first would imply success for the British assumption, built into political orthodoxy and public expenditure planning, that social expenditure should move as a component of economic growth and that its demands should fluctuate in line with economic success. The second would imply the primacy of pressures from within each area of social policy to secure growth whatever the economic circumstances. The third suggests a learning process among political actors in which economic growth is the independent variable either allowing or precluding social expenditure growth.

Graphs 26 and 27 show that social expenditure growth has a pattern similar to, but not coincident with, economic growth as a whole. There is no systematic pattern of leading or lagging, but it is worth noting that the peaks in social growth tend to be higher and that over time the differences between annual growth rates of GDP and social expenditure were increasing until the mid-1970s. The correlation of the two sets of annual growth rates (Table 29) is no higher than 0.26 and even this disappears when social expenditure is lagged, though in some pairs of years (1960-61, 1964-65 and 1973-74) a lagging relationship is observable. The second explanation - that of independent pressures for growth - seems to be the most likely on the basis of the relatively crude data assembled here.

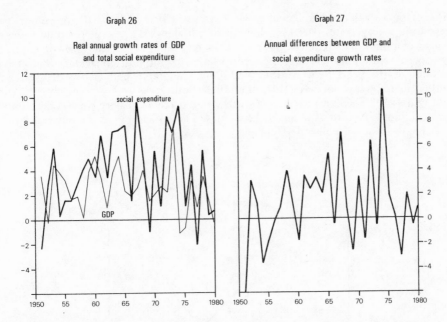

Graph 26

Real annual growth rates of GDP
and total social expenditure

Graph 27

Annual differences between GDP and
social expenditure growth rates

The pattern for individual services is more complex, and analysis is complicated by the lack of official time series at constant prices and by the occasional changes in classification. But Table 29 shows that the highest correlation with economic growth rates is for educational expenditure in the same year (0.47), suggesting that this service, with its mix of capital and current expenditure, is the most closely linked to economic, rather than demographic or political, factors. Housing has a correlation of 0.38 with a one-year lag, but those for health, personal social services and social security are even less significant. The negative correlation for social security may point to its tendency to increase during recessions, whereas the higher correlation for capital than for current expenditure suggests that the former is more dependent on economic growth, an observation which the experience over recent years would confirm.

Table 29   Correlations of annual real growth rates
                  of GDP and social expenditure items

	Lag 0	Lag 1	Lag 2
Total social expenditure	0.26	0.05	0.07
Social capital	0.30	0.05	-0.14
Social current	0.14	-0.25	0.26
Housing	0.21	0.38	-0.31
Health	0.18	-0.20	C.25
Education	0.47	-0.08	0.22
Personal social services	0.19	0.09	0.17

4. Phases in social policy development

The data do not yield a pattern of change in social expenditure which can be related to either institutional development or the phases of economic growth identified earlier. Graph 28 plots the annual growth rates of GDP and social expenditure on axes of the average rates over the whole period. It shows that the plots produce three clusters of points. Firstly, from 1952 to 1958 (excluding 1953) the growth rates of both social expenditure and GDP tended to be below the postwar average. Secondly, for most of the years between 1961 and 1968, they were both above the average. Thirdly, in four years between 1975 and 1980, both grew at 1 percent or less. The eight years when social expenditure growth was 7 percent or more were concentrated in two periods - 1961 to 1967 and 1972 to 1974. These stand out as the times of greatest emphasis on social policy development.

Graph 28

Relationships of GDP and social expenditure

annual real growth rates

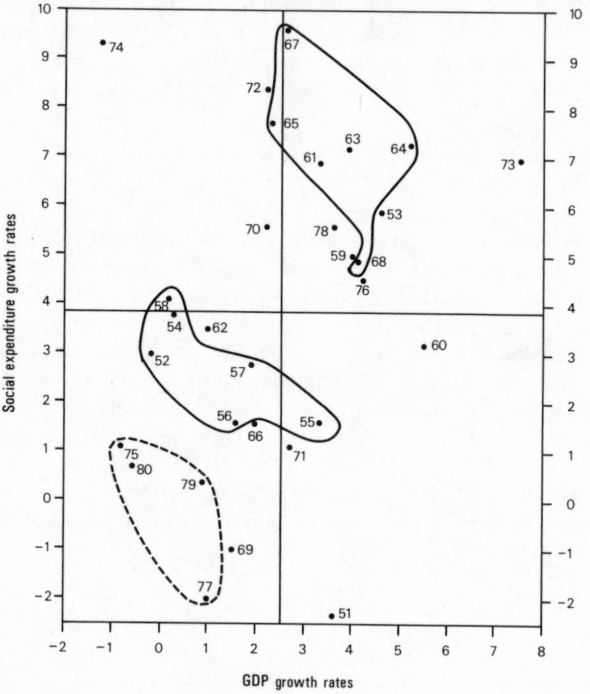

Summarising the data on growth, and relating them to developments in individual services, we see that during the 1950s the postwar welfare state was in place and there were virtually no institutional developments: social expenditure had a static share of GDP; real public expenditure and public employment were falling, and health, education and social security grew at comparable rates. During the 1960s public expenditure started to grow in real terms, and social expenditure increased its share of the total; educational provision was expanded, its growth rate outpacing that of health, and the real value of social security started to increase.

This growth continued until 1975, with a recessionary pause in 1969 after devaluation of the pound. There was steady growth in public non-industrial, and particularly social, employment relative to the total workforce. Social security became the fastest growing category as new benefits were introduced and the value of existing ones improved, and housing expenditure recovered as part of a general concentration on public investment.

From 1975 to 1980 public expenditure fell relative to GDP, and social expenditure was static. There was a sharp divergence of the growth trend between social security (which expanded at its fastest-ever real rate as indexation was accepted and the number of beneficiaries, including the unemployed, increased), and education and housing (which declined in real terms, and dramatically so in the case of public housing investment).

These periods are the retrospective and aggregated outcome of many separate policies, decisions and trends. British social policy making is prospective in that it reflects the supply of policies as well as the demand for them, and is often committed in advance of the availability of resources; they are at the same time sectional, in that discrete decisions are taken in demarcated policy areas. The results of policy are not readily correlated with economic variables, and it is in the political sphere that explanations may most readily be found.

5. Unemployment

There are several reasons for giving particular attention to unemployment. In political debate it is an even more salient indicator than economic growth, being published monthly and widely quoted in the media and parliament; it has become the principal indicator of the success or failure of economic policy; and the state is itself a major employer (of nearly one-third of the workforce) and is able to create or protect jobs. Unemployment was low in Britain for most of the postwar years, but rose to over 3 million, or 13 percent of the workforce, in the early 1980s as manufacturing employment contracted sharply and was not sufficiently replaced by the services sector. The creation of new jobs in the social services, especially for women working part-time, also slowed down as the control of public expenditure became an overriding preoccupation and prevented social policy from taking on a countercyclical character.

Component analysis is also useful here (see Graphs 29 and 30), though it can only be done on a full basis from 1959. The demographic ratio needs to be split into an activity ratio (the working population relative to the total population) and an unemployment ratio (unemployment relative to the employed labour force). The eligibility ratio (the proportion of the unemployed in receipt of unemployment benefit) is important, as is the transfer ratio (the extent to which average unemployment benefit replaces per capita GDP). The expenditure ratio (unemployment expenditure relative to GDP) is affected by cyclical movements in unemployment, though in the British case the relatively low rate of these movements does allow a pattern over time to become evident.

Expenditure on unemployment has risen from 0.14 percent of GDP in 1960 (a level also typical of the 1950s) to 0.48 percent in 1980. The most rapid growth occurred in 1967, 1971 and 1976, and an examination of the other ratios indicates the causes of this. The increase in 1967 is due to the coincidence of an increase in the transfer ratio from 0.26 to 0.43 on the introduction of an earnings-related supplement to unemployment benefits. In 1971 and 1976 the cause was an increase in the unemployment ratio, which was to be repeated from 1980 onwards. This increase has tended to obscure the decline in two other ratios: the eligibility ratio fell from 71 percent in 1972 to 48 percent in 1980 as fewer of the unemployed had a contributions record which would

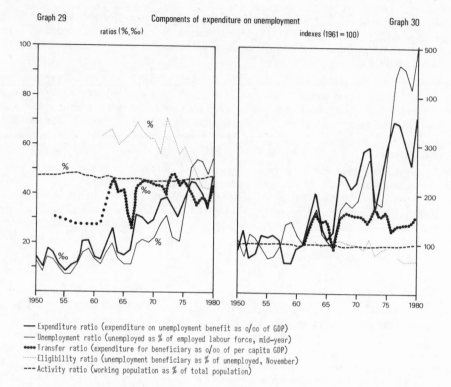

Graph 29   Components of expenditure on unemployment   Graph 30

ratios (%,‰)   indexes (1961 = 100)

— Expenditure ratio (expenditure on unemployment benefit as o/oo of GDP)
— Unemployment ratio (unemployed as % of employed labour force, mid-year)
•••• Transfer ratio (expenditure for beneficiary as o/oo of per capita GDP)
······ Eligibility ratio (unemployment beneficiary as % of unemployed, November)
--- Activity ratio (working population as % of total population)

entitle them to unemployment benefit; and the transfer ratio tended to fall from a peak of 50 percent in 1973, its level depending upon the number of long-term unemployed (who lost earnings-related supplement after six months) as well as the real level of benefit. Both these trends have intensified in the 1980s, as the proportion of those jobless for more than one year reached a third of the total, and as the earnings-related supplement was abolished in stages between 1980 and 1982. The component analysis reveals clearly that an increase in unemployment expenditure has been accompanied by a loss in the value of benefit to the claimant - a reversal of the policy approach of the 1960s.

6. The political context

The policies and electoral competition of the major parties are an important aspect of social policy change. In Britain, the definition of social policy from the nineteenth century onwards has been in terms of public legislation - public health acts, education acts, national insurance and social security acts. Once the franchise was extended to all adults (men in 1918, women in 1928), the social policies expressed by these Acts of Parliament became the most comprehensible areas of competition between the parties. Until World War II, the lack of fully alternating majority governments - for only the Conservative Party was able to form a majority government in the inter-war years - and the prevalence of old-fashioned balanced budget economics, reduced the scope for the party differentiation of policy. In the 1930s both Labour and Conservative governments were prepared to cut unemployment benefit; after a party split in 1931

the Labour government fell and a coalition government led by the Conservatives presided over a cut in government expenditure.

World War II fundamentally changed the shape of party competition over the welfare
state. By leading to the admission of Labour to a coalition government in 1940, it
gave the party credibility in office and a share in the wartime effort, thus paving the
way for Labour's victory in the 1945 general election. High public expenditure during
the war suggested that state activity could be increased while preserving economic stability. Keynesian economics gave an intellectual justification to countercyclical intervention by the state. The planning of reconstruction, even while the war was in progress, was inspired initially by a wish to rationalize the unsatisfactory administrative
arrangements of the 1930s. In practice, however, the resulting proposals - like the
1942 Beveridge Report and the 1944 Education Act - had broader social objectives
which all parties were prepared to accept, especially as more fundamental questions
regarding equality and class conflict were not asked. By the end of the war there was
a wide consensus on the objectives of policy. Conservatives emphasised individual initiative and Labour supporters social solidarity, but these were not reflected in radically
different policies.

After 1945, the Labour and Conservative Parties entered into two-party electoral competition, trading with the electorate in promises of public services, with diminishing
ideological emphasis. It was only at the end of the period - from 1979 onwards - that
the picture was altered by the strength of the Liberal/Social Democratic Alliance and
the rediscovery of ideological roots by both Labour and Conservative. Before then, it
is possible to assess party competition in the same terms as demographic or economic
variables.

The main source of information about party competition is the manifesto issued by
each party before a general election. These have a symbolic significance in Britain as
they define a mandate to which the winning party is committed and which the civil
service will do its best to implement. Manifestos are more significant than party policy
documents, which are issued regularly and usually do not commit the party to action
in government. In the field of social policy, Labour issued a notable document on
National Superannuation in 1957 which defined its pension policy, and during its
periods in opposition in the early 1970s and 1980s the party prepared comprehensive
future programmes; but all of these had to be incorporated into manifestos, when
some of the pledges were moderated.

Table 30 analyses the proportion of text devoted to social policy issues in each Conservative and Labour manifesto, and the main theme mentioned. It shows the
relatively low level of attention given to social policy objectives in postwar manifestos
- usually about 20 percent of the total space and never more than one-third - well
behind foreign, economic and industrial policy. Housing consistently came first early
in the period, especially as it was amenable to a 'numbers game' of promises
concerning housebuilding performance. Other services were neglected in terms of
policy detail, being confined to moral imperatives. The 1950 Labour manifesto had no
specifically social policy section at all, concentrating on production, agriculture and
the cost of living, and seeing social policy in terms of 'helping each other in time of
need' and the 'moral order'. In 1951 Labour spoke of social justice', and the Conservatives of 'value for money' - both being compatible with the organization of the postwar welfare state.

A change of emphasis may be traced from the mid-1950s onwards. Labour's sense of
social solidarity and faith in their post-1945 achievements were replaced by specific

Table 30   Social issues in electoral manifestos

Election	Relative weight of social issues (a)		Major social issue mentioned	
	Conservative L	Labour	Conservatives	Labour
1945	35	19	housing	housing
1950	16	17	housing	the 'moral order'
1951	5	33	housing	social justice
1955	12	19	housing	housing
1959	19	22	ending poverty in old age	education
1964	16	21	opportunities for youth	education
1966	18	17	providing most care for those in need	the family in the new welfare state
1970	23	30	homes for all	education and social equality
1974 Feb.	19	18	helping the pensioner	social justice
1974 Oct.	30	19	people and their homes	social justice
1979	19	17	helping the family	a fairer Britain
1983	21	19	responsibility and the family	helping families

proposals for reforming pensions (by an earnings-related element), social assistance (less stigmatic), and education (comprehensive organization) - all implicit repudiations of the Attlee government. Conservative minimalism and deference to the private sector were replaced by expansion, to be paid for by economic growth. By 1959, extensive programmes of hospital and housing construction, and of expansion in higher education, were promised by the Conservatives, together with a new undertaking to end poverty in old age in response to evidence that this had not been eradicated.

From 1964, political debate was dominated by Labour's idiom of 'fresh virile leadership' under Harold Wilson; policies were specified in increasing detail, including a wage-related scheme for retirement, sickness and unemployment aiming at half-pay benefits for those on average earnings. Promises became even bolder in 1966, when the Conservatives pledged themselves to 'remodel the welfare state' (no longer a term of abuse) by higher expenditure, and Labour promised to build 500,000 houses a year (the last of the 'numbers game' targets, and one that was never achieved). The spirit was the same in 1970, with pensions becoming a priority for both parties: promises about uprating headed each manifesto in February 1974.

In the 1970s both main parties rediscovered ideological roots that had been suppressed since the 1930s. Labour now sought a broader notion of social justice (including womens' rights), while the Conservative shift was even sharper. In 1970 under Heath, the manifesto stated that 'the fundamental problem of all Britain's social services - education, health, provision for the old and those in need - is shortage of resources'. By 1979 the theme had become that of 'helping the family', with the role of the welfare state being limited to one of supporting the discretion and responsibility of the citizen. This was signalled by maxims such as 'reviving the private rented sector' (in housing), 'standards in education', 'parental rights and responsibilities', and 'making sense of social security'. In 1983 the theme of responsibility for personal decisions was made even more explicit, though coupled with an attempt to claim political credit for high social expenditure. British social policy had come full circle as the notion of a consensual, technical, efficient welfare state based on high resource input had failed to blunt party ideology.

7. The party composition of government and welfare state development

The test of the impact of party competition on British social policy is the extent of the matching of the phases of welfare state development identified earlier, with the periods of government by each party. The main period of welfare state expansion in the 1960s straddles governments. Contraction from the late 1970s onwards, though much intensified by the Conservatives, must be regarded as a continuation of Labour's cutbacks of public expenditure (especially capital) and concern about public sector pay. Examination of growth rates by party gives weight to this cross-party view. From 1950 to 1980 the 17 years of Conservative governments had an average annual growth of 2.9 percent in GDP and 4.1 percent in social expenditure; the 13 years of Labour saw 2.0 percent annual growth in GDP and 3.5 percent in social expenditure. Conservative governments have raised social expenditure faster, despite what might be regarded as a lesser ideological commitment; but Labour has had a greater gap between the two growth rates. These approaches are typified by the 1970s, when in the Conservative government from 1970 to 1974, social spending grew by an annual 5.5 percent (the fastest of any postwar government) but was accompanied by a 4.1 percent growth in GDP; and the Labour government from 1974 to 1979, when social spending expanded twice as rapidly as GDP (3.2 percent as against 1.3 percent) [61].

Further evidence may be sought in the legislative field. It is not possible in Britain to distinguish 'core laws' from subsidiary legislation; a table of crude numbers of acts of parliament would be misleading. It is nevertheless noticeable that the most important legislation has occurred under two administrations - those of Attlee (1945-51) and Heath (1970-74). This is true of pensions and health and to some degree of housing. Pension policy remained largely unchanged from the 1946 National Insurance Act to the 1973 Social Security Act (which never came into effect, but was amended by Labour's 1975 Social Security (Pensions) Act). Health remained unchanged from the 1947 National Health Services Act to the 1973 National Health Services (Reorganization) Act. Housing has been the object of legislative action by all postwar governments, but the most radical change of course came with the 1972 Housing Finance Act. Education is a different case because its core law (the 1944 Education Act) has never been replaced; here policy has been altered largely through administrative advice (such as circular 10/65 on comprehensive reorganization), and public expenditure decisions. Despite frequent comment regarding adversarial policies in Britain, legislative changes are not a fully accurate indicator of the political input to social policy.

8. Pressure groups

Input to the social policy process does not come only from political parties. British politics has become increasingly marked by corporatist modes of operation in which the role of pressure groups in the policy process has both increased and changed. The traditional influence of the (Anglican) Church in education was reduced by the education settlement with the Churches in 1944; and that of the friendly societies and the voluntary hospitals was removed by the comprehensive nature of the health and social security reform in 1948. In their place, pressure groups based on occupational position have become dominant. This is especially true for professional associations such as the British Medical Association, and trade unions, which in Britain organize relatively more of the public than the private sector.

The 1974 Labour government marked the apogee of corporatism, with the so-called 'social contract' with the Trade Union Congress (TUC), which traded moderation in pay bargaining for social expenditure, especially on pensions and housing. Under both Heath and Wilson the employers organized in the Confederation of British Industry (CBI), were drawn in with the TUC and the government as corporate partners in economic planning. Both organizations took an interest in social issues, but chiefly as they affected their members (on matters like technical education and occupational health). Under the 1979 Conservative government the use of corporatist decision-making declined.

In the 1960s a more distinctive type of pressure group grew up, bringing informed comment, often from academics, into the debate, and for tactical reasons concentrating attention on the opposition of the day and seeking to win manifesto commitments from them. Most notable of these were Shelter (housing), the Child Poverty Action Group (campaigning for increased child benefit), and groups concerned with the disabled. The arguments of these groups are often better informed than those of traditional corporate interests, but they lack the central place in the policy process found, for instance, by pressure groups in agriculture, energy and employment policy.

Conclusion

Welfare state development in Britain, as elsewhere, is the product of demographic, economic and political factors. The relative influence of them is best expressed by a hierarchy of explanation, moving from the least to the most significant:

- the demographic base is relatively stable and, while significant for pensions, child allowances and educational policy, is less important than political decisions about coverage and value;

- political intervention by the parties is less than the clarity of two-party competition in Britain would suggest; party ideology has been expressed more in terms of symbols and rhetoric than in substantive policy change, at least until the 1980s; the 1940s, 1950s and 1960s provides an untypically consensual period in the history of the British party system;

- the economic situation has influenced social policy, but there is not a readily analysable relation between economic and social policy growth; a broad similarity of movement without precise correlation suggests that the two trajectories tend to fall into line despite attempts to plan them independently;

- some concept of a political and economic climate needs to be posited in order to explain the lack of similar periodizations of the welfare state and party government; what may be suggested is a learning process, which filters through the social services at different rates, and sets a climate of expectation about policy development, but at the same time imposes a sense of limitation through resource constraints and the perceived failure of some policies to achieve their objectives. The balance between the two changes over time, and the latter has become prominent at the end of the period; the point to emphasize is that the interplay between them is more subtle than a quantification of economic and social change would suggest.

V A crisis of the British welfare state?

The mood of politics and policy-making in the British welfare state changed sharply during the mid-1970s. For many bureaucrats and professionals, the change can be dated almost precisely to a package of cuts in public expenditure announced in December 1973 in the wake of the oil crisis. This marked the end of the Conservative government's attempts to solve what were seen as residual problems of social welfare by a higher resource input. Shortly after, the Heath government was voted out of office after failing to break a national coal miners' strike.

The incoming Labour government returned briefly to an expansionary policy, especially on housing and pensions, but its 'social contract' with the unions soon lost credibility as public expenditure, inflation, and public sector wage awards appeared to go out of control. A rigid pay policy was enforced in 1975, but further pressure on the currency and the balance of payments led to new rounds of cuts in 1976 under the tutelage of the International Monetary Fund. For the first time, aggregate targets for public expenditure and public sector borrowing came to determine policy, rather than the reverse.

The victory of the Conservatives under Thatcher in 1979 caused this principle to be proclaimed even more decisively, and showed that a moderate Labour administration was failing to meet the expectations of the electorate. The result had profound consequences: it seemed to give political justification to the right-wing, free market ideology adopted by the Conservatives; hastened a more left-wing definition for Labour, which precipitated the breakaway of the Social Democratic Party in 1981; and destroyed much of the structure of assumptions about public policy and the acceptability of policy changes to the electorate. The 1983 Conservative victory, with a share of the poll only slightly reduced, seemed to confirm the new dispensation.

Whether these developments may be regarded as a 'crisis' in more than a rhetorical sense is less clear. Crisis involves destabilization of the social structure and the re-evaluation of public priorities. In Britain both middle-income taxpayers and the poor and unemployed have seemed to accept rather than challenge the economic conditions of their lives. The atmosphere of 1981, with unemployment nearly doubling to three million and urban disturbances in racially mixed cities, was rapidly displaced by the jingoism of the Falklands war of 1982, which marked a reversion to nineteenth century concerns of security and national identity.

The motif of the 'cuts' has entered the vocabulary of the British social services, but this cannot be equated with real cuts in expenditure. During the first Conservative term (comparing 1983-84 with 1978-79), public expenditure increased by 7 percent in real (cost) terms because of the government's decision to increase expenditure on defence, law and order and social security; even securing the minimalist state proved to be expensive [62]. Ironically, the greatest sense of perceived cuts in terms of political and media attention have come in sectors where expenditure has been increased (social security and health). This suggests an interplay between public expectations and cost pressure as the main defining characteristic of recent social policy, and the one which this section seeks to explore.

1. A change in the orientation of social policy

In Britain, institutional reforms in public policy have been associated with times of expansion, the 1940s and 1960s. They have been seen as vehicles for extending the range and quality of services offered, but experience has tended to show that they incur transitional costs and fail to achieve more than a technical success in implementation. The Conservative Party gained a poor reputation for being associated with the reorganization of local government and the National Health Service in 1974. The latter reform in particular, with its elaborate hierarchies and consultative methods, became a symbol of the wrong turning taken by Conservatism under Heath. Conversely, institutional stability has been associated with retrenchment, and has been the preferred course under most Conservative governments.

Under Thatcher, public policy has sought to operate on a restricted range of variables, and the scope and pretensions of the public sector have been reduced. The concentration has been on matters such as rewards to employees, ownership and tenure, and the containment of rights to public services. In all of these, the Thatcher administration has secured a change far more substantive than the organizational devices of the Heath government.

The pay of public sector employees expanded rapidly in 1979-80 as comparability awards made by the Clegg Commission came into effect. These were an inheritance of the 'winter of discontent' of 1978-79, the industrial action by low-paid manual public employees, which was ended by the promise of a pay review. As a percentage of the private sector, public sector wages rose from 101.5 in 1979 to 108.8 in 1981. The Conservatives agreed to accept the Clegg awards, but subsequently imposed annual norms on public sector pay, linked to the planning of expenditure in cash rather than volume terms, which nearly eliminated the public sector pay advantage by 1985. Although the targets were not formally enforced and in practice were not always achieved, the 'squeeze' of cash-limited planning had a cumulative effect.

In terms of ownership and tenure, for the first time in the postwar years a British government sought seriously to alienate public assets and distance itself from the ownership of means of economic and social production. An increasingly bold programme of denationalization led to plans by 1984 to sell the majority of shares in almost all profitable state enterprises, including British Telecommunications and British Airways. Long-distance coach travel was deregulated by the 1980 Transport Act, and competition between airlines allowed to increase. This process marked a transfer of resources from producers and the state to owners and consumers as costs were reduced to increase profitability; it also allowed a higher level of public expenditure to be financed by the one-off benefit of asset sales, running at UKL 2 billion a year by 1984.

In the social field, the most important changes of ownership came from the statutory right given to public sector house tenants to buy their houses at a discount rising from 60 percent of the value according to their length of occupancy. By 1985, over 850,000 houses had been sold, reducing the public sector share of the housing stock by 6 percentage points. Moreover, the new owners became a source of political recruitment for the Conservative Party as Labour was slow to redefine its commitment to socialized housing. The sales also financed about half the cost of the much reduced programme of public housing construction, which was channelled increasingly through voluntary housing associations financed by the state, rather than through local authorities. The transfer of the payment of all means-tested housing benefit to local authorities in 1982 further benefited central government by reducing the size of the civil service and associating the unpopularity of the implementation of the change with authorities who were often controlled by Labour. Old notions of administrative optimality and social protection in housing as the responsibility of the state were replaced by an equally uncritical faith in private and voluntary provision.

A far more permissive framework for the social services is also evident in the interest in 'contracting-out' support services such as cleaning, catering and transport in the fields of health, social work and education. The Statutory Sick Pay scheme, introduced in 1983, transfers responsibility for paying benefit during the first eight weeks of sickness in a year, to employers, who deduct the cost from their national insurance contributions. Interest in a more liberal and personalized pension provision led to measures implemented in 1986 to protect the position of 'early leavers' from schemes and to allow contracting-out from company schemes.

This change of attitude may be seen as an alternative to institutional reform. Table 31 shows that the major reorganizations have been few. In 1980 the Supplementary Benefits Commission was abolished and the payment of social assistance vested directly in the Department of Health and Social Security, but this change had little practical effect and was the outcome of a review launched by the Labour government. The main reform was in health in 1982, when area and district authorities in England were merged into a single second tier. In 1983 health administration was further modified by the introduction of a National Health Service Supervisory Board and chief executive, with designated general managers in each authority. This showed a new interest in managerial control, but significantly the change was introduced after a brief and rapid inquiry (the Griffiths Report) undertaken by a food store executive [63]. The model of the retail chain store, with effective cost and stock control and responsiveness to changing consumer preferences, has come to symbolize the new Conservative welfare state. The old techniques of Royal Commissions and committees of enquiry with a balanced group of eminent persons, and of reorganizing central government as a symbol of policy priorities, have been almost totally abandoned. Instead, policy review has been undertaken inside existing departments, with considerable political input.

Table 31	Major institutional reforms, 1980–1986
1980	Social Security Act 1980: Supplementary Benefits Commission abolished; payment of supplementary benefit vested directly in Department of Health and Social Security
1982	Area tier in English health authorities abolished, under Health Services Act 1980
1982–83	Payment of housing benefit for supplementary benefit claimants transferred from Department of Health and Social Security to local housing authorities, under Social Security and Housing Benefits Act 1982
1983	Griffiths report on health service management: National Health Service Supervisory Board established, chaired by Secretary of State for Social Services
1984	Government legislation enacted to allow central government to set maximum levels for a local authority's rate (local property tax)
1986	Abolition of Greater London Council and metropolitan county councils in England and transfer of their functions to districts or joint boards

The overlap and complexity between the tax and benefit systems have prompted frequent suggestions of structural reform; but here too the political and administrative capacity to push changes through has been lacking. In 1972 the Heath government had proposed a tax credit system to introduce an element of negative income tax; the Liberals and Social Democrats, free of the constraints of office, have worked out a similar system; in 1984 the Institute for Fiscal Studies proposed a structure of tax credits and benefit credits progressively withdrawn as income increased or circumstances of social need were reduced [64]. Part of the problem is technical: the Inland Revenue and the Department of Health and Social Security failed to computerize their operations until the 1980s, though both now have plans to do so [65]. In addition a new system is likely to be less discriminatory - and thus the transitional period is likely to lead to either increased total expenditure or unacceptable losses for individuals. In previous years governments were prepared to finance the costs of change: now they are reluctant to bear them and prefer an immobility whose long-term inefficiency can be concealed from the immediate political agenda.

2. Marginal cuts in benefits

By 1979 the British welfare state appeared to have a stable structure of entitlements and expectations, some apparently guaranteed by law (national insurance benefits), others politically entrenched (public action on poor housing conditions, higher education for all qualified school leavers, access to advanced medical treatment). But equally, the government's parliamentary majority and the centralised control of public finance make it possible for government to execute rapid changes of policy, especially if the political salience of the services is less than was assumed by those with a vested interest in high expenditure and employment.

Table 32 shows that the major cuts in benefit came early in the Conservatives' first term. Previous Conservative administrations had been just as active as Labour in

Table 32   Changes in Benefit

Year	Change
1980	Long-term pensions and benefits to be indexed to prices, not to earnings if higher (saving UKL 500 million)
	Earnings-related supplement on short-term benefits abolished (in stages by 1982) and 1980 uprating abated by 5 percent as prelude to bringing the benefits into income tax (saving UKL 500 million)
	1980 uprating of benefits deferred by two weeks (saving UKL 100 million)
	Supplementary benefit additions for special circumstances and needs replaced by more restrictive single payments; maximum capital of UKL 2,000 allowed to be eligible for benefit
1981	1 percent overestimation of inflation in 1980 uprating recouped
	1981 uprating underestimated inflation by 2 percent - made up in 1982
1982	Contribution of general taxation to National Insurance Fund reduced from 18 to 13 percent
	Unemployed no longer required to register for work at a public employment agency
	Self-certification for the first 7 days of sickness introduced
	Housing benefit introduced (in two stages, November 1982 and April 1983): all housing assistance paid through local authorities
1983	Statutory Sick Pay introduced: benefit, on simplified scale, to be paid by employers for first 8 weeks of sickness in year and deducted from National Insurance contributions (saving UKL 400 million and 3,000 posts)
	Uprating of benefits each November to be based on May-May actual inflation rather than estimated November-November
	Women allowed to claim supplementary benefit on behalf of a household with an adult male if the principal breadwinner
1984	Supplementary benefit allowance for housing costs for non-householders aged 18-20 withdrawn
	Additions for child dependants on short-term national insurance benefits withdrawn
	Severely disabled allowance to replace non-contributory invalidity pension and remove test of fitness for household duties for married women (cost UKL 20 million)

extending the range of benefits, and the cuts represented a change of direction. The most significant cost saving was the indexing of retirement pensions to prices rather than to earnings - which is liable in the long-term to jeopardize the earnings-relation targets of state pensions. More politically controversial was the decision in 1980 to tax unemployment and sickness benefit, because this was the occasion of an immediate 5 percent cut in uprating to allow immediate implementation of the equivalent saving, and to abolish the earnings-related supplement on these benefits. Other changes, notably statutory sick pay, housing benefit and the system of single payments for non-routine needs under supplementary benefits, have made the system somewhat less generous and more rough-and-ready. Some additions payable on scale rates for children and other dependants have been trimmed. But two points need to be emphasised. The basics of the system and the annual uprating of benefits in line with prices have been maintained, with other cuts used to finance this in the public expenditure bargaining process. And the changes have been made directly by government on immediate political grounds without the need to consult employer or employee representatives or reckon with notions of actuarial equity.

These two points remained paramount even through a major review of social security by the government in 1984-85, and became known as the 'Fowler reviews' after the Secretary of State for Social Services, Norman Fowler. Proposals for discussion were issued in June 1985 and final government proposals in December 1985, which are intended to come into effect in April 1988 [66]. The centrepiece of the June 1985 proposals was the abolition of the State Earnings-Related Pension Scheme in favour of compulsory occupational insurance, but after widespread opposition this was withdrawn in favour of marginal cuts in pension benefits after the year 2000 and easier terms for contracting-out. Supplementary benefit is to be replaced by a similar Income Support scheme at rates more favourable to the disabled and families at the expense of pensioners and the young single childless. The difficulties of low-paid family heads in work are to be recognised by a Family Credit scheme offering better terms than Family Income Supplement. Some expenditure cuts will be involved - especially in housing benefit - but the main result is likely to be a modest technical improvement in the system and a clearer distinction between 'deserving' and 'undeserving' poor, in Conservative terms.

3.   Cost pressure on the welfare state

The paradox of social policy expenditure since 1975 is that perceived cuts have coincided with the growth of inflation-adjusted expenditure (see Table 33). From 1979 to 1985 social expenditure rose by 12 percent, despite the 46 percent fall in housing and near stability in education. Health and social services rose by 19 percent and social security by 30 percent. This represents the continuation of a trend evident during the 1974-79 Labour government, in which social expenditure rose by 15 percent, with social security up 33 percent and falls of between a quarter and a half in capital expenditure in other services being more than offset by a rise in current expenditure. It also contrasts with the rise of 21 percent in social expenditure in the three years of the Heath government. And yet so much of the learning experiences in British welfare had been in terms of increasing employment, increasing real rewards to employees, increasing support services to professions, and an increasing quality of equipment and physical stock, so that purely financial growth was of little political consolation. Moreover, the data are in cost terms and do not necessarily represent a greater volume of services.

Table 33	The growth of social expenditure by programme		
	(percentage change)		
	1970/1-1973/4	1973/4-1978/9	1978/9-1984/5
Housing	+52.6	-6.5	-46.0
Education	+21.0	+1.5	+0.5
Health and personal social services	+16.8	+19.4	+18.9
Social security	+14.0	-32.6	+30.0
Total social expenditure	+21.4	+15.0	+12.0
Total public expenditure	+17.2	+6.8	+11.5

A clue to the nature of this dilemma for government is given in official studies prepared in 1983-84. In 1983 a Treasury analysis was leaked to the press and became the basis of allegations about a 'secret manifesto', during the June 1983 election campaign. A carefully edited Green (discussion) paper on *The Next Ten Years: Public Expenditure and Taxation into the 1990s* was published in March 1984. This suggested that 'even if the public expenditure planning total is held flat in real terms up to 1988-89, the non-North Sea tax burden will, on the assumptions used here, be lower than 1983-84 but still slightly above its 1978-79 level' [67]. In short, the Conservative strategy of real tax reductions - excluding the windfall of revenues from North Sea oil taxation, which reached a peak in 1985 - cannot be achieved if there is any real increase in public expenditure.

The reason for this is indicated in the data by service given in Table 34. In the 1980s housing is likely to face the greatest upward cost pressures, because much less income from council house sales will be available. There is also an emergent problem of repair on much postwar housing, especially high-rise and industrialised building. This affects both the public sector (which is losing the best stock through sales) and owner-occupiers seeking improvement and repair grants from government.

Table 34	Cost pressures on the welfare state		
	(expenditure as % of GDP)		
Programmes with high cost pressure	1982-83	Projections for 1990-91 (a) optimistic	pessimistic
Housing	1.2	1.2	2.2
Defense	5.0	5.0	5.6
Health and personal social services	4.8	4.8	5.4
Employment	0.9	0.8	1.1
low cost pressure			
Education	4.5	3.5	4.2
Social security	11.3	9.7	11.1
Total public expenditure	44.0	39.3	46.8

(a) Optimistic projection based on 2.5 percent growth and 5 percent inflation, pessimistic projection on 0.5 percent growth and 10 percent inflation.

More pressure comes from health and social services, politically salient but dominated by a medical profession which tends to make the mix and prices of inputs inflexible. It is estimated that to keep pace with the demographic structure (the increasing number of elderly people) requires real spending growth of 0.7 percent a year; to meet 'inescapable innovations' another 0.5 percent; and to improve long-term care and meet demand for body repair through transplants and bone replacement a full 2 percent [68]. For instance, the number of operations carried out on those aged 75 and over increased by 49 percent between 1971 and 1979. Management devices such as performance indicators, assumed efficiency savings, and contracting-out cannot disguise this medical demand.

The other high pressure area relevant to social policy is employment and labour market policy, where spending on job subsidies and retraining rose by 61 percent in the first Conservative term. Funding and curriculum for further education is increasingly controlled by employment policy-makers. This is a sector particularly sensitive to economic assumptions, especially on the future level of unemployment.

These sectors are counterbalanced by low pressure from education, where the number of pupils is projected to fall from 8.9 million in 1984 to 8 million in 1991, and fulltime students from over 500,000 to under 450,000 as the falling birth rate reaches school-leaving age. More surprisingly, the immediate climate is benign for social security, as the number of persons of pensionable age rises only slowly through the 1980s; the number of unemployed may have peaked and fewer of them will have a full entitlement to national insurance benefits. But in the longer term there are problems for social security as the number of pensioners rises from 10.4 million in 1994 to 12.6 million in 2025: more of these (especially women) will be entitled to pensions in their own right, and the state earnings-related scheme will be paying full benefit from 1998 [69]. In addition, major items of social security reform - including comprehensive disability benefit, full equality of treatment for women, child benefit high enough to ease the poverty trap, and a higher long-term rate for the unemployed on supplementary benefit - remain unfulfilled. They are liable to be the object of political promises, but may have to be sacrificed to the cost of pensions. But, as the alternative projections in Table 34 emphasise, a good economic performance will avoid the necessity of social services taking up an increasing share of GDP.

4. The changing political agenda

While governments have been grappling with the long-term cost characteristics of each service, the public perception of welfare has been shifting, and imposing new forms of pressure. The evidence of opinion polls suggests the form that the new political agenda has been taking. Table 35 provides an indication of the shift of salience from inflation, strikes and taxes in 1979 to unemployment, peace and health in 1983 -

Table 35	Most important issues (a)		
Percentage mentioning the following issues	May 1979	June 1983	Percent change
Unemployment/jobs	27	72	+45
Defence/nuclear weapons/arms	2	38	+36
Health/hospitals/NHS	4	11	+7
Pensions/services for the old	7	8	+1
Welfare benefits	3	1	-2
Law and order/crime/vandalism	11	5	-6
Taxation	21	4	-17
Strikes/unions/industrial relations	20	3	-17

(a) Question: "Think of all the urgent problems facing the country at the present time. When you decided which way to vote, which two issues did you 'personally' consider most important? "

from the products of prosperity to the products of insecurity. Unemployment and defence have increased sharply - the latter from a very low priority, whereas taxation and industrial relations have been eclipsed, suggesting that the electorate's wishes may have been met by the Conservative government. The cost of living has halved in priority but remained high. Health has replaced pensions as the main social priority, but these, and especially welfare benefits, are well down on the list.

Additional clues to issue salience come from the data in Table 36 about approval of the government's handling of policies. This discloses a 'hard' political agenda of security and protection which corresponds to the electorate's views on priorities. Even though the Conservative government scores low on most social issues, this has not proved decisive in the electorate's overall judgment. Their best performance is on housing, where 41 percent approve of their record, and they have some support on pensions and education. Health is the area where the government's policies are disliked the most, with only 19 percent approving. A plurality of 18 percent (44 to 26 percent) ranked Labour rather than the Conservatives as the party with the best policies, a near reverse of the parties' share of the poll in 1983 [70].

Table 36   Approval of the government's record (a)

Percentage approving	October 1983
Defence and armaments	53
Common market	51
Strikes and labour relations	50
Law and order	49
Housing	41
Cost of living and prices	40
Old age pensions	34
Taxation	30
Education	28
Full employment	19
The health service	19

(a) Question: "In general, do you approve or disapprove of the way the Government is handling...? "

Still, substantial support appears to exist for the welfare state. On the central question of preference between more expenditure and lower taxes, opinion has moved since 1979 in favour of expenditure (Table 37). At the end of the Labour government the electorate was divided equally on this point; since 1981 half have positively wanted more services, and by late 1983 only 17 percent wanted more tax cuts.

Table 37   Taxes/spending choice

Percentage favouring	May 1979	March 1981	October 1983
taxes being cut, even if it means some reduction in government services, such as health, education and welfare	34	20	17
things should be left as they are	25	23	27
government services such as health, education and welfare should be extended even if it means some increase in taxation	34	49	50
don't know	7	8	6

Table 38 provides more evidence on this choice from the slightly different questions asked in the British Social Attitudes Survey of 1983. This showed a fairly stable pattern across social groups and party affiliation, with only 10 percent even of Conservative identifiers wanting lower social expenditure. Many more than in the Gallup survey wanted no change (half as against a quarter of the sample), suggesting that opinion on the issue may be sensitive to the wording of the concept.

Table 38	Priorities for higher expenditure				
	Percentage of respondents by party identification				
	Conservative	Labour	Liberal/ SPD Alliance	Non-aligned	Total
If government had to choose, should:					
Reduce taxes, spend less on health, education and social benefits	10	8	6	10	9
Keep at the same level as now	63	46	54	49	54
Increase taxes, spend more	24	42	36	29	32
None/other/don't know	3	4	4	12	5
Highest priority for extra government spending:					
Health	34	39	43	33	37
Education	24	24	24	25	24
Help for industry	20	13	16	13	16
Housing	5	10	6	10	7
Social security benefits	3	9	4	7	6
Defence	6	1	2	3	4
Police and prisons	4	2	2	1	3
Highest priority for extra government spending on social benefits:					
Retirement pensions	40	41	40	42	41
Benefits for disabled people	30	19	24	22	24
Benefits for the unemployed	11	25	20	15	18
Benefits for single parents	11	6	6	7	8
Child benefits	7	8	7	10	8
Highest priority for extra government spending on education:					
Less able children with special needs	28	37	27	41	32
Secondary school children	34	23	34	21	29
Primary school children	16	18	16	14	16
Nursery/pre-school children	9	13	8	9	10
Students at colleges, universities and polytechnics	11	7	11	9	9

When it comes to particular candidates for extra expenditure, health ranks remarkably high (37 percent naming it first) and housing and social security remarkably low (7 percent and 6 percent). Defence and the police - ranked highly as issues - are not seen as needing more expenditure. Within social security, retirement pensions score high, as do benefits for the disabled. But unemployment benefit is a low priority: only 18 percent ranked it top, with two-thirds of the unemployed themselves ranking another benefit as a higher priority. Benefits for children and single parents are even less favoured (8 percent each). Within education, 32 percent rank help for the less able and those with special needs as the highest priority, but only 10 percent place nursery and pre-school children top and only 9 percent students (see Table 38). Whatever the learning processes involved, this pattern of preferences does resemble the priorities of the Conservative government, which has drawn sharp distinctions between support for the health service and the retired and neglect of housing and the unemployed, rather than integrate them into a coherent social policy.

A final decision of analysis (see Table 39) is of the image of public services. The police are the most favoured public institution, but within the social services voters appear to rank the value of services in kind higher than those in cash. Voters perceive that the police, the health service and child benefits have been protected by the Conservatives, but satisfaction with most services fell between 1980 and 1983 and the government failed to get much credit for its expensive efforts to preserve the value of cash benefits. Conversely, housing and primary education seem to be just as highly regarded despite expenditure cuts. The message may be that the British welfare state is perceived as offering few success stories, and is perhaps never going to achieve the higher social goals posited in the 1940s. For instance, 41 percent of council tenants deny that 'council estates are generally pleasant places to live in', and 25 percent of respondents are very or quite dissatisfied with the National Health Service [71]. Voters may be prepared to spend more, but may have become resigned to a poor return from this spending.

Table 39   Opinion on public services (a)

Percentage saying to get good value from	April 1980	October 1983	Change
Police	81	76	-5
National Health Service – practitioners	74	71	-3
National Health Service – hospitals	74	67	-7
Family allowances (child benefit)	53	57	+4
Primary education	49	55	+6
Universities	49	49	0
Housing	42	44	+2
Secondary education	41	43	+2
Services for old people	44	39	-5
Sickness benefit	43	38	-5
Maternity benefits	40	36	-4
Unemployment benefit	43	34	-9
Pensions	44	34	-10

(a) Question: "...do you think you do, or do not, get value for money from...? "

5.   Conclusion: a pro-welfare backlash?

The evidence on institutional change, expenditure and public opinion suggests that the period since the oil crisis has seen the working-out of several previously implicit themes in British social policy. Instead of an undifferentiated welfare state, some services have been cut and others protected. The rhetoric of cuts has become commonplace, but major cash transfers, education and health services have been financed through taxation and enjoy solid popular support. Services perceived as less central to social priorities, like social assistance, council housing and social work services, are more vulnerable but do gain some protection from the existence of bureaucratic and professional interest groups, and, in many cases, from providing employment for the qualified middle-classes [72].

The change in recent years should not be exaggerated. Between 1976 and 1981 the relative proportions of public employees, public income recipients and private sector workers did not alter much: public employees fell from 21.4 to 20.0 percent, but benefit income recipients rose from 32.2 to 36.3 percent - in sum, more were receiving an income from the state [73]. Between 1979 and 1982, direct taxes, indirect taxes, cash benefits and the value of benefits in kind, such as education and health, all increased as a share of final incomes.

The main threats to the British welfare state are not political or sociological, but derive from physical and technical factors (normative standards of provision are enhanced and higher priced outputs demanded in fields like health and housing), and demographic entitlements (in which a rising share of an increasing client group demands the right to a service which public policy has previously conceded in principle, especially in pensions, health and social services for the elderly, and further and higher education).

For long, the Beveridge spirit seemed to protect social services from attack. But since 1979 this has been dispersed by the way that the Conservatives have been doing the unthinkable in welfare terms and retreating from some areas altogether - council housebuilding, school meals, sick pay. They have also broken the link between social policy and full employment so emphasised by Beveridge. The result is a much more discriminating structure of political consent, based on a cruder self-interest diffused throughout the electorate and without any great pretension to transfer between income groups.

Future Conservative thinking appears to envisage a replacement of collective provision by a mandated private responsibility. The most extreme statement of this kind suggests a complete withdrawal of the state from pensions, education and health in favour of insurance based schemes, with negative income tax as a fallback [74]. Many in the Thatcher government are influenced by the notion of restoring individual and family responsibility for the care of children and the elderly and for capital provision against contingencies. There is scepticism about the professionalization of social care tasks and a wish to encourage voluntary organizations. In short, the intellectual preferences of Conservative thinkers find much of the welfare state uncongenial, even though their policy decisions do not carry through this logic.

The British welfare state may have started to fragment into two sectors; a heartland of personal protection against ageing, and a marginal sector where the emphasis will be on flexibility and individual choice, a scepticism about value for money, and a preparedness to stigmatise recipients. Pensions, health services and school education will be in the first sector, housing, social work and other cash benefits in the latter. Already academic scepticism about monopolistic producers of welfare is beginning to affect the Labour Party and trade union movement, where an essentially individualistic model of consumption is displacing faith in social solidarity and collective allocation. The result is likely to be a redefined consensus about welfare which may come to acquire the resilience of the old, but represents a negative evaluation of the wider objectives of the postwar British welfare state.

Notes

1   Julia Parker, *Social Policy and Citizenship*. London, Macmillan, 1975; Vic George and Paul Wilding, *Ideology and Social Welfare*. London, Routledge and Kegan Paul, 1978; Graham Room, *The Sociology of Welfare*. Oxford, Martin Robertson, 1979; Robert Pinker, *The Idea of Welfare*. London, Heinemann, 1979.

2   David Riesman, *Richard Titmuss: Welfare and Society* London, Heinemann, 1977.

3   Hugh Heclo, *Modern Social Policy in Britain and Sweden*. New Haven, Yale University Press, 1974.

4   Beveridge Report, *Social Insurance and Allied Services*. London, HMSO, Cmd 6404, 1944. See also Jose Harris, *William Beveridge: a Biography*. Oxford, Clarendon Press, 1977.

5   Paul Addison, *The Road to 1945*. London, Jonathan Cape, 1975, Chapter 9.

6   See Ruth Levitt, *The Reorganised National Health Service*. London, Croom Helm, 1976; and Rudolf Klein, *The Politics of the National Health Service*. London, Heinemann, 1983.

7   But under the Conservative government the uprating of pensions was restricted, and it was proposed to restrict the benefits of the earnings-related pension scheme for workers retiring after 2000. See Part V below.

8   Department of Health and Social Security, *The Reform of Social Security*. London, HMSO, Cmnd 9517-9520, 1985.

9   Morris Beck, 'Public Sector Growth: a Real Perspective', *Public Finance*, 4:3 (1979), pp. 313-355.

10 This, the source of funding for contributors' pensions and benefits, is for most practical purposes part of central government revenue and expenditure, but is usefully treated separately in a study of social policy.

11 Department of Employment, *Employment Gazette*, 93:12 (December 1985), p. 494.

12 Frank Field, *Inequality in Britain: Freedom, Welfare and the State*. London, Fontana, 1981, pp. 52-53.

13 HM Treasury, *The Government's Expenditure Plans 1981-82 to 1983-84*. London, HMSO, Cmnd 8175, 1981, Table 2.4, line 4.7.

14 Social Security Advisory Committee, *Annual Report 1981*. London, HMSO, Table 1.1.

15 Department of Health and Social Security, *Social Assistance: Review of the Supplementary Benefits Scheme in Great Britain*. London, Department of Health and Social Security, 1978.

16 See Michael Hill, 'The Implementation of Housing Benefit', *Journal of Social Policy*, 13:3 (July 1984), pp. 297-320.

17 Merrison Report, *Royal Commission on the National Health Service*. London, HMSO, Cmnd 7615, 1979.

18 Robbins Report, *Higher Education*. London, HMSO, Cmnd 2154, 1963.

19 Various measures of this are available in Britain, including the 'public sector borrowing requirement' (PSBR), which is influenced by major capital items; the one used here is the difference between general government expenditure and revenue.

20 HM Treasury, *The Government's Expenditure Plans 1985-86 to 1987-88*. London, HMSO, Cmnd 9428-II, 1985, Table 2-18.

21 Brian Abel-Smith and Peter Townsend, *The Poor and the Poorest*. London, Bell, 1965.

22 Peter Townsend, *Poverty in the United Kingdom* Harmondsworth, Penguin, 1979.

23 Joanna Mack and Stewart Lansley, *Poor Britain*. London, George Allen and Unwin, 1985.

24 Muriel Brown and Nicola Madge, *Despite the Welfare State* London, Heinemann, 1982, p.13.

25 *Ibid.*, p.50.

26 *Ibid.*, p.53.

27 Townsend, *op.cit.*, p.88.

28 Townsend, *op.cit.*, p.261.

29 Townsend, *op.cit.*, Table 7.1, p.902ff.

30 Mack and Lansley, *op.cit.*, p.39 and p.107.

31 Townsend, op.cit., p.366f.

32 David Piachaud, 'Peter Townsend and the Holy Grail', *New Society* 57 (1981): 419ff.

33 Brown and Madge, *op.cit.*, p.157ff., see also David Donnison, *The Politics of Poverty.* Oxford, Martin Robertson, 1982.

34 Townsend, *op.cit.*, Table 16.5.

35 Townsend, *op.cit.*, Table 20.10.

36 *Social Trends 1984.* London, HMSO, Table 2.4.

37 Townsend, *op.cit.*, Table 20.10.

38 Townsend, *op.cit.*, Table 23.17.

39 Department of Health and Social Security, *Social Security Statistics 1984.* London, HMSO, p.267.

40 A.W. Dilnot, J.A. Kay and C.N. Morris, *The Reform of Social Security.* Oxford, Clarendon Press 1984, Table 2.20.

41 Central Statistical Office, *Social Trends 1985* London, HMSO, p.85.

42 R. Davies, L. Hamill, S. Moylan and C. H. Smee, 'Incomes in and out of Work', *Employment Gazette*, 90:6 (June 1982), pp. 237-243, p.239 and Table 2.

43 Julian Le Grand, *The Structure of Inequality.* London, George Allen and Unwin, 1982, p.14ff.

44 Frank Field, *Inequality in Britain: Freedom, Welfare and the State.* London, Fontana, 1981, p.26ff.

45 Central Statistical Office, 'The Effect of Taxes and Incomes on Household Benefits 1984', *Economic Trends December 1984* Table N.

46 *Ibid.*, Table D.

47 *Ibid.*, Tables B, E, X.

48 Le Grand, p.126ff.

49 Peter Townsend and Nick Davidson, *Inequalities in Health: the Black Report.* Harmondsworth, Penguin 1982, p.71.

50 A.H. Halsey, A.F. Heath and J.M. Ridge, *Origins and Destinations: Family, Class and Education in Modern Britain* Oxford, Clarendon Press, 1980, p.188.

51 Central Statistical Office, *Social Trends 1985* London, HMSO, Table 3.20.

52 Brown and Madge, *op.cit.*, p.96.

53 *Census 1981*, National Report Table 23.

54 Patrick Dunleavy, *The Politics of Mass Housing.* Oxford, Clarendon Press, 1981.

55 Central Statistical Office, *Annual Abstract of Statistics 1966.* London, HMSO, Table 12; see also John Ermisch, The *Political Economy of Demographic Change.* London, Heinemann, 1983.

56 Central Statistical Office, *Social Trends 1984 edition* London, Table 1.9.

57 *Ibid.*, Table 1.12.

58 The method is explained in more detail in the general introduction.

59 HM Treasury, *The Government Expenditure Plans.* various London, HMSO, various years.

60 Department of Education and Science, *Educational Statistics for the United Kingdom.* London, HMSO, various years.

61 The Conservative record is measured on the years 1971-73; the policies of Labour governments were predominant in 1970 and 1974.

62 HM Treasury, *The Government's Expenditure Plans 1986-87 to 1988-89.* London, HMSO, Cmnd 9702-II, 1986, Table 2.2.

[63] Griffiths Report, *NHS Management Inquiry*. London, Department of Health and Social Security, 1983.

[64] A.W. Dilnot, J.A. Kay and C.N. Morris, *The Reform of Social Security*. op. cit.

[65] Michael O'Higgins, 'Computerising the Social Security System: An Operational Strategy in Place of a Policy Strategy', *Public Administration*, 62:2 (Summer 1984), pp. 201-210.

[66] Department of Health and Social Security, *The Reform of Social Security: Programme for Action*. London HMSO, 1985.

[67] HM Treasury, *The Next Ten Years: Public Expenditure and Taxation into the 1990s*. London, HMSO, Cmnd 9189, March 1984, p. 18.

[68] Department of Health and Social Security, *Health Care and its Costs*. London, HMSO, 1983.

[69] HM Treasury, *op. cit.*, pp. 14-15.

[70] Gallup Poll, *BBC Election Survey 1983*, p. 5.

[71] Roger Jowell and Colin Airey, *British Social Attitudes: the 1984 Report*. Farnborough, Gower, 1984, p. 86 and 90.

[72] See Julian Le Grand, 'The Future of the Welfare State', *New Society*, June 1984, p. 385-6, and Peter Taylor-Gooby, *Public Opinion, Ideology and State Welfare*. London, Routledge and Kegan Paul, 1985.

[73] Richard Parry, 'The United Kingdom' in Richard Rose ed., *Public Employment in Western Nations*. Cambridge, Cambridge University Press, 1985, Table 2.12.

[74] Patrick Minford, 'State Expenditure: a Study in Waste', *Economic Affairs*, 4:3 April-June 1984.

Notes to and sources for tables and graphs

Table 1: Institutional Synopsis

Table 2: Richard Parry, 'Britain: Stable Aggregates, Changing Composition' in Richard Rose ed. *Public Employment in Western Nations*. Cambridge University Press, 1985.

Table 3: Department of Health and Social Security, *Social Security Statistics*. London, HMSO, 1975 Table 40.01 (flat-rate contributions 1950-74), Tables 40.04 and 40.05 (maximum graduated contributions 1961-74), *1982* Table 40.01 (contributions 1975-82) and 46.01 (average graduated contributions 1961-74).

Table 4: Central Statistical Office, *Annual Abstract of Statistics*. various years, London, HMSO; from appendix Tables 10 and 13.

Table 5: Department of Health and Social Security, *Social Security Statistics*. London, HMSO, 1980 and 1982, Tables 46.06 and 46.07. Calculation of benefits as percentage of earnings taken direct from source.

Table 6: Peter Townsend, *Poverty in the United Kingdom* Harmondsworth, Penguin, 1979, Table 7.1; Joanna Mack and Stewart Lansley, *Poor Britain*. London, George Allen and Unwin, 1985, p.184.

Table 7: Brian Abel-Smith and Peter Townsend (1960), Department of Health and Social Security (remainder), quoted by Vic George and Paul Wilding, *The Impact of Social Policy*. London, Routledge and Kegan Paul, 1984, Table 2.3.

Table 8: Central Statistical Office, *Social Trends 1985*. London, HMSO, 1985, Table 6.16.

Table 9: Inland Revenue, *Inland Revenue Statistics 1984*. London, HMSO, Tables 4.8 and 4.9.

Table 10: Royal Commission on the Distribution of Income and Wealth, *Report 7*. London, HMSO, Cmnd 7595, 1979, Tables A 1 and A 3; Central Statistical Office, *Economic Trends*, No 369. July 1984.

Table 11:   Central Statistical Office, *Economic Trends*, No 374. December 1984, Table B.

Table 12:   as Table 11, Table W

Table 13:   Central Statistical Office, *Economic Trends*, February 1971, November 1972, February 1978, January 1979, January 1980, January 1981, January 1982, Dezember 1982, November 1983, December 1984.

Table 14:   as Table 11, Table J

Table 15:   Central Statistical Office, *Annual Abstract of Statistics*, various years. London, HMSO; Department of Health and Social Security, *Health and Personal Social Services Statistics*, various years. London, HMSO.

Table 16:   Department of Health and Social Security, *Health Care and its Costs*. London, HMSO, 1983, p.37-38 and 41.

Table 17:   Central Statistical Office, *Annual Abstract of Statistics*, various years. London, HMSO.

Table 18:   Office of Population Censuses and Surveys, *General Household Survey 1982*. London, HMSO, 1984, Table 8.1.

Table 19:   Peter Townsend and Nick Davidson, *Inequalities in Health* The Black Report. Harmondsworth, Penguin, 1982, Table 7.

Table 20:   Department of Education and Service, *Educational Statistics for the United Kingdom*, various years. London, HMSO.

Table 21:   Central Statistical Office, *Social Trends 1985*. London, HMSO, 1985, Table 3.1; Department of Education and Science, *Statistics of Education* and Educational *Statistics for the United Kingdom*, various years. London, HMSO.

Table 22:   A.H. Halsey, A.F. Heath and J.M. Ridge, *Origins and Destinations* Family, Class and Education in Modern *Britain*. Oxford, Clarendon Press, 1980, Table 10.8.

Table 23:   Office of Population Censuses and Surveys, *General Household Survey 1982*. London, HMSO, 1984, Table 7 A.

Table 24:   Department of the Environment, *Housing Policy: Technical Volume Part I.* London, HMSO, 1977, Table I.12; *Housing and Construction Statistics 1974-1984* London, HMSO, Table 6.1, 8.3, 9.2.

Table 25:   Department of the Environment, *Housing Policy: Technical Volume Part I.* London, HMSO, 1977, Table I.5.

Table 26:   National Federation of Housing Associations, *Inquiry into British Housing* The Evidence. 1985, Information Paper 9, Table 1.

Table 27:   Appendix Table 1

Table 28:   Central Statistical Office, *Annual Abstract of Statistics*, various years. London, HMSO; Social Trends *1984*. London, HMSO, Table 4.7.

Table 29:   Appendix Tables 1 and 3

Table 30:   F.W.S. Craig, *British Parliamentary Election Manifestos*, various editions. Chichester, Political Reference Publications; *The Times Guide to the House of Commons*, various years. London, Times Books.

Table 31:   government legislation

Table 32:   HM Treasury, *The Government's Expenditure Plans* various years. London, HMSO; Social Security Advisory Committee, *Reports*, various years. London, HMSO.

Table 33:   HM Treasury, *The Government's Expenditure Plans* various years. London, HMSO.

Table 34:   HM Treasury, quoted in *Financial Times*, 6 October 1983, p.12.

Table 35:   Gallup Poll for BBC, June 1983.

Table 36:   *Gallup Political Index*, various months. London, Gallup Polls.

Table 37:   *Gallup Political Index* 278, October 1983, Table 9.

Table 38:   Roger Jowell and Colin Airey, *British Social Attitudes: the 1984 Report.* Farn-
                 borough, Gower, 1984, Tables 4.1 and 5.1

Table 39:   *Gallup Political Index*, October 1983, Table 9.

Graph 1:   Appendix Tables 1 and 2

Graph 2:   Appendix Tables 1, 3 and 4

Graph 3:   Appendix Table 2

Graph 4:   Appendix Table 2

Graph 5:   Appendix Table 2

Graph 6:   Appendix Table 4

Graph 7:   Appendix Table 3

Graph 8:   Appendix Table 4

Graph 9:   Appendix Table 5

Graph 10:   Appendix Table 5

Graph 11:   Appendix Table 6

Graph 12:   Appendix Tables 5 and 7

Graph 13:   Appendix Tables 5 and 7

Graph 14:   Appendix Tables 4 and 8

Graph 15:   Appendix Table 9

Graph 16:   Appendix Table 9

Graph 17:   Appendix Table 10

Graph 18:   Appendix Table 10, 11 and 12. 'Other benefits' include unemployment, sick-
                 ness, invalidity, non-contributory invalidity, injury and widows' benefit, mater-
                 nity allowance and war pension. Some estimates have been made to eliminate
                 double-counting and derive the number receiving benefit at a single time from
                 cases current during the year.

Graph 19:   Table 5

Graph 20:   Appendix Table 11

Graph 21:   Appendix Table 8

Graphs 22-23:   Appendix Tables 1, 5, 10 and 12

Graphs 24-25:   Appendix Tables 1, 5, 10 and 12

Graphs 26-28:   Appendix Tables 1 and 4

Graphs 29-30:   Appendix Tables 1, 5, 10 and 12

Ireland

MARIA MAGUIRE

e

Contents

I Historical synopsis

1. The legacy of the British regime and continuity in the new Irish state up to 1945

The foundations of a social service system had already been laid by the British administration by the time an independent Irish state was established in 1922. The new state inherited a variety of welfare institutions, including a poor relief system, an embryonic income maintenance system, some public health services, some housing measures and a school system which, although largely in clerical hands, received a substantial amount of state funding.

These structures had developed mainly from the 1830s onwards [1]. A poor relief system, providing care for the destitute in public workhouses, was established in 1838. The Poor Law also provided the basis for the development of public health services. The infirmaries for the sick poor which grew up alongside the workhouses gradually evolved into public hospitals, whilst in 1851 the Poor Law authorities were required to establish medical dispensaries and to appoint doctors to attend to the sick poor [2]. The dispensary system remained the basis of public general practitioner care until 1972. Preventive and sanitary services developed separately, within the local government system, following the Public Health (Ireland) Act of 1878. The scope of the health system was extended beyond the basic public assistance and preventive services shortly before independence, by the introduction in 1915 of a scheme permitting local authorities to provide medical care for expectant and nursing mothers and young children, and by a 1919 provision which required these authorities to establish a medical treatment service for children in primary schools.

The first steps in the field of social security came in the early part of the twentieth century. A Workmen's Compensation Act had already been passed in 1897, requiring employers to compensate workers according to fixed rates in respect of occupational injury. In 1908, a means-tested old age pension was introduced in Britain and Ireland. A social insurance scheme was established in 1911, providing unemployment and sickness compensation for certain categories of workers. The scheme was extended in 1920 to cover all manual workers (except those employed in agriculture and domestic service), and salaried employees with earnings below a specified ceiling. A means-tested pension for the blind was also introduced in 1920.

In the field of education, there was a considerable amount of private activity, mainly by the churches, in the eighteenth and early nineteenth centuries. The first major intervention by the state was the establishment of a uniform primary education system in 1831. In 1878 the state began to contribute towards the running costs of secondary schools, although the schools remained under private control. In 1892, school attendance became compulsory for children between the ages of six and fourteen.

A series of housing measures was enacted between 1850 and the end of the nineteenth century, of which the most important were the Labourers (Ireland) Act in 1883, which shifted the initiative for housing the rural poor from private individuals to the rural sanitary authorities, the Housing of the Working Classes Act in 1890, which attempted to deal with urban housing problems, and the 1899 Small Dwellings Acquisition Act, which enabled local authorities to provide loans for the purchase of private housing.

The period between the attainment of independence and the end of World War II saw few new developments in social policy. The existing institutions were taken over as they stood by the incoming regime and continued to operate in a relatively unchanged fashion for the following two decades. Social policy was low on the list of priorities of the newly independent state. A split in the nationalist movement over the terms of the treaty of independence led to the outbreak of civil war in the Spring of 1922. The party system which emerged from the civil war was dominated by the nationalist cleavage, with social cleavages being relegated to a minor role [3].

Apart from the problem of restoring law and order to the state, the *Cumann na nGaedheal* government, which held office from the end of the civil war in 1923 up to 1932, was faced with serious economic problems. This government pursued a policy of severe restriction on public expenditure and reduction of taxation [4]. Its social policy activities were confined almost exclusively to administrative reform. The poor relief system was remodelled in 1923, pending a detailed examination of the poor relief problem. The workhouses were abolished and home assistance became the normal method of poor relief. Two new government departments, for education and for local government and public health, were established in 1924 and the local government system was reformed in 1925. Enforcement of compulsory education was improved by legislation enacted in 1926, whilst the 1930 Vocational Education Act provided for the expansion of technical education. It should be noted that in spite of the cautious attitude towards social policy in this period, expenditure on social services accounted for a large proportion of total public expenditure. Old age pensions were one of the largest single items of state expenditure and it has been estimated that expenditure on social services represented about 37 percent of total central government expenditure in 1924, and about 36 percent in 1929 [5].

The Fianna Fail party, which formed a government in 1932, was more committed to social reform than its predecessor had been. The party's support was strongest in the poorer, western regions of the country and it was pledged to fight against unemployment and to increase state involvement in social welfare [6]. Under this government, housing was accorded particular priority: increased state funding was made available to the local housing authorities and housing output rose considerably in the period up to 1939. The income maintenance system was also improved. An unemployment assistance scheme was introduced in 1933 in response to the deteriorating employment situation as the international economic recession worsened. This measure was of particular importance to the large numbers employed in agriculture who were not covered by unemployment insurance. In 1935 another important group was removed from dependence on poor relief with the introduction of two pension schemes for widows and orphans. A compulsory insurance scheme covered those eligible for sickness insurance (i.e. all manual wage-earners and salaried employees below an earnings ceiling), whilst a means-tested pension catered for those outside the social insurance system. In 1942, insurance against intermittent unemployment due to bad weather was introduced for workers in the building industry, and in 1944 child allowances were introduced for all families with three or more children.

Although some progress was made during the 1930s and early 1940s, the social services which existed at the end of World War II differed little in their essential characteristics from those of the early 1920s. The social insurance system now included schemes for unemployment and sickness benefits, maternity grants and survivors' pensions. Coverage, nevertheless, was still limited to manual wage-earners and low-income salaried employees. Agricultural workers were excluded from unemployment insurance; the self-employed, who constituted over 40 percent of the active population at that time, were completely excluded from social insurance, and there was no provision for voluntary insurance. The income maintenance system still relied strongly on means-tested assistance schemes, survivors' pensions and unemployment assistance having been added to the old age and blind pension schemes already in existence when the state was founded. Payments under both social insurance and social assistance schemes were meagre and means-tests for social assistance were stringent.

The public assistance system, which had scarcely altered since the 1920s, retained many of the features of the old Poor Law. Assistance was minimal and the system was administered in a demeaning fashion [7]. Curative health services were still administered within the framework of the public assistance system, with entitlement determined by a severe means test. Maternity and child health services were available only in some parts of the country, and were also confined to poor patients. The school medical examination service and disease prevention services had developed only slowly during the 1920s and 1930s [8].

Despite considerable improvement in housing conditions during the 1930s, requirements in this area remained substantial. The education system remained largely in private hands. Most primary schools were vested in local trustees and managed by church authorities. Costs of school buildings were met through a combination of public funding and local contributions, whilst teachers' salaries were paid by the state. Secondary schools were privately owned, mainly by religious orders, although the state contributed to running costs and paid a substantial portion of teachers' salaries. The only public post-primary schools were the vocational schools administered by the local authorities, which had been established from 1930 onwards and which provided training mainly in practical subjects.

2. Growth and change in the postwar period

The period from 1945 to the early 1950s was a time of heightened interest and activity in the area of social policy. Even before the end of the war, pressure for reform had been mounting, fuelled by dissatisfaction with existing services and by the examples of the Beveridge Plan and proposals for a national health service in Britain [9]. Whyte notes that reforms taking place in Britain were of special relevance to Ireland since, given the mobility of labour between the two countries, it was likely that improved social services in Britain would add to the already high level of emigration from Ireland [10]. The health services attracted particular criticism on the grounds of their continuing association with the public assistance system, because they excluded the middle classes, and because health statistics at the time painted a grim picture of the health status of the population [11]. There was also pressure for extending the scope of the social insurance system to cover more risks and to include sections of the population excluded under the existing system, whilst housing statistics at this time showed that there were widespread problems of overcrowding and insanitary conditions [12].

Pressure for reform came from a variety of sources, including sections of the medical profession, the general public and members of the Roman Catholic hierarchy [13]. Clann na Poblachta, a new political party formed in 1946, adopted social policy reform as a major issue, and the Labour Party was similarly vociferous in its demands for improved social services. However, there were also signs of opposition to any major extension of the role of the state in the social sphere. Catholic social teaching in the 1940s and 1950s embodied a deep suspicion of state intervention and administrative centralisation, favouring the organisation of society along vocational lines, and these principles exerted a strong influence in Ireland at the time [14]. The leaders of the governing Fianna Fail party reacted unfavourably to calls for a comprehensive social insurance system, stressing that the economy could not support any considerable expansion of the social services and that the state should in any case avoid measures which might weaken individual initiative and responsibility [15].

The first reforms came in the area of health, with improvements in the organisation of the mental health service in 1945, the establishment of a separate department of health in 1946, and the 1947 Health Act, which provided for a comprehensive maternity and child health service free of charge for the entire population, for a compulsory school medical inspection service, and for sweeping measures to combat infectious diseases. The 1947 Act proved to be one of the most contentious pieces of social legislation in the history of the state, attracting strong criticism from the Roman Catholic hierarchy and the medical profession on the grounds that it represented an unjustifiable extension of the role of government [16]. Following a change of government in 1948, it fell to a coalition government including Fine Gael, Labour, Clann na Poblachta and some minor parties and independent members to implement the 1947 Act. The post of Minister for Health in the government was held by a member of the Clann na Poblachta Party. Efforts to establish the universal maternity and child health service, the so-called 'mother and child scheme', culminated in a crisis in 1951 when it became clear that the Roman Catholic hierarchy were adamantly opposed to the scheme. The cabinet withdrew its support for the scheme and the Minister for Health was forced to resign shortly afterwards.

In other areas of social policy, the coalition government succeeded in making considerable progress [17]. A major housing programme was launched in 1949, along with a seven-year hospital building plan. Tuberculosis, which was a very serious health problem in Ireland at the time, was virtually eradicated. Draft legislation for a new social insurance system was introduced in 1950 by the Minister for Social Welfare, who was a member of the Labour Party. Among the most important reforms contained in the Bill were that compulsory social insurance be extended to cover all employees and that a retirement pension be added to the benefits available under the system.

Before the Bill on social insurance could become law, the government fell, and was replaced by a Fianna Fail administration. The social security reforms enacted by this government were more limited than those proposed by its predecessor. The social insurance system was remodelled in 1952. The only extension of coverage, however, was the inclusion of male agricultural employees in the unemployment insurance scheme. Higher paid salaried employees and the self-employed remained excluded from the system. Child allowances were extended to the second child in 1952 and maternity allowances were introduced in 1953. The 1953 Health Act completed the process of health service reform which had begun in 1947. There was again considerable opposition from the Catholic hierarchy and the medical profession to proposed extensions of the services contained in the draft legislation. After a certain amount of amendment, the final Act provided for the extension of eligibility for public hospital services to about 85 percent of the population, the 15 percent in the highest income group being excluded [18].

Eligibility for hospital-based services was henceforth to be based on membership of one of four categories rather than on an individual means test. These included (i) persons insured under the social insurance system, (ii) persons with a family income of less than IRL 600 a year, (iii) farmers with farms valued at no more than IRL 50 and (iv) those outside these groups who could demonstrate undue hardship. The controver-

Table 1   Major institutional changes in the Irish welfare state, 1945-1980

Pensions

1960   Old age pension insurance for all manual wage earners and for salaried employees below an earnings
          ceiling; scheme provides flat-rate pensions at age 70.
1970   Retirement pension at age 65 and invalidity pension for same groups as insured for old age pension.
1973-77   Normal pensionable age reduced progressively from 70 to 66 years.
1973   Pension insurance extended to all employees as part of general expansion of social insurance system
          (effective 1974).

Sickness Cash Benefits

1947   Means-tested allowance for persons suffering from infectious diseases.
1952   Separate sickness insurance scheme becomes part of unified social insurance system; separate cash
          benefits for long- and short-term illness replaced by single benefit.
1954   Means-tested allowance for disabled persons.
1973   Sickness insurance extended to all employees; earnings-related component added to basic flat-rate
          sickness benefit (effective 1974).

Occupational Injuries

1966   Occupational injuries insurance for manual wage earners and for salaried employees below an earnings
          ceiling.
1973   Earnings-related component added to basic flat-rate short-term occupational injury benefit; coverage
          extended to all employees (effective 1974).

Unemployment

1952   Unemployment insurance scheme becomes part of unified social insurance system; insurance extended to
          male agricultural employees.
1965   Special unemployment assistance scheme for agricultural smallholders (effective 1966).
1966   Unemployment insurance extended to female employees in agriculture and domestic service.
1967   Redundancy payments scheme.
1973   Unemployment insurance extended to all employees; earnings-related component added to basic flat-
          rate benefit (effective 1974).

Families and Children

1952   Child allowance extended to second child (benefits previously available to families with at least
          three children); maternity allowance for insured women.
1963   Child allowance extended to first child.
1970   Means-tested allowance for unmarried mothers; social insurance benefit for deserted wives; maternity
          insurance extended to all female employees; earnings-related component added to basic flat-rate mater-
          nity benefit.
1974   Means-tested allowance for wives of prisoners.

Public Assistance

1975   Major reorganisation of public assistance system (effective 1977).

Health Services

1947   Administrative and financial reorganisation.
1953   Eligibility for public hospital services and maternity and child services extended to circa 85% of
          the population; health services removed from domain of public assistance.
1957   Voluntary health insurance scheme.
1970   Major administrative reorganisation; major reform of public general practitioner service provided to
          poor patients (effective 1972).
1971   Limited system of health insurance contributions; general revenues remain major source of finance.
1979   Eligibility for public hospital services extended to whole population; system of health contributions
          extended, but general revenues remain major source of finance.

Table 1 (contd.)

___

Education

1963   Establishment of state-owned comprehensive schools in areas of the country inadequately served by
        secondary schools.
1967   Free secondary education for all; free transport to school for pupils living more than three miles
        from nearest school; compulsory schooling extended to age 15 (effective 1972).
1968   Means-tested grants for university education.
1970   Beginning of rationalisation of post-primary school system.
1974   Revised scheme of state aid for primary schools; aid becomes conditional on management reforms.
1978   Extension of means-tested grants to wider range of third-level institutions.

Housing

1948-52 Improved state aid for private housing; increased aid from central government to local authorities
         for housing construction; local authorities given stronger powers to deal with special housing
         problems.
1957   Local authority housing loan scheme extended; loans now available for full cost of dwelling (scheme
         confined to those below a specified income ceiling).
1962   Rationalisation of state aid for private housing; special grants for housing of elderly and for indi-
         viduals or organisations building low cost prototype housing.
1965   Direct state provision for first time of public housing (prior to this public housing was sole respon-
         sibility of local authorities).
1966   Major revision of housing legislation; role of central government strengthened with regard to finan-
         cing, coordination and regulation of local authority housing.
1977   Special mortgage scheme for public tenants to purchase private housing; all existing grants for private
         housing replaced by pounds 1000 grant for all first time home-buyers (applies only to purchase of new
         houses).

___

sial 'mother and child' health scheme was also introduced in a modified form. The service was to be provided free of charge for the same groups who were eligible for hospital services, but the higher income group was to be charged a fee, and instead of being administered by the salaried public dispensary doctors as was originally intended, the scheme was to be run by private practitioners [19]. The 1953 Act also removed the public health services from the domain of public assistance, although free general practitioner services remained confined to low-income groups, with eligibility determined by a means test, and the service continued to be provided by salaried doctors through the public dispensary system established in the 1850s.

Following the reforms just discussed, the remainder of the 1950s was a time of virtual inactivity so far as the social services were concerned. This was a period of economic stagnation and the curtailment of social service development was just one facet of a more general restriction on public expenditure [20]. Although economic recovery began in 1959, priority was given initially to the promotion of economic growth, the policy being to postpone any further development of the social services until such time as the economy was again growing steadily [21]. The only noteworthy developments in this period were the establishment of a voluntary health insurance scheme in 1957 and the introduction in 1960 of an old age pension insurance scheme.

It was not until the early 1960s that the development of the social services resumed on any significant scale. The economic situation was considerably brighter by then, but there were also other factors at work [22]. The objective inadequacy of existing social services was highlighted in several ways. For instance, the 1961 census showed that much of the country's housing stock was in poor condition, whilst the collapse of a number of houses in Dublin in 1963 led to the declaration of a housing emergency.

With regard to the educational system, a study carried out under the joint auspices of the Irish government and the Organisation for Economic Co-operation and Development emphasised serious socio-economic and regional inequalities in access to education [23].

Both of the main opposition parties, Fine Gael and Labour, made reform of the health and social welfare systems a central issue in the general election of 1965 and the governing Fianna Fail party was forced to respond by promising improvements in these spheres. The trade union movement was more united from the beginning of the 1960s than it had been since the end of the war and it also began to place emphasis on the need for improvement of social services [24]. The attitude of the Catholic church towards the role of the state altered significantly during the 1960s, mistrust of state power being replaced by concern for more adequate public welfare provisions [25]. More generally, the increasing commitment to social objectives during this period can be placed in the context of rising expectations and rapidly changing social attitudes among the Irish public. Increasing awareness of developments in other European countries and the entry of Ireland into the European Economic Community in 1973 also contributed to pressure for reform.

Major reforms took place in the fields of education and housing during the 1960s and 1970s. State comprehensive schools were provided from 1963 in areas of the country poorly served by secondary schools. In 1967 free secondary education was introduced, whilst means-tested grants for third level education became available in 1968. The first half of the 1970s saw considerable expansion of third level institutions, as well as attempts to rationalise the secondary and tertiary systems. In housing, a major public building programme was launched in 1965 and the output of public housing rose rapidly up to the mid-1970s. Aid for private housing also increased during this period and in 1977 a scheme of universal grants for first time house buyers was introduced [26].

Reforms in the area of income maintenance came mainly in the 1970s, although child allowances were extended to all children in 1963, and 1967 saw the introduction of an occupational injury insurance scheme and a free travel scheme for old age pensioners. A series of new income maintenance schemes were introduced in the early 1970s, including invalidity and retirement pensions (1970), benefits for deserted wives (1970, 1973), benefits for unmarried mothers (1973) and benefits for prisoners' wives and elderly single women in poor circumstances (1974). Social insurance was extended to cover all employees in 1974, and an earnings-related supplement to the flat-rate benefit was made available for short-term risks, such as unemployment, sickness and maternity. The normal pensionable age was reduced from 70 to 66 years between 1973 and 1977. The extent of poverty in Ireland began to receive widespread attention in the early 1970s, resulting in efforts to raise the living standards of welfare recipients, while the public assistance system was also reorganised in 1977 [27].

The main reforms to the health services also came during the 1970s. The 1970 Health Act provided for the reorganisation of general practitioner services, with patients henceforth attending a private practitioner of their choice, rather than receiving treatment at a public dispensary. However, the service remained a means-tested one, confined to low income groups. The other major provision of the 1970 Act related to the reorganisation of the health system on a regional basis. In 1979, eligibility for free hospital services was extended to the entire population.

The period since the late 1970s has been characterised by efforts in Ireland, as elsewhere, to restrain public expenditure growth in the context of low economic growth. This period has seen restrictions on the further expansion of all the major social programmes. In recent years there has also been growing resistance among employees to increased taxation, as real disposable incomes have been progressively eroded by a combination of high inflation and heavier tax burdens. The major demand in this context has been for a more equitable distribution of the tax burden, with the farming community, the self-employed and industry bearing a larger share, rather than for a reduction in the level of public expenditure.

II Resources and clienteles: descriptions

1. The postwar growth of public and social expenditure and employment

The rate of growth of public expenditure in Ireland over the postwar period has been rapid by international standards. Between 1947 and 1980 the share of nominal public expenditure in nominal GDP more than doubled, rising from 26 to 55 percent, and over the period 1960-1980 the average growth rate of the public expenditure share was the fourth highest among the OECD countries [28].

This expansion in the GDP share of public expenditure did not, however, occur at a steady pace. Graph 1 shows total public expenditure and social expenditure as a percentage of GDP between 1950 and 1980. The years 1950-51 constituted the end of an expansionary phase in public expenditure which began in 1947 [29]. Following a decade of relative stability from 1952 to 1962, the share of public expenditure in GDP grew steadily between 1963 and 1971. After a pause in 1972-73, there was a very rapid rise in the period 1973-75, and following another pause in 1976-78, rapid growth resumed in the last two years of the 1970s [30].

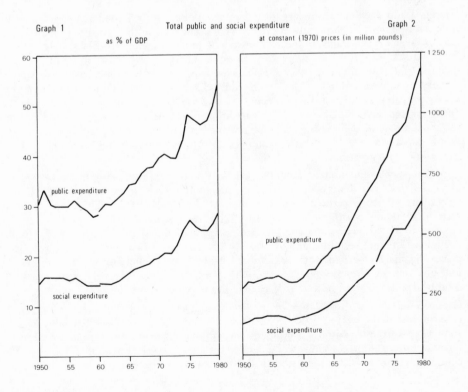

Graph 1   Total public and social expenditure   Graph 2

as % of GDP   at constant (1970) prices (in million pounds)

The growth pattern of social expenditure was very similar to that of total public expenditure. Kennedy's study of social expenditure in the period 1947-74 distinguishes three phases: an expansionary phase from 1947 to 1951, when the GDP share rose by almost six percentage points, albeit from a very low base; a regressive phase from 1952 to 1962, when the social expenditure share fell; and a phase of renewed and sustained growth from 1963 to 1975 [31]. Although growth resumed in 1963, it was not until 1965 that the GDP share of social expenditure surpassed its 1951 level. Thus, the recovery and expansion of social expenditure lagged behind that of total public expenditure by several years. As may be seen from Graph 1, expenditure rose particularly rapidly between 1973 and 1975. Following a pause in 1976-79, growth resumed at the end of the period.

Graph 2 describes the growth of public and social expenditure in real terms between 1950 and 1980. Here again, the pattern is one of virtually no change throughout most of the 1950s, a cutback in the years 1957-58, and a resumption of growth in 1959. Growth was fairly sustained throughout the remainder of the period up to 1980, apart from a marked deceleration from 1976 to 1977. Although total public expenditure and social expenditure have exhibited a broadly similar pattern of growth, Graph 2 shows that the pace of growth of the two series has varied during certain periods. Between 1950 and 1953, the social expenditure share rose from 49 percent to 52 percent of public expenditure. By 1958 this share had fallen back to 49 percent and there was a further displacement, to 47 percent, in 1961. Between 1962 and 1966 the social expenditure share rose gradually to 50 percent and remained at this level until the beginning of the 1970s. Between 1971 and 1974 social expenditure rose rapidly, going from 51 percent to 58 percent of public expenditure. Since the mid-1970s the social share has fallen again, to 53 percent in 1980.

Graphs 3 and 4, which disaggregate public expenditure by economic category and by function respectively, show how its structure has changed in the process of growth. As may be seen from Graph 3, the proportion of public expenditure devoted to investment fell sharply during the stagnatory phase of the 1950s, while the share of national debt interest rose and the other elements of expenditure remained relatively stable. Change was more limited in the 1960s and 1970s. The share of public consumption expenditure fell rather sharply between 1960 and 1969, rose again from 1969 to 1973, and remained stable thereafter. The share of national debt interest rose markedly in the second half of the 1970s. The other components of expenditure did not show any significant trend over the twenty year period, although their shares varied somewhat in the intervening period.

A functional classification of public expenditure is only available for the period since 1963. As shown in Graph 4, social and community services account for by far the largest proportion of expenditure, over half of the total in 1980. There was a clear shift in spending priorities between 1970 and 1973, with the share of expenditure devoted to social and community services rising and the share of economic services declining. In the second half of the 1970s, national debt interest absorbed an increasing share of expenditure, while that of social and community services fell. General government services and defence, which account for a relatively small share of total expenditure, have showed little change in the period since 1963.

Graph 5 shows the distribution of public expenditure among the different levels of government in the period 1953-1980. Approximately 60 percent of expenditure was channelled through central government throughout most of this period, 30 percent through local authorities and the remainder through the social insurance system. The central government share increased in the late 1950s at the expense of local govern-

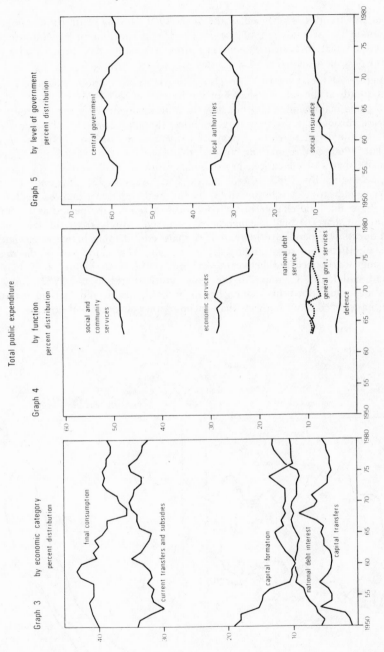

Total public expenditure

Graph 3   by economic category
percent distribution

Graph 4   by function
percent distribution

Graph 5   by level of government
percent distribution

ment, but this trend was reversed in the years 1969-74. The central government share rose again in the second half of the 1970s. The proportion of expenditure flowing through the social insurance system has risen gradually over time, levelling-off at around 11 percent after 1975.

The structure of social expenditure also changed in the period 1950-1980. Graph 6 describes trends in the relative shares of the four main social programmes - education, health, income maintenance and housing. Income maintenance was the largest area of expenditure throughout the period, accounting for approximately 32 percent of total social outlays in 1950, reaching a peak of 43 percent in 1958, declining to 36 percent by the late 1960s and remaining around that level for the rest of the period. The approximate shares of education, health and housing in 1950 were 20, 19 and 29 percent respectively. By 1980, these shares had become 22, 29, and 12 percent respectively, indicating a substantial rise in the health share, a marked decline in the housing share and little change in the education share over the period as a whole. The growth in the share of health expenditure occurred entirely from the late 1960s onwards. Education expenditure increased its share considerably between the late 1950s and the late 1960s, but subsequently declined again. The major part of the decline in the housing share occurred between 1953 and 1958, with further falls in the late 1960s and mid-1970s. Changes in the expenditure shares in the 1970s suggest that since the economic downturn which began in 1973, health and income maintenance spending has proved more buoyant than spending on education and housing.

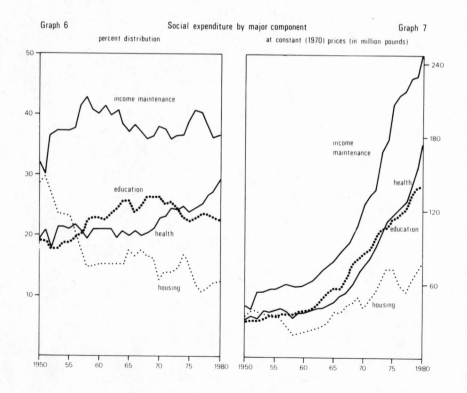

Graph 6   Social expenditure by major component   Graph 7
       percent distribution   at constant (1970) prices (in million pounds)

In order to gain a clearer picture of trends in the main elements of social expenditure, Graph 7 shows the development of expenditure at constant prices. It is evident from this graph that the expansion of social expenditure from the early 1960s onwards resulted from growth in all four major programmes. Health expenditure more than quadrupled in real terms, income maintenance expenditure increased three and a half times, and expenditure on housing and education approximately trebled. Expenditure on education, health and income maintenance has grown in a relatively sustained fashion, while the growth rate for housing expenditure has been more variable.

Graph 8

Income maintenance by major programme
percent distribution

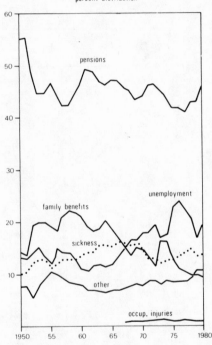

Turning to the largest element of social expenditure, namely income maintenance, Graph 8 shows that pensions account for by far the highest proportion of expenditure, although their relative weight has declined over time. Expenditure on family allowances rose significantly in relative terms during the 1950s, reaching over a fifth of total expenditure in 1958. However, its share fell almost continuously throughout the remainder of the period and by 1980 it had become one of the smallest income maintenance programmes. The share of expenditure on unemployment benefits rose rapidly in the second half of the 1960s and grew particularly fast following the first oil shock, reaching 24 percent of total income maintenance expenditure in 1976. This share declined between 1977 and 1979 but began to rise again in 1980 and unemployment benefits have remained the second largest element of income maintenance expenditure. Expenditure on sickness cash benefits account for a relatively small proportion of expenditure. Their share rose from 10 percent in 1950 to 16 percent in 1966 and declined slightly in the remainder of the period. Occupational injury benefits were only added to the social insurance system in 1967, and their relative share of expenditure is very small. The category 'other social programmes' includes public assistance and other miscellaneous programmes. The relative weight of this category has remained fairly stable over time at around 8 percent of total expenditure.

The growth of public expenditure has been accompanied by a substantial expansion in public service employment. Estimates by Rose, shown in Table 2, indicate that the proportion of the total labour force employed in the public sector grew from 14.5 percent in 1953 to 25.8 percent in 1978, and that the number of employees increased by 63 percent [32]. As in the case of public expenditure, most of this growth occurred after the mid-1960s.

Table 2 — Public employment by function

| | 1953 | | 1965 | | 1978 | | % change |
	1,000s	%	1,000s	%	1,000s	%	1953–1978
Defence	13	7.1	15	7.7	17	5.8	30.7
Health	27	14.8	31	15.5	57	19.4	211.1
Education	20	12.1	29	14.3	45	15.2	125.0
Social services	2	1.1	2	0.9	3	1.0	50.0
Agriculture	4	2.2	5	2.3	7	2.4	75.0
Police	7	3.8	7	3.3	9	3.2	28.6
Public corporations, utilities and services	62	34.1	76	37.8	107	36.1	72.6
of which:							
transportation	24	13.2	25	12.6	33	11.1	37.5
communications	17	9.3	19	9.3	32	10.9	88.2
gas/elec./water	11	6.0	11	5.5	13	4.4	18.2
other	10	5.4	21	10.0	29	9.7	190.0
Roads and highways	20	11.0	13	6.3	11	3.7	-45.0
General and tax administration	4	2.1	4	2.4	9	2.9	125.0
Other (a)	23	12.6	18	9.5	31	10.3	34.8
Total	182		200		296		62.6
As % of total labour force	14.5		17.9		25.8		

(a) Includes a variety of small functional categories, and some personnel that are not allocated to specific functions in national statistics.

The data in Table 2 also show how the structure of public employment has changed over time. Health care was the largest single category of employment during each of the years shown here, and was also one of the most expansionary sectors. The increase in health care personnel occurred mainly after the mid-1960s, and by 1978 approximately one in five public employees worked in this sector. Education was the third largest employment category in 1953 and the second largest in each of the two later years shown. The proportion of teachers and other education personnel increased most in the period 1953-65. Transportation and communication respectively are the next most important categories of public service employment after health and education. While the numbers employed in these sectors have grown considerably, their share of public employment has remained relatively stable. Both the numbers and proportion of public employees working in the roads and highways category have declined markedly over time. The numbers employed in the defence and police forces, in administration and in other functional categories have grown but their shares of public employment have diminished in the period shown here.

An analysis by Humphreys, covering the years 1970-1983, shows that total public service employment increased by 85,000 in this period, equivalent to a rise of 35 percent [33]. Table 3, which provides a disaggregation by broad functional category, shows that over 50 percent of this growth was in the social category. Employment in the education sector increased by 63 percent, health service employment grew by 53 percent and civil service employment related to the social services increased by 68 percent.

Table 3 — Functional changes in public employment

Public service group	1970	1975	1983	Change 1970–83	
	1,000s	1,000s	1,000s	1,000s	%
Economic/Infrastructural	126.2	125.4	142.4	16.2	12.8
Social	83.4	99.5	131.4	48.0	275.8
of which:					
health	40.4	47.0	62.0	21.6	53.5
education	37.7	46.2	61.6	23.9	63.4
civil servants	3.6	4.7	6.0	2.4	66.7
state sponsored bodies	1.7	1.5	1.7	0.0	0.0
Central service/Security	30.2	39.2	50.9	20.7	68.5
Total	239.8	264.1	324.7	84.9	35.4

2. Single programme development

Pensions

Pensions accounted for 16 percent of total social expenditure in 1980, making them the third largest item of expenditure after health and education. Their share of social expenditure has remained relatively stable over the period since 1950, while their weight within GDP has doubled, reaching 4.7 percent in 1980.

As shown in Graph 9, old age pensions are the largest component of total pension expenditure. In real terms, outlays on old age pensions have risen substantially since 1960 and the pace of growth was particularly rapid after 1973. Ireland, unlike other Western European countries, has not been subject to demographic pressure on the old age pension system in the postwar period. The number of elderly people has grown only slightly since 1960, and their weight within the total population has actually declined. There have, however, been a number of important improvements in pension provisions which have contributed to the rise in expenditure.

In 1961, a compulsory old age pension insurance scheme was introduced, covering all blue-collar employees and white-collar employees up to an earnings ceiling, and providing flat-rate pensions at the age of 70. Up until then the only general old age pension scheme was a means-tested one dating from 1908. In 1974, pension insurance was extended to all employees through the removal of the earnings limit for white-collar employees. Another new scheme, introduced in 1970, provided flat-rate retirement pensions at the age of 65 for employees, although the numbers availing themselves of this pension were low initially. The normal pensionable age was reduced from 70 to 66 between 1973 and 1977, considerably swelling the number of pensioners. The period from 1973 also saw significant improvements in real benefit levels.

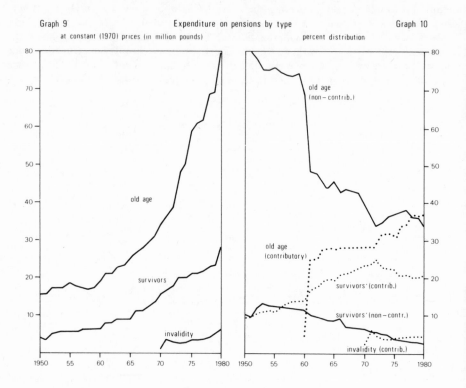

Graph 9 — Expenditure on pensions by type — Graph 10
at constant (1970) prices (in million pounds) — percent distribution

There are two schemes providing survivors' pensions, both dating from 1935: one an insurance scheme covering employees and the other a non-contributory scheme providing means-tested benefits. Real expenditure on survivors' pensions began to grow in 1960 and has increased by approximately the same magnitude as expenditure on old age pensions. The period of most rapid growth was from 1968 to 1973. Invalidity pensions were only introduced in 1970. Prior to that time there was a common benefit for both long and short-term disability.

Graph 10 shows the percentage distribution of expenditure among the various pension schemes. The old age pension schemes, taken together, accounted for 70 percent of total outlays in 1980, although their share has declined slightly since 1950, while that of survivors' pensions has increased. Invalidity pensions have also increased their share, although they accounted for only 6 percent of expenditure in 1980. The introduction of old age pension insurance in 1961 and the expansion of the social insurance system generally, is clearly reflected in the shift over time from expenditure on non-contributory, means-tested pensions to expenditure on contributory pensions.

Sickness and occupational injuries

As a proportion of total income maintenance expenditure, outlays on sickness benefits have remained relatively stable since the early 1950s, ranging between approximately 12 percent and 16 percent of the total. However, Graph 11 shows that in real terms expenditure on sickness benefits grew substantially between 1960 and 1980, rising particularly rapidly between 1973 and 1978.

Graph 11

Expenditure on sickness and occupational
injury benefits
at constant (1970) prices (in million pounds)

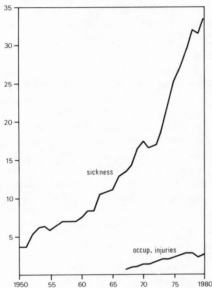

The growth of expenditure appears to be linked to several factors. Benefit levels improved gradually during the 1960s and the introduction of an earnings-related addition to the basic flat-rate benefit in 1974 increased the average replacement ratio relative to net earnings from around 40 percent to over 70 percent by 1976, although it subsequently declined to around 66 percent [34]. The proportion of the labour force insured for sickness benefits also increased as a result of the extension of social insurance coverage to all employees in 1974. More important, however, than the expansion of the social insurance system has been a substantial rise in both the frequency and duration of sickness benefit claims since the late 1960s, and particularly in the period since 1974 [35]. Analysis suggests that these increases in the incidence and duration of claims are linked to both improvements in the earnings-replacement ratio and a rise in the rate of long-term unemployment [36].

The occupational injuries insurance scheme was only introduced in 1967, and it accounts for a very minor proportion of income maintenance expenditure. Real outlays on this scheme rose gradually from the time of its introduction up to the mid-1970s and subsequently remained static.

Unemployment

Ireland has suffered high unemployment rates throughout most of the postwar period. Approximately 5 percent of the labour force were out of work during the 1950s and 1960s. The unemployment rate began to rise in the second half of the 1960s and it increased very rapidly in 1975 and 1976, reaching a peak of 8 percent in the latter year. Unemployment fell between 1977 and 1979 but has reached new high levels since 1980.

As might be expected, trends in expenditure on unemployment benefits have followed the trend of unemployment closely. Unemployment expenditure rose from 4 to 9 percent of total social expenditure in the period 1965-1976, becoming the second largest item in the income maintenance budget. As shown in Graph 12, real expenditure rose steadily between 1965 and 1974 and increased sharply in 1975-76. Expenditure fell between 1977 and 1979 in both real and relative terms, but began to rise again in 1980. Since 1980 the share of unemployment expenditure in the social budget has expanded considerably.

Institutional changes have also contributed to raising the level of expenditure. The maximum duration of benefits under the unemployment insurance scheme was doubled in 1968 and was further increased in 1976. The earnings-replacement ratio under this scheme was raised substantially in 1974 by the introduction of an earnings-related addition to the basic flat-rate benefit. Unemployment assistance is paid to those who have exhausted their entitlement to unemployment insurance, or who are ineligible for insurance benefits. Farmers are also eligible to apply for unemployment assistance, and those with smallholdings in designated areas of the country have, since 1966, had the option of having their means from the farm assessed on a more favourable basis than other applicants for assistance, although this system is now being phased out. The number of smallholders receiving unemployment assistance

Graph 12

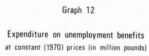

Expenditure on unemployment benefits
at constant (1970) prices (in million pounds)

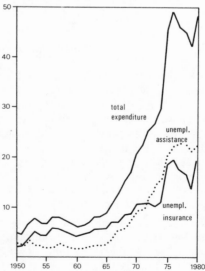

increased rapidly between 1966 and 1976. The real level of unemployment assistance payments also rose between the mid-1960s and the end of the 1970s. A redundancy payments scheme, introduced in 1968, also contributed to raising expenditure on unemployment benefits.

As may be seen from Graph 12, expenditure on unemployment assistance has grown more rapidly than that on unemployment insurance since the mid-1960s, becoming the larger programme in 1972. Among the factors which may have contributed to this change are the increase in long-term unemployment which has occurred since the mid-1960s, and particularly in the 1970s [37].

Since the mid-1960s, more emphasis has been placed on active manpower policy. Because this area is characterised by administrative fragmentation, it is difficult to arrive at an overall assessment of expenditure on manpower measures and this has not been included in the total shown in Graph 12. The principal policy measures have included reorganisation and expansion of industrial training activities and of the employment placement service, the introduction (1968) of a scheme of financial assistance for geographical relocation of the unemployed and, in the 1970s, the initiation of a series of youth employment schemes and wage subsidies [38].

Families and children

The decline in expenditure on families and children (including child allowances, maternity benefits and assistance to unmarried mothers) relative to other income maintenance programmes has been shown in Graph 8. Looking at Graph 13, it may be seen

Graph 13

Expenditure on family benefits
at constant (1970) prices (in million pounds)

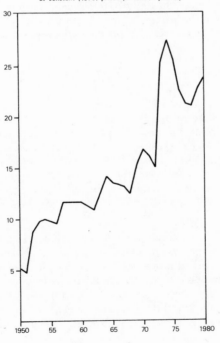

that in real terms expenditure more than quadrupled between 1950 and 1980, but its pattern of growth has been very uneven.

Child allowances, which account for the bulk of expenditure in this area, were introduced in 1944 for families with three or more children. The extension of allowances to the second child in 1952 and to the first child in 1963, as well as increases in benefit levels in 1952, 1957, 1963 and 1969, account for expenditure increases in those years. Maternity allowances for insured women were introduced in 1953. Real expenditure fell in the years intervening between these improvements because, although the number of beneficiaries increased, the nominal value of child allowances remained unchanged. Expenditure rose rapidly in 1973-74 when child benefit rates were raised considerably, eligibility was extended to dependent children between the ages of 16 and 18, a social assistance allowance for unmarried mothers was introduced and earnings-related benefits became payable with the basic flat-rate maternity benefit. Real expenditure fell between 1975 and 1978 as the value of child allowances was again eroded by inflation.

Developments in other areas, not included in the expenditure total shown in Graph 12, have also affected transfers to families. Provisions affecting the dependants of income maintenance beneficiaries were rationalised in 1952, when allowances became payable for adult dependants and up to two child dependants under most schemes. Allowances for the third child and any subsequent children were introduced in 1960, allowances for dependent children of old age pensioners were introduced in 1964, the age limit for dependent children was raised in 1969-70 and in 1974 an adult dependant's allowance was introduced in relation to the non-contributory old age pension. Benefits for deserted wives and for the wives of prisoners were introduced in the early 1970s and child dependant allowances for single parents were raised to a higher level than those for other income maintenance recipients. In real terms, benefits for dependants of income maintenance recipients have risen over time [39]. Tax relief is provided in respect of children under the age of 16. Revenue forgone on such relief was equivalent to approximately 58 percent of expenditure on child allowances in 1980. The real value of tax relief in respect of dependent children has declined considerably over time [40].

Public assistance and other social programmes

Expenditure on public assistance increased from 4 percent of total income maintenance in 1950 to 13 percent in 1980. Graph 14 shows that in real terms, expenditure remained relatively stable up to 1977. The number of public assistance recipients halved between 1950 and 1977, due at least in part to the expansion of social insurance and of categorical social assistance [41]. In 1977, public assistance was replaced by a supplementary welfare allowance scheme which, unlike the old system, conferred a statutory entitlement to benefit. Rates of benefit were also raised and standardised. The numbers receiving supplementary welfare allowance rose slightly in the late 1970s.

The category 'other social welfare expenditure' includes a variety of benefits and services, among the most important of which are services and benefits in kind for the aged and the disabled and cash transfers to deserted wives, prisoners' wives, elderly single women in poor circumstances and the disabled. Expenditure rose considerably from the mid-1960s, reflecting the introduction of a range of benefits for the elderly and the disabled, such as free travel on public transport, an allocation of free electricity or gas and a cash allowance in respect of care by a relative. The early 1970s saw the introduction of cash benefits for the categories of women mentioned above, whose only recourse up until then had been public assistance. The remainder of expenditure in this category includes miscellaneous small items, such as grants to voluntary welfare agencies and child welfare services.

Graph 14

Public assistance and other social
welfare expenditure
at constant (1970) prices (in million pounds)

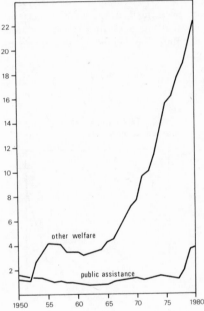

Health

Public expenditure on health increased from 2.8 percent of GDP in 1950 to 8.4 percent in 1980, nine-tenths of this increase having occurred since 1965. Graph 7 shows that in real terms, expenditure began to grow more rapidly after the mid-1960s, rising particularly fast in the years 1968-74 and 1978-80.

As noted in Section I, the second half of the 1940s was a time of considerable activity in the area of health policy, although the reforms actually achieved were less comprehensive than originally envisaged. An intensive campaign for the eradication of tuberculosis, a major health problem at the time, was launched after the war and a major hospital-building programme began in 1949. These programmes, along with the extension of eligibility for hospital-based services and maternity and child care services to a wider group in 1953, contributed to a substantial rise in expenditure in the years 1947-1953. However, health spending, like other areas of social expenditure, was severely restricted after 1953. No further reforms to the services were made until the early 1970s, while capital expenditure on health fell sharply between 1954 and 1958 and remained very low until the mid-1960s [42].

The renewed growth in expenditure after the mid-1960s was part of the general expansion in public and social expenditure. The curtailment of expenditure in earlier years had created a variety of pressing needs and the main thrust of health care policy in the period up to 1979 was to improve the standards and methods of delivery of existing services. Changes in financing arrangements between 1967 and 1977, which transferred an increasing share of health care costs from local to central taxation, provided a basis for increasing the resources available to the system. The 1970 Health Act provided for the complete reorganisation of the public general practitioner service, for the restructuring of health service administration on the basis of larger, regional units and for improvements in the child health services and in services for the aged and the chronically ill. In 1979, eligibility for free hospital services and for reimbursement of the cost of prescribed drugs over a certain amount per month was extended to the entire population, and an earnings-related health contribution was introduced [43]. Up until that time approximately 85 percent of the population had been eligible for hospital services.

Graph 15

Expenditure on health
at constant (1970) prices (in million pounds)

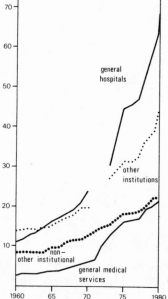

Graph 15 shows the development of expenditure on the health services in real terms by major programme over the period 1960-1980. Expenditure on general hospital services accounts for almost half of current expenditure and has been one of the most rapidly growing areas of expenditure. Hospital admission rates have risen considerably since 1960, although the average length of stay has fallen [44]. The numbers employed in hospitals have also grown, increasing by 47 percent between 1971 and 1980 [45]. The other area of expenditure which grew particularly rapidly in the 1970s is general practitioner services. The reorganisation of general practitioner care, implemented in 1972, replaced the then existing system of public dispensaries serviced by salaried doctors with a scheme operated by private practitioners and pharmacists who are paid on a fee-per-service basis. Utilisation rates, and particularly the consumption rate of pharmaceutical products, have risen appreciably during the time the new scheme has been in operation [46]. Eligibility for this service, which provides for general practitioner care and prescribed drugs free of charge, is limited to the lower income groups. Although the criteria for determining eligibility were not altered, the proportion of the population entitled to general practitioner services rose from 33 percent in 1973 to 38 percent in 1977, mainly as a result of higher unemployment rates. By 1980, entitlement had fallen again to approximately 35 percent of the population.

Education

Expenditure on education grew from 3 percent of GDP in 1950 to over 6 percent in 1980. As shown in Graph 7, real expenditure grew very slowly up to the early 1960s, increased rapidly from then up to the early 1970s and grew more slowly during the remainder of the period up to 1980.

The year 1963 marks the beginning of a period of major reform in the education system, the first since the foundation of the state in 1921. The role of the state in secondary education was greatly expanded through the provision of public comprehensive schools from 1963, the introduction in 1964 of building grants for private secondary schools - still the main type of second-level institution, and the introduction in 1967 of free secondary education for all and free transport for primary and secondary pupils living more than three miles from the nearest school. During the 1970s, secondary education policy concentrated on achieving a more efficient use of resources through breaking down the rigid separation between secondary schools, which traditionally provided an academic education, and vocational schools, which concentrated on technical subjects.

In the sphere of primary education, increased funds were made available for the construction, maintenance and equipping of schools from the mid-1960s. A policy of amalgamating smaller schools was pursued up to the mid-1970s, but was subsequently abandoned. Population growth has swelled enrolment in primary schools considerably since the beginning of the 1970s.

Higher education underwent major reforms during the late 1960s and 1970s. Means-tested grants for third level education were introduced in 1968 and these, along with increased access to secondary education have led to a significant rise in third-level enrolments. The early 1970s saw considerable expansion of the non-university sector, with particular emphasis on the provision of technological education. Adult education began to attract increasing attention during the 1970s, although this does not appear to have resulted in any marked investment of resources.

Housing

As noted earlier, the proportion of total social expenditure devoted to housing declined significantly between 1950 and 1980. In real terms, as shown in Graph 7, the pattern of housing expenditure varied considerably in this period. Kennedy, in her

analysis of developments in the period 1947 to 1970, identifies four major policy phases [47]. Ireland experienced severe housing problems after the war and the first policy
phase, from 1947 to 1951, was a time of rapid growth in housing expenditure. The
second phase from 1952 to 1958 began with a gradual decline in real expenditure, culminating in a severe cutback from 1956 to 1958. The economy was under strain
during these years, financial resources were scarce and, moreover, it was widely
believed that housing requirements had been largely satisfied. The third phase began
when the downward trend in expenditure was halted in 1959, and was characterised
by very slow growth up to the early 1960s, the emphasis in this period being on conservation of existing stock rather than new building.

The final phase identified by Kennedy, from 1962 to 1970, saw an acceleration of
growth in expenditure. Increased aid was provided for the construction, acquisition
and renovation of private housing from 1962. It became apparent in the early 1960s
that public housing requirements were also urgent due to the poor state of the
existing stock and the pressure of a growing urban population, and the output of
public housing rose rapidly from 1965. This expansionary phase continued up to the
mid-1970s and the rate of completion of new dwellings rose particularly quickly from
1972.

Real expenditure fell during the recessionary years following the first oil shock,
mainly due to a decline in house purchase loans and grants, although the output of
public housing also declined [48]. Expenditure began to rise again in 1978, but completions of public housing units continued to fall.

The main instruments of housing policy include direct provision of public housing for
low income groups, public authority loans for the purchase of private housing, and
subsidies, both explicit and implicit, to various tenure groups. There is no agreed
definition of what should be included in the category of housing subsidies, nor is it
possible to make a precise estimate of expenditure in this area [49]. Explicit subsidies
include a subsidy to the public housing sector which enables rents to be held below
market levels, allowances to public housing tenants who purchase their dwellings,
grants for first time purchasers of new houses and for the reconstruction and improvement of private housing, and intermittent subsidisation of building society mortgage
interest rates. Implicit subsidies include income tax relief on mortgage payments, discounts to public housing tenants who purchase dwellings, and occasionally charging
below market interest rates on local authority housing loans [50].

The official definition of housing expenditure does not include implicit subsidies.
According to an estimate for 1975, implicit subsidies to owner-occupiers amounted to
IRL 30.5 million, equivalent to 20 percent of total public housing expenditure, as officially defined [51]. Graph 16 shows a breakdown of the main elements of housing expenditure, as officially defined, in the period 1950-1980, distinguishing between capital
expenditure on public housing, grants and loans for private housing and subsidisation
of rents in the public housing sector. The 1950s saw a sharp decline in expenditure on
public housing relative to the other two categories of expenditure. This trend was reversed in the first half of the 1960s and since then the share of expenditure devoted to
provision of public housing has fluctuated around 40 percent. Loans and grants for
the private sector have accounted for around 30 percent of the total throughout most
of the period, although their share rose to 38 percent in 1975 and fell as low as 19
percent in 1977. The rent subsidy to the public housing sector has amounted to about
20 percent of expenditure throughout most of the period, although it rose to over 30
percent in the late 1950s.

Graph 16

Expenditure on housing
percent distribution

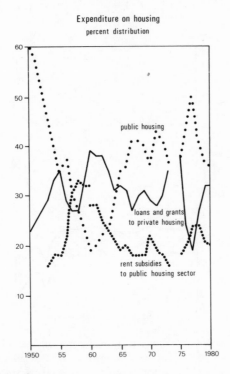

3. Public revenues and deficits

The growth of public expenditure since the early 1960s has been accompanied by marked changes in the sources of state revenue. The balance between taxation and borrowing has shifted in favour of the latter as a source of finance and the internal composition of taxation receipts has altered significantly.

Total public revenues grew from just under 24 percent of GDP in 1953 to 41 percent in 1980. As shown in Graph 17, revenues grew very slowly up to 1962, while between 1962 and 1971 there was a phase of sustained growth during which the share of revenues in GDP increased by 9.6 percentage points, reaching 35.5 percent in 1971. The development of revenues in the period after 1971 has been erratic, with growth in the GDP share confined to the periods 1975-76 and 1978-80. A comparison with the pattern of public expenditure growth (Graph 17 below and Graph 1) reveals that up to 1973 the expansion in expenditure was paralleled by a growth in revenues. Since 1973, however, the gap between revenues and expenditure has widened rapidly. This is illustrated by the trend in net lending of public authorities, shown in Graph 17. A negative balance in net lending indicates borrowing by public authorities [52]. Having remained relatively stable at about 5 percent of GDP throughout much of the period since 1953, public authority borrowing rose from 5.9 percent in 1973 to 14.6 percent in 1980. Looking only at the balance of current expenditure and revenue, shown in Graph 17 by the trend in public authorities' saving, net revenue slightly exceeded net current expenditure in 1973, whereas by 1980 revenue was falling substantially short of current expenditure, pushing the negative balance on the current account to 7 percent of GDP.

Graph 17

Total public revenue, saving and net lending
as % of GDP

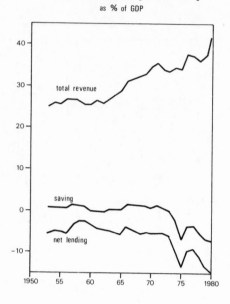

The rapid expansion of public expenditure in the period since 1973 has been financed to a considerable extent, therefore, by borrowing. Up to 1973 the public sector borrowing requirement was held relatively stable, at a level of around 5 percent of GDP and current expenditure was not allowed to exceed revenue. From 1974 onwards this policy was consciously abandoned in favour of allowing the current account budget deficit to expand and financing the shortfall from borrowing. As noted by one commentator, public expenditure could certainly not have risen as much as it did in the 1970s in the absence of this substantial growth in borrowing since the burden of taxation would have become unacceptably heavy [53]. In the early 1980s efforts have been made to reduce dependence on borrowing by imposing strict limits on the growth of public expenditure. This is discussed in the concluding section.

The internal composition of public revenues is shown in Graph 18. The share of indirect taxation has fallen considerably over time, from 63 percent in 1953 to 41 percent in 1980. However, indirect taxes in Ireland are still very high by international standards; in 1980 the average for the OECD area was 29 percent of total tax revenues. There has been a marked rise in the proportion of revenue drawn from direct taxation since 1960 and especially during the 1970s. This type of taxation accounted for 26 percent of the total in 1960 and for 33 percent in 1980. Social security contributions provide quite a small proportion of revenue by international standards, reflecting a relatively limited social security tax base and the importance of programmes financed from general revenues in the overall social security system. The share of social security contributions in total revenues has, however, grown quite substantially since 1960, climbing from 4.3 percent of the total in 1960 to 12.7 percent in 1980. Growth was particularly rapid in 1974 and 1975, reflecting the extension of the social insurance system and increased contribution rates. Social security taxes remained stable in terms of their contribution to total revenues between 1975 and 1980.

Graph 18

Total public revenue by major component
percent distribution

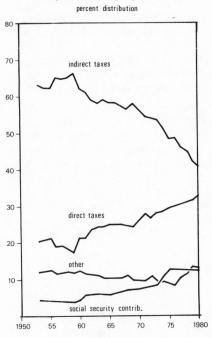

Other sources of revenue include trading and investment income, transfers from the rest of the world, capital taxes and other capital receipts. This category declined in importance during the 1960s and the first half of the 1970s, but has increased again since 1976.

A more detailed breakdown of taxation revenue, as shown in Table 4, indicates that the contribution of personal income tax has risen substantially since the mid-1960s whilst that of corporate income tax and taxes on property and wealth has fallen. The combined effect of increases in personal income taxation and in social security contributions means that the proportion of increasing revenue requirements borne by personal income has grown considerably. Continued reliance on a very high level of indirect taxation places an additional burden on disposable household income.

Table 4   Main types of taxation as percentage of total tax receipts

	1955	1960	1965	1970	1975	1980
Individual income tax	16.4	14.8	16.7	18.3	25.2	32.1
Corporate income tax	7.4	6.5	9.1	8.8	4.8	4.6
Social security contributions	4.6	4.9	6.5	8.2	13.8	14.3
Property taxes	19.7	19.6	15.1	12.2	9.6	5.2
Consumption taxes	47.7	49.8	49.1	49.4	44.4	42.9

4. Financing of welfare programmes

As indicated by Graph 19, social security programmes [54] are financed mainly by general revenues. The state contribution to total receipts of these programmes amounted to 61 percent of the total in 1980, far outweighing that of employers and the insured population. This heavy reliance on general revenues is accounted for by two factors. Firstly, the health services, which absorb a large proportion of social security expenditure (36 percent in 1980), are financed mainly from general revenues; and secondly, non-contributory income maintenance programmes are relatively important in overall social security spending (19 percent in 1980).

The share of total social security receipts drawn from general revenues has decreased somewhat over time, whilst contributions by employers and the insured have become more important. The displacement of general revenues by social security taxes occurred mainly at two points in time: In 1961, when the introduction of the old age pension insurance scheme increased the weight of contributory programmes in the social security system, and in 1974, when the coverage of the social insurance system was extended by the removal of the earnings limit for the insurance of white-collar workers. The introduction of employee contributions towards the cost of the health services in 1971 and the extension of the range of benefits provided under the social insurance system in the early 1970s also helped to shift the burden of financing away from general revenues.

Graph 19

Social security receipts by source
percent distribution

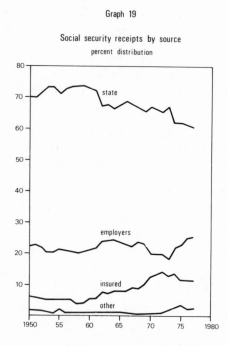

The proportion of receipts drawn from contributions by the insured population rose considerably in the period between 1959 and 1972 - particularly from 1968 onwards.

By contrast, the share borne by employers fell between 1964 and 1973. This trend was reversed in the period after 1973 when the employers' contribution to revenues rose and that of employees fell.

Turning to consideration of the financing of social insurance programmes alone, it will be seen from Graph 20 that the sources of revenue have changed markedly over time. The share of receipts drawn from general revenues rose rapidly between 1955 and 1957 and remained at a level of between 36 and 40 percent until 1967. Between 1967 and 1977 the state contribution declined to 18 percent. The stated policy since 1975 has been to decrease the state share of social insurance financing. Nevertheless, since 1978 this share has been rising again, possibly due to increasing unemployment and to resistance to further increases in the level of personal taxation. The share of social insurance revenue drawn from employer contributions has risen significantly since 1966, from 29.5 percent of the total in that year to 54.5 percent in 1980. The proportion of receipts drawn from the contributions of the insured has actually fallen since 1950, and accounted for 21.5 percent of the total in 1980.

Graph 20

Social insurance receipts by major source
percent distribution

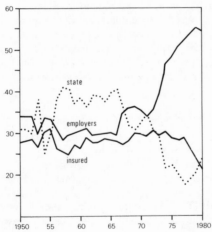

The institutional regulations with regard to the financing of social insurance programmes are as follows. Pensions, unemployment, maternity and sickness benefits are all financed from a single fund which draws its revenues from contributions by employers, employees and the exchequer. Up to 1974, contributions were flat-rate; in that year an earnings-related contribution was introduced to cover the cost of earnings-related supplements to certain benefits which were introduced at the same time. The flat-rate contribution was retained up until 1979 when the contribution system became fully earnings-related. The standard contribution rate in 1982 was 16.8 percent of earnings up to a ceiling of IRL 9,500 per annum, of which the employee paid 33 percent and the employer 67 percent.

Occupational injuries benefits are funded solely from employers' contributions. The contribution rate in 1982 was 0.3 percent of the employee's earnings up to a ceiling of IRL 9,500 per annum. The employer pays a further 0.01 percent of earnings, up to the same ceiling, to a redundancy payments fund. The Intermittent Unemployment Insurance scheme, which pays benefits to workers in the construction, civil engineering and painting trades in compensation for earnings lost due to bad weather, is financed by flat-rate contributions paid in equal parts by the employer and the employee.

As noted earlier, the health services are financed mainly from general revenues. However, reforms in the period since 1971 have led to some funding through contributions (see the Institutional Synopsis). All income earners, with the exception of those with full eligibility for free services (i.e. those on low incomes) and women in receipt of certain social welfare benefits, are liable for contributions. In the case of employees in the full eligibility category the employer is liable for the contribution. The contribution rate in 1982 was 1 percent of earnings up to a ceiling of IRL 9,500 per annum.

Thus, for private sector employees the combined earnings-related contributions in 1982 normally amounted to 18.11 percent of earnings up to the specified ceiling, with the employer paying 11.61 percent and the employee 6.5 percent. Women receiving widows' pensions and deserted wife's benefit or assistance are exempt from the employee's share of the contribution. Public sector employees pay reduced contributions, the rate depending on which of five categories of public sector employment the employee belongs to. In the case of permanent civil servants the contribution rate in 1982 was 3.75 percent, of which the employee paid 1.9 percent and the state 1.85 percent. Certain categories of private sector employees such as outworkers, persons aged 66 or over and those whose employment is of a subsidiary nature, are covered for a limited range of benefits and also pay reduced contributions (see the Institutional Synopsis). The self-employed are not eligible for social insurance.

5.   Fiscal policy: changing class relations

Since the mid-1960s, an increasing proportion of tax revenue has been drawn from income tax and social security contributions. Evidence is limited concerning the impact of this growing tax burden on the distribution of income among different social categories. However, an analysis by Rottman and Hannan examines relative gains and losses among social classes on the basis of Household Budget Survey data for the years 1973 and 1978 [55]. The data on which the analysis is based refer to urban households and only include the effects of direct taxes and cash transfers.

Increases in the proportion of direct income taken by direct taxation have been unevenly distributed across social classes. As shown in Table 5, the class with the highest direct income, professionals and managers, experienced the smallest growth in the proportion of income taken by taxation between 1973 and 1978 (19 percent), while the largest increase was felt by the lower middle-class, i.e. intermediate non-manual workers, whose tax burden grew 35 percent more than their direct income. The tax burden of skilled manual and service workers increased by 31 percent, whilst that of employers and owners grew by 30 percent. Semi-skilled and unskilled manual workers had an increase of 26 percent in the proportion of their income taken by taxation. As noted by Rottman and Hannan, increases in tax burdens appear to have been largely insensitive to the level of income earned, with lower income groups experiencing relatively large increases. The most outstanding anomaly of the distribution of tax burdens is the low level of taxation paid by employers and owners (11.5 percent in

1978), as compared to professionals and managers (20 percent), intermediate non-manual workers (19.2 percent), skilled manual and service workers (18.7 percent) and semi-skilled manual workers (17.9 percent). The analysis by Rottman and Hannan indicates that inflation has been the main force influencing changes in tax liabilities, with insufficient adjustment of tax bands and allowances ensuring that lower income groups paid an increasing proportion of their incomes in taxation.

Table 5   Changes in real income, direct taxes and direct transfers by social class (a)

Social class (c)	Changes 1973–1978 (b)				
	Direct income in 1973 at current prices, in pounds per week	Change in real direct income	Change in real direct transfers	Change in real direct taxes	Change in real disposable income
Employers and proprietors	51.52	1.18	1.03	1.53	1.14
Professionals and managers	67.25	1.03	0.74	1.23	0.98
Intermediate non-manual	47.39	1.15	1.13	1.55	1.08
Skilled manual and service workers	38.73	1.10	1.29	1.44	1.06
Semi-skilled and unskilled manual	31.55	1.06	1.51	1.34	1.10
All households	40.14	1.10	1.32	1.42	1.08

(a) Data refer only to urban households.
(b) Changes expressed as ratio of 1978 average to 1973 average.
(c) For definition of social class categories see Rottman and Hannan (1981).

Changes in real disposable income provide a clearer picture of the changing relativities among social classes. The analysis by Rottman and Hannan shows that employers and owners benefited most from the combined effect of increases in direct income, changes in direct transfers received and tax paid, whilst professionals and managers derived the least gain. This last group actually experienced a drop in real disposable income. Semi-skilled and unskilled workers also experienced an above-average gain in disposable income. Gains were more modest in the case of skilled workers and the lower middle class, as taxation burdens for these categories grew more rapidly than either direct income or direct transfers. The analysis shows that in redistributive terms, changes in the incidence of taxes and transfers during the 1970s have had uneven results. The lowest income category improved its relative position but redistribution to the intermediate income categories - the skilled working class and lower middle class - was slight. Rottman and Hannan note that the distribution of tax liabilities ensured that lower income categories bore a large share of the increasing cost of income transfers which they received. Conversely, the relatively low level of taxation applied to the incomes of employers and owners ensured that this category maintained its relatively privileged position within the income structure [56].

6. The expansion of welfare clienteles

The postwar period has seen a gradual evolution in Ireland from an essentially residual model of social policy to a system which, while retaining important elements of selectivity, incorporates a significant role for social insurance schemes as well as providing some services on a universal basis [57].

The summary in Table 6 (see below) of the extension of social security coverage by risk and by major social group shows that the situation in 1945 reflected a relatively minimalist interpretation of the role of the state in welfare provision. Compulsory social insurance for sickness and maternity benefits and for suvivors' pensions was confined to manual wage-earners and to lower-paid white-collar employees. Unemployment insurance existed for industrial workers and lower-paid white-collar employees. Old age pensions were means-tested. Means-tested assistance schemes also existed for unemployment and for survivors. Child allowances were payable to all families with three or more children, regardless of income. All of the above schemes provided flat-rate benefits. Employers were under statutory obligation to compensate workers on fixed scales in respect of occupational injury. Free medical services were provided for the poor, whilst those covered by sickness insurance were entitled to a range of medical care, excluding general practitioner care.

Reforms implemented during the postwar period reflect three distinct trends: 1) Social insurance was expanded to cover new groups and risks, and its effectiveness in replacing market earnings was improved; 2) the range of categorical social assistance programmes which underpin the social insurance system was expanded; 3) some benefits and services became available on a universal basis.

With regard to the growth of social insurance, a maternity allowance was introduced in 1953, old age pension insurance in 1960, an occupational injuries scheme in 1967, a redundancy payments scheme in 1968, invalidity and retirement pensions in 1970 and a deserted wife's benefit in 1973. Unemployment insurance was extended to cover male agricultural employees in 1953 and female agricultural and domestic employees in 1966. In 1974 compulsory social insurance coverage was extended to virtually all employees. Also in 1974, short-term social insurance benefits (unemployment, sickness, occupational injury and maternity benefits) became partially earnings-related, signalling an extension in the function of the income maintenance system from basic income support to proportional replacement of market earnings for some groups.

Graph 21

Insured persons
as % of labour force

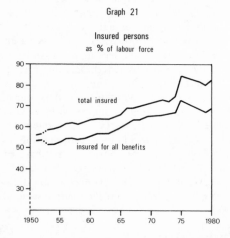

The growth of the insured labour force is shown in Graph 21, distinguishing between the number insured for all benefits available under the social insurance system and the total number insured. Some categories of employees, such as public service workers, for instance, are insured for a restricted range of benefits. The separate insurance schemes were unified in 1952 and the proportion of the labour force insured for all benefits under the unified system rose from approximately 52 percent to approximately 70 percent between 1953 and 1980. The total number of insured grew from around 59 percent to around 84 percent of the labour force in the same period. In addition to the effect of institutional reforms, the growth of the employed labour force has also contributed to increasing the size of the insured population. Between 1961 and 1981 the number of wage-earners and salaried employees rose from 61 percent to 76 percent of civilian employment. The proportion of the labour force insured has declined since the mid-1970s as a result of rising unemployment.

Given that social insurance is confined to employees, social assistance constitutes an important source of support for the self-employed and for those outside the labour force. As shown in Table 6, a range of new categorical assistance schemes have been added to the unemployment assistance, old age pension and survivor pension schemes existing in 1945. These schemes, many of which are targeted at relatively small groups, include allowances for those suffering from infectious diseases (1947), for the disabled (1954), deserted wives (1970), unmarried mothers (1973), elderly single women below retirement age in poor circumstances (1974), prisoners' wives (1974), and smallholders' unemployment assistance (1966).

Universal entitlement is confined to a few areas. Child allowances have, since the time of their introduction in 1944, been paid without reference to means or social insurance status, although an income tax 'claw-back' has operated at various times during the history of the scheme. The allowance was originally confined to families with three or more children, but was extended to the second child in 1952 and to the first child in 1963. Eligibility for free hospital services was extended to approximately 85 percent of the population in 1953, and to the entire population in 1979 [58]. In 1972, those eligible for free hospital care became entitled to reimbursement of the cost of prescribed drugs over a certain amount per month and in 1979 this scheme was extended to the whole population. Those with long-term illnesses became entitled to free drugs in 1971. Free secondary education became available in 1967, along with free transport to school for those living more than three miles from the nearest school. In 1972, all persons of pensionable age became entitled to free travel on public transport. In 1977, grants of IRL 1,000 were introduced for all first time buyers of new houses.

The expansion of social programmes has led to a considerable growth in the number of potential beneficiaries. A precise quantification of the numbers actually taking up benefits would need to include recipients of cash benefits and those utilising services, as well as, arguably, those benefiting from certain tax reliefs. Nevertheless, in the absence of satisfactory time series data on the last two groups, changes in the numbers benefiting from income maintenance schemes provide a useful indication of trends in the size of welfare clienteles. Table 7 shows beneficiaries under the major income maintenance schemes in absolute numbers and as a proportion of the population at risk. In order to facilitate comparison across schemes, Graph 22 shows beneficiary numbers as a proportion of the total population.

Looking first at the graph, it may be seen that the largest beneficiary group within the population are recipients of child allowances. The number of heads of households receiving child allowances increased from 5 percent of the population in 1951 to 12.7 percent in 1980. Pensioners and recipients of sickness cash benefits respectively are

Table 6 Social security coverage: extension by risk and by major social groups

Year	Pensions	Family and maternity allowances	Sickness cash benefits	Health services	Occupational injuries insurance	Unemployment	Year
1945(a)	Means-tested old age pension at age 70; means-tested survivors' pension; survivors' pension insurance for manual wage earners and for salaried employees below an earnings ceiling	Child allowances for all families with three and more children; maternity grants for poor mothers and for those insured for sickness benefits	Sickness insurance for wage earners and for salaried employees below an earnings ceiling	Hospital, general practitioner and maternity and child care for poor patients; hospital, dental and optical care for those insured for sickness cash benefits	Employers under statutory obligation to provide compensation on fixed scales	Unemployment insurance for industrial wage earners and for salaried employees below an earnings ceiling; insurance for manual workers in building industry against loss of earnings due to bad weather; means-tested general unemployment assistance	1945(a)
1947			Means-tested allowance for persons suffering from infectious diseases				1947
1952		Child allowance extended to second child				Unemployment insurance extended to male agricultural wage earners	1952
1953		Maternity allowance for insured women	Means-tested allowances for disabled persons	Hospital services and maternity and child care services for approx. 85% of population			1953
1957				Voluntary health insurance			1957
1960	Old age pension insurance for manual wage earners and for salaried employees below an earnings ceiling						1960
1963		Child allowance extended to first child					1963
1966					Manual wage earners and salaried employees below an earnings ceiling	Unemployment insurance for female employees in agriculture and domestic service; unemployment assistance scheme for smallholders	1966

Table 6 (cont.)

Year	Pensions	Family and maternity allowances	Sickness cash benefits	Health services	Occupational injuries insurance	Unemployment	Year
1970	Invalidity and retirement pension insurance for same groups eligible for old age pension insurance	Means-tested allowance for deserted wives					1970
1971				Reimbursement of cost of drugs over a certain amount per month for 85% of the population			1971
1973		Deserted wife's insurance benefit; means-tested allowance for unmarried mothers					1973
1974	Pension insurance extended to all employees	Means-tested allowance for prisoners' wives; earnings-related maternity benefit (b); maternity insurance extended to all female employees	Sickness insurance extended to all employees and earnings-related benefit introduced (b)		Insurance extended to all employees and earnings-related benefit introduced in certain circumstances (b)	Unemployment insurance extended to all employees and earnings-related benefit introduced (b)	1974
1978						Unemployment assistance for single women on same basis as for men	1978
1979				Free hospital care and reimbursement of cost of drugs over a certain amount per month for entire population			1979
1981		Fully earnings-related maternity benefit for women in full-time employment and entitled to resume same employment at end of maternity leave period					1981

(a) Provisions existing in 1945.
(b) Benefit now consists of basic flat-rate component and earnings-related supplement.

the next largest groups of beneficiaries. In both cases the numbers receiving benefits expanded rapidly during the first half of the 1970s. It should be noted that data for sickness refer to the number of cases for which benefit was paid, and, as such, there is some double counting of beneficiaries. The proportion of the population receiving unemployment benefits has almost doubled since the early 1970s, although in relative terms this group remains small.

Graph 22

Clienteles of the major welfare schemes
as a % of total population

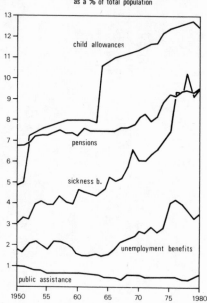

Table 7 provides a more detailed breakdown of beneficiary numbers under various schemes. As may be seen, old age pensioners are by far the largest group of pensioners. The proportion of the elderly population receiving pensions has risen quite considerably since the early 1970s as a result of the reduction of the normal pensionable age from 70 to 66, the introduction of a retirement pension for those over the age of 65, and an easing of the means-test for social assistance pensions. Eligibility for widows' pensions has also been extended through relaxation of age and income criteria.

With regard to sickness cash benefits, the expansion of sickness insurance has increased the numbers eligible for benefits, but the data in the table show that the claim rate has also risen markedly. As noted earlier, detailed analysis suggests that increases in the take-up rate have been significantly linked to improvements in the earnings-replacement ratio and to a rise in the rate of long-term unemployment [59]. The numbers in receipt of unemployment benefits have, of course, followed the trend in unemployment. However, research also suggests that the level of unemployment

Table 7   The clienteles of the major welfare schemes (a)

	1951	1956	1961	1966	1971	1976	1981
PENSIONS							
Old age pensioners (b)							
in thousands	157	165	154	154	164	210	229
as % of population 60+	35.8	37.2	34.5	34.3	35.3	43.1	45.2
Invalidity pensioners							
in thousands					12	10	19
as % of labour force					1.2	0.9	1.5
Survivors' pensioners (c)							
in thousands	44	48	57	65	71	76	85
as % of population 60+	10.0	10.8	12.8	14.5	15.3	15.6	16.8
UNEMPLOYMENT							
Recipients of cash benefits (d)							
in thousands	49	63	42	52	78	136	144
as % of the labour force	3.9	5.4	3.8	4.7	6.9	11.8	11.4
as % of unemployed	108.9	100.0	75.0	100.0	121.9	151.1	127.4
OCCUPATIONAL INJURIES							
Recipients of cash benefits (e)							
in thousands					3	6	7
as % of the labour force					0.3	0.5	0.5
SICKNESS							
Recipients of cash benefits							
in thousands	98	112	127	144	177	307	298
as % of insured (f)	14.5	16.6	19.2	20.2	23.9	37.2	31.6
as % of labour force	7.8	9.4	11.5	12.9	15.8	26.6	23.6
CHILD ALLOWANCES							
Supported children							
in thousands	346	587	601	942	990	1 153	1 200
as % of pop. 19 and under	31.6	53.0	54.1	81.2	82.6	89.1	87.9
Supported families (g)							
in thousands	147	227	225	317	342	402	436
as % of total population	5.0	7.8	8.0	11.0	11.5	12.5	12.7
PUBLIC ASSISTANCE							
Recipients of public assist. (h)							
in thousands	28	21	17	15	16	16	17
as % of total population	1.0	0.7	0.6	0.5	0.5	0.5	0.5

(a) Beneficiaries on last day of financial year in case of all benefits except unemployment, for which the weekly
    average number of beneficiaries throughout the year is used, and sickness benefits, for which the total number
    who received benefits during the year is used.
(b) Contributory and non-contributory old age pensions, retirement pensions.
(c) Contributory and non-contributory widows' and orphans' pensions.
(d) Unemployment benefit, unemployment assistance, smallholders' unemployment assistance.
(e) Injury benefit, disablement pension, death benefit.
(f) Calculated on number insured for disability cash benefit.
(g) Heads of household receiving child allowances.
(h) Home assistance/supplementary welfare allowance.

compensation has had some effect on the level of unemployment and on the duration of periods of unemployment [60]. It will be observed that the number of persons in receipt of benefits exceeds the numbers officially classified as unemployed. This is due to the fact that agricultural smallholders may apply for unemployment assistance to supplement earnings from farming, although they are not included in the numbers classified as being out of work in census and labour force survey data.

The proportion of those under age 19 receiving child allowances has almost trebled since 1951 as a result of extensions in coverage of the scheme. A rise in the birth rate in the 1970s contributed to increasing the absolute numbers receiving benefits. Finally, the number of people dependent upon general public assistance declined considerably between 1951 and the mid-1960s. However, during the remainder of the period considered here, the number of recipients rose slightly in absolute terms, while remaining stable relative to the total population.

Since there is relatively little overlap among the various income maintenance schemes, it is possible to arrive at a reasonably accurate summary estimate of how the numbers dependent upon the social welfare system have grown over time. Table 8 shows that the proportion of the population benefiting from income maintenance schemes has

Table 8   Estimated number of beneficaries of income maintenance benefits (a)

	1946	1961	1980
Recipients of long-term insurance benefits (b)	13	62	193
Recipients of short-term insurance benefits (c)	44	75	137
Total recipients of insurance benefits	57	137	330
As % of all recipients	21.3	44.9	60.0
Recipients of long-term assistance benefits (d)	172	149	153
Recipients of short-term assistance benefits (e)	38	19	67
Total recipients of assistance benefits	210	168	220
As % of all recipients	78.7	55.1	40.0
Total recipients			
as % of total population	9.0	10.8	16.1
as % of population 15+	12.5	15.7	24.1
Recipients of long-term benefits			
as % of total population	6.3	7.5	10.1
as % of population 15+	8.7	10.9	15.2

(a) In thousands; recipients on last day of financial year (i.e. 31 March in 1946 and
    1961, 31 December in 1980) in case of all benefits except unemployment benefits,
    for which the figure used is the average weekly number of beneficiaries in 1946 and
    1961 and the average monthly number in 1980, and maternity benefit, for which the
    figure used is the number who received benefits during the year.
(b) Old age, survivors', retirement, invalidity and occupational injury pension; desert-
    ed wife's benefit.
(c) Unemployment, sickness, maternity and occupational injury benefits.
(d) Old age and survivors' pensions; allowances for deserted wives, unmarried mothers,
    prisoners' wives and elderly single women.
(e) Unemployment assistance (including smallholder's unemployment assistance).

risen significantly in the period since 1961. By 1980, some 16 percent of the total population and some 24 percent of those aged 15 or over were in receipt of benefits of various types. The proportion of the adult population (15+) receiving long-term benefits rose from 9 percent in 1946 to 15 percent in 1980. These figures do not include the dependants of beneficiaries. Estimates for 1966 and 1981 put the total number depending on the income maintenance system, including both direct recipients and their adult and child dependants, at about 19 percent and 30 percent of the population respectively, with some 17 percent depending on long-term benefits in the latter year [61].

The growth of the social insurance system is clearly reflected in the changing balance shown in Table 8 between recipients of insurance benefits and recipients of assistance payments. In 1946, only 21 percent of beneficiaries were receiving insurance benefits. The proportion had increased to 45 percent by 1961 and to 60 percent by 1980, with a corresponding reduction in the importance of social assistance.

7. The development of benefits

The growth in the number of income maintenance beneficiaries has been accompanied by changes in the level and structure of benefits. Before going on to discuss these changes, it may be helpful to summarise the main features of the Irish system [62]. With the exception of benefits provided under the unemployment, sickness, maternity and occupational injury insurance schemes, neither insurance nor assistance benefits are earnings-related. The exceptions mentioned provide benefits which consist of a flat-rate and an earnings-related component. Insurance benefits are determined by the insurance record and assistance benefits are means-tested. Benefits are not automatically indexed, although in practice the rates are adjusted at regular intervals and have generally, in recent years, risen more rapidly than consumer prices.

Table 9 shows the development of standard benefits within the major schemes at constant prices and relative to average gross earnings in manufacturing industry. The real value of benefits rose only marginally between 1950 and the mid-1960s. However, the period since 1965 has seen a considerable improvement in real benefit rates, as increases in benefits have outstripped rising consumer prices. It is perhaps worth noting in this context that social policy was an important issue in the general elections of 1965 and 1973, and in each of these years the incoming government was pledged to raising the living standards of welfare recipients [63]. With regard to flat-rate benefits, the greatest improvement has been in the real value of pensions, which have risen substantially more than the flat-rate elements of unemployment, sickness and occupational injury insurance benefits since the late 1970s. In the case of pensions, means-tested benefits have risen slightly faster than insurance benefits and survivors' benefits have improved slightly more than old age benefits, the aggregate effect being to narrow the differentials among these various benefits. Child allowances do not conform to the general pattern of benefit growth. Benefits have risen more slowly and erratically than within other schemes and during some periods the real value of benefits has declined. However, benefits have improved substantially in the early 1980s. The relativities between families of different sizes have altered since 1970, with an improvement in the position of smaller families relative to larger ones.

The value of the standard flat-rate insurance benefits remained relatively stable in relation to average gross industrial earnings from the mid-1950s up to the late 1970s. The value of social assistance benefits has fluctuated rather more in relation to gross earn-

Table 9   Standard benefits of the major income maintenance schemes (a)

	1950	1955	1960	1965	1970	1975	1980	1982
SOCIAL INSURANCE PENSIONS								
Old age/retirement – personal rate(b)								
at constant (1975) prices	-	-	5.76(c)	6.02	7.67	10.50	12.68	14.77
as % of average gross earnings	-	-	25.0(c)	23.3	22.8	23.0	25.7	31.3
Addition for adult dependant(d)								
at 1975 prices	-	-	4.10(c)	4.50	6.52	6.65	8.10	9.43
Addition for child dependant								
at 1975 prices	-	-	none	1.57	1.44	2.65	3.31	3.05
Widow/deserted wife – personal rate(e)								
at 1975 prices	3.43	4.05	4.45	5.11	6.98	9.50	11.65	13.30
as % of average gross earnings	18.6	20.4	20.0	19.7	20.7	20.8	23.6	28.2
Addition for child dependant(f)								
at 1975 prices	1.37	1.18	1.19	1.92	1.56	3.15	3.88	3.58
Invalidity – personal rate(d)								
at 1975 prices	-	-	-	-	7.71(g)	9.40	11.41	13.03
as % of average gross earnings	-	-	-	-	21.7(g)	20.6	23.1	27.7
Addition for adult dependant								
at 1975 prices	-	-	-	-	5.39(g)	6.10	7.40	8.46
Addition for child dependant								
at 1975 prices	-	-	-	-	1.54(g)	2.65	3.31	2.99
SOCIAL ASSISTANCE PENSIONS								
Old age/blind – personal rate(b)								
at 1975 prices	3.73	3.61	4.06	4.53	6.98	8.85	10.87	12.64
as % of average gross earnings	20.2	18.2	18.3	17.4	20.7	19.4	22.0	26.8
Addition for adult dependant(h)								
at 1975 prices	none	none	none	none	none	4.40	5.46	6.35
Addition for child dependant								
at 1975 prices	none	none	none	1.23	1.17	2.35	2.95	2.68
Widow/deserted wife – personal rate(i)								
at 1975 prices	3.00	3.38	3.85	4.34	6.85	8.85	10.87	12.40
as % of average gross earnings	16.2	17.0	17.4	16.7	20.3	19.4	22.0	26.3
Addition for child dependant(f)								
at 1975 prices	1.29	1.01	1.19	1.20	1.16	2.95	3.57	3.23
UNEMPLOYMENT/SICKNESS INSURANCE								
Unemployment/sickness benefit – personal rate(k)								
at 1975 prices	4.81	4.05	4.45	5.11	6.98	9.40	10.58	11.61
as % of average gross earnings	26.0	20.4	20.0	19.7	20.7	20.6	21.4	27.4
Addition for adult dependant								
at 1975 prices	1.63	2.02	2.22	3.61	5.83	6.10	6.86	7.52
Addition for child dependant(f)								
at 1975 prices	0.52	1.18	1.19	1.57	1.44	2.65	3.08	2.75
UNEMPLOYMENT ASSISTANCE								
Unemployment assistance – personal rate								
at 1975 prices	3.43	3.04	2.82	3.49	5.72	7.70	8.80	9.64
as % of average gross earnings	18.6	15.3	12.7	13.5	17.0	16.9	17.8	19.0

Table 9 (contd.)

	1950	1955	1960	1965	1970	1975	1980	1982
Addition for adult dependant								
at 1975 prices	1.37	1.69	2.02	2.82	5.21	5.55	6.34	6.95
Addition for child dependant(f)								
at 1975 prices	0.52	0.84	0.89	1.20	1.17	2.35	2.74	2.40
OCCUPATIONAL INJURY INSURANCE								
Injury benefit - personal rate (1)								
at 1975 prices	-	-	-	-	11.73	13.10	14.60	15.98
as % of average gross earnings	-	-	-	-	34.8	28.7	29.6	33.9
Additions for adult and child dependants					same rates as for unemployment/			
at 1975 prices	-	-	-	-	sickness insurance			
Disablement benefit - personal rate(m)								
at 1975 prices	-	-	-	-	18.62	22.50	25.80	29.01
as % of average earnings	-	-	-	-	55.5	49.4	52.3	61.6
Additions for adult and child dependants					same rates as for unemployment/			
					sickness insurance			
CHILD ALLOWANCES								
Benefit for 1st child								
at 1975 prices	-	-	-	1.20	0.93	2.30	2.33	4.13
as % of average gross earnings	-	-	-	4.7	2.8	5.0	4.7	8.8
Benefit for 2nd child								
at 1975 prices	-	1.86	2.28	1.86	2.79	3.60	3.62	4.13
as % of average gross earnings	-	9.4	10.3	7.2	8.3	7.9	7.3	8.8
Benefit for 3rd and other children								
at 1975 prices	2.06	2.95	3.26	3.18	3.72	4.35	3.62	4.13
as % of average gross earnings	11.1	14.8	14.7	12.3	11.0	9.5	7.3	8.8

(a) All benefit rates shown here are maximum rates per week in Irish pounds in April of each year. Benefits at constant prices have been deflated by the consumer price index. Earnings-replacement rates have been calculated relative to average gross earnings (males, females and juveniles) in manufacturing industry.

(b) Under age 80. A slightly higher benefit is payable over age 80.

(c) 1961.

(d) Under age 66. A higher rate is payable over age 66.

(e) Under age 66. A higher rate is payable over age 66. Deserted wife's benefit introduced in 1973.

(f) Up to August 1960, the child addition was paid for a maximum of two children. Since that date an addition is paid for all dependent children.

(g) 1971.

(h) Dependant under pensionable age. Where both spouses are of pensionable age each may apply for a pension in own right.

(i) Deserted wife's allowance introduced in 1970.

(k) From 1974 an earnings-related supplement was payable. This raised the maximum benefit to approximately 39 percent of average gross earnings in 1975, 51 percent in 1980 and 53 percent in 1981. The full rate of earnings-related benefit is payable from the beginning of the third week of unemployment or sickness for up to 147 days. A gradually reduced rate is payable for up to 381 days, after which only the flat rate component of the benefit is payable.

(l) Benefit payable for a limited period (26 weeks). With the earnings-related supplement introduced in 1974 the maximum rate of benefit was equivalent approximately to 47 percent of average gross earnings in 1975, 59 percent in 1980 and 62 percent in 1981.

(m) Benefit payable in case of permanent disablement. Rates shown here are for 100% disablement and include the unemployability supplement which is normally payable in such cases.

ings and there was a clear upward shift in the benefit ratio between 1965 and 1970. Nevertheless, apart from this shift, there has also been quite a close association between assistance benefit rates and earnings. This would suggest that although there is no explicit indexation procedure for benefits, average gross industrial earnings have been used as a reference point for benefit adjustment, particularly in the case of insurance benefits. A detailed analysis by Hughes of the determinants of benefit rates during the period 1952-81 confirms that this has been the case [64]. This relationship between benefits and earnings appears to have weakened considerably since the late 1970s. As shown in Table 9, benefits rose appreciably faster than gross earnings in the period 1980-82. Old age pensions outstripped earnings by approximately 6 percent in this period, while unemployment and sickness benefits rose about 3 percent faster than earnings.

The introduction in 1974 of an earnings-related supplement to the flat-rate unemployment, sickness, maternity and occupational injury benefits has raised the value of these payments significantly. From the beginning of the third week of benefit, the earnings-related supplement becomes payable at the rate of 40 percent of earnings between specified upper and lower limits during the previous tax year. This rate of benefit is payable for 147 days, after which the earnings-related supplement falls to 30 percent of the reference earnings for a further 78 days, 25 percent for the next 78 days after that, and 20 percent for a final 78 days, after which both the flat-rate and earnings-related benefits cease. Between 1970 and 1980 the maximum rate of unemployment and sickness benefits, including the earnings-related supplement, increased approximately two-and-a-half times relative to average gross earnings, while the maximum rate of occupational injury benefit rose by almost three-quarters. Since 1980, however, maximum benefit rates have increased only slightly.

It should be noted that the data in Table 9 do not give an adequate description of the income level of social welfare beneficiaries relative to that of the employed population, since replacement rates have been calculated relative to gross rather than net earnings. Clearly, replacement rates are higher relative to net earnings and, moreover, rising rates of income taxation and social insurance contributions since the early 1970s have increased effective replacement rates more rapidly than the data in Table 9 would indicate. For instance, relative to the after-tax earnings of an employee earning the average male industrial wage, the contributory old age pension increased from 27 percent in 1975 to 40 percent in 1982, the non-contributory pension from 23 percent to 34 percent, flat-rate unemployment benefit from 24 percent to 31 percent and unemployment assistance from 20 percent to 26 percent [65]. As such, in recent years the net income of welfare beneficiaries has increased more rapidly than that of the working population.

Turning to the question of relativities between benefit rates, within the social insurance system, benefits are highest under the occupational injury scheme. Benefits under the sickness and unemployment insurance schemes are also relatively high for the period during which earnings-related benefits are payable, but the flat-rate component of these benefits is lower than the basic rates of both social insurance and social assistance pensions. In the case of pensions, social insurance pensions are only slightly higher than means-tested pensions. Old age pensions are paid at slightly higher rates than survivors' pensions which, in turn, are higher than the invalidity pension. Unemployment assistance payments are significantly lower than other means-tested benefits. There are also numerous small variations in the rates of benefit supplements for dependants.

Table 10 shows trends in average benefits under selected schemes in real terms and relative to average gross earnings. Movements in average benefits have, in general, followed trends in standard benefits, with increases in benefit levels reflecting improvements in both basic benefits and provisions for dependants [66]. These data do not, of course, give any clear indication of the distribution of benefits by value within a particular scheme. However, given that average benefit rates are relatively high in comparison to standard rates and given information on the number of dependants for whom increases are paid, it would appear that the majority of beneficiaries receive payments at, or close to, the maximum rate.

Table 10   Average benefits of the major income maintenance schemes (a)

	1950	1955	1960	1965	1970	1975	1980	1982
SOCIAL INSURANCE PENSIONS								
Old age/retirement pension								
at 1975 prices	-	-	6.60	8.05	10.22	13.18	15.63	18.01
as % of average gross earnings	-	-	30.6	31.1	30.3	28.9	31.7	38.2
Widow's pension								
at 1975 prices	4.42	4.70	5.46	5.71	8.19	10.20	12.25	13.90
as % of average gross earnings	23.9	23.6	24.6	22.0	24.3	22.4	24.8	29.5
Invalidity pension								
at 1975 prices	-	-	-	-	10.13	13.15	13.80	16.40
as % of average earnings	-	-	-	-	30.1	28.9	28.0	34.8
SOCIAL ASSISTANCE PENSIONS								
Old age/blind pension								
at 1975 prices	3.65	3.99	5.04	4.99	6.35	8.77	10.73	12.26
as % of average gross earnings	19.7	20.1	22.7	19.3	18.8	19.2	21.7	26.0
Widow's pension								
at 1975 prices	2.78	3.99	4.21	4.80	7.19	10.45	12.34	13.10
as % of average gross earnings	15.1	20.1	19.0	18.5	21.3	22.9	25.0	27.8
UNEMPLOYMENT								
Unemployment insurance (b)								
at 1975 prices	4.12	5.71	5.55	7.33	9.85	17.43	22.87	23.76
as % of average gross earnings	22.3	28.7	25.0	28.3	29.2	38.2	46.3	50.4
Unemployment assistance (c)								
at 1975 prices	2.83	2.97	3.26	5.37	8.08	10.80	12.09	13.63
as % of average gross earnings	15.3	15.0	14.7	20.7	24.0	23.7	24.5	28.9
CHILD ALLOWANCES								
Average benefit per family								
at 1975 prices	1.24	1.52	1.81	1.49	1.71	2.22	1.75	2.42
as % of average gross earnings	6.7	7.7	8.1	5.8	5.1	4.9	3.5	5.1

(a) Average weekly benefits in Irish pounds. Averages have been calculated by dividing annual axpenditure by the number of recipients on the last day of the financial year (i.e. 31st March up to 1975, 31st December from 1975 onwards) in the case of pensions and child allowances, and by the weekly average number of recipients (monthly average in 1980 and 1982) in the case of unemployment benefits. Benefits at constant prices have been deflated by the consumer price index. Earnings-replacement rates have been calculated relative to average gross earnings (males, females and juveniles) in manufacturing industry.

(b) Includes average benefit per recipient of earnings-related benefit from 1975.

(c) Including smallholder's unemployment assistance.

Despite the considerable improvements in coverage and benefits, there remain some important shortcomings in the income maintenance system. Since social insurance is confined to employees, and given that a relatively large minority of the labour force are self-employed, the proportion of the population dependent upon means-tested social assistance is high. The possibility of extending social insurance to the self-employed, and in particular the issue of financing, given that a majority of the self-employed are farmers, was examined in the late 1970s [67]. As yet, however, no steps have been taken to integrate the self-employed in the system. Another criticism is that the structure of the social welfare system, and particularly the social assistance system, is quite fragmented, with some schemes applying to very small groups within the population, and numerous small variations in benefit rates, for which it is difficult to find any rationale [68].

Although the introduction of earnings-related benefits has greatly improved short-term income replacement rates for unemployment, sickness, maternity and occupational injury benefits, benefits remain relatively low within the remaining schemes. There has been some discussion of the possibility of introducing an earnings-related pension scheme, but this has not so far produced any legislative proposals [69]. The value of pensions has, however, risen more rapidly since the late 1970s than the value of other benefits so that the purchasing power of pensioners has improved relative to that of other beneficiaries. On the other hand, at a time of rising unemployment and increasing long-term unemployment, the value of unemployment assistance has risen relatively slowly, implying a deterioration in the income of this group relative to that of other welfare beneficiaries. The position of all beneficiary groups has improved relative to average earnings in recent years, particularly when benefits are compared with net earnings.

8. Summary - the growth of the welfare state

The data on social expenditure, employment in the social services, welfare clienteles and social benefits presented here all point to a broadly similar pattern of development. Following a phase of expansion from a very low base in the late 1940s and early 1950s, the development of social programmes was virtually halted until the early 1960s. The period from then up to the mid-1970s saw rapid and sustained expansion of the welfare state, and while the pace of development slowed after 1975, the final years of the 1970s saw renewed growth.

The major expansionary phase of the welfare state which began in the early 1960s has been characterised by growth across all the main social programmes. While this growth occurred in the context of rapid economic development and a general expansion of the public sector, social expenditure has grown considerably faster than either GDP or total public expenditure. The expansion of the welfare state has also been marked by important institutional developments, with the establishment of new programmes, reform and expansion of existing ones and improvements in the living standards of welfare beneficiaries both in absolute terms and relative to the standard of living of the working population. The welfare state has become an important source of support for a sizeable section of the population as well as being a major employer.

This expansion has left Ireland at the beginning of the 1980s with a relatively high level of social expenditure by international standards. In 1960, social expenditure amounted to 11.7 percent of GDP compared with an average of 13.1 percent across

OECD countries. By 1981 the Irish expenditure share had risen to 28 percent, compared with an OECD average of 25.6 percent [70]. The growth of social spending is particularly impressive considering that Ireland is not an especially wealthy country by OECD standards. In 1981, Ireland ranked twentieth in the OECD area in terms of per capita GDP, but eighth in terms of the GDP share of social expenditure.

The expansion of the welfare state has been underpinned by a substantial increase in taxation, particularly in income tax and social security contributions, leading to an appreciable increase in the financing burden borne by the working population and in non-wage labour costs. Moreover, the available evidence suggests that the burden of increased taxation has been unevenly distributed among the various social classes, with the lower paid and the employee classes in general bearing a relatively large share, while the tax burden of employers and proprietors has remained relatively light. More recently, high levels of public and social expenditure have been sustained by heavy public borrowing for current as well as capital purposes. Again, the dimensions of the financing burden are placed in perspective by comparison with other OECD countries. In 1980, current government receipts (consisting mainly of direct and indirect taxes and social security contributions) amounted to 41 percent of GDP in Ireland, compared with an OECD average of 37 percent, while the general government budget deficit in Ireland was 11.9 percent of GDP, as against an average of 2.4 percent in other OECD countries [71].

III   Achievements and shortcomings: evaluations

The earlier sections of this study have underlined the considerable expansion in resources channelled to social programmes in the post-war period, to improvements in social benefits and to the growth in beneficiary numbers. The following section attempts to evaluate the achievements of a welfare system which currently spends close to 31 percent of Gross Domestic Product [72]. Some basic indicators of the achievements and shortcomings of the major income maintenance schemes and of the health, education and housing systems are presented, the findings of some recent studies of the social programmes are reviewed and the major issues of the current debate on the merits and flaws of Irish social policies are discussed.

Three major aims of Irish social policy in the post-war period have been identified by Kennedy on the basis of official documents and policy statements: the relief of poverty and the provision of a minimum standard of living for all, equalisation of opportunity, and increased productivity and economic growth [73]. The first of these aims has been shown by Kennedy to underpin all of the major social programmes, whereas the second and third aims have been enunciated chiefly in relation to educational policy [74]. A fourth aim, which can be discerned in a number of official policy statements in the 1960s and 1970s, is that social policy should reduce inequalities and should ensure that all sections of the community, particularly the weaker groups, benefit from increasing national prosperity [75]. In the course of the following discussion consideration will be given to the extent to which the above objectives have been achieved, beginning with the issues of poverty and income inequality and then going on to assess the performance of the social services.

1. Poverty and the adequacy of the income maintenance system

The extent of poverty

Although the relief of poverty and the provision of a minimum standard of living for the entire community are explicitly stated aims of social policy, there is no official poverty line in Ireland. The 'supplementary welfare allowance' (introduced in 1977), which is intended to provide a guaranteed minimum income, may be said to represent an implicit poverty line, although its level has been fixed in an arbitrary fashion. As noted by O'Cinneide, the lowest incomes maintained by the social security system have not been justified as being adequate, nor has there been any officially sponsored research designed to establish what an adequate minimum income might be [76]. Prior to the introduction of the supplementary welfare allowance, public assistance was provided on a discretionary basis. The proportion of the population receiving assistance declined from 2.6 percent in 1946 to 0.9 percent in 1976. The proportion receiving supplementary welfare allowances rose from 0.9 percent in 1977 to 1.2 percent in 1981 [77].

Following the 'rediscovery' of poverty in the early 1970s, there have been a number of studies which indicate that the extent of poverty is substantially greater than might be suggested by the numbers receiving the supplementary welfare allowance. The rediscovery of poverty dates primarily from a conference on the topic organised in 1971 by the Council for Social Welfare, an advisory body established by the Roman Catholic hierarchy [78]. Widespread concern was aroused at the time by the main finding of the conference, that at least 20 percent of the population were in poverty [79]. The elimination of poverty became an important issue in the 1973 General Election and the National Coalition government which subsequently took office made substantial increases in income maintenance payments [80].

Prior to 1976, when the results of the 1973 Household Budget Survey (HBS) were published, attempts to estimate the extent of poverty were hampered by the lack of satisfactory data on income distribution [81]. Since then there have been several studies of poverty based on the 1973 HBS as well as one based on the more recently published 1980 HBS [82]. These studies have arrived at estimates of the numbers in poverty ranging between 8 percent and 30 percent of the population in 1973 and between 5 percent and 13 percent in 1980 [83]. The discrepancies in the estimates arise from variations in the choice of poverty line and in the weighting of household composition.

One report, commissioned by the EC as part of the European Programme of Pilot Schemes and Studies to Combat Poverty, used three alternative poverty lines to estimate the extent of the problem in 1973 [84]. The basic poverty line (A) was set at the level of the lowest social assistance benefit available at the time, rural unemployment assistance. This was also the level at which public assistance payments were unofficially set [85]. The other two poverty lines (B and C) were set at levels of 120 percent and 140 percent respectively of the basic line. The methodology used in this study was replicated in an analysis by Roche [86], based on the 1980 HBS and using updated poverty lines, thus permitting a direct comparison of the extent of poverty at two points in time (see Table 11). It should be noted that the lowest poverty line used in the 1980 study was 16 percent less than the basic rate of supplementary welfare allowance in force from April 1980 and is therefore a very conservative line [87].

Table 11   Relationship of poverty lines to selected income maintenance payments
and average net male earnings, 1973 and 1980 (a)

	1973 % of poverty line			1980 % of poverty line		
	A	B	C	A	B	C
Contributory old age pension	143	119	102	176	147	126
Non-contributory old age pension	122	102	87	151	126	108
Unemployment benefit	130	108	93	147	122	105
Unemployment assistance (b)	106	88	76	122	102	87
Supplementary welfare allowance (c)	100	83	72	118	99	85
Average net male industrial earnings (d)	544	454	390	551	459	394

(a) Data refer to July 1983 and April 1980. Poverty lines, benefit rates and net earnings shown
here refer to a single person.
(b) Urban rate.
(c) The Supplementary Welfare Allowance did not exist in 1973. The figures shown here for 1973
are based on the rural rate of Unemployment Assistance. The Supplementary Welfare Allowance
has been set at this rate since its introduction in 1977.
(d) Gross earnings less income tax and social insurance contributions, and less health contribution in 1980.

Roche's findings concerning trends in poverty between 1973 and 1980 are summarised
in Table 12. In 1973, 8 percent of the population had disposable incomes below the
lowest poverty line, while 21 percent had incomes below the highest line. The extent
of poverty had fallen considerably by 1980, to 5 and 13 percent of the population
below the lowest and highest poverty lines respectively. However, there are grounds
for arguing that the lowest poverty lines used in the studies just discussed do not
represent a reasonable definition of adequate income.

Table 12   Percentage of households and population poor in Household Budget Survey sample
1973 and 1980 (a)

Poverty Line	Households		Adults		Children (b)		Total persons	
	1973	1980	1973	1980	1973	1980	1973	1980
A	9.8	4.3	7.5	4.0	9.2	6.1	8.2	4.9
B	15.3	7.5	12.2	6.8	15.2	11.1	13.4	8.6
C	22.7	12.3	18.8	10.9	24.0	17.0	21.0	13.4

(a) The Household Budget Survey sample included 7,709 households in 1973 and 7,163 in 1980.
(b) Persons under age 18.

Roche has estimated a minimum income line based on the average expenditure on
food of the lowest 30 percent of the income distribution in 1980 relative to the food
expenditure of the fifth and sixth deciles of the distribution [88]. This approach gave a
minimum income which was more than twice the level of the lowest poverty line used
by Roche and was 1.6 times above the highest poverty line. O'Cinneide and Rottman

et al. have also argued in favour of a poverty line which is higher than the minimum lines used in the 1973 and 1980 poverty studies [89].

As such, the estimates of poverty based on the higher lines shown in Table 12 may provide a better guide to the numbers subsisting on inadequate incomes. These estimates must, however, be regarded as tentative for several reasons. First, income is typically understated in household budget surveys, with the result that the numbers apparently in financial poverty may be inflated [90]. On the other hand, Roche points out that the HBS excludes some groups who would almost certainly be poor, such as those without a permanent residence and those living in certain types of institutions [91]. Second, the HBS provides a static picture of the financial situation of respondants and it is possible that for a proportion of the poor, poverty is a transitory state. Finally, Kennedy has drawn attention to the sensitivity of estimates of the extent and distribution of poverty to the equivalence scales used to standardise for household composition [92].

Notwithstanding these caveats, it would appear that although considerable progress was made in reducing the level of financal poverty between 1973 and 1980, a sizeable minority of the population were still subsisting on inadequate incomes in the latter year. Given these findings, it is clear that the income maintenance system only partially succeeds in preventing poverty. Moreover, Roche has shown that the poverty gap, that is the extent by which the income of the poor falls below the poverty line, is relatively wide for a substantial proportion of poor households [93].

Information concerning the risk and distribution of poverty is useful in identifying where the shortcomings in the social security system may be (see Table 13). With regard to the livelihood status of the head of household, in both 1973 and 1980, households headed by an unemployed person were most at risk of poverty, being over five times more susceptible than the average household in the latter year. The poverty risk for farm households in 1980 was over three times higher than the average at the lowest poverty line and almost twice the average at the highest line. The risk in 1980

Table 13   Risk of poverty classified by livelihood status of head of household, 1973 and 1980

Livelihood status of head of household	% of households poor 1973 poverty line			% of households poor 1980 poverty line		
	A	B	C	A	B	C
Self-employed, non-farmer	4.6	8.6	13.6	2.3	3.3	6.0
Self-employed, farmer	10.3	15.0	21.8	13.2	17.1	21.8
Employee	1.5	4.2	9.1	0.6	1.3	3.2
Total at work	4.9	8.6	14.6	3.7	5.1	7.7
Ill	28.9	44.7	58.5	6.8	23.2	40.7
Unemployed	49.5	59.5	68.2	23.2	50.7	60.4
Total out of work	40.9	53.3	64.1	16.8	40.0	52.7
Retired	14.0	24.0	36.5	2.2	4.5	13.0
Home duties	24.9	35.7	40.1	2.5	6.3	17.0
Other	28.8	39.7	57.7	13.2	22.6	32.1
Total outside labour force	19.9	24.5	43.0	2.7	5.7	15.2
All households (a)	9.8	15.3	22.7	4.3	7.5	12.3

(a) A small number of households in the 1973 sample could not be classified owing to missing data; the total number of classified households was 7,591 in 1973 and 7,162 in 1980.

for households headed by an ill person was one-and-a-half times the average at the lowest poverty line, but was considerably increased at the higher lines. The poverty risk for households headed by an economically inactive person, retired or engaged in homes duties, was reduced dramatically between 1973 and 1980. In the latter year this group had a below average risk at the two lower poverty lines and only a slightly above average risk at the highest poverty line.

Analysis by Roche of the demographic correlates of poverty has shown that in 1980 families with children were at greater risk than families without children, a reversal of the situation in 1973 [94]. The risk of child poverty was found to be highest in households where the head was out of work. The risk was also relatively high in farm households and in larger families. The risk of poverty for single parent families was found to have been considerably reduced between 1973 and 1980, reflecting improvements in income maintenance arrangements for this group, although such families still had an above average risk at the higher poverty lines in 1980 [95]. The risk of poverty among the elderly was found to have been reduced markedly between 1973 and 1980, a period in which benefits for this group were improved considerably, although elderly persons living alone still had a relatively high risk of poverty at the highest poverty line in 1980 [96].

Turning to the distribution of poverty, Table 14 shows that in 1980, households in which the head was working accounted for 60 percent of all poor households at the lowest poverty line and for 44 percent at the highest line. Between a fifth and a quarter of poor households, depending on the poverty line used, were headed by an unemployed person, while 15 percent at the lowest poverty line and 29 percent at the highest line were headed by a person outside the labour force. There has been a considerable shift in the incidence of poverty between 1973 and 1980 [97]. The proportion of poor households with an economically inactive head was substantially lower in 1980 than in 1973, while the proportions where the head was at work or unemployed

Table 14   Incidence of poverty in 1973 and 1980 classified by livelihood status
of head of household

Livelihood status of head of household	1973				1980			
	% of poor households poverty line			% of all sampled households	% of poor households poverty line			% of all sampled households
	A	B	C		A	B	C	
Self-employed, non-farmer	3.0	3.7	3.9	6.6	3.6	3.0	3.2	6.8
Self-employed, farmer	23.5	21.8	21.4	22.6	49.7	36.6	28.3	16.1
Employee	6.6	11.6	17.0	43.2	6.9	8.0	12.1	47.2
Total at work	33.1	37.1	42.3	72.4	60.1	47.7	43.7	70.1
Ill	6.1	6.0	5.3	2.1	3.9	7.7	8.2	2.5
Unemployed	14.4	11.1	8.6	2.9	21.2	26.5	19.1	3.9
Total out of work	20.5	17.1	13.9	5.0	25.4	34.2	27.3	6.4
Retired	15.1	16.6	17.0	10.7	7.2	8.2	14.5	13.7
Home duties	27.1	25.0	22.6	10.9	5.2	7.7	12.6	9.1
Other	2.9	2.6	2.6	1.0	2.3	2.2	1.9	0.7
Total outside labour force	45.1	44.2	42.2	22.6	14.7	18.1	29.0	23.5
All households (a)	98.7	98.4	98.4	100.0	100.0	100.0	100.0	100.0

(a) Balance in 1973 relates to unclassifiable poor households; see Table 13.

rose markedly. Roche suggests that this shift in the incidence of poverty reflects the effects of improved benefits for those outside the labour force as well as the impact of a sharp drop in farm incomes in 1979-80 and rising unemployment [98]. Roche has also shown that the incidence of child poverty rose between 1973 and 1980, with children constituting over half of the poor at each poverty line in the latter year [99].

To summarise the situation, approximately one percent of the population were in receipt of the supplementary welfare allowance in 1980, but analysis of household budget survey data has indicated that the numbers in poverty are considerably higher, with possibly as many as 13 percent of the population living below what might be termed a low income threshold. The groups with the highest risk of poverty were found to be the unemployed and farmers, while families with children, particularly larger families, also ran a high risk. Roche's comparison of the situation in 1973 with that in 1980 shows that the income maintenance system has been much more succesful in reducing the risk of poverty for the economically inactive population than for other groups [100].

The persistence of poverty indicates that there are serious shortcomings in the income maintenance system. The following sections examine income support arrangements for three important groups - the unemployed, families with children and the elderly.

Unemployment compensation

Ireland has experienced high unemployment rates over much of the postwar period. With the exception of the early 1950s and the period from 1962 to 1966, the level of unemployment has not fallen below five percent since 1951. The employment situation

Table 15   Employment and unemployment, 1951–1983

	1951	1961	1971	1975	1977	1979	1980	1981	1982	1983 (f)
Total employment (in 1,000s) (a)	1 217	1 053	1 055	1 073	1 083	1 145	1 156	1 146	1 148	1 125
Unemployed (in 1,000s) (a)	45	56	65	73	89	74	74	106	123	155
Seeking first job (b) (in 1,000s) (a)				20	16	14	17	20	25	29
Labour force (c) (in 1,000s)	1 262	1 108	1 120	1 146	1 172	1 219	1 230	1 252	1 271	1 280
Unemployment rate A (in %) (c)	3.6	5.0	5.8	6.4	7.6	6.1	6.0	8.5	9.7	12.1
Unemployment rate B (in %) (d)				8.0	8.8	7.1	7.3	9.9	11.4	14.1
Registered unemployed (in 1,000s) (e)			57.3	96.2	106.4	89.6	101.5	127.9	156.6	192.7
Insured unemployed (in 1,000s) (e)			42.4	75.4	81.9	66.4	73.7	96.1	117.8	148.7

(a) Figures refer to mid-April. Data for 1951, 1961 and 1971 are based on the population censuses of those years. Later figures are based on the labour force surveys of 1975, 1977, 1979 and 1983, on the population census of 1981 and on Central Statistics Office estimates.
(b) Data on first time job seekers not available before 1975.
(c) Excluding first job seekers.
(d) Including first job seekers.
(e) Annual average; figures are not comparable to those measured on a census and labour force survey basis.
(f) Official estimate.

deteriorated sharply in 1975 following the first oil shock and although unemployment was reduced somewhat between 1977 and 1979, the numbers out of work have risen very rapidly in the early 1980s, with the unemployment rate reaching an estimated 14 percent in 1983 if first-time job seekers are included (Table 15).

With rising unemployment, the numbers claiming unemployment benefits have increased sharply. Unemployment compensation is provided through two schemes: an insurance scheme covering virtually all employees provides benefits for a maximum of 390 days to those who have fulfilled the necessary contribution conditions; an assistance scheme provides means-tested benefits for most of those who do not qualify for unemployment insurance benefits [101]. The coverage of the unemployment insurance system was expanded considerably in 1974 when the earnings ceiling which had disqualified higher paid employees from insurance was removed. Increases in the duration of benefit have also contributed to a rise in the numbers eligible for benefits. Gaps in the unemployment assistance scheme have also been filled, most notably through the removal of restrictive conditions applying to female applicants. However, married women without dependants are still effectively excluded from the scheme, although this situation should be remedied when the European Communities Directive on equal treatment between the sexes in matters of social security is implemented [102].

Despite improvements in the coverage of the unemployment insurance system, the proportion of beneficiaries receiving unemployment benefit has fallen from 60 percent in 1975 to 51 percent in 1982, so that an increasing proportion depend on the lower unemployment assistance payments [103]. This development can be attributed largely to the upward trend in long-term unemployment. The number of persons on the unemployment register for over a year has risen from 17 percent in 1971 to 39 percent in 1984 [104]. Thus, an increasing proportion of beneficiaries have exhausted their entitlement to unemployment benefit. It is likely that the growth in youth unemployment has also contributed to this trend. Between 1980 and 1984 the proportion of the registered unemployed aged less than 25 years rose from 25 percent to 31 percent [105].

As shown in Table 9, the purchasing power of unemployment benefit and assistance remained relatively stable between 1950 and 1965 but has risen appreciably since the latter year. For a single person the real value of the flat-rate unemployment benefit more than doubled between 1965 and 1982 and the value of unemployment assistance increased 2.8 times. For a family consisting of husband, wife and two children the respective increases were 2.0 and 2.5. Benefits have also been improved by the introduction in 1967 of a redundancy payments scheme providing lump sum severance payments, by increases in the maximum duration of unemployment benefit from 156 days in 1967 to 390 days in 1976, and by the introduction in 1974 of earnings-related benefits, payable with the basic flat-rate unemployment benefit from the fourth week of unemployment [106]. The long-term unemployed, those who have been registered for more than one year, have since 1983 received unemployment assistance at a rate which is five percent higher than the standard rate.

But while the real value of unemployment benefits has improved considerably over time, attention has been drawn to the fact that since the late 1970s the unemployed have received much smaller benefit increases than the retired population, although both groups have fared better than the working population [107]. Between 1979 and 1983 the contributory old age pension increased by 32 percent in real terms, the noncontributory pension increased by 33 percent, unemployment benefit increased by 18 percent and unemployment assistance increased by 19 percent, while average gross male industrial earnings fell by 7 percent (Table 16).

Table 16   Trends in the real value of unemployment benefits, old age pensions
                  and average gross male industrial earnings, 1970-83 (a)

	Unemployment benefit	Unemployment assistance	Contributory old age pension	Non-contributory old age pension	Average gross male industrial earnings (b)
1970	6.98	5.72	7.67	6.98	44.43
1973	9.26	7.14	10.18	8.70	51.09
1976	9.24	7.54	10.30	8.69	56.76
1979	9.82	8.05	11.38	9.67	59.30
1980	10.58	8.80	12.65	10.87	58.73
1981	10.55	8.77	13.18	11.29	56.63
1982	11.61	9.63	14.77	12.64	54.55
1983	11.56	9.60	14.98	12.82	55.12
Change (%)					
1970-79	+40.7	+ 40.7	+ 48.4	+ 38.5	+ 33.5
1979-83	+17.7	+ 19.3	+ 31.6	+ 32.6	- 7.0

(a) Weekly rates in Irish pounds at 1975 prices, deflated by consumer price index.
(b) Transportable goods industries.

Replacement ratios of unemployment benefit and assistance relative to net industrial earnings in 1983 for various categories of recipients are shown in Table 17. Since benefits increase with family size, the initial phase of unemployment, during which only the basic flat-rate unemployment benefit is payable, does not bring a very severe drop in disposable income for large families. For smaller families, childless couples and single persons the income reduction is much greater. The earnings-related supplement boosts replacement ratios considerably, although benefits for single persons and childless couples remain relatively low. The exhaustion of insurance benefits brings a severe reduction in income for all but very large families [108].

Table 17   Replacement ratios of unemployment benefit and unemployment assistance
                  in mid-1983 (a)

	% of average net male industrial earnings replaced (b)				
	Single person	Married couple	Married 2 children	Married 4 children	Married 8 children
Basic unemployment benefit (c)	33	47	60	72	91
Unemployment benefit and pay-related benefit (d)	57	68	81	85	91
Unemployment assistance	27	41	53	62	78

(a) Tax rebates are not included in the calculations.
(b) Transportable goods industries.
(c) First three weeks of unemployment.
(d) Pay-related supplement is limited so that it will not lead to replacement ratios in excess of 85%; however, the basic rate of benefit may not in any circumstances be reduced; from the fourth week up to 141 days, with a lower rate of supplement for a further 234 days.

Thus, for the majority among the growing numbers of long-term unemployed, unemployment assistance provides an income which cannot be regarded as providing for anything more than bare subsistence needs. Roche has shown that although the risk of poverty for the unemployed was reduced between 1973 and 1980, this group was still extremely vulnerable to poverty in the latter year [109]. The unemployed constituted between a fifth and a third of the total poor population in 1980, depending on the poverty line applied. It appears unlikely that the risk of poverty for the unemployed has altered very much since 1980, given that up to 1984 real increases in the value of unemployment benefits were relatively small.

Unemployment levels are likely to remain high for the next several years at least. At a time when the living standards of the working population are falling and when the cost of social benefits already imposes a heavy burden it may be difficult to make any major improvement in the real value of social welfare payments. However, there is a strong case for improving the level of assistance for the long-term unemployed, accompanied by the development of policies to enhance their labour market prospects.

Income support for families

Despite a sustained decline in fertility since the mid-1960s, the Irish birth rate, at 21 per 1000 in 1981, remains high by Western European norms. The average family size has also declined, but is still much higher than in many other European countries. Another trend of relevance for income maintenance policy is the growing number of single parent families. The 1979 Census of Population estimated the number of such families at 12 percent of all family units and it is thought that this estimate is probably too low due to the problems of identifying unmarried parents as separate family units [110]. The proportion of illegitimate births has risen from 3.7 percent in 1975 to 6.8 percent in 1983 [111]. There are no accurate estimates of the rate of marital separation, but the growing number of claims for deserted wives' benefits points to an upward trend. The issue of family income support has attracted increasing attention in

Table 18   Value of child allowances and child tax relief, 1971 and 1984 (a)

	1971		1984		
	Nominal	Value at 1975 prices	Nominal	Value at 1975 prices	% change 1971–84
Child allowance					
First child	0.11	0.19	2.63	0.81	+ 326
Second child	0.35	0.60	2.63	0.81	+ 35
Third child	0.52	0.89	2.63	0.81	− 9
Tax saving (b)	26,25% marginal tax rate		35% marginal tax rate		
First child	0.68	1.16	0.67	0.21	− 82
Second child	0.60	1.03	0.67	0.21	− 80
Third child	0.59	1.01	0.67	0.21	− 79
Total family income support					
First child	0.79	1.35	3.30	1.02	− 24
Second child	0.95	1.63	3.30	1.02	− 37
Third child	1.11	1.90	3.30	1.02	− 46

(a) Weekly benefits in Irish pounds; data refer to April each year; the 1971 figures have been deflated by the consumer price index average for the year, the 1984 figures have been deflated by the consumer price index for the second quarter of the year.

(b) For standard rate tax payer; the 26,25% tax rate was the equivalent of the standard tax rate of 35% when allowance was made for earned income relief.

recent years, with particular focus on the high level of child poverty and on the problems of larger, low-income families and single parent families [112].

Income support is provided for families with children through a universal child allowance scheme, through tax relief for dependent children and through dependants' additions to the standard social insurance and assistance benefits. Important changes have taken place in state support for families since the early 1970s. The problems of single parent families have received explicit recognition through the introduction of benefits for deserted wives and unmarried mothers and through improvements in benefit rates for children of single parents relative to rates for children of other welfare recipients. On the other hand, Table 18 shows that the net result of trends in the level of child allowances and child tax relief has been to reduce substantially the real value of total income support in respect of children between 1971 and 1984.

Data from the Household Budget Survey, shown in Table 19 indicate that in the period 1973-80, households with children experienced a much smaller increase in real disposable income than households without children. Larger families fared worst of all and households consisting of two adults and four or more children actually experienced a decline of 1.5 percent in average real disposable income. When disposable income in 1980 was standardised for household composition, the lowest income households were those consisting of several adults and a number of children. Large two-adult families also had a relatively low average income. Given these trends it is hardly surprising that the risk of poverty in 1980 was found to be substantially higher in households with children than in those without, and to be particularly high for larger families.

Table 19   Average weekly disposable income (in Irish pounds) classified by household composition
1973 and 1980

Household composition	At 1975 prices (a) 1973	1980	% change 1973-80	Nominal value per adult (b) 1980
1 adult	17.84	23.30	+ 30.6	45.01
2 adults	37.36	42.64	+ 14.1	49.93
3 adults	51.54	58.21	+ 12.9	48.89
4 adults	69.57	82.77	+ 19.0	54.21
Other households without children	85.97	111.58	+ 29.8	53.71
2 adults with 1 child	48.38	53.16	+ 9.9	52.94
2 adults with 2 children	52.88	58.02	+ 9.7	50.27
2 adults with 3 children	55.17	59.40	+ 7.7	46.46
2 adults with 4 or more children	59.10	58.22	− 1.5	39.17
3 adults with children	61.44	62.58	+ 1.9	40.24
4 adults with children	66.18	71.32	+ 7.8	38.13
Other households with children	83.57	91.15	+ 9.1	(c)
All households	51.31	55.10	+ 7.4	(c)

(a) Deflated by consumer price index.
(b) Equivalent unit weighted according to the equivalence scale implicit in the unemployment benefit scheme, April, 1980: adult=1.0, additional adult=0.65, first child=0.29, second child=0.29, each additional child=0.24.
(c) Household composition unknown.

Table 20 provides an overview of the horizontal redistribution produced by state interventions in 1980. Disposable income was lower than direct income for all household types except those consisting of one or two adults. The position of households consisting of three adults and of larger households with children was altered only

Table 20

Incidence of state taxes and benefits by household composition in 1980 (a)

Household composition (b)	Average weekly direct income	Cash benefits	Direct taxes	Disposable income	Non-cash benefits	Indirect taxes	Total benefits less total taxes	% of sample households
1 adult	42.27	10.96	8.22	45.01	7.64	7.19	3.19	16.4
2 adults	80.52	16.96	15.10	82.38	11.40	14.24	- 0.98	20.2
3 adults	113.09	19.84	20.48	112.46	16.30	20.36	- 4.70	7.2
4 adults	173.24	17.84	31.16	159.92	21.74	29.71	-21.29	4.1
Other households without children (5.6)	245.27	16.68	46.37	215.58	33.94	37.33	-33.08	3.3
2 adults with 1 child	119.39	4.88	21.55	102.71	8.58	19.44	-27.53	6.2
2 adults with 2 children	126.22	6.37	20.49	112.10	14.84	18.27	-17.55	10.2
2 adults with 3 children	124.78	9.64	19.66	114.76	22.09	20.03	- 7.96	7.4
2 adults with 4 or more children (6.7)	114.12	14.98	16.63	112.47	35.31	19.27	14.39	6.5
3 adults with children (5.5)	121.90	17.09	18.08	120.91	35.77	21.31	13.47	7.0
4 adults with children (6.4)	139.77	18.37	20.85	137.79	45.58	21.94	21.66	4.3
Other households with children (7.3)	182.79	23.23	29.92	176.10	50.65	29.20	14.76	7.3
All households (3.7)	111.74	14.26	18.95	106.45	20.85	18.31	- 2.15	100.0

(a) Estimated from the 1980 Household Budget Survey; amounts in Irish pounds.
(b) Figures in brackets refer to the number of persons in the household.

slightly by transfers and direct taxes. Thus the overall effect of transfers and direct taxes was to redistribute income from households with children to those consisting of one or two adults. Income inequalities among families with different numbers of children were reduced in so far as the net income loss of smaller families was substantially greater than that of larger families. Households with children benefited more from non-cash benefits than households without children, with larger families benefiting particularly from education services. When all taxes and benefits are balanced, large families are seen to have benefited substantially, while single adults also made a net gain. Households with fewer children and households consisting solely of a number of adults were net contributors to the redistributive system.

Attention has been drawn by the National Economic and Social Council to the existence of unemployment and poverty traps, particularly for larger families, caused by the structure of the tax-benefit system [113]. A principal cause of the unemployment trap has been the fact that social welfare benefits are increased according to the number of dependants, with the result that for large families with low earning potential, replacement rates in excess of 100 percent are possible, particularly in the short term. The poverty trap results from a situation where, due to increasing taxes and withdrawal of benefits as earnings increase, low earners may be unable to increase their final income even if gross earnings rise.

A new Family Income Supplement was introduced in late 1984 as a remedy for the unemployment trap. This benefit, which is worth more than the child allowance and which is payable to the families of low income employees, alleviates the unemployment trap by increasing the net gain from taking up low paid employment. It is planned to make a fundamental change in the family income support system in 1986 by replacing all the existing benefits and tax relief with an increased child benefit, accompanied by a reduction in the level of child dependant supplements for social welfare recipients. The proposed scheme is to be welcomed in so far as it will eliminate the regressive child tax relief and is intended to be neutral with regard to employment decisions. Since benefits are to be taxed the scheme also has the potential to target resources to lower income families. The National Economic and Social Council has suggested, however, that the scheme will not succeed in removing the poverty trap unless accompanied by a more graduated imposition of taxes and withdrawal of benefits as earned income rises [114].

In conclusion, although the period since the early 1970s has seen considerable improvements in provisions for single parent families, the real value of income support in respect of children generally has declined. And while the tax-benefit system effects a substantial redistribution to larger families, the financial position of households with children has deteriorated relative to childless households during the 1970s, with larger families experiencing the most severe relative decline. Overall, the system of family income support has been marked by a lack of coherence, leading to anomalies such as the unemployment and poverty traps discussed above. While the introduction of the family income supplement in 1984 appears to have alleviated the unemployment trap, it remains to be seen whether the proposed new child benefit scheme will succeed in significantly improving the structure of family income support.

The adequacy of pensions

The proportion of those aged 65 and over drawing state pensions has increased from an estimated 51 percent in 1960 to approximately 82 percent in 1981 [115]. This increase is attributable to the expansion of the pension system and relaxation of eligibility criteria as well as to a trend towards earlier retirement. The introduction of old age pension insurance for low paid employees in 1961, the expansion of this scheme to all employees in 1974, the introduction in 1970 of a retirement pension payable at age 65, and reductions in the general pensionable age from 70 to 66 years between 1973 and 1977, have been among the most important institutional developments contributing to growth in the numbers receiving pensions. The network of other state cash and non-cash benefits, which constitute an important supplement to pensions, has also been expanded [116].

Benefits provided under state pension schemes are flat-rate. As shown in Table 9, the purchasing power of pensions has risen substantially over time. Relative to gross average industrial earnings, pensions have risen quite markedly since the late 1970s. In recent years, pensioners have fared considerably better than both the unemployed and the working population (see Table 16). Ratios of pensions in 1983 relative to average net male industrial earnings are shown in Table 21. For single pensioners the contributory pension amounts to just over two-fifths of net earnings, while for couples the pension is equivalent to almost two-thirds of earnings. Non-contributory pensions are considerably lower for single persons and for couples where one partner is below pensionable age. Little consideration has been given in Ireland to the question of what an appropriate earnings replacement ratio for state pensions might be. A recent report by the National Council for the Aged suggests that a pensioner couple would need between 65 percent and 80 percent of pre-retirement net income in order to maintain purchasing power [117]. On this basis, it would appear that pension rates for couples are almost sufficient in the case of the average earner to provide the minimum income considered necessary. This is not true in the case of the non-contributory pension for a person with an adult dependant under pensionable age, and it is also questionable whether a replacement ratio of 36 percent for a single non-contributory pensioner represents an adequate income.

Table 21   Rates of old age pension relative to average industrial earnings, 1983 (a)

	Single rate (b)	Pensioner couple (c)	Pensioner with adult dependant under pensionable age (c)
Contributory pension	42%	64%	60%
Non-contributory pension	36%	63%	47%

(a) Benefit rates in July 1983 as a proportion of average net male earnings in transportable goods industries in 1983.
(b) Calculated on net earnings of a single person.
(c) Calculated on net earnings of a married person.

To what degree are these standard replacement ratios likely to be representative of the pensions actually received by the majority of pensioners? In 1983, some 79 percent of non-contributory pensions were paid at the maximum rate [118]. Data on the distribution of contributory pensions are not available, but a comparison of the standard and average pension rates, which are shown in Tables 9 and 10 respectively, provides some indication of how representative the standard rates may be. Average pensions are in fact higher than the standard rate, presumably reflecting the addition of supplements for dependants and other supplements to the basic benefit. In 1983, 44 percent of old age and retirement pensioners received the higher contributory pension.

Furthermore, the adequacy of state pensions should be considered in connection with the question of to what extent the elderly have other soures of income. Table 22 summarises the findings of three studies [119]. The studies are not directly comparable since they cover different groups of elderly and refer to different years. Among all persons aged 65 and over in 1977, state pensions were the major source of income, accounting on average for over half of the total. Income from farming was also important, accounting for more than one fourth, while occupational pensions contributed 12 percent. The situation of recently retired employees is rather different. For this group, occupational pensions provide a much greater proportion of income than for the elderly population as a whole, partly due to the growth in coverage of occupational pension schemes [120]. The third group, households headed by an elderly person, derive a substantial portion of their income from earnings, since such households may also contain non-elderly persons.

Table 22   Average weekly income of elderly persons and households (a)

Source of income	Persons aged 65 and over 1977		Households headed by a person aged 65 and over 1980		Recently retired employees 1983	
	pounds	%	pounds	%	pounds	%
State pension or allowance	12.12	51.4	19.40	27.4	46.60	55.2
Pension from previous employer	2.87	12.2	8.7	12.3	31.68	38.4
Income from farming	6.49	27.5	13.3 (b)	18.8 (b)	-	-
Income from self-employment	0.23	1.0			-	-
Income from employment	0.59	2.5	21.5	30.3	1.54	1.9
Income from interest	0.88	3.7	2.8	3.9	3.57	4.3
Income from other sources	0.39	1.7	5.2	7.3	0.20	0.2
Total all sources	23.57	100.0	70.9	100.0	82.59	100.0

(a) Income from different sources in Irish pounds in nominal terms.
(b) Including other miscellaneous sources of indirect income, such as value of own garden/farm produce.

When all sources of income are taken into account, the financial situation of elderly and/or retired persons, on average, compares favourably with that of other sections of the community. Whelan and Whelan's 1983 survey of recently retired people found that the average ratio of post-retirement income relative to pre-retirement income in the sample population was 73 percent [121]. Analysis of Household Budget Survey data for 1980 has shown that the average per capita disposable income, in adult equivalent terms, of households headed by an elderly person was 78 percent of that of households headed by a non-elderly person [122]. Given the rapid rise in pension levels relative to average earnings since the late 1970s, it is probable that the income gap between elderly and non-elderly households has narrowed since the 1980 survey.

The above information provides a relatively reassuring picture of the financial circumstances of the elderly. However, broad averages may mask important variations among different sub-groups of elderly persons. Several recent studies have highlighted the heterogeneity of the elderly population [123]. Groups experiencing economic problems include those living alone, those depending on state pensions for the bulk of their incomes and the very elderly [124]. Pension dependent households, which in 1980 accounted for 42 percent of all elderly households, are the poorest group. With an average size of 1.6 persons, these households received in 1980 only 50.6 percent of the income of all households headed by persons aged 65 and over, where the average size was 2.2 persons [125]. The relative position of this group may, however, have improved since 1980 given the upward trend in pension rates.

To summarise, there has been a marked improvement in the economic circumstances of the elderly population since the early 1970s, which must be attributed in large part to better state pension provisions. The continuing expansion of occupational schemes has also contributed to this improvement and can be expected to bring about a further rise in the incomes of the elderly in the future. The risk of poverty among the elderly has been reduced considerably and the gap between the average disposable income per capita of elderly and non-elderly households now appears relatively narrow. Despite this encouraging picture, there are substantial minorities within the elderly population whose needs are not being met satisfactorily at present. As such, there appears to be a good case for the view expressed in Whelan and Whelan's recent study, that a more differentiated approach to provision of financial support for the elderly is required in order to direct aid to the groups with the greatest problems [126]. Such a strategy may be particularly important in times of budgetary constraint and high unemployment, when the overall level of resources available for support of the elderly population is likely to be limited.

2. Income inequality

As a result of the rapid growth of social expenditure and the concomitant increase in taxation since the early 1960s the state has assumed an increasingly significant role in determining the life chances of individuals. In 1980, state transfer payments accounted for over 11 percent of average gross household income, while transfers and non-cash benefits together represented almost one-third of average final income [127].

This section of the study examines the redistributive effects of state taxes and benefits on household incomes. Estimates of these effects relating to the years 1973 and 1980, based mainly on data collected in the Household Budget Survey, have been published by the Central Statistics Office [128]. The discussion below also draws on analyses by Nolan, by O'Connell and by Rottman et al. of the 1973 data and by Roche of the 1980 data which provide useful insights on various aspects of the redistributive process [129].

In the course of the following discussion reference will be made to four income concepts. Direct income is defined as all income accruing to the household before the deduction of taxes or the addition of state benefits. Gross income is defined as direct income plus cash benefits. Disposable income is defined as gross income minus direct taxes. Final income is defined as disposable income plus the value of non-cash benefits and minus indirect taxes.

Table 23 shows the average weekly direct, disposable and final income of households in 1980 and the average weekly incidence of direct and indirect taxes and benefits classified by direct weekly income. Cash benefits amounted to 13 percent of average direct income, non-cash benefits to 19 percent, direct taxes to 17 percent and indirect taxes to 16 percent of this income. Cash benefits increased as incomes fell, while direct taxes decreased. Non-cash benefits accrued in approximately equal amounts over most of the income range but increased for households in the higher direct income groups. Indirect taxes increased with income. Overall, the tax-benefit system produced a net gain for all households with incomes of less than IRL 90 per week - the bottom 47 percent of the income distribution - and a net loss for all other households.

Table 24 gives the decile distributions of direct, gross and disposable weekly household income in 1973 and 1980. The distributions are unlinked, which is to say that

Table 23   Average weekly income, taxes and benefits of all households in 1980,
classified by direct weekly income (a)

Direct weekly income	Direct income	Cash benefits	Direct taxes	Disposable income	Non-cash benefits	Indirect taxes	Final income	Total benefits less taxes
Less than 20	3.79	31.66	0.32	35.12	18.46	7.32	46.26	+ 42.48
20-30	24.63	21.97	0.93	45.67	19.57	8.98	56.26	+ 31.63
30-40	34.55	19.41	1.25	52.71	18.36	9.54	61.53	+ 26.97
40-60	49.97	15.81	3.26	62.52	20.00	12.73	69.79	+ 19.82
60-80	70.18	11.23	7.15	74.26	18.96	14.63	78.59	+ 8.41
80-90	84.56	9.09	10.56	83.09	20.03	16.53	86.59	+ 2.03
90-100	95.05	8.44	12.68	90.80	18.18	16.82	92.16	- 2.88
100-120	109.11	8.56	16.20	101.46	20.44	19.04	102.86	- 6.25
120-140	129.73	7.14	21.02	115.85	20.07	20.45	115.48	- 14.25
140-170	153.91	7.14	25.68	135.38	22.03	22.79	134.62	- 19.29
170-200	183.50	6.85	34.80	155.56	23.71	27.07	152.19	- 31.31
200-230	213.19	5.97	42.43	176.72	22.31	31.26	167.78	- 45.41
230 and over	322.58	6.90	66.71	262.77	27.74	36.04	254.47	- 68.11
All households	111.14	14.26	18.95	106.45	20.85	18.31	108.99	- 2.15
% of average direct income	100.0	12.8	17.0	95.8	18.8	16.5	98.1	

(a) All amounts in Irish pounds.

Table 24   Percent distribution of direct, gross and disposable weekly household income
by decile shares, 1973 and 1980

Decile of households	1973			1980		
	Direct income	Gross income	Disposable income	Direct income	Gross income	Disposable income
Bottom decile	} 1.19	1.53	1.67	} 0.5	1.5	1.8
2		3.02	3.28		3.0	3.5
3	3.78	4.80	5.02	2.8	4.5	5.0
4	6.07	6.40	6.52	5.7	6.1	6.5
5	7.64	7.67	7.85	7.7	7.6	7.9
6	9.26	9.15	9.21	9.4	9.1	9.3
7	11.26	10.88	10.86	11.5	10.9	11.0
8	13.83	13.14	12.99	14.2	13.3	13.0
9	17.69	16.62	16.16	18.4	16.9	16.2
10	29.28	26.79	26.44	29.8	27.0	25.8
Gini coefficient (a)	.448	.380	.370	.469	.386	.363
Ratio of income share of top 20% to share of bottom 40%	4.25	2.76	2.58	5.36	2.91	2.50

(a) Normalised Gini in the closed interval (0.1) adapted for group data.

households have been re-ranked according to their incomes after each stage of the redistributive process to show the actual distribution of each income type among all households. As the published redistribution data do not include calculations of the actual distribution of final income it has not been possible to include this in the table. Analysis of final income distributions by O'Connell and by Roche on the basis of unpublished data are dicussed below [130].

The distribution of direct income is very unequal and as shown by the Gini coefficient this inequality has become more pronounced between 1973 and 1980, a trend which Roche attributes to the depressing effect of rising unemployment and the sharp fall in farm incomes in 1979-80 on the share received by the lower deciles [131]. A comparison of the distributions of direct and gross income reveals the redistributive effect of cash benefits, which raised the income shares of each of the bottom four deciles in 1980. The redistributive effect of cash benefits was greater in 1980 than in 1973, raising the share of the bottom 40 percent of households by 6.1 percentage points in the later year as compared with a rise of 4.7 points in the earlier year. However, this was insufficient to compensate for the increased inequality in the distribution of direct income so that gross income was less equally distributed in 1980 than in 1973. The redistributive impact of direct taxation may be gauged by comparing the distributions of gross and disposable income. The impact was progressive in both 1973 and 1980 and the degree of progressivity increased between the two points in time. In both years, however, the redistributive effect of direct taxation was considerably weaker than that of cash transfers.

The redistributive impact of non-cash benefits and indirect taxation on household income in 1973 has been analysed by O'Connell, whose calculations are shown in Table 25 [132]. Non-cash benefits taken into account in the analysis include medical services, education, housing, social benefits-in-kind and subsidies on food, postal and telephone services and public transport. Indirect taxes taken into account include rates on dwellings, motor taxation, value added tax, fiscal duty and other indirect taxes such as licences [133]. As may be seen from Table 25, the net effect of non-cash benefits and indirect taxation is regressive, rendering the distribution of final income less equal than that of disposable income. O'Connell's analysis indicates that this regressive effect resulted from the incidence of indirect taxes rather than from that of non-cash benefits [134].

Table 25   Percent distribution of disposable and final weekly
             household income by decile shares in 1973

Decile of households	Disposable income	Final income
Bottom decile	1.67	1.42
2	3.28	3.18
3	5.02	4.77
4	6.52	6.30
5	7.85	7.16
6	9.21	9.79
7	10.86	11.05
8	12.99	13.21
9	16.16	16.28
10	26.44	26.84
Gini coefficient	.370	.381

It is likely that the use of social services and other non-cash benefits is strongly conditioned by household composition. The distribution of income in 1980 adjusted for household composition has been analysed by Roche, whose estimates are shown in Table 26 [135]. Here the net effect of non-cash benefits and indirect taxation is shown to be progressive, resulting from the incidence of social services, while subsidies and indirect taxation had a slightly regressive effect.

Table 26   Percent distribution of different types of weekly household income
per capita, by decile shares, in 1980 (a)

Decile	Disposable income	Disposable income plus social services (b)	Final income
Bottom decile	{ 7.8	{ 9.9	{ 9.1
2			
3	5.8	6.7	6.8
4	6.7	7.5	7.5
5	7.8	8.3	8.2
6	9.1	9.2	9.2
7	10.5	10.4	10.5
8	12.4	11.9	11.9
9	15.4	14.3	14.4
10	24.4	21.9	22.5
Maximum equalisation percentage	22.7	18.5	19.3

(a) Household income per adult equivalent unit.
(b) Non-cash benefits included here are as follows: medical services, education, subsidised rents in public housing and social benefits-in-kind. Subsidies on food, transport, postal and telephone services and mortgage interest relief are not included here, but are included in the calculation of final income.

Estimates of the progressive or regressive effects of individual taxes and benefits in 1973 and 1980 are shown in Table 27, along with the average weekly value of each tax or benefit to all households. The effect of each cash benefit is measured in relation to the distribution of direct income, the effects of direct taxes are measured in relation to the distribution of gross income and those of non-cash benefits and indirect taxes in relation to the distribution of disposable income [136].

Looking at Table 27 it will be seen that all cash benefits were progressive, the greatest reduction in the Gini coefficient being produced by pensions. Income tax had a modest progressive effect, while the impact of social insurance contributions on the Gini coefficient for gross income was negligible. Among the non-cash benefits, medical services had a discernable progressive impact, indicating that they tended to favour lower income households. Educational services, which accounted for a relatively high average expenditure, had no significant redistributive impact. Housing benefits and other non-cash benefits also left the Gini coefficient virtually unchanged. The regressive effect which has been found for indirect taxation appears to be due largely to the impact of fiscal duty.

Table 27   Progressive and regressive effects of individual taxes and benefits
in 1973 and 1980

Tax or benefit	Average weekly value to household (a)		Change in Gini coefficient (b)	
	1973	1980	1973	1980
Cash Benefit				
Child allowances	0.71	1.80	-.005	-.006
Pensions	1.90	6.71	-.039	-.052
Unemployment benefits	0.78	2.87	-.016	-.023
Other cash benefits	0.83	2.88	-.016	-.021
Direct taxes				
Income tax	3.12	16.15	-.015	-.028
Social insurance contributions	0.83	2.80	+.001	-.002
Non-cash benefits				
Medical services	1.80	8.19	-.022	-.026
Education	3.09	9.12	+.002	-.006
Housing	0.40	0.96	-.004	-.006
Other non-cash benefits	0.41	2.55	-.004	-.006
Indirect taxes				
Rates	0.91	}0.15 (c)	+.004	}.000 (c)
Motor taxation	0.26		.000	
Value added tax	2.22	6.88	+.003	+.003
Fiscal duty	3.93	10.76	+.009	+.011
Licences	0.14	0.51	+.001	+.001

(a) Irish pounds in nominal terms.
(b) A negative value indicates a reduction in the Gini coefficient and, therefore, progressivity;
a positive value indicates regressivity.
(c) Rates and motor taxation were terminated in 1978; figures shown for these headings in 1980
include local water charges and motor registration fees.

The redistributive effects of the tax-benefit system operate on the horizontal distribution of income among households of varying composition as well as on the vertical distribution. These may be considered simultaneously by using equivalence scales to adjust for differences in household composition. Table 28 shows the distribution of direct, gross and disposable income in 1980 per adult equivalent unit as calculated by Roche [137]. While the degree of inequality in the distribution of direct income, as meas-

Table 28   Percent distribution of direct, gross and disposable weekly
household income per capita, by decile shares, in 1980 (a)

Decile of households	Direct income	Gross income	Disposable income
Bottom decile	}0.7	}6.8	}7.8
2			
3	3.5	5.1	5.8
4	5.7	6.2	6.7
5	7.5	7.4	7.8
6	9.3	8.8	9.1
7	11.2	10.4	10.5
8	13.9	12.7	12.4
9	18.0	16.1	15.4
10	30.1	26.5	24.4
Gini coefficient	.471	.357	.319

(a) Household income per adult equivalent unit.

ured by the Gini coefficient, does not differ significantly from that of the corresponding unadjusted distribution presented in Table 24, the distributions of gross and disposable income appear less unequal for the adjusted distributions, confirming that vertical redistribution is reinforced by horizontal redistribution [138].

The 1973 Household Budget Survey has been used by Rottman et al. to examine the income differentials associated with social class and to assess the effect of direct taxes and transfers on households of different social classes [139]. This study showed that redistribution took place primarily from the higher income categories of employees to the semi-skilled and unskilled working class and to marginal farm households. The property owning classes were found to be relatively unaffected by taxation with the result that proprietors of large and medium-sized farms were net beneficiaries from the tax-transfer system and large non-farm proprietors, who had the highest direct income of any of the class categories examined, experienced only a slight loss in disposable income.

The published data for the 1980 Household Budget Survey also provide some indication of how different groups are affected by the tax-benefit system (see Table 29). A comparison of direct and disposable income shows that the two groups with the lowest direct incomes, semi-skilled/unskilled manual workers and farmers/agricultural workers/fishermen made a net gain from direct taxes and cash transfers while all other groups were net losers. The most advantaged group in this context were the farmers and other primary producers who paid relatively little direct tax while receiving substantial cash transfers. A comparison of direct and final income shows that the net effect of all taxes and benefits was to increase the incomes of the two groups with the lowest direct incomes by similar amounts, to leave the position of the 'other non-manual' group unchanged and to decrease the incomes of the remaining groups.

Table 29   Average weekly income, taxes and benefits (in Irish pounds) of households in 1980, classified by social group of head of household

Social group	Direct income	Cash transfers	Direct taxes	Disposable income	Non-cash benefits	Indirect taxes	Final income	Disposable/ direct inc.	Final/ direct inc.
Higher professional, lower professional, employer or manager	189.21	5.47	40.50	154.53	18.76	24.80	148.49	0.82	0.78
Salaried employee, intermediate non-manual worker	132.77	8.81	24.21	117.37	17.78	19.64	115.51	0.88	0.87
Other non-manual worker	103.91	15.14	18.29	100.75	22.00	18.69	104.07	0.97	1.00
Skilled manual worker	123.69	12.29	22.81	113.17	21.83	20.60	114.40	0.91	0.92
Semi-skilled and unskilled manual worker	79.54	22.53	13.77	88.29	23.76	15.79	96.26	1.11	1.21
Farmer, farmer's relative or farm manager, other agricultural worker or fisherman	84.15	17.96	6.35	95.77	22.58	16.68	101.67	1.14	1.21
Unknown	22.78	21.69	2.34	42.13	16.92	5.06	53.99	1.85	2.37
All households	111.14	14.26	18.95	106.45	20.85	18.31	108.99	0.96	0.98

Finally, Table 30 shows the incidence of taxes and benefits according to livelihood status. Substantial redistributive flows to the unemployed and the economically inactive population take place as a result of the transfer of resources from employees, while the self-employed also make a slight net gain from the system. Households headed by a self-employed person pay the smallest proportion of their direct income in direct taxes of any of the groups shown here and, in contrast to employees, receive more in cash transfers than they pay in direct taxes. As a proportion of disposable income, indirect taxation bears most heavily on unemployed and retired households, while the self-employed and employees both pay about the same proportion. The net effect of indirect taxation and non-cash benefits is to further improve the position of the self-employed and of unemployed and inactive households, while leaving that of employees more or less unaltered.

Table 30   Average weekly income, taxes and benefits (in Irish pounds) of households in 1980, classified by livelihood status of head of household

Livelihood status	Direct income	Cash transfers	Direct taxes	Disposable income	Non-cash benefits	Indirect taxes	Final income	Disposable/ direct inc.	Final/ direct inc.
Self-employed	111.36	12.57	10.19	113.74	22.62	19.30	117.06	1.02	1.05
Employee	154.87	5.12	31.22	128.78	20.76	22.28	127.25	0.83	0.82
Out of work	28.98	45.38	5.10	69.25	29.11	14.18	84.18	2.39	2.91
Retired	43.46	27.51	5.96	65.01	16.94	11.44	70.53	1.50	1.62
Other	48.74	23.34	7.68	64.40	17.22	9.21	72.41	1.32	1.49
All households	111.14	14.26	18.95	106.45	20.85	18.31	108.99	0.96	0.98

To summarise, the distribution of direct income became more unequal between 1973 and 1980, whereas the distribution of disposable income became slightly less unequal, indicating that the redistributive effect of state interventions increased between the two points in time. Even after the allocation of direct taxes and cash benefits, however, the distribution of income remained very unequal. When household composition was taken into account the redistributive impact of direct taxes and cash benefits appeared more pronounced. Of the non-cash benefits, only medical care spending had a progressive impact, while indirect taxation and subsidies were found to be regressive. With regard to social class relativities, the tax-benefit system appears to redistribute income mainly within the employee sector, from the high to the lower income categories, while leaving the position of the proprietorial classes and the self-employed relatively unaltered.

3.   The adequacy of social services

As documented in Sections I and II of this study, the social services have undergone important reforms over the past two decades, while the share of GDP expended on the three major services - health, education and housing - has more than doubled. The achievements of the health, education and housing systems are discussed below. In the case of each programme some conventional input and intermediate output indicators are presented. Based on secondary evidence the programmes are then assessed in terms of their main stated goals and/or objectively defined criteria.

Health

Public expenditure on the health services increased from 3.0 percent of GDP to 8.4 percent between 1960 and 1980. Real per capita expenditure on health services almost quadrupled in the same period. Employment in the public health service quadrupled in absolute terms between 1970 an 1981, going from 1.4 percent to 5.0 percent of the labour force [140]. Other conventional input indicators, shown in Table 31, also attest to the expansion of the health care system.

Table 31   Health care resources – selected indicators, 1961–1975

		1961	1971	1975
Doctors:	total number	2 952	3 565	3 758
	per 10,000 pop.	10.5	12.0	12.0
Dentists:	total number	576	659	869
	per 10,000 pop.	2.0	2.2	2.8
Nurses:	total number	15 230	19 284	19 475
	per 10,000 pop.	54.0	64.7	62.3
Hospital beds:	per 1,000 pop.	6.2	6.1 (a)	5.8 (b)
Mean length of stay in hospitals:	number of days	19	13 (a)	11 (b)
Cases treated per bed per year		19	22 (a)	28 (b)

(a) 1970.
(b) 1976.

In assessing the achievements of health care policy, it is proposed to focus on three issues. These are first, trends in the health status of the community; second, the extent to which the health care system is an equitable one, and third, whether the system is efficient in its use of resources.

Some indication of trends in health status may be gained from the data on life expectancy and mortality shown in Tables 32 and 33 respectively. Since 1950, life expectancy at birth has risen by five years for men and by almost eight years for women, while life expectancy at age 65 has risen by 0.3 years for men and by almost two years for women. Infant mortality rates and maternal death rates have fallen dramatically over time, as has the death rate from tuberculosis. These trends are almost certainly attributable in large measure to improvements in standards of living,

Table 32   Expectation of life at selected ages, 1950–1960

	Age	1950–52	1960–62	1970–72	1978–80
			Life expectancy		
Males	0	64.5	68.1	68.8	69.5
	25	44.8	46.4	46.3	46.4
	45	27.0	27.8	27.6	27.7
	65	12.1	12.6	12.4	12.4
	75	6.8	7.1	7.3	7.1
Females	0	67.1	71.9	73.5	75.0
	25	46.6	49.5	50.5	51.4
	45	28.9	30.7	31.4	32.1
	65	13.3	14.4	15.0	15.4
	75	7.6	8.1	8.5	8.8

but health care policy has also played a significant part. At the end of the Second World War, the infant mortality rate and the death rate from tuberculosis were very high by Western European standards and improvement of health care in these areas became a major policy priority [141]. Since then there has been a shift in the causes of mortality away from those such as infant mortality and infectious diseases, which appear to be commonly associated with lower levels of economic development, towards those such cancer which are relatively more prevalent in developed societies.

Table 33   Mortality rates by selected causes of death, 1961 - 1983

	1961	1971	1983
Crude death rate (per 1,000 pop.)	12.3	10.7	9.3
Infant mortality rate (per 1,000 live births)	30.5	18.0	9.8
Maternal death rate (per 100,000 live births)	45	25	13
Tuberculosis death rate (per 100,000 pop.)	14.7	6.1	2.2
Cancer death rate (per 100,000 pop.)	166.9	190.7	182.3
Diseases of circulatory system (per 100,000 pop.)	606.6	547.3	470.7

Data on preventive health care provide an indirect indication of trends in health status since more effective coverage of the target population presumably reduces the incidence of disease and disablement. Rates of immunisation against certain infectious diseases have risen considerably since the mid 1970s, to virtually total coverage of the target population in the case of diphtheria and rubella, although coverage in the case of poliomyelitis was still only 79 percent in 1982. Following the recommendations of an official study group on the child health services which reported in 1968, a medical screening service for young children was established in the early 1970s [142]. However, the service is mainly confined to towns with populations of 5,000 and over and even in these centres only 75 percent of eligible children received a six months examination in 1982. Moreover, there are marked regional variations in the proportion of eligible children receiving examinations [143]. The health authorities are obliged to provide a medical examination for all children entering primary school. In 1982, 82 percent of new entrants were examined in the country as a whole, but again there were regional variations in the coverage rate. Coverage was particularly low in the Eastern and South-Eastern regions [144]. Thus while preventive care has improved, the services have not yet reached targeted standards.

Turning to the issue of equity, this may be interpreted in the context of health care to imply that there should be equality of financial and physical access to services of comparable quality for all, regardless of ability to pay or social status [145]. While provision of a free national health service has never been an objective of health care policy in Ireland, the structure of eligibility is intended to ensure that inability to pay is not a barrier to access [146]. There are three categories of eligibility, with membership determined by income. Category I includes all those deemed unable without 'undue hardship' to provide general pracitioner care for themselves and their dependants. The members of this category, about 38 percent of the population in 1984, are entitled to receive all medical care free of charge. Those in Category II, about 47 percent of the population in 1984, receive free hospital care but their eligibility for out-patient care is restricted to specialist care, maternity and infant care and subsidisation of pharmaceutical expenses. Category III includes the top 15 percent of the income distribution and persons in this category are entitled only to free hospital accommodation, subsidisation of pharmaceutical expenses and free specialist out-patient care at public clinics (excluding consultants' fees).

While the structure of eligibility would appear to ensure that the poorer sections of the community have unimpeded financial access to health care, it is not entirely free of inequities. One major anomaly to which attention has been drawn by Tussing is that dependants are taken into account in determining the income guidelines for Category I eligibility, whereas no allowance is made for dependants in setting the income limit dividing Categories II and III [147]. A second anomaly is that although uniform income guidelines are set down for determining Category I eligibility, membership of this category is at the discretion of the regional health authorities. This is thought to give rise to regional disparities, particularly in the treatment of farmers and of special hardship cases whose incomes are above the limits set by the guidelines [148].

There is a regressive element in the funding of health care arising from the fact that while those on higher incomes qualify for only a restricted range of public services, they receive subsidies for private services. These include provision of private and semi-private accommodation in public hospitals and use of facilities in public hospitals for private patients without commensurate charges to the patient, and tax relief on private health insurance premiums. Tussing has suggested that in the early 1980s over half of the cost of private care was funded, directly or indirectly, by the state [149]. The level of subsidisation has been reduced since 1983 through the discontinuation of public subventions for patients in private hospitals and an increase of 50 percent in charges for private and semi-private accommodation in public hospitals.

With regard to quality of health care, patients in all three eligibility categories receive care from the same providers. Up to 1972, those who qualified for free general practitioner care, that is the poorer sections of the population, received such care in public clinics from doctors employed by the health authorities. Since 1972, however, this system has been replaced by one whereby patients are free to attend the general practitioner of their choice. While it would, therefore, appear that in general the health care system now makes available care of the same quality to all sections of the community regardless of income, some doubts have been raised concerning the care actually received by low income patients and the physical access to services by such patients, especially in rural areas [150].

What little evidence there is on patterns of morbidity by socio-economic status in Ireland indicates that those in the lower socio-economic groups generally have a higher level of illness, with respect, for example, to the risk of heart disease, diseases of the respiratory and circulatory systems, neoplasms and accidents [151]. A survey on the incidence of gastro-enteritis in Dublin in the mid-1960s showed that children affected by this illness were more likely to come from low income families with relatively poor living conditions [152]. There is also a significant social class differential in admission rates to psychiatric hospitals, with unskilled manual workers having an admission rate of more than twice the national average in 1977 [153]. Such social class differentials in health status are, however, more likely to result from disparities in living and working conditions than from inequalities in access to health care.

Information on inequalities in the use of health services is also scanty. Utilisation rates of general practitioner services are significantly higher among low income groups than in the rest of the population [154], but there is no information on the use of hospital services and preventive services by different income groups and it is not clear to what extent variations in health status are being adequately catered for. However, there is some evidence that a minority of low income persons are not receiving adequate care. A 1978 survey of elderly poor people in Dublin uncovered a high incidence of undiagnosed treatable illnesses [155]. A separate survey by Tussing found that about five percent of persons with full eligibility for free health care had not seen a doctor for at least five years [156].

With regard to the economic incentive structure operating within the health care system, Tussing notes that the Irish system contains perverse incentives for both the clients and the providers [157]. As in many health care systems, the clients bear very little direct cost for the use of services and so have little incentive to economise. In the case of general practitioner care, almost 40 percent of the population receive free care and free prescription pharmaceuticals, while the remainder are liable for only a portion of pharmaceutical costs and may insure privately for general practitioner fees exceeding a relatively low floor. In the case of hospital care and specialist out-patient care, 85 percent of the population are eligible for free services and the remainder can insure privately for the total cost of hospitalisation. Not only is there little incentive for economising behaviour in the use of these services, but Tussing has pointed out that the structure of charges in the health care system as a whole tends to encourage utilisation of higher cost resources over lower cost ones [158]. For instance, the large segment of the population who are liable for the costs of general practitioner care have an incentive to use more expensive hospital-based services which they receive free of charge.

These remarks should not be taken as a recommendation for the imposition or raising of user charges for medical services. The implications of any change in health care pricing for access to services by poorer patients would require careful consideration. Changes which might discourage early access by this group would clearly run counter to the equity objectives of health care policy. Tussing has noted, however, that a valuable contribution of user charges in the Irish context could be to encourage the use of lower-cost and/or high priority services over higher-cost and/or low priority ones [159].

Turning to the providers of health care, Tussing has noted that the payment systems used in Ireland for doctors and hospitals do not appear to be particularly conducive to efficiency [160]. General practitioners are paid on a fee-for-service basis, a method of payment which is thought to encourage unnecessarily high consultation rates and a pattern of frequent consultations of short duration, with heavy reliance on drug therapy [161]. The payment system for doctors participating in the public scheme is currently under review [162]. Hospitals are paid on an individual budget basis, determined annually in advance through negotiation with the health authorities. Most hospital consultants are paid for in-patient services on a patient-day basis, a system which, Tussing notes, provides an incentive to extend patient stays [163].

With regard to the allocation of resources among the different sectors of the health care system, it is recognised in Ireland as elsewhere that there may be considerable potential for efficiency gains through promotion of community care and preventive care over more expensive institutional care [164]. However, despite a commitment in principle to shift resources away from institutional services, expenditure on hospital services has actually increased relative to expenditure on community-based services in recent years and admission rates to acute hospitals rose at a rate of over 4 percent per annum during the 1970s [165].

In conclusion, it would appear that the health care system is on the whole an equitable one, providing access to good quality care for most sections of the community. As such, the system may be said to be reasonably successful in providing a minimum standard for all. There are, however, some anomalies in the structure of eligibility and some problems of outreach. Particular areas of concern appear to be the child health services, care for the elderly and provision of services in rural areas. The major criticism of the health care system is that it contains many inefficiencies. The evidence reviewed here points to the existence of perverse incentives for both the consumers and providers of care and over-reliance on expensive institutional care. At a time when the health care system is under severe financial pressure improvements in efficiency are clearly a matter of some urgency.

Education

The Irish educational system has undergone considerable change and expansion since the mid-1960s under the impetus of a series of important reforms and the pressure of a growing school age population. The share of educational expenditure in GDP doubled between 1961 and 1981, reaching 6.6 percent in the latter year. The proportion of the population in full-time education rose from 22 percent in 1964 to 26.5 percent in 1981 and about 4 percent of the labour force were employed in teaching in the early 1980s [166].

Among the most significant of the educational reforms were the introduction of free secondary schooling in 1967, the raising of the minimum school leaving age to fifteen in 1972 and the introduction of a grants scheme for university students in 1968. Extensive institutional development has also taken place, including the introduction of comprehensive and community schools at second level and the expansion of technological education at third level [167]. The main impetus for these reforms came from a comprehensive survey of the educational system undertaken jointly by the Irish authorities and the Organisation for Economic Cooperation and Development in the early 1960s [168].

The major objectives of the educational reforms undertaken during the 1960s and 1970s were to reduce inequalities in educational participation and to adapt the system to the manpower needs of the rapidly industrialising economy through expansion of the vocational/technical sector [169]. In addition, the provision of a minimum standard for all has also been an implicit goal of educational policy [170]. This section examines the extent to which these three objectives have been achieved.

Total enrolments in the educational system grew at an annual average rate of over two percent during the period 1966-1981 (see Table 34). The growth rate has slackened since the mid-1970s due to slower growth in enrolments at primary and secondary levels, but enrolment in third level education has continued to expand at the rate of almost five percent per annum. While a large proportion of enrolment growth is attributable to growth in the school age population, it has been estimated that about 29 percent of the total enrolment growth recorded in the period 1971-1981 was due to rising participation rates [171].

The introduction of free secondary education and improvements in the financial aid available to third level students clearly led to a marked improvement in post-compulsory participation rates. Within the 15 to 24 age group, increased participation accounted for 56 percent of the rise in enrolments in the period 1971-81 [172].

Table 34   Rates and growth of enrolment by level of education

Level	Enrolment rates				Average annual growth rate of enrolment		
	1965/66	1970/71	1975/76	1980/81	1966–71	1971–76	1976–81
First level	504.9	526.8	550.1	568.4	0.9	0.9	0.7
Second level	142.9	208.5	271.0	300.6	7.8	5.4	2.1
Junior cycle	110.0	152.1	186.9	199.7	6.7	4.2	1.3
Senior cycle	32.9	56.4	84.1	100.9	11.4	8.3	3.7
Third level	20.7	26.2	33.1	41.9	4.8	4.8	4.8
Total	668.5	761.5	854.2	910.9	2.6	2.3	1.3
% population	23.2	25.6	26.5	26.5			

As shown in Table 35, the participation rate for 15-year olds rose from 54 percent in 1966 to 87 percent in 1981 and there have also been very marked increases in the rates for the 16 to 19 age group. Participation rates in the 20 to 24 age group have remained relatively stable over time, reflecting perhaps the fact that a large proportion of students have completed third level education by age 20 [173].

Table 35   Educational participation rates by age, 1966 – 1981

Age	1966	1971	1974	1981 (a)
6–13	95.8	98.6	99.8	99.3
14	68.7	84.7	92.5	96.9
15	54.2	70.7	77.5	86.9
16	39.0	55.0	60.4	70.7
17	27.3	39.4	43.1	51.3
18	14.7	20.8	22.4	27.4
19	9.6	12.1	12.5	15.7
20–24	7.2	7.5	6.8	7.6

(a) Estimates.

Despite the expansion in educational participation, there are some indications that a proportion of pupils may be failing to reach minimum standards of literacy and numeracy. Although there is no direct evidence on this point, Breen has estimated that between 10 and 20 percent of each age cohort leave the school system either without sitting for any public examination or having performed very poorly in examinations in the basic areas of English and Mathematics [174]. Breen points out that it must, therefore, be questioned whether the objective of providing a minimum standard of education for all has been achieved.

In spite of significant improvements in access to education, the available evidence indicates that there are still pronounced social class differentials in participation rates. Estimates by Rottman et al. indicate that although post-compulsory second level participation rates increased more rapidly among those from working class backgrounds than among those from the middle classes in the period 1961-71, in the latter year the participation rate for working class children was still less than half the rate for children from upper middle class backgrounds [175]. More recent estimates by Breen show that of the 1976/77 cohort of boys entering secondary education, those from upper middle class backgrounds were at least six times more likely to complete the secondary cycle than those from lower working class backgrounds; among girls the class differential was considerably less, although still substantial [176].

Class inequalities are further magnified at entry to third level education. A comparison of the results of Nevin's survey of the 1965 cohort of university entrants and Clancy's survey of the 1980 cohort, as shown in Table 36, reveals that although class differentials have narrowed over time there are still major inequalities [177]. Class inequalities are greatest in the university sector. Students from lower socio-economic backgrounds are more highly represented among entrants to colleges of technology and other non-university institutions. With regard to fields of study, class disparities are most marked within the professional faculties such as medicine and law [178].

Table 36   Entrants to higher education and potential students by social group in 1965 and 1980

Percent distributions

Social group	Universities				Other third level instit.
	Entrants	Potential (a) students	Entrants	Potential (b) students	Entrants
	1965	1965	1980	1980	1980
Farmers	17.3	25.4	16.4	20.3	24.4
Agricultural workers	0.4	7.4	0.6	4.3	1.1
Higher professionals	13.2	1.9	16.3	3.0	8.5
Lower professionals	11.2	2.1	7.7	3.1	6.7
Employers and managers	18.0	3.8	14.9	7.1	22.7
Salaried employees	7.7	2.1	11.4	2.7	5.4
Intermediate non-manual workers	20.3	9.7	17.6	10.0	6.5
Other non-manual workers	2.8	9.6	4.8	11.7	6.7
Skilled manual workers	5.9	15.4	6.8	21.4	13.8
Semi-skilled manual workers	0.8	7.7	2.6	5.5	2.8
Unskilled manual workers	0.4	10.2	1.0	10.9	1.4
Total	98.2 (c)	95.3 (c)	100.0	100.0	100.0

(a) Based on the social group distribution of the 0–14 age group in the 1961 Census of Population.
(b) Based on the social group distribution of the 0–14 age group in the 1971 Census of Population.
(c) Persons who cannot be allocated to above social groups excluded.

Significant sex differentials also persist within the educational system. At second level the take up of scientific and technical subjects among girls is very low and has increased only slightly since the mid-1960s [179]. The proportion of female students entering higher education is also less than the proportion of male students. In 1980, female students constituted 57 percent of candidates in the Leaving Certificate examination but only 46 percent of entrants to third level institutions. Women constituted only 38 percent of entrants to the technological sector in 1980, while 48 percent of university entrants and 84 percent of entrants to teacher training colleges were female [180].

The *Investment in Education* report, published in the mid-1960s, drew attention to the existence of serious regional disparities in educational participation[181]. Between 1966 and 1974, fifteen comprehensive schools were established in various areas of the country with the objective of counteracting such disparities. The introduction of free school transport services in 1967 and the establishment since 1969 of nine Regional Technical Colleges, offering continuation and third level courses, may also be assumed to have contributed to reducing regional disparities. With regard to participation in second level education, there are no precise data available on regional differentials [182]. Clancy's survey of entrants to higher education in 1980, however, has revealed the persistence of large regional disparities in participation rates at third level [183].

A major objective of educational policy since the mid-1960s has been to move the system away from a heavily academic bias and to promote the vocational/technical sector. Among the steps taken to achieve this aim were the establishment of comprehensive schools and community schools, broadening the traditional secondary school curriculum to include more scientific, technical and commercial subjects, and the establishment of the Regional Technical Colleges and of two National Institutes for Higher Education in order to strengthen the technological sector at third level [184].

Efforts to reorientate the educational system towards a more vocational/technical emphasis have been only partially successful. Breen has shown that traditional secondary schools rather than the vocational sector benefited from the growth in second level enrolments after 1967 and that although take up of technical, scientific and commercial subjects at second level has increased, a high proportion of senior cycle school leavers lack qualifications in such subjects [185]. At third level, however, there has been a marked expansion of the technological sector [186]. Breen has pointed out, however, that since industrial employment grew more slowly than had been expected, while the service sector expanded rapidly, labour market demand and educational supply remained more or less in balance during the 1970s [187].

In conclusion, the educational policies pursued since the mid-1960s have met with mixed success. There has been a significant growth in participation rates at post-compulsory levels, but there are indications that a sizeable minority of pupils fail to obtain minimum educational competencies. Despite some narrowing of class differentials in participation rates, substantial inequalities persist at both second and third level. Regional disparities in participation rates also persist at third level. Differences in participation rates of males and females are relatively small, but there are marked differences in the sectors and fields of study chosen by the two sexes. The objective of moving the educational system towards a more vocational emphasis has been achieved only to a limited extent. Although this shortcoming did not prove serious in the 1970s due to the rapid expansion in white-collar employment, soaring unemployment rates in the early 1980s have led in Ireland, as elsewhere in Europe, to a questioning of the role of the educational system vis-a-vis the labour market.

Housing

Housing conditions have improved considerably over the postwar period. In 1981, some 25 percent of dwellings were less than ten years old, a further 28 percent had been built between 1941 and 1971 and only 30 percent dated from before 1919. This compares very favourably with the situation in 1961, when 58 percent of the housing stock had been erected before 1919, and the situation in 1971 when pre-1919 dwellings comprised 45 percent of the stock [188].

The modernisation of the housing stock is reflected in improvements in basic household amenities, shown in Table 37. The proportion of dwellings with a piped water supply inside rose from 39 percent in 1946 to 92 percent in 1981 and the proportion with a fixed bath or shower rose from 15 percent to 82 percent. The proportion with indoor sanitary facilities rose from 23 percent in 1946 to 91 percent in 1981. The average size of dwellings rose from 4.12 rooms in 1946 to 4.97 rooms in 1981, while the density of occupation fell from 1.01 persons per room to 0.74. In 1946, 25 percent of the population lived in overcrowded conditions whereas in 1981 the proportion had fallen to about 6 percent.

Table 37   Selected indicators of housing standards, 1946-1981

	1946	1961	1971	1981
Percentage of dwellings with				
piped water inside	38.7	51.0	73.8	92.1
fixed bath/shower	15.4	33.2	55.8	82.0
sanitary facilities inside	23.1	42.7	62.9	90.8
Average number of rooms per dwelling	4.12	4.42	4.56	4.97
Occupants per room	1.01	0.90	0.86	0.74
Percentage of households with				
2 or more persons per room	25.0	17.8	14.8	6.0 (a)

(a) Estimate.

Despite the very substantial improvements in housing conditions over the past decade, some problems of overcrowding and unfitness persist. The measure of overcrowding used in Ireland, an average of two or more persons per room, is relatively conservative [189] and the incidence of overcrowding is considerably above the national average in inner city areas. In the Dublin inner city in 1971 an estimated 29 percent of the population lived in overcrowded conditions [190]. The waiting list for public housing has grown steadily since 1979, to 31,000 families in 1983, and it can be assumed that a high proportion of those on the housing list live in unfit or overcrowded conditions. An estimated 2,000 to 3,000 people are homeless [191].

Although the proportion of the housing stock lacking basic amenities has fallen markedly over the past decade or so, the fact that in 1981 as high a proportion of households as 18 percent still lacked a fixed bath or shower and 7 percent lacked sanitary facilities of any sort gives ground for concern. Particular disquiet has been expressed about the housing conditions of elderly people living alone. A sample survey carried out in 1978 found that an extraordinarily high proportion of this group lacked basic water facilities [192]. A scheme of home improvement grants aimed at relieving problems of overcrowding and unfitness came into operation in late 1981, and it can be assumed that this has contributed to further improvement in housing conditions since that date.

Owner occupation is the dominant form of housing tenure in Ireland. The rate of owner occupation has risen from 59 percent of the population 1971 to 68 percent in 1981. In the latter year, just over 20 percent of dwellings, accommodating 23 percent of the population, were publicly owned, being rented or acquired from local authorities. This form of tenure has declined since 1971 and the proportion of new dwellings provided directly by public authorities has fallen in recent years. Private rented accommodation accounted for 7 percent of total occupancy in 1981 [193].

Several commentators have drawn attention to serious inequities in the housing system [194]. Inequities arise between different tenure groups due to the structure of financial support. Of the three main tenure sectors - owner-occupation, local authority housing and private rented accommodation - the first two receive substantial public subsidies while the last receives very little. It has been estimated that in 1980 public subsidies to housing amounted to IRL 157.1 million, of which about 56 percent went in various forms to the owner-occupied sector and about 40 percent to the local authority sector in form of rent subsidies [195]. The local authority sector also benefits from a subsidy which is not included in the above estimate: Sales of local authority houses to tenants at substantial discounts constitute a subsidy which in 1981 was estimated to be in the region of IRL 50 million [196]. Subsidisation of the private rented sector is minimal. Following a Supreme Court ruling in 1981 that rent control regulations - which applied at the time to about one-third of the private rented sector - were unconstitutional, a rent allowance was introduced for tenants who would otherwise have suffered hardship through the derestriction of their rents. The only other subsidy to tenants in this sector takes the form of income tax relief in respect of rent for elderly people.

The inequalities between different tenure groups show up clearly when income and housing costs are compared across tenure types as in Table 38 [197]. Average weekly disposable income is significantly higher among home owners with mortgages than among other groups. The private rentel group, which receive the lowest level of public subsidisation, have a relatively low average disposable income. Comparing housing expenditure within income groups, it will be observed that expenditure is very low for those who own their houses outright and is relatively low for local authority tenants. Expenditure is much higher for home owners with mortgages and is highest of all for those in the private rented sector.

Table 38   Average weekly expenditure on housing classified by gross income and tenure, 1980

Gross weekly household income (Irish pounds)	As % of total expenditure			
	Owned outright	Owned with mortgage	Rented from Local Authority	Rented from private owner
Under 60	2.7	9.6	4.5	14.1
60 and under 100	2.7	13.1	6.9	16.1
100 and under 150	2.3	11.7	5.7	10.7
150 and over	2.6	9.8	3.6	11.0
Average weekly disposable income (Irish pounds)	97.55	134.20	78.15	92.60

There are also inequities associated with the functioning of subsidies within tenure groups. While tax relief on mortgages provides important assistance for first-time home buyers, it is a form of subsidy which is likely to have a directly regressive impact since it is of most value to those with the highest marginal tax rates and largest mortgages and the size of loan taken tends to vary directly with income [198]. In 1983 the maximum value of mortgage interest repayments eligible for tax relief was reduced and this change will have reduced the degree of regressivity in the system. Within the local authority sector, the operation of a differential rents system - relating the rent to household income - is intended to distribute rent subsidies in a progressive manner. However, the scheme does not appear to operate in a systematically progressive fashion [199]. Attention has also been drawn to the likely regressive aspects of sales of local authority housing to tenants at large discounts, since higher income tenants are most likely to avail of the scheme [200].

There are clear disparities in access to the various tenure sectors by different socio-economic groups. As shown in Table 39, owner occupation is most common among the higher socio-economic categories, while local authority tenancy is mainly a feature of the working class categories. Home ownership without a mortgage is most common among farming households and private rental is most common among the lower middle classes. Baker and O'Brien note that the major problem of access to housing concerns those who cannot afford to buy houses and who are unable to qualify for local authority housing [201]. Waiting lists for local authority housing indicate that there is considerable pressure on this sector, particularly in the cities and aspiring entrants must meet a variety of administrative conditions. Small families and single people, those who lack certain residential qualifications, and those who lead unconventional lifestyles are among the groups unable to qualify for local authority tenancies [202].

Table 39   Households classified by nature of tenure and socio-economic group of head of household, 1981 (a)

Percent distributions (c)

Socio-economic group of head of household	Nature of tenure						Total (b) (in 1,000)
	Rented from local authority	Rented from private owner	Being acquired from local authority	Owner occupied with mortgage	Owner occupied without mortgage	Occupied rent free	
Farmers, farmers' relatives and farm managers	1.6	–	1.2	7.3	86.6	1.9	150.6
Other agricultural occupants and fishermen	17.7	–	17.4	9.6	41.5	7.1	28.2
Higher professional	–	13.7	–	52.6	24.6	7.6	34.2
Lower professional	2.4	20.7	3.0	41.2	30.6	–	46.8
Employers and managers	–	8.4	1.9	53.6	32.5	2.2	63.3
Salaried employees	–	5.6	–	55.4	27.2	–	21.3
Intermediate non-manual workers	7.9	19.4	5.4	32.9	32.0	2.1	101.8
Other non-manual workers	19.7	12.1	13.0	25.8	26.9	2.3	94.3
Skilled manual workers	15.5	9.3	10.9	34.6	27.7	1.7	156.5
Semi-skilled manual workers	28.8	10.2	14.8	20.2	24.1	–	43.1
Unskilled manual workers	32.3	8.0	16.4	10.8	29.2	1.8	66.5
Unknown	19.5	13.0	8.8	8.2	45.3	4.0	87.9

(a) Private households in permanent housing units.
(b) Including nature of occupancy not stated.
(c) Figures do not sum up to 100% due to exclusion of households which cannot be classified in any of the categories below.

A comprehensive study of the housing system by Baker and O'Brien has concluded that the system works efficiently in so far as the majority of households can obtain separate dwellings in the tenure group they prefer and a reasonable choice of accommodation within that group [203]. It is clear, however, that the basic housing needs of some groups are not being adequately met by present policies. Moreover, the system contains many inequitable features. Baker and O'Brien conclude that the principal inequity in the housing system results from the interaction between the financial requirements for entering the owner-occupied sector, the social criteria for becoming a local authority tenant, and the cost of private renting and that for a significant proportion of poorer households the system intensifies rather than reduces disadvantages [204].

4. The Irish welfare state - a success?

The data and analysis presented here indicate that the achievements of social programmes, particularly over the past two decades, have been considerable. The expansion of the income maintenance system and improvements in the benefits provided
have led to increased security against a range of social risks. In addition to providing
better protection against long-recognised contingencies such as old age and unemployment, the system has also succeeded in accommodating new demands, such as the
need to provide support for the growing number of single parent families. The data
on health and housing standards point to a general improvement in levels of service in
these areas, while educational participation has expanded markedly since the late
1960s.

Despite the achievements outlined in this section, it is evident that a range of problems remain unsolved. The basic objective of providing a minimum standard of living
for all has not yet been attained. Although considerable progress has been made in
reducing the level of financial poverty, the persistence of the problem attests to
serious shortcomings in income maintenance arrangements. More generally, the persistence of poverty highlights the failure of social and economic policy to come to
grips with the underlying causes of the problem which lie in inequalities in command
over resources and in life chances in Irish society.

One clear shortcoming in income maintenance policy is the lack of some objectively
defined social minimum which could serve as a benchmark against which to assess
income adequacy. There is also an obvious need for better integration of the tax and
benefit systems and for changes in both in order to avoid the problems of unemployment traps and poverty traps. It remains to be seen whether recent reforms in this
area will be successful in eliminating these traps. Changes in the relative levels of
benefits provided for various beneficiary groups since the late 1970s and the deterioration in living standards of the working population raise questions concerning the
appropriate relativities between different categories of income maintenance payments
and the appropriate relationship between levels of income from work and welfare
benefits. These are issues which have received very little explicit consideration in official circles in Ireland.

Turning to specific areas where income maintenance arrangements appear inadequate,
support for the long-term unemployed, for pensioners whose major source of income
is the state pension and for the elderly living alone are areas of particular concern.
Although the record on family income support is rather poor, recent and planned
changes in this area should improve the situation of low income families where the
parent or parents are in work as well as that of families depending on welfare benefits. However, it remains to be seen whether the new child benefit scheme will completely solve the problem of family poverty. Despite improvements in income maintenance for single parent families, the indications are that such families tend to live
close to the poverty margin. The high level of financial poverty found among farm
households in 1980, although likely to be a temporary phenomenon, calls into question the ability of the income maintenance system to respond to fluctuations in the
economic fortunes of this group.

With regard to the social services, the objective of providing a minimum standard for
all appears to have been achieved to a large extent in the area of health, but not in
the areas of housing or education. The persistence of problems of overcrowding and
unfitness in housing conditions, the long waiting lists for public housing, the poor
housing standards endured by sub-groups such as those in certain inner city areas and

the elderly living alone and the continuing problem of homelessness all attest to inadequacies in the housing system. With regard to education, it would appear that a substantial minority still leave the school system lacking in basic educational skills.

Turning to the issue of inequality, the extent to which social programmes have contributed to a more equal sharing out of the fruits of economic progress must be questioned. Inequality of income and opportunity remain pronounced in Ireland. Although the net redistributive impact of direct taxes and cash benefits increased slightly between 1973 and 1980, the distribution of disposable income was still very unequal in the latter year. With the exception of medical services, non-cash benefits fail to contribute to the redistributive process and indirect taxes are regressive. Such evidence as is available indicates that the redistributive process operates unevenly from a social class perspective, treating the property owning classes in a relatively favourable fashion.

It has been shown that both the education and housing systems contain serious inequities. Despite the considerable expansion in educational participation since the late 1960s, the contribution to equalisation of opportunity appears to have been marginal. Post-compulsory participation, particularly at third level, remains closely linked to social class, with the higher socio-economic categories making a disproportionately high use of the system. Regional differentials in participation rates also persist, although these have weakened over time. Although participation rates for the two sexes are very similar, there are marked differences in the subject areas pursued which, presumably, serve to reinforce gender-based occupational segregation in Irish society. The inequities in the housing system stem from the uneven impact of public subsidies both between and within different tenure groups. Of particular concern are the very substantial subsidies flowing to the relatively privileged owner-occupied sector and the failure of housing policy to address the problems of those who cannot afford to become owner-occupiers and who do not qualify for accommodation in public housing.

The health care system, by contrast, appears to operate in a reasonably equitable fashion, although there are some anomalies in the eligibility structure and the questions of the outreach of services to the poorer sections of the population and the subsidisation of the private health care sector require attention. The major shortcoming of the system is that it contains many inefficiencies leading to wasteful distribution of resources within the system as well as to problems of control of the overall level of health care expenditure.

The problems just outlined are thrown into sharp relief by current economic constraints which place a severe restriction on the resources which can be devoted to social programmes in the coming years. In the context of budgetary limitations it is crucial that the available resources be used in the most effective and efficient manner possible and that the priorities of social programmes be clearly defined. Prospects for the social programmes through the remainder of the decade are taken up in the final section of the study.

IV   Correlates and causes: explanations

This section of the study considers how the expansion of the welfare state in Ireland in the postwar period has been influenced by certain features of the economic, social and political context. It may be useful to begin by summarising the major phases of development of the welfare state, based upon the changes in expenditure and services discussed in earlier sections of the study. We shall then go on to assess the importance of demographic, economic and political factors respectively, for its growth.

1. Phases of welfare state development

The postwar period from 1947 to 1951 was a phase of rapid expansion of social expenditure, beginning from a very low base. As shown in Table 40, real social expenditure grew at an average rate of almost 13 percent per annum, increasing its share of GDP from 10 percent to 16 percent. The predominant concerns in this period were housing and health services: increased expenditure on housing accounted for over two-thirds of the rise in the GDP share of total social expenditure, whilst growth in expenditure on health accounted for a further 23 percent.

Table 40   Phases of growth of real social expenditure

Phases of development		Annual growth rate (a)
Post-war expansion	1947-51	12.7
Stagnation	1952-62	1.8
Major expansion	1963-75	8.8
Slackening growth	1976-80	4.8
Average	1947-80	6.3

(a) Average compound growth rates of total social expenditure
at 1970 prices.

The phase of stagnation which lasted from 1952 to 1962 saw the average growth rate of real social expenditure reduced to 1.8 percent per annum. Expenditure declined in real terms in the years 1957-58 and the 1956 level was only regained in 1961. The share of social expenditure in GDP also declined and did not recover to its 1951 level until 1964. The most marked cutback was in housing expenditure, which was virtually halved in real terms between 1951 and 1958. Real health expenditure also declined sharply in the years 1957-58, mainly due to a decrease in capital expenditure [205]. This phase began with reforms of the social insurance system (1952) and health services (1953), both of which had already been planned during the earlier expansionary phase. In the event, neither reform was as far-reaching as originally intended [206]. Apart from the establishment of a voluntary health insurance scheme in 1957 and the introduction of old age pension insurance in 1961, there were no further reforms of the social services during this phase.

The major expansionary phase of the welfare state extended from 1963 to 1975. In real terms social expenditure grew at an average rate of 8.8 percent per annum in this period, increasing its share of GDP from 15 percent to 27 percent. The expansion of social expenditure was part of a general expansion of the public sector, sustained by rapid economic growth. However, social expenditure was by far the fastest growing area of public expenditure, increasing its share of the total from 48 percent in 1963 to 56 percent in 1975. All of the major social programmes underwent expansion and reform during this phase. The social insurance system expanded to cover new risks and groups, income maintenance benefits generally were improved and the numbers receiving benefits rose significantly. The 1960s and 1970s saw important reforms at all levels of the educational system, considerable displacement of private expenditure by public expenditure and a marked rise in participation at the secondary and tertiary levels. Support for both public and private housing increased and housing output rose rapidly. Reform of the health services during this period concentrated on the administrative structure, on the delivery of services and on upgrading of existing services.

The final phase of development, spanning the years 1976 to 1980, began with a dramatic decline in the growth rate of real social expenditure in 1976-77. However, growth rates recovered to near the levels of the early 1970s during the remaining years of the period and the average growth rate for the period was 4.8 percent. Relative to GDP, social expenditure recovered to near its 1975 share by 1979 and increased its share to 29 percent in 1980. This period was characterised by abrupt changes in budgetary policy [207]. There was a severe cutback in public expenditure in 1976, followed by a mildly expansionary budget in 1977. However, following a change of government in 1977 the policy of public expenditure restraint was replaced by an expansionary stance, underpinned by a decision to allow the public sector deficit to grow. Although a somewhat more restrictive budgetary stance was adopted in 1979-80, public expenditure exceeded budgeted targets by a considerable amount. Health was by far the fastest growing area of social expenditure during this phase, increasing at approximately twice the rate of expenditure on education and income maintenance in real terms, while expenditure on housing remained static over the period as a whole. There were few policy innovations during this period, apart from the extension of eligibility for public hospital-based services to the entire population in 1979. The phased reduction of the pensionable age from 70 to 66 years which had begun in 1973 was completed in 1977. Income maintenance benefits continued to improve in real terms, with the exception of child allowances. Expenditure on unemployment benefits, which had registered a sharp rise in 1975-76 as unemployment increased in the wake of the first oil shock, fell in the years 1977-79 as the employment situation improved. However, expenditure began to rise again in 1980 as unemployment worsened once more.

2. The impact of demographic factors

Since the details of Irish demographic development are documented elsewhere, only the major features need be outlined here [208]. The population of Ireland declined steadily from the 1840s up to the early 1960s, going from 6.5 million in 1841 to 2.8 million in 1961 [209]. This decrease resulted from a very high emigration rate, since the rate of natural increase was relatively high throughout the period [210]. Since the early 1960s, the population has been growing rapidly. The rate of emigration decreased markedly in the inter-censal period 1961-66 and the period 1971-79 recorded net immigration. At the same time, the rate of natural increase has risen, reaching an annual average of 11.1 per thousand during the inter-censal period 1971-79 and 11.9 per thousand during the period 1979-81.

The age structure of the population has remained relatively stable during the postwar period. In 1946, 28 percent of the population were under the age of 15, whilst almost 11 percent were aged 65 or over; in 1981 the comparable proportions were 30 percent and 11 percent. By Western European standards Ireland has a large young population and a relatively small proportion of elderly people. In 1981, the population under the age of 15 represented 21 percent of the total in the EEC area, whilst 14 percent were aged 65 or over [211]. Ireland also has a very high dependency ratio. Defining the dependency ratio in the conventional way, as the ratio of those aged under 15, and 65 and over, to those aged between 15 and 64, there were in 1946 six dependants for every ten persons of working age. By 1981 the ratio had risen to seven to ten. The comparable ratio for the EEC countries in 1981 was five to ten. The actual ratio of dependants to workers is considerably higher than the demographic ratio. The total labour force participation rate has declined in Ireland over the postwar period, female participation rates are relatively low by international standards and the unemployment rate has remained relatively high throughout the postwar period. In 1951 there were approximately 14 inactive persons to every 10 workers and by 1981 this ratio had risen to 2 to 1.

The demographic features just outlined have important implications for the demand for social services, as well as for the availability of resources to meet these demands. All other things being equal, a high dependency ratio implies increased pressure on child support and education. It also tends to increase the demand for certain types of health services [212]. On the other hand, given the relatively small elderly population, the Irish pension and health care systems have not been subject to the pressures which ageing populations have created for these systems in many other Western European countries. With regard to the supply side of the welfare state, a high dependency ratio implies a relatively narrow tax base with the result that the expansion of social expenditure is likely to place a heavy burden on the working population. In Ireland, the problem of an already narrow tax base is further compounded by the difficulty of finding an appropriate method of taxing the substantial minority of households whose income is derived from farming and other forms of self-employment [213].

In order to assess the contribution of demographic factors to the growth of social expenditure, programmes for which such factors appear to be of particular relevance - old age pensions, child allowances and education - have been analysed using a growth accounting framework developed by the OECD [214]. Changes in the share of GDP devoted to expenditure on a given programme are the product of changes in demography (i.e. the size of the population relevant to the programme), eligibility (the proportion of the relevant population who actually benefit from the programme), and level of benefit (the average benefit or cost per beneficiary). Using this accounting identity, changes in the ratio of expenditure to GDP may be decomposed into a demographic ratio (the ratio of the relevant population to total population), an eligibility ratio (ratio of beneficiaries to relevant population), and a transfer ratio (ratio of average benefit or cost per beneficiary to per capita GDP).

Expenditure on old age pensions grew from 1.9 to 3.5 percent of GDP between 1951 and 1981 [215]. The relevant population group in this instance is taken to be the population aged 65 and over. As may be seen from Graph 23, the size of this group relative to the total population has varied very little during the period under review. The proportion of the elderly population receiving pensions rose markedly in the period 1973-78, reflecting the progressive reduction of the pensionable age from 70 to 66 years. The transfer ratio has fluctuated considerably but has followed an upward trend over the period as a whole, indicating an improvement in the average pension relative to per capita GDP. The most marked improvements in this ratio occurred in the years 1973-75 and 1980-81.

As is clear from Graph 24, expenditure on old age pensions has grown mainly as a result of changes in the transfer and eligibility ratios, with demographic change exerting a minimal influence. The transfer ratio improved by 49 percent and the eligibility ratio by 24 percent during the period under review. Changes in eligibility only contributed significantly to expenditure growth during the 1970s with the reduction in the pensionable age, and the eligibility ratio actually declined from the mid-1950s to the mid-1960s.

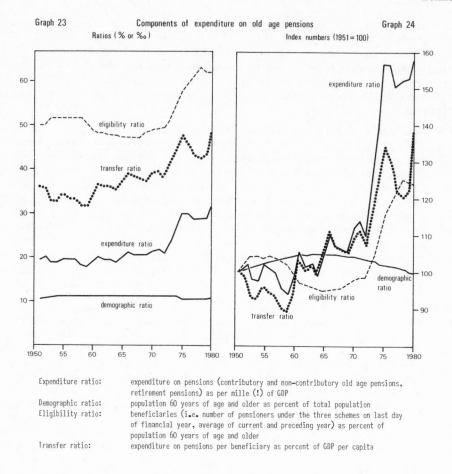

Graph 23   Components of expenditure on old age pensions   Graph 24

Ratios (% or ‰)   Index numbers (1951 = 100)

Expenditure ratio:	expenditure on pensions (contributory and non-contributory old age pensions, retirement pensions) as per mille (!) of GDP
Demographic ratio:	population 60 years of age and older as percent of total population
Eligibility ratio:	beneficiaries (i.e. number of pensioners under the three schemes on last day of financial year, average of current and preceding year) as percent of population 60 years of age and older
Transfer ratio:	expenditure on pensions per beneficiary as percent of GDP per capita

In the case of child allowances, the relevant population is taken to be the 0 to 19 age group [216]. The share of GDP devoted to expenditure on child allowances rose from 0.6 percent in 1951 to 1.3 percent in 1974, declining thereafter to 0.9 percent by 1981. As may be seen from Graph 25, the proportion of the population in the 0-19 age group rose slightly over the period 1951-81, going from 37 percent to 40 percent. The proportion of this age group for whom allowances are paid has grown dramatically, reflecting extensions in the coverage of the scheme. By contrast, the average benefit has fallen sharply relative to per capita GDP. Graph 26 shows that changes in eligibility accounted for most of the increase in expenditure in the period 1951-74, whilst the effect of demographic change was slight. The deterioration in the transfer ratio operated to offset the effect of extensions in eligibility so that expenditure did not rise as much as would have been the case had the transfer ratio improved or remained static. The decrease in the expenditure share since 1975 is due almost entirely to deterioration in the transfer ratio.

In the case of education the analysis is confined to the period 1963 to 1973 due to deficiencies in the available data. This period was characterised by major institutional changes in the educational system and the GDP share of public expenditure on educa-

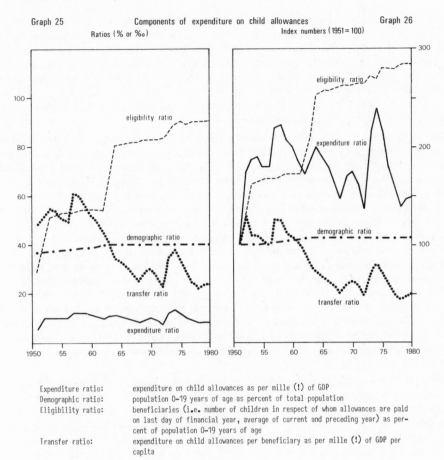

Graph 25   Components of expenditure on child allowances   Graph 26
        Ratios (% or ‰)   Index numbers (1951 = 100)

Expenditure ratio:	expenditure on child allowances as per mille (!) of GDP	
Demographic ratio:	population 0–19 years of age as percent of total population	
Eligibility ratio:	beneficiaries (i.e. number of children in respect of whom allowances are paid on last day of financial year, average of current and preceding year) as per cent of population 0–19 years of age	
Transfer ratio:	expenditure on child allowances per beneficiary as per mille (!) of GDP per capita	

tion rose by 45 percent, from 3.7 percent to 5.4 percent of the total. Table 41 shows that cost per student rose by 23 percent, accounting for the largest proportion of expenditure growth. Enrolment rose by 11 percent and the demographic ratio, based on the 5-24 age group, rose by 6 percent.

Table 41   Components of growth of education expenditure, 1963–73 (a)

	Change in share of GDP (b)	Demographic changes	Due to: Eligibility (enrolment) changes	Cost ratio changes
1963–73	1.450	1.060	1.107	1.232

(a) Ratio of end year to initial year.
(b) This column equals the product of the next three columns.

The components of change in the GDP share of expenditure on primary, vocational and university education respectively in the period 1961-79 have been examined by O'Hagan and Kelly [217]. This analysis indicates that for the vocational and university sectors, enrolment changes were the dominant cause of expenditure growth, demographic changes were next in importance and changes in the cost ratio (i.e. expenditure per student) were relatively unimportant. In the case of primary education, changes in the cost ratio were the main factor contributing to expenditure growth, with demographic change playing a very minor role.

The analysis so far indicates that demographic factors have been relatively unimportant for the growth of expenditure on old age pensions and child allowances, although they have had some significance for the growth of education expenditure. For all of the programmes examined here, changes in eligibility have been a major factor contributing to increased expenditure. In the case of old age pensions and education, changes in the average benefit or cost per recipient have also contributed significantly to expenditure growth, whilst in the case of child allowances the deterioration in the average benefit has operated to restrain expenditure. Given that changes in eligibility and average benefits reflect, at least to some extent, policy changes, these findings indicate that decisions to expand and improve social programmes have been of more significance for the growth of expenditure than has demographic change. This conclusion needs to be qualified by recognition of the fact that shifts in the eligibility and transfer ratios may also reflect non-policy factors, such as changes in utilisation rates and relative price effects. In this context, analysis indicates that whilst relative price effects have not been of much importance in the case of cash transfers, they may have contributed significantly to observed changes in average cost per beneficiary in education [218].

Although from a diachronic perspective demographic factors do not appear to have been particularly influential with respect to the growth of social expenditure, the demographic structure may have important implications for the internal composition of expenditure and for its overall level. Thus, Ireland's relatively young population - by Western European standards - may provide at least a partial explanation as to why education expenditure accounts for a higher share of total social expenditure and pensions a much lower share than in other European countries [219]. The fact that Ireland has a very high dependency ratio may also help to explain why the share of GDP devoted to social expenditure in Ireland is similar to that in countries at a much higher level of economic development [220].

The component analysis method can also be used to examine the determinants of growth of expenditures which lack any clearly defined demographic component, such as expenditure on unemployment compensation. Given that unemployment compensation has been one of the most rapidly growing areas of social expenditure in recent years, reaching 2.5 percent of GDP in 1981, it is a programme which merits closer examination [221]. In this case the demographic ratio has been subdivided into the ratio of the labour force to the total population and the ratio of the unemployed to the labour force, thus separating changes in the unemployment rate from changes in the participation rate [222].

Between 1951 and 1981 expenditure on unemployment compensation went from 0.5 percent to 2.5 percent of GDP. The unemployment rate rose by 107 percent during the period, contributing most to expenditure growth. However, improvements in the transfer ratio, which rose by 82 percent were also an important factor in increasing the level of expenditure. Eligibility changes were less important, the eligibility ratio having risen by 36 percent. The activity ratio fell, reflecting a declining participation rate. Graphs 27 and 28 show that the influence on expenditure growth of the unemployment, transfer and eligibility ratios has varied considerably over time. During the phase of expenditure growth from 1951 to 1958 the main factor at work was rising unemployment. However, during the second growth phase of expenditure, from 1965 to 1976, eligibility changes were the most important factor, although the unemployment and transfer ratios also rose quite rapidly. It is important to note in this context that the rise in the eligibility ratio cannot be accounted for solely by deliberate extensions in the coverage of unemployment compensation schemes; increases in the claim rate were also important [223]. During the final phase of expenditure growth in 1980-81, rising unemployment was again the main factor contributing to growth, although improvement in the transfer ratio was also important.

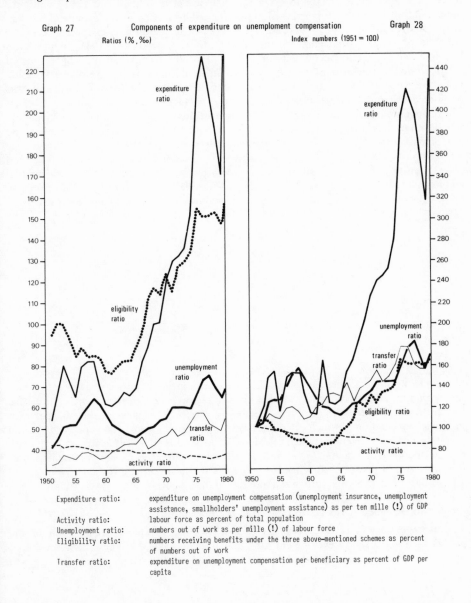

Graph 27   Components of expenditure on unemployment compensation   Graph 28
Ratios (%, ‰)   Index numbers (1951 = 100)

Expenditure ratio:	expenditure on unemployment compensation (unemployment insurance, unemployment assistance, smallholders' unemployment assistance) as per ten mille (!) of GDP
Activity ratio:	labour force as percent of total population
Unemployment ratio:	numbers out of work as per mille (!) of labour force
Eligibility ratio:	numbers receiving benefits under the three above-mentioned schemes as percent of numbers out of work
Transfer ratio:	expenditure on unemployment compensation per beneficiary as percent of GDP per capita

3. Economic correlates of social expenditure growth

Irish economic development in the postwar period has diverged considerably from the general Western European pattern. Following a period of expansion in the late 1940s, economic growth was well below the European average during the 1950s [224]. The economy grew rapidly during the 1960s and 1970s, but per capita GDP in 1981 was second lowest among the European Community countries and the Irish economy still remains more heavily dependent on the primary sector than other Western European countries [225].

The change in the pace of economic development from the late 1950s is clearly reflected in the structure of GDP and employment, shown in Table 42. The contribution of the agricultural sector to GDP was halved between 1961 and 1981, whilst the industrial and service sectors grew in importance. The service sector expanded particularly rapidly during the 1970s and early 1980s. Agricultural employment declined from 36 percent of total employment in 1961 to 17.5 percent in 1981. In the latter year the service sector accounted for over half of total employment. The results of rapid economic transformation are also evident in the increasing rate of urbanisation since the early 1960s, although it was not until 1971 that the urban population outnumbered the rural one. The rural population, at 44 percent of the total in 1981, is still relatively large. Economic growth and industrialisation have brought about important changes in the class structure of Irish society. A recent study by Rottman and O'Connell notes three points of particular interest: self-employment has increasingly given way to wage employment; the balance in the employed workforce has shifted from semi-skilled and unskilled labour towards white collar and skilled manual employment; however, there still remains a substantial proportion of the workforce in marginal categories, particularly agricultural smallholders and unskilled labourers [226].

Table 42   Sectoral structure of GDP and employment, 1946 – 1981

	% share of GDP at current factor cost					% share of employment				
	1949	1961	1966	1971	1981	1946(a)	1961	1966	1971	1981
Agriculture	29.5	24.5	19.6	16.3	11.4	46.0	36.0	31.3	25.9	17.5
Industry	25.7	31.3	34.0	36.1	34.5	14.9	24.6	27.5	30.6	31.3
Services	44.7	44.2	46.4	47.6	54.1	39.1	39.5	41.2	43.5	51.2

(a) Percentage of economically active population.

There can be little doubt that the marked acceleration in economic growth rates since the beginning of the 1960s has been a crucial factor in the development of the Irish welfare state. Without the resources created by economic expansion, the rapid growth in social expenditure which characterised the period from 1963 onwards could certainly not have been sustained. Real social expenditure in 1980 was equivalent to over 60 percent of real GDP in 1960. At the same time, the process of industrialisation has created pressures and needs for increased social service provision, to meet the aspirations of a growing, urbanised middle and skilled working class, to provide a well trained and educated pool of labour for the expanding economy, and to protect those who find themselves disadvantaged in the market place.

The average growth rates of real GDP and real social expenditure in each of the phases of welfare state development are compared in Table 43. These data show that both the postwar expansionary phase of social expenditure and the major growth phase from 1963 to 1975 occurred in the context of relatively rapid economic growth, whilst the phase of low expenditure growth from 1952 to 1962 took place against a background of low economic growth rates. While the slackening of social expenditure growth in the period 1976-1980 occurred in the context of relatively high average economic growth rates, this was a period of fluctuating growth and rising fiscal imbalances. Table 43 also shows that the income elasticity of social expenditure - that is the ratio of the growth rate of real social expenditure to the growth rate of real GDP - has varied considerably from one period to another. Both of the expansionary phases of social expenditure were characterised by high income elasticity. Social expenditure expanded at 3.7 times the rate of GDP during the years 1947-51 and over twice as fast as GDP during the years 1963-75. By contrast, expenditure grew more slowly than GDP during the years 1952-62 and only slightly faster than GDP during the years 1976-80. Thus, not only were the expansionary phases of social expenditure underpinned by high economic growth, but they were also characterised by an apparent willingness to channel an increasing proportion of national wealth to the welfare state.

Table 43	Average annual growth rates of real GDP and real social expenditure by period		
Period	Average annual growth rate		Income elasticity of social expenditure
	GDP	Social expenditure	
1947-51	3.4	12.7	3.74
1952-62	2.1	1.8	0.86
1963-75	4.2	8.8	2.10
1976-80	4.4	4.8	1.12

Graphs 29 and 30 provide a more detailed picture of the relationship between the annual real growth rates of GDP and social expenditure over the period 1950 to 1980. Changes in the growth rates of the two series from year to year appear to be directly related to a moderate extent. In seventeen of the thirty-one years examined, a shift up or down in the growth rate of GDP was accompanied by a movement in the same direction in the growth rate of social expenditure. In the remaining years the two growth rates moved in opposite directions. Graph 30 confirms that social expenditure began to grow considerably faster than GDP from 1963 onwards and that its growth rate remained well above that of GDP throughout the period up to 1975. It is also evident that the reduction in the income elasticity of social expenditure in the period after 1975, shown in Table 43, reflected the very low growth rates of social expenditure relative to GDP in the years 1976-77. During the last three years of the period, social expenditure expanded considerably more rapidly than GDP again.

The correlation coefficients of annual changes in real GDP and real social expenditure over the period 1950-1980 are shown in Table 44. As already indicated by Graph 29, there is a significant positive correlation between the two series (.64). However, a fairly significant positive correlation still persists when GDP growth rates are lagged one year, indicating that variations in economic growth rates continue to be reflected in social expenditure growth rates after one year. As shown in Table 44, different types of social expenditure appear to be affected to varying degrees by variations in economic growth rates. Annual growth rates of income maintenance expenditure correlate very weakly with those of GDP, whilst in the case of health expenditure there is quite a strong positive correlation (.58) and in the case of housing and educa-

Graph 29

Real annual growth rates of GDP
and total social expenditure

Graph 30

Annual differences between GDP and
social expenditure growth rates

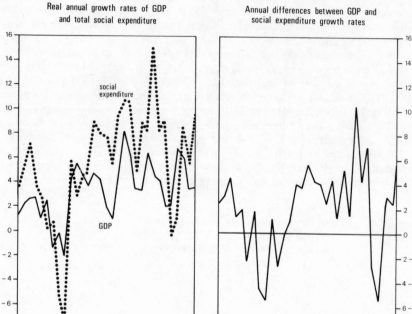

tion expenditure moderately strong positive correlations (.45 and .42 respectively). The weak correlation between the growth rates of income maintenance expenditure and GDP may reflect the relatively inelastic nature of income maintenance expenditure in the short term, given that the greater part of this consists of current expenditure on statutory social insurance and social assistance benefits. It may also reflect the fact that dependence on income maintenance benefits may tend to increase during periods of low economic growth, due to rising unemployment rates.

Table 44   Correlation of annual growth rates of real GDP and
                  real social expenditure, 1950–1980

| | Annual growth of GDP | | |
Annual growth of	Lag 0	Lag 1	Lag 2
Total social expenditure	+0.64	+0.56	+0.36
Income maintenance	+0.21	+0.25	+0.15
Health	+0.58	+0.44	+0.44
Education	+0.42	+0.42	+0.02
Housing	+0.45	+0.42	+0.25

The scatterplot in Graph 31 illustrates the moderately strong overall correlation
between the growth rates of social expenditure and GDP. But it also shows that the
overlap between phases of economic growth and phases of social expenditure growth
has not been perfect. The postwar expansionary phase of social expenditure from
1947 to 1951, was marked by very large fluctuations in the annual growth rates of
social expenditure. The years of highest growth, 1948 and 1949, coincided with a
period of rapid economic growth. It is generally accepted that 1949 marked the end
of the postwar recovery phase for the economy but social expenditure continued to
grow quite rapidly up to 1952 [227]. It should be noted that the high growth rate in
1952 was due solely to growth in income maintenance expenditure; health, education
and housing expenditure did not expand in real terms in this year. The growth rate of
social expenditure fell steadily in the years 1953 to 1955, although economic growth
rates did not deteriorate further during these years. The period 1956-58 saw a sharp
fall in economic growth rates, accompanied by a severe cutback in social expenditure
in 1957-58 [228]. Although economic recovery began in 1959, it will be observed that
social expenditure growth rates remained relatively low until 1963.

Graph 31

Relationship of GDP and social expenditure
annual real growth rates

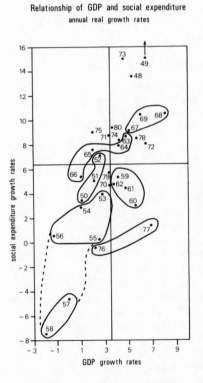

The delay in the recovery of social expenditure reflects a deliberate policy decision to
postpone development of the social services until such time as economic growth
should be deemed to be well established. Economic recovery took place in the context
of a state-stimulated plan for expansion and industrialisation, two central tenets of

which were a reduction in direct taxation and a shift in the balance of public invest-ment from 'non-productive' spheres, such as social services, to 'productive' pro-jects [229]. Although the displacement of social expenditure over the period of the *First Programme for Economic Expansion*, covering the years 1958-63 was in fact slight, it was not until towards the end of the programme period that social expenditure began to expand on any marked scale [230].

From 1963 to 1975, with the exception of the years 1966 and 1970, the growth rate of social expenditure lay well above the average for the postwar period. During much of this period economic growth rates were also buoyant and there was a relatively close association between movements in the growth rates of the two series. However, the relationship became less systematic from the early 1970s. Social expenditure grew very rapidly in the period 1971-75, despite quite marked annual fluctuations in the growth of GDP and low growth in 1971 and 1975. It was not until 1976 that the growth of social expenditure was curtailed in response to the economic downturn. The period 1976-80 was characterised by relatively large fluctuations in the annual growth rates of both GDP and social expenditure and a relatively weak association between the two.

In conclusion, therefore, economic factors can provide only a partial explanation for the pattern of expansion of the welfare state. While the economic upturn from the late 1950s was clearly a necessary prerequisite for the rapid growth of social expendi-ture, it is also evident that policy decisions were influential in determining both the timing and pace of this growth.

4. The political context of welfare state development

The foregoing discussion of the role of demographic and economic factors in shaping the development of the Irish welfare state has shown that while these have had a sig-nificant influence, it is also important to investigate the political environment within which they have operated. Analysts of the influence of political factors on the develop-ment of the welfare state have generally tended to emphasise the role of class and ideology, operating through the party system and through major interest associations within the society [231]. Among the range of possible issues which could be taken up in this context, the discussion here focusses on three factors which appear to be of partic-ular interest in the Irish context. These are the respective roles of political parties, the trade union movement and the Roman Catholic church. Finally, the role of and the diffusion of social policy ideas from abroad is considered. Perhaps the most outstanding feature of the Irish party system from a comparative perspective is that it is not rooted in any of the major social cleavages - class, religion or territoriality - which have been identified as powerful influences on the development of party sys-tems in other Western European countries [232]. The two major parties, Fianna Fail and Fine Gael, derive from a split within the nationalist movement over the terms of the Treaty of Independence in 1921. The polarisation of the party system over the treaty issue effectively prevented social class from playing a significant role during the forma-tive period of the party system. Though there was a slight tendency for Fianna Fail to find support among the less privileged sections of society and for Fine Gael to gain support among the better-off classes, the main political opposition was, nevertheless, primarily an expression of a strictly political as opposed to social cleavage. The Labour Party, which is a class based party, did not succeed in mobilising any signifi-cant section of Irish society during the early years of the state, and during the postwar period the Labour Party has had the lowest average vote of any European social democratic party [233].

For a variety of reasons the terms of the major political opposition have changed during the postwar period. During the first two decades of independence Fianna Fail and Fine Gael confronted one another, with the Labour Party attempting to establish an independent alternative. However, the decline in Fine Gael's vote since the 1930s has led to a situation where Fianna Fail now confronts all the other parties in a bi-polar opposition. As such, the governmental alternatives in postwar Ireland have been a Fianna Fail single party government on the one hand or a non-Fianna Fail coalition on the other, involving primarily Fine Gael and the Labour Party [234].

The characteristics of these alternative governments are in some crucial respects similar: Fianna Fail is a populist, catch-all party which draws support in virtually equal proportions from all sections of society; Fine Gael's support base is somewhat more skewed towards the higher socio-economic groups, whilst the Labour Party is oriented primarily towards the working class. The net effect of a Fine Gael/Labour Party coalition is to produce a government which is as heterogeneous in terms of its support base as is Fianna Fail. The result of this situation for party competition is that rather than particular parties emphasising particular issues, all issues are accessible to all governments. And while this is less true at party level - for instance the Labour Party is certainly more oriented towards social policy issues than the other main parties - the heterogeneous nature of the two governing alternatives ensures that there is little distinction between the issues which are accessible to each. As such, one might not expect to find any significant connection between governmental alternation and the development of the welfare state.

Furthermore, it is important to note that there has, in fact, been very little alternation in government in the postwar period. Since 1945 there have been twelve administrations, of which Fianna Fail have formed eight. Whilst this bias in favour of Fianna Fail may not appear particularly striking when expressed in these terms, a count of the number of years spent in office by each administration shows that out of the 37 years from 1945 to 1982 (excluding the most recent government which took office in December 1982), Fianna Fail governed for over 25 years.

The political salience of social policy

Before examining the implications of the party composition of government for the development of the welfare state, it may be useful to consider briefly the salience of social policy in the political arena. The political salience of social policy has increased considerably over the postwar period. This much is clear from a variety of indicators, including election manifestos of the parties, official policy documents and parliamentary records. A recent study of party election manifestos indicates a relatively clear association between the salience of social policy issues in electoral rhetoric and the different phases of welfare state development [235]. During the period 1948-61, the average proportion of references by the three main parties to social policy issues in their election manifestos was of the order of 15 percent of the total documents. During the period 1965-82 the corresponding figure was 22 percent. Again, over the period 1948-61 issues relating to the social services ranked fourth in the list of leading issues in election manifestos, whilst issues relating to social justice ranked seventh. In the period 1965-82 social justice was the second most important issue on average, whilst issues relating to the social services followed closely in third place.

Increasing interest in social policy has not been confined to the electoral arena. In policy making circles too, social issues have gained increasing prominence. One indicator of this trend is the number of policy documents on social policy topics emanating from the administration. Between 1947 and 1962, four major policy documents (white papers) were published, dealing respectively with housing, social insurance, and the health services. After this, no further policy documents relating to the social services appeared until 1964. The period 1964 to 1980 saw an unprecedented outpouring of official reports and discussion papers. During these years sixteen white papers, discussion papers and reports of official committees and study groups appeared, and these ranged over a broad variety of social topics.

Another useful indicator of official policy priorities is the annual budget statement of the Minister for Finance. Analysis of these statements over the postwar period reveals that the proportion of space devoted to social policy issues remained insignificant throughout the period 1946-64; at no time during this period did discussion of social policy exceed 9 percent of the budget statement, and during the period 1952-55 the space devoted to social issues was minimal. The year 1965 marks a turning point after which considerably more prominence has been given to social policy in budget statements. This turning point was aptly highlighted by the Minister for Finance at the time, who described the budget in 1965 as a 'social services budget' [236]. The period 1965-74 was characterised by a sustained emphasis on social issues in budget statements, although the years since 1975 have seen a waning of the prominence afforded to such issues.

Whilst evidence concerning the political salience of social policy issues may not say much about the actual impact of political factors on the development of the welfare state, it does highlight the fact that such development did not occur in a political vacuum. Instead, the major developmental phase of the Irish welfare state has been marked by a clear rise in the political prominence of social policy issues.

Party composition of government and welfare state development

Although the features of the Irish party system noted earlier suggest that the party composition of government may not have very much explanatory power with regard to the development of the welfare state, analysis of party election manifestos reveals some noteworthy variations in the emphasis which the different parties place on social policy issues [237]. As might be expected, the Labour Party has consistently placed much greater emphasis on social policy than have Fianna Fail and Fine Gael. Over the period 1948-82 as a whole, the average proportion of Labour Party election manifestos devoted to social policy issues was over 26 percent, compared with 15 percent in the case of Fine Gael and 14 percent in the case of Fianna Fail. It is important to note that whilst the Labour Party has consistently emphasised social policy issues and Fianna Fail has consistently paid less attention to such issues, Fine Gael's policy stance underwent a major change in the mid-1960s. The proportion of Fine Gael election manifestos devoted to discussion of social policy went from an average of 10 percent in the period 1948-61 to 19 percent in the period 1965-82. Thus, in the period since 1965 particularly, there has been quite a marked difference in emphasis on social policy by the two governing alternatives - Fianna Fail on the one hand and Fine Gael and the Labour Party on the other.

Despite the partisan variations in emphasis on social policy issues to be found in election manifestos, there does not appear to be any particularly clearcut association between political phases and phases of welfare state development. As shown in Table 45, a coalition government (in which Fine Gael and Labour were the major partners) presided over the postwar expansionary phase of social expenditure. Whilst Fianna Fail held office during most of the phase of social expenditure stagnation from 1952 to 1962, it is also the case that Fianna Fail presided over the greater part of the major expansionary phase of the welfare state from 1963 to 1975. The last three years of this expansionary phase, during which a Fine Gael/Labour coalition governed, saw rapid expansion of social expenditure and important policy reforms. Again, the slackening of welfare state expansion since 1975 has occurred in the context of governmental alternation.

Table 45   Party composition of government and phases of welfare state development

Government	Phase of welfare state development
Fianna Fail 1944-48 Coalition 1948-51 (a)	Post-war expansionary phase 1947-51
Fianna Fail 1951-54 Coalition 1954-57 (b) Fianna Fail 1957-61	Stagnation in social policy and expenditure 1952-62
Fianna Fail 1961-65 Fianna Fail 1965-69 Fianna Fail 1969-73 Fine Gael/Labour 1973-77	Major expansionary phase 1963-75
Fianna Fail 1971-81	Slackening growth 1976-

(a) Fine Gael, Labour, National Labour, Clann na Poblachta, Clann na Talmhan.
(b) Fine Gael, Labour, Clann na Talmhan.

The relationship between the party composition of government and the expansion of the welfare state is examined in a more systematic fashion in Table 46, which compares average growth rates of real social expenditure under different administrations. The average growth rate of expenditure was 7.2 percent per annum under coalition governments and 5.4 percent per annum under Fianna Fail governments. However, since economic growth rates have varied considerably during the periods of office of different governments, a comparison of the income elasticity of social expenditure under the various administrations will provide a more accurate picture of partisan variations. As shown in Table 46, real social expenditure grew, on average, at 1.5 times the rate of real GDP under Fianna Fail administrations, whereas under coalition governments, social expenditure grew 2.3 times as fast as GDP. Thus, it would appear

Table 46   Average growth rate and income elasticity of real social expenditure by party composition of government

Period	Fianna Fail government		Coalition government	
	Annual growth rate of real social expenditure	Income elasticity (a)	Annual growth rate of real social expenditure	Income elasticity (a)
1948-51			12.7	3.7
1951-54	4.8	2.3		
1954-58			1.3	1.9
1957-61	0.02	0.01		
1961-65	6.7	1.7		
1965-69	8.7	2.0		
1969-72	8.0	1.7		
1973-77			6.6	1.7
1977-80	6.2	1.3		
Average over total years government	5.4	1.5	7.2	2.3

(a) Ratio of growth rate of real social expenditure to growth rate of real GDP.

that party composition of government has had an impact on the rate of expansion of social expenditure, with expenditure growing more rapidly under coalition governments. However, these results must be treated with caution since there are only eleven observations relating to coalition governments. Moreover, the higher average growth rate of expenditure under coalition governments is to a substantial extent a reflection of the very rapid expansion of expenditure under the first inter-party government in the years 1948-51. If these years are omitted, the income elasticity of social expenditure under coalition governments has been only slightly higher than under Fianna Fail governments [238].

Another indication of the impact of party composition of government on the development of the welfare state is the number of core laws relating to the social services passed by different governments. Fianna Fail governments were responsible for a total of 35 core laws relating to income maintenance and health services in the period 1945-80, whilst coalition governments passed a total of 17 core laws [239]. Standardised by length of time in office, these totals are equivalent to 1.37 laws per year in the case of Fianna Fail and 1.63 laws per year in the case of coalition governments. As such, there has been very little difference in legislative activity under the two types of government.

Graph 32   The growth of Social Expenditure by Party Composition of Government   Graph 33

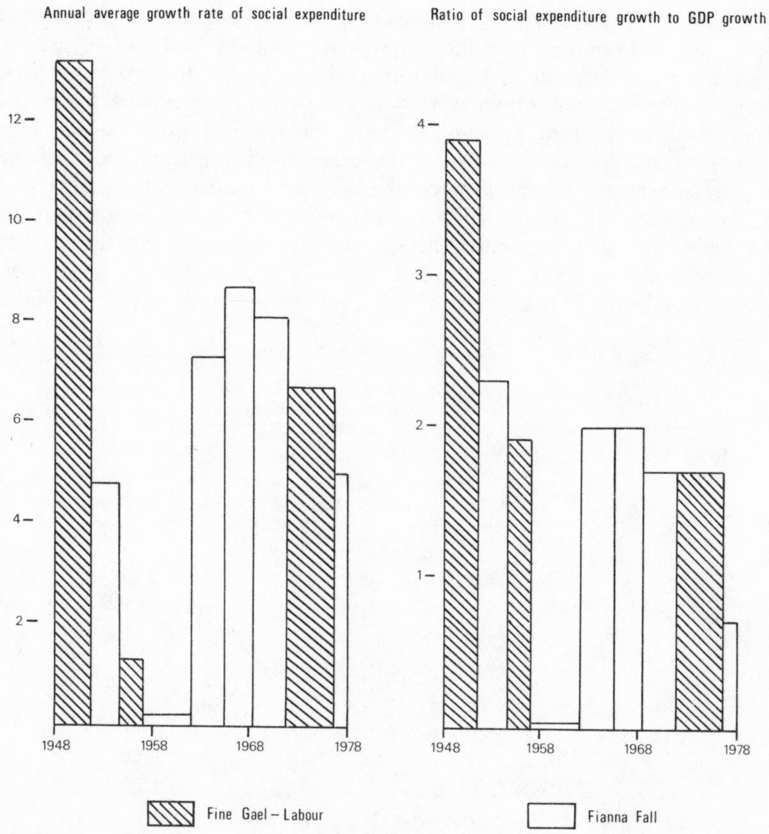

Annual average growth rate of social expenditure   Ratio of social expenditure growth to GDP growth

Fine Gael – Labour   Fianna Fall

Over the postwar period as a whole, party alternation in government does not appear to have played a very significant role in the development of the welfare state. As noted at the beginning of this discussion, there is little to distinguish the two governmental alternatives in terms of electoral support or political ideology and, moreover, there was relatively little alternation in government over most of the postwar period. However, as is clear from the discussion of the political salience of social policy, the major developmental phase of the welfare state was characterised by the emergence of social policy as an element in party competition. It is worth exploring briefly the circumstances of this change.

As noted earlier, the year 1958 marked a crucial turning point in Irish economic policy with the adoption by the Fianna Fail government of a programme for state-induced economic development. Expansion of the social services was, in general, accorded low priority in both the first and second programmes for economic expansion, covering the periods 1958-1963 and 1964-1970 respectively. The exception was education which was accorded more emphasis in the second programme, being viewed as an important element in the process of industrialisation. However, capital expenditure on education and housing exceeded planned targets in most of the years from 1962/63 up to 1970 and one commentator has noted that the expansion of social expenditure in this period took place in apparent contradiction to officially stated policy [240]. The view has been advanced by Bew and Paterson that the expansion of the social services, particularly the growth in social investment, from the early 1960s, was to a significant extent the result of a pragmatic strategy on the part of the Fianna Fail government to ensure the retention of its mass support base [241]. There appears to be some substance to this view. Certainly, the decision to begin expanding social expenditure in 1963 appears to have been linked to some extent to the introduction of a new form of indirect taxation which proved highly unpopular and which brought sharp criticism from the Irish Congress of Trade Unions [242]. However, the crucial turning point in Fianna Fail's attitude to social policy appears to have come in 1965.

In 1964, Fine Gael had produced a comprehensive policy document entitled *The Just Society* which placed major emphasis on social welfare and called for much higher levels of spending on social programmes. Both Fine Gael and the Labour Party made social policy a central issue in the general election campaign of 1965. Bew and Paterson note that although Fianna Fail had not put forward any proposals on social policy issues at the start of the election campaign, the party responded by promising improvements in the social services [243]. Although Fianna Fail increased its vote in the 1965 election, the Labour Party made major gains in the Dublin region and continued to gain strength in the second half of the 1960s. The Labour Party produced a more radical programme in 1967, its membership rose, its relations with the trade union movement improved and it made substantial gains in all major urban areas in the 1967 local elections. The 1969 general election saw the Labour Party making further advances in the Dublin region [244]. Fine Gael also increased its share of the poll, although it did not gain any additional seats.

From 1965 onwards Fianna Fail demonstrated a stronger commitment to the expansion of the social services, as evidenced by the expansion in social expenditure and the quickening pace of reforms. The third programme for economic development, covering the period 1969-72, also accorded much greater prominence to social policy than the two previous programmes had done [245]. It seems likely that this increasing concern with social policy on the part of Fianna Fail was to some degree prompted by a concern to retain the party's urban support base in the face of a strong challenge from the Labour Party. Fine Gael's newly found concern with social policy from the mid-1960s also appears to have influenced Fianna Fail's stance. Thus, the expansion of the welfare state from the mid-1960s can to some extent be explained in terms of the exigencies of party competition.

Trade unions and social policy

The role of interest groups in the development of the welfare state has attracted a good deal of attention from social policy analysts, with a particular focus on the influence of organised labour [246]. As shown above, the expansion of the welfare state in Ireland has coincided with important changes in the structure of the economy. The period since the early 1960s has seen the growth of a large, urbanised, employee workforce, with a predominance of white-collar and skilled manual workers. The labour force is also relatively highly organised, with some 58 percent of employees belonging to trade unions in 1979 [247]. And although the trade union movement is quite fragmented, with 85 different unions in 1979, the majority of these are affiliated to the Irish Congress of Trade Unions, which represents about 93 percent of union membership [248]. Given the rapid changes which have taken place in the structure of the labour force and the strength of the trade union movement, it is clearly of relevance to investigate whether organised labour has influenced the development of the welfare state in Ireland.

The role of the trade union movement in the policy-making process has altered significantly over the period since 1960. From the early 1960s, the trade unions, along with employers' representatives, began to be incorporated in the policy formulation process through participation in a series of newly established consultative bodies, such as the National Industrial and Economic Council, the Committee on Industrial Organisation and the National Productivity Committee [249]. During this period the unions and employers also established a joint consultative body, the Employer-Labour Conference. The emergence of what some commentators have termed 'corporatist' tendencies played an important role in the strategy for economic development and industrialisation [250]. There is little indication, however, that the trade union movement attempted to broaden the dialogue with government beyond economic policy during the 1960s. Nevertheless, the unions evinced a general commitment to improved social services and increased social expenditure from the early 1960s. In 1964, for instance, the Irish Congress of Trade Unions criticised the government's failure to put forward plans for the development of the social services, and welcomed an increase in the social capital budget in that year [251]. But there is no evidence that the union movement developed a coherent policy with regard to the development of the welfare state, or actively pursued specific social policy aims at this stage.

The 1970s were marked by new departures in government/trade union relations, prompted by efforts to achieve pay restraint in the interests of economic expansion. From 1970 onwards, free wage bargaining by the unions was replaced by centralised collective bargaining between the Irish Congress of Trade Unions and the employers' representatives. Although the government did not play any formal role in the conclusion of National Wage Agreements during the first half of the 1970s, it has been noted that budgetary policy and tax concessions played an important part in wage determination [252]. From 1976 the role of the state became more formalised, with the government taking part in tripartite discussions with the unions and employers, and offering a package of tax and other measures in return for pay restraint. This pattern was repeated in the following two years. In 1979 and 1980 wage agreements were incorporated into formal National Understandings for Economic and Social Development, negotiated between the government, the Irish Congress of Trade Unions and employers' representatives. These 'understandings' included, for the first time, agreements on social policy reforms as well as on economic policy, thus providing an important channel of influence for labour, as well as prompting the unions to give closer consideration to what their priorities in social policy might be [253]. The 1979 and 1980 National Understandings included commitments to increase social welfare benefits at least in line with the standard of living, to draw up a government white paper on a new national pension plan and to review the system of family income support, the child health services, income support for the disabled and house purchase finance. It was also agreed that the income limit for eligibility for health services would be increased and that additional real resources would be provided for education. Since 1980, however, there have been no further national understandings.

The other major official channel which the trade union movement has for articulating social policy aims is the National Economic and Social Council, formed in 1972. The Irish Congress of Trade Unions, along with the government, the agricultural sector and employers' organisations, nominates representatives to the Council. This body has come to play an important advisory role to government with regard to the development of the social services.

In conclusion, therefore, the role of the trade union movement during the 1960s appears to have been a fairly modest one of adding its voice to those calling for expansion of the social services. In the 1970s the union movement has played a more active role through the National Economic and Social Council and through the social policy reforms sought in the context of the national understandings. Since the late 1970s the unions have also played an important part in orchestrating tax protests by the employee sector. This last development is taken up in Section V.

The influence of the Catholic church on social policy

The influence of the Roman Catholic church on the development of the welfare state merits particular attention in the Irish context. Some 95 percent of the population belong to the Roman Catholic religion and although there is evidence that Irish society is becoming increasingly secular, surveys carried out in the early 1970s indicated that over 90 percent of the population attended church regularly [254]. The Constitution of Ireland, drawn up in 1937, clearly echoes Roman Catholic social philosophy of the time [255]. The sections dealing with principles of social policy emphasise the role of private enterprise and undertake to ensure that citizens are able to provide for their needs through their occupations. However, concentration of ownership and wealth is condemned and the state undertakes to safeguard the economic interests of the weaker sections of the community. But in terms of setting out principles for the achievement of the latter objective, the state merely undertakes to contribute, 'where necessary' to the support of the infirm, the widow, the orphan and the aged [256].

Notwithstanding the constitutional commitment to a relatively minimal role for the state in social policy, the postwar years brought a rapid expansion of all of the major social programmes except education (see Section II). Whyte's analysis of church-state relations shows that during the 1940s and 1950s the Catholic hierarchy were strongly opposed to expansion of the welfare state and there was tension between Church and state over social policy issues on several occasions during this period [257]. For instance, one bishop, who at the time was chairman of the National Health Insurance Society, published in 1944 a plan for the reorganisation of the health and social insurance systems along vocational lines [258]. This met with a hostile reaction from government ministers and when the bishop's term of office as chairman came to an end he was not reappointed.

The plans for reform and expansion of the social insurance system published by the government in 1949 met with strong criticism from members of the clergy and the hierarchy on various grounds. Whyte documents that the objections to the plans included the following: some critics were opposed to the extension of the role of the state implied by the proposed reforms, others thought the government should concentrate on achieving a wider distribution of property rather than on expansion of social insurance, yet others were concerned that the scheme neglected the problems of small farmers and other self-employed people [259]. Whyte points out, however, that while the above episodes aroused a good deal of attention at the time, none had an impact on policy outcomes [260].

The most noteworthy incursion by the Church in the social policy arena, and one of the few occasions when the hierarchy have actively intervened in the legislative process, was in connection with the health care scheme for mothers and children referred to in Section I [261]. Outline provision for a universal scheme providing free ante- and post-natal care, as well as health care for children up to the age of 16, was made in the Health Act of 1947. However, subsequent attempts to implement the scheme met with opposition from the hierarchy on the grounds that it represented an unwarranted incursion by the state on the rights of the individual. In particular, the hierarchy were critical of the universal nature of the proposed scheme and of the fact that it was to be administered by publicly employed doctors rather than private practitioners. The scheme was withdrawn by the inter-party government in 1951 in the face of this criticism. It finally passed into law in 1953, having been modified to meet some, although not all, of the hierarchy's objections [262].

Whyte notes that the area where the church has exerted most influence is education [263]. The school system is characterised by a high degree of clerical control and there can be little doubt that this was an important reason for the absence of any major intervention by the state prior to the 1960s. The 1960s and 1970s have, however, seen a significant expansion in the role of the state in the educational sphere. Whyte points out that whilst there has been some tension between church and state on issues of educational reform, the changes have, on the whole, met with cooperation on the part of the hierarchy [264].

Whyte has underlined an important change in the attitude of the Church towards social policy during the 1960s [265]. From this period onwards, the Church became, to an increasing extent, a force for, rather than against, reform of the social services. In the late 1960s members of the clergy began to call for increased state action to help the disadvantaged sections of society and the hierarchy played a central role in placing the issue of poverty on the public agenda in the early 1970s. As noted earlier, the hierarchy's Council for Social Welfare organised a conference on poverty in 1971 which attracted widespread attention and which appears to have contributed to making poverty and social justice an issue in the general election campaign of 1973. In 1977, the hierarchy published a joint pastoral letter which identified unemployment and poverty as two major social problems and urged policies to remedy these problems [266]. In contrast, therefore, to the inhibiting role which the Church played during the postwar expansionary phase of the social services, during the period of major development of the welfare state the church has contributed to the social consensus in favour of this development. Diffusion of social policy ideas from abroad

Several writers have drawn attention to the role of diffusion of ideas and policies between countries in the development of social programmes [267]. The notion of a 'demonstration effect' as a determinant of public sector growth has also been proposed by a number of commentators [268]. There are good reasons why developments in neighbouring countries might be expected to have influenced the growth of the welfare state in Ireland. By the time of independence, in 1921, Ireland already had a set of social programmes which were closely modelled on the British ones, since many of the social policy reforms enacted in Britain were also extended to Ireland. Commentators have suggested several factors which might have led to developments in the United Kingdom exercising a strong influence in Ireland since independence. Given the mobility of labour between the two countries, relative levels of social benefits and provision of social services might be expected to have an important impact on migration flows [269]. Moreover, Northern Ireland has remained within the United Kingdom and has developed its social services at the same pace as mainland Britain and, as noted by O'Hagan, this renders differentials in provision between Ireland and the United Kingdom particularly visible [270]. Indeed, Fitzgerald has suggested that discrepancies in standards of social services between the two parts of Ireland may constitute an obstacle to reunification of the country [271]. As such, it has been noted that the desire for reunification might provide an additional impetus for Ireland to strive for parity with the United Kingdom in social service provision [272].

Membership of the European Community may provide another source of diffusion of social policy developments. Although the EC actually imposes only a few definite requirements on member states in the field of social policy, increased awareness of provisions in other Community countries might be expected to lead to pressures for similar levels of provision in Ireland. O'Hagan suggests that the demonstration effect might be particularly important in the case of a small, less economically developed country such as Ireland [273].

With regard to the overall growth of the public sector, O'Hagan has found evidence of a strong demonstration effect from the United Kingdom to Ireland in the period 1953-76, indicating that this may have been an important factor contributing to public expenditure trends [274]. Turning to the specific area of social policy, there is a good deal of associative evidence to suggest that developments in Ireland in the field of social insurance were influenced by developments in Britain. There can be little doubt that the Beveridge Report and the British National Insurance Act of 1946 added significantly to pressure for reform in Ireland in the late 1940s [275]. A motion on reform of the social security system proposed in the Dail by two Labour Party members in 1946 displayed a clear concern with the gap which would open up between the two countries when the British scheme was implemented [276]. The proposals of the inter-party coalition government for reform of the social insurance system, published in 1949 and incorporated in the Social Welfare (Insurance) Bill of 1950, reflected many elements of the British reforms [277]. Although the Bill differed from the British National Insurance Act, 1946, in excluding the self-employed from insurance, it proposed to extend insurance to all employees, to introduce a retirement pension payable at the same ages for women and men as in Britain, to provide a death benefit and to adhere to the principle of flat-rate benefits.

In the event, the inter-party government fell before the Social Welfare Bill became law. The Fianna Fail government which assumed office in 1951 had shown itself during its previous period of office, from 1944 to 1948, to be opposed to any major development of the social services, stressing that reforms being implemented elsewhere were not necessarily appropriate for Ireland and that the country could not in any case afford a substantial expansion of the social services [278]. But while the reform of the social insurance system implemented by the Fianna Fail government in 1952 was less comprehensive than that envisaged in the Social Welfare Bill of 1950, several commentators have drawn attention to parallels between the system introduced in 1952 and that adopted in Britain in 1946 [279]. While the Irish scheme was much more limited in scope than the British one, it followed the British pattern in setting up a centralised, unified social insurance system, based on the principle of providing a basic flat-rate benefit. Moreover, Hughes has noted that the household equivalence scales, adopted in 1952, to determine the relative rates of benefit for different family members within the Irish unemployment and sickness benefit schemes, closely approximate those proposed by Beveridge and used in the United Kingdom since 1946 [280].

The slow rate of development of the Irish social services from the early 1950s up to the early 1960s led to a situation whereby levels of provision in Ireland lagged considerably behind those in the United Kingdom. Since the mid-1960s, however, the gap between benefit rates in the two countries has narrowed appreciably and several of the extensions of the Irish social insurance system introduced in this period appear to have been modelled on British schemes. Kaim-Caudle notes that the Redundancy Payments Act, 1967, had several features in common with three British schemes, namely the Contracts of Employment Act, 1963, the Redundancy Payments Act, 1965, and the earnings-related supplement to unemployment benefit introduced in 1966 [281]. The occupational injury insurance scheme introduced in Ireland in 1966 also bore a close resemblance to the scheme which had operated in Britain since 1946 [282]. More recently, the earnings-related supplements to unemployment and sickness benefits introduced in 1974 also closely resemble the British scheme of supplements introduced in the mid-1960s.

In areas other than social insurance, the Irish services have been much less influenced by British developments. Although British plans for establishment of a national health service in the 1940s must certainly have contributed to the pressure for reform in Ireland, the measures which were enacted in the Health Act, 1953, fell far short of the British reforms and in the period since then the two health systems have diverged considerably [283]. Nor was the expansion of education in postwar Britain matched by a similar development in Ireland. In fact, in contrast to the interest aroused by British advances in the areas of social insurance and health services in the 1940s, the parallel reforms taking place in the educational sphere appear to have been largely ignored in Ireland.

The decision in 1961 to apply for membership of the European Community heightened the awareness of the Irish authorities of the gap which had opened up between Ireland and other Western European countries in the sphere of social service provision. Although the aspiration to join the EC was not to be realised for more than a decade, the desire to catch up with the rest of Western Europe appears to have exercised an influence on policy makers from the early 1960s onwards. For instance, in two speeches delivered in 1963 Prime Minister Lemass emphasised the need to build the social services up to the levels of those in other European countries, while the Fine Gael party in its 1965 election programme drew unfavourable comparisons between the Irish health services and those in other Western European countries [284]. The *Third Programme for Economic and Social Development*, which set out plans for development in the period 1969-72, explicitly recognised that a reappraisal of the social services would be required if Ireland joined the EC and established the objective of bringing the income maintenance system up to the level set by international practice [285]. Academic commentators in this period also drew attention to discrepancies between provisions in Ireland and those in other European countries [286].

Thus, the expansion of the welfare state since the early 1960s appears to have been prompted to some extent by a wish to emulate other, more advanced, systems. More recently, there has also been evidence of an interest in the social security systems operating in other countries. Two discussion papers published by the Department of Social Welfare in the late 1970s, on options for an income-related pension scheme and on social insurance for the self-employed, reviewed schemes operating in other European countries [287]. Although policies have not to date been developed in either area, both documents display an awareness of the potential for adopting ideas from other countries.

5.   Correlates and causes - a summary

It is only since the early 1960s that the Irish social services have developed in a rapid and sustained fashion. This development has occurred in the context of a comprehensive transformation of the Irish economy and society. The most active phase of welfare state growth, from the early 1960s to the mid-1970s, coincided closely with a period of rapid economic growth, significant changes in the structure of production and employment, rapid urbanisation, a growing secularisation of Irish society and increasing contact with other Western European countries.

Clearly, economic growth has been an essential prerequisite for the expansion of the welfare state. It can hardly be coincidental that the emergence of a developed welfare state only occurred after the economy began to grow in a sustained fashion, or that the economic recessions of the mid-1970s and early 1980s have been accompanied by slackening growth of social programmes. Without the increase in national income which occurred in the 1960s and 1970s, it certainly would not have been feasible to raise the additional tax revenues necessary to support the growth of social expenditure, and of the public sector in general, which took place during that period. Financing by way of public borrowing, as has happened in recent years, can scarcely be regarded as a viable long-term option.

In addition to providing resources, economic growth also created demands for the expansion of social programmes. The educational reforms of the 1960s appear to have been prompted to a significant degree by the perceived need to adjust the education system to the manpower requirements of a rapidly industrialising economy. The growth in wage employment which accompanied industrialisation led automatically to an increase in the numbers covered by the social insurance system. Moreover, with an increasing proportion of the labour force in wage employment, there were also pressures to expand the social insurance system to cover a wider range of contingencies. Finally, it seems likely that rising standards of living in the 1960s and 1970s led to rising expectations concerning provision of social services.

This is not to suggest that there is a simple one-way causality between economic growth and the expansion of the welfare state. The short-lived expansion of social programmes in the late 1940s and early 1950s and the more sustained growth from the early 1960s to the mid-1970s were both marked by a willingness to allow social expenditure to rise much faster than output. The explanation for this willingness to channel an increased share of national resources to the welfare state, as well as for the time lag between renewed economic growth in the late 1950s and the renewed expansion of social programmes from the early 1960s, must be sought in factors other than economic growth.

The decomposition of expenditure growth on selected social programmes into demographic factors and other components, such as coverage rates and average levels of benefit, has provided some valuable insights into the proximate determinants of growth. This has shown that, in general, 'automatic' factors such as demographic change and relative price effects have been less influential in increasing expenditure than have increases in coverage and average benefits, which can, to a large extent, be attributed to policy decisions to expand social programmes. Thus, while the decomposition procedure cannot of itself identify the underlying causes of expenditure growth, it would seem to indicate that the expansion of the welfare state must, to a significant degree, be regarded as the outcome of intentional political actions.

In this context, the party composition of government has been shown to have little explanatory power, aside from the late 1940s and early 1950s when the accession to power of the first inter-party coalition government led to a perceptible increase in the pace of social policy reform. Otherwise, there has been little difference in the pace of growth and institutional development under alternative governments. However, the development of the welfare state has clearly been linked to a rise in the political saliency of social policy. From the mid-1960s onwards, social policy issues occupied a more prominent place in electoral platforms and became an important element in electoral counterbidding. The shift in attitude of the governing Fianna Fail party, from relegating social policy to a very secondary position in the late 1950s and early 1960s, to according it increased priority from around 1963, appears to some extent to be explicable in terms of the exigencies of party competition. Both of the main opposition parties were at this time placing considerable emphasis on the need for improvements in social programmes, and the trade union movement was also beginning to be more concerned with social policy. There appears to be a good deal of validity to the thesis that Fianna Fail's change in policy was to some extent prompted by a desire to consolidate its mass support base.

But there were also other factors at work in stimulating policy makers to devote more concern to social policy during the 1960s. There was objective evidence of the need for improvements in the social services, most notably in the declaration of a housing crisis in Dublin in 1963 and in the numerous shortcomings in the educational system revealed in the joint Irish-OECD report, *Investment in Education* published in 1966. More recently, the 'rediscovery' of poverty in the early 1970s has provided an impetus for the continuing development of social programmes. The shift in attitude of the Roman Catholic church, from one of antipathy towards state intervention in the 1940s and 1950s to one of support and even pressure for development of social programmes from the 1960s onwards, has also been influential.

A desire to close the gap which had opened up between Ireland and other Western European countries in the realm of welfare state development was another factor in the renewed emphasis on social policy from the early 1960s. Developments in the United Kingdom have provided an important stimulus for development of Irish provisions. The aspiration towards membership of the European Community from the early 1960s also disposed Irish policy makers to look more critically at social programmes. There is, clearly discernable in policy statements in the 1960s and 1970s, a wish to catch up with the more advanced welfare states in neighbouring countries.

V   Current problems and policy choices

The two decades to 1980 witnessed a substantial expansion of public social programmes in Ireland. By the end of this period the share of national output devoted to
the welfare state was close to the European norm, notwithstanding the fact that per
capita GDP in Ireland was well below the European average [288]. Up to the early
1970s, the expansion of the welfare state took place in a context of sustained high
levels of economic growth. Since 1973, however, the decline in economic growth rates
engendered by two oil shocks, and the emergence of large public sector deficits have
placed severe strains on the public finances. In Ireland, as in many other Western
countries, the ability to sustain high levels of public expenditure and the desirability of
so doing have begun to be questioned. In this context, the welfare state, as one of the
largest items of public expenditure, has become a focus of particular attention. Commentators and analysts in a number of countries have in recent years suggested that
the welfare state is facing an economic and political crisis [289]. This final section of our
study examines the problems facing the Irish welfare state at the present time and
assesses the prospects for the medium term.

1.   The changing macro-economic context and its implications for social policy

Following over a decade of virtually uninterrupted economic expansion, Ireland began
to experience serious economic problems after the 1973-74 oil crisis. The period since
1973 has been characterised by declining real growth rates, record levels of inflation
and unemployment, and the emergence of severe fiscal imbalances. The rate of
growth of real GDP declined from an average of 4.4 percent per annum in the period
1961-73 to 3.4 percent in the 1974-84 period. The downturn in growth rates
following the first oil shock was succeeded by a strong recovery in the years 1977-78,
with real GDP growth averaging almost 8 percent per annum. Growth rates deteriorated sharply again, however, from 1979 with real GDP expanding at less than 2.0
percent per annum between 1979 and 1984.

Although the downturn in economic growth rates in the post-1973 period has not
been as severe in Ireland as in many other Western economies, the levels of inflation
and unemployment reached during the past decade are high by international standards [290]. Inflationary pressures accelerated rapidly in the early 1970s, with the annual
rise in the Consumer Price Index going from 9 percent in 1972 to 21 percent in 1975.
Having been brought back to 8 percent by 1978, inflation began to climb sharply
again in 1979, peaking at over 20 percent in 1981. Since 1981, efforts to control inflation have met with some success and by 1984 the inflation rate had fallen to under 9
percent. The unemployment situation deteriorated significantly during the economic
recession which followed the first oil shock, with the unemployment rate rising from
6 percent in 1972 to 9 percent in 1977 [291]. Unemployment had fallen back to 7 percent by 1979, but in the period since then, continuing growth of the labour force and
falling employment have combined, pushing the unemployment rate to almost 16 percent in 1984.

As noted in Section II, the period since 1973 has also seen the emergence of large
fiscal imbalances. The current budget went into deficit in 1974 and by 1975 the deficit
had reached 7 percent of GNP. Between 1973 and 1975 the Exchequer Borrowing
Requirement (EBR) rose from 7 percent to almost 16 percent of GNP. The government deficit was reduced in the two years up to 1977, but a return to expansionary
fiscal policies led to a further major deterioration in the public finances in the Period
up to 1981 (see Table 47) [292]. Exchequer expenditure rose from 48 percent of GNP in

1977 to 63 percent in 1981, mainly due to large increases in current expenditure. Although taxation also rose significantly in this period, this was insufficient to prevent a wide gap from opening up between revenues and expenditure. By 1981 the current budget deficit had reached 7.6 percent of GNP, the EBR had risen to over 16 percent of GNP and the total public sector borrowing requirement stood at 21 percent of GNP. In 1981 interest payments on the national debt accounted for 8 percent of GNP and for 17 percent of central government current spending.

Table 47   Government revenue and expenditure
                                                (as % of GNP)

	1977	1978	1979	1980	1981	1982	1983	1983(a)	1984
Current expenditure of which:	35.4	38.4	38.7	41.9	45.2	48.8	50.1	47.7	48.5
Debt interest	(5.5)	(6.1)	(6.5)	(6.9)	(7.9)	(9.8)	(10.1)		(10.6)
Current revenue	31.8	32.1	31.7	35.7	37.6	40.6	42.9	39.5	41.3
Current deficit	3.6	6.3	7.0	6.2	7.6	8.2	7.2	8.2	7.2
Capital expenditure	12.5	13.4	13.8	14.8	17.9	16.5	14.1	14.1	13.3
Capital resources	6.3	6.8	7.3	7.2	9.2	8.6	8.1	8.3	7.8
Capital deficit	6.2	6.6	6.5	7.6	8.7	7.9	6.0	5.8	5.4
Exchequer borrowing requirement	9.8	12.9	13.4	13.8	16.3	16.1	13.2	13.9	12.6
Public sector borrowing requirement	12.7	15.6	16.7	17.6	20.9	20.4	17.1		16.4
Total tax revenue	34.5	33.2	33.0	36.5	38.1	41.0	42.5		44.0

(a) A reclassification of accounts arose from the transfer in 1984 of the day-to-day operations of the postal and telecommunication services from central government. Data for 1983 are shown on both bases to indicate the magnitude of these changes.

Since 1981 budgetary policy has become more restrictive in an effort to correct these large fiscal imbalances. Meanwhile, however, the outstanding national debt had risen to 128 percent of GNP by 1984, the highest in the OECD area, while interest repayments on the debt had mounted to 11 percent of GNP and 20 percent of current government expenditure [293]. As Table 47 shows, fiscal adjustment in the period 1981-84 was achieved mainly by increasing taxation rather than reducing expenditure. The share of total tax revenues rose from 38 percent to 44 percent of GNP in this period. The exchequer expenditure share was reduced slightly as a result of a reduction in the ratio of capital expenditure. However, current expenditure continued to expand up to 1984 under pressure of rising debt interest payments and transfers to the rapidly increasing numbers of unemployed.

At mid-decade, therefore, the economic situation remains difficult. Although inflation has moderated, economic growth rates are still quite low and major problems persist in the forms of severe fiscal imbalances and very high unemployment. The remainder of this sub-section examines how social programmes have fared during these years of economic difficulty in order to see whether economic constraints have led to institutional curtailments and to cuts in social expenditure or whether the welfare state has passed relatively unscathed through the economic recession.

Although the pace of institutional development of social programmes has decreased since the onset of economic difficulties, social legislation has by no means been at a standstill in the post-1973 period. As noted in Sections I and II, the years up to 1980 saw several important reforms, including the introduction in 1974 of earnings-related supplements to short-term benefits, reduction of the pensionable age from 70 to 66 years between 1973 and 1977, reform of the public assistance system and of the system of state housing grants in 1977 and extension of eligibility for free hospital care and reimbursement of drug costs in 1979.

As shown in Table 48, development of social programmes in the period since 1980 has been confined mainly to marginal improvements in existing schemes, although there have been several innovations in the area of income maintenance. An earnings-related maternity benefit for women in full-time employment was introduced in 1981. The introduction in 1982 of a rent allowance for tenants in formerly rent controlled accommodation was designed to prevent this relatively small group from suffering hardship due to rent increases following a Supreme Court decision that rent control of private lettings was unconstitutional. The Family Income Supplement, introduced in 1984, for low income families with one or both parents in full-time employment was designed primarily to enhance work incentives [294]. The Enterprise Allowance Scheme introduced in 1984 aimed at boosting employment by encouraging unemployed persons to establish their own businesses. With regard to improvement of existing schemes, various categories of pensioners have benefited from the extension of eligibility for a number of supplementary allowances and benefits and there has been some easing of means-tests for social assistance payments. In the area of housing policy, state support for purchase of private dwellings has been improved, particularly for lower income groups.

Table 48   Institutional reforms, 1981-1984

Income maintenance

1981   Earnings-related maternity benefit introduced for women in full-time employment.
        Fifteen years residence requirement for non-contributory old age pension removed.
        Free telephone rental scheme for pensioners extended to invalidity pensioners and recipients of
        disabled person's maintenance allowance.
        Allowance for care by relative extended to survivor pensioners aged 66 or over.
        Definition of adult dependant of contributory old age pensioner and retirement pensioner extended.
        Definition of child dependant of invalidity or retirement pensioner who is a widow extended to cover
        children between ages 18 and 21 in full-time education.

1982   Rent allowance scheme for tenants who would otherwise suffer hardship as a result of a Supreme Court
        decision that rent control of private tenancies is unconstitutional.
        Free telephone rental scheme extended to blind pensioners under age 66.
        Unemployment assistance scheme extended to married women without dependent children who are separated
        from and not supported by the husband.
        Easing of means test for social assistance allowances for widows, deserted wives, unmarried mothers
        and prisoners' wives.

1984   New family income supplement for families with at least one parent in full-time employment with an
        income of less than IRL 90 per week.
        Free travel on public transport extended to all blind pensioners.
        Enterprise allowance scheme providing income support for unemployed persons setting up their own
        businesses.

Housing

1981   Mortgage subsidy for first time purchasers of new houses.
        New loan and mortgage scheme for local authority tenants.
        Income limit for local authority loans for private house purchase increased and limit on amount
        of loan raised.
        Increased grants to disabled for alterations to and reconstruction of housing.

1982   Housing Finance Agency established to provide mortgages for low earners.

1984   Grant of IRL 5,000 to local authority tenants as incentive to purchase private housing

The period since 1980 has also seen some cuts in social programmes however, culminating in a series of cost saving measures in 1983. As shown in Table 49, earnings-replacement ratios of unemployment, sickness and maternity benefits have been reduced through cuts in the level of the earnings-related supplement and reductions in the maximum level of benefits payable under the sickness and maternity benefit schemes. The

Table 49   Cuts in social programmes, 1980–1984

Sickness cash benefit

1980   Waiting period of three days for benefit, which was formerly waived for claims separated by not more
       than thirteen weeks, extended to all claims except in cases where the claimant becomes ill while
       receiving unemployment benefit or, having been in receipt of sickness benefit, suffers a relapse
       within three days of returning to work.

1981   Waiting period of twelve days for earnings-related supplement to benefit, which was formerly
       waived in cases of claims separated by not more than thirteen weeks, now applied in the same way
       as the waiting period for the flat-rate sickness benefit.

1982   Strengthening of team of medical referees and more intensive investigation of sickness benefit claims.

1983   Reduction in earnings-related supplement to benefit from 40% of reference earnings to 25% for the
       first six months of benefit, from 30% to 20% for the next three months and from 25% to 20% for the
       following three months.
       Maximum rate of benefit, including the flat-rate and earnings-related elements, reduced from 100%
       to 75% of reference earnings.
       Waiting period for earnings-related supplement extended from twelve to eighteen days.
       Increase in the amount of earnings disregarded in the calculation of earnings-related benefit.

Unemployment

1982   Closer checks on benefit claims.

1983   Waiting period for earnings-related supplement extended from twelve to eighteen days. Earnings-
       related supplent no longer paid to workers on short-time and flat-rate benefit for such workers
       reduced. Change in method of assessing eligibility of smallholders for unemployment assistance.
       Assessment on a national basis related to valuation of the farm discontinued.
       Earnings-related benefit reduced in same way as for recipients of sickness benefit.

Maternity

1983   Maternity grant of IRL 8 discontinued.
       Maternity benefit reduced from 80% to 70% of reference salary.
       Earnings-related benefit reduced in same way as for recipients of sickness benefit.

Health

1983   Cut in funding of private care; increase in threshold over which cost of prescribed medicines is
       refunded; cut in list of drugs which can be prescribed for patients eligible for free general
       practitioner care and free pharmaceuticals.
       Restriction of eligibility of students for free medical care.

Education

1983   Charges introduced for school transport; increase in pupil-teacher ratios; increase in teaching hours.
       Increase in examination fees and in fees in teacher training colleges.
       Abolition of fee waiver for children of staff in third level institutions.
       Reduced provision for running costs of schools.

Housing

1984   Decision to raise rents in local authority housing and to shift cost of minor repairs and routine
       maintenance to tenants.

waiting periods for both the flat-rate and earnings-related elements of sickness and unemployment benefits have been increased and checks on claimants have been tightened. For workers on short-time the earnings-related benefit supplement has been abolished and the flat-rate benefit reduced.

In the area of health services the main targets of retrenchment have been public subventions for private care and expenditure on drugs. Public funding of private care has been reduced, the list of drugs available to those eligible for free general practitioner services has been restricted and the threshold for refunds of the cost of prescribed drugs for the remainder of the population has been raised considerably. Eligibility of students for public health services has been restricted. There have also been cuts in educational services through measures such as raising of pupil-teacher ratios, increases in teaching hours for some categories of teachers, introduction of charges for school transport and reductions in provision for running costs and materials in schools. With regard to housing, a decision was taken in 1984 to raise rents for public housing and to shift maintenance costs to tenants.

Trends in the level of social benefits also provide an indication of the pace and direction of change in social programmes. Tables 9 and 16 above show that standard cash benefits rose rapidly in real terms in the late 1970s and early 1980s. Between 1975 and 1982, old age pensions increased by over 40 percent in real terms, while unemployment benefits went up by over 25 percent. Table 50 shows that the rate of benefit increase declined sharply in 1983, leading to a fall in the real value of unemployment benefits and child allowances. All benefits fell slightly in real terms in 1984. However, while the rapid growth of real transfer payments has been halted since 1983, the substantial improvements made in the late 1970s and early 1980s have not so far been significantly eroded.

Table 50	Trends in real benefits, 1975-84			
	1975	1982	1983	1984
	Irish pounds per week			
Old age contributory pension	10.50	14.77	14.98	14.75
Old age non-contributory pension	8.85	12.64	12.82	12.63
Unemployment/sickness benefit	9.40	11.61	11.56	11.39
Unemployment assistance	7.70	9.63	9.60	9.45
	Irish pounds per month			
Child allowance: 1st child	2.30	4.13	3.74	3.69
2nd child	3.60	4.13	3.74	3.69
3rd child	4.35	4.13	3.74	3.69

Trends in social expenditure and public employment support the impression that social programmes have only come under strong pressure for restraint since 1982. As shown in Section II, the expansion of social expenditure was halted temporarily in the period 1976-78 and the GDP share of expenditure fell by over two percentage points. Growth resumed, however, in 1979 and by 1981 the GDP share of social expenditure was over four percentage points above its 1978 level [295]. At the time of writing, National Accounts data on social expenditure are not available for the period since 1981. However, the budgetary data shown in Table 51 indicate that expenditure continued to grow relative to GDP up to 1982, increasing its ratio by almost three percentage points in the two years from 1981. The growth rate decreased in 1983, however, and the expenditure share fell in 1984. In real terms, social expenditure also continued to grow quite rapidly until 1982, with a sharp decrease in the growth rate in 1983 and a virtual halt in 1984. Current expenditure continued to grow up to 1984, albeit at a reduced rate, while capital expenditure fell sharply in 1984.

Table 51		Social expenditure, 1980–84 (a)			
	1980	1981	1982	1983	1984
At constant (1975) prices					
Health	337.9	333.3	342.8	345.0	332.5
Education	259.2	283.0	303.3	301.3	303.0
Housing	125.5	145.1	156.1	165.0	164.1
Income maintenance	439.2	494.9	601.8	639.7	653.6
Total	1 162.8	1 256.3	1 404.0	1 451.0	1 453.2
Currant	1 021.8	1 093.9	1 234.0	1 283.0	1 296.7
Capital	141.0	162.4	170.0	168.0	156.5
As % of GDP					
Health	7.4	7.1	7.0	7.0	6.6
Education	5.7	6.0	6.2	6.1	6.0
Housing	2.8	3.2	3.3	3.5	3.4
Income maintenance	9.6	10.6	12.4	13.0	13.0
Total	25.5	26.9	28.9	29.6	29.0

(a) Data are on a budget basis and are not, therefore, comparable with the national accounts data shown in Appendix Table 3.

The disaggregation of expenditure by programme shown in Table 51 reveals that health care spending has come under most pressure in recent years, having fallen by almost 4 percent in real terms in 1984 and having declined by almost one percentage point relative to GDP since 1980. Expenditure on education has remained more or less static in real terms since 1982 and has fallen slightly, relative to GDP. Housing expenditure continued to grow up to 1983 and fell slightly in 1984. Expenditure on income maintenance programmes continued to grow in real terms up to 1984, although its growth rate was reduced markedly from 1983 and its share of GDP stabilised.

The rapid expansion in public sector employment during the 1970s has been discussed in Section II. The details of annual changes in the numbers of public sector employees shown in Table 52 reveal that the rate of expansion accelerated from 1977 and remained very rapid up to 1981. During this six year period public sector employment grew at an average rate of over 3 percent per annum. The rate of expansion decreased in 1982 and there was virtually no growth in 1983. With regard to employment in the social services, health service employment showed no growth in 1982 and fell in 1983 while employment in the educational sector continued to expand up to 1983.

On balance, the welfare state has fared relatively well in the period since 1973. Indeed, social expenditure, employment in the social services and living standards of welfare beneficiaries all rose rapidly in the late 1970s and early 1980s. The year 1982

Table 52   Annual change in public service employment
1973–1983
(in %)

	Total public employment	Health	Education
1973	2.5	3.6	4.1
1974	3.4	3.9	5.4
1975	2.3	4.9	2.7
1976	2.4	1.5	3.0
1977	3.1	7.1	1.7
1978	3.2	7.0	6.2
1979	3.5	6.0	3.7
1980	3.2	3.4	4.3
1981	3.2	4.2	2.3
1982	2.2	0.2	4.7
1983	0.2	- 1.0	3.3

clearly represents a turning point for the welfare state, with the adoption of restrictive budgetary policies and the implementation of cuts in social programmes in the following two years. However, the impact of the measures taken to date has been to halt the expansion of the welfare state rather than to bring about any significant dismantling of social programmes. Social expenditure, public sector employment and real transfer payments have all fallen back slightly, but the substantial gains made in the period to 1982 have not to date been eroded.

2. Medium-term prospects for social programmes

Although social programmes did not suffer any major retrenchment up to 1984, the prospects for the remainder of the decade do not appear encouraging. Budgetary policy is now under severe constraint due to the necessity of achieving correction of fiscal imbalances without incurring further increases in the already high tax burden. As such, public expenditure, of which social expenditure is a major element, will be under greater pressure in the coming years than has been the case up to now. A further constraint on expenditure will arise from the still increasing share of resources absorbed by interest payments on the public debt.

Policy in relation to the social programmes in the period 1985-87 has been set out in the Government's recently published economic and social plan [296]. A key objective of the Plan is the achievement of substantial reductions in the budget deficit and public borrowing (Table 53). In contrast to policy in the period up to 1984, fiscal adjustment in the coming years is to be achieved via reductions in public expenditure rather than on the basis of further increases in taxation.

As shown in Table 53, the share of taxation in GNP is projected to remain at its existing level up to 1987, while the share of current expenditure is projected to fall by over 2 percent and that of capital expenditure by almost 3 percent. Since expenditure on Central Fund services (consisting mainly of debt service payments and contributions to the EC budget) is not projected to fall, the entire reduction in current spending is to be borne by public consumption expenditure and expenditure on transfers and subsidies. Reductions in expenditure on public service pay constitute a central element of planned expenditure restraint, accounting for three-quarters of the projected drop in current expenditure. The Exchequer allocation for pay is to increase by 4.4 percent annually over the period of the Plan, implying a reduction in real public service pay when the Plan's assumptions concerning inflation rates are taken into account [297].

Table 53   Target budget profile, 1984–1987

As % of GNP

	Budget provision 1984	Planned provision 1987
Total current expenditure	48.25	46.00
Central fund	13.25	13.25
Supply services	35.00	32.75
Total revenue	40.75	41.00
Tax	36.50	36.50
Non-tax	4.25	4.50
Current budget deficit	7.50	5.00
Public capital programme	12.30	9.60
Borrowing for capital purposes	5.25	4.75
Exchequer borrowing requirement	12.75	9.75
Public sector borrowing requirement	17.00	11.25

Details of projected expenditure on the social programmes are shown in Table 54. Expenditure on health, education and income maintenance is projected to fall by 1.2 percent of GNP between 1985 and 1987, the bulk of the reduction being borne by current rather than capital expenditure. Capital expenditure on housing is projected to fall by 0.4 percent of GNP. The largest reduction is to be in health expenditure, while income maintenance expenditure is projected to fall only slightly. Since pay accounts for all but a small portion of current expenditure on education and for about two-thirds of expenditure on health, planned restraint on public service pay will account for a large part of the savings in these areas. In the case of health, further payroll savings are to come from redeployment of staff and an overall reduction in staffing levels [298].

Table 54   Projected expenditure on social programmes, 1984–1987

As % of GNP

	Budgeted 1984	Planned 1985	Provision 1986	1987	Change 1984–87
Current expenditure					
Education	5.75	5.43	5.32	5.34	− 0.41
Health	6.59	6.51	6.34	6.07	− 0.52
Income maintenance	8.56	8.59	8.46	8.34	− 0.22
Total	20.90	20.53	20.12	19.75	− 1.15
Capital expenditure					
Education	0.57	0.61	0.63	0.62	+ 0.05
Health	0.38	0.37	0.34	0.33	− 0.05
Housing	2.57	2.45	2.34	2.22	− 0.35
Total	3.52	3.53	3.31	3.27	− 0.25

The implications of these expenditure plans for the social programmes have not been explored in the Plan. The general strategy articulated therein emphasises greater selectivity of services, increased efficiency and cost effectiveness, and reductions or abandonment of services and structures no longer appropriate to current needs. However, an assessment of the Plan by the National Economic and Social Council points out that it contains little in the way of specific policy measures for attaining these objectives [299]. In the case of cash transfers, the Government have made a commitment to index long-term payments in line with inflation and short-term payments in line with net earnings [300]. Thus, a deterioration in living standards of welfare beneficiaries would appear to be excluded. However, projections by the National Economic and Social Council indicate that without any changes in programme coverage, increases in beneficiary numbers are likely to add between 2 percent and 3 percent per annum to expenditure on income maintenance schemes in the period 1985-87 [301]. On the assumption that net earnings will at least keep pace with inflation and given the projected rate of increase in consumer prices during the period of the Plan, indexation of benefits will add an additional 6.5 percent per annum to expenditure. As nominal GNP is expected to increase at a rate of 8 percent per annum, unless unemployment falls there is clearly going to be considerable tension between the objectives of containing the GNP share of expenditure and maintaining levels of benefit.

With regard to health and education, the proposed expenditure reductions imply increased efficiency if current levels of service are to be maintained. However, the National Economic and Social Council has pointed out that the Plan contains no proposals for achieving efficiency gains [302]. Indeed, given the stringent limits set on public service salaries in the Plan, the possibility of a productivity loss cannot be ruled out. The extent to which public service salaries can be held in line with the limits set in the Plan will be central to the attainment of the expenditure targets set for health and education. Achievement of the degree of salary restraint sought would represent a marked departure from experience since the late 1970s [303]. To the extent that salary targets are exceeded, levels of service may come under additional pressure in an effort to keep expenditure within the projected limits.

A more concise assessment of medium term prospects for social programmes is possible using the expenditure decomposition technique developed by the OECD [304]. As discussed in Section IV, changes in expenditure on a given programme can be decomposed into changes in demography, coverage and average benefit. Additionally, the effect of changes in input prices can be distinguished from that of changes in real average benefit by incorporating both general price inflation and relative price inflation in the social services into the growth accounting framework [305]. Thus, the growth rate of nominal social expenditure may be decomposed into the growth rates of five principal components:

(i) General inflation, measured by the GDP/GNP deflator;

(ii) Relative prices, measured in the case of health and education by changes in the deflators for these services relative to the GDP/GNP deflator, and in the case of cash benefits by relative changes in the private consumption deflator, which are taken as an indication of changes in the cost of maintaining living standards of beneficiaries [306];

(iii) Demography, changes in the size of the population relevant to a particular programme;

(iv) Coverage, changes in the proportion of the relevant population which actually benefits from the programme;

(v) Average real benefit.

As shown in a recent OECD study, this decomposition technique can be used not only to examine the determinants of past growth in social expenditure, but also to provide some perspective on possible future developments [307]. Given the necessary assumptions concerning economic trends and the policy stance of government in the medium-term, in conjunction with demographic projections, an assessment can be made of the pressures to which social programmes may be subject during the remainder of the decade. The limitations of this type of exercise have been clearly spelled out by the OECD [308]. Economic developments in the medium-term are uncertain and the policy stance of governments can change significantly over time. Moreover, while the decomposition of expenditures into their constituent parts can identify possible pressure points, it does not purport to show how social demands and economic constraints might ultimately be reconciled. However, despite the speculative nature of the exercise, it provides an informative illustration of the implications of evolving economic and demographic forces for social programmes.

The expenditure decomposition technique is used here to examine prospects for the major social programmes in the period 1984-1990. The economic scenario used in this context is based on the most recent short-term forecast by the OECD [309]. As this only runs to 1986, some assumption had to be made concerning developments over the remainder of the decade. The assumption is that the growth rate of GNP and the rate of inflation will remain at their 1986 levels for the period up to 1990 and that unemployment will continue to rise, although at a slower rate than in the first half of the decade. Thus, over the period 1984-1990 it is assumed that real GNP will grow at a rate of 2.5 percent per annum, that the GNP deflator will rise at an average rate of 5.5 percent per annum and that the private consumption deflator rises at the same rate as the GNP deflator. Projections of unemployment up to the beginning of the 1990s have been made by the National Economic and Social Council [310]. The one adopted for the purposes of our scenario assumes that unemployment will continue to rise, although at a much slower rate than during the first half of the decade [311].

As shown by the OECD, prospects for social programmes in the context of this economic scenario may be assessed in either of two ways [312]. Some assumption can be made about the level of social expenditure relative to GNP that government is prepared to accept and in the light of projected demographic developments the implications for provision of social services and cash benefits can be demonstrated. Alternatively, some assumption can be made concerning the demand for social programmes and the impact on the ratio of social expenditure to GNP traced through. Here the first approach is adopted since this reflects the current policy stance of government, that the level of social expenditure should be determined in relation to the supply of economic resources. To implement this approach, it will be assumed that the planned reduction of 1.2 percentage points in the share of social expenditure in GNP in the period 1985-87 will be implemented and that the social expenditure share will then be held constant for the remainder of the period up to 1990. The assumption of tight budgetary policies over the remainder of the decade seems reasonable in view of the fact that even if the targets set in the National Plan are attained, substantial imbalances in the public finances will still remain in 1987.

To complete the scenario, it is assumed that price inflation in the social services can be held down to the level of general inflation during the period under consideration, giving a zero relative price effect. In the case of cash benefits the relative price effect is also zero since the private consumption deflator is assumed to change at the same rate as general inflation. The growth rates of the relevant population groups are derived from demographic projections made by the National Economic and Social Council. It is assumed that programme coverage does not change. Given these assumptions and the projected growth rate of real GNP, the residual element in the scenario - the growth rate of average real benefit across the major programmes taken together - can be estimated [313].

A decomposition of social expenditure growth for five programmes in the period 1984-1990 in terms of the above scenario is shown in Table 55. As may be seen, the average real benefit across the five programmes could increase only very slightly - at 0.1 percent per annum. This is considerably less than the growth rate of real GNP (2.5 percent per annum) because demographic changes absorb most of the permitted growth in social expenditure. It is also substantially less than the growth rate of real GDP per capita, which averages 1.4 percent per annum, implying a relative fall in standards of welfare provision [314]. The change in average real benefit need not necessarily be the same across all programmes as has been assumed in Table 55 for the sake of convenience. However, to the extent that real benefits increased more quickly under some programmes, this would have to be offset by a slower increase or even a decrease under other programmes.

Table 55   Decomposition of the growth of social expenditure, 1984-1990 (a)

| | Initial expenditure share (b) | Deflated expenditure (c) | Relative prices (d) | Real expenditure | of which | | | Final expenditure share |
					demography (e)	coverage	average real benefit	
	1984			Annual growth rates (%), 1984-90 (f)				1990
Education	6.3	0.8	0.0	0.8	0.7	0.0	0.1	
Health	7.0	1.2	0.0	1.2	1.1	0.0	0.1	
Old age pensions	3.9	0.8	0.0	0.8	0.7	0.0	0.1	
Unemployment compensation	3.8	4.6	0.0	4.6	4.5	0.0	0.1	
Sickness benefits	2.1	0.9	0.0	0.9	0.8	0.0	0.1	
Total	23.1	1.6	0.0	1.6	1.5	0.0	0.1	21.9

(a) For details of methodology see OECD, Social Expenditure 1960-1990. Paris, 1985, p.44.
(b) Budgeted expenditure in 1984 as % of GNP.
(c) Deflated by GNP deflator which is assumed to increase at an average rate of 5.5 percent per annum.
(d) Relative prices assumed to increase at same rate as GNP deflator.
(e) Relevant population for education is 4-24 age group, for health the total population, for old age pensions the population aged 65 and over, for unemployment compensation the number of unemployed and for sickness benefits the insured labour force.
(f) Average annual compound growth rates.

Thus, in event of a continuation of relatively slow economic growth, it should be possible for social programmes to absorb projected demographic pressures without relinquishing the gains in coverage and benefit levels made since the 1960s, provided that no further reduction is sought in the GNP share of social expenditure after 1987 and that the relative prices of education and health services increase no faster than general inflation. However, while any major dismantling of social programmes appears unlikely within the scenario drawn here, the implied halt in improvements in coverage and benefits during the remainder of the decade would represent a significant departure from experience during the 1960s and 1970s, when programmes expanded rapidly and real levels of service and benefit improved substantially.

The conclusions drawn from this type of analysis can only be as firm as the assumptions upon which they rest [315]. With regard to the economic scenario, faster growth in real GNP would be capable of supporting a concomitant increase in the growth rate of social expenditure while slower growth would require a concomitant reduction. Under either scenario, however, average real benefits would still grow more slowly than real per capita GNP. Trends in the unemployment rate will also be influential in determining the degree of pressure on social programmes. A smaller increase or a fall in the unemployment rate would free additional resources for improvements in levels of benefit. If anything, however, the scenario presented above may err on the side of optimism, particularly concerning trends in programme coverage and relative prices of the social services. It may be quite unrealistic to expect that there will be no further increases in coverage. There will almost certainly be increasing demands on social programmes through the remainder of the decade. For instance, there is scope for further increases in post-compulsory education participation rates [316]. There is also scope for increases in the coverage of the social insurance system, for demands from sections of the community whose needs are at present inadequately met and for the emergence of new needs and demands. Within the economic and policy scenario outlined in Table 55, any expansion in programme coverage would have to be offset by reductions in average real benefits.

For relative prices of health services and education to increase no faster than general inflation, as has been assumed above, would represent a significant departure from experience in the period since the late 1970s, when the average rate of increase in the price of social services has exceeded that of general inflation [317]. Trends in the coming years will depend mainly on the development of public service salaries. While efforts to restrain salary increases have met with some success in recent years, it is likely to be difficult to achieve the degree of restraint implied by the scenario in Table 55 throughout the remainder of the decade [318]. Within the assumed budgetary constraint, any relative price increases in the social services would have to be traded off against reductions in average real benefits.

A final element of over-optimism in the scenario presented here may be the assumption that no further reductions will be sought in the social expenditure share of GNP after 1987. Given that a substantial budget deficit will still remain by then, the possibility of additional retrenchment in social spending during the final years of the decade cannot be ruled out of the question. Thus, it would appear that at best social programmes can be maintained at their existing levels up to 1990. This would, however, imply a fall in levels of welfare provision relative to general standards of living in the community, given that the projected increase in real levels of benefit and service is considerably less than that of real per capita GNP. There is unlikely to be any scope for expansion of the welfare state and there could well be considerable pressure on levels of service and benefit.

3. The changing political context

The future of the welfare state will be shaped not only by economic constraints but also by political factors. It is important therefore to investigate whether there are any signs of political strains emerging over issues of social policy. This section of the study explores whether there are any symptoms in Ireland of either declining support for the welfare state or conflict over attempts to curtail social programmes. Following a brief discussion of potential constellations of welfare interests, some evidence from public opinion polls on attitudes towards social policy issues is examined. The section concludes with an exploration of whether welfare interests have been reflected in political activity in recent years.

As shown in Section II, the welfare state has become a major source of support for a sizeable section of the population, with some 17 percent of the adult population depending on benefits as a long-term source of income in 1981 [319]. In addition to this, health, education and housing services represent a substantial benefit for certain categories of households [320]. Presumably, those sections of the population which are major beneficiaries of the welfare state have a strong interest in the expansion of social programmes, or at least in maintaining the *status quo*. The financing of social programmes has, however, placed an increasing tax burden on the economically active population, although sections of this population may also derive sizeable benefits from the welfare state. Nevertheless, to the extent that immediate costs in the form of income tax and social insurance contributions exceed immediate benefits, groups within the economically active population may have an interest in seeking a reduction of their tax burden and/or improvements in the benefits which they receive.

An approximate indication of the size of potential welfare interest constituencies is provided by Table 56, which shows the economic status of the adult population in 1981. Some 16 percent of the adult population were either unemployed, unable to work due to permanent disability or retired. It can be assumed that the majority of these persons were in receipt of cash transfers from the state and so would have a strong interest in the welfare state. It is difficult to identify any clear welfare interests among the remaining groups who were economically inactive - students, those engaged in home duties and those looking for a first job - who comprised 36 percent of the adult population. Doubtless, these groups contained a proportion of welfare beneficiaries. For instance, almost a fifth of those engaged in home duties were aged 65 or over and presumably a large proportion of these were in receipt of state pensions [321]. A proportion of those aged under 65 in this group would also have been receiving survivors' pensions or other benefits of various types. A small proportion of those seeking their first job would have been in receipt of unemployment assistance. It is also likely that a small proportion of those in the economically active group would have been receiving benefits. For instance, there is no retirement condition attached to the contributory old age pension, nor are recipients of widows' contributory pensions and deserted wife's benefit precluded from working.

Table 56   Population aged 15 and over classified by economic status in 1981

Economic status	(000)	%
At work	1 150.7	47.8
employers and self-employed	(243.1)	(10.1)
assisting relatives	(29.7)	(1.2)
employees	(877.9)	(36.5)
Unemployed	112.9	4.7
Unable to work (a)	83.0	3.5
Retired	194.1	8.1
Looking for first regular job	19.7	0.8
Students	203.1	8.4
Home duties	638.1	26.5
Other	4.0	0.2
Total	2 405.6	100.0
Memorandum:		
Public sector employees	317.0	13.0
White-collar employees	510.0	21.0
Skilled manual employees	196.0	8.0
Semi-skilled and unskilled		
manual employees	172.0	7.0

(a) Unable to work due to permanent sickness or disability.

A clearer impression of the size of the welfare beneficiary group can be obtained by taking the information contained in Table 56 in conjunction with data on the number of welfare recipients. At the end of 1981, some 14 percent of the adult population were in receipt of state pensions of various types, 7 percent were in receipt of unemployment compensation and 3 percent were in receipt of sickness cash benefits [322]. The adult dependants of these beneficiaries constituted a further 6 percent of the adult population, bringing the total proportion in receipt of benefits to about 30 percent. While a percentage of these would have been transient recipients, it is nevertheless evident that a substantial minority of the adult population are likely to have a strong interest in maintaining existing levels of welfare provision. The size of this group is likely to have increased since 1981 due to rising unemployment.

The interest structure within the working population is likely to be rather complex. Analysis by Hannan, O'Connell and Rottman has revealed important variations in the impact of social expenditure and taxation on different socio-economic classes [323]. Employers and proprietors are in a relatively favourable position, being taxed very lightly while benefiting to a moderate extent from social programmes. The working classes derive substantial benefits from the welfare state, but for all except the most marginal categories this is counterbalanced by their tax burden. Moreover, the position of this group is complicated by the fact that except in the case of unskilled workers, welfare gains tend to be concentrated in the later stages of the life cycle while younger households tend to be net contributors to the system. Middle class employees are heavy contributors to the tax system, while receiving little in the way of cash transfers. However, the middle classes derive major benefits from the educational system, and also receive sizeable subsidies through the housing and health systems.

A detailed breakdown of the working population into social class categories in 1981 is not feasible. However, turning again to Table 56, it will be seen that the self-employed, employers and assisting relatives constituted 11 percent of the adult population in that year. Given the advantageous position of this group under existing arrangements, it seems reasonable to assume that they would tend to defend the *status quo*. However, since their advantage lies more in their relatively light tax liability than in their gains from the welfare state, attempts to increase the tax burden of this group could conceivably lead to their demanding a reduction in public expenditure. This group also contains employers, whose non-wage labour costs have risen considerably in recent years as a result of increases in social insurance contributions and who might, therefore, favour a reduction in social expenditure.

Employees comprised 36 percent of the adult population in 1981. With regard to the class structure of the employee group, approximately two-fifths were manual workers and three-fifths were in white collar occupations. Given the present distribution of taxes and benefits, it might be expected that white collar employees and the skilled working class, who comprised about 30 percent of the adult population in 1981, would have an interest in seeking a reduction of their tax burden, or at least a change in the present pattern of gains and losses to achieve a more favourable balance for themselves. It is less likely, however, that these groups would favour a curtailment of social programmes. Over a third of employees work in the public sector and presumably a large proportion of these have an interest in defending the welfare state. Among private sector employees there could be some ambivalence towards the welfare state. Middle class employees might possibly support retrenchment in the more visibly redistributive programmes, such as cash transfers and some sectors of the health services, while resisting curtailment in the areas of expenditure which benefit them most, such as education and the social subsidies channelled though the taxation system. Within the working class, the differentiation between contributing and beneficiary households could weaken support for the welfare state among skilled and semi-skilled workers.

On balance, a substantial minority of the adult population have a strong interest in the welfare state as a source of either transfer income or employment. As such, there is a relatively large constituency which might be expected to resist attempts to curtail social programmes. On the other hand, there is also a relatively large group of skilled working class and middle class employees on whom rising public expenditure has imposed a heavy tax burden and who could constitute a potential source of protest against taxation. It is less likely, however, that this group would support cuts in social programmes. While the self-employed would appear to have an interest in defending the *status quo*, this interest would appear to lie more in resisting increases in their tax burden than in defending the welfare state.

The mere fact of being able tentatively to identify potential welfare interest constellations within the population does not necessarily imply that such interests are actually clearly perceived by the groups involved or that they will be translated into political action. Attitude surveys and public opinion polls can provide an indication of how issues related to the welfare state are perceived by different groups. Unfortunately, survey evidence of this type is extremely limited in Ireland. Nevertheless, such evidence as does exist merits examination.

A national random sample survey of 2,359 adults carried out in 1976/77 by Davis et al. examined attitudes towards poverty and related social issues [324]. This survey included a question tapping beliefs about improving social welfare benefits, respondants being asked to rate this issue on a series of scales. The results are summarised in Table 57, which shows that the sample population were generally supportive of improving benefits. The responses also indicated a high degree of awareness of this issue. However, there was also a strong perception that improvement of benefits would be difficult, controversial and expensive. The survey found little relationship between socio-demographic characteristics and beliefs about improving benefits. The characteristics considered included sex, age, urban/rural location, income and education. Only educational attainment showed a consistent correlation with attitudes towards this issue, with those of lower educational attainment, who are likely to have lower incomes and to rely more on benefits, considering improvement of benefits to be more important and more feasible [325]. There was some indication that rural respondants thought improvement of benefits to be less important than did urban respondants. Age also showed a slight correlation with attitudes, with older respondants tending to be more positively disposed towards improving benefits.

Table 57   Attitudes towards improving social welfare benefits

Percent distributions

To improve social benefits is		neutral		To improve social benefits is
Important	88.5	4.3	7.3	Unimportant
Desirable	87.7	6.9	5.4	Undesirable
Relevant	83.5	9.8	6.7	Irrelevant
Fair	58.5	14.9	26.5	Unfair
Easy	17.6	6.8	75.5	Difficult
Non-controversial	8.5	10.9	80.7	Controversial
Cheap	2.3	3.2	94.4	Costly

Since the survey by Davis et al. was carried out in 1976/77, the results may now be somewhat dated. However, to the extent that the survey found strong support for improving benefits, it might be expected that attempts to curtail social programmes would meet with some opposition. On the other hand, the authors of the survey point out that in view of the fact that there was a widespread perception of improvements in benefits being difficult and expensive to achieve, there could be considerable resistance to funding social programmes if this were to lead to increases in taxation [326].

Some indication of the perceived political salience of social policy issues is provided by opinion surveys carried out during recent general election campaigns. Table 58 reports the relevant results of an opinion poll conducted during the 1981 general election campaign [327]. When asked to choose the most important election issue from the list shown here, only a tiny proportion of respondants picked pensions/social welfare, housing or taxation. Not surprisingly, given the high levels of unemployment and inflation at the time, these latter issues were considered to be by far the most important ones. However, when asked to indicate other important issues, only 20 percent of respondants chose pensions/social welfare and only 16 percent chose housing, while about a third chose taxation. A poll conducted during the November 1982 general election campaign provides a similar picture [328]. Only 15 percent of respondants considered provision of social welfare and health benefits to be an important election issue, while 12 percent chose provision of a fairer tax system and 14 percent chose sorting out the public finances.

While the perceived salience of social policy and taxation as election issues appears to be generally rather low, there is some evidence that attitudes vary according to age and social class. As may be seen from Table 58, older respondants, those approaching or over retirement age, placed more emphasis on provision of social benefits than did younger respondants. Conversely, taxation was seen as a more important issue by younger respondants than by older ones. With regard to social class, concern about provision of social benefits was stronger among the semi-skilled and unskilled working class and marginal farmers than among other groups. This is consistent with the fact that the lower socio-economic groups rely heavily on the welfare state [329]. Farmers were generally less concerned with improvement of benefits than were the non-agricultural classes. Concern about taxation was also stronger among the non-agricultural classes than among farmers and among the higher socio-economic groups than among the lower ones.

There have been two very limited surveys of attitudes towards curtailment of social programmes. These cannot be taken as being representative of general opinion since neither was based on random sample survey methods and the sample group in each case was relatively small. Nevertheless, the results are of some interest. A survey carried out in 1983 by one of the main daily newspapers, The Irish Times, invited readers to give their opinions of which areas of public spending should be subjected to cuts and which should be protected [330]. This elicited 599 responses, predominantly from male employees in the 20-40 age group. Given that the readership of the newspaper tends to be drawn mainly from the higher socio-economic groups, it can be assumed that the respondents belonged mainly to the middle classes. Broadly speaking, therefore, the sample was drawn predominantly from middle class employees, a group which has tentatively been identified as a potential source of tax protests. However, social programmes came low on the list of areas favoured by this group for spending cuts, with curtailment being preferred in areas such as defence, foreign aid, transport and agriculture.

The second survey of attitudes towards public spending cuts involved senior figures in the business community [331]. One hundred chief executives of major companies and financial institutions were included in the survey. Social welfare and health came very high on the list of areas favoured by this group for spending cuts, notwithstanding the

Table 58

Perception of important election issues by sex, age and social class, 1981

Percentage of issues called most important (important)

	Total	Sex		Age					Class					
		male	female	18–24	25–34	35–49	50–64	65+	Professionals, employers, managers	Salaried employees	Other non-manual	Manual workers	Large farmers	Small farmers
Unemployment/jobs for young people	48 (83)	47 (80)	49 (86)	63 (92)	45 (83)	42 (79)	44 (83)	43 (74)	49 (87)	54 (90)	49 (84)	47 (81)	38 (77)	43 (77)
Prices/inflation/food prices	27 (74)	27 (72)	27 (76)	24 (64)	29 (74)	24 (80)	31 (79)	28 (74)	28 (76)	26 (78)	26 (73)	28 (69)	31 (74)	26 (80)
Strikes and industrial relations	3 (21)	2 (22)	4 (20)	3 (20)	2 (21)	3 (20)	3 (23)	6 (22)	4 (21)	3 (21)	4 (21)	3 (23)	2 (19)	1 (18)
Northern Ireland/ security	6 (25)	5 (26)	6 (24)	6 (27)	7 (30)	6 (26)	6 (21)	3 (18)	4 (35)	8 (23)	6 (23)	4 (29)	6 (14)	7 (21)
Crime in the streets	3 (20)	3 (18)	3 (21)	1 (17)	3 (17)	2 (19)	4 (23)	4 (23)	5 (21)	1 (21)	5 (25)	3 (18)	2 (18)	1 (9)
Agriculture	3 (17)	4 (21)	2 (14)	2 (8)	2 (16)	3 (18)	4 (24)	5 (23)	0 (4)	0 (6)	1 (8)	0 (8)	17 (56)	13 (50)
Taxation	5 (32)	7 (35)	3 (30)	7 (38)	6 (39)	5 (34)	3 (27)	2 (21)	9 (40)	4 (34)	4 (37)	5 (30)	3 (29)	4 (24)
Pensions and social welfare	3 (20)	2 (18)	3 (21)	1 (12)	2 (14)	1 (18)	3 (25)	9 (36)	0 (14)	1 (14)	2 (19)	6 (29)	0 (9)	2 (18)
Family law reform	6 (9)	0 (7)	1 (11)	0 (8)	2 (12)	1 (10)	0 (7)	0 (3)	2 (12)	2 (12)	0 (10)	1 (9)	0 (1)	0 (2)
Housing (costs/provision)	1 (16)	1 (15)	1 (17)	2 (22)	1 (20)	1 (16)	0 (10)	0 (9)	0 (16)	1 (16)	2 (18)	2 (20)	0 (3)	0 (8)
Others	1 (1)	1 (2)	1 (-)	1 (1)	1 (1)	1 (3)	1 (-)	0 (1)	1 (4)	0 (1)	1 (2)	1 (1)	0 (0)	2 (2)
Do not know/no reply	1 (0)	1 (0)	1 (0)	1 (0)	1 (0)	1 (0)	1 (0)	0 (0)	0 (0)	1 (0)	1 (0)	2 (0)	0 (0)	0 (0)
Respondents (N)	1 050	523	527	226	236	231	209	148	105	185	249	297	94	120

fact that it was recognised that curtailment of these programmes would be likely to have a strong detrimental impact on the poorer sections of the community. Cuts in educational expenditure proved less popular as it was felt retrenchment in this area could have adverse consequences for business and industry.

Given the limited nature of the available evidence, it is not possible to draw any firm conclusions concerning attitudes towards the welfare state. Notwithstanding the widespread support for improvements in social benefits found by Davis et al. in the late 1970s, social policy issues do not appear on the whole to have been considered particularly salient in the electoral arena in the early 1980s, although taxation was somewhat more salient. Since the two political opinion polls discussed above took place before the series of curtailments of social programmes implemented in 1983, there is no way of knowing whether the political salience of social policy issues changed subsequent to the cuts. There is some evidence that attitudes vary according to age and social class, with those in older age groups and lower socio-economic classes placing more emphasis on the provision of social benefits and less emphasis on taxation than do younger age groups and higher socio-economic classes. There is also some evidence that the farming community tends to be less concerned than other groups with social policy and taxation issues, and that the business community would tend to favour curtailment of social programmes. Thus, it would appear that to some extent attitudes towards the welfare state and related issues do tend to vary along the lines of interest discussed earlier. Confirmation of this would, however, require much more careful investigation than has been carried out to date.

Turning to the question of the political articulation of welfare interests, there have been some signs of mobilisation in recent years. At the mass level the major event has been the emergence of strong discontent within the employee sector with the current structure of taxation. The main point of contention has been the heavy burden of taxation borne by employees compared to the self-employed, the farming community and industry. In 1982, the employee sector contributed approximately 87 percent of income taxation, while the self-employed contributed 11 percent and the farming community less than 2 percent [332]. Between 1976 and 1983, the average tax rate for a single employee rose from 30 percent to almost 36 percent, while that for a married worker with a dependent spouse and two children rose from 20 percent to 25 percent. Marginal tax rates rose from 38.5 percent to 63.5 percent in the case of a single employee and from 38.5 to 43.5 percent in the case of a married one [333].

The first tax protests, in 1979, were sparked off by increases in income tax and social insurance contributions and by the failure of the government to undertake tax reforms sought by the trade union movement. Following the establishment of an official commission to examine the taxation system there was relative quiescence until 1982. Tax protests flared up again in this year and in 1983 in the wake of the announcement of further increases in taxation and social insurance contribution rates, with public demonstrations, work stoppages and the withholding of taxes for a period by employees in some firms. The discontent of the employee sector was intensified by the announcement of a wage freeze in 1983, by revelations concerning tax evasion and late payment of taxes by the non-employee sectors and by the persistent unresponsiveness of government to lobbying by the trade union movement for tax reform. The protests resulted in the introduction of a special tax relief for employees to offset partially the increase in the social insurance contribution rate. Efforts were also made to curb tax evasion.

The Irish tax protests have not included to any discernable extent the element of welfare backlash seen in a few Western countries in recent years. Although they attracted considerable support at the time, the protests failed to crystallise into a sustained mass campaign or to develop any organised political structure. Since 1983 the protests have died down again, although the tax system has not undergone any major reform. The protest campaign was coordinated by the trade union movement, which was careful to emphasise that the demand was for a more equitable distribution of the tax burden rather than a reduction in the overall level of taxation. Moreover, it was stressed at the time that the protests should not be used as an excuse to implement cuts in social expenditure. The Irish Congress of Trade Unions also sought to discourage withholding of taxes as a form of protest because of the possible adverse effects on welfare beneficiaries.

At the associational level there have been signs of polarisation between industry and labour over the welfare state and issues of fiscal policy. Apart from coordinating the tax protests, the trade unions, particularly those representing social service workers have been vocal in condemning cuts in social programmes. The major teachers' union threatened to strike over cuts in education, although such action did not actually materialise. However, plans to introduce charges on school buses had to be modified significantly following strong representations by educational bodies and government backbenchers. The main business organisations, by contrast, have repeatedly called for reductions in the levels of public expenditure and taxation and have criticised what they perceive as the *ad hoc* expansion of social programmes. Submissions to government by the representative bodies of employers and industry have emphasised that high levels of taxation and social transfers create disincentives for employment, have warned against the dangers of a financial crisis of the social security system and have advocated cost-containment measures and sharp reductions in public expenditure [334]. The business organisations have also been critical of the effect on private sector wage bargaining of what they perceive as excessive wage settlements in the public sector.

Issues relating to the future of the welfare state have also had some effect on party competition in recent years. To the extent that social class cleavages have only a minor impact on patterns of partisanship in Ireland, it is unlikely that either of the two main parties, Fianna Fail and Fine Gael, would seek to appeal to sectional welfare interests. Although opinion polls suggest that Fine Gael is weaker among working class voters and small farmers than Fianna Fail, and is stronger among the middle class and large farmers, both parties draw support in substantial proportions from all sections of the community [335]. Moreover, both parties seek to present themselves as classless, catch-all parties [336]. The Labour Party has a more discernable class basis, drawing support disproportionately from the working class. However, with only 9 percent of the vote, the electoral impact of this party is relatively minor.

The emergence of acute fiscal imbalances since the late 1970s has brought issues concerning the public finances to the forefront of the electoral arena, forcing the parties to take a stance on the subject [337]. The Fine Gael-Labour coalition government fell in January 1982, having been defeated in a parliamentary vote on the severe budget which it was proposing to introduce. However, in the ensuing election campaign, Fine Gael continued to stress the need for fiscal rectitude in order to eliminate the current budget deficit and reduce dependence on foreign borrowing. Fianna Fail responded by announcing that it too would adopt austere budgetary policies if elected. The Fianna Fail minority government which was elected only remained in office until November 1982 and the second general election campaign of the year saw further convergence between the two main parties on the necessity for fiscal austerity. Just prior to losing office, the Fianna Fail government had published a plan proposing severe cuts in public expenditure and this plan became a major element of its electoral platform [338]. Fine Gael also remained strongly committed to its well publicised stance on the need for budgetary restraint. Thus, while public expenditure has become a major electoral issue in the early 1980s, the positions of the two main parties on the issue have converged rather than diverged. There have, however, been signs of strain within the Fine Gael-Labour coalition which was returned to office in November 1982. While the senior coalition partner, Fine Gael, has pressed ahead with its policy of expenditure retrenchment, Labour has sought, albeit without much success, to limit the extent of cuts in social programmes.

With regard to electoral support, there has been no indication to date of an electoral backlash against parties advocating fiscal restraint. Although the Fine Gael-Labour coalition which had pursued restrictive budgetary policies was defeated in the general election of February 1982, the Fine Gael vote actually increased slightly in this election. The defeat of Fianna Fail in the November 1982 election was probably due more to signs of serious disunity within the party and the damaging effect on the party's image of a series of scandals which came to light during its period of office, than to its adoption of austere budgetary policies [339]. In any event the Fine Gael-Labour government which was returned to office on this occasion was proposing equally severe budgetary measures.

On the basis of the evidence presented here, it would appear that while there have been some signs of strain in recent years, the welfare state has not to date given rise to major political conflicts. It is possible to identify a number of potential welfare interest constellations and there is some evidence that attitudes towards social programmes and taxation tend to vary along these interest lines. However, while there has been some polarisation at the associational level between business and labour over issues of social policy and public finance, there is little other sign of interest constellations crystallising into politically articulate groupings in support of or opposition to the welfare state.

At the level of the party system the weak influence of social class on partisanship would appear to preclude any restructuring of support around welfare interests. Moreover, social policy issues are not apparently considered by the electorate to be of major importance. There have been tensions within the Fine Gael-Labour coalition government over curtailment of social programmes, but the two main parties, Fine Gael and Fianna Fail appear to be firmly committed to a policy of fiscal restraint. Attempts to curtail social programmes have not so far met with major opposition. Although there have been some objections, the government has succeeded in implementing most of the planned curtailments without major difficulty. As such, it would appear that the political limits to retrenchment have not yet been reached.

The main conflict to date has been over taxation and there is clearly potential for further tension over this issue. Attempts to increase the tax burden of the farming community, the self-employed and industry are likely to meet with strong opposition and could well give rise to pressure for reductions in public expenditure. On the other hand, failure to implement reforms is likely to lead to further tax protests from employees and could well alienate some groups within the employee sector from the welfare state. Moreover, reform of the taxation system would appear to be a crucial factor in establishing a firmer basis for the public finances.

4. The future of the Irish welfare state

As a result of the rapid expansion of the welfare state in the 1960s and 1970s the share of national resources devoted to social expenditure in Ireland has risen to a level comparable to that found in much wealthier European countries. This expansion has been underpinned by the imposition of a heavy tax burden and, more recently, by public borrowing on a substantial scale. The limits to the growth of the welfare state now appear to have been reached, at least for the time being. The pressing need to restore order to the public finances has already led to curtailment of social expenditure, with further cuts planned over the coming years. The scenario developed above in this section suggests that social programmes will be under considerable pressure during the remainder of the decade. The magnitude of the imbalances in the public finances and the limited scope for increases in tax revenues will impose severe constraints on public expenditure. In addition to this budgetary constraint, social programmes will be under pressure from demographic developments, high unemployment and heavy public sector payroll costs. While the future of the welfare state will be closely dependent on economic developments, it appears unlikely that conditions will improve sufficiently in the medium term to permit any expansion of existing social programmes and the scope for accommodating the new social demands which will inevitably emerge in the coming years is likely to be extremely limited.

Within the limits imposed by economic constraints, the future of the welfare state will also depend on political developments. Although there is no evidence of a welfare backlash supported by a significant section of the population, the political limits to the expansion of social programmes appear also to have been reached for the present. The resistance to taxation which has developed in recent years will impose a significant limitation on the level of public expenditure which can be sustained in the future. Moreover, both of the main political parties, Fianna Fail and Fine Gael, are now placing strong emphasis on the need for expenditure restraint until such time as fiscal balance is restored. Although the Labour Party has sought to reduce the extent of expenditure cuts, its efforts have not met with any marked degree of success so far. The existence of large groups within the community who derive substantial benefits from the welfare state will probably preclude any large scale dismantling of social programmes, but the success of the government in implementing restrictive policies since 1982 has demonstrated that limited cuts are politically feasible in the current economic climate.

The limit on the share of national resources which can be devoted to the welfare state in the medium term poses a major challenge for social policy in Ireland. As shown in Section III, there are serious shortcomings in the effectiveness and efficiency of the existing social programmes. The impact of expenditure restraint will depend to a significant degree on whether or not the functioning of these programmes can be improved. In a situation where the welfare state is under considerable financial pressure, it is essential that priorities and costs be carefully examined with a view to putting the available resources to the most effective use. While some erosion of real levels of welfare provision may be unavoidable, the main danger is that expenditure will be curtailed in an *ad hoc* fashion, with little consideration for the distributional consequences or the effect on the efficient functioning of social programmes.

The establishment of social policy priorities is, of course, a matter for political decision. However, in view of the tight limits on social expenditure which are likely to continue for the foreseeable future, it would appear to be essential that the available resources be concentrated on those most in need. There is considerable scope for improving the redistributive impact of social programmes. The analysis in Section III has shown that while cash transfers effect a significant redistribution of income, the same is not true of expenditure on the social services. Expenditure on education benefits higher income groups disproportionately because of their relatively greater participation in post-compulsory education. The housing and health systems also contain important elements of regressivity. Social benefits channelled through the tax system in the form of tax reliefs are another example of expenditures which are of most benefit to the higher income groups.

Improving the redistributive impact of the welfare state will require not only changes in the incidence of social benefits but also reform of the taxation system. Among the major criticisms which can be levelled at the existing system are the inequitable distribution of the direct tax burden among different groups in society, the heavy reliance on indirect taxation which has a regressive impact, and the narrowing of the tax base which has resulted from the virtual elimination of taxes on capital and wealth over the years and the provision of a wide range of tax reliefs.

Given the extent to which the current distributional outcomes of the welfare state are embedded in the social class structure, reforms aimed at achieving greater redistribution could give rise to conflict. The more advantaged groups are likely to resist attempts to erode their benefits or increase their tax liability. Increasing the selectivity of social programmes also carries the risk of rendering them more vulnerable to attack by non-benefiting groups. Nevertheless, the current financing problems of the welfare state and the shortcomings in existing provisions make it imperative that reforms be undertaken. During the 1960s and 1970s, high economic growth rates enabled successive governments to expand social programmes simultaneously on a range of fronts, largely avoiding the need to choose between competing demands or to confront issues of programme effectiveness and efficiency. If social needs are to be satisfactorily met and social expenditure is to be kept within affordable limits in the more difficult economic climate of the 1980s, important technical and political choices will have to be made. It will be necessary to specify the objectives of social programmes much more clearly than has been done in the past, to establish the priorities among these objectives, to improve the functioning of programmes and to enhance their flexibility in responding to new pressures and demands. Finding the political will to institute the necessary reforms will be the main challenge for policy makers in the coming years.

Notes

[1] For details of the early development of the public health system see Brendan Hensey, *The Health Services of Ireland*. Dublin, Institute of Public Administration, 1979 (3rd edition); the development of the Poor Law system is dealt with in Seamus O'Cinneide, 'The development of the home assistance service', *Administration*, 17 (1969), pp. 284-308; the growth of social insurance and social assistance have been documented in Desmond Farley, *Social Insurance and Social Assistance in Ireland*. Dublin, Institute of Public Administration, 1964; the history of the housing system is described in P.J. Meghan, *Housing in Ireland* Dublin, Institute of Public Administration, 1964; the early history of the education system is dealt with in J. Coolahan, *Irish Education: Its History and Structure*. Dublin, Institute of Public Administration, 1981, and in D.H. Akenson, *The Irish Education Experiment: The National System of Education in the Nineteenth Century*. London, Routledge and Kegan Paul, 1970, and *A Mirror to Kathleen's Face: Education in Independent Ireland 1922-1960*. Montreal and London, McGill and Queen's University Press, 1975.

2   Publicly funded dispensaries had been gradually growing up around the country during the first half of the nineteenth century, but the 1851 legislation provided for the establishment of a uniform and consolidated service. See F.S.L. Lyons, *Ireland Since the Famine* Fontana, 1973 (revised edition), pp. 77-79, and Hensey, *op. cit.*, p. 8.

3   See, for instance, Basil Chubb, *The Government and Politics of Ireland.* Stanford, Stanford University Press, 1982 (2nd edition), p. 13.

4   See James Meenan, *The Irish Economy Since 1922* Liverpool, Liverpool University Press, 1970, pp. 35-36, 245-246.

5   J.C.M Eason, 'An analysis showing the objects of expenditure and the sources of revenue during the financial years 1924/25 to 1929/30', *Journal of the Statistical and Social Inquiry Society of Ireland* 1930/31, pp. 1-13, cited in Finola Kennedy, *Public Social Expenditure in Ireland.* Dublin, Economic and Social Research Institute, 1975, p. 1.

6   E. Rumpf and A.C. Hepburn, *Nationalism and Socialism in Twentieth Century Ireland.* Liverpool, Liverpool University Press, 1977.

7   See, for instance, Most Rev. J. Dignan, 'Social security: outlines of a scheme of national health insurance', pamphlet published 11th October 1944, cited in J.H. Whyte, *Church and State in Modern Ireland 1923-79.* Dublin, Gill and Macmillan, 1984 (2nd edition, paperback), pp. 101-103.

8   Hensey, *op. cit.*

9   For a discussion of pressures for reform in this period see Hensey, *op. cit.*, p. 19, Whyte, *op. cit.*, pp. 125-127, Lyons, *op. cit.*, p. 660.

10 Whyte, *op. cit.*, p. 126.

11 *Ibid.*, pp. 125-126.

12 Dignan, *op. cit.*; also, in early 1946 two Labour Party deputies introduced a motion in the Dail (parliament) calling for a comprehensive social insurance system covering all gainfully employed persons, see *Dail Eireann, Parliamentary Debates, Official Report*, Vol. XCIX, January 1946, Cols. 143-176. The *Report of the Commission of Inquiry into the Housing of the Working Classes of the City of Dublin, 1939-43*, Dublin, Stationery Office, 1944, and the *Census of Population of Ireland, 1946* both drew attention to housing needs.

13 Whyte, *op. cit.*

14 *Ibid.*

15 See, for instance, statement to the Dail by the Taoiseach (Prime Minister), Eamon de Valera, *Dail Eireann Parliamentary Debates, Official Report* Vol. XCIX, January 1946, Cols. 171-172. For an analysis of attitudes within Fianna Fail towards social service reform see Paul Bew and Henry Paterson, *Sean Lemass and the Making of Modern Ireland.* Dublin, Gill and Macmillan, 1982.

16 See Whyte, *op. cit.*

17 See Kennedy, *op. cit.*, and Lyons, *op. cit.*, pp. 571-572.

18 The estimate of 85 percent is given in *The Health Services and their Further Development.* Dublin, Stationery Office, 1966, p. 12. The higher income group was defined as those with means exceeding IRL 800 per annum or, in the case of farmers, the rateable valuation of whose farms exceeded IRL 50.

19 For a detailed comparison of changes in the proposed mother and child scheme see Whyte, *op. cit.*, pp. 292-294.

20 See Kennedy, *op. cit.*

21 See *Economic Development.* Dublin, Stationery Office, 1958, and Capital Investment Advisory Committee, *Third Report.* Dublin, Stationery Office, 1958.

22 On this point see also Kennedy, *op. cit.*, and Anthony McCashin, 'Social policy: 1957-82', in Frank Litton (ed.), *Unequal Achievement. The Irish Experience 1957-82.* Dublin, Institute of Public Administration, 1982.

23 *Investment in Education.* Dublin, Stationery Office, 1966.

24 See, for instance, Bew and Paterson, *op. cit.*

25 See Whyte, *op. cit.*

26 The grants were confined to purchasers of new houses.

27 The rediscovery of poverty is documented in Seamus O'Cinneide, 'Poverty and inequality in Ireland', in Vic George and Roger Lawson (eds.), *Poverty and Inequality in Common Market Countries.* London, Routledge and Kegan Paul, 1980, pp. 124-160.

28 Public expenditure as defined throughout this chapter includes the following items: final consumption expenditure of public authorities, current transfers and subsidies, national debt interest, gross physical capital formation of public authorities, gross capital transfers and capital transfers to the rest of the world. For a comparison of trends in the public sector share of GDP in Ireland and other OECD countries, see *OECD Economic Outlook, Historical Statistics 1960-82* Paris, OECD, 1984. The definition of public expenditure used by the OECD differs slightly from that used in this chapter.

29 See Appendix Table 1.

30 For a more detailed examination of public expenditure trends in the period 1953-1976, see John O'Hagan, 'Demonstration, income and displacement effects as determinants of public sector expenditure shares in the Republic of Ireland', *Public Finance*, 35:3 (1980), pp. 425-435.

31 Kennedy, *op. cit.*

32 Richard Rose, *Changes in Public Employment: a multi-dimensional comparative analysis.* Glasgow, Centre for the Study of Public Policy, University of Strathclyde, 1980.

33 Peter C. Humphreys, *Public Service Employment.* Dublin, Institute of Public Administration, 1983.

34 See Gerard Hughes, *Social Insurance and Absence from Work in Ireland.* Dublin, Economic and Social Research Institute, 1982.

35 *Ibid.*

36 *Ibid.*

37 See Mary O'Mahony, 'The length of spells of unemployment in Ireland', *Economic and Social Review* 14:2 (1983), pp. 119-136.

38 See Denis Conniffe and Kieran A. Kennedy (eds.), *Employment and Unemployment Policy for Ireland.* Dublin, Economic and Social Research Institute, 1984.

39 See Eithne Fitzgerald, *Alternative Strategies for Family Income Support.* Dublin, National Economic and Social Council, 1980.

40 *Ibid.*

41 See Section II, part 6.

42 Finola Kennedy, *op. cit.*, notes that capital expenditure on health was actually less than planned between the late 1950s and the mid-1960s.

43 Those whose earnings exceed a specified ceiling, set at IRL 7,000 in 1980, (about 15 percent of the population), are eligible for free hospital accommodation but are required to pay for consultants' services. The health contribution, payable by all income earners, amounts to 1 percent of earnings up to the same ceiling as for social insurance contributions. In 1982, 6.3 percent of funding for the health services came from this source.

44 See *Statistical Information Relevant to the Health Services,* Dublin, Stationery Office, various issues. It is reported that the number of hospital admissions per 1,000 population rose from 106 in 1960 to 162 in 1976, whereas the mean length of stay fell from 19 to 11 days. Between 1977 and 1981, the discharge rate for acute hospitals, which account for the bulk of expenditure on general hospital services, rose from 161.6 to 175.5 per 1,000 population and the average length of stay fell from 10.9 to 9.4 days.

45 See Humphreys, *op. cit.*, p. 75.

46 See *Report of the General Medical Services Payments Board,* Dublin, published annually.

47 Finola Kennedy, 'Public expenditure on housing in the postwar period', *Economic and Social Review,* 3 (1971-72), pp. 373-401.

48 See T.J. Baker and L.M. O'Brien, *The Irish Housing System. A Critical Overview*. Dublin, Economic and Social Research Insitute, 1979.

49 For a detailed discussion of housing subsidies see National Economic and Social Council, *Report on Housing Subsidies*, Report No. 23, Dublin, 1977; and Baker and O'Brien, *op. cit*

50 The above mentioned report by the National Economic and Social Council also includes in the definition of housing subsidies the cost to the exchequer of stamp duty exemption on the purchase of new houses, rates remission on new and reconstructed houses and tax relief on capital gains.

51 National Economic and Social Council, *op. cit.*

52 The notion of 'net lending' as used here is the same as in the OECD *National Accounts Statistics*. Negative net lending is equivalent to net borrowing and the further net lending falls below the zero line the greater the public sector borrowing requirement.

53 Kieran A. Kennedy, 'Poverty and changes in the socio-economic environment in Ireland 1971-1981', *In* The Council for Social Welfare, *Conference on Poverty 1981*. Dublin, 1982, pp. 1-54.

54 The definition of social security programmes used here is that used by the International Labour Organisation in compiling the publication *The Cost of Social Security*, Geneva, ILO, various years. Included are the following: Social insurance and assimilated schemes, family allowances, public employee schemes, public health services, public assistance and assimilated schemes and administrative expenditure.

55 D.B. Rottman and D.F. Hannan, 'Fiscal welfare and inflation: winners and losers', *In* Economic and Social Research Institute, *The Irish Economy and Society in the 1980s*. Dublin, ESRI, 1981.

56 Since the discussion here refers only to cash flows and does not include consideration of non-cash benefits, it does not give a complete picture of redistributive effects.

57 For a delineation of the 'residual' and other broad models of social policy, see Richard M. Titmuss, *Social Policy: an Introduction*. London, George Allen and Unwin Ltd., 1974.

58 Nevertheless, those whose incomes exceed the maximum earnings upon which social insurance contributions are payable (approximately 15 percent of the population) are liable for consultants' fees when in hospital.

59 See Hughes, *op. cit.,* 1982.

60 See Brendan M. Walsh, 'Unemployment compensation and the rate of unemployment: the Irish experience', *In* Herbert G. Grubel and Michael A. Walker (eds.), *Unemployment Insurance: Global Evidence of its Effects on Unemployment.* Vancouver, The Fraser Institute, 1978; and Gerard Hughes and Brendan M. Walsh, 'Unemployment duration, aggregate demand and unemployment insurance: a study of Irish live register survival probabilities, 1967-1978', *Economic and Social Review*, 14:2 (1983), pp. 93-118. In both cases the authors stress that the results of the analysis should be treated with caution.

61 Figure for 1966 is taken from National Economic and Social Council, *Towards a Social Report*, Report No.25. Dublin, 1977, Table 8.7. Figure for 1981 is from Damien Courtnay and Anthony McCashin, *Social Welfare: the Implications of Demographic Change*. Dublin, National Economic and Social Council, 1983, Table A.2.

62 For a detailed description of the system see the Institutional Synopsis.

63 See for instance, Cornelius O'Leary, *Irish Elections 1918-1977*. Dublin, Gill and Macmillan Ltd., 1979.

64 Gerard Hughes, *Payroll Tax Incidence, the Direct Tax Burden and the Rate of Return on State Pension Contributions in Ireland*. Dublin, Economic and Social Research Institute, 1985.

65 These benefit ratios are calculated relative to the net earnings of an unmarried male earning the average wage in transportable goods industries. The benefit rates are those in force in April of the relevant years, while earnings are an annual average.

66 Variations in average benefit levels may also reflect changes in various characteristics of the recipient group, such as, for instance, family circumstances.

[67] See *Social Insurance for the Self-employed,* discussion paper published by the Department of Social Welfare, Dublin, Stationery Office, 1977.

[68] For a discussion of this point, see for instance, Laraine Joyce and A. McCashin (compilers), *Poverty and Social Policy.* Dublin, Institute of Public Administration, 1981.

[69] See *A National Income-Related Pension Scheme* discussion paper published by the Department of Social Welfare, Dublin, Stationery Office, 1976.

[70] These data are from OECD, *Social Expenditure 1960-1990* Paris, 1985, Table 1. Housing expenditure is excluded from the OECD figures. Comparative data on per capita GDP are shown in OECD, *Economic Surveys 1983/84 - Ireland.* Paris 1983.

[71] Data on receipts are from OECD, *Economic Outlook,* No. 36, Paris, December 1984, Table R.9. Data on government deficits are from OECD, *Economic Surveys 1984/85 - Ireland.* Paris, 1985, Table 12 and OECD, *Economic Outlook, op. cit.,* Table 2. Data are on a SNA basis. The OECD average excludes Iceland, Ireland, Luxembourg, New Zealand, Portugal, Switzerland and Turkey.

[72] This figure is an estimate for 1983 based on data given in *Comprehensive Public Expenditure Programmes 1984* Dublin, Stationery Office, 1984.

[73] Finola Kennedy, 1975, *op. cit.*

[74] *Ibid.*

[75] See speech on the Budget, 1965, *Dail Eireann, Parliamentary Debates, Official Report,* Vol. 215, 1965, cols. 976 and 988; *Ibid.,* Vol. 273, 1974, Col. 1325; *The Third Programme: Economic and Social Development 1969-72.* Dublin, Stationery Office, 1969, Chap. 16; *Programme for National Development 1978-1981.* Dublin, Stationery Office, 1979.

[76] Seamus O'Cinneide, 'Poverty and Inequality in Ireland'. *In* Vic George and Roger Lawson (eds), *Poverty and Inequality in Common Market Countries.* London, Routledge and Kegan Paul, 1980.

[77] Including recipients and their dependants. Source, *Report of the Department of Social Welfare, op. cit.* various years.

[78] For a more detailed account of the rediscovery of poverty see O'Cinneide, 1980, *op.cit.*

[79] This was the conclusion of a paper presented at the conference by Seamus O'Cinneide and later published as 'The Extent of Poverty in Ireland', *Social Studies* 1:4(1972), pp.381-400.

[80] See O'Cinneide, 1980, *op.cit*

[81] Central Statistics Office, *Household Budget Survey 1973.* Dublin, Stationery Office, 1976. The HBS is intended primarily as an investigation of expenditure patterns but it also collects data on incomes.

[82] See Eithne Fitzgerald, 'The Extent of Poverty in Ireland'. *In* Stanislaus Kennedy (ed.), *One Million Poor.* Dublin, Turoe Press, 1981; Joyce and McCashin, *op. cit.;* John D. Roche, *Poverty and Income Maintenance Policies in Ireland 1973-80.* Dublin, Institute of Public Administration, 1984; David B. Rottman et al, *The Distribution of Income in the Republic of Ireland: A Study in Social Class and Family Cycle Inequalities.* Dublin, Economic and Social Research Institute, 1982, Chap. 5.

[83] The figure of 8 percent is from Joyce and McCashin, *op.cit.;* the figure of 30 percent is from Fitzgerald, *op.cit.;* the figures of 5 percent and 13 percent are from Roche, *op.cit.*

[84] Joyce and McCashin, *op.cit.*

[85] *Ibid.,* p.10.

[86] Roche, *op.cit.*

[87] The poverty line for a single person was 16 percent lower than the supplementary welfare allowance. The discrepancy was less in the case of larger households due to differences in the household weighting systems used in determining the poverty line and the rate of supplementary welfare allowance. For a family consisting of two adults and three children the poverty line was almost equal to the rate of the supplementary welfare allowance and for larger families the poverty line exceeded the allowance.

[88] Roche, *op.cit.,* pp.219-222.

89   O'Cinneide, 1980, *op.cit.*; Rottman et al, *op.cit.* p.138.

90   For a comparison of the numbers in poverty using income and expenditure data see Joyce and McCashin, *op.cit.* Table A2.1. Roche, *op.cit.*, Table 1B.4 shows the income and expenditure data for households at different income levels in 1980.

91   Roche, *op.cit.*, p.77.

92   Kieran A. Kennedy, *op. cit.*; Roche, *op.cit.*, Appendix 4C, also explores the sensitivity of poverty estimates to alternative equivalence scales.

93   Roche, *op.cit.*, pp. 126-132.

94   Roche, *op.cit.*

95   *Ibid.*

96   *Ibid.*

97   *Ibid.*

98   *Ibid.*, p. 151.

99   *Ibid.*, pp. 75, 113.

100 *Ibid.*, p. 152.

101 For details of the schemes see Institutional Synopsis.

102 The Directive is due for implementation by December 1984.

103 See *Report of the Department of Social Welfare* 1972-75 and 1981-82, *op.cit.*

104 The 1971 figure is from Conniffe and Kennedy, *op.cit.* p. 15; the 1984 figure is from National Economic and Social Council, *Economic and Social Policy Assessment* Report No. 79. Dublin, 1985, Table 20.

105 European Communities, *Employment and Unemployment* Luxembourg, 1985, Table IV/8.

106 Earnings-related benefit was originally payable from the beginning of the third week of unemployment but the waiting period was lengthened in 1983.

107 See also Gerard Hughes, 'Contributory State Pensions for the Elderly: Indexation and Cost'. *In* Economic and Social Research Institute, *Public Social Expenditure - Value for Money?*, Papers presented at a conference on 20 November 1984. Dublin: ESRI, 1984, pp.63-83.

108 For very large families with below average earnings, the replacement ratio can approach or even exceed 100 percent giving rise to an unemployment trap. See National Economic and Social Council, *Economic and Social Policy 1983: Aims and Recommendations*, Report No.75. Dublin, 1983, Table 2.10. However, large families constitute a very small proportion of beneficiaries. See National Economic and Social Council, Report No. 79, 1985, *op.cit.*, Appendix 1. This issue will be discussed below in the context of family income support.

109 Roche, *op.cit*

110 Central Statistics Office, *Census of Population of Ireland 1979*. Dublin, Stationery Office, 1983, Vol.III, Part II, Table 2 and p.vii.

111 Central Statistics Office, *Quarterly Report on Births, Deaths and Marriages*. Dublin, Stationery Office, December 1983, Table 2 and *Statistical Abstract of Ireland 1981*. Dublin, Stationery Office, 1983.

112 See, for instance, Fitzgerald, *op. cit.*, Joyce and McCashin, *op.cit.*, Roche, *op.cit.*, Rottman et al, *op.cit.*

113 National Economic and Social Council, *Irish Social Policies: Priorities for Future Development*, Report No. 61. Dublin, 1981 and Report No. 79, 1985, *op.cit.* Appendix 1.

114 National Economic and Social Council, Report No. 79, 1985, *op. cit.*

115 The 1960 figure is from B.J. Whelan and R.N.Vaughan, *The Economic and Social Circumstances of the Elderly in Ireland*. Dublin, Economic and Social Research Institute, 1982, Table 3.6. The 1981 figure has been calculated on the basis of beneficiary data provided in the *Report of the Department of Social Welfare 1981-82*, *op.cit.* The figure given here assumes that 55 percent of those in receipt of widows' contributory pensions are aged 65 and over; this is the same assumption as made by Whelan and Vaughan. The adult depend-

ants of old age contributory pensioners and retirement pensioners are included, along with all blind pensioners; this may give rise to some over-estimation as a proportion of these may be under age 65. Retired civil servants are not included.

116 See the Institutional Synopsis for a description of the various schemes.

117 National Council for the Aged, *Incomes of the Elderly in Ireland*. Dublin, 1984, p.112.

118 Department of Social Welfare, *Statistical Information on Social Welfare Services 1983*. Dublin, Stationery Office, 1984, Table 8.

119 National Council for the Aged, *op.cit.*; Whelan and Vaughan, *op.cit.*; C.T. Whelan and B.J. Whelan, 'Adjustment to Retirement: Economic and Social Influences' in Economic and Social Research Institute, *Public Social Expenditure - Value for Money?*, 1984, *op.cit.*, pp.39-62.

120 For estimates of the coverage of occupational pension schemes see Department of Social Welfare, *A National Income-Related Pension Scheme*, *op.cit.*, Chap. 6 and National Council for the Aged, *op.cit.*, pp. 54-55.

121 Whelan and Whelan, *op.cit.*, p.59.

122 National Council for the Aged, *op.cit.*, p.77.

123 National Council for the Aged, *op.cit.*; Roche, *op.cit.*, Whelan and Vaughan, *op.cit.*; Whelan and Whelan, *op.cit.*

124 *Ibid.*

125 National Council for the Aged, *op.cit.*

126 Whelan and Whelan, *op.cit.*

127 Central Statistics Office, *Redistributive Effects of State Taxes and Benefits on Household Incomes in 1980*. Dublin Stationery Office, 1983, Table 1.

128 *Ibid* and *Redistributive Effects of State Taxes and Benefits on Household Incomes in 1973*. Dublin Stationery Office, 1980.

129 Brian Nolan, 'Redistribution of Household Income in Ireland by Taxes and Benefits', *Economic and Social Review*, 13:1(1981), pp.59-83; Philip J. O'Connell, 'The Distribution and Redistribution of Income in the Republic of Ireland', *Economic and Social Review* 13:4(1982), pp.251-78; Roche, *op.cit.*; Rottman et al, *op.cit.*

130 O'Connell, *op.cit.*; Roche, *op.cit.*

131 Roche, *op.cit.*

132 O'Connell, *op.cit.*

133 See *Redistributive Effects of State Taxes and Benefits on Household Incomes in 1973*, *op. cit.*, pp.58-61, and O'Connell, *op.cit.*, p. 255.

134 O'Connell, *op.cit.*, p. 265.

135 Roche, *op.cit.*

136 This procedure is suggested by O'Connell, *op.cit.*, who has applied it to the 1973 data.

137 *Ibid.*, p. 157.

138 O'Connell, *op.cit.* found this to be the case in 1973 also.

139 Rottman et al., *op.cit.*, Chap.3.

140 Humphreys, *op.cit.*, Table 31.

141 See Whyte, *op.cit.*, pp. 125-126.

142 *The Child Health Services*, Report of a Study Group appointed by the Minister for Health. Dublin, Stationery Office, 1971.

143 *Statistical Information Relevant to the Health Services 1984*, *op.cit.*, Table B.1 and p.18.

144 *Ibid.*, Table B.4.

145 See, for instance, Peter Townsend and Nick Davidson, *Inequalities in Health, The Black Report* Harmondsworth, Penguin, 1982, Chap. 4; L.A. Aday et al, *Health Care in the U.S., Equitable for Whom?* Beverly Hills, Sage, 1980.

146 See, for instance, John Curry, *The Irish Social Services*. Dublin, Institute of Public Adminis-
     tration, 1980, p. 145.

147 A. Dale Tussing, 'Health, Education, and Redistribution to the Poor'. *In* Council for Social
     Welfare, *Conference on Poverty 1981*, *op.cit.*, pp. 198-213.

148 *Ibid.*

149 *Ibid.*

150 A. Dale Tussing, 'Poverty and the Development of the Health Services'. *In* Stanislaus
     Kennedy, (ed.), *One Million Poor?*, 1981, *op. cit.*, pp. 218, 232 and John Curry, 'Rural
     Poverty'in Stanislaus Kennedy, (ed.), *op.cit.*, pp.102-105.

151 Joyce and McCashin, *op.cit.*,p.42.

152 Survey carried out by the Medical Research Council of Ireland, reported in R.C. Geary and
     F.S. O'Muircheartaigh, *Equalisation of Opportunity in Ireland: Statistical Aspects*. Dublin,
     Economic and Social Research Institute, 1974, pp.83-88.

153 Joyce and McCashin, *op.cit.*, p.43.

154 *Report of the Working Party on the General Medical Service*. Dublin, Stationery Office,
     1984, pp.29-32.

155 B. Walsh, 'Previously Unrecognised Treatable Illness in an Irish Elderly Population',
     Journal of the Irish Medical Association, 73:2 (1980), pp.62-67.

156 Tussing, 1982 *op.cit.*, p.201.

157 A. Dale Tussing, 'Financing the Health Services', *New Exchange* (University College Dub-
     lin), 1982, pp.3-10.

158 A. Dale Tussing, 'Efficiency and Control of Irish Medical Care Expenditures'. *In* Economic
     and Social Research Institute, *Public Social Expenditure - Value for Money?*, 1984, *op.cit.*,
     pp.21-38.

159 *Ibid.*

160 Tussing, 'Financing the Health Services', *op. cit.* and 1984, *op. cit.*

161 *Report of the Working Party on the General Medical Service*, *op.cit.*, Chap. 6; A. Dale
     Tussing, 'Physician-Induced Demand for Medical Care: Irish General Practitioners', *Eco-
     nomic and Social Review* 14:3 (1983), pp.225-247.

162 *Report of the Working Party on the General Medical Service*, *op.cit.*

163 Tussing, 1984, *op.cit.*

164 *Report of the Working Party on the General Medical Service*, *op.cit.*, p.152.

165 National Economic and Social Council, *Economic and Social Policy 1982: Aims and Recom-
     mendations*, Report No. 70. Dublin, 1983, pp.42-43 and Table 3.21.

166 Data on enrolments in 1964 from National Economic and Social Council, Report No.25,
     op. cit., Tables 5.1, 5.3 and 5.5; enrolments data for 1981 from Department of Education,
     Statistical Report 1980-81. Dublin, Stationery Office, Table 1. Data on employment in edu-
     cation from Humphreys, *op.cit.*, Table 39.

167 For a more full description of educational reforms in this period see J. Sheehan,
     Educational Expenditure in Ireland. Dublin, National Economic and Social Council, Report
     No.12, 1976, Chap.1; A. Dale Tussing, *Irish Educational Expenditures - Past, Present and
     Future* Dublin, Economic and Social Research Institute, 1978, pp.64-67; Coolahan, *op.cit.*,
     Chap. 5.

168 *Investment in Education*. Dublin, Stationery Office, 1964-65.

169 See Coolahan, *op.cit.*, Chap. 5; Maurice Craft, 'Economy, Ideology and Educational Devel-
     opment in Ireland', *Administration*, 18:4 (1970), pp.363-74; Richard Breen, 'Irish
     Educational Policy: Past Performance and Future Prospects'. *In* Economic and Social
     Research Institute, *Public Social Expenditure-Value for Money?*, 1984, *op.cit.* pp.99-128.

170 Breen, *op.cit.*; Finola Kennedy, 1975, *op.cit.*

171 Dennis Murphy, *Education: The Implications of Demographic Change*. Dublin, National
     Economic and Social Council, Report No.71, 1983, p.2.

172 *Ibid.*

173 See P. Clancy, *Participation in Higher Education* Dublin, Higher Education Authority, 1982, pp.18, 52, and Murphy, *op.cit.*, p.10.

174 Breen *op.cit.*, p.102.

175 Rottman et al, *op.cit.*, pp.51-52.

176 Breen, *op.cit.*, p.105.

177 Monica Nevin, 'A Study of the Social Background of Students in Irish Universities', *Journal of the Statistical and Social Inquiry Society of Ireland* 21:6 (1968), pp. 201-225; Clancy, *op. cit.*, Tables 6 and 7.

178 Clancy. *op. cit.*, Tables A11 and A12.

179 See Breen, *op.cit.*, pp.108-111 and Tussing, 1978, *op.cit.*, Table 3.4.

180 Data on candidates in Leaving Certificate examination from Department of Education, *Statistical Report 1979-80, op. cit.*, Table 12.1; Data on university entrants from Clancy, *op. cit.*, Table 1.

181 *Investment in Education, op.cit.*

182 However, Clancy's analysis indicates that there are regional disparities in second level post-compulsory participation rates. Clancy, *op.cit.*, pp.48-50.

183 *Ibid.*, pp. 31-33.

184 See Breen, *op.cit.*, p.108 and Sheehan, *op.cit.* pp.34-37.

185 Breen, *op.cit.*

186 *Ibid.*

187 *Ibid.*

188 See Central Statistics Office, *Census of Population of Ireland 1961*, Vol. VI, Table 22A and *Census of Population of Ireland 1981*, Five Percent Sample Estimates Housing and Households. Dublin, Stationery Office, 1983, Table F.

189 See National Economic and Social Council, Report No. 25, *op.cit.*, Chap.6. John Blackwell, *Housing Requirements and Population Change, 1981-1991*, Dublin, National Economic and Social Council, 1983, discusses the sensitivity of estimates of overcrowding to the cut-off point chosen.

190 Joyce and McCashin, *op.cit.*, Table A5.12.

191 Annual number on waiting list shown in National Economic and Social Council, Report No. 75, *op. cit.* Table 2.1; Blackwell, *op.cit.*, Chap. 6 gives estimates of the numbers on Local Authority Housing lists who were living in unfit or overcrowded conditions: the approved Local Authority waiting list for dwellings in 1980 was 27,700; in September 1980 an estimated 11,000 of those on the list were living in unfit dwellings, while an estimated 15,000 were living in overcrowded conditions. An estimate of the number of homeless is given in Blackwell, *op.cit.*, p. 37.

192 Brian Power, *Old and Alone in Ireland.* Dublin, Society of St. Vincent de Paul, 1980.

193 *Census of Population of Ireland 1981, op. cit.*, Table H.

194 John Blackwell, 'Do Housing Policies Show a Redistribution to the Poor?'. *In* Council for Social Welfare, *Conference on Poverty, 1981*, 1982, *op.cit.* pp.214-230; Brian Dillon et al, 'Poverty and Housing'. *In* Stanislaus Kennedy, (ed.), *One Million Poor?*, 1981, *op.cit.*, pp. 58-75; T.J. Baker and L.M.O'Brien, *op.cit.*

195 National Economic and Social Council, Report No. 70, *op.cit.*, Table 3.6.

196 *Ibid.*

197 Disparities in costs between tenure types are discussed in Baker and O'Brian, *op.cit.*, Chap.10 and Blackwell, 1982, *op. cit.*

198 Baker and O'Brian, *op.cit.*, pp.60-61, 244-245. These authors point out, however, that in an inflationary period many large mortgages tend to be held by recent purchasers and in such a situation mortgage tax relief may have a progressive impact by aiding most the less well off younger households which are paying a large share of their income for housing. Neverthe-

less, Baker and O'Brian note that, in general, mortgage tax relief is not a satisfactory instrument for assisting first-time buyers since it creates inequalities simultaneously with this more equitable result.

199 National Economic and Social Council, Report No. 75, *op.cit.*, p.25.

200 National Economic and Social Council, Report No. 23, *op.cit.*, Report No. 75, *op.cit.*

201 Baker and O'Brien, *op.cit.*, Chap. 10.

202 Baker and O'Brien, *op.cit.*, p. 222; T.J. Baker, 'Housing-Market or Social Service'. *In* Economic and Social Research Institute, *Public Social Expenditure - Value for Money?*, 1984, *op.cit.*, p. 91.

203 Baker and O'Brien, *op.cit.*, pp. 223-226.

204 *Ibid.*

205 See Appendix Table 4 and Finola Kennedy, 1975, *op. cit.*, Chap. 2.

206 See Section I of this chapter.

207 See Moore McDowell, 'Irish budgetary policies', *National Westminster Bank Quarterly Review*, August 1981, pp. 22-35.

208 See, for instance, Brendan M. Walsh, 'Ireland's demographic transformation: 1958-70', *Economic and Social Review*, 3, 1971, pp. 254-70 and 'Recent demographic changes in the Republic of Ireland', *Population Trends*, 21, 1980, pp. 4-9.

209 These figures relate to the area which is now the Republic of Ireland.

210 See *Census of Population of Ireland 1981*. Dublin, Stationery Office, 1982, Vol. I., Tables J and K.

211 See *Eurostat Demographic Statistics*. Luxembourg, Office of Official Publications of the European Communities, 1984.

212 See, for instance, National Economic and Social Council, *Health Services: The Implications of Demographic Change*, Report No. 73. Dublin, 1983.

213 David Rottman and Damian Hannon, 'The impact of state taxation and transfer policies on income inequality in the Republic of Ireland' *In* Mary Kelly et al. (eds.) *Power, Conflict and Inequality*. Dublin, Turoe Press, 1982, pp. 116-130 show that in 1972/73 a relatively low proportion of households deriving income primarily from property paid direct income tax.

214 OECD, *Public Expenditure on Income Maintenance Programmes*. Paris, 1976.

215 Including expenditure on contributory old age pension, non-contributory old age pension and retirement pension.

216 Allowances are payable for children up to the age of 18 who are in full-time education, otherwise the age limit is 16. However, the 0-19 age group is the most suitable age disaggregation available from the census.

217 John O'Hagan and Morgan Kelly, 'Components of growth in current public expenditure on education and health', *Economic and Social Review*, 15:2, 1984. Vocational schools provide education in technical as well as academic subjects and accounted in 1981 for approximately 23 percent of full-time second level enrolments.

218 See Maria Maguire, 'Components of growth of income maintenance expenditure in Ireland 1951-1979', *Economic and Social Review*, 15:2, 1984, pp. 75-85, and O'Hagan and Kelly, *op. cit*

219 For a comparison of social expenditure shares by programme see Maria Maguire, 'Social expenditure in Ireland and other European OECD countries', *In* Economic and Social Research Institute, *Public Social Expenditure - Value for Money'*, 1984, *op. cit.*, pp. 1-20.

220 See footnote 70.

221 Including expenditure on unemployment benefit, pay-related benefit paid with unemployment benefit, unemployment assistance and redundancy payments.

222 The unemployment ratio has been calculated on the basis of a three-year moving average of the unemployment ratio in order to reduce the effect of short-term cyclical fluctuations.

[223] It will be observed that the eligibility ratio exceeds unity from 1967 onwards. This is due to the fact that the official estimates of the numbers out of work apply a more restrictive definition of unemployment than does the register of benefit recipients (the Live Register). In particular, the Live Register includes agricultural smallholders claiming unemployment assistance, whereas this group is not included in the estimates of numbers unemployed taken from census data and from labour force survey data. For a discussion of factors which may have contributed to the rise in the eligibility ratio between 1965 and 1976 see Maguire, 'Components of growth of income maintenance expenditure in Ireland 1951-1979', *op. cit*

[224] See Kieran A. Kennedy and Brendan R. Dowling, *Economic Growth in Ireland: the Experience Since 1947*. Dublin, Gill and Macmillan, 1975, Chap. 16.

[225] For comparative data on the structure of the economy see OECD, *Economic Surveys, Ireland, op. cit*

[226] David B. Rottman and Philip J. O'Connell, 'The changing social structure' *In* Litton, 1982, *op. cit*. pp. 63-88.

[227] For a discussion of phases of economic growth in the postwar period see Kennedy and Dowling, *op. cit*

[228] This point is brought out clearly by Finola Kennedy,1975, *op. cit.*

[229] See for instance, Garret Fitzgerald, *Planning in Ireland*. Dublin, Institute of Public Administration, 1968.

[230] See Finola Kennedy, 'Social expenditure of public authorities and economic growth 1947-66', *Economic and Social Review*, 1:3, 1970, and 1975, *op. cit.*, Chaps. 1 and 2.

[231] See for instance, Peter Flora and Arnold J. Heidenheimer (eds.), *The Development of Welfare States in Europe and America*. New Brunswick, New Jersey, Transaction Books, 1981; Arnold J. Heidenheimer et al., *Comparative Public Policy*. London, Macmillan, 1976; Francis G. Castles (ed), *The Impact of Parties* London, Sage Publications Ltd., 1982.

[232] See Seymour M. Lipset and Stein Rokkan, 'Cleavage structures, party systems and voter alignments: an introduction', in Lipset and Rokkan (eds.), *Party Systems and Voter Alignments: Cross-National Perspectives*. New York, The Free Press, 1967.

[233] For a discussion of the development of the party system during the early years of the state, see Brian Farrell, *The Founding of Dail Eireann*, Dublin, Gill and Macmillan, 1971; Peter Mair, 'Labour and Irish party system revisited: party competition in the 1920s', *Economic and Social Review*, 9, 1977. Comparative data on electoral support for social democratic parties in Western Europe are given in Stefano Bartolini, 'The European left since World War I: size, composition and patterns of electoral development', *In* Hans Daalder and Peter Mair (eds.), *Western European Party Systems: Continuity and Change* London, Sage Publications Ltd., 1983, pp. 139-176.

[234] See Peter Mair, 'The autonomy of the political; the development of the Irish party system', *Comparative Politics*, 11:4, 1979, pp. 445-465.

[235] See Peter Mair, *The Changing Irish Party System* London, Frances Pinter, 1985 (forthcoming).

[236] See *Dail Debates*, Vol. 215, 1975, Col. 976.

[237] Peter Mair, *The Changing Irish Party System, op. cit*

[238] Frank Gould, 'The growth of public expenditure in Ireland, 1947-77', *Administration*, 29:2, 1981 found a similar pattern with regard to the growth of total public expenditure under different administrations.

[239] Core laws are defined as including major administrative changes, major changes in financing, changes in the benefit structure, introduction of new schemes, extension of duration of benefit, extension of eligibility.

[240] See Finola Kennedy, 1975, *op. cit.*, Chaps. 1 and 2.

[241] Bew and Paterson, *op. cit.*

[242] *Ibid.*, pp. 159-160.

[243] *Ibid.*, pp. 161-162.

[244] See Cornelius O'Leary, *Irish Elections 1918-1977* Dublin, Gill and Macmillan, 1979, p. 72.

[245] See *The Third Programme: Economic and Social Development 1969-72.* Dublin, Stationery Office, 1969.

[246] See, for instance, Heidenheimer et al., *op. cit.* Ramesh Mishra, *Society and Social Policy.* London, Macmillan, 1977; Harold Wilensky, *The Welfare State and Equality.* Berkeley, University of California Press, 1975.

[247] Chubb, *op. cit.*, Table 7.1.

[248] *Ibid.*

[249] See for instance, Bill Roche, 'Social partnership and political control: state strategy and industrial relations in Ireland', in Mary Kelly et al., (eds.), *op. cit.*; see also J.J. Lee 'Sean Lemass', *In Ireland 1945-70.* Dublin, Gill and Macmillan, 1979.

[250] Lee, *op. cit.*

[251] See Bew and Paterson, *op. cit.*, p. 163.

[252] See Roche, *op. cit.*

[253] In 1981 the Federated Workers Union of Ireland organised a seminar to discuss trade union priorities in social policy. According to a statement delivered at this seminar by the representative of the Irish Congress of Trade Unions, this was the first occasion on which a trade union in Ireland had had a major discussion on social policy. See Federated Workers Union of Ireland, *Trade Union Priorities in Social Policy.* Dublin, F.U.E., 1981.

[254] Chubb, *op. cit.*, pp. 32-33; Whyte, *op. cit.*, p. 382.

[255] Basil Chubb, *The Constitution of Ireland.* Dublin, Institute of Public Administration, 1963, pp. 20, 34.

[256] *Bunreacht na hEireann* (Constitution of Ireland), Dublin, Stationery Office, Article 45.

[257] Whyte, *op. cit.*

[258] *Ibid.*, Chap. IV.

[259] *Ibid.*, pp. 180-181.

[260] *Ibid.*, Chaps. IV and VI.

[261] *Ibid.*, Chaps. V-IX.

[262] *Ibid.*, pp. 292-297.

[263] *Ibid.*, p. 375.

[264] *Ibid.*, Chaps. XI and XIII.

[265] *Ibid.*

[266] *Ibid.*, pp. 396-397.

[267] See Vladimir Rys, 'The sociology of social security', *Bulletin of the International Social Security Association*, 17:1/2, 1964, pp.3-34; James Midgley, 'Diffusion and the development of social policy: evidence from the third world', *Journal of Social Policy*, 13:2, 1981, pp.167-84; Joan Higgins, *States of Welfare.* London, Basil Blackwell and Martin Robertson, 1981.

[268] For a survey of the literature on the 'demonstration effect' see John W.O'Hagan, 'Demonstration, income and displacement effects as determinants of public sector expenditure shares in the Republic of Ireland', *Public Finance/Finances Publiques*, 35:3, 1980, pp.425-35.

[269] *Ibid.*; Whyte, *op.cit.*, p.126; P.R. Kaim-Caudle, *Social Policy in the Irish Republic.* London, Routledge and Kegan Paul, 1967, pp.22-23.

[270] O'Hagan, *op.cit.*

[271] Garret Fitzgerald, *Towards a New Ireland.* Dublin, Gill and Macmillan, 1973.

[272] O'Hagan, *op.cit.*; Kaim-Caudle, *op.cit.*, p.105; Lyons, *op.cit.*, p.742.

[273] O'Hagan, *op.cit.*

[274] *Ibid.*

[275] Whyte, *op.cit.*, p.126; Lyons, *op.cit.*, p. 660.

[276] *Dail Eireann, Parliamentary Debates, Official Report* Vol. XCIX, January 1946, Cols. 143-174.

[277] Kaim-Caudle, *op.cit.*, Chap.4.

[278] *Dail Eireann, Parliamentary Debates, Official Report* Vol. XCIX, January 1946, Cols.171-172.

[279] Kaim-Caudle, *op.cit.*, Chap. 4; Hughes, 1985, *op.cit.* p.88.

[280] Hughes, 1985, *op.cit.*, p.88.

[281] P.R.Kaim-Caudle, *Comparative Social Policy and Social Security.* London, Martin Robertson, 1973, pp.213-4.

[282] *Ibid.*, p.83.

[283] Hensey, *op.cit.*, p.19; Whyte, *op.cit.*, p.126.

[284] Speech reported in the *Irish Times*, 10 May, 1963, cited in P.R.Kaim-Caudle, *Social Security in Ireland and Western Europe.* Dublin, Economic and Social Research Institute, 1964, p.1; *Dail Eireann, Parliamentary Debates, Official Report*, Vol.202, 24 April, 1963, Cols.320-321.

[285] *The Third Programme, Economic and Social Development 1969-72, op.cit.*

[286] Kaim-Caudle, 1964, *op.cit.*, 1967, *op.cit.*

[287] Department of Social Welfare, *A National Income-Related Pension Scheme, op.cit.*, *Social Insurance for the Self-Employed, op.cit.*

Sources for tables and graphs

Table 1

Report of the Department of Social Welfare, 1947-49 to 1979-80. Dublin, Stationery Office; *Report of the Department of Health*, 1945-58. Dublin, Stationery Office; Brendan M. Hensey, *The Health Services of Ireland.* Dublin, Institute of Public Administration, 1979; John Coolahan, *Irish Education: Its history and structure.* Dublin, Institute of Public Administration, 1981; P.J. Meighen, *Housing in Ireland.* Dublin, Institute of Public Administration, 1964; John Curry, *The Irish Social Services.* Dublin, Institute of Public Administration, 1980.

Table 2

Richard Rose, *Changes in Public Employment: A multi-dimensional comparative analysis.* Glasgow, Centre for the Study of Public Policy, University of Strathclyde, 1980.

Table 3

Peter C. Humphreys, *Public Service Employment.* Dublin, Institute of Public Administration, 1983, Tables 48 and 50.

Table 4

Organisation for Economic Co-operation and Development, *Long-Term Trends in Tax Revenues of OECD Member Countries 1955-1980.* Paris, 1981.

Table 5

D.B.Rottman and D.F.Hannan, 'Fiscal welfare and inflation: winners and losers' *In* The Economic and Social Research Institute, *The Irish Economy and Society in the 1980s* Dublin, 1981, pp.80-112, Table 5.

Table 6

Report of the Department of Social Welfare, 1947-49 to 1981-82. Dublin, Stationery Office; Brendan M. Hensey, *The Health Services of Ireland.* Dublin, Institute of Public Administration, 1979; John Curry, *The Irish Social Services* Dublin, Institute of Public Administration, 1980.

Table 7

Report of the Department of Social Welfare, various years. Dublin, Stationery Office; *Census of Population of Ireland* various years. Dublin, Stationery Office; Appendix Table 10.

Table 8

As for Table 7.

Table 9

Report of the Department of Social Welfare, various years. Dublin, Stationery Office; International Labour Organisation, *Yearbook of Labour Statistics,* various years. Geneva, ILO; *Statistical Abstract of Ireland,* various years. Dublin, Stationery Office.

Table 10

As for Table 9.

Table 11

Report of the Department of Social Welfare, 1972-75 and 1979-80. Dublin, Stationery Office; John D. Roche, *Poverty and Income Maintenance Policies in Ireland 1973-80.* Dublin, Institute of Public Administration, 1984, Appendix Table 4A; Central Statistics Office, *Irish Statistical Bulletin,* various issues. Dublin, Stationery Office; *Annual Report of the Revenue Commissioners,* 1973/74, 1980. Dublin, Stationery Office.

Table 12

John D. Roche, *Poverty and Income Maintenance Policies in Ireland 1973-80.* Dublin, Institute of Public Administration, 1984, Table 4.1.

Table 13

As for Table 12, Table 4.3.

Table 14

As for Table 12, Table 4.4.

Table 15

Central Statistics Office, *The Trend of Employment and Unemployment,* various years. Dublin, Stationery Office; Central Statistics Office, *Labour Force Survey, 1979 Results.* Dublin, Stationery Office, 1981; Department of Finance, *Economic Review and Outlook,* various years. Dublin, Stationery Office.

Table 16

Report of the Department of Social Welfare, various years. Dublin, Stationery Office; Central Statistics Office, *Irish Statistical Bulletin,* various issues. Dublin, Stationery Office.

Table 17

National Economic and Social Council, *Economic and Social Policy: Aims and Recommendations,* Report No. 75. Dublin, NESC, Table 2.10.

Table 18

Eithne Fitzgerald, 'Trends in family living standards and family income support' *In* Council for Social Welfare, *Conference on Poverty 1981.* Dublin, The Council for Social Welfare, 1982, pp.188-197, Table 2; Department of Social Welfare, *Rates of Payment,* 1983, 1984. Dublin, Stationery Office; *Budget,* 1984. Dublin, Stationery Office.

Table 19

Central Statistics Office, *Redistributive Effects of State Taxes and Benefits on Household Incomes,* 1973 and 1980. Dublin, Stationery Office, 1980 and 1983.

Table 20

Central Statistics Office, *Redistributive Effects of State Taxes and Benefits on Household Incomes in 1980.* Dublin, Stationery Office, 1983.

Table 21

Department of Social Welfare, *Rates of Payment,* 1983. Dublin, Stationery Office: Central Statistics Office; *Budget,* 1983. Dublin, Stationery Office.

Table 22

B.J. Whelan and R.N. Vaughan, *The Economic and Social Circumstances of the Elderly in Ireland*. Dublin, Economic and Social Research Institute, 1982, Table 3.2; National Council for the Aged, *Incomes of the Elderly in Ireland*. Dublin, 1984, Table 12; C.T. Whelan and B.J. Whelan, 'Adjustment to retirement: economic and social influences' *In* Economic and Social Research Institute, *Public Social Expenditure - Value for Money?*, papers presented at a conference, 20 November, 1984. Dublin, ESRI, 1984.

Table 23

As for Table 20.

Table 24

Philip J.O'Connell, 'The distribution and redistribution of income in the Republic of Ireland', *Economic and Social Review*, 13:4,1982, Table 4; John D. Roche, *Poverty and Income Maintenance Policies in Ireland 1973-80*. Dublin, Institute of Public Administration, 1984, Appendix Table 5A; Central Statistics Office, *Redistributive Effects of State Taxes and Benefits on Household Incomes in 1980*. Dublin, Stationery Office, 1983, Tables 1,10,11.

Tables 25

Philip J.O'Connell, 'The distribution and redistribution of income in the Republic of Ireland', *Economic and Social Review*, 13:4, 1982, Table 4.

Table 26

John D. Roche, *Poverty and Income Maintenance Policies in Ireland 1973-80*. Dublin, Institute of Public Administration, 1984, Table 5.20.

Table 27

Philip J.O'Connell 'The distribution and redistribution of income in the Republic of Ireland', *Economic and Social Review*, 13:4, 1982, Table 6; Data for 1980 calculated from Central Statistics Office, *Redistributive Effects of State Taxes and Benefits on Household Incomes in 1980*. Dublin, Stationery Office, 1983, Tables 1,10,11.

Table 28

John D. Roche, *Poverty and Income Maintenance Policies in Ireland 1973-80*. Dublin, Institute of Public Administration, 1984, Table 5.1 and p.163.

Table 29

Central Statistics Office, *Redistributive Effects of State Taxes and Benefits on Household Incomes in 1980*. Dublin, Stationery Office, 1983, Table 7.

Table 30

As for Table 29, Table 6.

Table 31

Department of Health, *Statistical Information Relevant to the Health Services 1984*. Dublin, Stationery Office, 1984, Tables G11, G12, H2.

Table 32

As for Table 31, Table A6.

Table 33

As for Table 31, Table A15.

Table 34

Department of Education, *White Paper on Educational Development*. Dublin, Stationery Office, 1980, Table 1; Department of Education, *Statistical Report 1980-81*. Dublin, Stationery Office, Table 1.

Table 35

A. Dale Tussing, *Irish Educational Expenditures - Past, Present and Future*. Dublin, Economic and Social Research Institute, 1978, Table 4.6; D. Murphy, *Education: The Implications of Demographic Change*. Dublin, National Economic and Social Council, 1983, Table A.1.

Table 36

Monica Nevin, 'A study of the social background of students in Irish Universities', *Journal of the Statistical and Social Inquiry Society of Ireland*, 21:6, 1968, pp.201-225, Tables 3 and 4; Patrick Clancy, *Participation in Higher Education*. Dublin, The Higher Education Authority, 1982, Tables 6,7.

Table 37

Central Statistics Office, *Census of Population of Ireland 1946*, Vol. IV; *Census of Population of Ireland 1971*, Vol. VI; *Census of Population of Ireland 1981*, Bulletin No. 41 and Five Per Cent Sample Estimates. Dublin, Stationery Office, 1983, 1984.

Table 38

Central Statistics Office, *Household Budget Survey 1980*, Vol. I. Dublin, Stationery Office, 1982, Table 4; Vol.2, 1984, Table 11.

Table 39

Central Statistics Office, *Census of Population of Ireland 1981*, Five percent sample estimates housing and households. Dublin, Stationery Office, 1983, Table 9.

Table 40

Appendix Table 4.

Table 41

Central Statistics Office, *Census of Population of Ireland*, various years. Dublin, Stationery Office; Department of Education, *Statistical Report*, various years. Dublin, Stationery Office; Higher Education Authority, *Annual Report*, various years; Central Statistics Office, *National Income and Expenditure*, various years. Dublin, Stationery Office; Central Statistics Office, *Statistical Abstract of Ireland*, various years. Dublin, Stationery Office.

Table 42

Central Statistics Office, *National Income and Expenditure*, various years. Dublin, Stationery Office; Central Statistics Office, *Census of Population of Ireland*, various years. Dublin, Stationery Office.

Table 43

Appendix Tables 1 and 4

Table 44

Appendix Tables 1 and 4.

Table 45

Cornelius O'Leary, *Irish Elections 1918-1977*. Dublin, Gill and Macmillan, 1979; Michael Gallagher, *Political Parties in the Republic of Ireland*. Manchester, Manchester University Press, 1985.

Table 46

Table 45 and Appendix Table 4.

Table 47

Budget, various years. Dublin, Stationery Office; *National Income and Expenditure*, various years. Dublin, Stationery Office; OECD, *Economic Surveys, Ireland*, various years. Paris.

Table 48

Report of the Department of Social Welfare, 1979-80, 1981-82. Dublin, Stationery Office; Commission of the European Communities, *Report on Social Developments*, 1980, 1981, 1982, 1983, 1984; National Economic and Social Council, *Economic and Social Policy 1981: Aims and Recommendations*; *Economic and Social Policy 1982: Aims and Recommendations*; *Economic and Social Policy 1983: Aims and Recommendations,* Reports No. 62,70,75. Dublin, NESC, 1981, 1983, 1984; *Budget,* 1982, 1983, 1984. Dublin, Stationery Office; *Report of the Department of the Environment,* 1980, 1981, 1982. Dublin, Stationery Office.

Table 49

As for Table 48.

Table 50

Report of the Department of Social Welfare, 1972-75, 1981-82. Dublin, Stationery Office; Department of Social Welfare, *Rates of Payment,* 1983, 1984. Dublin, Stationery Office.

Table 51

Budget, 1980 to 1984. Dublin, Stationery Office; *Economic Review and Outlook,* 1984, 1985. Dublin, Stationery Office.

Table 52

Peter C. Humphreys, *Public Service Employment.* Dublin, Institute of Public Administration, 1983, Table 41.

Table 53

Building on Reality 1985-1987. Dublin, Stationery Office, 1984, Chap. 7.

Table 54

As for Table 53.

Table 55

As for Table 53; Dennis Murphy, *Education: The Implications of Demographic Change.* Dublin, National Economic and Social Council, Report No.71, 1983; D. Courtney and A.McCashin, *Social Welfare: The Implications of Demographic Change.* Dublin, National Economic and Social Council, Report No.72, 1984.

Table 56

Census of Population of Ireland 1981, Vol.4. Dublin, Stationery Office, 1985; *Census of Population of Ireland 1981,* Five percent sample estimates - age, marital status and labour force. Dublin, Stationery Office, 1983; David B. Rottman and Philip J.O'Connell, 'The changing social structure' In Frank Litton (ed.), *Unequal Achievement: The Irish Experience 1957-1982.* Dublin, Institute of Public Administration, 1982, pp.63-88, Table 1; Peter C.Humphreys, *Public Service Employment.* Dublin, Institute of Public Administration, 1983.

Table 57

E.E.Davis, Joel W. Grube and Mark Morgan, *Attitudes Towards Poverty and Related Social Issues in Ireland.* Dublin, Economic and Social Research Institute, 1984, Table D 27.

Table 58

Irish Marketing Surveys Ltd., Political opinion poll prepared for *The Irish Times,* June 7-8, 1981.

Graph 1

Appendix Tables 1 and 3.

Graph 2

Appendix Tables 1 and 4.

Graph 3

Appendix Table 2.

Graph 4

As for Graph 3.

Graph 5
As for Graph 3.

Graph 6
Appendix Table 3

Graph 7
Appendix Table 4.

Graph 8
Appendix Table 5.

Graph 9
As for Graph 8.

Graph 10
Central Statistics Office, *National Income and Expenditure* various years. Dublin, Stationery Office; *Report of the Department of Social Welfare*, various years. Dublin, Stationery Office.

Graph 11
Appendix Table 5.

Graph 12
Central Statistics Office, *National Income and Expenditure* various years. Dublin, Stationery Office; *Report of the Department of Social Welfare*, various years. Dublin, Stationery Office.

Graph 13
Appendix Table 5.

Graph 14
Appendix Table 5.

Graph 15
Central Statistics Office, *Statistical Abstract of Ireland* various years. Dublin, Stationery Office.

Graph 16
Central Statistics Office, *National Income and Expenditure* various years. Dublin, Stationery Office; Finola Kennedy, *The Growth and Allocation of Public Social Expenditure in Ireland Since 1947*, unpublished Ph.D. thesis, University College, Dublin, 1971, Tables A.3.2., A.3.3. (data used by kind permission of Mrs. Finola Kennedy); *Quarterly Bulletin of Housing Statistics*, various issues. Dublin Stationery Office; National Economic and Social Council, *Report on Housing Subsidies*, Report No.23. Dublin, NESC, 1977; National Economic and Social Council, *Economic and Social Policy 1982: Aims and Recommendations*, Report No.70. Dublin, NESC, 1983.

Graph 17
Appendix Table 6.

Graph 18
Appendix Table 6.

Graph 19
Appendix Table 6.

Graph 20
Appendix Table 7.

Graph 21
Appendix Table 7.

Graph 22
Appendix Tables 7,8,9.

Graph 23

National Income and Expenditure, various years. Dublin, Stationery Office; *Report of the Department of Social Welfare,* various years. Dublin, Stationery Office; Appendix Tables 8,10.

Graph 24
As for Graph 23.

Graph 25

National Income and Expenditure, various years. Dublin, Stationery Office; *Report of the Department of Social Welfare,* various years. Dublin, Stationery Office; Appendix Tables 9,10.

Graph 26
As for Graph 25.

Graph 27

National Income and Expenditure, various years. Dublin, Stationery Office; *Report of the Department of Social Welfare,* various years. Dublin, Stationery Office; *The Trend of Employment and Unemployment,* various years. Dublin, Stationery Office; *Economic Review and Outlook,* Summer 1981. Dublin, Stationery Office, Appendix Tables 7,9.

Graph 28
As for Graph 27.

Graph 29
Appendix Tables 1,4.

Graph 30
As for Graph 29.

Graph 31
As for Graph 29.

Graph 32 and 33
Table 46.

Italy

Maurizio Ferrera

Contents

I Historical synopsis

1. The Catholic and Fascist heritage and the missed opportunity of 1948

In spite of the secular imprint of the new unitary state born in 1861, social policy in Italy remained almost exclusively the monopoly of the Catholic Church until the end of the nineteenth century. Basic poor relief was provided by a number of national and local charitable institutions, and confessional schools represented the commonest form of education, especially in the Centre and South of the country. The state limited itself to a mild overall regulation of the activities of the Church and voluntary associations (mainly workers' mutual aid societies) and its boldest social reform was the introduction of compulsory education from six to nine years of age in 1877.

In the last two decades of the century, however, the 'social question' gradually moved to the forefront of political attention. The incipient industrial take-off was slowly causing the traditional social fabric to disintegrate; the masses started to mobilize, with the emergence of the first industrial and agrarian unions in the North and the official birth of the Italian Socialist Party in 1892. A group of progressive intellectuals and politicians began to publicly denounce the dramatic conditions of the *Mezzogiorno* (the southern part of the country), calling for state action [1]. In its turn, Leo XIII's encyclical *Rerum Novarum* impressed a more advanced orientation upon the Church's policy and sensitized Catholic consciences to the new 'workers' problem' [2]. Social policy thus gained greater emphasis on the agenda of all political movements. Formerly opposed, on different grounds, to any state reform, Socialist and Catholic movements now started to favour and actually press for active intervention. Partly echoing the German example, the Liberal government took some primary measures towards the improvement of working conditions and social protection: in 1890 a comprehensive law regulated the sector of poor relief, bringing all the charitable institutions (*opere pie*) under rigid state control; in 1898 compulsory insurance against industrial accidents was introduced, as well as a state-subsidized voluntary scheme for old age and invalidity insurance.

It was, however, only in the twentieth century that spontaneous activism, intellectual and political debate and the government's new 'social attention' were translated into a concrete social policy. By the end of the nineteenth century, the process of industrialization was well under way, rapidly changing the composition of the labour force and the pattern of urbanization [3]. The new liberal leader, Giolitti, was guiding the country towards democratization (universal male suffrage was introduced in 1912) and he inaugurated a 'new deal' of interventionist social policies. Numerous new laws improved the protection and assistance of migrant workers, as well as working conditions. The state began to subsidize voluntary insurance funds and all life insurance was nationalized. Economic and social infrastructures were greatly improved, especially in the South, and a small public housing programme was initiated. Two measures in 1904 and 1911 led to a reorganization of the educational system [4] and illiteracy began to rapidly decline.

The first major steps in welfare reform, however, took place after World War I. In the wake of the social disruption and material destruction resultant upon this conflict, social policy became the major topic of the day. The government introduced compulsory insurance for old age, invalidity and unemployment (1919). Several draft bills were submitted by various factions to parliament for the establishment of compulsory sickness insurance and a Parliamentary Commission even came to propose a single global insurance scheme for all (white- and blue-collar) employees. Party and union activism in this field greatly increased, with the Socialist and Popular (Catholic) parties competing against each other in organizing conferences and proposing changes [5]. This social insurance legislation represented one of the last and greatest achievements of the Italian era of Liberalism.

The advent of Fascism marks in fact a neat turning point. Besides a general suppression of political debate and social conflict, the new regime initially restrained expansion of the welfare state. The plans for the introduction of sickness insurance were dropped, as was the promised extension of unemployment insurance to agriculture; eligibility criteria were tightened.

With the foundation of a Corporatist state in 1927, social policy did, however, regain political momentum and it acquired a high ideological status. The regime began to consider and use it as a privileged tool for the creation and maintenance of social consensus. This consensus was based on the corporatist cooperation between capital and labour, under the wings of the National Fascist Party [6].

Thus, the 1930s and early 1940s witnessed a great increase in welfare programmes, especially in the field of sickness and family policy (both aimed at improving the physical and moral 'health of the race'). In 1933/1934 a scheme for family allowances was created, and nine years later (in 1943) compulsory sickness insurance was finally introduced for all workers. Social assistance was also given much attention with new party and ad hoc organizations complementing the traditional Catholic charities [7].

But the most peculiar characteristic that Fascism impressed on the Italian welfare state was an overall bureaucratization of its structures and their use, as mentioned, as instruments of social control. Three large national insurance agencies were set up, surrounded by a variety of smaller institutes (*enti*) for special categories. The welfare state soon became an arena of clientelistic exchanges, through the provision of selective benefits to social clients whose consensus had to be secured or preserved [8].

Thus, at the outset of the Second World War, the Italian welfare state existed as a fairly well articulated institutional system. From a quantitative viewpoint, social expenditure represented some 15-17 percent of the state budget, two and a half times as much as the 1922 figure [9]. Besides state welfare, however, the Church was still very active in poor relief and education.

In contrast to some other European countries, in Italy the war years gave rise to sharp internal divisions rather than national solidarity: the country even remained split into two separate polities from 1943 to 1945. Thus national solidarity had to be re-established after the war, upon the ruins of the Fascist state. Although not so apparently relevant as other issues [10], the theme of welfare soon claimed the attention of all political organizations due to the gravity of the economic and social situation. 'Reconstruction' thus became the motto of the post- and anti-Fascist leadership, the target of a massive effort to reorganize and rebuild the economic and social infrastructure. Some urgent steps also had to be taken to assist those people who had been most severly hit by the war damages and to support the pensioners' income [11].

Meanwhile, a vast 'constitutional' debate began in the newly born Republic on the overall approach to be chosen for the social security system. All parties favoured a transformation of the Fascist legacy, but interests and preoccupations diverged. The Left pressed for workers' and union self-management and control and for drastic reforms; the Catholic party opposed a dismantling or secularization of the Church's social assistance network and feared a communist take-over. The smaller liberal-democratic parties shared the same fear, and although attracted by the Beveridge reforms, were also preoccupied with the economic and financial situation and its constraints upon social reforms [12].

The welfare issue fuelled the debate on the new Constitution. Finally, two specific references were included, one with regard to health as being a 'fundamental right of the citizen' and the other with respect to social assistance being guaranteed to the poor and to workers in certain circumstances [13]. At the same time, a Parliamentary Commission, chaired by the Socialist senator D'Aragona, was charged in the Spring of 1947, to examine in detail the question of social security. A year later, the commission submitted its proposals for a thorough restructuring of the existing system. The main points of these proposals were: 1) institutional simplification and centralization, according to a one-risk-one-scheme approach; 2) extension of coverage to all employees and self-employed for health care, old age, invalidity and accident insurance and to all employees for unemployment, sickness and family cash benefits; 3) introduction of a single scheme for old age pensions to all employees, providing a basic pension to be supplemented with occupational or private schemes; 4) introduction of earnings-related benefits for all other schemes [14]. The Commission's proposals were not a Beveridge plan; nevertheless, their approach was markedly innovative and inspired by principles of equity and efficiency.

The change of political climate resulting from the 1948 election (which greatly strengthened the Christian Democratic Party and its centre and right allies, at the expense of the Communist-Socialist Popular Front) and the beginning of the Cold War, coupled with a decline in the economic situation, prevented these proposals from materializing. The new centre coalition led by the Christian Democrats opted for a restoration of the pre-war institutional framework. Although not intended as a mere defence of the status quo (relevant changes would soon be introduced), this choice did, however, rule out, after 1948, any strategy for radical change. Thus, the traditional traits of the Italian welfare state were maintained and the 'natural' continuation of the pre-war experience was promoted. The welfare issue soon moved back to the periphery of political debate and competition, with social policy remaining for two decades a fragmented arena of marginal adjustments, additive expansions and clientelistic exchanges.

2. Two decades of institutional continuity and the reforms of the 1970s

The institutional framework inherited by the new Republican regime divided social security into three separate parts: social insurance (*previdenza*), health and sanitation (*sanità*), and assistance (*assistenza*).

Social insurance included six major schemes (for pensions, unemployment, tuberculosis, family allowances, sickness and maternity, occupational injuries and diseases), administered by a number of separate agencies and funds for selected occupational categories, often with diverse eligibility and benefit regulations. The central position was, however, occupied by the three big agencies set up during the fascist period: INPS, INAM and INAIL [15]. Insurance coverage was limited to employees, thus excluding the self-employed; most benefits were flat-rate or related to previous contributions [16].

The provision of health services relied heavily on the private sector. Some insurance funds (e.g. INAM) had their own medical centres, but basic medical and pharmaceutical assistance was mostly contracted-out through agreements with doctors' and pharmacists' associations. Hospitals were subject to state control, but with large administrative and financial autonomy. The state itself provided public sanitation through local offices in charge of the maintenance of minimum hygenic standards.

Finally, a plethora of public agencies provided social assistance for the needy at a national, provincial and local level, paralleled by private and church charities.

This institutional setting remained basically unaltered throughout the 1950s. If we exclude coverage extensions, the only noteworthy innovations during this period were the introduction of maternity benefits and protection in 1950 and the pension reform of 1952 (see Table 1). The underlying trend was therefore substantial continuity in the basic institutional principles and regulations, as well as in organizational and administrative patterns.

Table 1   Major institutional changes in the Italian welfare state

Social Insurance

1950	Job security and earnings-related maternity benefits granted to women
1952	Pension reforms: improvement of pension formula and establishment of minima
1955	Family allowances reform
1965	Schemes for occupational injuries and diseases coordinated
1968	Special earnings-related benefits for full employment introduced; protection against temporary or partial unemployment extended to cases of sectoral crisis, restructuralizations and conversions
1969	Pension reform: introduction of earnings-related and social pensions; cost of living indexation; unions gain administrative control over INPS
1975	Pensions linked to minimum contractual wage in industrial sector; the positions of the unions strengthened within unemployment schemes

Health

1968	Reform of administrative and financial regulations for hospitals
1974	Hospital assistance transferred to regions
1978	Establishment of National Health Service (Servizio Sanitario Nazionale, SSN) covering all citizens; liquidation of all existing public insurance funds and agencies

Education

1962	School leaving age raised to 14; introduction of unified post-elementary curriculum (scuola media unificata)
1969	Access to higher education greatly expanded
1972	Some responsibilities transferred to regions
1974	Creation of student/parent/union representative boards

Housing

1949	Special fund created for economic housing construction
1962	Controls on construction market introduced
1971	Housing reform: liquidation of public housing agencies and funds; new decentralized housing programmes; centralization of funds
1978	Rent controls tightened; tenant protection increased

Social assistance and services

1972	Jurisdiction over social assistance and services transferred to regions
1977	Social assistance agencies and funds liquidated; jurisdiction transferred to local authorities

The same holds true for education, which continued to operate until the early 1960s along the criteria set out in 1923 by the Gentile reform [17]. Housing was perhaps the only field characterized by some immediate innovation after the war. Besides a strengthening of tenant protection and rent control, the state set up a special insurance fund to finance programmes for economic housing. This step represented an institutional novelty and enhanced the status of housing within the Italian welfare state.

The 1960s were a decade of ambitious plans and sweeping programmes. As a result of a rapid economic boom, the country had finally achieved a level of relative affluence. The cultural and political climate was changing. A group of leading economists and sociologists began to denounce the imbalance of the country's economic and social development and to call for a programme of thorough reforms [18]. The new Centre-Left coalition was formed precisely on these reformist grounds and pledged itself to a full modernization of the Italian economic and social structure. In a 'supplementary note' to the 1962 budget, the minister Ugo La Malfa (leader of the small but influencial Republican Party) stated certain principles which can be considered as the first public acknowledgement of the welfare state and its tasks in Italy:

> In order to guarantee to everyone a decent standard of living, the direct intervention of the state must be strengthened - in as much as it is its jurisdiction. Under state authority are in fact (besides education) health assistance - which must be adequate and effective for all citizens, regardless of their financial conditions - and social insurance, which must guarantee everyone a minimum security for life [19].

Numerous lengthy documents and some concrete programmes followed this impressive entree, but the record of actual reforms was quite poor until the end of the decade (as Table 1 shows). The National Council for Economy and Labour (*Consiglio Nazionale dell'Economia e del Lavoro*, CNEL) drafted a comprehensive plan for a reform of the social security system, proposing the introduction of a basic uniform pension (to be supplemented by occupational pensions) and a National Health Service [20]. Both proposals provoked harsh conflicts within the coalition and in the end neither materialized. Various attempts were made in order to rationalize the chaotic housing sector, but with little success (in spite of the important step taken in 1962). Perhaps, the only major institutional change of this period was the educational reform of 1962, which finally raised the age limit of compulsory education to 14 and equalized educational curricula.

From 1968 onwards, however, the institutional profile of the Italian welfare state started to change rapidly, in the wake of new and heated social conflicts and under popular and union pressures [21]. Hospital care was thoroughly revised in its administrative and financial status. Within social insurance, a new link was established between pensions, previous earnings and the cost of living (the link with the wage index was postponed until 1975); unemployment protection was strengthened and a new housing policy instituted in 1971.

This reformist zeal continued and indeed deepened throughout the 1970s. This important decade, which witnessed a process of general secularization and modernization of Italian society [22], thoroughly reshaped the welfare state. Administrative decentralization has transformed the regions and the local authorities into the main loci of welfare policy, gradually suppressing the national sickness insurance and assistance funds [23]. Social assistance, health care, housing and vocational training have become the competence of regional and local authorities and successful manifestations of institutional initiatives. New social and personal services were organized, new housing and transport programmes launched and active labour market policies inaugurated. 'Client' participation and control were fostered, especially in education. In 1978 a sweeping change led to the establishment of the National Health Service (SSN), which replaced all previous separate occupational insurance funds.

At the end of the 1970s, the Italian welfare state emerged as distinct from its historical 'predecessors'. Although still fragmented, the sector of social insurance provided better benefits, most of which were indexed and earnings-related [24]; the formerly dispersed and separate sectors of health and assistance had been replaced by a unitary and integrated system of social and health services; education had been reformed and greatly expanded, and housing broadly decentralized. A process of thorough secularization, moreover, has accompanied these institutional transformations, thus greatly reducing the role of the Catholic Church in social policy and clearly disconnecting the notion of 'welfare' from that of 'christian charity'. The complex of welfare policies and institutions represents a major feature of the contemporary Italian state, and is a red-hot issue in the current debate on its prospects.

II Resources and clienteles: descriptions

1. The postwar growth of public and social expenditure: a summary

The relative growth of public expenditure as a percentage of GDP since the early 1950s has been impressive (see Graph 1): commencing from a rate of 24.8 percent in 1951, it reached 44.4 percent or even 45.7 percent, according to different sources, in 1980 [25]. This rapid growth in the 1950s and early 1960s, after a leap in 1965, followed a less linear trend, with some marked jumps and oscillations. If we look, however, at the absolute figures at constant prices (Graph 2) a continuous and sustained growth is revealed from 1951 to 1980.

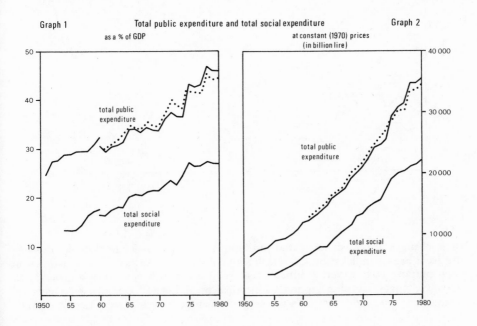

Graph 1   Total public expenditure and total social expenditure   Graph 2
          as a % of GDP   at constant (1970) prices
                              (in billion lire)

At a preliminary level of disaggregation, we can analyse public expenditure growth by economic category, as shown by Graph 3 [26]. Transfers and subsidies display a generally upward trend from the mid-1950s until the mid-1970s; they have hence declined in relative terms. Public consumption markedly declined during the 1950s, increased in the early 1960s and then began to decline again. Public investment is characterized by a slow relative decline for the whole period. Finally, interest on public debt, declining in the early 1960s, then witnessed a noticeable growth.

Graph 4 reports the distribution of public expenditure by level of government. Until the mid-1970s the overall trend showed a marked increase in the share of local government and social security funds at the expense of central government [27]. Since 1975 this trend clearly reverts, pointing towards a relative re-centralization of expenditure.

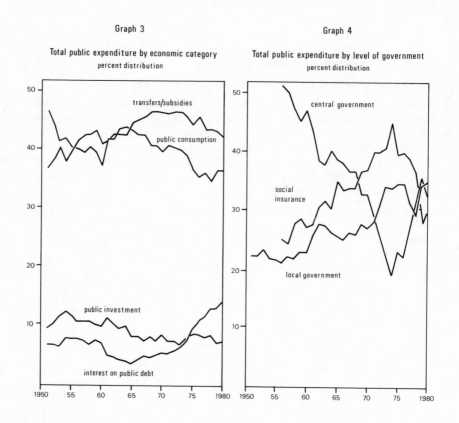

Graph 3

Total public expenditure by economic category
percent distribution

Graph 4

Total public expenditure by level of government
percent distribution

These changes in the economic and institutional composition of total public expenditure have been paralleled by sizeable functional changes. An accurate breakdown by major purpose is, however, a difficult task [28]. In order to have at least a general idea of these changes, Graph 5 reports a functional breakdown of central government expenditure, based on W. Rostow's typology [29]. Welfare appears as the largest expenditure category, revealing a strong growth pattern from the 1950s until 1971, when it sharply declined. Expenditure for the promotion of economic growth grew rapidly from the mid-1950s to the early 1970s, when it began to decline. However, it is probable that this is only the appearance of decline; the massive increase of financial transfers (counted under 'others' in the graph) suggests that economic growth has continued to be 'promoted' during the 1970s, although in different ways (for instance, through the subsidization of enterprises in crisis). In contrast to welfare and growth promotion, spending on defence and constitutional order has steadily declined.

Graph 5

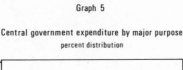

Central government expenditure by major purpose
percent distribution

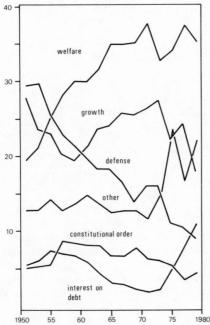

Social expenditure, as shown by Graphs 1 and 2, has been a major component of public expenditure growth [30]. Its share within the GDP has more than doubled, rising from some 13 to almost 27 percent. The internal composition of social expenditure (see Graph 6) reveals that income maintenance has always been the largest component. Within income maintenance expenditure, a major shift has taken place, with family allowances rapidly loosing their prominence and pensions doubling their relative share from 40 to 80 percent (see Graph 7). Education and health expenditures have grown considerably; education from the early 1950s to the early 1960s, and health continuously until the mid-1970s. In contrast, public assistance lost ground throughout the whole period and housing has witnessed a dramatic fall.

Graph 6

Social expenditure by major component
percent distribution

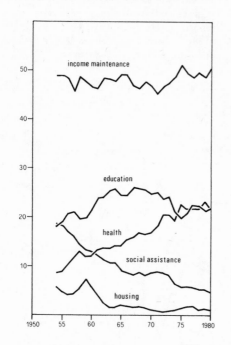

Graph 7

Expenditure on income maintenance
by major component
percent distribution

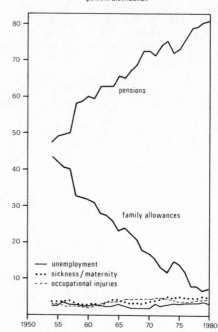

A substantial increase in the size of public employment has accompanied expenditure growth, as indicated by Table 2. At the beginning of the 1950s, the size of public employment was fairly low in Italy by international standards (some 10 percent of the total labour force). To a large extent, Italy was still a pre-industrial country, with an extensive agricultural sector. But between 1951 and 1976, public employment more than doubled, reaching 22 percent of the labour force. The figures on its internal composition show that typical welfare sectors such as education and health witnessed the largest relative growth.

Table 2			Size and structure of public employment					
	1951		1961		1971		1976	
	in 1,000	%	in 1,000	%	in 1,000	%	in 1,000	%
Defence	262	13.5					273	6.2
Administration a.o	597	30.9					1 034	23.6
Agriculture								
Industry								
Services a.o.	648	33.5					1 513	34.5
Health	115	5.9					453	10.3
Education	272	14.1					1 008	23.0
Social services	38	2.0					98	2.2
Total public employment	1 932	100.0	2 502	100.0	3 599	100.0	4 379	100.0
As % of labour force	10.3		12.0		18.9		22.0	

2. The development of single programmes: expenditure and institutional change

Pensions

Pensions are by far the most important item within social expenditure. In 1980, they came to represent 24.3 percent of total public expenditure and 11 percent of GDP in relative terms (starting from 8.5 percent and 2.1 percent respectively in the early 1950s); moreover, they absorb about 80 percent of income maintenance expenditure. In absolute terms, the real growth has been constant and sustained (see Graph 9). As shown by Graph 8, old age pensions are the largest component of total pension expenditure since the mid-1950s. In relative terms they grew during the 1950s and started to decline thereafter. In real terms (see Graph 9), they have witnessed a substantial increase, especially in 1965 and in the early 1970s, due to some important reforms, which greatly improved benefits.

Expenditure for invalidity pensions has risen very sharply since the mid-1950s in both real and relative terms. This is largely the consequence of a massive expansion in the number of beneficiaries, above all within the agricultural sector and the South in general. Through the relaxation of eligibility criteria and of their control, invalidity pensions have increasingly been used as an indirect subsidy for underdeveloped areas with limited employment opportunities, supplementing or more often substituting for a very low, flat-rate unemployment indemnity. In the early 1970s, this link between invalidity pensions and employment opportunities was even institutionalized [31]. For public employees, it is not possible to distinguish between old age and invalidity pensions. They have their own pension scheme which has not been substantially changed since

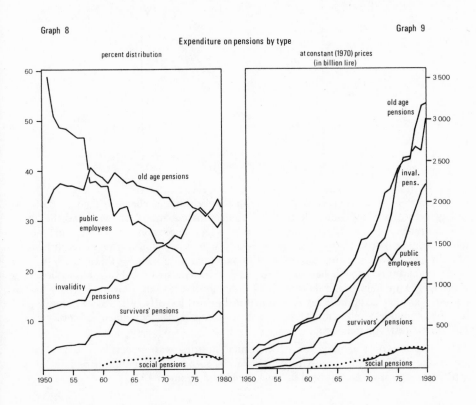

Graph 8

Graph 9

Expenditure on pensions by type

percent distribution

at constant (1970) prices
(in billion lire)

World War II. Although pension expenditure for public employees has grown steadily in real terms, its relative position within total pension expenditure sharply declined until the mid-1970s. Since 1976 this trend has reverted, probably due to the improvement of indexing regulations. Survivors' pensions expenditure displays almost linear patterns of growth in both real and relative terms. Finally, since their introduction in 1969, social pensions have witnessed a modest absolute growth and have maintained their relative share of total pension expenditure.

Sickness, maternity and occupational injuries

As a percentage of total income maintenance, expenditure on cash benefits for sickness, maternity and occupational injuries has remained relatively stable, reaching 9 percent at the end of the 1970s. In real terms, however, it has witnessed a substantial growth since the early 1960s, reflecting an extension of insurance coverage as well as improvements in benefit levels (see Graph 10).

Graph 10

Cash benefits for sickness, maternity,
and occupational injuries
at constant (1970) prices (in billion lire)

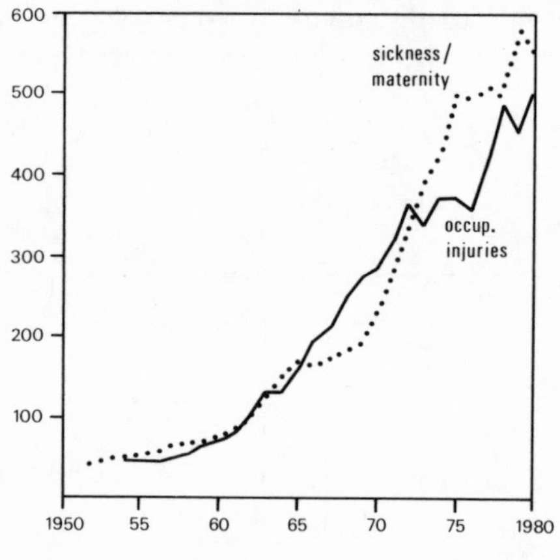

The extension of coverage was less a result of institutional changes, than of the relative growth of the dependent labour force, due to occupational changes and the 'institutionalization' of the labour market (i.e. a wider application of contractual norms and insurance registration). This is especially true for sickness and maternity insurance, which have increased almost continuously, pausing only in the mid-1970s. The rapid expenditure growth between 1969 and 1975 is also probably a consequence of the changes in industrial relations, which occurred between 1968 and 1972. In this period, workers acquired greater protection against lay-offs, wage continuation paid by the employers was introduced, and controls loosened, thus diminishing the individual 'costs' of sickness.

The extension of eligibility for occupational injuries was especially relevant in the 1950s and 1960s. With respect to benefit levels, substantial upgradings of minima and replacement ratios were granted in 1963, 1965 and again in 1975.

Unemployment

Unemployment is the smallest item within income maintenance expenditure (2-3 percent in the 1950s and 1960s and 3-4 percent in the 1970s). This type of expenditure
is, of course, closely related to the business cycle and employment levels. This is most
obvious for 1965, 1971, and 1975, years of economic downswing or real recession
(see Graph 11). The sharp increase in expenditure since 1970, however, is not simply
a consequence of higher unemployment levels, but also a result of institutional
changes.

Graph 11

Expenditure on unemployment

at constant (1970) prices (in billion lire)

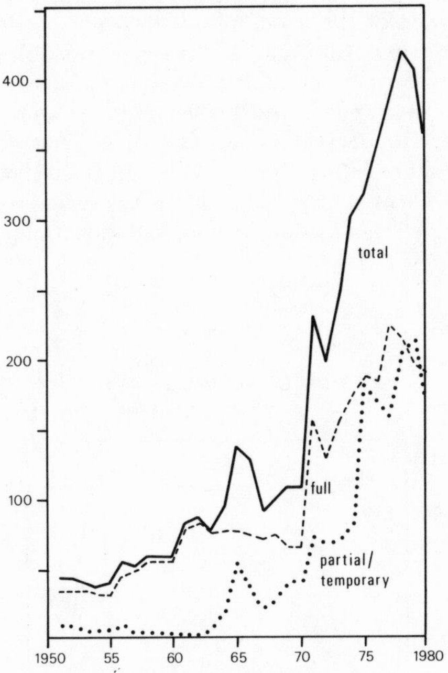

Until the early 1960s almost the only type of unemployment expenditure was flat-rate
full unemployment benefits. Their real value stagnated in the 1960s, but increased
rapidly in the 1970s, when special earnings-related benefits were introduced (1968,
1970, 1972, 1977) and the flat-rate indemnity doubled (1974).

Since the mid-1960s a new form of unemployment expenditure - benefits for partial
and temporary unemployment in employment crises of single enterprises or whole sectors - has gained increasingly in absolute and relative importance, as a consequence of
coverage extensions (1963, 1970, 1971, 1972) and benefit improvements (1968, 1972,
1975).

More recently greater emphasis has been placed on active labour market policy as a
complement to unemployment insurance, but this has not resulted in any conspicuous
expenditure.

An overall assessment of Italian employment policy would also, of course, have to take into account other factors, such as the subsidization of private enterprises risking bankruptcy or the use of public enterprises for employment purposes, but such an assessment would be very difficult in quantitative terms [32].

Family allowances

Although their relative importance has constantly diminished, family allowances still represent an important component of income maintenance. Graph 12 reports the evolution of real expenditure, distinguishing between the private and public sectors. In the former, real expenditure for family allowances grew very rapidly in the 1950s, more than doubling between 1951 and 1962 (see Graph 12). This was mainly due to a high birth rate, some improvement in benefits, and the relative increase of the dependent labour force. Between 1962 and 1964 expenditure fell in real terms, probably as a consequence of the economic downswing of 1963/64, since the unemployed did not receive family allowances. The extension of eligibility to the unemployed in 1965 [33] and to farmers in 1967 as well as the improvement of benefit levels explain the new rise in expenditure between 1964 and 1968. After 1968 the accelerating inflation and a decreasing number of eligible persons produced a new fall. In 1974 the expenditure jumped to a much higher level when pensioners became entitled to family allowances which, in addition, were improved in 1974 and 1975. After 1975 expenditure fell again, due to high inflation (family allowances not being

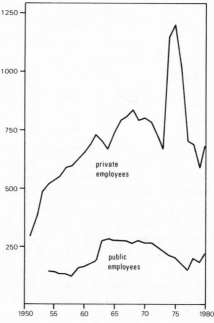

Graph 12

Expenditure on family allowances
at constant (1970) prices (in billion lire)

indexed) and probably also as a result of an increasing number of unemployed not registered and therefore not entitled to this kind of benefit.

In the public sector, expenditure grew between the mid-1950s and the mid-1960s, and declined thereafter. Benefit levels were equalized in the two sectors in 1977 and were substantially raised in 1979, as reflected in the graph.

Besides family allowances, the Italian welfare state provides a number of other benefits and services to the family such as tax credits, kindergartens, recreation and counselling facilities and various ad hoc subsidies in cash and kind. Unfortunately, it is not possible to quantify the aggregate size of tax credits. Family services have only become important in the last decade, as a consequence of regional and local initiatives. The various ad hoc subsidies have been counted here under public assistance.

Public assistance and social services

The great heterogeneity and disparity of the Italian social assistance system makes it very difficult to analyse its postwar development in quantitative terms. Even the reforms of the 1970s, which simplified the system, have not led to more detailed and reliable statistical information. In spite of these problems, Graph 13 presents a time series of data which include the most important benefits provided by central and local government and other public agencies: services for various target groups (old people, handicapped, orphans, single parents etc.), school and unemployment assistance (food and clothing supplies, pupil care etc.) and cash benefits to support insufficient incomes (war pensions and other regular assistance allowances, various ad hoc subsidies etc.).

Graph 13

Expenditure on health, education
and social assistance
at constant (1970) prices (in billion lire)

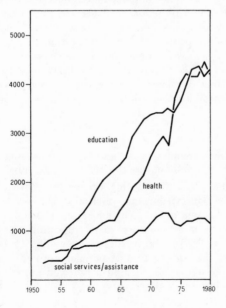

Although declining in relative terms, expenditure on social services and public assistance has been growing in real terms since the mid-1950s. The fall in expenditure in 1974 is mainly explained by the hospital reform of that year, which introduced free hospital care to all citizens, thus relieving local authorities of the responsibility of providing this type of assistance to the poor. Furthermore, cash benefits (and especially war pensions) began to decline in real terms around the mid-1970s.

Health

Health expenditure grew dramatically from the early 1950s until the mid-1970s. In the 1950s and 1960s this growth can be primarily related to an extension of health insurance coverage and to an increased utilization of public health services by consumers. The end of the 1960s, however, saw a massive increase in production costs, especially in hospital care. The hospital reform of 1968 exacerbated this problem, authorizing an almost unlimited increase in personnel and assistance fees. As a result of this measure, hospital expenditure soared in the early 1970s, pushing up total health expenditure to unprecedented heights. It must be noted that the total figures given in Graph 13 do not reflect the real economic size of the health sector in the early 1970s: they do not include, in fact, the huge deficit accumulated by the social security funds and by hospitals - an enormous sum, amounting to some 6,500 billion lire or almost 5.2 percent of the 1975 GDP. In 1974 a new law abolished the 1968 regulations and brought about a general restructuring of the hospital sector, as a first step towards the establishment of a National Health Service. In the period 1950-1980, real expenditure seems to have become more stable [34].

Education

Expenditure for education and culture [35] grew constantly in real terms until the mid-1970s (see Graph 13). This growth was especially rapid during the 1960s, primarily due to the major reform of 1962. This produced in fact higher enrolment ratios and, consequently, a higher number of teachers and other school personnel (especially at the middle school or *scuola media* level), thus claiming an increasing share of resources for this sector. New impetus was also given to expenditure growth at the end of the 1960s by the opening of higher education to all students holding a high school degree and, to a lesser extent, by the introduction of pre-elementary state schools. After the mid-1970s educational expenditure increased again. Regional and local expenditures account for most of this increase, owing to the transference of certain functions from central government in 1972.

Housing

As already noted, public expenditure on housing has witnessed a sharp relative decline in the postwar period, especially during the 1970s (see Graph 14).

Expenditure during the 1950s was the highest for the postwar period. As a result of the need to restore the national housing stock after the war and in order to promote employment, housing became in fact a major concern of the policy makers. The early 1960s saw a swift decline in expenditure, mainly due to the gradual exhaustion of the investment plans of the 1950s. The legislative provisions of 1962 and 1963 (when a new public agency for the construction of popular housing was set up) and the anti-cyclical measures of the mid-1960s, caused a renewed growth of expenditure, which, however, began to decline again after 1968.

Graph 14

Expenditure on housing
at constant (1970) prices (in billion lire)

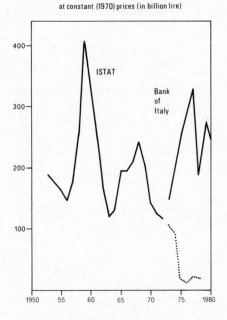

In 1972 a comprehensive reform attempted to give renewed impetus to the housing sector, decentralizing responsibilities and expenditure from central government to the regions and local authorities. Unfortunately, the available data do not allow a reliable assessment of the results of this reform. ISTAT data (thick line, dotted after 1974) seem to point toward a dramatic fall in expenditure, which is, however, mainly due to lack of information. Other data provided by the Bank of Italy seem, on the contrary, to point toward a substantial increase: these data are not, however, homogeneous with those of ISTAT and therefore cannot be compared with them [36]. In 1978 a new investment plan, again centred on the regions, was launched, in the hope of catching up with a constantly rising demand.

3. State revenues and public deficits

A complete picture of the growth of the Italian welfare state requires at least a cursory consideration of its revenue side, i.e. the way in which the massive expansion of public and, particularly, social expenditure, has been financed. We can start by looking at the development of total public revenues as a percentage of GDP. As Graph 15 shows, public revenues grew rapidly during the 1950s, remaining at just over 30 percent until the mid 1970s, after which time they increased again, reaching some 38 percent in 1980 [37]. The growth pattern for total public revenues and for public expenditure (Graph 1) are quite different. The comparison between the two allows us to distinguish two distinct phases in the evolution of Italy's public sector: a first phase of 'balanced growth' (1950-1964), in which the expansion of public expenditure was largely matched by a parallel expansion of public revenues and a second

phase of 'unbalanced growth' (1965-1980), in which the gap between expenditure and
revenues gradually widened, thus creating growing fiscal problems. The contrast
between the two phases is also underlined by trends in public saving and net lending
(Graph 15): in fact both point clearly downwards after 1964, especially during the
first half of the 1970s [38].

Graph 15

Total revenues, saving and net lending as % of GDP

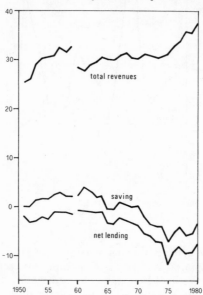

The shift from balanced to unbalanced growth was the product of a more or less
deliberate choice by policy-makers of the Centre-Left coalition. This choice followed
a long debate on the correct interpretation of Article 81 of the Italian Constitution
which states that any law involving the disbursement of public money, must indicate
the source of the necessary financial coverage in advance. The debate consisted of
two conflicting interpretations of this point: a 'conservative' one, which interpreted
this prescription as an obligation to balance expenditure with real revenues (i.e. with
no resort to borrowing), and a 'Keynesian' one, which accepted the notion of deficit
spending in cases where this would stimulate unexploited productive resources, especially through an increase of public investment. The 'Keynesian' interpretation prevailed, given strong support by Republicans and Socialists, and deficit spending
became the current practice [39].

The development during the subsequent decade did not, however, correspond to the
intentions and expectations of the Keynesian school. It was not public investment that
grew, but current expenditure (transfers and subsidies, as already seen in Graph 3
above), leading to a dramatic erosion of public saving. Thus, the deficit served increasingly to finance the growth of the welfare state: a trend which reached a peak during
the mid-1970s, when the Treasury had to bear the enormous debt accumulated by

social security funds for the provision of health services (equal to some 6,500 billion lire, i.e. ca. 5.2 percent of GDP). The situation seems to have improved after 1975. In 1973 a major fiscal reform greatly simplified the Italian tax system, by almost completely centralizing the levy of taxes and introducing automatic tax-deductions for the wages of dependent workers. This simplification has resulted in a renewed relative growth of overall revenues which, coupled with other important expenditure provisions, at least arrested the further worsening of fiscal imbalances until 1980.

Graph 16 provides a picture of the internal composition of public revenues. During the 1950s and 1960s, indirect taxes constituted by far the largest component of public revenues. However, as a result of a constantly downward trend they ranked below the other two components by the end of the 1970s. Direct taxes remained the smallest component until the end of the 1970s; their rapid growth after 1974 is largely attributed to the effect of the 1973 fiscal reform. Social security contributions grew impressively between the 1950s and the mid-1970s, as a consequence of continuous upgradings of statutory rates and the growing size of the dependent labour force. However, their relative weight declined during the second half of the 1970s.

Graph 16

Total revenues by major component
percent distribution

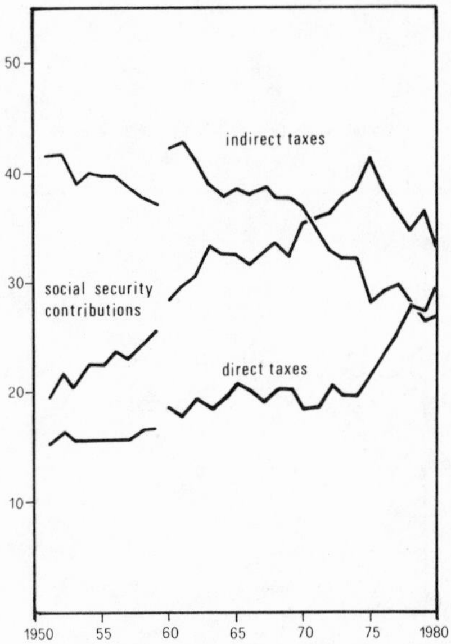

4. **Financing of welfare programmes and their growing deficits**

As indicated by the heavy incidence of this type of taxation, social security contributions constitute the main source of finance for the Italian welfare state. This is especially true for income maintenance programmes and health (although, the major reforms of the 1970s gradually increased the latter's share of financing through general revenues). Conversely, education, housing and public assistance have always been financed directly out of general revenues.

Graph 17 provides a breakdown of the receipts of social security programmes by major source. As may be seen, employers' contributions have been by far the major component of total receipts - although their share has tended to gradually decrease. The insured population's contributions grew rapidly during the 1950s and early 1960s and tended to decline in relative terms during the 1970s. They represent the smallest component of social security receipts.

Finally, the state contributes a sizeable share of total receipts. Generally declining until the mid-1960s, this share has tended to increase thereafter, due to repeated ad hoc interventions of financial support from the state to social security funds. On the one hand these interventions have resulted from the aim of relieving the employers of part of their contributions, in order to reduce labour costs in periods of crisis: this is well indicated by the parallel oscillations which can be observed in Graph 17. On the other hand, the state has been forced to cover the growing deficits of social security funds [40]. Ever since the mid-1960s, the aggregate balance between statutory contributions and benefits began to be negative for most sickness and pension funds. As already mentioned in the case of health, the deficit started to reach worrying proportions around the mid-1970s and the trend has not changed since that time. Given that social security funds enjoy an unlimited and automatic access to the Treasury for their financial requirements, their growing deficit can be held as largely responsible for the fiscal imbalances of Italy's public sector.

Graph 17

Social security receipts by major source
percent distribution

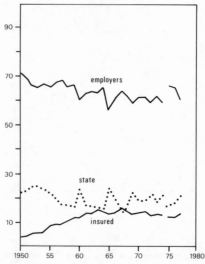

The institutional regulations regarding the financing of the various social insurance programmes are relatively simple in Italy. Pension contributions are paid for two-thirds by the employers and one third by the insured. As shown in Table 3, the contribution rate has been constantly rising and amounted to 24.31 percent of gross wage in 1980. The self-employed pay a flat-rate yearly contribution. In addition to the already mentioned ad hoc interventions, the state pays statutory 'solidarity' contributions to the social fund of INPS and to the pension of the self-employed.

Table 3   Pension schemes, contribution rates

	Employees (a) (general scheme)	farmers		Self-employed (b) artisans		traders	
1952	9.00	-		-		-	
1958	9.00	4 995	(1.15)	-		-	
1959	11.60	4 995		7 728	(1.67)	-	
1960	11.60	4 995		7 728		-	
1961	15.75	4 995	(0.75)	7 728		-	
1962	15.75	6 708	(0.86)	7 728		-	
1963	19.40	6 708		7 728		-	
1964	19.40	6 708		7 728	(0.80)	-	
1965	19.40	6 708		14 928	(1.36)	-	
1966	19.40	6 708		14 928		14 928	(1.27)
1972	19.40	6 708		14 928		14 928	
1973	19.40	6 708	(0.27)	14 928	(0.60)	14 928	(0.60)
1974	19.80	14 976	(0.50)	30 528	(1.01)	30 528	(1.01)
1975	21.60	46 800	(1.30)	72 528	(2.01)	72 528	(2.01)
1976	21.60	58 136	(1.35)	87 408	(2.02)	87 408	(2.02)
1977	23.50	65 936	(1.21)	99 672	(1.58)	99 672	(1.58)
1978	23.50	78 416	(1.24)	119 112	(1.88)	119 112	(1.88)
1979	23.50	110 968	(1.48)	290 428	(3.89)	286 928	(3.84)
1980	24.31	188 596	(2.06)	432 736	(4.73)	429 236	(4.69)

(a) Contributions are constituted by a fixed percentage of wages.

(b) Contributions are constituted by a flat-rate lump sum per annum. The figures in brackets express these sums as percentages of average gross wage (58-59: industrial sector; 60-80: all sectors).

Sickness insurance contributions are paid mainly by employers. In 1980 the contribution rate amounted to 13.15 percent of gross wage (in the industrial sector), of which 12.85 percent was paid by the employers. The state pays sickness contributions for its own employees, and in addition it regularly supported the sickness funds for the self-employed until their liquidation. The 1974 hospital reform and the establishment of the SSN in 1978 have gradually modified the system of financing for the entire health sector, considerably increasing the role and amount of financing through general revenues (cf. the Institutional Synopsis).

Finally, unemployment, maternity, TB and family allowance insurance are financed through contributions paid by employers, with rates which vary according to the economic sector (for industry, respectively 1-4 percent, 0.53 percent, 2.01 percent and 6.20 percent in 1980). The state only pays minor statutory contributions to these schemes.

5. Financial transfers across schemes: 'winners' and 'losers'

Whether deliberately or not, the financial procedures designed to cover the growing deficits accumulated during the 1970s have generated a net of redistributive flows across insurance schemes - and therefore, indirectly, across social groups. A detailed and precise balance is obviously difficult to reach, given the low transparency of the financial transactions involved. Social insurance contributions are often pooled or transferred from one scheme to another. Moreover, the increasing amount of state contributions and interventions makes it very difficult to trace the redistributive flows. In turn these flows produce a number of contrasts (between generations, sexes, different sectors of the labour market and even between different risks), so that 'winners' and 'losers' cannot be easily identified. Some data are however available to indicate at least the major gains and losses resulting from the combination of the contribution and benefit sides of welfare programmes.

Graph 18 draws up the balance sheet of family allowances and pension schemes (INPS). As may be seen, the aggregate balance between contributions and benefits has been almost constantly negative for pension schemes since the mid-1960s, while it has been almost constantly positive and largely increasing in the case of family allowances (the same is also true for the TB and full unemployment schemes). In other words: expenditure on income maintenance for pensioners exceeds that originally earmarked for this purpose, whereas expenditure allocated for compensation of income losses deriving from the burden of a large family, TB and unemployment, has not been fully utilized. The intricate flows of internal financial INPS transfers do not allow us to establish clearcut connections between the surplus of one scheme and the deficit of another. Whatever the procedures, the result is quite clear: whilst old age pensioners, invalids and survivors have 'gained' in terms of income maintenance, dependent workers suffering from TB, those with many family dependents and the unemployed

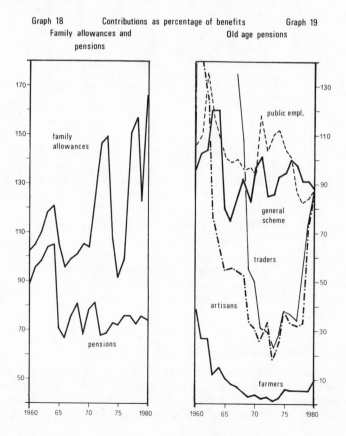

Graph 18   Contributions as percentage of benefits   Graph 19
Family allowances and
pensions   Old age pensions

have 'lost' part of what they paid - and, as we will see, unemployment benefits and family allowances have in fact been kept at low rates, thus losing increasing ground in relative terms (Table 7 below).

As regards old age pensioners, however, some groups have gained more than others. As shown in Graph 19, the retired self-employed (particularly retired farmers) receive a much greater 'gift' than retired dependent workers. Soon after their introduction (and in the case of farmers from the very beginning) the schemes for the self-employed have rapidly widened the gap between benefits and contributions: the former were in fact payable according to constantly upgraded statutory minima, whilst the latter were kept at very low flat rates (Table 3). On the contrary, the general scheme for dependent workers and the various schemes for public employees have operated either with 'moderate' deficits or clear surpluses: as Table 3 shows, pension insurance has been considerably more 'costly' for dependent workers than for the self-employed.

As shown in Graph 19, the situation seems to have gradually changed in the second half of the 1970s. Growing fiscal problems have in fact brought about an increased awareness of welfare state burdens, thus making the favours accorded to the self-employed more visible. In 1974 and 1979 the contributory status of artisans, traders and, to a lesser extent, farmers, was substantially revised (especially under pressure from the left) in the direction of a more equitable distribution of the benefits and burdens of social security.

6. The rise of the welfare clienteles

An obvious cause of the massive growth in social expenditure has been the extension of the welfare system to more and more social groups. With respect to the employment and occupational structure, we can observe a general tendency across schemes, though with a different timing (see Table 4). At the outset, only industrial employees were usually covered (agricultural employees lagging somewhat behind), reflecting the original aim of social insurance to protect this crucial group of industrial society. Gradually, however, welfare entitlements were extended to other categories of the economically active population and finally to economically non-active groups. Thus, the self-employed (farmers, artisans, and eventually traders) came under pension and health insurance between the mid-1950s and the mid-1960s, and under maternity insurance in 1971. Insurance against occupational injuries was made available to artisans in 1963, and family allowances were granted to farmers in 1967. Among the economically non-active, pensioners were the first to receive other benefits (health insurance in 1953-55), followed by housewives (pensions in 1963), the unemployed (health insurance in 1966, family allowances in 1968), and finally to marginal groups such as the impoverished elderly (pensions in 1969, health insurance in 1972) or part-time agricultural workers (unemployment benefits and family allowances in 1977).

This extension meant also a quantitative growth of insurance membership (see Graph 20) [41]. In the period from 1950 to 1963 we can observe a general extension of membership in all schemes, but especially for health and pension insurance. The years 1964 and 1965 saw a general shrinking of membership, due to the rising number of unemployed. Paradoxically, however, unemployment insurance seems to have substantially extended its reach in those very years. Although our data may not be fully reliable, this fact could be linked to a tightening of controls on the side of INPS as well as to the lowering of social security contribution for unemployment, which occurred in 1965. The period 1966 to 1980 was then characterized by diverse developments: a growing coverage of health and sickness insurance (with a slight decline in the late 1970s), a stagnation in unemployment insurance, a decline in the membership of pension schemes, and a very marked decrease in the coverage of work injuries insurance. Coverage ratios tended to decline during recession years (due to the fact that the unemployed were not covered by some schemes), as in the mid-1960s and mid-1970s. The growth in the number of young people in search of a first job (who are not covered by social insurance), partly explains the decline of coverage ratios in recent years.

Table 4   Social insurance coverage: extension by social category

Year	Pensions(a)	Family Allowances	Maternity	Health	Year
1945(b)	Employees below income ceiling	Employees	Employees (industry)	Employees	1945
1949			(agriculture)		1949
1950	All employees				1950
1953				Public employees (retired)	1953
1954				Farmers (active)	1954
1955				Pensioners	1955
1956				Artisans (active)	1956
1957	Farmers				1957
1958	Fishermen				1958
1959	Artisans			Traders (active)	1959
1963	Housewives (voluntary)			Artisans (retired)	1963
1966	Traders			Traders/Farmers (retired)/Unemployed	1966
1967		Farmers			1967
1968		Unemployed			1968
1969	Impoverished elderly above 65				1969
1971			Farmer/Artisans/Traders		1971
1972				Impoverished elderly above 65	1972
1974		Pensioners		All citizens (hospital assistance)	1974
1977		Part-time workers (agriculture)			1977
1978				All citizens (medical/pharmaceutical assistance)	1978

Year	Sickness(c)	Occup. Injuries	Unemployment full	partial/temporary	Year
1945(b)	Employees	Manual workers (industry)	Employees (industry)	Employees (manufacturing)	1945
1949			(agriculture)		1949
1959		(agriculture)			1959
1963		Artisans		(construction/mining)	1963
1968			(manufacturing)(d)		1968
1970			(construction/mining)(d)		1970
1972			(agriculture)(d)	(agriculture)	1972
1977			Part-time workers (agriculture)(d)		1977

(a) Old age, invalidity and survivors' pensions
(b) Initial situation as resulting from regulations existing in 1945
(c) Cash benefits
(d) Introduction of special earnings-related benefits

Graph 20

Social insurance coverage
(members of social insurance schemes
as percentage of the labour force)

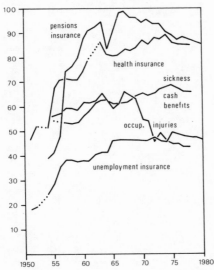

A precise quantification of the number of actual recipients of welfare benefits is diffi-cult. Official statistics report only the total number of benefits or 'cases', thus giving too high figures, since the same person may receive more than one benefit at a time (e.g. more than one pension) or several benefits in a given year (e.g. unemployment or sickness cash benefits). The data presented in Table 5 allow nevertheless an approxi-mate assessment of the quantitative development of the various welfare clienteles (in absolute terms and as a percentage of relevant reference groups).

In order to allow a comparison across programmes, Graph 21 reports the evolution of beneficiaries/benefits as a percentage of total population. Pensioners (pensions) appear as the largest class of beneficiaries (benefits). As is seen, the group of invalidity pensioners has been characterized by a real proliferation, even coming to surpass that of old age pensioners since 1971. Besides the already mentioned link between the expansion of invalidity pensions and territorial and sectoral disequilibria, a number of institutional factors have also played an important role. In fact, the lower contribution requirements, the absence of an age threshold (in comparison to old age pensions) and the weighting of the medically ascertained disability rate according to the socio-economic conditions of the applicant's area of residence have represented a great incentive for the demand for this type of pension, especially on the side of the self-employed in agriculture. The other groups of pensioners have grown at a slower pace, even slightly declining (as in the case of old age pensioners) in more recent years.

A similar pattern of moderate growth has characterized the clientele of occupational injuries benefits. The number of family allowances sharply increased in 1974 when this type of insurance was extended to pensioners. The number of unemployment

Table 5   The major clienteles of the welfare state

	1951	1955	1960	1965	1970	1975	1980
PENSIONS							
Old age pensions (a)							
in thousands	1324	1951	3249	3532	3868	4175	4165
in % of population 60+	22.9	32.2	49.6	47.2	45.8	44.5	44.1
Invalidity pensions (a)							
in thousands	501	732	1224	2145	3415	4959	5314
in % of population 60+	8.7	12.1	18.7	28.6	40.5	52.9	56.3
Survivors' pensions (a)							
in thousands	172	330	851	1186	1550	1967	2394
in % of population 60+	3.0	5.4	13.0	15.8	18.4	20.1	25.4
Pensions to government employees (b)							
in thousands	486	526	655	754	902	1035	1413
in % of population 60+	8.4	8.7	10.0	10.1	10.7	11.0	15.0
Social pensions							
in thousands					766	824	708
in % of population 60+					9.5	8.8	7.5
OCCUPATIONAL INJURIES							
Pensions							
in thousands	183	311	460	592	775	924	1135
in % of labour force	0.9	1.5	2.3	3.0	4.0	4.7	5.5
SICKNESS							
Recipients of cash benefits (c)							
in thousands	1875	2253	2944	3631	4282	6802	n.a.
in % of insured	n.a.	20.6	24.0	29.2	32.1	47.2	
UNEMPLOYMENT							
Recipients of cash benefits (d)							
in thousands	841	883	1458	1934	1558	1791	n.a.
in % of the labour force	4.1	4.4	7.2	9.9	8.1	9.1	
FAMILY ALLOWANCES							
Dependants receiving benef.							
in thousands	n.a.	n.a.	n.a.	n.a.	13527	17419	16173
in % of non-working population					39.6	49.4	45.6
Heads of households receiv. benef.							
in thousands	n.a.	n.a.	n.a.	n.a.	5548	8177	7485
in % of total population					10.4	14.9	13.3
PUBLIC ASSISTANCE							
War pensions							
in thousands	931	1104	1101	1049	990	901	n.a.
in % of population 60+	16.1	18.2	16.8	14.0	11.8	9.7	
Other social assist. recipients (e)							
in thousands	2803	2695	2508	2034	1618	1185	n.a.
in % of total population	5.9	5.6	5.1	4.0	3.0	2.2	

(a)INPS general and special schemes
(b)Old age, invalidity, and survivors' pensions
(c)Single cases of sickness compensated with cash benefits within the INAM general scheme (thus excluding government
    employees and other employees insured with special schemes).
(d)Cases of full unemployment compensated with ordinary or special benefits (as explicitly acknowledged in the official
    source, some degree of overlap may have occured).
(e)Number of people assisted by the ECA (Enti Comunali di assistenza or local authorities assistance agencies).
    n.a. = not available

Graph 21

Welfare clienteles
(recipients of cash benefits as a % of total population)

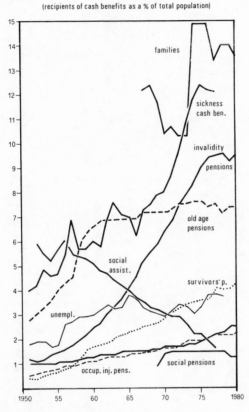

benefits has also increased since the early 1950s (and especially since 1956, when the insurance was extended to agriculture), with a trend closely connected with the fluctuations of the economic cycle. During the postwar period, sickness cash benefits have grown outstandingly, particularly since 1970. Besides the extension of coverage, this massive growth is due to a wider use of this type of insurance by its members, resulting from the already mentioned changes in industrial relations. Social assistance recipients are the only clientele which has substantially declined throughout the postwar period. Although our data do not include all groups of recipients, this process is not surprising, given the institutional changes which have gradually brought also the weakest population groups within the reach of the major insurance schemes (such as pensions and health).

7. The improvement of benefits

The development of standard (flat-rate or earnings-related) benefits reveals some common trends despite their great variation across schemes, and particularly with regard to unemployment benefits (see Table 6). Firstly, there has been a clear shift from flat-rate or actuarial benefits (i.e. based on the revaluation of contributions), to

Table 6   Flat-rate benefits and earnings-replacement ratios

Year	Standard pension	Sickness benefits (180 days)			Maternity benefits (150 days)			Full unemployment benefits (180 days)		Partial/temporary unempl. benefits (40 hours a week)	Year
		industry/ commerce	public empl.	agri-culture	industry/ commerce	self-empl.	agri-culture	ordinary benef.	special benefits manuf. constr. agric.	manuf. constr. agric.	
1945					Lit.1.000(d)					66%(h)	1945
1946		50%		Lit.28-60(c)							1946
1948			50%								1948
1949								Lit.200(17%)(f)			1949
1950					80%		Lit.12.000-25.000(d)				1950
1953			80%(b)								1953
1957								Lit.230(13.6%)(f)			1957
1958		66%(a)									1958
1960								Lit.300(16%)(f)			1960
1963				50%							1963
1966								Lit.400(12.7%)(f)		80%	1966
1968	65%								66%	80%	1968
1969	74%										1969
1970									50%(g)		1970
1971					80%(e)	Lit.120.000					1971
1972										80%(i)	1972
1974				66%(a)					60%(g)	66%(k)	1974
1975	80%							Lit.800(8.6%)(f)	66%		1975
1977									66%(g)	80%(j)	1977
1979										80%(k)	1979
1980									80%		1980

(a) 50% for 20 days starting from the 4th day of sickness and 66% for the other 160 days.
(b) 80% for the first 30 days and 50% for the remaining 150 days.
(c) Flat rate daily benefit, higher for men and lower for women and minors.
(d) Lump sum, meant to compensate for 4 months of earnings.
(e) Plus an additional voluntary period of 180 days at 30% of previous earnings.
(f) Flat rate sum: the figure in brackets expresses this sum in percentage of the average gross industrial earnings of that year.
(g) For 90 days.
(h) For a maximum of 16 hours a week for 90 days.
(i) Extendable beyond 180 days.
(j) For a maximum of 270 days in two years.
(k) For a maximum of 90 days.

earnings-related benefits (with the only exceptions being full ordinary unemployment benefit and family allowances). Secondly, the earnings replacement ratio has been upgraded step by step for most programmes, passing from 50-66 percent in the 1960s to 80 percent in the 1970s. A major exception to this rule is the sickness cash benefits, which may be explained by the fact that most collective contracts foresee wage continuation. Thirdly, the duration of most benefits has settled at 180 days per year, though this statutory limit is often surpassed in practice.

Largely as a consequence of these institutional improvements, the average amount of most benefits has constantly grown in real absolute terms. Table 7 illustrates this process for pension benefits and family allowances. All types of pensions have substantially increased since 1950. The figures in constant prices show that the average pension has gradually augmented its purchasing power. Also with respect to the average wage we can observe a relative improvement for most benefits, especially in the 1950s and 1970s. As the table indicates, public employees' pensions have always been the highest (although the difference seems to have decreased in the last decade): this is primarily due to the fact that public employees were granted earnings-related pensions long before the other categories, with a fairly high replacement rate (up to 80 percent since 1958). The other types of benefit do not differ as widely: invalidity

Table 7	Average benefits: pensions and family allowances (a)						
	1951	1955	1960	1965	1970	1975	1980
PENSIONS							
Old age (b)	54	91	128	273	409	986	2861
at constant (1970) prices	101	153	187	311	409	576	770
in % of the av. gr. wage (c)	16.5	24.5	27.7/20.1	24.9	24.9	27.3	31.2
Invalidity (b)	52	90	146	248	338	814	2144
at constant (1970) prices	98	151	214	282	338	475	577
in % of the av. gr. wage (c)	16.0	24.2	30.9/23.8	22.6	20.6	22.5	23.4
Survivors (b)	47	76	95	222	290	662	1680
at constant (1970) prices	88	127	139	252	290	386	452
in % of the av. gr. wage (c)	13.9	20.4	20.1/15.5	20.3	17.6	18.3	18.3
Public employees (d)	253	432	605	980	1286	2382	5961
at constant (1970) prices	476	725	885	1116	1286	1390	1604
in % of the av. gr. wage (c)	78.1	116.1	128.2/98.8	89.5	78.2	66.0	65.1
Social pensions					154	499	1318
at constant (1970) prices					154	291	355
in % of the av. gr. wage (c)					9.4	13.8	14.4
Occupational injuries (e)	43	44	58	163	196	417	1318
at constant (1970) prices	81	74	85	185	196	243	355
in % of the av. gr. wage (c)	13.3	11.8	12.3/9.5	14.9	11.9	11.5	14.4
Family allowances	n.a.	n.a.	n.a.	47(f)	59	119	156
at constant (1970) prices				51	59	69	42
in % of the av. gr. wage (c)				3.7	3.6	3.3	1.7

(a) Average benefits are derived by dividing aggregate expenditures by the number of benefits. Figures refer to annual payments in 1000 lire.
(b) INPS schemes.
(c) 1951 and 1955: industrial sector; 1965-1980: all sectors. For 1960, the first data refer to the industrial sector, the second data to all sectors.
(d) All types of pensions.
(e) INAIL pension scheme for permanent disability.
(f) 1967
n.a. = not available

and survivors' pensions have always been lower than old age pensions, due to the different formula and the preponderance of minimum pensions (see below) within these two categories. Only social pensions fare well below: however, their relative position seems to have improved during the 1970s.

To some extent, the real and relative growth of the average pension can be related to the improvement of the pension formula, especially after the introduction of earnings-related pensions in 1968. It must however be noted that, so far at least, the principle of earnings replacement has not applied in practice to a large number of Italian pensions: only a few workers have in fact achieved the necessary contribution requirements for the new formula (which is not applicable, at any rate, to the self-employed). Therefore, the most important factor 'explaining' the real growth of average benefits is the upgrading of pension minima, i.e. of the statutory minimum amounts guaranteed to every recipient regardless of his or her contributory status. These sums were occasionally revised in 1958, 1959, 1962, 1965, 1968 and 1969 (as reflected in Graph 22) and have been automatically indexed to the cost of living since 1971 (1973 for social pensions) and to the industrial wage in 1976 (for the general scheme). As Graph 22 demonstrates, the trend of the average pension closely follows that of pension minima. Minima have differed across schemes, being highest for the general scheme and lowest for social pensions. However, the relative distance has decreased in the last decade: as established by the 1969 reform, the minima for dependent workers and for the self-employed were gradually equalized, until in 1975 and 1976 they coincided. Since 1977 they have again diverged, as a result of the new indexation mechanism introduced for the general scheme. With respect to the average wage, we can observe that minima substantially improved their position in the second half of the 1950s, underwent a (slight) decline during the 1960s, and started to regain ground during the 1970s.

Graph 22

Old age pensions as % of average gross wage (a)

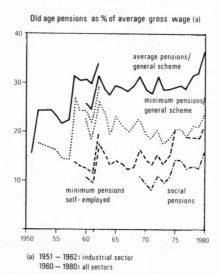

(a) 1951 – 1962: industrial sector
    1960 – 1980: all sectors

As to family allowances, our data show that they grew in real terms in the decade between 1965 and 1975 and have drastically declined thereafter under inflationary erosion: moreover, they have progressively represented a smaller proportion of the average wage.

Our summary analysis of the evolution of standard and average benefits clearly indicates that welfare clients have been able to improve their economic position both with regard to the initial situation and, generally, with regard to the active population. The only groups to have remained behind seem to be the unemployed (or better, those compensated with the ordinary benefit) and those with family dependents, whose benefits have lost considerable ground in relative and real terms. In the other cases, upgrading of the legal earnings replacement rates has allowed all employees exposed to various risks to maintain a progressively higher proportion of their income and the indexation of long-term benefits has safeguarded them against the attacks of inflation and against otherwise relentless relative losses with respect to active income-earners. The increase of minima has provided in its turn a 'subsistence net' for those people ineligible for insurance benefits. Furthermore, although great fragmentation of benefits still exists, some steps have certainly been made in the direction of greater uniformity.

The welfare state has grown to represent today an important component in the income of Italian households, the main or even the only source of income for a sizeable part of them. According to a survey by the Bank of Italy, transfer incomes constituted, in 1979, some 16.3 percent of the income of a representative sample of families. More than 16 percent of these families drew more than two-thirds of their total income from transfers and another 16 percent of families still drew one-third of their total income from them [42].

III Achievements and shortcomings: evaluations

1. The development of health, education and housing

During the three decades between 1950 and 1980, significant progress was made in the field of health and educational services. Their infrastructures (e.g. hospitals and schools) were expanded both in absolute numbers and capacity, and the amount of both personnel and clients was increased. The national housing stock also improved in size and quality - although the specific contribution of the state is difficult to isolate, given the large role still played by the market in this sector.

Table 8 presents data on the development of the hospital sector, i.e. the largest and most relevant one within the public health system. Although decreasing in absolute numbers in the last twenty years, public hospitals have greatly expanded their capacity in terms of beds (especially between 1961 and 1971), as larger and new institutions

Table 8	Output indicators for health			
	1953	1961	1971	1980
No. of hospitals	1 419	1 495	1 342	1 137
No. of hospital beds	317 884	386 813	478 688	468 550
per 1 000 population	6.7	7.6	8.8	8.3
No. of hospital in-patient treatments	2 635	4 281	7 538	9 121
per 1 000 population	55.4	84.6	139.2	162.3
No. of hospital doctors	15 639	24 346	38 869	68 951
per 1 000 treatments	5.9	5.7	5.2	7.6
No. of paramedical staff	41 668	53 153	119 247	227 050
per 1 000 treatments	15.8	12.4	15.8	24.9

have replaced older, smaller and less well equipped ones. The number of cases of in-patient treatment more than tripled in the period under consideration. Although the processes of 'medicalization of health' and of 'professionalization of medicine' certainly have something to do with it, this growth must be largely connected with the already examined expansion of health insurance through various sectors of the population.

Table 9 presents some output indicators for public education. Most of these point towards quantitative and qualitative growth. The only exceptions are the number of elementary schools and pupils: the former sharply declined between 1961 and 1978 (a large number of closures involved institutions located in unsuitable buildings), whereas the latter displays an oscillatory trend, largely connected with demographic changes. The enrolment ratio has constantly increased: in 1978, 96.9 percent of the population between the ages of 6 and 13 (i.e. the period of compulsory education), attended a public institution. The number of schools has expanded at the middle and secondary level, especially between 1961 and 1971, as a consequence of the 1962 school reform. Similarly, the number of middle, secondary and higher education pupils/students has constantly increased. This increase is more accurately explained in terms of higher enrolment ratios than in terms of demographic changes, as shown by our figures. Finally, the number of teachers has increased at all levels. However, this growth only resulted in lower pupil/teacher ratios at the elementary level, while at the other levels these ratios increased in the 1950s (middle and secondary) and 1960s (secondary). The growth in the number of secondary and university teachers in the 1970s is quite remarkable: during this period, the educational system functioned as an absorber of 'intellectual' unemployment [43].

Table 9	Output indicators for education			
	1951	1961	1971	1978
Elementary				
No. of schools	34 837	37 984	34 496	29 554
No. of pupils (in 1,000)	4 307	4 024	4 501	4 318
No. of teachers (in 1,000)	158	181	210	259
Pupil/teacher ratio	27.3	22.2	21.4	16.7
Middle				
No. of schools	2 109	4 602	7 969	9 069
No. of pupils (in 1,000)	572	11 257	2 066	2 813
No. of teachers (in 1,000)	49	102	187	246
Pupil/teacher ratio	11.7	12.3	11.0	11.4
Secondary				
No. of schools	1 258	1 730	4 903	5 359
No. of pupils (in 1,000)	291	628	1 475	2 037
No. of teachers (in 1,000)	29	51	116	197
Student/teacher ratio	10.0	12.3	12.7	10.3
Higher				
No. of universities	27	29	42	44
No. of students (in 1,000)	231	268	681	996
No. of teachers (in 1,000)	4	6	9	24
Student/teacher ratio	58.5	44.7	75.7	41.5
Enrollment rates				
Elementary and Middle	72.6	81.1	92.9	96.9
Secondary and Higher	5.8	10.3	24.7	34.1

As shown in Table 10, the national housing stock developed constantly during the period 1951-1981. The total number of rooms and dwellings almost doubled between 1951 and 1981 and the proportion of 'unsuitable' dwellings tended to decline. The role of the state in this process has mainly consisted of a policy of regulation and subsidization of private housing (cf. Institutional Synopsis, Appendix Volume). Direct public housing construction programmes played an important role only during the 1950s: as shown by the expenditure data in section II/2 above, the state contribution to the growth of the national housing stock has been small and declining, especially during the 1970s.

As regards the social services, the reforms of the 1970s have greatly expanded this sector, especially through the introduction of services for new target groups: counselling units for young couples and families; kindergartens for children of employed women; personal services and home help for the elderly, handicapped and invalids; assistance centres for drug addicts etc. Although these new services are still experimental and controversial, they represent an important achievement in Italian social policy and witness its capacity to adapt to the rapid changes of societal needs [44].

Table 10	Output indicators for housing			
	1951	1961	1971	1981
No. of occupied dwellings (in 1,000)	10 756	13 032	15 301	17 509
No. of occupied rooms (in 1,000)	35 063	43 424	56 242	71 465
Rooms per dwelling	3.3	3.3	3.7	4.1
Occupants per dwelling	4.3	3.8	3.5	3.2
No. of unsuitable dwellings (in 1,000)		164	79	96
as % of occ. dwellings		1.3	0.5	0.5

2. The record on poverty

Owing to the economic and social backwardness of a large part of the country, poverty has always been a serious national problem in Italy. Until World War II, however, its political visibility remained quite low. State intervention in the field of social assistance greatly increased in the first half of this century; but in public debate the theme of poverty tended to be perceived rather as a competence of the Catholic Church than as a matter of state concern.

As we have already mentioned, the Republican Constitution made explicit references to poverty, recognizing the right of the needy to assistance, and thus giving the fight against poverty the status of a constitutional aim. Soon after the reconstruction period, the dramatic living conditions in the Southern and/or rural areas attracted the attention of policy makers. A Parliamentary Commission was set up in 1951 to investigate the problem of 'destitution' and ways of combating it [45]. This was the first important step which aimed at carrying out a large-scale, national quantitative and qualitative assessment of this phenomenon. The Commission surveyed the housing, nutrition and clothing conditions of Italian families and identified four different standards of living: 'destitute', 'in hardship', 'middle' and 'high'. Table 11 summarizes the findings of this survey, showing that some 23.3 percent of Italian families, i.e. some 12.1 million people still lived in conditions of 'hardship' or 'destitution', i.e. with appallingly low and inadequate levels of consumption, housing, hygiene and sanitation. Destitute families could hardly afford to buy foodstuffs such as meat, sugar or wine; they lived in overcrowded dwellings (often with more than four people per room), and only had very poor clothing. This huge mass of poor tended to be concentrated in the South (where 18.3 percent of the resident families were 'destitute' and 20.6 percent 'in hardship') and in the islands (24.8 percent and 20.6 percent respectively, as against 1.5 percent and 4.3 percent in the North). Poverty was widespread in large families, in the agricultural sector, among the old, the disabled and especially the unemployed. Lack of work (or irregular and underpaid work) was given by the Commission as the principal cause of destitution: a fact which received further corroboration by the dramatic findings of a second Parliamentary Inquiry on Unemployment (which counted in 1953, 1,716 million unemployed, i.e. 9 percent of the labour force).

Table 11	Families according to their standard of living, 1951	
Standard of living	1,000	%
'destitute'	1 357	11.7
'in hardship'	1 345	11.6
'middle'	7 616	65.7
'high'	1 274	11.0
Total	11 592	100.0

These data had a strong impact on public opinion and gave rise to a heated debate. The Commission's recommendations, however, were rather general, being limited to advocating a greater coordination of the various public assistance schemes and agencies, a more rigorous expansion of both social assistance schemes and agencies, and social insurance.

The period of rapid economic growth which started around the mid-1950s, together with the improvement in welfare benefits and services profoundly changed the dramatic situation depicted by the 1951 Commission. Average per capita income grew some 2.5 times between 1950 and 1970 and economic affluence had a spill-over effect, albeit somewhat limited, which affected the more backward and poor areas of Italy. The increase of employment opportunities offered 'poor' families a greater chance of earning a market income though often at the price of migration to more developed areas. The growth of minimum pensions, the introduction of social pensions and the universalization of health assistance, moreover, represented a tangible improvement for these families.

During the late 1950s and 1960s, the visible and generalized increase of material welfare gradually obscured the issue of poverty in public discussions and political programmes, but the 1970s witnessed a 'rediscovery' of poverty. The economic crisis suddenly brought to the surface the persisting and profound geographical imbalances and high economic and social vulnerability of the South (not only the rural areas, but also large metropolitan areas such as Naples or Palermo). The restructuring and decentralization of social services and assistance stimulated a new social activism by the political parties, trade unions and the Catholic Church, all aimed at improving the living conditions of particular groups (the handicapped, the elderly, drug addicts, the disabled), and at a more effective response to 'social needs' [46].

The results of some of the first sociological investigations started to contribute empirical evidence on the widespread persistence of absolute poverty, i.e. of family and individual situations characterized by precarious subsistence levels [47].

At the end of the 1970s a more systematic empirical inquiry on poverty was carried out by G. Sarpellon, for the European Community research project on this topic. The research findings were published in 1982 and represent the first comprehensive picture of the Italian 'poor' since 1951 [48]. Sarpellon's investigation focused on 'relative' rather than 'absolute' poverty, as defined by the international standard-of-poverty line, and measured at two points in time, 1973 and 1978 [49]. In order to take into account the large disparities of consumption patterns and living conditions between North and South, Sarpellon and his colleagues decided to draw two different poverty lines: a 'destitution' line (*miseria*) and a higher 'in need' line (*indigenza*). On the basis of these two lines, they arrived at three estimates of the poor population: a minimum estimate, comprising all families under the 'destitution' line (1,625,000 families, or 9.4 percent of all Italian families); a maximum estimate, comprising all families under the 'in need' line (3,626,000, or 20.4 percent of all families); and an intermediate (and probably more realistic) estimate, comprising all 'destitute' families plus those living 'in need' in the North and Centre of the country (2,593,000, or 15 percent of all families). As in 1951, poor families still tended to be massively concentrated in the South (Table 12).

Table 12   Poverty in Italy, 1978

Families in	No. of families in 1,000			as % of all families		
	North/ Centre	South	Total	North/ Centre	South	Total
'destitution'	621	1 004	1 625	5.3	18.0	9.4
'need'	968	1 033	2 001	8.2	18.6	11.5

Table 13 gives the most interesting findings as regards the main factors of poverty and its territorial distribution.

Table 13   Destitute families (a) by cause of poverty and family size
                         percent distribution

Poverty due to:	No. of family members					
	1	2	3	4-5	6+	Total
(1) Insufficient market income						
Centre/North	1.1	8.0	16.1	24.4	5.6	55.2
South	1.1	7.3	10.5	26.9	14.2	60.0
(2) Unemployment						
Centre/North	–	0.3	0.5	0.4	–	1.2
South	–	0.4	0.4	0.6	0.6	2.0
(3) Low pensions						
Centre/North	19.2	21.6	1.0	0.9	–	43.6
South	14.6	19.0	3.0	1.0	0.4	38.0
Total						
Centre/North	20.3	29.9	18.5	26.7	5.6	100.0
South	15.7	26.7	13.9	28.5	15.2	100.0

(a) See table 12.

The table groups poor families according to the employment condition of its members. Group (1) comprises all poor families with at least one gainfully employed member: this is by far the largest group and its poverty is due to the inadequacy of the market income earned by these members. Group (2) comprises all poor families whose active members were in search of a job (at the moment of the survey): these families do not earn market incomes and probably survive as a result of assistance payments and subsistence activities. Poverty due to lack of work of all family members is relatively limited. Group (3), finally, comprises all poor families with only economically inactive members: in this case poverty is mainly due to inadequacy of the pensions.

The breakdown of the aggregate figures by family size and geographical area allows us to single out some important differences. In the North and Centre, there are a greater number of smaller sized families (one or two members), living on a low (social or minimum) pension: in this case poverty is the effect of widowhood, old age and invalidity in an industrial and probably urban environment. Conversely, in the South there are a greater number of large families, earning a market income which is insufficient to guarantee a relatively decent standard of living. Under these circumstances poverty is primarily the effect of the scarcity of work opportunities and the inadequacy of market remunerations (especially in the 'irregular' and black sectors) [50].

The income maintenance system bears a heavy responsibility with respect to the persistence of poverty. Social and minimum pensions are unable to guarantee a decent standard of living when they are the sole source of family income, and the same applies for full employment benefits and assistance payments. The high frequency of poverty among large families indicates moreover that the existing system of family allowances is not adequate to satisfactorily compensate the 'risk' of family dependents, especially where labour market conditions are backward or depressed.

In addition to 'vertical' or economic poverty, new forms of 'horizontal' poverty have emerged. Censis and Sarpellon have documented serious disparities in living standards and life chances as a result of the geographical distribution and organization of services, together with changes in the social and human environment. The main contrasts are between large and medium or small urban concentrations, and secondly between urban and rural areas. This contrast consists of several factors, of which housing conditions is the most significant: the availability, price, size and quality of housing is worse (and still deteriorating) in metropolitan than in rural areas. In large cities the availability of reasonable housing and the frequently excessive prices of such housing constitute an acute problem, especially for low-income and young families.

In the Censis survey the provision of virtually all publicly provided amenities (water, electricity, transport, health services etc.), varies between areas of high and low population density/urban and rural.

Poverty, although still widespread, and 'rediscovered' by social research, does not occupy a top position on the political agenda. According to Sarpellon, the financial resources necessary to lift all poor families above the poverty line would amount to around 1 percent of GDP (at 1978 prices). In institutional terms, the best instrument to fight poverty would be (again, according to Sarpellon), a gradual reform of income maintenance directed towards the establishment of a guaranteed social minimum. However, neither the present political nor the economic climate offer much prospect of such a programme.

3. The record on inequality

Empirical evidence regarding the extent and distribution of inequality within Italian society is rather limited, and very little is known about the redistributive effectiveness of social policies.

Table 14 reports the available evidence on the distribution of post-tax household incomes for selected points in time, contrasting three different strata [51]. With respect to the initial situation, an overall (if slight) improvement of distribution can be observed: the top 10 percent seems to have lost ground (-4 percentage points), while the lower 60 percent seems to have obtained the highest relative gain (+2.4 percentage points). The years 1948-1958 and 1968-1978 stand out as the periods with the greatest redistribution.

Table 14	The distribution of household incomes after tax				
	1948	1958	1968	1978	1980
Top 10% decile X	33.9	30.6	29.3	27.4	29.9
Middle 30% deciles IX-VII	34.7	35.2	39.0	38.3	35.3
Lower 60% deciles VI-I	31.4	34.1	31.7	34.3	33.8

It would be impossible to clearly sort out the determinants of these relative modifications, especially as their empirical basis is already uncertain [52]. We can, however, say at least a few words on the change of inequalities in terms of wages and salaries, and in terms of pensions.

At the level of factor distribution, the most relevant development in the postwar period has certainly been the increase of the employees's share of national income, which passed from 49 percent in 1950 to 67 percent in 1979. This suggests that wage and salary inequality now constitutes a major part of total inequality. According to a famous piece of research carried out by Gorrieri at the beginning of the 1970s, the Italian wage system (especially as it had developed in the 1960s) was extremely fragmented and was to a great extent responsible for the reproduction and persistence of economic inequality [53]. However, wage inequality has decreased during the 1970s, as a consequence of the egalitarian wage policy pursued by the trade unions and automatic indexations. Thus, there seems to be evidence of an increasing degree of equality, at least within the employees' sector [54].

Also on the expenditure side of the pension system there are a few elements pointing towards redistributive effectiveness. In fact, despite the link between earnings and pensions (which in principle tends to reproduce market inequalities), institutional regulations have increasingly directed the pension system towards 'vertical' redistribution, especially through the upgrading of minimum pensions and the introduction of social pensions. In addition, the indexation mechanisms, introduced during the 1970s, favour the lower level pensions (particularly those slightly above minima, as shown by Table 15).

Table 15   The effects of indexation on pension levels

	1975	1977	1979	1981
Pension level	Absolute figures in lire			
Below minimum	50 000	68 000	84 400	91 200
Minimum	55 950	76 650	122 300	188 250
Above minimum	60 000	109 000	190 300	313 300
	200 000	265 400	367 000	504 200
	500 000	603 450	745 750	913 450
	Index numbers (1975=100)			
Below minimum	100	137	169	182
Minimum	100	142	219	336
Above minimum	100	182	317	522
	100	133	184	252
	100	121	149	183
Cost of living index	100	137	178	249

The effects of social policies go well beyond the distribution of income and have a considerable effect on the non-economic aspects of inequality. Unfortunately there is virtually no empirical information on this topic.

The only empirical indications available refer to educational policies. Evaluation research carried out in this field seems to suggest the following conclusions:

- in spite of the massive expansion of educational resources and access, little progress has been made in reducing the influence of class backgrounds on school achievement, i.e. in equalizing educational opportunities for different socio-economic groups;
- compensation policies have failed to provide effective support to lower income pupils and students, and have instead had a regressive effect on redistribution [55].

The second point deserves closer examination. Compensation policies (under the form of tax exemptions, cash transfers, free travel and books, extra tuition etc.) became increasingly important in Italy during the 1960s and 1970s. According to a detailed study by Padoa Schioppa, they have not been effective [56]. Most resources have in fact been spent at university level rather than at the level of compulsory education; benefits in kind (e.g. free books), have not been concentrated selectively at lower income levels, but have been distributed according to universalistic criteria; cash transfers have been fully inadequate and, again, owing to a high income threshold, have also been granted to students who were not in need. In 1977 a Census survey reported that over 20 percent of secondary school students dropped out of education due to financial difficulties [57]. A recent study by Bernardi and Trivellato has confirmed that families in lower socio-economic classes are markedly under-represented in the educational system, in terms of both access and resources [58].

4. The disparity of treatments

As has already been stressed, the legislative framework governing the provision of welfare benefits is extremely fragmented. For each standard risk there is a wide variety of schemes, with different regulations governing the structure of benefits, their financing and administration. The result of this situation is a marked disparity of treatments across sectors and categories, which has recently become one of the major indictments against the Italian social security system.

The simplification of structures and harmonization of schemes and regulations have long been central themes in the Italian debate on social policy. The D'Aragona Commission advocated changes in these directions as early as in 1947 and during the 1960s the CNEL repeatedly called for a comprehensive rationalization of the welfare system, to enhance both equity and efficiency. The reforms of the 1970s achieved some of these recommendations with the transfer of social services and assistance to local authorities and the establishment of the SSN. Equity of treatments - at least *de jure* - has now been fully achieved as regards these two important sectors. In the field of income maintenance (*previdenza*), however, little progress has been made, except for family allowances, which were fully equalized across sectors at the end of the 1970s: during the last decade the organization and coverage in this field have increased greatly, especially as a consequence of the introduction of various indexing mechanisms.

Some significant examples of 'unequal treatment' have already emerged in previous sections (e.g. the low contributions paid by the self-employed and the higher benefits for public employees). Given more specific references to institutional regulations, we can briefly survey some of the major disparities and distortions, i.e. those which are the focus of the current discussion. Given its size and importance, the pension system bears the heaviest indictments, regarding the following factors [59]:

- Pensionable age. The self-employed retire at the age of 65 (60 for women); private sector employees retire at 60 (55 for women), or after 35 years' contributions; public employees have practically no age threshold and are allowed to retire after 20 years' service (and in some cases after 14 or even 11 years as a result of some special privileges).

- The earnings-replacement rate. This is set at 80 percent after 40 years' contributions for dependent workers (general scheme). The same formula should apply, in general, to public employees: however, again as a result of various 'exceptions' and privileges, their pensions often amount to 100 percent of earnings after 40 years' service. The selfemployed do not qualify for earnings-related pensions.

- Pensionable earnings. This is an important aspect, as earnings vary at different stages of one's career and at different paces in different careers. For private employees, pensionable earnings consist of the average earnings of the best five years, revalued according to the cost of living index. For public employees, pensionable earnings are those of the last month of service. As shown by Castellino [60], the regulations for private employees tend to favour careers which are most dynamic in terms of earnings towards their end - normally those of white-collar employees. As regards public employees, their privileged position is evident: the last month's salary is very likely to be the highest possible of one's career (if only for indexation) and the practice in the public sector is often to grant a career advance in proximity to retirement. It must be added that private employees have a ceiling on pensionable earnings, whereas there is no such ceiling for public employees.

- The cumulation of pensions and earnings. Pensions are temporarily discontinued or only paid at the minimum amount to retired private employees starting a new dependent occupation, whilst public employees are entitled to seek re-employment (for instance, in the private sector), without forfeiting their pension.

- The indexation mechanisms. There is little difference between sectors, but a serious contrast between minimum pensions, pensions which are slightly above the minimum, and higher pensions. Minimum pensions are indexed to the minimum contractual wage of the industrial sector (which is in turn indexed to the cost of living); for all other pensions, there is a mixed system of flat-rate adjustments determined by the wage indexation mechanism (*scala mobile*) and graduated adjustment, at a rate equal to the difference between the wage index and the cost of living index. As shown in Table 15 above, this system of indexation favours those pensions which are slightly above the minimum. The rationale behind this complex and differentiated mechanism was the assumption that pensions slightly above the minimum were the most representative of a 'typical' working life of an Italian employee with a full contribution record, and that it was consequently 'fair' to guarantee stronger protection for these pensions. It is common conviction today, that the effects of such mechanisms during years of high inflation have gone well beyond the intentions of policy-makers in the mid-1970s, by under-protecting minimum pensions and flattening higher pensions.

All the issues discussed above are currently the subject of heated debate. A Study Commission established by the Ministry of the Treasury has recently produced a report, containing detailed proposals in order to eliminate unjustified privileges and harmonize legislation along the model of the general scheme of INPS [61]. A draft bill is also under examination by parliament.

Although no proposal explicitly refers to 'acquired entitlements', but only to future ones, there is strong opposition to reform by the categories involved (especially public employees and the self-employed). Given the great economic interest at stake and the change of the economic climate in the 1980s, the reform of the pension system will certainly prove more difficult to achieve than the health reform of the late 1970s.

In addition to the pension system, unemployment insurance is characterized by marked disparities of treatment, which heavily discriminate between 'types' of risk (full versus partial or temporary unemployment), and between sectors (industry versus agriculture).

As the Institutional Synopsis in the Appendix Volume illustrates in detail, the degree of economic compensation granted to various typical cases of unemployment displays a great range of variation. Limiting ourselves to extreme cases, 'full' unemployment (i.e. that resulting from cessation of the employment contract) is reimbursed with a low flat-rate benefit (equal to some 6 percent of the average net industrial wage at the end of the 1970s) for a duration of six months, whilst 'temporary' unemployment (i.e. that resulting from the suspension of the employment contract), is normally compensated, in the industrial sector, with earnings-replacement benefits, amounting to 80-90 percent of previous earnings, for a duration of up to several years. It must be noted that obtaining a given benefit is not only a consequence of the occupational sector to which a worker belongs, but also of the bargaining power of its unions.

This high fragmentation of provisions has recently come under attack and a number of proposals for harmonization are awaiting to be reviewed by parliament. In the political debate (especially on the side of the trade unions and left parties), the idea of a radical reform is gaining increasing ground, i.e. the replacement of the existing system with a National Labour Service, with the task of an overall 'active' coordination of the labour market [62].

5. The differential access to welfare

The above section on the growth of the welfare clienteles has shown that access to welfare schemes and programmes has been greatly extended in the postwar period, gradually including all the active members and even some inactive members of the population. The reforms of the 1970s universalized access to health and social services. In the field of income maintenance, however, entitlements are still linked to occupational conditions and this causes a number of direct and indirect access differentials.

In the first place, some occupational categories have no access at all to some insurance schemes. Thus, the self-employed are excluded from unemployment and sickness (cash benefits) insurance, family allowances (except for farmers), and work injuries (except for artisans). This exclusion is often cited by the groups affected and their political spokesmen, in defence of their favourable contribution/benefit ratio.

Another important occupational category which remains totally outside social insurance is constituted by young people in search of a first job. This category is practically non-existent as regards the income maintenance system. Persons over the age of 18 no longer have the status of 'dependents' (receiving family allowances and covered by the head of the household's health insurance) and may only 'enter' the income maintenance system if they find 'regular' employment. During the transitional period, they have no entitlements: a situation which has created resentments and problems, owing to increased youth unemployment.

Full access to income maintenance is thus only granted to employees. Even within this group, however, a subtle differentiation of access can be observed, resulting from the peculiar characteristics of the Italian labour market.

In order to gain full welfare entitlements, employees must fulfill the following preconditions: 1) be officially registered as members of the respective insurance schemes, and 2) have completed the required contribution period.

The fulfillment of these two preconditions is no easy task, given the character of the Italian labour market. Only 'regular' jobs allow this fulfillment, i.e. stable employment which is in accordance with the Compulsory Insurance and National Contract regulations (the so-called 'institutional' labour market). 'Regular' workers are immediately registered with the compulsory schemes, thus acquiring all the important welfare entitlements: sickness and maternity benefits, family allowances, access to the National Health Service (formerly health assistance), for themselves and their dependents. The 'regularity' of employment and consequently of the employee's contribution record leads to an earnings-related pension and minimizes the risk of unemployment; where unemployment does occur, it is normally of a partial or temporary nature and is compensated with earnings-related benefits.

The size of the 'institutional' labour market has expanded significantly between 1950 and 1980, thus widening the access to full insurance entitlements. The supply of 'regular' jobs, however, has always been lower than the demand for employment: the Italian labour market thus includes large sectors of 'irregular' workers, i.e. active members of the labour force who have only occasional access to the 'institutional' labour market or remain segregated in the 'black' sectors of the economy. It is obviously difficult to quantify the size of the non-institutional, 'irregular' or 'black' sector. Studies carried out at the end of the 1970s have suggested a minimum estimate of 2,542,000 workers: (the maximum and most comprehensive estimate being approximately seven million people) [63]. These workers have no or only limited access to welfare benefits. By definition, social insurance does not reach into the 'black' sector: only public assistance benefits are therefore available to 'black' workers in cases of extreme need. Occasional access to the institutional labour market confers welfare entitlements during the time of 'regular' employment; after the termination of employment workers are only entitled to a low unemployment subsidy for six months, after which time all entitlement expires.

Needless to say, an 'irregular' employment record does not allow an earnings-related pension to mature, and will only produce a minimum pension. This type of 'irregular' labour market is fairly extended in some sectors, such as agriculture and the building industry in underdeveloped areas, particularly in the South [64]. Here unemployment and under-employment are high, and 'black' labour is widespread; 'regular' employment tends to be offered only on a temporary basis (i.e. some days or months per year), given the seasonal character of production. Thus, the workers of these sectors may continuously fall in and out of the insurance system, and the benefits derived from it are set at minimum levels: ordinary full unemployment benefits, minimum (invalidity) pensions and, until the mid-1970s, only limited access to the health system. It must be noted that the 'regular', 'irregular' and 'black' sectors do not strictly correspond to three separate and distinct compartments of the labour force, but should rather be understood as 'typical' working situations, which tend to be more frequent in some areas, often with the same individual worker combining 'regular' and 'black', or 'irregular' and 'black' employment [65]. Moreover, the effects of these employment conditions on income security should be measured against the family situation: if at least one family member participates in the 'institutional' labour market, income losses of the other members in 'black' or 'irregular' occupations are less dramatic; in addition, these members may qualify as 'dependents', thus gaining family allowances and automatic access to the SSN. Thus, due to the segmentation of the Italian labour market the social security system displays a dual character: it only grants full and 'strong' protection to a core group of workers, whilst providing merely 'weak' subsidization to peripheral or marginal groups of the labour force. In order to have a quantitative idea of this phenomenon, Table 16 gives some figures on the number of some typical 'weak' welfare benefits.

Table 16   Some typical 'weak' welfare benefits

Number of	1970	1978
Invalidity pensions	3 415 000	5 355 000
Social pensions	766 000	801 000
Full unemployment benefits	1 540 627	1 913 467
of which:		
agriculture	845 112	1 301 520
other sectors	695 515	611 947

This dualism of income maintenance is one of the major structural problems of the Italian welfare state, and the current economic crisis has aggravated its effects. In the 'institutional' sector, social insurance regulations (especially those of the partial or temporary unemployment insurance) impose severe constraints on economic performance (for instance, discouraging and even preventing labour mobility and encouraging absenteeism). On the other hand, the crisis may leave a sizeable number of workers and families with inadequate income in the 'irregular' and 'black' sectors. There is currently a debate on how to homogenize the system. This would obviously entail a redistribution of entitlements between 'strong' and 'weak' sectors of the labour force. The political conditions for such a reform are, however, quite feeble. The 'institutional' sector is highly unionized and the Italian unions seem neither ready nor capable of imposing sacrifices on their 'strong' members to the advantage of their 'weaker' colleagues. The latter constitute a fragmented and heterogeneous category, with seemingly scarce aggregational capacity and diverse interests.

6. Social policies and Southern underdevelopment: has there been a redistribution?

Redressing the balance between an advanced North and an underdeveloped South has always been one of the major preoccupations of Italian social and economic policies. The way in which the state has brought about a redistribution of resources and its extent, is a major research question for students of the Italian welfare state. Although systematic historical analyses of geographical redistribution are lacking, empirical evidence collected during the 1970s suggests, that in the aggregate, the public sector produces a transfer of resources from North to South [66]. Table 17 gives a geographical breakdown of general revenues and expenditure by major areas. As may be seen, the

Table 17	General revenues and expenditure by major geographical areas, 1973					
	in 1,000 lire per capita			as % of GDP of respective area		
	Revenues	Expend.	Balance	Revenues	Expend.	Balance
North West	678	626	52	40.0	37.0	3.0
North East	487	618	-131	33.9	43.1	-9.1
Centre	523	679	-156	37.0	48.1	11.0
South	276	549	-272	27.9	59.1	-29.0
Islands	303	644	-341	30.6	65.1	-34.3
Italy	477	619	-142	35.8	46.4	-10.6

overall balance is highly favourable to the South and the Islands. The same pattern and redistribution characterizes the social security sector (Table 18). It should be noted, however, that per capita social security benefits tend to be lower in the South. This is basically the consequence of the dual character of the Italian income maintenance system described above. Given the depressed conditions of the labour market, Southern workers and pensioners only manage to obtain 'weak' welfare entitlements.

Table 18	Revenues and expenditure of all social security funds, 1973					
	in 1,000 lire per capita			as % of GDP of respective area		
	Contrib.	Expend.	Balance	Contrib.	Expend.	Balance
North West	243	242	1	14.3	14.2	0.1
North East	178	211	-33	12.4	14.7	-2.3
Centre	175	207	-32	12.4	14.7	-2.3
South	105	165	-60	11.3	17.7	-6.4
Islands	114	169	-55	11.5	17.0	-5.5
Italy	171	203	-33	12.8	15.2	-2.4

The following tables illustrate this phenomenon for unemployment and pension benefits. Table 19 gives the geographical distribution of unemployment benefits in the industrial and agricultural sectors, standardized for the size of the respective occupational groups. In the industrial sector, differences between North and South are not outstanding. In agriculture, however, they are quite marked: in the South and the islands there is a widespread use of flat-rate benefits, owing to the large size of the 'irregular' sector, and a relatively small diffusion of earnings-replacement benefits, characteristic of 'regular' employment situations; in Northern areas, the opposite is true. This contrast represents a typical example of the differentiated response of the income maintenance system to the occupational problems of North and South.

Table 19   Unemployment benefits
                                          by type and geographical area, 1978

| | Full unemp. benefits (flat-rate)(a) | | Temp./partial benefits (earnings-related)(b) | | Active workers (in 1,000) | |
	Industry	Agric.	Industry	Agric.	Industry	Agric.
North West	2.3	3.7	37.9	75.9	3 034	441
North East	3.0	19.8	45.5	609.6	1 607	579
Centre	2.1	15.9	37.7	579.4	1 353	439
South	3.4	63.8	56.5	51.9	1 129	1 169
Islands	4.3	77.0	42.3	121.6	509	460
Italy	2.9	42.0	42.5	245.1	7 632	3 088

(a) Number of cases compensated as a percentage of the active workers in the respective sector.

(b) Number of working hours (industry) or working days (agriculture) compensated per 100 active workers.

One can also observe a marked contrast between North and South in terms of pension expenditure per capita. As Table 20 shows, this is due to the combination of various factors. In the first place, there are variations in the demographic structure: in the North and Centre there are more elderly people than in the South and the islands. Secondly, in the North and Centre there are an over-proportionate number of benefits in comparison with the South (but not the islands), thus indicating that access to the pension system is wider.

Table 20   Pension expenditure
                               and its components by geographical area, 1977

	pension exp. per capita(a)	pop. 60+ as % of total pop.	pension(er)s as % of total pop.	average pension(a)	GDP per capita(a)
North West	440	18.4	28.5	1 551	4 449
North East	427	18.8	28.9	1 477	3 846
Centre	483	18.3	28.4	1 699	3 378
South	292	14.6	21.7	1 342	2 245
Islands	376	15.8	24.8	1 517	2 253
Italy	404	17.3	26.5	1 523	3 357

(a) In 1,000 lire, annual amounts.

Finally, on average the level of benefits tends to be lower in the South. This is largely a consequence of the type of pensions predominating in this area. As seen in Table 21, the relative share of old age pensions (a relatively 'strong' benefit, typical of the 'institutional' labour market) decreases to the advantage of invalidity pensions (a 'weaker' benefit typical of the 'irregular' sector, with high unemployment) as one moves from North to South. Social pensions (another typical 'weak' subsidy), are also higher in the South and the islands.

Table 21   Pensions by type and geographical area
                                              percent distribution

Type of pension	North West	North East	Centre	South	Islands	Italy
Old age	40.0	33.0	22.5	19.8	17.2	28.6
Invalidity	24.3	31.2	37.5	47.4	43.9	35.0
Survivors	18.9	15.7	12.6	13.2	13.5	15.3
Social	4.9	4.2	6.0	6.6	8.1	5.6
State	12.0	16.0	21.5	13.1	17.4	15.5
Total	100.0	100.0	100.0	100.0	100.0	100.0

These data show that the pension system in the South tends to provide only weak subsidization: it certainly plays an important role (at times even crucial) in maintaining
the income of the Southern population (or just keeping it above subsistence), but pays
lower benefits than in the North and Centre. As the per capita GDP figures reveal
(Table 20), the gap between North and South still exists, and continues to represent a
major policy problem. The 'subsidizing' role of transfer policies is frequently criticized as being responsible for the reproduction of socio-economic backwardness in
the South. Certainly, a sprinkling of subsidies just above subsistence levels cannot be
expected to exert a dynamizing effect on the economic and social structure. The real
failure to arrest Southern underdevelopment, however, should be attributed to economic policies rather than social policies. Despite repeated ad hoc interventions, mobilizing sizeable amounts of resources, the former have in fact been unable to 'trickle
down' economic development, thus leaving social policy a vacuum to fill.

IV Correlates and causes: explanations

1. The impact of demographic change

As in most industrialized countries in the postwar period, the Italian demographic
structure has undergone significant changes [67]. Rather than a single and uniform
trend, two distinct periods can be observed: the first includes the 1950s and the first
half of the 1960s, and is characterized by an increasing population growth and
increasing fertility and marriage rates; the second period, starting from the mid-1960s,
is characterized by a rapid inversion of these trends.

The rate of natural increase of the population averaged 8.5 percent per annum in the
period 1952-1964. Since the mid-1960s, however, this rate has started to decline
rapidly, reaching 2.3 percent in 1979, thus indicating a trend towards zero growth or
even a contraction in the near future. Given the near stability of the mortality rate,
this trend must be primarily imputed to the fertility rate, which tended to increase
until the mid-1960s and has been constantly falling thereafter (Graph 23).

Graph 23

Mortality and fertility
(deaths and births per 1 000 inhabitants)

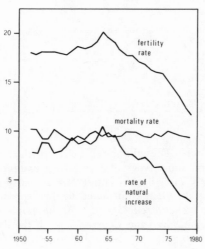

The age structure of the population has witnessed a gradual and considerable increase of older age groups (over 60) and a relative decline of younger ones (Table 22). In addition to the decline of the fertility rate, this change of the age structure is also partly a result of the increase of average life expectancy. In 1950-1953, this averaged 65.5 at birth and 16.8 at the age of 60; in 1974-1977 the corresponding values had risen to 72.8 and 18.5 respectively. As a consequence of these changes, the dependency ratio (i.e. the proportion of predominantly inactive age groups vis-a-vis active ones) has passed from 62.1 in 1951 to 69.5 in 1971. The decline between 1971 and 1981 reflects the changing trend of fertility, but it is also contingent upon entry into old age of the thin age groups born in the 1915-1918 period.

Table 22   Changes in the age structure of the Italian population

Age group	1951	1961	1971	1981
0–14	26.1	24.5	24.4	21.6
15–59	61.7	61.6	59.0	61.0
60+	12.2	13.9	16.6	17.4
Dependency ratio (a)	62.1	62.3	69.5	64.0

(a) Population 0–14 and 60+ as a percentage of population 15–59.

Important changes have also characterized the family structure. Marriage rates remained fairly stable throughout the 1950s and 1960s (around the value of 7.5 weddings per 1,000 inhabitants) but tended to decline during the 1970s (1978 = 5.9). The average number of members per family also steadily declined, passing from 4.0 in 1951 to 3.3 in 1971 and 3.0 in 1981. Family units have tended to become smaller not only due to the lower number of children, but also due to the increase in the number of one-member or two-member families, which passed respectively from 12.9 percent and 22.0 percent of the total number of families in 1971 to 17.9 percent and 23.8 percent in 1981. The majority of these families consist of old people living alone. A series of indicators seem moreover to point towards a higher instability of the traditional family, as revealed by the increase of illegitimate births and legal separations (the first step towards attaining a divorce) (Table 23).

Table 23   Illegitimate births and legal separations

	1961	1971	1981
Illegitimate birth per 100 live births	2.4	2.3	3.9
Legal separations per 100.000 inhabitants	9.6	21.8	45.6

These changes must be taken into serious consideration in order to explain the growth of social expenditure. Thus the modification of the age structure has had an immediate repercussion on some types of transfer expenditure such as pensions and family allowances: in these cases benefit entitlement is tied directly to age. The baby boom of the 1950s and early 1960s contributed to the expansion of education during these periods, while the generalized 'ageing' of the population has increased the burden on the health system, given the J curve shape of the demand for health of the various age groups [68].

In addition to these changes, the changes in the size and composition of the family have certainly exerted a less direct, but nonetheless important effect on social expenditure, especially if looked at against the background of the changing pattern of sexual roles and division of labour. The decline of the extended family and of kinship networks - the *parentela*, a very important trait of the traditional Italian society [69] - have brought about serious structural problems especially as regards the care of the elderly and children: the introduction of social pensions in 1969 and the reform of the assistance sector in the 1970s can be partially seen as responses to these newly emerged problems.

Although intuitively relevant, the specific impact of demographic changes on social expenditure growth cannot be easily determined, since these changes often require the mediation of political factors to actually effect policies (e.g. the introduction of new types of benefits or of special services for the elderly etc.).

We can, however, try to isolate the impact of demographic factors on a type of expenditure which is most typically and immediately affected by them, i.e. that for old age pensions: an increase in the number of old people produces an 'automatic' expansion of benefits, other things being equal.

Following a method first developed by the OECD studies on resource allocation [70], Graphs 24 and 25 report the evolution of pension expenditure (expressed as percentage of GDP) and its components: the demographic ratio (i.e. the percentage of

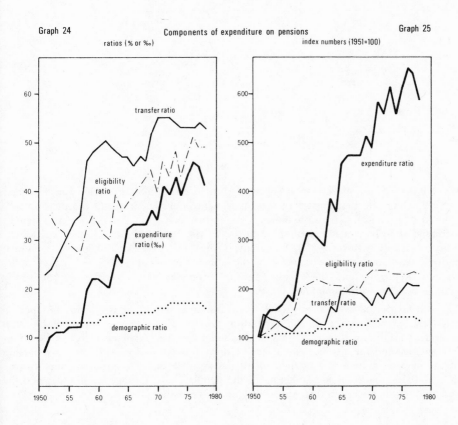

Graph 24

ratios (% or ‰)

Components of expenditure on pensions

index numbers (1951=100)

Graph 25

people aged 60 or above with respect to total population); the eligibility ratio (i.e. the percentage of beneficiaries with respect to old people); and the transfer ratio (i.e. the average benefit as a percentage of GDP per capita).

As shown in Graphs 24 and 25, the expenditure ratio witnessed a massive growth, passing from some 0.7 percent of GDP in 1951 to 4.1 percent in 1978. The demographic ratio was characterized by a linear growth, thus showing an expansion of the potential demand for pensions. The eligibility ratio had an even more dynamic evolution, more than doubling in the period under review. Finally, the transfer ratio was marked by an oscillatory trend, which appears ascending in the aggregate: it passed from 24 percent of GDP per capita in 1951 to 49 percent in 1978.

In order to facilitate comparisons, Graph 25 expresses the various ratios as index numbers. A simultaneous reading of the curves allows us to identify a number of phases characterized by a different combination of the various components. Table 24 attempts a periodization of growth: for each phase, the growth of the GDP share of expenditure is reported (in percentage points) and disaggregated in three components, reflecting the independent effect of demographic, eligibility and transfer changes.

Table 24   The growth of expenditure on old age pensions and its components

Phases	Change in % share of GDP	Due to(a)		
		Demographic change	Eligibility change	Transfer change
1952–1957	0.18	0.04	0.40	− 0.28
1958–1959	0.99	0.02	0.46	0.42
1960–1962	− 0.17	0.15	0.04	− 0.34
1963–1966	1.23	0.26	− 0.20	1.17
1967–1970	0.15	0.12	0.68	− 0.60
1971–1976	1.13	0.24	− 0.15	1.03
1977–1978	− 0.40	− 0.16	− 0.02	− 0.23
1952–1978	3.11	0.67	1.25	1.17
%	100.0	21.5	40.2	37.6

(a) Because of the interactions not included here, the three components do not
    add up to the total change in percentage share of GDP

We will now give a more detailed illustration of the various stages. Our analysis starts in 1952, when the first important reform was introduced, improving the pension formula and establishing pension minima. As shown in Graph 25, the average benefit increased sharply as a result of this reform. In the 19521957 period, the expenditure ratio only grew by a modest 0.18 percent; Table 24 reveals that this growth is almost entirely attributable to the increase in the number of beneficiaries; the demographic effect is negligible and the average pension even decreased, as most of the newly granted benefits were minimum pensions.

The second period covers only two years, but it is important to isolate this period given the great increase in the expenditure ratio (almost 1 percentage point with respect to GDP). In this case, growth resulted from the combined effect of increases in eligibility and the rise in benefit levels. In fact, at the end of 1957 the membership of the pension system was opened up to the agricultural self-employed, and to artisans in 1959 (immediately blanketing-in the people above the age threshold); in 1958 and 1959 minima were in their turn substantially revised.

A third phase began in 1960, characterized by a relative decline in the expenditure ratio, resulting from a considerable decrease in the average benefit. This was not the product of a deliberate decision, but rather of a 'non decision', i.e. the failure to revise minima to keep pace with the continual increases in the standard of living. No significant change occurred in terms of eligibility, while demographic factors started to exert a tangible effect on expenditure.

Between 1963 and 1966 expenditure boomed again. Growth resulted from the considerable increase in the number of elderly as well as from the improvement of the average benefit (minima were upgraded again in 1962 and 1965). It is interesting to note that eligibility decreased in this period, indicating that the pension system was unable to absorb the growing number of old people: many categories still remained in fact excluded from access to the system (most notably traders and, more generally, all those with an irregular employment or contribution record).

The situation changed in the subsequent period. The extension of coverage to traders in 1967 and the introduction of social pensions in 1969 greatly opened the pension system and this immediately reflected itself in expenditure levels. Demographic changes continued to exercise their effect but the average benefit decreased. This may be surprising, given that minima were again revised in 1968 and 1969, in the context of a reform which greatly improved the pension formula. However, the low level of social pensions 'pulled down' the average, so that the aggregate impact of transfer changes during this period turned out to be 'negative'.

A new phase started in 1971, characterized by an oscillating growth of expenditure. This resulted primarily from the improvement of the average benefit, due to the effects of the 1969 reform and especially of the cost of living indexation which started to operate in 1971. The increase of older age groups also explains this growth to some extent. Conversely, eligibility is marked by a slight decline, which is probably connected with the parallel 'explosion' of invalidity pensions which occurred in those years (i.e. with the fact that a growing share of old people were granted invalidity rather than old age pensions).

In the last two years, the combined decline of transfer and demographic ratios produced a visible (but certainly temporary) shrinkage of expenditure levels.

As Table 24 shows, in the aggregate period demographic factors account for 21.5 percent of the growth of pension expenditure, whilst eligibility changes account for 40.2 percent and improvements of the average benefit for 37.6 percent.

2. The modifications of the employment structure and the increasing costs of unemployment

Demographic changes have been paralleled by dramatic modifications of the employment structure. At the beginning of the 1950s, Italy was to a large extent still an agrarian country. The agricultural sector employed the majority of the active population, with a high number of small self-employed farmers (Graph 26) [71]. By 1960, however, the industrial labour force had imposed itself as the predominant occupational group and since the mid-1960s this role has been taken up by the tertiary sector, which constantly and rapidly grew throughout the 1970s, getting closer to the 'post-industrial' threshold of 50 percent. Largely as a consequence of the growth of industrial and tertiary occupations, the mass of employees has steadily increased within the total labour force, passing from 44.7 percent in 1952 to 66.2 percent in 1980. It must however be noted that the number of self-employed is still quite high in Italy by international standards (26 percent of the labour force in 1980).

Graph 26

Sectoral composition of labour force
percent distribution

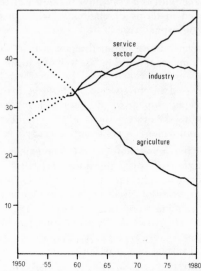

This rapid sectoral modification of the employment structure has been accompanied by significant changes in the overall activity rate, which increased during the 1950s, but underwent a steady decline thereafter - at least until the early 1970s (Graph 27).

Graph 27

Employment and unemployment rates
percentages

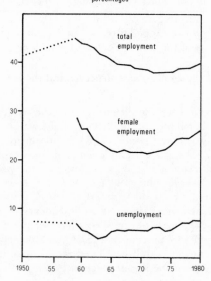

This decline is partly in contrast with the European trend, and is mainly a reflection of the growth of the 'hidden economy'. As numerous studies have illustrated, the massive transfer from agriculture to the industrial and tertiary sectors has resulted in the statistical 'disappearance' of a large number of marginal workers (especially women) into the parallel ('black' or 'irregular') economy [72]: the inclusion of the parallel sector would raise the official activity rate by some 4-5 percentage points during the 1970s. This hypothesis is also supported by the declining trend of women's activity rates. To some extent, this phenomenon may be attributed to the general improvement of economic conditions and to urbanization, which have allowed (and pushed) an increasing number of women to stay at home; to another extent, however, it probably reflects the transformation of marginal female workers registered in agriculture into unregistered workers of the 'hidden' industrial sector [73]. It must however be added that women's participation in the labour market changed dramatically during the 1960s and 1970s: in 1959 the proportion of female employees amounted to 27.4 percent of total employees, whereas this proportion had risen to 31.8 percent in 1980 (32.2 and 55.1 respectively for the tertiary sector alone).

At the beginning of the 1950s unemployment was both massive and widespread, but declined constantly during the economic boom until 1963. During the mid-1960s and early 1970s it tended to rise, and has been increasing constantly since 1974. During the last fifteen years, the internal composition of the unemployed has undergone a great change. The number of 'typical' unemployed (i.e. formerly employed workers seeking another job) has in fact constantly declined in both relative and absolute terms, whilst the bulk of the unemployed is now made up of young people in search of a first job or by non-employed people (e.g. housewives, students, pensioners) seeking work. The latter two categories constituted 85.7 percent of total unemployment figures in 1980. The decline of 'typical' unemployment despite the economic crisis of the latest period may appear surprising. However, it should be noted that the growing rigidity of the institutional labour market has made dismissals very difficult, thus 'freezing' a large number of potentially unemployed workers in their jobs and subsidizing them through the *Cassa Integrazione* (see the Institutional Synopsis). A precise estimate of the size of the unemployed population in Italy should therefore undergo a twofold correction, to take account of both 'hidden' and 'frozen' employment [74].

All these changes in the employment structure have greatly effected the growth of social expenditure. The shift from agriculture to the industrial and tertiary sectors and the expansion of employees have in fact put heavier burdens on the Italian social security system in a number of ways. With respect to the self-employed, employees enjoy in fact wider entitlements (e.g. to family allowances and sickness/maternity cash benefits). In the industrial and tertiary sectors, moreover, welfare entitlements have tended to be introduced at an earlier stage than in the agricultural sector, and normally with more favourable formulas or flat-rate levels, as in the case of unemployment benefits, sickness and maternity cash benefits and family allowances (Tables 3 and 4 above). Finally, industrial and tertiary workers have tended to enjoy a greater degree of job security (most notably during the 1970s): this has in turn meant a greater stability and a wider use of welfare entitlements.

We can attempt to illustrate some of these relationships in more detail by examining the growth of expenditure on sickness, maternity and full unemployment benefits in the 1959-1977, or 1978 period, with a method similar to that used for pensions. Sickness/maternity and unemployment expenditure, expressed as a ratio to GDP (expenditure ratio) can be considered as the result of four distinct components: an activity ratio (i.e. the proportion of active within total population); a composition ratio (i.e. the proportion of the respective target occupational group within the active population: all employees in the case of sickness, female employees in the case of maternity, the unemployed in the case of unemployment); an eligibility ratio (i.e. the proportion of benefits/beneficiaries within the target population); and finally a transfer ratio (i.e. the average benefit, expressed as a percentage of GDP per capita) [75].

Graph 28 gives the evolution of the relevant ratios for sickness cash benefits in the form of index numbers. As shown, the expenditure ratio grew in 1960-1964, declined between 1965 and 1968 and then increased sharply again during the 1970s [76]. The decline of the activity ratio exerted a negative pull on expenditure until the mid-1970s; conversely, the growing share of employees positively contributed to it. The eligibility ratio displays a constantly upward trend, particularly rapid during the 1970s. Since no significant change has taken place during this period in either coverage or morbidity rate, this growth reflects the increasing 'use' of this type of benefit by employees, resulting from the introduction of wage continuation and from

Graph 28

Components of expenditure
on sickness cash benefits
index numbers (1959 = 100)

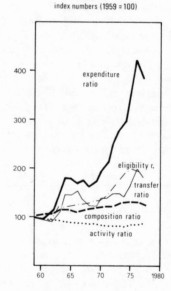

a greater degree of job security in general [77]. Finally, the transfer ratio displays an oscillatory upward trend. The sharp increase in the early 1960s reflects the extension of earnings-replacement benefits to the agricultural sector (1963); the subsequent oscillations, however, are not the result of institutional modifications (regulations remained in fact unaltered), but rather reflect the trend of the average wage with respect to per capita GDP: if benefits are earnings-related, their average amount is, in fact, largely a function of the average wage. Table 25 singles out different phases of growth. As may be seen, the increase of expenditure in the early 1960s is mainly explained by the improvement of the transfer ratio and, to a lesser extent, of the eligibility and composition ratios. The decline between 1965 and 1968 was the result of the combined effect of activity and transfer changes, only partially counteracted by an increase of the composition and eligibility ratios. Finally, the rapid expenditure growth of 1969-1976 resulted from the combined positive effect of all (but especially the eligibility and transfer) ratios.

Table 25   The growth of expenditure on sickness cash benefits and its components

Phases	Change in % share of GDP	Due to (a)			
		Activity change	Composition change	Eligibility change	Transfer change
1960–1964	+ 0.102	– 0.011	+ 0.019	+ 0.021	+ 0.075
1965–1968	– 0.020	– 0.010	+ 0.001	+ 0.025	– 0.030
1969–1976	+ 0.319	+ 0.003	+ 0.022	+ 0.122	+ 0.174
1977	– 0.051	+ 0.006	+ 0.001	– 0.013	– 0.046
1960–1977	+ 0.350	– 0.012	+ 0.043	+ 0.155	+ 0.017

(a) See note to Table 24.

Graph 29 gives the evolution of the relevant ratios for maternity benefits. The expenditure, activity and composition ratios are characterized by a pattern similar to that of sickness benefits. The transfer ratio displays two sharp increases, in 1963 and 1972, which correspond neatly to the two major institutional improvements regarding this type of benefit, i.e. the increase of the flat-rate benefit for agricultural workers in 1963 and the improvement of benefits in 1972 (most notably the introduction of earnings replacement benefits for agricultural workers and the extension of benefit duration). These two institutional changes are also reflected in the evolution of the eligibility ratio: in fact, both provisions strengthened coverage requirements (and controls) for female employees. It should be noted that the number of beneficiaries is also

Graph 29

Components of expenditure
on maternity cash benefits
index numbers (1959 = 100)

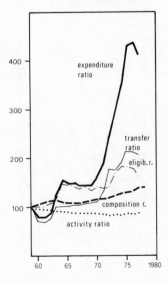

(and obviously) affected in this case by the fertility rate. As we know, the latter has been rapidly declining since the mid-1960s, and this trend is reflected in the decline of the eligibility ratio seen before and after the effects of the 1972 provisions. Table 26 distinguishes the various phases of growth. As in the case of sickness benefits, eligibility and transfer changes tend to play a more important role in accounting for short-term expenditure variations. In the long-term, however, the expansion of the number of female employees within the labour force appears as the second important factor of expenditure growth, in addition to the increase in average benefits.

Table 26   The growth of expenditure on maternity benefits and its components

Phases	Change in % share of GDP	Due to (a)			
		Lab. force activity change	Lab. force composition change	Eligibility change	Transfer change
1960–1963	+ 0.021	– 0.003	+ 0.003	+ 0.020	+ 0.002
1964–1969	– 0.003	– 0.036	+ 0.001	– 0.005	+ 0.005
1970–1976	+ 0.114	– 0.007	0.017	+ 0.028	+ 0.065
1977	– 0.009	+ 0.002	+ 0.009	– 0.016	– 0.003
1960–1977	+ 0.123	– 0.004	0.030	+ 0.027	+ 0.069

(a) See note to Table 24.

Finally Graph 30 gives the evolution of the relevant ratios for full unemployment benefits. After a swift increase in 1961, the expenditure ratio underwent a constant

Graph 30

Components of expenditure
on unemployment benefits
index numbers (1959 = 100)

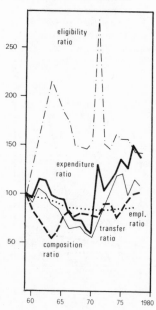

decline during the 1960s and started to increase again rapidly, with some oscillations, during the 1970s. The eligibility ratio seems to follow an awkward pattern, which should be explained with reference to both institutional change and to unemployment, especially in the agricultural sector, as flat-rate allowances were mainly used to subsidize marginal workers in this sector. During the early 1960s total unemployment tended to decrease, but the number of unemployed marginal workers in agriculture entitled to insurance remained fairly constant, thus producing an increase in benefits per unemployed person. In the period 1964-1970, total unemployment grew again, but an increasingly large share of these unemployed were not entitled to insurance benefits, i.e. young people in search of a first job or marginal workers without the necessary contribution record. The increase in absolute numbers of unemployment benefits during this period was not proportionate to the increase in total unemployment, and this fact helps to explain the decline in the eligibility ratio. The rise in the eligibility ratio in 1971 is, in turn, the result of a precise institutional intervention, namely the relaxation in 1970 of contribution requirements in the agricultural sector. The decline of eligibility during the remainder of the 1970s is largely explained, again, by the rapid growth of youth unemployment and of other categories of unemployed not entitled to benefits (e.g. housewives, students, etc.). Finally, the trend of the transfer ratio closely reflects institutional changes, i.e. the rise of benefit levels in 1960, 1966 and 1974 in addition to the introduction of special earnings-related benefits in 1971-1972, and 1977.

Table 27 singles out the distinct phases of growth and the relative weight of the various ratios. In the aggregate, changes in eligibility and unemployment ratios appear as the most relevant growth factors. It is interesting to note that during the 1970s the 'potential' effects of rising unemployment on expenditure levels were completely cancelled out by the closure of eligibility vis-a-vis the increasing number of young unemployed and nonemployed looking for work. It should also be noted that the expenditure considered here is only a part of total unemployment expenditure, and that a vast amount of resources have in fact been spent on partial and temporary unemployment, which do not appear in official statistics.

Table 27   The growth of expenditure on full unemployment benefits

Phases	Change in % share of GDP	Due to (a)			
		Activity change	Unemployment change	Eligibility change	Transfer change
1960-1961	+ 0.032	− 0.007	− 0.051	+ 0.087	+ 0.014
1962-1970	− 0.115	− 0.021	+ 0.012	+ 0.026	− 0.112
1971	+ 0.141	− 0.000	− 0.000	+ 0.093	+ 0.027
1972-1978	+ 0.017	+ 0.003	+ 0.089	− 0.131	+ 0.115
1960-1978	+ 0.076	− 0.025	+ 0.050	+ 0.075	+ 0.044

(a) See note to Table 24.

All these analyses demonstrate that the change of the socio-economic environment (and more particularly of the demographic and occupational structures), have had a significant influence on the growth of the Italian welfare state. It is true that in our operationalizations, socio-economic factors prove less helpful in explaining short-term, annual expenditure variations than institutional changes which improve the coverage or the amount of benefits. Nevertheless, socio-economic change takes place at a slow rate and it should not therefore be surprising that the effects of such change take time to manifest themselves.

3. The advantages and constraints of economic growth

In the first two decades after World War II the Italian economy underwent a process of remarkable growth - one of the highest in Europe. This growth rapidly enabled the country to gain a quite respectable position among the top industrialized powers and is commonly referred to as the economic miracle (*miracolo economico*). During the 1970s, however, Italy entered into a state of permanent crisis (one of the most serious among advanced countries), characterized by slower growth, rocketing inflation and public deficits, balance of payments problems and high unemployment [78].

The start of the 'economic miracle' may be dated to around the mid-1950s. The reconstruction (*ricostruzione*) of the productive apparatus had been completed by 1950, accompanied by a policy of monetary stabilization and by some important steps to modernize the backward economic structure of the South, such as the agrarian reform and the establishment of the Fund for the South (*Cassa per il Mezzogiorno*), both in 1950. Aggregate economic growth boomed in the years 1955-1963 especially as a result of international trade and the penetration of foreign markets. The real annual growth rate averaged 6.0 percent during this period, reaching an unprecedented (and unparalleled) peak of 7.9 percent in 1961 (see Graph 31). This massive increase in output was accompanied by monetary stabilization and balance of payments equilibrium.

By the beginning of the 1960s, however, this situation was starting to change. There was a sharp increase in industrial conflicts in the period 1961-1962; prices became increasingly unstable and the balance of payments became negative. In 1963-1964 a policy of severe monetary restraint caused the first and marked deceleration of growth since 1950, with the growth rate falling to 2.8 percent in 1964 and 3.3 in 1965.

Starting from 1966, the economy accelerated again. The private industrial sector began a process of technological and financial rationalization; the public industrial sector was greatly expanded, in the context of a 'Keynesian' economic policy oriented towards planning and moderate nationalization. However, this new expansion did not last long. In 1969 there was a climate of instability which was the result of both international and domestic factors (the crisis and subsequent collapse of the dollar standard, the increase of raw material prices, the 'hot autumn' of social conflicts). A new money 'squeeze' in 1970 provoked a marked downswing of growth in 1971 (1.6 percent). Throughout the rest of the 1970s, the pattern of growth was characterized by marked oscillations, with years of 'boom' (such as 1973 and 1976), and sudden decelerations (such as 1977), or even falls (such as 1975, when real output fell by 3.6 percent). This decade witnessed a mounting rate of inflation and an overall deterioration in the productive structure of the Italian economy. In the years 1977-1979 an attempt was made to recuperate economic stability by means of a policy of wage restraint and financial control. This policy, however, only proved effective in the short-term and the 1980s have again opened with worrying symptoms of instability.

In order to clarify the relationship between economic and social expenditure growth, we shall observe the concomitant variations of their real annual growth rates [79].

As Graph 31 shows, social expenditure has tended to grow at a faster rate than GDP. This was especially true during the 1950s and 1960s. In the period 1955-1969 the difference between the two growth rates (reported in Graph 32), averaged 3.2 percent, whilst it declined to 2.0 percent (0.8 excluding 1975) in the subsequent years. We can see that the annual variations in the growth pattern of social expenditure do not closely follow those of GDP: however, the overall trend points downwards for both variables (r = 0.45 for GDP, and -0.53 for social expenditure), thus showing a common tendency for growth to decelerate over time. A comparison between the two slopes indicates moreover that social spending has decelerated to a greater extent (b = -0.13 and -0.26 respectively). As revealed by Graph 31, social expenditure growth rates have fallen substantially during the 1970s (with the exception of the years 1975 and 1976) with respect to the high peaks of the 1950s and 1960s. The higher deceleration of social expenditure growth with respect to economic growth is further documented by the trend line in Graph 32 (r = -0.21 and b = -0.12).

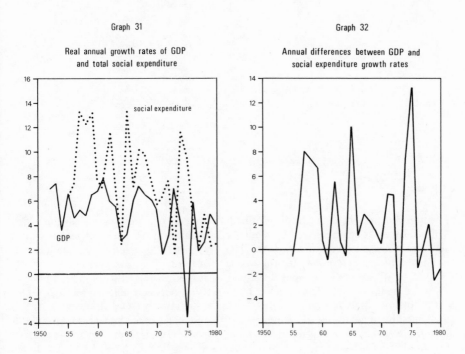

Graph 31

Real annual growth rates of GDP
and total social expenditure

Graph 32

Annual differences between GDP and
social expenditure growth rates

Table 28 gives the result of a correlation analysis between GDP and social expenditure growth rates. As may be seen, the relationship between the two variables is virtually nil, and this tends to be true for all its components, with the exception of education. The correlation coefficients tend, however, to increase when the GDP growth rates are lagged by one (health, education), or by two years (income maintenance, housing). This suggests that the pattern of economic growth on the short-term variations in social expenditure has been slight, and that this influence has only manifested itself after a time lag of two years. Since most of the coefficient signs are positive, the (weak) relationship between economic growth and social expenditure growth can be assumed to have been of a cyclical nature, i.e. social expenditure has tended to expand following years of high economic growth. Only housing expenditure seems to have grown countercyclically, i.e. expanding in periods of economic downswing or recession and vice versa: public investment in this sector has in fact been used as an instrument to stimulate the economy and to absorb unemployment.

The weakness of the relationship between economic surplus and social spending is further confirmed if we take into account the development of total revenues (Table 28). The latter appear in fact to be closely associated with GDP, thus showing that economic growth has indeed yielded an increasing fiscal 'dividend' to the state. Social expenditure, however, seems to have developed quite independently of the availability of this 'dividend'.

Table 28   GDP, social expenditure, and total revenues:
                  correlation of annual real growth rates

	Annual growth of GDP		
Annual growth of	lag 0	lag 1	lag 2
Social expenditure (a)	0.06	0.26	0.41
Income maintenance (a)	− 0.15	0.17	0.40
Health (b)	0.11	0.20	0.18
Education (c)	0.40	0.23	0.10
Housing (d)	− 0.09	− 0.20	− 0.35
Public assistance (a)	0.26	− 0.01	− 0.31
Total revenues (e)	0.56	− 0.19	− 0 20
	Annual growth of social expenditure		
Total revenues (a)	− 0.11	0.12	− 0.01

(a) 1955-1980; (b) 1953-1980; (c) 1952-1980; (d) 1954-1980; (e) 1953-1980,
   excluding 1960.

The scatterplot presented in Graph 33 finally allows us to identify some distinct 'constellations' of years characterized by similar coordinates on the two dimensions of economic and welfare expenditure growth. The graph is divided into four quadrants by two lines which correspond to the average values of growth over the period 1955-1980. The various years appear as quite scattered throughout the plot, thus indicating once again the absence of a linear correlation between the two variables. Despite this disorder two clusters of years can be tentatively singled out: the first is located mainly in quadrant III (high growth) and comprises the periods 1955-1963 and 19661969; the second is located mainly in quadrant I (low growth), and comprises the 1976-1980 period. The mid-1960s and the first half of the 1970s do not cluster together, but are spread in different quadrants.

The period 1955-1963 (predominantly in quadrant III), was characterized, as we know, by the economic miracle and by an expansionist wave of social policy, in terms of both coverage and benefit improvement. These were the 'happy years' of the Italian economy, which produced a growing surplus available for social uses: as we have seen in section II/1 above, the current balance of the state budget remained positive until 1964. The measures taken in 1963-1964 suddenly interrupted this positive syndrome. In 1964 (quadrant I) the economy decelerated sharply as did all types of welfare expenditure, with the exception of housing. This did not mean that benefits were crushed: deceleration resulted in the inflationary erosion of non-indexed (and non revised) benefits, in addition to a slackening of social investments. In 1965 (quadrant IV) economic growth remained low, but social expenditure grew at a rate similar to that of the late 1950s: this was the 'Keynesian' year of spending expansion which witnessed a substantial revision of transfer programmes (most notably pensions), and larger investments in health and especially housing. The period 1966-1969 (predominantly in quadrant III), was then characterized by renewed economic growth together with new social policy commitments: the extension and improvement of the pension system and of other income maintenance benefits; continuing investments in the sectors of health (especially hospitals) and education.

The years 1970-1975 do not seem to follow a common pattern, and are situated within the 'less coherent' quadrants II and IV (with the exception of 1970). The years 1972, 1974 and 1975 are characterized by the unstable and 'dangerous' combination of higher than average social spending and lower than average economic growth. The scattered and unstable coordinates of this period indicate that it probably witnessed a break in the 'easy co-existence' between economic growth and social expenditure (in both its 'pre-Keynesian' and 'Keynesian' versions), and the search for a new equilibrium. The economic environment drastically changed during these years, displaying wide annual oscillations but in a direction of substantial deterioration, while social policy remained on an expansionist drive, largely due to commitments undertaken in the late 1960s (e.g. the regional reform of 1972, the 1974 hospital reform, and the improvement of the pension system in 1975). After the shock of 1975, the years 1976-1980 seem to have recovered some sort of coherence. The growth rate for social expenditure decreased markedly and economic performance displayed signs of stabilization and renewed growth.

Graph 33

Relationships of GDP and social expenditure
annual real growth rates

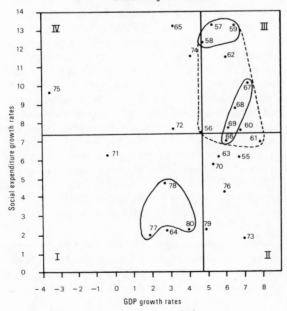

Our analysis is far too crude to allow any generalization concerning the nexus between economic growth and social expenditure. We must therefore limit ourselves to concluding that, in the overall period reviewed here, the former generally appears as a weak predictor of the latter's yearly variations.

The relationship between the economy and the welfare state is mediated (and often distorted) in the short run by a high number of intervening factors. Earlier on we illustrated the weight of demographic and occupational dynamics on the expansion of some welfare programmes. The same analyses have also shown the close relationship between institutional changes and short-term expenditure variations. It is to these changes and their political determinants that we must now turn, in order to get a deeper understanding of welfare expansion.

4. Electoral competition and the role of clientelism

As Regonini has recently put it, 'in Italy it can be easily shown that in the proximity of each great electoral confrontation there has always been a political bargain on pensions at stake' [80].

Thus, in 1958, the extension of pension entitlements to the self-employed (notably artisans), played an important role in the campaign, especially for the Christian Democrats (DC): this electoral commitment was put into action immediately after the election, and the law was passed two months later. In the 1963 elections, the proposal to establish a national insurance system was again an important theme (together with education and housing), especially in the union and leftist campaign. Two months before the elections, the housewives' pension issue was rapidly settled and the government granted generous gifts in the form of pension extension to some minor professional categories. However, it was the 1968 election deadline which was crucial as regards political bargaining on welfare issues. Two 'hot' welfare issues were at stake: the introduction of earnings-related pensions and the hospital reform. In the former case, the elections resulted in a violent polarization of the actors: the PCI (*Partito Comunista Italiano*) and its union CGIL (*Confederazione Generale Italiana del Lavoro*), on the one side and the centre-left government together with the other two unions, CISL (*Confederazione Italiana dei Sindacati dei Lavoratori*) and UIL (*Unione Italiana del Lavoro*), on the other. The government's plan was passed two months prior to the elections and the opposition called a general strike and mobilized the workers against it (a year later, the law had to be changed in line with the basic requests of the opposition: see the Institutional Synopsis). In the case of hospitals, the elections had the opposite effect, i.e. the rapid agreement (after years of discussion) on a reform in which all the interested actors had something to gain (see below). In both cases, the 'electoralistic' attitude of the parties involved was widely lamented by the press. The elections of 1972 and 1976 were less important in the development of social policy. In 1979, however, the electoral campaign again gave high priority to the reform of the pension system (as well as to the first timid 'cuts'). In 1983, the campaign was dominated by the need for stringent welfare austerity, with special emphasis on pensions and health.

The influence of elections in moulding the development of the welfare state is likely to have manifested itself not only at the political-institutional level, but also at the financial (i.e. expenditure) level. With the help of some aggregate quantitative data, we can therefore try to test the hypothesis of an 'electoral cycle' in the growth of welfare expenditure [81].

Table 29 presents a simple breakdown of public expenditure real growth rates by electoral and non-electoral years. Transfers and subsidies (within total public expenditure) and income maintenance (within total social expenditure), have been selected as the most likely expenditure components to be manipulated for electoral purposes. As may be seen, in both cases, the average for electoral years tends to be higher than that for non-electoral years: and this is not merely due to a single (or a couple of) 'exceptional years' - five out of seven (i.e. ca. 71 percent) electoral years in the case of transfers and subsidies and four out of six electoral years (i.e. ca. 67 percent) in the case of income maintenance, witnessed an over-proportionate increase in expenditure (see bracketed figures). The divergence could also be interpreted as the consequence of the economic cycle, with elections occurring haphazardly in 'rich' years or periods. The bottom half of the table shows however that this is not the case. If in both groups of years expenditure tends to increase at a faster rate than GDP (whichever the latter's speed), this is particularly true for electoral years, thus corroborating the hypothesis of an extra-economic influence (such as that of elections).

Table 29   Real annual growth rates of expenditure by electoral and
                  non-electoral years

Expenditure category	Electoral years	Non-electoral years	All years
	Average growth rates (a)		
Transfers and subsidies	9.1 (5/7)	7.5 (8/21)	7.9 (13/28)
Income maintenance	9.3 (4/6)	8.3 (7/19)	8.5 (11/25)
	Average difference between expenditure growth rates and GDP growth rates		
Transfers and subsidies	3.6	3.0	3.1
Income maintenance	4.3	3.7	3.8

(a) Bracketed figures report the number of years above the average over the
    total number of years for each column.

The relationship between economic welfare and voting is commonly understood in general and impersonal terms and not as an immediate/personal one, i.e. as a 'real' exchange of individual votes against individual benefits. In Italy, however, the latter type of relationship may well provide a rationale as valid as the former type for the existence of an electoral cycle/pull of welfare expansion. As numerous studies have shown, besides issue voting (*voto d'opinione*) and voting according to party and/or sub-cultural identifications (*voto d'appartenenza*), a third type of electoral behaviour has played a prominent role in Italy: voting in exchange for individual benefits (*voto di scambio*) [82]. This is particularly, but not exclusively, widespread in the South among the DC electorate. The DC can largely be seen (as Graziano has put it) as a real 'mass patronage' party [83]. In order to gain votes, this type of party provides its clients with individual benefits in a number of ways: for instance, granting them job opportunities in the public sector or assisting them in obtaining a subsidy from the welfare bureaucracy. The 'control' of the exchange on the side of the party mainly occurs through the market of preference votes, in ways which are not necessarily (or better, only occasionally) illegal [84]. The extended area of *sottogoverno* (under-government, i.e. the various spoils represented by state enterprises, public agencies of different sorts, social security funds etc.), has been the main locus of these clientelistic exchanges and welfare benefits are one of their privileged currencies.

The clientelistic use of the welfare state for electoral purpose has taken two main forms: the *lottizzazione*, i.e. the (mainly informal) partisan apportionment of the welfare administration (even in its middle and lower posts), and the establishment and consolidation of a parallel organizational network based on patronage institutions (*patronati*) to attend the various welfare clienteles.

The system of partisan allocation in the Italian public sector has been the object of extensive empirical research. A recent study by Bonaccorsi has explored this phenomenon in the social security sector [85]. Table 30 reports the most interesting (and summarized) findings of the study. As may be seen, a large majority of posts have partisan links, but this is especially true for the DC.

Table 30   The distribution of post-years (a) in the executive boards of social security funds by party, 1945-1975

Periods Parties	1945-47	1948-54	1955-62	1963-69	1970-75	Total
DC	25.1	31.5	35.7	38.0	38.5	36.3
PCI	8.7	5.3	4.0	4.1	4.1	4.3
PSDI	6.4	6.5	7.1	5.3	4.7	5.8
PSI	5.9	4.3	4.2	5.4	8.4	5.6
PLI	5.0	7.2	4.1	3.5	2.3	4.0
PRI	0.9	3.5	3.5	3.6	3.3	3.5
MSI	0.5	1.6	2.1	2.5	1.7	2.0
N.i. (b)	47.5	40.1	39.3	37.6	37.0	38.5
Total	100.0	100.0	100.0	100.0	100.0	100.0
(N)	(219)	(2 019)	(3 822)	(4 028)	(3 453)	(13 541)

(a) In order to control for the length of tenure (the same person may hold office for several years), the units of analysis are posts per year.
(b) Not identified (i.e. the post-holder has no party affiliation or, more probably, his party affiliation is uncertain).

The table refers to all social security funds, but, as Bonaccorsi has shown, the relative shares for the various parties differ according to the type of fund, with each party trying to penetrate more extensively those funds which are closer to their electoral base. Thus, the DC has an over-proportionate representation (39.7 percent; 47.7 percent in 1970-1975) in social assistance funds (the Catholic poor have long constituted a pool of electoral support for the DC), and more generally in funds paying benefits to public employees (48.9 percent and 50.1 percent) and to agricultural workers (39.6 percent and 43.2 percent); the left parties are relatively better represented in social insurance and health funds for employees and the smaller parties in funds for professional categories. As revealed by Table 30, the size of partisan allocation has tended to increase (the absolute number of posts has increased massively) as has its extent (the number of non partisan posts has shrunk).

Although Bonaccorsi's analysis ends in the mid-1970s, there are indications that the phenomenon has in fact intensified in more recent years. In particular the 1978 health reform stimulated the clientelistic behaviour of Italian parties. The management committees (*comitati di gestione*), the new organs created by the health reform and charged with the task of overall administration, have been literally assaulted by parties, as shown in Table 31 (with the DC, the PSI and the PCI securing for themselves the greatest shares). The economic crisis of recent years has in fact made it even more essential for parties to avail themselves of fresh resources in their competition.

Table 31   Distribution of posts within the management committees
by party, 1983

	Presidents	Vice-Presidents	Members	Votes in 1980 local elections
DC	53.8	27.6	39.6	35.7
PSI	20.9	34.9	19.0	14.1
PCI	19.8	21.1	25.3	30.0
PSDI	3.9	9.0	7.7	5.3
PRI	0.6	1.4	4.0	3.7
PLI	0.2	2.0	1.5	2.6
MSI-DN	-	-	0.7	4.8
Independents	0.6	1.1	1.3	-
Other parties	0.2	2.9	0.9	3.8
Total	100.0	100.0	100.0	100.0

If the system of partisan allocation has provided parties with the necessary resources to attract votes in exchange for individual benefits, the articulated network of patronage institutions has provided them with the necessary channel to distribute these resources to their clients. *Patronati* are quasi-partisan institutions, headquartered in Rome but with numerous offices at regional, provincial and communal level which offer personal assistance to welfare applicants (such as information on opportunities and procedures; preparation of the necessary documents; urging the competent administration in cases of delay; administrative and court actions if an application is rejected etc.). In other words, it is the grass-roots institution which regulates individual access to welfare. The first *patronati* were founded in the late 1940s, e.g. ACLI (*Azione Cattolica dei Lavoratori Italiani*), and INCA (*Istituto Nazionale Confederale di Assistenza*), which are the largest Catholic and Communist institutions respectively. Their numbers gradually increased as the welfare system extended to cover new social categories (with a peak in 1968-1972, i.e. the period of substantial re-organization in the social security system). In addition to these large sub-cultural *patronati*, (e.g. ACLI or INCA), there are smaller institutions for special or professional categories (farmers, artisans, traders, agricultural employees etc.). Needless to say, these patronage institutions are under the control, either direct or indirect, of the political parties. The *patronati* offer an efficient organizational network for the vote-benefit exchange. Invalidity pensions (especially in the South) represent the typical target of *patronati*'s activity: in fact the latter are held as largely responsible for the massive expansion of this type of benefit, especially in the early 1970s. An indirect measure of this fact is given in Table 32, which reports the number of actions brought against the INPS administration to obtain (invalidity) pensions in the period 1968-1977. Although the sources do not specify whether these actions have been initiated by the *patronati*, it is almost certain that this has been the case. As may be seen, the number of actions has tended to increase, especially in the early 1970s, as a consequence of both the proliferation of *patronati* and the re-organization of INPS, which made it more permeable to external pressures. The vast majority of actions concerned invalidity pensions, but only a fraction of these were successful. This high failure rate has not constituted a great disincentive for at least two reasons. Firstly (and more importantly) the *patronato* receives a reimbursement for each action by the Ministry of Labour. Secondly, starting an action has a value *per se* vis-a-vis the client (who feels that his needs are being taken care of). Incidentally, it may be worth noting that the rate of success tends to be higher than average in election years (1968, 1972 and 1976). Actions regarding other types of pensions are much less frequent: old age and survivors' pensions are in fact less amenable to clientelistic/electoral manipulations, as they depend on more objective criteria. In the case of other pensions, the awkward pattern revealed by the data may however conceal a phenomenon similar to that for invalidity pensions. As we already know, 1969 witnessed the introduction of social pensions: this may explain the relative fall of total actions (in percentage terms) until 1970 (the total number of pensions rose), and the subsequent increase (social pensions may well have become a new target of action, given again their rather 'manipulable' character).

Table 32   Actions brought against INPS due to rejected pension
                   applications, 1968–1976
                   (in 1,000)

	Invalidity pensions		Other Pensions	
	Total actions	Successful actions	Total actions	Successful actions
1968	415 (119)	163 (47)	59 (20)	36 (10)
1969	480 (157)	135 (44)	95 (11)	20 (2)
1970	454 (129)	150 (42)	38 (7)	21 (4)
1971	704 (169)	263 (63)	-	-
1972	614 (143)	194 (46)	193 (37)	64 (12)
1973	738 (192)	187 (49)	147 (38)	48 (12)
1974	798 (176)	181 (40)	176 (36)	46 (9)
1975	778 (157)	155 (31)	168 (34)	45 (9)
1976	773 (253)	157 (51)	164 (35)	64 (14)
Total	5 754 (165)	1 585 (45)	1 040 (25)	344 (8)

(a) Bracketed figures express absolute numbers as a percentage of the total
number of new pensions liquidated in that year.

The data and information presented make it quite clear that the *patronati* have exerted a significant influence on the expansion of welfare benefits. Their activism has served the purpose of feeding the various parties' clienteles, of providing job opportunities for lower party cadres and (last but not least) hidden sources of party financing.

5. The welfare record of different coalition formulas: has the Centre-Left been important?

Italy has a multi-party system characterized by a high degree of fragmentation (multiplicity of parties), factionalism (factions within the parties) and polarization (high ideological distance between parties, especially between 'opposition' and 'government' parties) [86]. The centre of the political spectrum is occupied by the DC (Christian Democracy). This is a composite inter-class party which is traditionally very close to the Catholic Church and characterized by overall moderate orientations on economic and social policy, and by a strong Atlantic loyalty on foreign policy. Since the 1948 elections, this party has always obtained the majority of the vote (ranging from 48.5 percent in 1948 to 32.9 percent in 1983), thus playing a key role in the development of postwar Italy. The three minor centre parties - PLI (Liberal Party), PRI (Republican Party) and PSDI (Social Democratic Party) - have an aggregate electoral strength which has never exceeded 14-15 percent; but despite their smaller size, these parties have played an influential role as essential partners with the DC in most of the experimented coalitions. The right-wing has always been monopolized by an anti-system party, the MSI-DN (Social Movement-National Right), which has oscillated between 2 and 9 percent of the vote and, given its neo-fascist outlook and orientation has never taken part in any coalitions, remaining segregated as part of the opposition. The Left comprises the PSI (Socialist Party) and PCI (Communist Party). In the 1948 elections (where they gained 31 percent of the vote), these two parties joined to form a popular front but have subsequently followed quite different routes, bringing the former gradually closer to the centre and pushing the latter into a permanent anti-system opposition. In electoral terms, the PSI underwent a steady decline between 1958 (14.2 percent) and 1976 (9.6 percent) and has only recently started to regain ground (1983 = 11.9 percent). The PCI, on the contrary, has witnessed a constant increase of its vote, passing from 22.6 percent in 1953 to a peak of 34.4 in 1976 (1983 = 29.9 percent).

Despite the relative gains and losses of the various parties at different times, electoral change has never produced major governmental shifts. Thus since 1948 Italy has always been governed by coalition cabinets, constantly led (until 1981) by the DC and encompassing - in all the possible combinations - the other four 'pro-system' parties (PLI, PRI, PSDI, PSI). Four types of coalition formulas have been tried since 1948: 'centrism' (DC together with minor centre parties), 'Centre-Left' (DC, PRI, PSDI and PSI), 'National Solidarity' (DC, PRI, PSDI, PSI and the parliamentary support of the PCI) and 'Penta-Party' (DC, PLI, PRI, PSDI and PSI). Centrism reached a peak during the period of the first legislature [87] (1948-1953), when the DC leader De Gasperi obtained 48.5 percent of the vote and the absolute majority of parliamentary seats and could thus govern almost uncontested by his smaller coalition partners. The centrist formula survived throughout the whole of the second legislature (1953-1958) but started to show crisis symptoms during the third (1958-1962). A gradual *rapprochement* was in fact taking place between the DC (which was increasingly breaking loose from the Catholic Church and witnessing the emergence of a new generation of more progressive cadres), and the PSI (which was in turn gaining greater autonomy from the PCI, especially on foreign policy grounds).

In February 1962 the first centre-left coalition was formed, with the PSI granting support or abstaining, but never voting against the government. The birth of the Centre-Left represented a very significant event in the early 1960s, both for the enormous hopes (of the Socialists), and the enormous fears (of Catholic and entrepreneurial interests) to which it gave rise. The Centre-Leftbecame 'organic' during the fourth legislature (1963-1968), with the PSI participating directly in the cabinet and holding important ministerial posts, e.g. for the Budget, Public Works, Labour and Social Security and Health. The failure of the socialist unification (*unificazione socialista*), i.e. the merger between the PSDI and the PSI, at the 1968 elections, and especially the increasing contrasts in policy between the two parties, exacerbated by the waves of social conflict during the same year, gradually undermined the centre-left formula, which came to a sudden end with the 1972 elections (called one year in advance due to the extent of the conflict between the coalition partners). Thus, the fifth legislature (1972-1976) witnessed a short-lived resurrection of centrism, followed by a new centre-left experiment (1973-1974). Following the outstanding success of the PCI in the 1976 national elections (as well as the major strategic shift, which brought this party to offer the DC a 'historical compromise', i.e. a broad reformist alliance), a new formula was inaugurated: that of National Solidarity, with the PCI firstly abstaining, and subsequently supporting the two DC-led governments in parliament, without holding cabinet posts. However, this formula did not last long and was replaced by the Penta-party formula during the 1979-1983 legislature.

Given the wide ideological spectrum of the Italian party system, the differences between the various parties' social policy profiles are quite significant. The PCI has always displayed a markedly pro-welfare attitude: however, in the 1950s and 1960s the Marxist-Leninist orthodoxy pushed this party to pursue a policy of short-term defence of the (core industrial) workers' interests (as in the case of pensions), in a substantial distrust of welfare reforms (and in the hope of a capitalist collapse). Only in the 1970s has this party adopted a strategy which (albeit still basically anti-capitalist), gives high priority to social reforms and to the consolidation of the welfare state. Since the mid-1950s, the PSI has in its turn always pursued (at least in its programmes) a strategy of 'social reformism' aimed at modernizing and rationalizing the Italian welfare system along the lines of the Anglo-Saxon or Scandinavian models, i.e. through the creation of a 'real' social security system, based on national insurance and emphasising the need for social consumption and investment. The smaller centre parties display a mixed social policy profile. The PSDI has pursued a policy of social reformism similar (though more moderate) to that of the PSI. In more recent years, this party has adopted the role of overtly defending some welfare clients (most notably, pensioners). With its constant emphasis on 'planning', the PRI has pressed for a thorough rationalization of welfare, seen as an instrument to achieve both social equity and capitalist efficiency. The PLI has traditionally been the least pro-welfare party: now substantially aligned with the PRI position, this party displayed fierce opposition to social reforms during the centre-left period, in defence of the free market and individual freedom. Finally, the DC displays a twofold social policy profile: on the one hand, it has systematically slackened (if not overtly opposed) the expansion of the welfare state, especially where this involves drastic and widespread changes of the *status quo*; on the other hand, it has promoted sectoral solidarity on Catholic charity grounds, favouring the development of a public assistance network and the survival of church and private charitable institutions.

Though quite visible and relevant at electoral level, ideological contrasts have been less influencial at policy level, where party behaviour has been directed less by ideals and programmes than by the logic of the coalition game (with its internal trade-offs and compromises). The participation in highly fragmented and ideologically divided coalitions (such as the first centre-left, National Solidarity and the penta-party) have made it difficult for each partner to promote and implement its 'own' social policy fully. The Italian welfare state has thus developed through a proliferation of *leggine* (minor laws) for selected problems/clients, which a single party had a specific interest to pass and no party a specific interest to oppose. Moreover, all important reforms involving structural change have been systematically delayed, in a roll-over process of small counter-adjustments needed to integrate the interests of all the coalition partners.

Given the characteristics of the Italian party system and its policy-making, it is difficult to trace the impact of single parties on any dimension of welfare expansion. A few general observations can however be made on the expenditure and institutional record of the various coalition formulas, with special emphasis on the Centre-Left, i.e. the most significant postwar political experiment, for both its 'political colour' and duration.

A substantial expansion of the public sector (especially through public consumption and investments) and the overall improvement of the welfare state were among the major themes of the Centre-Left. The PSI saw in the former an instrument with which to 'tame' capitalism and in the latter an instrument to raise the living standards of the popular masses and to fully integrate them into the political system. Table 33 allows us to measure the extent to which the Centre-Left actually succeeded in carrying out its stated goals in quantitative terms. The table compares the growth rates of various public/social expenditure components under different coalition formulas. The centre-left period has been subdivided into two phases: a 'pure' centre-left phase (1962-1972) and the crisis of the Centre-Left (1972-1976), which includes less stable centre-left cabinets together with a centrist one. The most fruitful comparison is probably that between centrism and the Centre-Left, given the overall similarity of the economic background of these two political phases (at least until 1970). The contrast of real growth rates (top half of the table) reveals that the Centre-Left actually witnessed an acceleration of total public expenditure with respect to the centrist period, especially as a result of public consumption.The rate of growth of social expenditure tended on the contrary to slightly decelerate, with the exception of income maintenance and public assistance. The second phase of the centre-left period witnessed a general slackening of public sector growth (except for public investment, as confirmed also by housing). It is interesting to note that it was during the crisis of the Centre-Left that the public debt increased at its highest rate, as a consequence of the pattern of 'unbalanced public sector growth' which has been illustrated earlier (see Section III/1 above).

A comparison of simple growth rates may however conceal variations in terms of economic backgrounds. In order to control for these variations, the bottom half of the table 'standardizes' expenditure growth rates for the growth rate of GDP: the remaining variation can thus be taken as a gross indicator of the non-economic, pre-

Table 33   Growth rates of public/social expenditure by component
                                        and coalition type

	Centrism (1953-1961) (a)	Centre-Left (1962-1971)	Centre-Left Crisis	National Solidarity (1977-1979)	Total
Average growth rate of:					
Total public exp.	6.1	6.6	5.3	4.1	5.9
– Transfers and subsidies	9.0	8.7	4.3	4.3	7.4
– Public consumption	3.4	4.4	3.2	2.2	3.6
– Public investment	9.6	3.5	5.7	3.4	5.6
– Interests on debt	8.9	8.7	22.3	12.3	11.8
Total social exp.	9.6	7.9	7.0	3.0	7.6
– Income maintenance	8.8	9.2	9.0	4.7	8.5
– Health	13.6	10.1	9.6	1.9	10.3
– Education	11.1	6.3	3.5	1.2	6.8
– Housing	7.3	-4.1	19.6	5.8	5.1
– Public asst.	3.5	6.1	-1.5	1.4	3.3
Average difference between exp. growth rates and GDP growth rates of:					
Total public exp.	0.4	1.5	1.9	0.9	1.2
– Transfers and subsidies	3.2	4.4	1.0	1.1	3.0
– Public consumption	-2.3	-0.7	-0.1	-1.6	-1.1
– Public investment	5.0	0.3	2.4	-0.4	2.8
– Interests on debt	3.2	3.6	19.0	10.3	7.2
Total social exp.	3.5	2.8	3.7	0.2	2.9
– Income maintenance	2.8	4.2	5.7	1.8	3.8
– Health	7.6	5.1	6.4	-1.3	5.4
– Education	5.1	1.2	0.2	-2.0	1.9
– Housing	7.9	-9.0	16.3	2.6	2.3
– Public asst.	-2.6	1.1	-4.7	-1.7	0.0

(a) For total public expenditure and its components, 1961 is excluded; for social expenditure, income maintenance and public assistance, 1953 and 1954 are excluded; for housing, 1953 is excluded.

sumably 'political' influence on expenditure growth. As may be seen, the impact of the Centre-Left is revealed to an even greater extent if measured in relation to GDP growth. The relative expansion of the public sector was highest in the periods 1962-1971 and especially 1972-1976, owing to an acceleration of both transfers and subsidies (1962-1971) and public consumption (1962-1976). In comparison, public investment lagged somewhat behind, witnessing a sizeable deceleration (despite the emphasis on housing policy). With respect to social expenditure, the Centre-Left exerted a great impact especially on income maintenance, but did not promote an over-proportionate expansion in the sectors of education and health, only investing in the latter during its second and 'critical' phase.

To summarize, it can be said that the role played by the Centre-Left experiment made a modest, but not negligible difference to the quantitative expansion of Italy's public economy. Its impact on expenditure growth was however only partly consistent with its stated goals. On the one hand, it promoted aggregate public consumption, but was unable to stimulate two socially relevant components, i.e. health and particularly education. Moreover, the Centre-Left was incapable of maintaining the rate of expansion of capital expenditure, in spite of the increased efforts of the early 1970s. As regards welfare policy the Centre-Left exerted most influence in the area of income maintenance.

Let us turn to a brief examination of the institutional record. The Centre-Left was born with the aim of greatly modernizing Italian society through a strategy of 'structural reforms' in the economic sphere (planning, public enterprises, a new agricultural policy); in the sphere of state administration (regional decentralization, public order and judicial procedures, state bureaucracy); and especially in the social sphere (education, housing and social security). 'Social reformism' became the much repeated motto (in both cultural and political terms) of the coalition, the real *leitmotiv* of the 1960s in Italy. Many of the promised reforms were in fact implemented, although not without some delay: for instance, the nationalization of the electrical power industry and the expansion of public enterprises; the revision of the budgetary process and inauguration of economic planning; and the establishment of administrative regions. The record is even more impressive in the field of social policy. Elementary and secondary education underwent a sweeping change, access to higher education was expanded and public pre-elementary education was introduced. Pensions were repeatedly and substantially improved and the whole pension system was broadly reformed in 1968/1969. Important steps were taken towards the establishment of a national health service (a core objective of the PSI) by means of two broad reforms of the hospital sector (1968 and 1974). In the wake of the regional reform, housing and the social service sector were drastically re-organized. In addition to these 'structural reforms', other minor but significant provisions were made: the improvement of sickness and maternity insurance in agriculture (1963); the improvement of work injuries' benefits (1963 and 1965); the extension of health insurance to some categories of pensioners and the unemployed (1967); the introduction of housewives' and social pensions (1963 and 1968); the thorough reform of maternity insurance (1971); and the improvement of unemployment insurance (1968-1972). These social insurance provisions were paralleled by important changes introduced in the system of work and industrial relations, such as the universal enforcement of national contracts, the strengthening of union rights and the legal constraints placed on dismissals: changes which culminated in the 1971 Workers' Statute (*Statuto dei Lavoratori*).

On the basis of this sporadic but substantial record, the institutional impact of the Centre-Left can be tentatively summarized as follows: it tended to re-shape the Italian welfare state along universalistic lines, i.e. granting access to all citizens regardless of their socio-economic status (e.g. in education, health and social services/assistance); it tended to strengthen the position of private employees on the labour market (especially for women and those employed in backward sectors); it tended to grant some sort of inclusion in the welfare system of inactive categories (housewives, the unemployed, pensioners, students, the poor, elderly etc.). It is true that these changes involved actors (most notably, trade unions), other than the governing parties, but it must also be acknowledged that the PSI had an important part in promoting this process. Despite its internal tensions and ambiguities, this party was seriously committed to social reforms and fought a restless and at times violent battle against its opponents (including both right-wing and some DC factions). The fact that both the first and the second centre-left 'organic' cabinets fell on welfare issues (in 1964 and 1966), due to harsh conflicts between the DC and the PSI, may be taken as an indicator of this commitment [88].

Has the Centre-Left succeeded in terms of its welfare achievements? The political and social science debate has long been dominated by severe and critical judgements [89]. Some reforms have been implemented, but, it is alleged, with a frustrating (and at times detrimental, as in the case of housing) delay and with such alteration with respect to their original 'universal' and 'rational' aims so as as to make little difference vis-a-vis the previous situation; a typical example of this being the 1968 hospital reform. Furthermore, it was during the period of centre-left government that some of the worst traits of the contemporary welfare state (e.g. partisan allocation, the patronage system, and the pattern of 'unbalanced growth') developed. Recent debate however, has started a gradual rehabilitation of the Centre-Left without wholly clearing it of responsibility for these failures. The negative evaluations (especially those coming from its socialist protagonists) are in fact largely self-inflicted, in that they tend to use as a yardstick, aims and ideals rather than the initial situation and its constraints. As has been recently stated, 'if the achievements of the Centre-Left are confronted with the hopes and, symmetrically, the fears originated in Italy by its appearance, it is legitimate to speak about a failure. But if the conditions in which that governing experience has emerged and developed are taken into account, then ... the Centre Left has pursued and achieved that much of reformism which its initial constraints allowed' [90].

6. The politics of welfare interests: the case of health reform

Electoral competition and party ideologies and programmes are a prominent, but certainly not the sole political determinant of welfare expansion. To a large extent, this expansion can be seen as the result of a complex interplay which involves other important actors besides parties, i.e. unions, professional and consumer associations, bureaucracies, social groups and movements etc. The role of these actors is not easily testable by means of strict empirical analysis, but its importance can be ascertained or assessed by an informed reconstruction of the decision-making process which underlies various policy decisions.

In order to give at least the flavour of the constellation of interests and forces underlying the Italian welfare state, we can briefly survey the development of one important policy area, i.e. the health sector. This choice is based on three considerations. Firstly, this sector has undergone significant changes during the postwar period, culminating in a sweeping reform which is unparalleled in Europe, i.e. the establishment of a national health service, (*Servizio Sanitario Nazionale*, SSN). Secondly, health reform has been a major theme in the development of the Italian welfare state and thus offers a representative instance of the strains and alliances which have formed around social issues. Thirdly, this policy area involves a multiplicity of actors and is thus particularly suitable for an illustration of the wider 'politics of welfare' [91].

In addition to government, parliament and political parties, there are at least five other actors who have played an important role in the evolution of the health sector: workers' unions (especially the two largest, CGIL and CISL), doctors (especially through their professional and union associations), the health funds (*mutue*), regions and CNEL. Though not equally influential, all these actors have had some significant stake or interest in health policy and have therefore actively participated in its formation.

The postwar history of health policy can be subdivided into three distinct phases. The first phase started in 1948, with the new centrist government's rejection of the D'Aragona Commission's recommendations for a thorough reform of the social security system, including the extension of health insurance to all workers, pensioners and dependents. Following this choice for the maintenance of the *status quo*, during the 1950s the system developed in a fragmented and uncoordinated way through the proliferation of separate health funds (under strict DC control) for each professional category. By the end of the 1950s, the health funds had become a major pillar of the welfare patronage system. The establishment of a Ministry of Health in 1958 did not substantially curb their powers (at least until the mid-1960s): as was said at the time, the real Minister was not a member of the cabinet, but the president of INAM. The doctors were the strongest allies of the DC and its policy, and actively participated in the system of public health insurance (*mutualita*), although being in principle opposed to it. The government guaranteed to maintain their private professional status and lured them into acceptance by means of generous monetary and normative rewards. Placing reliance on the Catholic background and orientation of most doctors, the DC allowed them to share in the health spoils (posts on the health boards and other health agencies, research funds, etc.). Doctors often acted as patrons in the vote relationship, especially in the South and the countryside. At this time the Left opposition was active but still quite uninfluential. In its 1956 Congress, the PCI demanded a thorough reform of the health system which largely repeated the proposals of the D'Aragona Commission. At the same time the PSI was gradually elaborating the idea of a national pension and health insurance. In 1957, CGIL submitted a law proposal for the establishment of a national health service: the first to be presented to parliament. In 1959 CNEL (a composite organ which represented the views of the top levels of ministerial bureaucracy and the academic intelligentsia) timidly proposed the universal extension of hospital insurance, but immediately qualified this by warning of the financial burdens involved. The idea of a health reform was slowly, but tangibly gaining ground.

The birth of the Centre-Left opened the second phase of the history of Italian public health. The theme of a health reform occupied a top position in the first planning documents prepared by La Malfa (PRI) and Saraceno (PSI) [92]. In 1963 CNEL publicized its plan for a reform of the social security system, which contained a fuller formulation of the 1959 proposal of a national hospital insurance, coupled with a comprehensive rationalization of the health funds. From their new stronger position, the unions renewed their pressures on the government and in 1965 the PCI submitted its own reform proposal for a national health service to parliament. In the same year, parliament approved the first five-year plan, prepared by the socialist Minister for the Budget Giolitti, and approved by the entire Centre-Left cabinet. The plan explicitly committed itself to the realization of a national health service and the Socialist Minister for Health, Mariotti, subsequently drafted a more concrete proposal. Conditions seemed to favour the establishment of a national health service, but this was not entirely the case.

The plan (especially in its health section) was the object of heated debate. The PRI, the Bank of Italy, and CNEL all expressed their serious misgivings as to the financial aspects of such a development. But it was the DC in particular which withheld support, under pressure from the health funds' bureaucracy, the doctors (and less overtly the entrepreneurs). Though not openly opposing the idea of a national health service, the DC tried to give a very restrictive interpretation of this notion, i.e. not as a national insurance system, broadly decentralized and replacing the health funds, but as a complement to them, in the form of a national agency with the task of prevention, coordination and sanitation controls. At most, the DC was prepared to accept a rationalization of public health insurance, by fusing the numerous existing funds into three large health funds (*supermutue*), which would cover private and public employees and the self-employed respectively. The attempt by the DC to guarantee the survival of the health funds was obvious. During the first half of the 1960s, the latter had in fact witnessed a gradual weakening of their powers, owing to the new political and institutional climate: as a member of the coalition the PSI was particularly influential in the Ministry of Health; autonomous regions were particularly active in the health field and the coalition was committed to establishing ordinary regions, to which the Constitution entrusted jurisdiction over health policy. Acting through the DC, the health funds were thus strenuously fighting to regain and preserve their institutional and political strength, and fiercely opposed any reform plan which would entail a restriction of their competence, let alone their abolition. The doctors viewed the establishment of a national health service as a powerful threat to their professional autonomy and economic privileges. Though none of the reform plans (and certainly not the governmental one) envisaged the transformation of doctors into salaried employees, the medical associations denounced the 'manoeuvre to nationalize the profession' and submitted a memorandum to CNEL in which they thoroughly criticized the Mariotti plan. The opposition to the establishment of a national health service was then still quite strong and included (in addition to those forms of opposition already mentioned), the right-wing parties, the PLI, the Monarchists, the MSI, and the entrepreneurial associations, (especially in the pharmaceutical industry).

If the reformist front was still too weak to impose the introduction of a national health service, it was however sufficiently strong to impose a hospital reform. The state of the Italian hospital system was continually worsening as a result of the increasing demand for hospital care and services. Still formally considered as charitable institutions, Italian hospitals were run in an inefficient and uncoordinated way, and encountering growing financial problems. A thorough revision of their status had been proposed (together with universal coverage for this type of assistance) even by a 'neutral' organization such as CNEL, and evidently some sort of change was also in the interests of counter-reformers. The financial situation of the health funds was deteriorating rapidly, largely due to increasing hospital costs. Their deficit amounted to 250 billion lire in 1965 and had increased to 500 billion lire in 1967. Doctors were in turn starting to suffer from the chaotic and inefficient functioning of the hospitals. Moreover, younger hospital doctors were developing a more modern and socially oriented outlook - their main goal being to obtain security of job tenure (very difficult to obtain given the regulations at that time). Given this situation a concrete bargain could reasonably start on hospital reform, in which all actors expected some gain. The left parties and the unions saw it as a first step after a series of long and frustrating debates and as an important improvement *faute de mieux*. The health funds were badly in need of financial relief from their debts vis-a-vis the hospitals and were by this time prepared to accept a change in the situation. Doctors (and, more generally, health workers' unions) hoped to gain power and jobs. Provided that a few 'vital' conditions were met (e.g. the protection of private and catholic clinics, and the autonomy and status of top medical staff), the DC was not opposed to a reform, from which it hoped to draw fresh spoils to spend on the vote market. The electoral deadline completed the process, and in February 1968 the law was passed to everybody's satisfaction. The 'only small inconvenience of it', as Michele Salvati commented, was that 'hospital costs tripled in five years' [93].

The hospital reform marks the end of the second phase. The third is characterized by the entry of new and powerful actors: ordinary regions, whose councils were first elected by popular votes in 1970. The birth of the regions greatly strengthened the constituency for the national health service. Immediately after their establishment, the regions initiated a fight against the central administration in order to force it to accomplish the transfer of functions (first of all, health policy) foreseen by the Constitution. This transfer offered a unique institutional and political opportunity for a thorough reorganization of the health system, the abolition of the health funds and the establishment of a national health service. Not surprisingly, however, resistance to this idea was slow to wither away. The regional elections had revealed the much feared strength of the left in local government, which had resulted in the appearance of some 'red regions'. In this context, a health reform was not merely a matter of health funds, doctors and costs: it was a political question, involving the 'gift' (or 'conquest') of substantial resources for the opposition. Thus central government (but again especially the DC), engaged itself in a battle to delay the institutional transfer and to bring a positive halt to the reformist trend. The DC attempted a last move in defence of the health funds, (now experiencing critical financial difficulties, largely as a result of the regulations introduced in 1968), with a plan to transfer hospital assistance to the regions, thus relieving the health funds of their most costly burden, while at the same time delaying the transfer of other types of assistance and postponing *sine die* the liquidation of the health funds. The plan was supported by the smaller centre parties, which were not particularly in favour of the health funds, but were at the same time concerned (and given subsequent events, not without reason) about the spending and administrative capacity of the regions. Nevertheless, the plan failed due to the strength of the reformist front. The unions, regions, the left (especially the PCI), and the overall social and political temperature of the early 1970s, together created such pressure for reform, that in 1974 a law was passed which contained extraordinary provisions to repay the hospital deficit, transfer jurisdiction for hospital assistance to the regions and (the most disputed point), fix a deadline (June 1977) for the definitive liquidation of the health funds. This law was the result of one of the most heated parliamentary struggles of the whole history of the Italian welfare state. Not long afterwards the government itself submitted its own reform proposal for a national health service. The parliamentary proceedings lasted four years: not only because they were interrupted by the anticipated end of the legislature, but because, at this point, every actor was fighting to maximize gains. The PCI (which became a member of the coalition majority in 1976, and saw the national health service as a 'socialist reform in a capitalist setting'), pressed for the extension of decentralization and democratic (i.e. union/party) participation. The DC fought to limit the extent of the 'nationalization of health' and to preserve the status of private clinics and institutions and the professional character of medical services (as well as the level of their fees). Only CNEL, the PRI (from within the coalition) and the PLI (from the outside) tried (and failed) to equip the reform with some adequate tools to stimulate and control economic and administrative efficiency. The Health Reform Law was passed in December 1978. At half a decade's distance, it is now considered to have been an enormous 'failure' - an inefficient and ineffective band-wagon, manipulated by the political parties (see Table 31) and consuming an inordinate amount of public resources.

V Current conflicts and future prospects

1. The need for welfare austerity and its conflict potential

As has already been mentioned, the 1970s ended with a relative improvement both in terms of public sector balance and of equilibrium between economic performance and welfare expenditure. Public deficit seemed to follow a descending trend (Graph 15), and the growth rates of GDP and welfare expenditure became more consistent, in comparison to the previous period. The early 1980s, however, have witnessed a rapid and dramatic deterioration of this scenario. In the wake of world recession, real economic growth fell to .1 percent in 1981, -.3 percent in 1982 and -1.5 percent in 1983, whilst social expenditure grew by ca. 7 percent in 1981 and 1.3 percent in 1982 in real terms. The balance of the public sector has again started to deteriorate, with general government deficit reaching its postwar peak of 12 percent of GDP in 1983. Public debt reached 81 percent of GDP in 1983 (in 1973 it amounted to 61 percent), this being by far the highest among the major industrial countries; the debt service has absorbed 3.8 percent of GDP in the same year.

As recent research has illustrated in detail [94], welfare financing is the major root of public sector imbalance. The pension and health systems bear the heaviest responsibility. Largely as a result of system-inherent pressures (illustrated above), these two sectors continued to expand, thus putting great strain on a public purse already hit by economic recession. Experts and policy makers now seem to agree on the immediate need for a stringent welfare 'austerity' [95]: a broad reform of social policy institutions is regarded as the first and most vital step towards the recovery and stabilization of the Italian economy in the 1980s.

As shown in Table 34, initial measures in this direction have already been taken. The table starts with 1978 - although extraordinary or temporary provisions of financial restraint had been introduced prior to this date [96] - because provisions introduced during this year marked a turning point. Even given their modest institutional scope and financial effect, they were publicly presented and perceived as the first permanent restriction of welfare policy after three decades of almost uninterrupted expansion.

Cutback provisions have mainly affected pensions, health, education and, more recently, family allowances. In the field of pensions, cuts have been limited to curbing the most unnecessary and inequitable privileges stemming from a lax and cost-unconscious application of institutional regulations: multiple indexations (1978), minimum pensions granted to beneficiaries not in need (1981 and 1983), abuse of the invalidity pension system (1983), and the so-called 'baby pensions' granted to married female employees in the public sector after only 12 years' service without an age threshold (1983). In health policy, restrictions have basically concentrated on the regulation of demand via the introduction of fees for the use of services (drugs, prescriptions, medical tests). An effort to restrain the so-called supplier induced demand (i.e. that stimulated by doctors) has been undertaken via the introduction of medical review systems. The expansion of health personnel has also been halted. In almost every sector

Table 34   Cuts of welfare benefits, 1978-1983

1978	Restriction of indexing: for beneficiaries in receipt of more than one pension, indexation only applies to one pension. Introduction of prescription fee.
1981	Restrictions applying to minimum pensions: where beneficiaries' income equals twice minimum benefit, pensions lower than the minimum not raised automatically; (decree, not converted into law). Increase of prescription fees. No further expansion of health sector personnel. Increase of all school fees. Introduction of an income-related university fee (decree, not converted into law). No further expansion of school sector personnel.
1982	Introduction of a medical test fee. Restriction of medicines available per prescription. Full cost of dental, optical and aural services/treatment to be born by patients.
1983	Restriction of minimum pension regulations (as in 1981, but with an income threshold set at three times the minimum). Increased eligibility requirements for invalidity pensions. Restriction of special rights for female public employees. Tighter controls of the payment of social security contributions and sickness leave. Abolition of family allowances for higher-income beneficiaries. Increase of prescription and medical test fees. Introduction of additional fixed prescription fee. Restriction of number of medicines available free of charge. Introduction of controls of doctors' medical standards and minor restrictions of benefits.

of social security, contributions have been substantially raised and stricter controls enforcing payments have been placed on employers. Fees have been raised in the educational sector in addition to the introduction of severe restrictions on the number of personnel and the expansion of schools, courses, classes, etc. Regarding family allowances, an important revision took place at the end of 1983: entitlement to allowances has been tied to income, with families of employees earning 28-34 million per year (i.e. 150-190 percent of the average household income), loosing one or more allowances according to the number of children, and employees earning above 34 million loosing all entitlement.

In the period under review the frequency and extent of cuts has remained quite limited. The trend emerging from Table 34 is that of curbing 'excessive' benefit levels (e.g. pensions), discouraging 'excessive' demand for services (e.g. the health sector), raising fees or contributions (both as a means of financing and as a means of making beneficiaries more cost-conscious), and 'freezing' the quantitative size of service supply. Some measures have introduced income thresholds for benefit entitlements (minimum pensions, family allowances), thus strengthening the element of selectivity in social security.

However, it must be noted that these restrictive efforts have been paralleled by significant improvements in other respects. Thus, the frequency of pension indexation reviews was increased in 1980, 1981 and 1982, and the pension formula was redefined in 1982 to take account of inflation (see Institutional Synopsis). At the beginning of 1983 family allowances were substantially increased for lower income beneficiaries with many children. The establishment of the SSN (National Health Service), in 1978 greatly extended coverage and improved benefit entitlements. A reform of higher education in 1980 brought about a sizeable expansion in the number of personnel by granting tenure to a large number of junior staff. All these improvements have to a large extent counteracted the effects of the mild restrictive measures listed in Table 34, in terms of finance and public perception. It can thus be said that until 1983 welfare 'austerity' was more a financial objective and political slogan than a tangible reality.

Despite their modest scope and effects, however, these first cuts have provoked harsh political conflicts. They have been enforced by eleven separate acts. In seven cases, the legislative instrument chosen by government has been a decree. This is a direct governmental decision with immediate validity even without previous parliamentary consent. Parliament must transform the decree into a law within 60 days, otherwise it is invalidated. However, it may be repeatedly renewed by government. According to the Italian Constitution (Art. no. 77), government can issue a decree in 'extraordinary cases of necessity and urgency'. The frequent resort to 'cutting' decrees thus underlines their 'urgent' character. It also indicates the wish to confront parliament with *faits accomplis*, in the hope of thwarting conflict. In three out of the seven cases, governmental decrees have not been approved by parliament within the deadline and have thus been re-issued one or more times (with minor modifications) before actually becoming law. This occurred four times in the cases of the 1981 education provisions and the 1983 provisions on pensions and health. In other instances, either the whole decree or its most controversial parts, have never obtained parliamentary approval, e.g. 1981 decree on minimum pensions (which was again presented to parliament for approval two years later, but with a higher income threshold), and the article covering income-tested and income-related university fees contained in the 1981 education provisions (this was dropped during the parliamentary proceedings). Parliamentary 'resistance' to these governmental decrees was accompanied by lengthy debates and harsh opposition between the various parties (even among coalition members).

The issue of welfare restraint presently occupies a top position in the political agenda. The experience of the first cuts demonstrates that the conflict potential of this issue is very high and that the political resistance to change is strong and stubborn, largely reflecting the new constellation of interests which has emerged in almost four decades of welfare expansion.

2. The new constellation of welfare interests

The welfare state and in particular the social security system are today a major source of income maintenance for large sectors of the Italian population (particularly pensioners, the unemployed, the disabled etc.). We may assume that, in principle, these sectors should favour an expansion of welfare. In the present situation, they presumably have a strong interest in at least maintaining the status quo by avoiding cuts. The financing of welfare has, on the other hand, placed increasing burdens (in terms of both social security contributions and personal taxation) on other population groups (basically the economically active population). For these groups, the aggregate costs of welfare are likely to exceed benefits - and this is especially true if immediate costs are compared with immediate benefits. This discrepancy is likely to be exacerbated by the emerging trend towards selectivity. These people may develop an interest in altering the status quo in two ways: on the one hand, they may press for a diminution (or at least no further expansion) of taxes and contributions; on the other hand, they may press for an improvement of their welfare 'balance' by demanding higher or more benefits (or at least resisting cuts, especially cuts in their immediate benefits, such as family or sickness allowances).

Thus, in the present climate of austerity, the constellation of interests linked to the structure of the Italian welfare state appears highly conflictual. It should be stressed, however, that the focus of these structural contrasts is not the welfare state *per se*, but only the present distribution of benefits and costs. Thus, 'winners' and 'losers' should be simply taken as potential supporters/opposers of the existing distributive *status quo*, but not necessarily as 'pro-welfare' and 'anti-welfare' constituencies. A closer empirical examination of this constellation may provide interesting insights into the potential political strains surrounding welfare and the constraints and prospects for change.

The task is obviously very difficult, and is exacerbated by the highly fragmented character of Italian social and fiscal policies (for some quantitative estimates, see Tables 35 and 36). According to 1981 census data, the vast majority of the Italian population was economically inactive (see Table 35). Only around 34 percent were active and employed, whilst around 6 percent were in search of employment. Thus, roughly one third of the population produced the national product, part of which was consumed by the other two thirds. As we know, this transfer of resources between 'producers' and 'non-producers' is massively regulated by the welfare state. Table 36 offers a breakdown which may be more significant for our purposes. The table focusses on the adult population over the age of 18 (which corresponds to the enfranchised population). It distinguishes between three different groups. The first comprises the employed population, i.e. 'producers' earning a 'market' income in either the private or the public sector. The second group comprises all the economically inactive with a 'transfer' income. Housewives over the age of 60 have been included here because this group has the highest concentration of survivor and social pensioners. The third group comprises all the economically inactive without personal income (either from the productive sector or the transfer system). The most relevant groups for our analysis are obviously the first (where interests against the maintenance of the status quo are more likely), and the second (where interests for the maintenance of the status quo are more probable). The heterogeneity and instability of the third group make it very difficult (and probably not very significant) to identify its interests vis-a-vis the welfare state [97].

Table 35   Total population by employment status, 1981

Employment status	(in 1,000)	%
Economically active	22 272	39.8
employed	18 980	33.9
unemployed	1 007	1.8
in search of 1st job	2 285	4.1
Economically inactive	33 657	60.2
pupils/students	10 735	19.2
housewives	10 060	18.0
pensioners	7 603	13.6
disabled	556	1.0
others	4 702	8.4
Total	55 929	100.0

The 'transfer constituency', (i.e. the economically inactive with transfer income) represents 29.4 percent of the enfranchised population. This means that one third of the Italian electorate has a direct structural interest in the welfare state. The 'producer constituency' (i.e. the economically active with market income) amounts to 44.6 percent. However, public employees also draw their income from the state and are highly privileged by existing welfare regulations. Therefore, we may assume that in principle they too are interested in the maintenance of the status quo. Added to the 'transfer constituency' the potential 'pro-welfare' group would amount to 39 percent of the electorate. However tentative, this figure gives an idea of the potential extent of opposition to changes in the status quo.

Table 36   Enfranchised population by major source of income, 1981

	(in 1,000)	%
Persons with market income	18 289	44.6
private sector	14 337	35.0
public sector	3 952	9.6
Persons with transfer income	12 061	29.4
pensioners	7 596	18.5
housewives (60+)	2 422	5.9
unemployed	934	2.3
disabled	541	1.3
others	568	1.4
Persons without personal income	10 642	26.0
students	1 679	4.1
in search of 1st job	1 568	3.8
housewives (up to 60)	7 395	18.0
Total	40 992	100.0

Without public employees, the 'producer constituency' only amounts to 35 percent of the electorate. We may assume that this group is in principle interested in altering the status quo along the lines illustrated above. The interest structure within this group is, however, rather complex. The self-employed for instance, find themselves in an ambiguous position. On the one hand, they are highly favoured by present fiscal arrangements: they pay quite low contributions (see Section III/3) and tend to be large-scale tax evaders [98]. On the other hand, their welfare entitlements are more limited (see Section V/4). Given that their present balance is strongly positive, they are likely to support the status quo. A revision of their fiscal status might, however, rapidly transform them into vocal supporters of expenditure cuts, i.e. a curtailment of benefits to which they have only partial access. It must also be noted, that for statistical purposes, employers are also included under the category of 'self-employed'. Given the high contributions paid by this group, it is reasonable to assume that they would support a curtailment of welfare.

Even in the case of the employed in the private sector, interests are not uniform. As illustrated in Table 37, private employees in lower income brackets avail themselves of a number of selective benefits/advantages (most of which have been introduced in recent years, thus confirming the trend towards selectivity). The only group which seems to be the real 'loser' in the contemporary Italian welfare state is that of the private employees in middle/higher income brackets. The combined effect of taxes and transfers reduces their disposable income with respect to taxable income (which normally corresponds to earned income given the impossibility of tax evasion); they are deprived of various privileges to which lower income employees are entitled (entailing a further curtailment of income). There is evidence that during the last decade this group has suffered the highest relative deprivation in economic terms [99]. Thus, this group is likely to be in favour of lower income taxation/contributions, against selectivity in benefits, and for a shift of cuts and burdens to other categories (the self-employed, public employees and the economically inactive generally).

Table 37		The welfare balance of private employees (a), 1983	
Annual taxable income in mill. lire	Disposable income as % of taxable income	Benefits	Loss of benefit
5	131	Free health assistance Free elementary/secondary education Higher education allowance No income tax Lower legal rents Special housing allowance Family allow., special family supplement	
8	119.4		Fees for elementary/secondary educ. Prescription and medical test fees Income tax payable
9	113		Lower special family supplements Legal rents Lower special housing loan
12	104.4		
15	99.2		
20	88.7		Loss of special family supplement
28	84.4		Loss of special housing loan
30	82.0		Only one family allowance
32	81.4		Loss of family allowance
34	81.0		
60	74.7		

(a) Figures refer to a typical family of four persons where both the husband and wife are employed (one income = half of the other).

It is difficult to estimate the size of this group. We can take net household income of 20 million lire (above which disposable income decreases significantly in relation to taxable income) as a relevant threshold. According to a Bank of Italy survey carried out in 1982 [100], 31.7 percent of Italian households earned an income of this size. This figure drops to 14 percent if only households whose head is a private employee are selected, i.e. roughly 2.6 families. Supposing that each household has, on average, two votes, we would arrive at a (very tentative) estimate of some 5.2 million persons, i.e. ca. 13 percent of the electorate. If there is a potential constituency for an Italian 'tax-welfare backlash' - besides the employed and some of the self-employed - this occupational group appears as the likeliest candidate.

3. The welfare state, political mobilization and party mobilization

In order to assess the likelihood of socio-economic categories transforming themselves into political constituencies, either supporting or opposing the present pattern of welfare distribution, we must first look for empirical evidence showing: (1) whether welfare interests are actually perceived by the involved groups, being reflected in public attitudes, and (2) whether these interests are politically articulated and aggregated, being reflected in collective forms of behaviour [101].

Survey evidence on attitudes to welfare programmes is unfortunately very limited. Table 38 reports the distribution of answers to three welfare-related questions asked in two different surveys [102]. In the first question, a sample of 5,000 respondents was asked at two points in time about their willingness to accept higher contributions in order to bring pensions up to a 'decent' (*dignitoso*) level. In general, the level of 'willingness' was very high, although it declined from 1978 to 1982. Not surprisingly, a breakdown by age reveals that central age groups (i.e. those predominantly employed and paying pension contributions) are much less in agreement than older age groups

Table 38   Public opinions on some welfare issues

Items	% of agreement		
	Total	age 18–54	age 55+
1) Social security contributions may well increase as long as pensions are raised to a 'reasonable' level			
– 1978	61.2	57.9	76.4
– 1982	56.2	52.5	71.6
– Difference	–5.0	–5.4	–4.8
2) How much waste (and thus higher possibility for a reduction of expenditure) is there in the following sectors (1982):			
– Pensions			
no waste	24.3	23.1	26.7
a little waste	19.9	19.7	20.3
a lot of waste	45.2	47.0	41.4
don't know	10.6	10.2	11.6
– Health			
no waste	18.6	19.5	16.7
a little waste	22.4	22.3	22.5
a lot of waste	48.7	49.5	47.0
don't know	10.3	8.7	13.8
– Education			
no waste	32.6	35.1	27.5
a little waste	27.0	28.9	23.1
a lot of waste	21.7	21.4	22.3
don't know	18.6	14.5	27.0
3) Which of the following proposals for reducing health expenditure do you consider the most fair for reducing health expenditure:			
– not paying the first day of sickness	30.9	28.9	35.0
– charging consumers 20% of prescription costs	30.7	31.2	29.7
– charging a fixed fee for medical consultations	22.3	24.5	17.8
– restricting free prescriptions to cases of serious illness, with full cost being payable for minor illness	49.4	50.0	48.0
– granting only indirect care (i.e. reimbursible care) to families with net monthly income in excess of 1.5 mill. lire	31.3	29.2	35.6
– don't know	21.6	20.4	24.1

(i.e. those either in receipt of a pension or approaching pensionable age). Nevertheless, we should note that even in the first group there is a clear majority in favour of increasing pension contributions.

In the second question (1983), a sample of 2,000 respondents was asked to indicate which sectors of public expenditure were more 'wasteful', and therefore more amenable to cuts. The health sector turned out to be perceived as the 'most wasteful' (48.7 percent of respondents), closely followed by pensions (45.2 percent); education was perceived as much less wasteful. The breakdown by age again revealed some differences between central and older age groups. The former tended to judge the health and especially the pension system (in which they have a less immediate interest) as more wasteful (and therefore more amenable to expenditure cuts) than the latter. In the case of education, the opposite is true - a result which may reflect the reduced importance of this sector for older age groups.

In the third question the same sample of respondents was asked about their willingness to accept a number of possible cuts to health expenditure. Younger respondents tended to oppose a reduction of sickness cash benefits or the introduction of 'indirect care' (i.e. the reimbursing of health costs) for higher income groups (i.e. two cuts which would affect them immediately and noticeably), more than older respondents. On the other hand, they tended to be more in favour of general charges for health services, which they normally use more seldom than the old. Although these data still indicate a high consensus on welfare policy (especially the first question), and a strong opposition to cuts (especially the third), they tend to reveal a divergence between younger and older respondents.

With respect to collective behaviour, we can observe a growing political activation of welfare interests. The middle and higher income brackets of private employees, identified above as the most penalized 'welfare group', have in recent years witnessed an increasing mobilization based on welfare claims. This process started in the 1970s, when the socalled *quadri intermedi* (i.e. the upper middle echelon of private employees) began to organize in the larger enterprises of the industrial North, speaking out against the erosion of wage and status differentials. A number of smaller sectoral/local unions were formed, which confederated in 1977 into the *Confederquadri*. In 1975 the *Unionquadri* was founded, i.e. a professional association aiming not only at a defence of their economic interests, but also at a promotion of their 'values', (i.e. 'professional skill', 'merit', 'efficiency', 'creativity', 'individual responsibility'). Among the several claims advanced by both the union and the association, the top priorities are: (1) a reform of existing national contract regulations, not recognizing a contractual status for this category; (2) a reform of the social insurance system, modifying penalizing mechanisms (such as the ceiling on pensionable earnings, pension indexation and social security contributions, see Section V/4); and (3) a reform of the fiscal system, shifting burdens to favoured categories such as the self-employed.

The political activism of the *quadri intermedi* has rapidly increased in recent years. In October 1980, 40,000 of their members demonstrated in Turin, and ever since, both have become respected partners in the various government-union consultations on economic, social and fiscal policy. Although their prime objective (i.e. a reform of contract legislation) has not yet been achieved, the pressure of this group has already had significant results in other respects. In September 1983, they succeeded in preventing the introduction of 'selectivity' within the health system, i.e. the exclusion of higher income families from free health care, and in December of the same year they obtained a substantial reform of pension indexation. They declare themselves in favour of welfare austerity, as long as this is not 'one-sided', i.e. devised to 'penalize those who are now paying for all the others' [103].

Within the 'transfer constituency', there are parallel signs of growing political mobilization. Besides a number of occasional or local phenonema such as the Neapolitan movement of the *disoccupati organizzati* (the organized unemployed) in the late 1970s, the most relevant development is the organization of pensioners. During the 1970s the rate of unionization of this category within the larger unions (CGIL and CISL) increased rapidly and in 1979 a political party was formed, the National Pensioner Party (*Partito Nazionale dei Pensionati*, PNP). In the subsequent years PNP has developed an organizational network, with sections in practically every major city, and at the 1983 elections it obtained 1.4 per cent of the vote [104].

The reform of the pension system in favour of a substantial increase of lower (social and minimum) pensions, together with a lower taxation of pensions, is the top item in the party's political agenda. The party also advocates a higher involvement of the aged in public affairs, especially at the local level, through the formation of 'popular commissions' for the control of public services and public order. They propose a general increase of all welfare payments and fiercely oppose welfare cuts (especially in the health sector). On other issues the party displays moderate centre orientations.

Although mainly representing the interests of lower/middle income pensioners, the PNP tried in their 1983 election campaign to reach all important 'transfer constituencies', i.e housewives, the unemployed, disabled and even young people in search of a first job. It presented itself as a possible catalyst of the resentment and protest of welfare clients against unreliable and 'dishonest' politicians and bureaucrats. To a large extent, the PNP phenomenon must be interpreted in the light of increasing political distrust and cynicism among the Italian electorate, and of the state of acute crisis of the party system. To some extent at least, it also reflects genuine interests and the new conflicts: besides complaining against 'politicians and bureaucrats', the PNP explicitly points its finger at economically active categories who pay low contributions and avoid taxes.

As we can see, there are some symptoms indicating that the new structure of welfare interests is increasingly important in moulding and activating mass political attitudes and behaviour. What is the impact of this development on the Italian party system? To what extent, and in what ways does the welfare state affect the behaviour of, and competition between parties?

In recent years the Italian party system has undergone significant changes [105]. Ideological polarization has decreased, the traditional class and sub-cultural bases of the various parties have been progressively eroded, transforming the latter into more secularized, catch-all parties. Issue voting has become increasingly important and the segmented Italian electorate has gradually become a more homogeneous political market, in which all parties are able to compete more freely for voters across the political spectrum. It is difficult to assess the extent to which the welfare state (i.e. the new socio-economic differentiations resulting from fiscal and social policies), has contributed to these developments. However determined, the present state of fluidity offers a favourable ground for at least a partial realignment of the party system. Given its structural and functional relevance, the welfare state may well serve as a lever for such a process.

The experience of the 1983 electoral campaign offers some interesting insights in this respect. Owing to the acute fiscal crisis, all parties were forced to take a stand on welfare issues (more precisely, on welfare 'cuts'). Party strategies had to be elaborated under a threefold pressure: the 'functional' need of welfare austerity; the need to defend the interests of traditional party electorates and the objective of capturing new electoral groups by a reshuffling of welfare 'gains' and 'losses'. The effort to reconcile all this resulted in ambiguous party programmes. As widely lamented by the press and in public debates [106], the various 'welfare packages' were highly incoherent. Clearly, all parties were trying to influence disparate socio-economic constituencies, and not surprisingly, both the *quadri intermedi* and pensioners were among the most important.

Table 39 may help to explain the difficulties of political parties to develop unambiguous strategies. The table reports a breakdown of party electorate by 'welfare constituency', similar to that presented in Table 36. Given the limited size of the sample and the high number of non-respondents, these data must be read with extreme caution [107]. As is seen, all parties tend to attract votes from all sides, and the confrontation between producer and transfer constituencies is fairly balanced. This is particularly true for left parties (PCI and PSI and, with some marked internal differences, the Radicals, PR, and to the extreme left PDUP). The DC and the PSDI which have a similar composition, show an over-proportionate representation of transfer constituencies (especially pensioners). The PRI and PLI, on their side, are the parties with the highest relative concentration of 'producers', especially of self-employed. Finally, the extreme right (MSI-DN) appears to be quite split between producers and transfer recipients.

Table 39   Party electorates by employment status and source of income, 1982

	DC	PCI	PSI	MSI DN	PSDI	PRI PLI	PR PDUP	n.i.	Total
Economically active (market income)	39.3	49.0	48.4	51.5	39.3	58.2	48.6	44.9	46.8
self-employed entrepreneurs,	12.5	10.4	11.4	20.9	14.4	25.4	11.4	15.7	13.9
professionals farmers, artisans	0.5	1.4	1.4	–	1.8	9.0	–	2.8	2.0
and traders	12.0	9.2	10.0	20.9	12.6	16.4	11.4	12.9	11.9
employees	26.8	38.4	37.0	30.6	24.9	32.8	37.2	32.1	32.9
blue-collar	13.0	24.6	24.4	12.9	8.9	6.6	2.9	19.5	18.3
teachers	3.6	3.9	2.2	3.2	7.1	4.1	11.4	2.8	3.5
white-collar	10.2	9.9	10.4	14.5	8.9	22.1	14.8	9.8	11.1
Economically inactive (transfer income)	60.7	51.0	51.6	48.4	60.7	41.8	51.4	52.5	53.2
pensioners	26.8	19.5	24.7	24.2	26.8	23.8	5.7	18.6	21.9
housewives	27.0	23.0	20.1	8.1	21.4	11.5	11.4	25.0	22.6
unemployed	3.6	4.1	4.3	4.8	7.1	1.6	8.6	3.9	4.0
students	3.3	4.4	2.5	11.3	5.4	4.9	25.7	5.0	4.7
Total: %	100	100	100	100	100	100	100	100	100
n	422	435	279	62	56	122	35	544	1955

With all the necessary methodological caveats, a number of interesting observations can be drawn from this table. No party appears to represent a single constituency to such a disproportionate extent as to make a clearcut choice in favour of this or that group politically convenient. There are, however, some significant differences, especially when contrasting those parties which find themselves at the centre of the political spectrum (DC-PSDI and PRI-PLI). These parties have always been traditionally very close and allied in government coalition. In recent years, however, the electoral competition between parties has increased markedly, largely on welfare issues. The difference in the social bases of these parties revealed by our data indicates that this competition is now structurally grounded and is doomed to increase if the crisis of the welfare state worsens. It is interesting to note that the major surprise of the 1983 elections concerned precisely these parties, and especially the DC (-5.4 percent) and the PRI (+2.1 percent). Both parties presented an electoral programme mainly based on the theme of austerity, advocating a thorough rationalization and limitation of the welfare state. If for the PRI this appeal was coherent with both its historical and cultural tradition and its socio-economic constituencies, in neither respect was this true for the DC: the new austerity image which this party tried to put on had probably the negative effects of alarming its transfer constituencies whilst not convincing the producer ones.

More detailed information would obviously be needed for a more thorough assessment of the effect of the newly emerged welfare interests on the Italian party system, on its interference with the traditional, class based social roots of parties and its impact on the 'normal' left-right dimension of party coalitions.

Given the paucity of data and the fluidity of situation, we must limit ourselves to concluding that there are visible signs of a growing impact of the welfare state on party behaviour and that this is especially true for the centre of the political spectrum, where a visible and structurally grounded party differentiation is taking place. It is possible that this formerly homogeneous area will undergo an internal restructuring, with the PRI and PLI increasingly emphasizing their appeal to a welfare rationalization more favourable to producers, and the DC and PSDI trying to more overtly defend transfer interests. Considering its half-way location in terms of social base and its present political dynamism, the PSI is also likely to intervene in the game, taking a role of mediation between the two sides. In whichever direction this situation may evolve, it is sure that welfare competition will represent a hampering factor for the stability of the present 'penta-party' coalition formula.

The present problems of the welfare state do not only constitute powerful electoral stimuli for Italian parties, but also a serious structural challenge requiring responsible action. Whichever their electoral interest, all parties seem therefore well aware of the functional need for a broad institutional restructuring. A vast debate on this theme has started in Italy with the participation of all relevant elite groups. If the ideological and programmatic contrasts are still high and significant, the will for a profound change is generalized and a common basis seems to be gradually emerging. A closer look at this debate may therefore cast some light on the probable future profile of the Italian welfare state.

4. The intellectual debate and the future of the welfare state

Until the second half of the 1970s, the welfare state remained a rather marginal topic in Italian academic research and intellectual debate. In the wake of international discussion, however, and under the growing pressure of structural problems, the 'welfare crisis' has rapidly gained attention in recent years.

Academic research on this subject has largely been based on work done outside Italy. We can distinguish between three basic approaches: neo-marxist, neo-liberal, and 'rad-

ical catholic'. The neo-marxist was the first to be imported, largely due to the strong
leftist leaning of Italian social science, at least until the second half of the 1970s.
Thus, James O'Connor and Claus Offe's diagnoses of welfare crisis have become very
popular, and now largely inspire the cultural/ideological stance of the Left on the subject. Italian neo-marxists, in the same way as their foreign colleagues, interpret the
current problems of the welfare state as a fundamental, structural crisis, ultimately
reflecting the incompatibility between capitalist accumulation and social redistribution.
The solution to the crisis is a 'moving beyond welfare capitalism' to a 'third road'
which is distinct from both social democracy and socialism. Although never clearly
defined, this 'third road' is basically an 'intensive' Keynesian welfare state, with a high
degree of economic planning and public control over capitalist accumulation, a high
degree of redistribution via the fiscal and transfer systems, and basic universal services
coupled with higher self-management at the social level. The Scandinavian (especially
Swedish) debate on 'economic democracy' has recently become influential among
Italian neo-marxists [108].

The second approach, that of neo-liberalism, has rapidly gained consensus in recent
years, in the wake of its international revival. It must be noted that Italian neo-liberals
tend to formulate their critique in quite moderate tones, and seem to be more inspired
by a Rawlsian type of 'social liberalism' than by radical 'free market' liberalism. Thus,
Italian neo-liberals call for a more efficient and de-regulated, but still solid and conspicuous, welfare system, based on a mix (but still a mix) of market and state. Outright neo-conservative attacks on the welfare state have been few and far between [109].

The third approach is 'Radical Catholic', and is inspired by various traditions ranging
from neo- and 'radical' marxism (e.g. Agnes Heller's theory of 'radical needs') to
structuralist sociology, and from German phenomenology to contemporary social doc-
trine in the Catholic Church. Radical Catholic authors criticize the alienating
character of welfare provisions based on either monetary transfers or bureaucratic
and professional services and their disruptive effects on individual and familiar *Lebens-
welten*. Basically anti-capitalist, these authors are less interested in altering property
relations or shifting the mechanisms of economic control than in a radical re-definition of the boundaries between public and private. They advocate a general retrenche-
ment of the state in favour of the 'social private' sphere, i.e. the network of voluntary
private and local solidarities [110].

Scholarly evaluations constitute a general background for the present debate on the
future of the welfare state and are thus important in order to grasp the overall
cultural climate which nourishes this debate. Given their high level of generality and
abstraction, these evaluations obviously have only a very vague and distant bearing
upon actual policy choices. It is therefore useful to briefly survey also non (or less)
academic, and more policy-oriented evaluations and proposals, illustrating some of
their most interesting and relevant themes and ideas.

'Rationalization' is perhaps the commonest and most consensual theme at this level of
debate. It implies a substantial revision of existing welfare arrangements in order to
achieve a higher level of 'equity' (i.e. equal treatment for all those with similar objective needs/risks) and higher 'efficiency'. Analysts and ideologues from all sides seem
to agree on the need for a more equitable distribution of fiscal burdens and transfer
benefits, for a more rational set of incentives for welfare suppliers and consumers,
and for a general administrative simplification and harmonization of programmes and
regulations. Commissions set up by the Treasury have recently formulated a variety of
proposals for the reform of specific welfare sectors [111].

A second recurrent theme is that of 'flexibility'. The provision of welfare through rigid compulsory insurance is regarded as inappropriate with respect to an increasingly multi-faceted and changeable demand. A more flexible pattern of welfare provision is recommended, allowing a much greater 'personalization' of benefits and services. Liberal-democratic authors and ideologues couple the issue of higher flexibility with that of 'privatization' or 'liberalization'. They suggest that the role of private welfare be extended to the sectors of health and education, possibly by the use of voucher systems [112]. The public versus private issue is much debated also in the case of pension reform. Most reform proposals share a common basis: the new system should distinguish between two (or even three) separate 'pillars': a basic flat-rate, universal scheme which guarantees a 'decent' minimum, and an additional occupational, earnings-related scheme (and possibly a third voluntary scheme). All parties agree that the first pillar should remain the sole competence of the state, but regarding occupational pensions we can distinguish between a 'liberist' and an 'etatist' interpretation: the former favours a competitive system including public and private schemes, whilst the latter would like to concentrate this type of pension within the public sector (merging everything into INPS) [113].

A third and increasingly important theme is that of 'selectivity'. During the 1970s, the commonly held view (especially on the side of the Left) was that welfare progress was conditional upon a broad universalization of social security and a shift from a particularistic and fragmented system to an 'institutional redistributive' system -the Swedish welfare state normally being taken as an example. At the moment this approach is being substantively revised. There has been some disillusion regarding the actual welfare achievements of Northern European countries in terms of both redistribution and economic efficiency. Above all, however, the first Italian experiences of universalization (e.g. health) have created enormous organizational and financial problems and proved to be largely ineffective. Thus, social scientists are increasingly shifting their focus from universalism back to selectivity, as being a more adequate means of redistributing welfare resources and reaching target groups. This growing emphasis on selectivity is not interpreted as a return to a 'residual' model of welfare. What it purports is rather an Italian version of the Beveridge model, characterized by basic, universal welfare entitlements based on citizenship (rather than the present occupational status), but which only gives full protection for the less well-off, while the better-off are either 'selectively' deprived of some benefits or charged a fee for services.

The issue of selectivity is discussed especially in relation to the National Health Service, but, as has already been mentioned, is also applicable to other types of insurance (e.g. family allowances, sickness cash benefits, housing loans). There is a good degree of consensus regarding the general rationale underlying the idea of selectivity, but within this consensus we can distinguish between two different interpretations of the principle. On the one hand, there is a 'strong' interpretation, according to which the better-off should be 'locked-in' as contributors to social insurance programmes, and subsequently be excluded from some benefits or charged relatively high fees (in other words, they should pay without receiving or pay twice to receive). On the other hand, there is a 'weak' interpretation, according to which the better-off should be given some sort of compensation for their exclusion from benefits or free services, allowing them to 'opt out' (after payment of a solidaristic earmarked contribution) of public programmes, or by granting them a higher margin of choice within public welfare (e..g. with respect to the type of services) [114]. What lies at the basis of these two different interpretations of positive selectivity (and, more generally, of the whole welfare debate) is the old issue of equality vs. meritocracy, i.e. the relative weight to be assigned to 'needs' and 'merits' in the distribution of welfare. After having been banished for a long time from political and intellectual discussion, the notion of merito-cracy has recently been relegitimized not only within liberal-democratic circles, but also within the Socialist Left, which even launched the political slogan of a new 'alli-ance between merits and needs' [115].

A final theme of the current debate is that of welfare 'moralization'. As has been illus-trated above, party control of welfare institutions and the discretionary use of welfare benefits are among the most peculiar traits of the Italian welfare state. Massimo Paci has recently coined the notion of a 'particularistic-clientelistic' model of welfare, in order to describe the format of Italian social policy in a comparative perspective [116]. The system of welfare patronage has come under increasing attack in recent years and an energetic campaign for a 'moralization' (i.e. a less personalized and partisan management) of the welfare apparatus is under way, especially in the media. What is demanded is the definition of precise boundaries to 'party government', i.e. the limita-tion of the role and competence of political parties in the administration of public (and especially welfare) institutions. This would imply, for example, a profound revi-sion (or even the suppression) of the various 'political committees' operating in the social insurance (e.g. INPS) and especially, health sectors (see Section VI/4) and an overall retrenchment of 'politics' from the welfare arena, placing greater emphasis and responsibility over the bureaucracy (which in turn should be made less partisan, through appropriate recruitment procedures and efficiency controls) and over consumer self-management.

As may be seen, the current welfare debate is characterized by many interesting sug-gestions and reveals at least a clear awareness of the problems and an effort to devise reasonable solutions; most contributions are moreover marked by a pragmatic orienta-tion. These can certainly be taken as encouraging signs, but they must not be over-esti-mated. It is probably reasonable to expect that some 'rationalizing' and 'moralizing' measures will be taken in the coming years, correcting some of the most outstanding shortcomings of the current welfare system in order to maintain at least a minimum of financial and political viability. It is, however, unlikely that welfare reform may pro-ceed beyond the level of 'minimum viability'. As our analysis has shown, the roots of the present problem are deep and far-reaching. The high and persisting degree of structural differentiation of Italian society will in fact pose severe constraints upon any serious project of comprehensive rationalization and reform: this structural back-ground will in fact work to reproduce the prevailing 'particularistic' format of welfare provision. Selectivity may well become the new political *leitmotiv*, thus shifting the traditional emphasis on univeralism or institutional redistribution as preferable and ideal welfare objectives. The structural obstacles to a succesful implementation of such a new political project are likely to prove as powerful as those which were responsible for the failure of universalization at the end of the 1970s. What kind of selective poli-cies are possible in those sectors which are still characterized by high institutional frag-mentation? And, even in those sectors which already offer universal benefits, how are target groups to be singled out, given the present tax system? Does not the very idea of selectivity immediately lend itself, in the Italian context, to 'particularistic' interpre-tations and manipulations?

These questions raise serious doubts about the actual prospects of many reform pro-posals. Certainly, ideological depolarization and increasing pragmatism at the elite level, coupled with gradual improvements in the country's socio-economic homogeni-zation may slowly prepare the conditions for a future, more fundamental change in the institutional and political profile of the Italian welfare state. In the medium term, how-ever, the striving to safeguard 'minimal viability', in a context of persisting struc-tural disequilibria, is likely to remain the gloomier, but more realistic welfare scenario.

Notes

1 The best report on the beginning of the 'southern question' in the new state is: G. Fortunato, *Il Mezzogiorno e lo Stato Italiano*. Laterza, Bari 1911. Fortunato, a progressive southern land-owner, was one of the most prominent voices in favour of social reform during this period. For an overall picture of social policy during the first decades of the new Italian state, see especially V. Fargion, 'L'assistenza pubblica in Italia dell'unita al fascismo: primi elementi per un'analesi strutturali', in *Rivista Trimestrale di Scienza dell'Amministrazione*, forthcoming, and D. Marucco, *Mutualismo e Sistema Politico*, Milan, Franco Angeli, 1982.

2 See A. C. Jemolo, *Chiesa e Stato in Italia negli Ultimi Cento Anni.* Turin, Einaudi, 1948.

3 According to Gerschenkron, the Italian 'take-off' took place between 1880 and 1914, reaching a peak in 1886-1908, when the yearly growth rate of industrial output surpassed 6 percent. See A. Gerschenkron, 'Notes on the rate of industrial growth in Italy, 1881-1913', *The Journal of Economic History*, Vol. 15 (1955), pp. 360-375. See also R. Romeo, *Breve Storia della Grande Industria in Italia.* Milan, La Nuova Cappelli, 1961.

4 The first measure raised the age limit for compulsory education to 12; the second transferred to central government the responsibility for elementary education, and established new agencies for the assistance of poor pupils in all local authority areas.

5 See A. Cherubini, *Storia della Previdenza Sociale.* Rome, Editori Riuniti, 1977, especially chapter V.

6 'Corporatist state' is a definition first used in the *Carta del Lavoro*, a party document published in 1927, stating the new fascist understanding of social and economic relations. Social insurance was considered as a prominent manifestation of the principle of collaboration between the various social 'bodies', through their cooporative organizations. According to its theorists, the fascist state was 'beyond' social policy because it presented in itself a preventive cure for all social ills. See again A. Cherubini, *op. cit*, chap. VI.

7 In spite of its thorough social penetration and suppression of pluralism, Fascism did not substantially curb the sphere of influence of the Catholic Church. See A. C. Jemolo, *op. cit.*, and D. A. Binchy, *Church and State in Fascist Italy.* Oxford, Oxford University Press, 1941.

8 For a thorough account of the Fascist regime see the works of R. De Felice, especially his *Mussolini il Fascista*, Vol. II and *Mussolini il Duce*, Vol. I., Turin, Einaudi, 1968 and 1974.

9 These figures only refer to central government expenditure on social security, public health, housing and education (the expenditure of social insurance funds is thus excluded). Source: Peter Flora et al., *State, Economy and Society in Western Europe 1815-1975*: A data handbook, 2 Vols. Frankfurt a.M and London, Campus and Macmillan, 1983.

10 In the immediate aftermath of the war, the struggle between the various political factions concerned the very fundamentals of the new political system: the political (monarchy vs. republic) and the socio-economic (free market vs. planning) institutional framework, and the international position of the country.

11 See the legislative provisions listed in the institutional synopsis, especially for pensions, sickness, unemployment and housing.

12 For a survey of the positions of the various parties, see again A. Cherubini, op. cit.

13 Articles No. 32 and 38 of the Constitution. A less debated article (No. 33) also made reference to education, for which 'the Republic establishes general rules ... and institutes state schools at all levels...'. See *Costituzione della Repubblica Italiana*, Istituto Poligrafico dello Stato, Rome, 1976.

14 See Commissione per la Riforma della Previdenza Sociale, *Relazione sui Lavori della Commissione*, Ministero del Lavoro e della Previdenza Sociale, Rome, 1948.

15 INPS = *Istituto Nazionale della Previdenza Sociale* (National Institute for Social Insurance); INAM = *Istituto Nazionale per l'Assicurazione contro le Malattie* (National Institute for Sickness Insurance); INAIL = *Istituto Nazionale per l'Assicurazione contro gli Infortuni sul Lavoro* (National Institute for Occupational Injuries Insurance).

[16] The only notable exceptions were earnings-related cash benefits for sickness and partial unemployment. See below paragraph No. IV/2.

[17] The basic structure of the Italian education system can be traced to this reform, in its four separate layers (elementary, lower middle, upper middle, and higher education) as well as in its programmes and curricula. Gentile was a leading Italian philosopher of the idealist school of thought, who saw in the Fascist State the incarnation of the Hegelian ethical State.

[18] These were the years when the vast debate on the 'Italian pattern of development' began to articulate itself, building on the first results of empirical economic and social research. Among the most prominent academic voices, we should mention G. Fua, F. Momigliano, C. Napoleoni and P. Sylos Labini as economists, F. Alberoni and A. Pizzorno as sociologists. A book published in 1959 (*Aspetti e Problemi Sociali dello Sviluppo Economico in Italia*, Bari, Laterza), including contributions by some of them, served to stimulate the debate and addressed it towards the 'programmazione', i.e. deliberate social and economic planning by policy-makers. For a good picture of the academic and political debate of this period, see M. Centorrino (ed.), *Consumi Sociali e Sviluppo Economico in Italia*. Rome, Coines, 1976, and G. Manin Carabba, *Un Ventennio di Programmazione*. Bari, Laterza, 1977.

[19] See Ministero del Bilancio, 'Problemi e prospettive dello sviluppo economico italiano', in *La Programmazione Economica in Italia*, Rome, 1967, p. 126.

[20] See Consiglio Nazionale dell'Economia e del Lavoro (CNEL), *Osservazioni e Proposte sulla Riforma della Previdenza Sociale*, Istituto Poligrafico dello Stato, Rome. The CNEL is an influential constitutional body of experts, charged with the task of counselling the parliament and the government about relevant economic and social problems: its 1963 proposals echoed, in many respects, the D'Aragona Commission's recommendations of 1948.

[21] In Italy, the period from 1968 to 1972 was characterized by a sharp increase in social conflict, which reached a peak in the 'hot Autumn' of 1969. The improvement of the welfare state became a major target of union action, which overtly pressed, in a series of strikes, for reforms in the pension, housing, health, education, transport and tax systems. For a comprehensive analysis of the relationship between trade unions and the political and social systems, see A. Pizzorno et al., *Lotte Operaie e Sindacato: Il Ciclo 1968-1972*. Il Mulino, Bologna, 1978 and (for a shorter survey) M. Regini, 'Labour unions, industrial action and politics', *West European Politics* Vol. 2, No. 3 (1979), pp. 51-66.

[22] Major changes occurred during this period: divorce was legalized in 1971 and, significantly, retained after a referendum promoted by the Catholic Church in 1974; family law was thoroughly revised and fully modernized in 1975; the age of majority was lowered to 18 in 1975; equal treatment between men and women with respect to work was introduced in 1977 and abortion was legally authorized under certain circumstances in 1978.

[23] This process started with housing in 1971 and continued with social assistance in 1976-77 and health in 1978. For more details see the Institutional Synopsis in the Appendix Volume.

[24] A few projects for a thorough reform of social insurance (again in the direction of administrative simplification) have been discussed in Parliament since 1978, but no decision seems imminent because of the violent contrasts between the parties on the matter.

[25] There is some discrepancy between the time series of expenditure data presented by OECD and ISTAT (Istituto Centrale di Statistica - Central Bureau of Statistics): for earlier years, in spite of its more comprehensive definition, the ISTAT series lies beneath the OECD one, because its figures for final consumption are somewhat lower than those of OECD. Given its wider temporal extension, we have decided to take the ISTAT series when using total public expenditure as a denominator in the following graphs. Graph 1 shows also a break in the trend line between 1959 and 1960, due to a change in the GDP data series (for which there is no difference between OECD and ISTAT). For the period after 1960 in fact, the value of GDP has been re-computed, trying to take into account the 'black' economy.

[26] Only for this Graph we have used the OECD total and breakdowns for the 1961-1978 period, because we think they provide a more accurate figure for public consumption (see note 25).

27 This graph is based on tentative breakdowns which are not entirely mutually exclusive. For precise definitions, see the Appendix Volume.

28 The consolidated account of total public expenditure only reports breakdowns by economic category. A precise functional classification would therefore have to start from very detailed institutional breakdowns.

29 See W. Rostow, *Politics and the Stages of Growth*, Cambridge, Cambridge University Press, 1971. For precise definitions, see the tables in Appendix Volume.

30 An accurate quantification of the growth of social expenditure is difficult to present. Only recently has the very notion of social expenditure gained the attention of official statistical publications. Detailed accounts (with functional and institutional comprehensive break-downs) only exist, so far, for the period 1975-1979 (ISTAT, I conti della protezione sociale 1975-1979, *Supplemento al Bollettino Mensile di Statistica*, 1981, No. 8). Drawing on different sources we have constructed a time-series of relatively homogeneous data covering the following functions: income maintenance (i.e. cash benefits for old age, invalidity, survivors, sickness, maternity, occupational injuries, unemployment and family dependents), education, health (benefits in kind), housing and public assistance (in cash and kind). We have taken into account central and local government expenditure, social security funds and a few other separate agencies of the Italian public sector, re-aggregating it according to our five functions.

31 It was in fact decided that, in order to establish the degree of invalidity, the socio-economic conditions of the area of residence - and in particular the available chances of finding a job - should be taken into account. On the special role of invalidity pensions in the Italian welfare system, their sectoral and territorial distribution, see especially A. Becchi Collida, *Sussidi, Lavoro e Mezzogiorno*, Franco Angeli, Milan 1978 and *Politiche del Lavoro e Garanzia del Reddito*, Il Mulino, Bologna 1979; G. Morcaldo, 'Analisi della struttura dei trattamenti pensionistici e della sua evoluzione', in *Contributi alla Ricerca Economica*, Banca D'Italia, Dicembre 1977, pp. 77-162.

32 On this topic, see especially G. Brosio, 'I trasferimenti alle imprese', pp. 153-182 in E. Gerelli, F. Reviglio (eds.), *Per una Politica della Spesa Pubblica in Italia*, Franco Angeli, Milan 1978 and E. Portarollo, *Il Salvataggio nell'Europa della Crisi*, Il Mulino, Bologna 1976.

33 Although the legal entitlement to family allowances was only granted to the unemployed in 1968, this type of benefit was in fact paid to them starting from 1965, thanks to ad hoc provisions.

34 Debt repayment, the creation of a National Hospital Fund to finance the regions, the gradual liquidation of social security funds and the establishment of a National Health Service initiated a storm of financial transfers between 1975 and 1980, so that an accurate reconstruction of yearly expenditure data is extremely difficult for this period. see 'Rapporto sanità', in *Relazione Generale sulla Situazione Economica del Paese*, Rome 1980, Vol. III, pp. 163-182.

35 Unfortunately, official statistics only report an aggregate figure for 'education and culture' and it is not possible to disaggregate one from the other. Needless to say, education absorbs by far the largest share of the total, i.e. some 85 percent-90 percent. For a good survey on the availability and quality of data on education, see S. Bruno, '*La spesa pubblica per istruzione e cultura in Italia: andamento, problemi e prospettive*', pp. 109-130 in E. Gerelli, F. Reviglio (eds.), *op.cit.*

36 In 1975, the ISTAT data series ceased, in fact, to report the data relative to the expenditure of GESCAL (the public agency created in 1963 and abolished in 1971), even if part of it was still continuing. Moreover, data relative to regional and local authorities expenditure appear underestimated through the 1970s, due to the delay and disorder of regional and other local financial accounts. ISTAT data refer to actual expenditure for all state housing constructions in a given year: the Bank of Italy provides data only on the total amount of public investments for state housing in a given year.

[37] As was the case with public expenditure, there is a discrepancy between ISTAT and OECD data on public revenues. This discrepancy is mainly due to a difference of definition: ISTAT includes capital transfers received within total revenues, while the OECD only gives the balance. We have used the OECD data in Graph 1 for the period 1960-1980 and ISTAT data (the only data available) for the period 1951-1959. The break in the line is also due to the break in the GDP data series. The same sources have been used for Graph 1.

[38] A 'negative' net lending is equivalent to positive net borrowing. We have used the notion of negative net lending as it is found in the OECD National Account Statitics. If net lending 'goes down' (i.e. below the zero line), this means that the borrowing requirement of the state increases correspondingly.

[39] For a more thorough discussion of these points, see G. Amato, *Economia, Politica e Istituzioni in Italia*, Bologna, Il Mulino, 1976.

[40] The 1960 jump in the state share of welfare programme financing is due to a lump transfer from the state to social security funds, compensating for unpaid contributions during previous years. The Graph has a break at 1974-75 due to the change of the data series. This change (and the lack of data for the period 1978-1980), makes it difficult to see clearly the increase of the state share to cover deficits.

[41] Data on the membership of social insurance schemes are not very reliable. Due to the great number of seasonal, part-time and marginal workers, yearly figures are estimated (and normally turn out to be overestimated). Data on members of pension insurance do not include public employees. Despite this, the percentage figure is very high with respect to the labour force especially during the 1960s. This probably results from the fact that a great number of self-employed appeared as active members of the insurance, but were not reported as active workers in the labour force surveys. The decline of coverage in the 1970s is also due to the relative increase in the number of public employees within the labour force.

[42] See 'Reddito, risparmio e patrimonio immobilare delle famiglie italiane nell'anno 1979', *Bollettino della Banca d'Italia*, Vol. XXXV, No.s 3-4, 1979, pp. 311-374.

[43] On this phenomenon, see M. Barbagli, *Disoccupazione Intellettuale e Sistema Scolastico in Italia*, Bologna, Il Mulino, 1973 and M. Dei and M. Rossi, *Sociologia della Scuola Italiana*, Bologna, Il Mulino, 1978.

[44] On the development of social services during the 1970s, see M.C. Bassanini, C. Lucioni, P. Pietroboni, E. Ranci-Ortigosa, *I Servizi Sociali: realtà e riforma*, Bologna, Il Mulino, 1977; M. La Rosa, E. Minardi and A. Montanari, (eds), *I Servizi Sociali tra Programmazione e Participazione*, Milan, Franco Angeli, 1978; C. Trevisan, *Per una Politica locale dei Servizi Sociali*, Bologna, Il Mulino, 1978.

[45] For a thorough reconstruction of the Commission's works and a selected presentation of its reports, see P. Braghin, (ed.), *Inchiesta sulla Miseria in Italia (1951-1952)*, Turin, Einaudi, 1978.

[46] The attitude and strategy of Italian parties, trade unions and of the Catholic church with respect to poverty are reviewed by P. Pombeni, R. Scaldaferri, F.G. Cammarano, G.P. Cella, S. Negrelli and E. Bace in the anthology edited by G. Sarpellon, *La Povertà in Italia*, 2 Vols., Milan, Franco Angeli, 1982.

[47] See especially C. D'Apice, 'La povertà in Italia. Note introduttive a una ricerca', in *Economia e Lavoro*, 1975, Vol. IX, No. 2, pp. 221-238 and No. 4, pp. 503-522; Censis, *Indagine sulla Povertà*, Rome, 1979.

[48] G. Sarpellon, *op. cit.*

[49] As is known, absolute poverty is measured with respect to a yardstick which is fixed by the observer, estimating the minimum income necessary for subsistence, whilst in the case of relative poverty the yardstick usually corresponds to some average indicator: in Sarpellon's analysis, average consumption expenditure per capita.

[50] See *infra* for a more detailed discussion of this point.

[51] The contrast between the middle 30 percent and the lower 60 percent seems most suited for an aggregate analysis of income distribution across time, as suggested by F. Kraus in 'The historical development of income inequality', in P. Flora and A.J. Heidenheimer, *The Devel-*

opment of Welfare States in Europe and North America, New Brunswick, Transaction, 1981. In fact 'in almost all countries ... the income share of the sixth decile is smaller than 10 percent, while that of the seventh decile is greater at least since World War II. The two income strata are thus divided by a hypothetical equality line, defined by this proportionate income share of 10 percent.' (p. 195).

52 For a critical discussion on the reliability of those data, see P. Roberti, 'Le variazioni nella distribuzione personale del reddito in Italia 1948-1966', in *Rassegna Economica*, Vol. XXXV (1971), No. 4, pp. 801-832 and C. D'Apice, 'La distribuzione del reddito nelle indagini della Banca d'Italia', in G. Pinnaro, (ed.), Lavoro e Redditi in Italia 1978-1979, Rome, Editori Riuniti, 1981, pp. 215-243.

53 See E. Gorrieri, *La Giungla Retributiva*, Bologna, Il Mulino, 1972.

54 For a detailed empirical analysis of this point, see G. Faustino, 'Reddito e consumi delle famiglie negli anni dell'impoverimento', in G. Sarpellon, *op. cit*, second volume, pp. 19-208. Evidence which points in the same direction is also given by the periodical surveys of the Bank of Italy: 'Reddito e risparmio delle famiglie Italiane nell'anno ...', *Bollettino della Banca d'Italia*, Rome, various years.

55 Evaluation research in in the field of education is relatively developed. Among the main studies, we may mention: M. Barbagli, (ed.), *Scuola, Potere, Ideologia*, Bologna, Il Mulino, 1972; M. Braghin, *Le Disegualianze Sociali - Anlisi Empirica sulla Situazione della Diseguaglianza in Italia*, Milan, Sapere, 1973; M. Livolsi et al., *La Macchina del Vuoto. Il Processo di Socializzazioni nella Scuola Elementare*, Bologna, Il Mulino, 1974; F. Padoa Schioppa, *Scuola e Classi Sociali in Italia*, Bologna, Il Mulino, 1974; and M. Dei and M. Rossi, *op. cit.*

56 F. Padoa Schioppa, *op. cit.*

57 F. Censis, *I Drop-outs nella Scuola Secondaria*, Rome, 1976 (mimeo).

58 See L. Bernardi and U. Trivellato, 'Istruzione e povertà: un condizionamento reciproco', in G. Sarpellon, *op. cit.*, second volume, pp. 471-568.

59 The following survey of the 'ills' of the pension system is based on Censis, *Spesa Pubblica e Politica Sociale*, Milan, Franco Angeli, 1983, as well as on the Institutional Synopsis (see the Appendix volume).

60 See O. Castellino, *Il Labirinto delle Pensioni*, Bologna, Il Mulino, 1975.

61 See Ministero del Tesoro, *La Spesa Previdenziale e i suoi Effetti sulla Finanza Pubblica*, Rome, Istituto Poligrafico dello Stato, 1981.

62 See the special issue in this topic of the *Quaderni della Rivista Trimestrale*, 1980, Nos. 62-63. See also C. Dell'Aringa, *L'Agenzia per la Mobilita della Manodopera*, Milan, Vita e Pensiero, 1981.

63 For a survey of these studies and new updated estimates see R. Brunetta, 'Marginalita e precarietà nel mercato del lavoro italiano', in G. Sarpellon, *op. cit.*, second volume, pp. 209-306.

64 See A. Bagnasco, *Tre Italie*, Bologna, Il Mulino, 1977; A. Becchi Collida, *op. cit.*, and R. Brunetta, *op.cit.*

65 See L. Gallino, (ed.), *Occupati e Bi-occupati*, Bologna, Il Mulino, 1982.

66 See Francesco Forte et al., *La Redistribuzione Assistenziale*, Milan, Etas, 1978.

67 For a short but comprehensive survey of these changes, see Istituto della Enciclopedia Italiana, *Rapporto sulla Popolazione*, Rome, Istituto Poligrafico dello Stato, 1980.

68 A recent survey by ISTAT has in fact shown that the use ratio of health services for the elderly is considerably higher than that for central age groups. See ISTAT 'Indagine statistica sulle condizioni di salute della popolazione e sul ricorso ai servizi sanitari', special supplement to the *Bollettino Mensile di Statistica*, 1982, No. 12. On the use of health services, see also M. Ferrera, 'Crescita da domanda o crescita da offerta? Un'analisi delle spese sociali in Italia', in *Rivista Italiana di Scienza Politica*, Vol. XII, 1982, No. 2, pp. 297-331.

69 On the Italian family structure and its relationship to social policy, see L. Balbo, *Stato di Famiglia*, Milan, Etas, 1976; P. Donati, *Famiglia e Politiche Sociali*, Milan, Franco Angeli, 1982; G.Rossi, *La Famiglia Assistita*, Milan, Franco Angeli, 1982.

[70] See OECD, *Public Expenditure on Income Maintenance Programmes*, Paris, 1976.

[71] Reliable and comparable data on the Italian labour force are only available since 1959, when ISTAT started its periodical survey. Graphs 26 and 27 report data also for 1952 in order to give an idea of the overall trend.

[72] See R. Brunetta, *op. cit.*

[73] Official registration is in fact more 'costly' in the industrial sector both for employers, who have to pay higher contributions and for workers who have to pay higher contributions and income taxes.

[74] Estimates in this direction have been made by the Bank of Italy; see Banca d'Italia, *Relazioni Annuali*, Rome, various years.

[75] This method is again borrowed to a large extent from the OECD studies on resource allocation (which do not include, however, a composition ratio). It should be noted that the eligibility ratio is based on *benefits* and not on the eligible people, and should therefore be more properly referred to as 'benefit rate': we have retained the OECD term for the sake of analogy.

[76] Data for sickness and maternity expenditure only refer to INAM (see Institutional Synopsis). There is a change in the series in 1977, and this is the main cause of the decline of the expenditure and transfer ratios in this year.

[77] The burden of wage continuation exceeding the statutory replacement rate is borne directly by the employers and is therefore not reflected in the transfer ratio.

[78] For a summary of the development of the Italian economy, see A. Graziani, (ed.), *L'Economia Italiana*, Bologna, Il Mulino, 1979.

[79] Following the current procedure in the literature, economic growth is operationalized using the rate of GDP growth.

[80] See G. Regonini, 'Stato e sindacati nella formazione della politica della sicurezza sociale. Il caso delle pensioni', in *Quaderni della Fondazione Feltrinelli*, No. 10, 1980, p. 99.

[81] In recent years the electoral business cycle has been the subject of an increasing amount of empirical research. Santagata has for instance suggested the existence of such a cycle in the evolution of the Italian political economy in the 1953-1979 period. More particularly, he has shown that in the four-monthly period immediately preceeding an election there seems to be an acceleration in the growth rate of GDP, total money supply, public consumption expenditure and local government expenditure, combined with a deceleration in the rate of inflation. See W. Santagata, 'Ciclo politico-economico: il caso italiano, 1953-1979', in *Stato e Mercato*, Vol. 1, 1982, No. 2, pp. 257-299.

[82] See A. Parisi and G. Pasquino, 'Relazioni partiti-elettori e tipi di voto', in A. Parisi and G. Pasquino, *Continuità e Mutamento Elettorale in Italia*, Bologna, Il Mulino, 1977, pp. 215-249.

[83] See. L Graziano, *Clientelismo e Sistema Politico: il Caso dell'Italia*, Milan, Angeli, 1980.

[84] For a description of these systems and, more generally, on the electoral-patronage system, see A. Ancisi, *La Cattura del Voto*, Milan, Angeli, 1976; P.A. Allum, *Politics and Society in Postwar Naples*, Cambridge, Cambridge University Press, 1973, especially ch. 6.

[85] See M. Bonaccorsi, 'Gli enti pubblici nel settore della sicurezza sociale', in F. Cazzola (ed.), *Anatomia del Potere DC*, Bari, De Donato, 1979, pp. 57-149.

[86] On the Italian party system, see G. Sartori, *Teorie dei partiti e caso Italiano*, Milan, Sugarco, 1982; P. Farneti (ed.), *Il Sistema Politico Italiano*, Bologna, Il Mulino, 1973, and *Il Sistema dei Partiti in Italia*, Bologna, Il Mulino, 1983. For a good survey of the postwar evolution of Italian parties and of government coalitions, see also A. Marradi, 'Italy: from Centrism to Crisis of the Centre-left coalition', in E. Browning and J. Dreiymans (eds.), *Government Coalitions in Western Democracies*, London, Longman, 1981, pp. 33-70.

[87] The term 'legislature' here refers to the inter-election period, in which there may be cabinet shifts, but the composition of parliament remains unaltered.

[88] The first Moro cabinet fell on an issue regarding the financing regulation of private middle schools; the second Moro cabinet fell on an issue regarding the establishment of pre-elemen-

tary education. For an overview of the programmes of the different cabinets see Centro Romano Editoriale, *I Programmi dei Governi Reppubblicani dal 1946 al 1978*, Rome, 1978.

89 See 'Centrosinistra rivisitato', special issue of *Biblioteca delle Libertà*, Vol. XIX (1982), No. 87.

90 See the interview with A. Giolitti, *ibid.*, p. 129-134.

91 On the development of Italy's health policy see, G. Berlinguer, *Medicina e Politica*, Bari, De Donato, 1973 and *Una Riforma per la Salute*, Bari, De Donato, 1973; S. Caruso, *Il Medico della Corporazione* Milan, Feltrinelli, 1977; S. Delogu, *Sanità Pubblica, Sicurezza Sociale e Programmazione Economica*, Turin, Einaudi, 1977 and *La Salute dietro l'Angolo*, Rome, Napoleoni, 1978; D. Francesconi, *Lavoratori e Organizzazione Sanitaria*, Bari, De Donato, 1978; A. Piperno, 'La politics sanitaria', in U. Ascoli (ed.), *Welfare State all'Italiana*, Bari, Laterza, 1984, pp. 153-183.

92 For a complete collection of all the documents on planning and its priorities, see Ministero del Bilancio, *La Programmazione Economica in Italia*, cit.

93 M. Salvati, *Alle Origini dell'Inflazione Italiana*, Bologna, Il Mulino, 1978, p. 110.

94 Cf. E. Gerelli and A. Majocchi (eds.), *Il Deficit Pubblico: Origini e Problemi*, Milan, Franco Angeli, 1984.

95 A strong recommendation in this sense was formulated in October 1983 by the annual report on Italy by the IMF.

96 Such as the freezing of hospital personnel in 1974 and the severe restrictions on local government expenditure imposed in 1977.

97 In general, this group is also likely to have pro-welfare interests: students often derive cash tranfers or scholarships from the state; young people in search of a first job may rely on the state for an easier access to the labour market; housewives do not pay contributions but are eligible for a wide array of benefits if married to an employee.

98 See V. Visco, 'Erosione ed evasione dell'imposta sul reddito delle perone fisiche', in *Rivista Milanese di Economia*, 1983, No. 7, pp. 101110.

99 See the series of articles on this topic which appeared in the weekly magazines *L'Espresso*, 30 October 1983, and *Il Mondo*, 24 October 1983.

100 See Banca d'Italia, 'I bilanci delle famiglie italiane nell'anno 1982', in *Supplemento al Bollettino*, 1983, No. 57.

101 It must be noted that for the formation of political groupings and conflicts surrounding the welfare state. The constellations of socio-cultural identities and movements may in fact represent another important basis for the structuring of welfare politics. In this second respect the Italian landscape of the 1980s seems characterized by a relative quiet. The big wave of welfare mobilization on the side of various 'conscience constituencies' (especially women and students) which unfolded itself during the 1970s seems to have come to and end - or at least appears now as highly fragmented and dispersed in different institutional arenas (school councils, family counselling units, and more generally, neighbourhood and local government). As Ergas has recently suggested, the institutional response which these movements have received through the social reforms of the 1970s has partly contributed to their political integration and destructuralization. See Y. Ergas, 'Allargamento della cittadinanza e governo del conflitto: le politiche sociali negli anni settanta in Italia', in *Stato e Mercato*, 1982, No. 6, pp. 429-464.

102 These data have been kindly provided by Prof. F. Calvi of Eurisko and Prof. G. Urbani of Bocconi University.

103 For an interesting survey of the claims of this category, see the periodical magazines *Quadri* (published by the *Unionquadri*), and *Noiquadri* (published by the *Conferderquadri*).

104 Due to the regulations of the Italian electoral mechanism, depite its fairly high number of votes the PNP did not gain parliamentary representation.

105 On these changes, see especially A. Parisi and G. Pasquino, *op. cit.*

106 See for instance *Il Mondo* of 13 June 1983.

[107] These data have been drawn from a survey carried out in 1982 by G. Urbani in collaboration with the daily newspaper *Il Sole* and the Doxa Institute. The survey contained a wide array of quesitons (two of which have been reported in Table 38), including 'for which party do you think it would be better to vote'. The small size of the sample and the high number of non-respondents to this item put its statistical representativeness seriously in question.

[108] For a survey of the Italian neo-marxist debate on the welfare state see especially P. Barcellona, *Oltre lo Stato Sociale*, Bari, De Donato, 1981; P. Barcellona and M. Carrieri, 'Governo dell'economia e controllo operaio nelle strategie della sinistra europea', in *Democrazia e Diritto*, 1982, No. 4, pp. 5-32; C. Donolo and M. Fichera (eds.), *Il Governo Debole*, Bari, De Donato, 1981; E. Fano, S. Rodota, and G. Marramao (eds.), *Il Welfare State come Problema Politico e Teorico*, Bari, De Donato, 1983. For a thorough reconstruction of the debate, see especially the journals *Democrazia e Diritto*, *Critica Marxista*, and *Rinascita*.

[109] For a survey of the neo-liberal debate, see especially the anthology volume *Il Welfare State Possibile*, Florence, Le Monnier, 1984. A neo-conservative attack is contained in *La Crisi dello Stato Assistenziale*, Rome, CREA, 1984.

[110] For a survey of 'radical catholic' positions, see especially A. Ardigo, *Crisi di Governabilità e Mondi Vitali*, Bologna, Cappelli, 1980; *Pubblico e Privato: Fine di un'Alternativa?*, Bologna, Cappelli, 1978; also G. Rossi and P. Donati (eds.), *Welfare State, Problemi e Alternative*, Milan, Angeli, 1982.

[111] See for instance, Ministero del Tesoro, *La Spesa Previdenziale, op. cit.*

[112] The issues of 'flexibility' and 'personalization' are stressed particularly by the Roman research centre CENSIS, directed by the sociologist G. De Rita. See especially, *Spesa Pubblica e Politica Sociale, op. cit.* On the use of vouchers in the educational sector, see *Il Finanziamento dell'Istruzione in una Libera Democrazia: il Buono-Scuola - Opinioni a Confronto*, Rome, CREA, 1982.

[113] For the debate on this issue see the anthology volume *Previdenza Integrativa*, Milan, Mondadori, 1984.

[114] The issue of selectivity has been recently discussed in U. Ascoli (ed.), *Welfare State all'Italiana*, Bari, Laterza, 1984. With reference to the health sector, see M. Ferrera and G. Zincone (eds.), *Rapporto sulla Domanda Sanitaria in Italia*, Turin, Centro Einaudi, 1984.

[115] See F. Reviglio, 'Meritocrazia e stato sociale', in *Mondoperaio*, 1982, No. 7, pp. 125-129.

[116] An articulate debate has recently started in Italy on the Italian 'type' of welfare state. Ascoli and Paci have suggested the notion of a 'particularistic-clientelistic' type of welfare, which would constitute a southern variant of Titmus' 'meritocratic-particularistic' type. As is known, the latter is one which reproduces in the public system of services and (especially) transfers the differentiations of the market place. In the corporatist variant (e.g. Germany), a clearcut boundary exists between the political system and the welfare system and especially between parties and the welfare bureaucracy. In the clientelistic variant (e.g. Italy), there is on the contrary, a subordination of the main public mechanisms of resource distribution to the general clientelistic logic which seems to regulate the functioning of the political system: more particularly, political parties have a direct access to, and control over the distribution of welfare benefits. See U. Ascoli, 'Il sistema italiano di welfare', in U. Ascoli (ed.), *op. cit.*, pp. 5-51, and M. Paci, 'Il sistema di welfare italiano fra tradizione clientelare e prospettive di riforma', in U. Ascoli (ed.), *op. cit*, pp. 297-326.

Sources to tables and graphs

Table 1:   Institutional Synopsis.

Table 2:   A. Cendali Pignatelli, 'The State as Paymaster: The Italian Experience 1951-1976', paper presented at the ECPR Joint Sessions of Workshops, Florence, March 1979.

Table 3:   O. Castellino, *Il Labrinto delle Pensioni*, Bologna, Il Mulino, 1975; and *Lavoro e Previdenza Oggi*, Rome, various years.

Table 4:   Institutional Synopsis.

Table 5:   Appendix Tables 8, 9, 10.

Table 6:   Institutional Synopsis.

Table 7:   Institutional Synopsis and Ministero del Lavoro e della Previdenza Sociale, *Statistiche del Lavoro*, Rome, various years.

Table 8:   ISTAT, *Annuario Statistico Italiano*, Rome, various years.

Table 9:   *Ibid.*

Table 10:   *Ibid.*

Table 11:   P. Braghin, *Inchiesta sulla Miseria in Italia (1951-1952)*, Turin, Einaudi, 1978.

Table 12:   G. Sarpellon (ed.), *La Povertà in Italia*, Rome, Franco Angeli, 1982.

Table 13:   *Ibid.*

Table 14:   P. Roberti, 'Le Variazioni nella Distribuzione Personale del Reddito in Italia 1948-1966, in *Rassegna Economica*, No. 4, 1971, pp. 801-832; and Banca d'Italia, 'Reddito Risparmio e Patrimonio delle Famiglie Italiane nell'anno ...', *Bollettino della Banca d'Italia*, Rome, various years.

Table 15:   Censis, *Spesa Pubblica e Politica Sociale*, Milan, Franco Angeli, 1983.

Table 16:   Ministero del Bilancio and Ministero del Tesoro, *Relazione Generale sulla Situazione Economica del Paese*, Rome, various years.

Table 17:   F. Forte (ed.), *La Redistribuzione Assistenziale*, Milan, Franco Angeli, 1978.

Table 18:   *Ibid.*

Table 19:   ISTAT, *Annuario Statistico Italiano*, cit., 1979 edition; Ministero del Bilancio and Ministero del Tesoro, *Rel. Gen. Ec. Sit. Paese*, cit. 1979 edition.

Table 20:   *Ibid.*, 1977 editions.

Table 21:   *Ibid.*

Table 22:   ISTAT, *Annuario Statistico Italiano*, cit. various years.

Table 23:   *Ibid.*

Table 24:   Appendix Tables 5, 8, 10.

Table 25:   *Ibid.*

Table 26:   *Ibid.*

Table 27:   *Ibid.*

Table 28:   Appendix Tables 1, 3, 7.

Table 29:   Appendix Tables 1, 2, 3.

Table 30:   M. Bonaccorsi, 'Gli Enti Pubblici nel Settore della Sicurezza Sociale', in F. Cazzola (ed.), *Anatomia del Potere DC*, Bari, De Donato, 1979, pp. 57-149.

Table 31:   Centro di Ricerca e Documentazione 'Luigi Einaudi', Turin, internal unpublished report.

Table 32:   A. Forni, *Il Pianeta Previdenza*, Bari, De Donato, 1979.

Table 33:   Appendix Tables.

Table 34:   Institutional Synopsis.

Table 35:   ISTAT, *Censimento della Populazione 1981*, Rome, 1983.

Table 36:   *Ibid.*

Table 37:   *Il Mondo*, 24 October, 1983.

Table 38:   Centro di Politica Comparata, Università L. Bocconi, Milan and Eurisko, Milan.
Table 39:   Centro di Politica Comparata, Università L. Bocconi, Milan.

Graph 1:   Appendix Tables 1 and 4.
Graph 2:   Appendix Tables 1 and 3.
Graph 3:   Appendix Table 2.
Graph 4:   Ibid.
Graph 5:   Ibid.
Graph 6:   Appendix Table 4.
Graph 7:   Appendix Tables 5 and 6.
Graph 8:   Ibid.
Graph 9:   Appendix Table 6.
Graph 10:   Ibid.
Graph 11:   Ibid.
Graph 12:   Ibid.
Graph 13:   Appendix Table 3.
Graph 14:   Ibid.
Graph 15:   Appendix Table 7.
Graph 16:   Ibid.
Graph 17:   J. Alber, 'Social Security', in P. Flora, *State, Economy and Society in Western Europe 1815-1975*, Frankfurt/London/New York, Campus and Macmillan, 1983; Appendix Table 7.
Graph 18:   ISTAT, *Annuario Statistico Italiano*, various years; Ministero del Bilancio and Ministero del Tesoro, *Relazione Generale sulla Situazione Economica del Paese*, Rome, various years.
Graph 19:   Ibid.
Graph 20:   Appendix Table 9.
Graph 21:   Appendix Table 10.
Graph 22:   Ministero del Bilancio and Ministero del Tesoro, *Rel. Gen. Sit. Ec. Paese*, cit., various years.
Graph 23:   ISTAT, *Annuario Statistico Italiano*, various years.
Graph 24:   Appendix Tables 1, 5, 8, and 10.
Graph 25:   Ibid.
Graph 26:   Appendix Table 8.
Graph 27:   Ibid.
Graph 28:   Appendix Tables 1, 5, 8 and 10.
Graph 29:   Ibid.
Graph 30:   Ibid.
Graph 31:   Appendix Tables 1 and 3.
Graph 32:   Ibid.
Graph 33:   Ibid.

Appendix

Pension politics and pension policy in Italy: an institutional analysis of pension bills and laws

Ezio Maestri

Introduction

In Italy, as in most industrialized countries, public expenditure on pensions has become an increasingly heavy financial burden on the state. This is partly accounted for by such large-scale factors as the ageing of the population, but in addition, the complexity and fragmentation of the Italian pension system is said to have further contributed to its financial crisis. As shown by Maurizio Ferrera in the preceding chapter, the Italian pension system consists of a great variety of schemes for different occupational groups, with enormous variations in financing, eligibility criteria, benefit levels, etc. It will be argued here that this fragmented structure reflects the workings of a political system in which the relationship between political parties and social classes and/or occupational groups is relatively close, thus inviting clientelistic exchanges [1].

The purpose of this short appendix to the chapter on Italy is to shed some light on these complex relationships, by presenting some results of a much broader study of the impact of political factors on Italian pension lawmaking in the first eight legislatures of the Italian Republic from 1948 to 1983 [2]. It is based on an extensive analysis of the total set of approximately 2,900 pension draft bills and the 600 resulting pension laws. As pension policy is principally pursued through legislation, it is useful to first review the basic characteristics of the legislative process in Italy.

The Italian Parliament consists of the Senate (315 members) and the Chamber of Deputies (630 members). Legislation can be initiated independently in either chamber. Draft bills, on the other hand, may be introduced by cabinets as well as MPs. In order to become law, a draft bill must be passed in both parliamentary chambers, either in restricted parliamentary committees or in the General Assembly, according to their political importance [3].

The main question to be dealt with here is how political actors have 'used' pension policy for their own political purposes and thereby influenced pension lawmaking in Italy. In order to obtain some insights into this intricate question, attention has been focused on the whole range of the legislative process. Firstly, draft bills and subsequent laws have been coded according to a variety of aspects (person introducing the bill, population group affected, final output, policy sub-sector, party voting attitudes, policy content, etc.). Only a few of these can be discussed here, with emphasis on the more general trends which emerged in the research. Secondly, pension draft bills have been categorized according to the parliamentary activities of the four most important Italian policy-makers in this field, i.e. the Christian Democratic Party (DC), the Italian Communist Party (PCI), the Italian Socialist Party (PSI), and the respective cabinets. The three political parties represent on average about 80 percent of the parliamentary seats.

For the analysis of the social/occupational groups affected by the bills/laws, seven population categories have been distinguished: (a) the general population, (b) pensioners, (c) dependent workers of the private sector, (d) public employees, (e) the self-employed, (f) professionals, and (g) a 'residual' category of persons formally outside the labour market such as veterans, housewives, refugees, poor elderly, etc.

One should be aware that the following quantitative analysis of the pension bills/laws is limited in at least three respects: (a) it necessarily gives a 'mechanistic' view of legislative processes, (b) the implementation of pension laws is not dealt with [4], and (c) the form and extent to which 'beneficiary' groups really 'benefit' from the respective bill/law is not exactly specified.

As to the first limitation, it is obviously rather difficult to confute the argument that the complexity of a legislative process involving a great number of actors (parties, cabinets, pressure and interest groups, fractions) cannot be fully grasped by a longitudinal study dealing with hundreds of bills and laws. In this regard, case studies would seem by and large more suitable. On the other hand, given the highly fragmented structure of the Italian pension system, a longitudinal and extensive study of the entire legislative process is likely to provide more systematic insights into the relationship between policy-makers and class structure in pension politics and policies.

As regards the second limitation, concentrating on the making of pension laws, and thereby neglecting their implementation, does not entail an irremediable loss of information about their specific welfare effects because pension provisions are essentially cash benefits. Furthermore, as there are no significant private pension schemes in Italy today, a study of the decision-making in the social transfers arena is even more relevant from a theoretical as well as political point of view [5].

Finally, the present analysis is also limited in the sense that 'beneficiary' groups in reality mean 'target' groups. In principle, a group of citizens affected by pension bills or laws may either benefit or be penalized by them. Empirical evidence shows that at least the party-sponsored bills in this policy sector have been almost without exception favourable for their 'beneficiaries' [6]. This is not true to the same degree, however, for draft bills introduced by cabinets, especially in times of economic crises.

1. The incidence and salience of pension lawmaking

As a political issue, the relevance of the pension system in Italy has varied. A first indicator of this variation is the 'incidence of pension bills in the total number of bills introduced' in the Italian parliament both by political parties and cabinets. Graph 1 shows that this incidence averaged more than 5 percent, ranging from 3.5 percent in the first legislature to 6.9 percent in the seventh. The higher levels were reached as from the fifth legislature, most likely as a consequence of the increasing politicization of the pension issue followed by the wave of strikes in that period [7].

Studying the mere incidence of pension bills is only a first step in an analysis of the pension issue in post-World War II Italy. Other characteristics such as the 'demographic weight' and the 'institutional weight' of the pension draft bills and laws must also be taken into account. The 'demographic weight' is a measurement of the sectors of population affected by pension legislation. Graph 2 shows that since the sixth legislature there has been an increasing difference between the demographic weight of bills

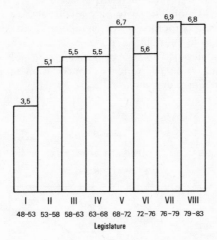

Graph 1

The incidence of pension bills

(as % of all bills)

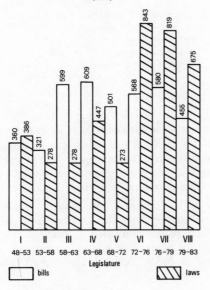

Graph 2

The 'demographic weight' of pension bills/laws

(index)

and that of subsequent laws. Since 1972 pension laws have tended to affect larger population categories than those targeted by the respective bills. The most likely reason for this shift lies in the modification of relationships between the Italian unions and the government after the unprecedented strike cycle of 1969-1972. Since then and throughout the seventies, unions began to play a considerable role in pension policy [8]. The emergence of a 'neo-corporatist' pattern in the 1970s was accompanied by a parallel decline of the role of political parties. The increasing 'political exchange' between unions and cabinets led to a less particularistic policy on the government's part, whereas MPs, being excluded from the 'concertation process', went on as usual with more fragmented political demands.

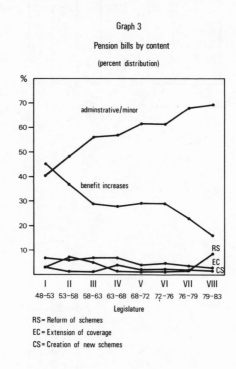

Graph 3

Pension bills by content

(percent distribution)

RS= Reform of schemes
EC= Extension of coverage
CS= Creation of new schemes

The 'institutional weight' of pension draft bills is an evaluation of the importance of the pension laws passed. The pension provisions have been grouped into five content categories: (1) minor administrative, (b) increase in benefit levels, (c) extension of pension coverage and eligibility to new social groups, (d) reform of schemes, and (e) creation of completely new schemes and/or programmes.

Graph 3 shows that the bulk of pension bills deals with minor administrative provisions. It also shows that the relative incidence of bills proposing an increase in benefits has decreased since the sixth legislature, probably explained by the unprecedented fiscal crisis [9], and that reform bills had their relative peak number in the eighth legislature, reflecting Italian public opinion about the inadequacy of the pension system structure [10].

2. The role of parties and cabinets

The pension system has become a relevant political issue, notably since the late 1960s. To what extent did this attract the parliamentary activity of the different parties and cabinets? Graph 4 clearly shows that political parties have been the most active in pension lawmaking, introducing nearly 90 percent of the relevant bills. The DC has played the most active role, with almost 40 percent of the total set of pension bills. Since the rise of the new Centre-Left majorities in the fourth legislature (1963-1968), essentially characterized by the alliance between the DC and the PSI, there has been a symmetry between the parliamentary initiatives of these parties and those of the PCI. Both the DC and the PSI have tended to increase their activity in the pension area considerably, while the PCI did the opposite. This general trend continued until the seventh legislature (1976-1979), when the DC and the PSI slowed down their quantitative commitment while the PCI increased its own.

Graph 4

Pension bills by party/cabinet

(percent distribution)

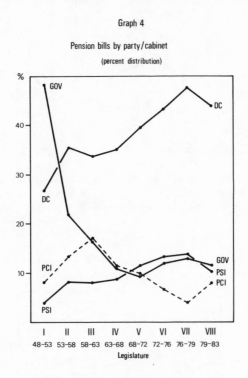

If one takes into account that during the seventh legislature the DC and the PCI had their minimum and maximum number of parliamentary seats respectively, it is possible to infer a change in their political strategies. The seventh legislature was characterized by the formation of a majority which included the PCI for the first time since 1947 [11]. The DC's behaviour could be seen as a reaction to the new threat posed by increasing activity on behalf of its traditional clienteles, while the PCI attempted to limit the normal range of pension initiatives in order to finally 'rationalize' policy intervention in the pension system. This interpretation is further supported by a comparison of the relationships between the parties' parliamentary strength and their production of pension draft bills (see Graph 5).

Graph 5 shows that since the sixth legislature, there has been a striking symmetry in the development of the three main Italian parties. In this period the PCI reached its highest parliamentary and institutional strength but its minimum in quantitative commitment. On the contrary, the DC and the PSI moved in exactly the opposite direction.

Graph 5

Pension bills and parliamentary strength

(percent distribution of bills and seats by party)

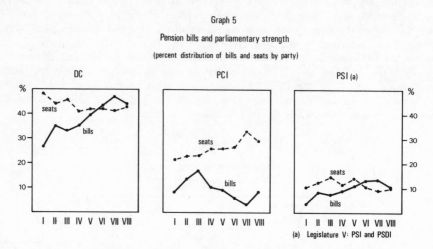

(a) Legislature V: PSI and PSDI

Of course, in addition to the number of bills, their 'demographic weight' and 'institutional importance' must also be considered. Graph 6 shows that the average 'demographic weight' (measured in terms of the size of the different socio-professional groups concerned) has been about 500,000 persons in the 35 years considered here. The most striking figure concerns the PCI. During the crucial seventh legislature, it pursued a

Graph 6

The 'demographic weight' of pension bills by party

(index)

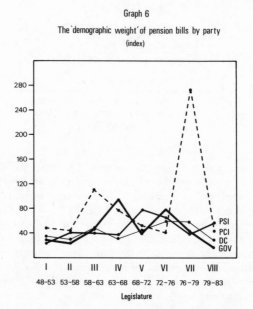

Legislature

rationalization of the Italian pension system, mainly by reducing the number of schemes. This is demonstrated by the fact that in this legislature the PCI's average 'demographic weight' reached its highest point with nearly 2,800,000 versus the DC's 600,000 persons.

Graph 7

Pension bills by party/cabinet and content

(percent distribution)

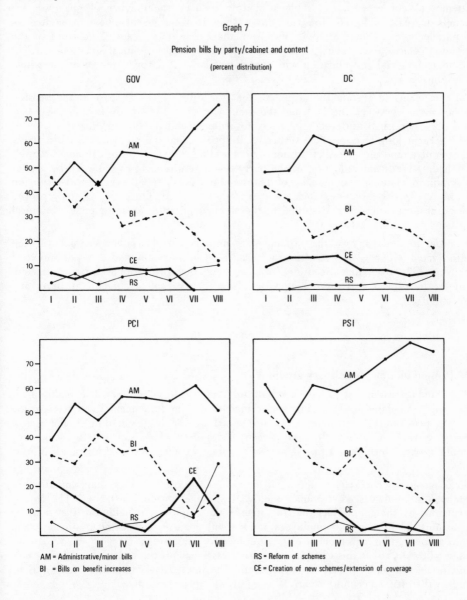

AM = Administrative/minor bills

BI = Bills on benefit increases

RS = Reform of schemes

CE = Creation of new schemes/extension of coverage

As regards the 'institutional weight' of the pension bills, Graph 7 shows a general increase - at least until the seventh legislature - of the minor administrative bills [12], probably as a result of the growing 'maturity' of the pension system [13]. As regards bills proposing increases in cash benefits, the PCI followed the majority parties in decreasing the number of this kind of pension draft bill up to the seventh legislature. However, when the PCI returned to the opposition in the eigth legislature, it not only increased the number of its reform bills, but also the number of its bills aiming at benefit improvements. The other three actors followed different strategies. In their attempt to cut expenditure, cabinets sharply reduced the number of proposals for benefit increases. The DC followed this strategy to some extent, but compensated by a parallel increase in draft bills proposing the extension of existing schemes or the creation of new ones. The PSI, finding itself in an uneasy political situation, tried to combine financial consolidation with the claim of the PCI for a reform of the whole pension system.

All this seems to sustain the argument that the difference - at least in the pension policy area - between the PCI and the other parties of the Centre-Left majority [14] is not only a 'normal' difference between government and opposition, but also a result of divergent long-term political strategies. It appears that the pursuit of a substantially cooperative and non-conflict strategy by the PCI (of the 'historical compromise') implied a significant reduction of the party's 'competitiveness', as indicated by a considerable decline in the number of pension bills dealing with very short-term and highly competitive requests such as increases of benefits. Once this strategy proved to be unsuccessful, the PCI shifted in the eighth legislature to a competitive political strategy.

In order to find out how the parliamentary initiatives in this policy sector have been interrelated with the class structure, we shall look in more detail at the distribution of pension bills over time according to: (a) the socio-professional groups affected, (b) the introducer and the 'beneficiaries', and (c) the 'policy content' by party and group(s).

3. Pension bills and beneficiary groups

The Italian pension system has been built up along professional lines. It is highly intricate and dominated by 'particularistic' principles [15]. This fundamental character of the Italian pension system is very likely explained by the fragmentation of the Italian party system [16]. Graph 8 gives the percent distribution of pension bills by socio-economic group affected, as a first impression of their varying 'potential for political pressure'.

Two categories have clearly attracted most of the parties' parliamentary initiatives in the pension policy sector: public employees and the 'residual' category. The first is explained by the simple fact that the state is the employer. In addition, the 'political proximity' of most public employees' unions with majority parties must also be taken into account. The high number of pension bills for the residual category may be attributed to the fact that this category (and to a lesser extent, the pensioners) is not easily identifiable in political and electoral terms. The inter-party competition may thus be higher than for other more clearly aligned groupings of citizens.

The decreasing number of the pension bills relating to traditional dependent workers might be accounted for both by the 'maturity' of their schemes and by the 'victory' of Italian unions in the general reform of the pension system in 1969 [17]. In the case of the self-employed, the decreasing trend may be explained by the increasing hostility of large sectors of Italian public opinion over the large public subsidies for the self-em-

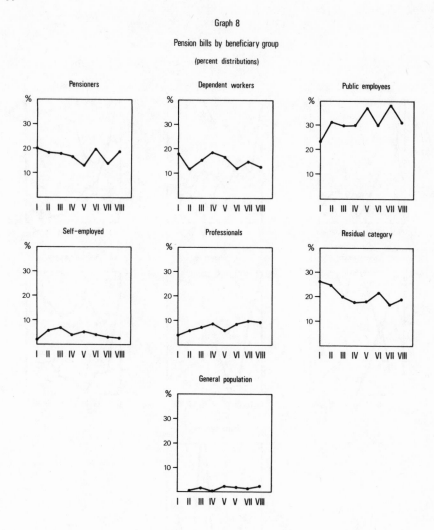

Graph 8

Pension bills by beneficiary group

(percent distributions)

ployed (notably that of the farmers). The increasing number of the bills dealing with professionals, on the other hand, is probably related to the large number of pension schemes (about 25 versus 3 for the self-employed), of the relatively slow extension of coverage, and of the high capacity for political pressure of this category [18].

4. Pension bills and party clienteles 1948-1983

In which ways did political actors utilize the pension issue for their different strategies? As a first step, this question may be dealt with by studying the distribution of the pension bills by social category and political party (see Graph 9).

Graph 9

Pension bills by beneficiary group and party/cabinet

(percent distributions)

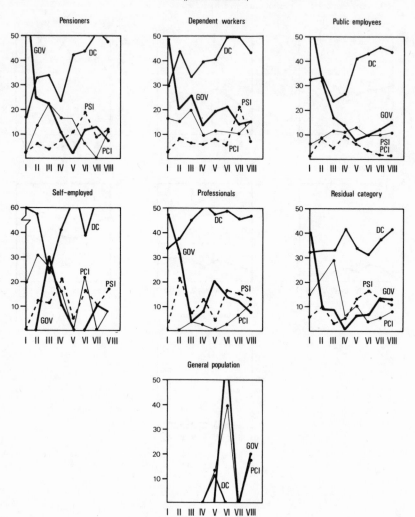

The DC has been the most active party in pension policy on the whole, introducing on average nearly half of the relevant draft bills for all the six specific social categories. The PCI instead acted mainly on behalf of the pension schemes for dependent workers of the private sector. The PSI and the government were more active than the PCI in sponsoring bills dealing with the pension schemes of the public employees, self-employed, professionals and residual categories.

On the basis of Table 1, which gives the rank-order of the different 'beneficiaries' of pension bills submitted by the three parties and the government for the entire period

Table 1   The relevance of social categories for
           parties in pension policy, 1948-1983 (a)

Pension bills introduced for	Pension bills introduced by			
	GOV	DC	PCI	PSI
General population	7	7	7	-
Pensioners	3	3	3	3
Dependent workers	2	4	2	4
Public employees	1	1	4	1
Self-employed	6	6	5	6
Professionals	5	5	6	5
Residual category	4	2	1	2

(a) Rank order of social categories by the number of
    pension bills introduced on their behalf by the
    cabinet and the three major parties.

1948-1983, three different patterns of specific interest representation can be identified. Firstly, the DC and the PSI, with basically the same structure of interest representation, concentrated their pension initiatives on public employees and the residual category, relatively neglecting the dependent workers. This seems to support the argument that the PSI is more a Centre than a Left party [19]. Secondly, the PCI showed its strongest commitment to the residual category and the dependent workers of the private sector, neglecting the public employees. Lastly, the cabinets acted chiefly on behalf of public employees and dependent workers, showing a minor commitment for the residual category. Thus, despite their essentially conservative majorities, the cabinets devoted an important part of their pension bills to the traditional working class. Among the parties, however, the PCI clearly has the strongest roots in this class. All this suggests that cabinets have the same 'degree of freedom' in their decision-making as political parties. Unlike the latter, however, they must pay more attention to the 'power relationships' among classes and groups.

5. Pension lawmaking and policy content

Of course, the various pension 'benefits' brought in by the draft bills do not all have the same intrinsic importance or political relevance. If one analyses the distribution of pension bill by type of content (Table 2), it appears that there is a close relationship between the type of provisions proposed in the pension bills and party strategies.

Both the DC and the PCI concentrated most of their parliamentary activities on eligibility extension. Here too, the DC acted essentially as an inter-class party by distributing its pension bills on eligibility extension relatively evenly among the various population categories, whereas the PCI concentrated almost half of its bills on the dependent workers of the private sector. The Italian governments proceeded in pension policy by increasing the benefits level for pensioners and public employees, extending eligibility on behalf of the self-employed, and finally, by creating new schemes for residual category. As for the PSI, as already noted, the most striking aspect concerns its rather weak policy commitment to the traditional working class.

The political dynamics roughly sketched out here suggest that the assumption of an irreversible emergence of party systems, characterized by the model of the 'catch-all party', is not so easily applicable in the Italian case [20].

Table 2   Percent distribution of pension bills by content, party, and beneficiaries (a)

Increase of benefits

Legislature	GOV GP	PE	DW	PU	SE	PR	RE	Total	DC GP	PE	DW	PU	SE	PR	RE	Total	PCI GP	PE	DW	PU	SE	PR	RE	Total	PSI GP	PE	DW	PU	SE	PR	RE	Total	GOV	DC	PCI	PSI
I	–	45	16	25	–	2	12	100	–	17	4	18	–	–	61	100	–	67	–	–	–	–	33	100	–	25	–	–	–	–	75	100	56	25	7	4
II	–	48	16	20	–	–	16	100	–	31	12	29	–	2	26	100	–	31	8	23	8	–	30	100	–	25	17	33	22	17	41	100	21	36	11	10
III	–	42	16	19	10	10	3	100	–	48	–	21	7	7	21	100	–	37	13	17	10	3	20	100	–	22	20	33	22	23	23	100	26	24	25	8
IV	–	36	21	36	–	7	–	100	–	27	15	26	8	8	15	100	–	56	19	12	–	3	13	100	–	20	20	10	10	30	30	100	11	32	13	8
V	–	17	33	33	–	17	–	100	–	38	4	31	8	2	23	100	–	50	7	14	–	–	29	100	–	41	18	24	6	11	11	100	10	41	11	14
VI	–	74	13	–	–	13	–	100	–	31	5	42	3	9	11	100	–	33	–	15	–	2	50	100	–	67	12	25	–	–	8	100	13	39	5	10
VII	–	57	40	40	–	–	–	100	–	59	–	10	17	13	–	100	–	33	–	25	100	–	–	100	–	37	12	20	–	–	32	100	13	49	1	10
VIII	–	–	–	29	5	6	10	100	–	–	–	–	77	7	–	100	–	–	44	6	17	13	31	100	–	–	8	17	5	2	20	100	10	47	6	7
Average	–	35	19	25	5	6	10	100	–	35	6	25	4	5	25	100	–	41	–	15	2	13	23	100	–	37	8	17	5	2	31	100	20	37	10	9

Extension of eligibility

Legislature	GOV GP	PE	DW	PU	SE	PR	RE	Total	DC GP	PE	DW	PU	SE	PR	RE	Total	PCI GP	PE	DW	PU	SE	PR	RE	Total	PSI GP	PE	DW	PU	SE	PR	RE	Total	GOV	DC	PCI	PSI
I	–	17	17	–	–	–	66	100	–	33	67	–	–	–	–	100	–	–	–	–	25	–	75	100	–	–	–	100	–	–	–	100	43	21	29	7
II	33	–	33	–	33	–	74	100	–	11	11	17	50	–	33	100	–	50	50	–	50	–	30	100	–	–	33	33	–	–	–	100	16	32	11	16
III	–	–	50	–	–	44	–	100	–	11	11	6	44	19	22	100	–	12	38	–	12	–	38	100	–	–	–	100	–	–	–	100	7	32	29	7
IV	–	–	100	–	100	–	–	100	–	6	12	8	25	32	–	100	–	50	50	–	–	–	–	100	–	33	–	–	–	33	33	100	3	52	6	10
V	50	–	–	–	–	50	–	100	26	17	8	8	33	–	–	100	–	100	–	–	–	–	–	100	–	–	–	–	–	100	100	100	6	67	6	6
VI	–	–	–	50	–	–	–	100	15	8	8	54	–	–	–	100	–	67	–	–	–	–	33	100	–	–	–	–	–	–	100	100	11	68	16	6
VII	–	–	–	–	–	–	–	–	25	12	13	38	–	–	–	100	–	100	–	–	–	100	100	100	–	–	–	–	–	100	–	100	–	50	17	5
VIII	–	–	13	6	9	25	–	100	74	9	7	33	–	31	100	–	–	44	6	17	13	31	100	–	–	17	17	9	29	100	100	–	75	17	–
Average	–	4	8	13	19	6	25	100	5	2	20	9	7	7	33	100	–	2	44	6	17	13	31	100	–	4	8	17	17	9	29	100	11	50	16	6

Creation of new scheme

Legislature	GOV GP	PE	DW	PU	SE	PR	RE	Total	DC GP	PE	DW	PU	SE	PR	RE	Total	PCI GP	PE	DW	PU	SE	PR	RE	Total	PSI GP	PE	DW	PU	SE	PR	RE	Total	GOV	DC	PCI	PSI
I	–	–	100	–	–	–	–	100	–	–	–	–	100	–	–	100	–	100	–	–	–	–	–	100	–	–	–	100	–	–	–	100	43	29	74	–
II	–	33	–	33	34	–	60	100	–	–	22	33	45	–	40	100	–	–	60	–	–	–	–	100	–	–	33	33	34	–	–	100	74	43	24	–
III	20	–	20	20	–	–	–	100	–	–	22	44	74	–	–	100	–	–	–	50	12	38	–	100	–	–	–	–	100	74	33	100	23	41	–	5
IV	–	40	40	40	–	100	–	100	–	–	20	80	–	–	–	100	–	100	–	–	–	–	–	100	–	–	–	–	–	100	33	100	45	45	–	9
V	–	–	–	–	50	50	–	100	–	–	–	100	–	–	54	100	–	100	–	–	–	–	33	100	–	–	–	100	–	–	100	100	33	33	–	–
VI	–	50	50	50	–	–	50	100	–	–	–	100	–	–	50	100	–	100	–	–	–	–	100	100	–	–	–	100	–	100	100	100	40	40	–	–
VII	–	–	–	–	–	–	–	–	–	–	–	100	–	–	–	100	–	100	–	–	–	–	–	100	–	–	–	100	–	–	100	100	–	50	–	20
VIII	40	–	–	–	–	50	–	100	–	–	–	100	60	–	100	100	–	100	–	–	100	–	100	100	–	–	–	100	100	100	100	100	–	62	17	17
Average	–	3	29	8	–	13	24	100	5	–	–	77	8	10	–	100	–	13	–	–	8	13	18	100	–	–	–	13	25	13	–	100	25	43	8	6

(a) Content: increase of benefits, extension of eligibility, creation of new schemes; party: GOVernment, DC, PCI, PSI; beneficiaries: general population (GP), pensioners (PE), dependent workers (DW), public employees (PU), self-employed (SE), professionals (PR), residual category (RE).

Table 3   Percent distribution of pension bills by party and beneficiaries (a)

Legis-lature	Party	GP	PE	DW	PU	SE	PR	RE	Total	GP	PE	DW	PU	SE	PR	RE
I	GOV	-	29	20	27	-	5	18	100	-	71	49	55	-	56	40
	DC	-	13	19	26	6	6	32	100	-	17	30	32	60	33	32
	PCI	-	6	35	6	6	-	47	100	-	2	16	2	20	-	15
	PSI	-	13	13	38	-	-	38	100	-	2	3	6	-	-	6
	Total (b)									-	92	98	95	80	89	93
II	GOV	-	23	11	48	-	9	10	100	-	25	21	33	-	32	9
	DC	-	18	15	31	7	6	24	100	-	33	44	33	56	37	33
	PCI	-	14	12	19	16	-	40	100	-	13	15	9	31	-	23
	PSI	-	13	10	30	7	13	27	100	-	7	8	9	13	21	10
	Total (b)									-	78	88	84	100	90	75
III	GOV	-	25	22	30	12	1	10	100	-	23	26	17	30	4	9
	DC	-	19	16	29	7	10	19	100	-	35	34	24	30	50	33
	PCI	-	28	17	10	7	1	36	100	-	23	19	5	26	4	29
	PSI	-	10	13	50	10	7	10	100	-	4	6	12	11	7	4
	Total (b)									-	85	85	58	97	65	75
IV	GOV	-	16	27	42	4	4	7	100	-	11	15	14	11	8	1
	DC	-	12	22	24	6	17	20	100	-	23	39	28	42	62	42
	PCI	-	27	20	31	7	2	13	100	-	16	10	10	16	3	7
	PSI	-	15	13	39	10	13	10	100	-	8	6	11	21	13	5
	Total (b)									-	58	70	63	90	86	55
V	GOV	-	5	36	31	-	18	10	100	-	4	19	8	-	20	7
	DC	1	13	16	39	9	7	16	100	11	42	40	42	71	56	74
	PCI	3	26	23	28	-	-	21	100	11	16	13	7	-	-	10
	PSI	-	13	13	47	2	2	22	100	-	11	8	13	5	4	13
	Total (b)									22	73	80	70	76	80	64
VI	GOV	6	18	28	28	-	10	10	100	60	11	22	10	-	14	8
	DC	-	21	15	30	4	13	17	100	-	44	51	44	39	58	31
	PCI	12	12	23	19	15	4	15	100	40	6	12	4	22	3	4
	PSI	-	28	6	22	6	11	28	100	-	19	6	10	17	17	17
	Total (b)									100	80	91	68	80	92	60
VII	GOV	-	15	23	35	3	8	18	100	-	13	15	13	10	13	13
	DC	-	16	16	40	5	11	12	100	-	52	50	46	70	50	37
	PCI	-	-	39	23	-	15	23	100	-	-	10	2	-	6	6
	PSI	-	10	25	33	3	13	18	100	-	9	21	10	10	16	13
	Total (b)									-	74	96	71	90	95	69
VIII	GOV	4	12	14	41	2	6	21	100	20	8	15	16	8	8	13
	DC	-	21	13	31	4	11	19	100	-	49	43	44	67	54	42
	PCI	6	24	24	9	3	12	21	100	20	10	15	2	8	10	9
	PSI	-	20	9	34	5	11	20	100	-	12	8	12	17	13	11
	Total (b)									40	79	81	74	100	85	75
Total	GOV	1	22	22	35	3	7	13	100	19	18	21	17	9	14	11
	DC	0	17	16	32	6	11	19	100	4	37	41	37	51	53	35
	PCI	2	21	21	18	7	3	27	100	19	12	14	6	16	4	13
	PSI	-	17	12	36	6	10	20	100	-	9	8	11	13	12	10
	Total									42	76	84	71	89	83.	69

(a) Party: GOVernment, DC, PCI, PSI; beneficiaries: general population (GP), pensioners (PE), dependent workers (DW), public employees (PU), self-employed (SE), professionals (PR), residual category
(RE).
(b) Excluding pension bills introduced by other parties.

6. Political factors and pension politics: a preliminary view

It has been shown that the four political actors under consideration clearly differ in their respective long-term policy (and political) options [21]. However, there has been some significant variation over time (see Table 3). The most important changes were related to the rise of the first Centre-Left majority at the beginning of the fourth legislature (1963-1968), the entry of the PCI into the majority (although not into the cabinet) in the course of the seventh legislature (1976-1979), and to the influence of the strike wave of 1969 upon the pension lawmaking process.

In an explanation of these changes, the inter-party competition [22] and, ultimately, the balance of forces between major social classes [23] seems to be highly significant. The changes in the fourth legislature, when the PSI for the first time since 1947 entered the government coalition, could be regarded as the result of a new pattern of inter-party competition between the PSI and the PCI. The PCI considerably increased its parliamentary activity on behalf of the civil servants, likely in an attempt to neutralize the potential threat to its traditional electorate coming from the PSI.

In the fifth legislature the inter-party competition was heavily influenced by the strike wave of that period. All parties tended to introduce more pension bills for public employees, while the government increased the number of its bills affecting the dependent workers of the private sector. In a climate in which the industrial unions' claims for a more egalitarian pension system prevailed [24], the public employees' unions activated a process of more or less conscious particularistic platforms on pension matters that eventually led to a greater concentration of party competition on the schemes for the civil servants than on those for the traditional working class which was in general far more involved in the strike movement of that period [25].

In the seventh legislature, the entrance of the PCI into the majority produced an unprecedented competition between the PCI and PSI on pension schemes for dependent workers. The PCI's increase in pension bills for the dependent workers could be read as an attempt to smooth the strong resistance within its rank and file against the 'historical compromise' with the DC. The reaction of the PSI, on the other hand, might be interpreted as an endeavour to profit politically from those difficulties in order to counterbalance the loss of 'centrality' following the entry of the Communist Party into the majority.

7. Legislative outputs and interest representation

Lawmaking is, needless to say, a highly complex process in which the relevance of interest representation is evident both on the input and the output side. Therefore, in order to reach a more comprehensive understanding of interest representation in pension lawmaking, the different 'rates of transformation' of pension draft bills into laws should be examined.

Table 4 shows that political parties generally did not have a strong influence on pension legislation. Almost 70 percent of the enacted pension laws have been introduced by the various cabinets in power, while political parties have proposed only 10 percent of the related draft bills. The DC has followed a decreasing trend over time while both the PCI and the PSI - except in the fifth and seventh legislatures - have had a relatively stable trend in pension lawmaking. In the course of the fifth legislature, the 'rate of transformation' of the PCI was null whilst that of the PSI was 'normal'. By contrast, the PCI reached its maximum transformation rate during the seventh legislature whereas that of the PSI was null.

Table 4   Transformation rate of pension bills into laws, by beneficiaries and party (a)

Beneficiaries	General population				Pensioners				Dependent workers				Public employees			
Legislature	GOV	DC	PCI	PSI	GOV	DC	PCI	PSI	GOV	DC	PCI	PSI	GOV	DC	PCI	PSI
I	-	-	-	-	72	29	100	0	75	40	0	0	70	14	0	67
II	-	-	-	-	94	25	0	0	88	29	40	0	94	31	13	11
III	-	-	-	-	71	12	0	33	60	36	8	0	95	8	0	0
IV	-	-	-	-	71	17	17	0	83	9	0	0	79	11	14	7
V	100	0	0	-	100	9	0	17	29	8	0	0	67	6	0	5
VI	0	-	0	-	44	0	0	7	50	19	17	0	93	4	0	0
VII	100	-	-	-	17	8	-	0	22	4	0	0	29	0	0	0
VIII	50	-	0	-	50	5	13	11	0	8	0	0	40	4	0	7
Total	60	0	0	-	69	10	7	8	55	16	7	0	74	8	6	6

Beneficiaries	Self-employed				Professionals				Residual category				All categories			
Legislature	GOV	DC	PCI	PSI	GOV	DC	PCI	PSI	GOV	DC	PCI	PSI	GOV	DC	PCI	PSI
I	-	33	0	-	40	33	-	-	67	18	13	67	70	24	12	50
II	-	25	0	0	100	57	-	75	86	33	6	38	93	32	9	23
III	50	0	0	0	100	36	100	0	86	8	8	0	75	16	6	3
IV	100	11	0	0	50	24	0	20	100	26	17	0	82	16	11	5
V	-	0	-	0	14	25	-	0	50	4	0	10	46	7	0	7
VI	-	0	0	0	60	9	0	0	100	13	50	7	64	7	12	4
VII	100	0	-	0	33	0	0	0	43	13	33	0	33	3	16	0
VIII	0	0	0	0	67	25	0	20	80	24	14	0	45	7	6	7
Total	58	6	0	0	53	19	11	18	75	16	12	12	67	12	7	8

(a) Pension laws passed as percentage of pension bills introduced for beneficiary groups (general population, pensioners, dependent workers, public employees, self-employed persons, professionals and a residual category) by party or cabinet (GOVernment, DC, PCI, PSI); hyphens indicate that no pension bill was introduced.

It appears also that the degree of parliamentary and legislative 'collaboration' between Centre and Centre-Left majorities and the PCI's opposition - measured by the transformation rates - has varied considerably according to the different sectors of population affected. In general the degree of collaboration in pension lawmaking is lower when draft bills affect large and politically well established categories of the population such as dependent workers, public employees, and the self-employed. On the contrary, when they deal with smaller and politically less identifiable categories such as the general population, the pensioners, and the 'residual' category, the degree of collaboration tends to increase considerably [26].

Conclusion

The aim of this contribution has been to point out the importance of political factors in accounting for the persistent and ever-growing intricacy of the Italian pension system. The pension policy area has become a rather relevant political issue in the Italian party system. Its relevance increased principally during periods of intense strain on the political system - the fifth, seventh and eighth legislatures. The DC and the PSI acted essentially as interclass parties (the DC as the most active party in pension policy), while the PCI was more linked to the traditional working class and to the less favoured sectors of citizenry. The 'collaboration' between the majority and the PCI varied both according to the 'political strength' of the cabinets and the sector of population affected.

The particularistic drive in the Italian pension system can be regarded principally as an effect of the fragmentation and polarization of the party system in Italy. The direct consequences of this constitutive character of the Italian polity are both a sharp intensification of the inter-party competition and a fragility of governmental coalitions. This encourages parties to emphasize their role by introducing a high number of bills to ensure the best 'political visibility'. All this may account for what occurred on the 'input' side. However, to understand what happened on the 'output' side, the role of government is essential. Its selective action revealed its 'sensitivity' not only to party and/or traditional lobby pressures, but also to mass strike movements.

Notes

[1]   L. Graziano, 'A conceptual framework for the study of clientelistic behaviour', *European Journal of Political Research*, 4 (1976), pp.149-174; and idem, Clientelismo e *sistema politico. Il caso dell'Italia*. Milano, F. Angeli, 1980.

[2]   A study carried out for a doctoral dissertation at the European University Institute, Florence.

[3]   See G. Di Palma, *Surviving without Governing. The Italian Parties in Parliament*. Berkeley, University of California Press, 1977; F. Cantelli et al., *Come lavora il Parlamento* Milano, Giuffré, 1974.

[4]   See for a theoretical discussion, I. Burton and G. Drewry, *Legislation and Public Policy: Public Bills in the 1970-1974 Parliament*. London, Macmillan, 1981; T. Raison, Power and *Parliament*. Oxford, Blackwell, 1979.

[5]   See F. G. Castles, 'How does politics matter? Structure or agency in the determination of public policy outcomes', *European Journal of Political Research*, 9 (1981), pp. 119-132.

[6]   See Burton and Drewry, *op. cit.*

[7]   See M. Regini and G. Esping-Andersen, 'Trade unions strategies and social policy in Italy and Sweden', *West European Politics*, 3,1 (1980); G. Regonini, 'Stato e sindacati nella formazione della politica della sicurezza sociale. Il caso delle pensioni', *Quaderni della Fondazione Feltrinelli*, 10 (1980).

[8]   See M. Regini and G. Regonini, 'La politica delle pensioni in Italia: il ruolo del movimento sindacale', *Giornale di Diritto del Lavoro e di Relazioni Industriali*, 3, 10 (1980), pp. 217-242.

[9]   See I. Gough and A. Steinberg, 'The welfare state, capitalism and crisis', *Political Power and Social Theory*, 2 (1981), pp. 141-171.

[10]   See the declarations of the Italian minister for social security in the report presenting his draft bill (not passed) on the reform of the pension system in: *Previdenza Sociale*, 34 (1979), pp. 1789ff.

[11]   Formally, this occurred in 1978, but there had been substantial political agreement between the DC and the PCI ever since the seventh legislature in 1976.

[12]   See G. Di Palma, 'Contenuti e comportamenti legislativi nel Parlamento italiano', *Rivista Italiana di Scienza Politica* 6 (1976), pp. 3-39.

[13]   See H. L. Wilensky, *The Welfare State and Equality. Structural and Ideological Roots of Public Expenditures* Berkeley, University of California Press, 1975.

[14]   See F. Bartolotta, *Parlamenti e governi d'Italia*. Roma, Vito Bianco Editore, 1972; M. Calise and R. Mannheimer, *I governi misurati*. Bologna, Il Mulino, 1982.

[15]   See O. Castellino, *Il labirinto delle pensioni*. Bologna, Il Mulino, 1976.

[16]   See G. Sartori, *Correnti frazioni e fazioni*. Bologna, Il Mulino, 1973; E. Vitiello, 'Pluralismo polarizzato e sistema politico italiano', *Rivista Italiana di Scienza Politica*, 11 (1981), pp. 483-515.

[17]   See Regini and Regonini, *op. cit.*

[18]   See O. Castellino, *op. cit.*

[19]   See G. Pasquino, 'Mass media, partito di massa e trasformazioni della politica', *Il Mulino*, (1983), pp. 559-579.

[20]   See Pasquino, *op. cit.*

[21]   See D. Hine, 'Thirty years of the Italian Republic', *Parliamentary Affairs*, 34 (1981), pp. 63-80.

[22]   See I. Budge and D. Farlie, *Voting and Party Competition* London, Wiley, 1977.

[23]   For more details see E. Maestri, 'Partiti e sistema pensionistico in Italia. Un' analisi dell' azione parlamentare della DC e del PCI (1953-1975)', *Rivista Italiana di Scienza Politica*, 14 (1984), pp. 125-159.

[24]   See Regini and Regonini, *op. cit.*

[25]   See S. Caruso, *Burocrazia e capitale in Italia. Struttura e ideologia.* Verona, Bertani, 1974.

[26]   See S. Belligni (ed.), *La giraffa e il liocorno. Il PCI dagli anni '70 al nuovo decennio.* Milano, F. Angeli, 1983.

Authors' biographical sketches

ALBER, JENS, University Assistant of Sociology, Forschungsinstitut für Soziologie, University of Cologne, 1983-; born 1947; M.A., University of Constance, 1972; Dr. phil., University of Mannheim, 1979; Research Fellow, European University Institute, Florence, 1980-83; Stein Rokkan Prize in Comparative Social Science Research of the International Social Science Council, 1983; author: Vom Armenhaus zum Wohlfahrtsstaat. Analysen zur Entwicklung der Sozialversicherung in Westeuropa, 1982; Der Sozialstaat in der Bundesrepublik Deutschland 1950-1983, 1986; various articles on the welfare state and political sociology in professional journals and collections.

FERRERA, MAURIZIO, Lecturer in Political Science, University of Pavia, 1984-; born 1955; Laurea in Philosophy, University of Torino, 1977; M.A. in Political Science, Stanford University, 1979; Doctor in Political and Social Science, European University Institute, Florence, 1984; editor: Lo Stato del Benessere: Una Crisi senza Uscita? (The Welfare State: A Crisis without Exit?), 1981; author: Il Welfare State in Italia, 1984; various articles in professional journals and collections.

FLORA, PETER, Professor of Sociology, Director of the West European Data Arachive (WEDA), University of Mannheim, 1982-; born 1944; M.A., University of Constance, 1969; Dr. rer. soc., University of Constance, 1973; Habilitation in Sociology, University of Mannheim, 1976; Associate Professor of Sociology, University of Cologne, 1976-79; Professor of Sociology, European University Institute, Florence, 1979-82; co-editor of Zeitschrift für Soziologie, 1979-82; author and editor: Modernisierungsforschung, 1974; Indikatoren der Modernisierung, 1975; Quantitative Historical Sociology, 1976; The Development of Welfare States in Europe and America (with A.J. Heidenheimer), 1980; State, Economy, and Society in Western Europe 1815-1975, vol. I, 1983, vol. II (with Franz Kraus and W. Pfenning), 1986; Westeuropa im Wandel, 1986; various articles in professional journals and collections.

MAGUIRE, MARIA, Administrator, Directorate for Social Affairs, Manpower and Education, Organisation for Economic Co-operation and Development, Paris, 1984-; born 1954; B.C.S., National Institute for Higher Education, Limerick, Ireland, 1977; M.A. in Politics, University College Dublin, 1980; Doctor in Political and Social Science, European University Institute, Florence, 1985; author: various articles on social policy, comparative politics and Irish politics in professional journals and collections.

MAESTRI, G. EZIO, Doctoral candidate at the European University Institute, Florence; born 1953; Degree in Sociology, University of Trento, 1979; Diplome d'Etudes Supérieures Européennes and Diplome d'Etudes Approfondies en Sciences Politiques, University of Nancy, 1980; author: articles on Italian politics in professional journals.

PARRY, RICHARD, Lecturer in Social Policy, University of Edinburg 1983-; born 1953; M.A. in Politics, University of Edinburg 1974; Civil servant, Department of the Environment 1974-78; Research Officer, Centre for the Study of Public Policy, University of Strathclyde, 1978-81; M.S.C. in Politics, University of Strathclyde, 1981; Research Fellow, Department of Politics, University of Edinburgh 1981-83; author: 'Britain', in: Rose (ed.), Public Employment in Western Nations, 1985; 'Social Policy', in: Drucker (ed.), Development in British Politics, 1986; 'The Scottish Office', in: Rose (ed.), Ministers and Ministries, 1986; articles in professional journals and collections.

Growth to Limits

The Western European Welfare States
Since World War II

A Series under the Editorship of
Peter Flora

Volume 1:
Sweden, Norway, Finland, Denmark

Volume 2:
Germany, United Kingdom, Ireland, Italy

Volume 3:
Austria, Switzerland, Netherlands, Belgium

Volume 4:
Appendix, (Synopses, Bibliographies, Tables)

Volume 5:
Unity and Diversity — A Comparison
